Practical Guide to Partnerships and LLCs

Sixth Edition

Robert Ricketts
Larry Tunnell

Wolters Kluwer
CCH

Editorial Staff

Production . . . . Christopher Zwirek

ISBN: 978-0-8080-3479-7

©2013 CCH Incorporated. All Rights Reserved.
4025 W. Peterson Ave.
Chicago, IL 60646-6085
800 248 3248
CCHGroup.com

Printed in the United States of America

SUSTAINABLE FORESTRY INITIATIVE
Certified Sourcing
www.sfiprogram.org
SFI-01234
SFI label applies to the text stock

This book is dedicated to Frank M. Burke, truly a legendary figure in the field of taxation. A former partner and member of the board of directors of Peat, Marwick, Mitchell & Co. (now KPMG), Frank drafted the original Wyoming LLC statute in 1976 and obtained the first ruling from the IRS in support of partnership status for LLCs. Among his many legacies, Frank is thus the father of the modern partnership, the most popular form of organization for new businesses.

A graduate of both the BBA and the MBA programs at Texas Tech University, and the SMU Law School, Frank spent a very productive lifetime advising clients and governments on tax and business issues. He negotiated the entry of KPMG into China, established the firm's first offices in Beijing and in Brunei, and assisted the Guatemalan government in the preparation of its petroleum law in the 1970s. He was an influential voice in the development of tax policy, oil and gas policy, and in the years following Enron, in establishing policies for the corporate boardroom. Few people have influenced their professions as significantly as Frank influenced ours. He was also a loyal and tireless supporter of education, and his support of the Texas Tech accounting program will forever be appreciated. It has been said that we all stand on the shoulders of giants. In the field of taxation, Frank Burke was one of those giants.

Preface

Practical Guide to Partnerships and LLCs will help readers understand the many facets of partnership and LLC taxation in a practical way. This book includes detailed reference material for the federal income taxation of partnerships and LLCs taxed as partnerships. It also discusses the taxation of state law partnerships with a separate commentary on the taxation of LLCs when there are actual or perceived issues that arise in applying Subchapter K of the Internal Revenue Code of 1986 to LLCs. In five parts, *Practical Guide to Partnerships and LLCs* covers the critical concepts and issues of partnership and LLC practice. Individual parts focus on partnership characteristics, funding, taxation of operations, partner's share of partnership debt, disposition of partnership interest, and distributions. From choice of entity considerations to sales and liquidations, the breadth of partnership and LLC taxation is covered. Special attention is given throughout to the complex inner-workings of rules that bind, tax, and control these entity operations.

Practical Guide to Partnerships and LLCs explains in detail the most important points of this challenging practice. The book is a mix of detailed explanations, illustrative examples and computations, and practical insights. Thoroughly foot-noted to authority and organized to lead the reader from the basics to the complex, the book will assist those of all levels of experience.

Please visit *http://www.cchgroup.com/Resources* for any periodic updates or clarifications that may become available related to the *Practical Guide to Partnerships and LLCs* as well as CCH's Daily Tax Day News, Tax Briefings and other items of interest.

August 2013

About the Authors

Robert Ricketts is Director of the School of Accounting, and Frank M. Burke Chair in Taxation, at the Rawls College of Business at Texas Tech University. Larry Tunnell is Professor of Accounting at the College of Business at New Mexico State University. Both are authors of numerous publications in the taxation area.

Contents

Contents in Detail

Please visit *http://www.cchgroup.com/Resources* for any periodic updates or clarifications that may become available related to the *Practical Guide to Partnerships and LLCs* as well as CCH's Daily Tax Day News, Tax Briefings and other items of interest.

PART I

BASIC PARTNERSHIP OPERATIONS

Chapter 1

What Is a Partnership?

¶ 101 Introduction

For legal purposes a business activity may be conducted in various forms, ranging from a sole proprietorship to a partnership to a corporation. Along that continuum, a jointly held activity can be conducted as a tenancy in common, a general partnership, a limited partnership, a limited liability company, a limited liability partnership, a limited liability limited partnership, a professional corporation, a C corporation, or a publicly traded partnership. The array of available entities in which a business can operate is more diverse than ever, and taxpayers should take into account both tax and nontax considerations when selecting the entity for their business.

A partnership is an association between two or more persons who join to carry on a trade or business for profit. Each person contributes money, property, labor or skill, and expects to share in the profits and losses of the business. As indicated above, the laws of different states provide for several different kinds of partnerships. A *general partnership* is one in which every partner has unlimited liability for the debts of the partnership. A *limited partnership* is one in which at least one partner's liability for the debts of the partnership is limited to that partner's investment in the partnership. Any partner with such limited liability is a limited partner, and any partner with unlimited liability is a general partner. Unlike limited partners, general partners also are able to participate in the management of the partnership.

A *limited liability partnership* (LLP) is a type of general partnership in which all of the partners (all of which are general partners) are protected at a minimum from personal liability for negligent acts committed by other partners or by employees not under his or her direct control. Some states allow general partners in an LLP essentially the same protection as limited partners would have. The use of this type of partnership is often restricted to professional partnerships such as law firms and accounting firms. A *limited liability limited partnership* (LLLP) is generally a limited partnership that elects to become an LLP as well, thus affording the general partners the same protection from liability as an LLP does. A *limited liability company* (LLC) is an extremely popular type of entity whose owners can all participate in the management of the business, but who also are all given protection from the liabilities of the LLC (except to the extent of their investment in the LLC). Although not legally a partnership, most LLCs are treated as partnerships for tax purposes.

Just because an entity is *legally* a partnership does not mean that it will be taxed as a partnership. The legal treatment of an entity is determined under state and local laws, while the federal income tax treatment is determined under the federal income tax laws. Often a business will have the same entity for both federal income tax purposes and legal purposes, but many businesses have different entities for federal income tax and legal purposes. A business that is classified as a partnership under state law, for example, can generally elect to be treated as a corporation for federal income tax purposes, if the owners don't want it to be taxed as a partnership. In addition, joint owners of property may be classified as tenants-in-common for legal purposes but as a partnership for federal income tax purposes.

It should also be noted that while the income tax system defines certain categories of entities that exist only for income tax purposes, such as S corporations, many types of legal entities do not have a separate, specifically defined counterpart for income tax purposes. Limited liability companies and limited liability partnerships, for example, exist under state law but are usually treated for federal income tax purposes much the same as any partnership would be. This is true even though they share many characteristics with corporations (*e.g.*, limited liability, unlimited life, etc.).

There are three general sets of regulatory rules that classify entities as a partnership for tax purposes versus something other than a partnership (*e.g.*, a corporation, trust or sole proprietorship):

- The rules which are commonly referred to as the "check-the-box" classification rules;[1]

- The "anti-abuse" rules;[2] and

- Rules which allow investment joint venturers to choose whether to be partnerships or tenancies-in-common.[3]

The check-the-box regulations are by far the most important of these, and they allow taxpayers to choose whether to treat partnerships and other unincorporated entities which are not partnerships (*e.g.*, LLCs) as either corporations or partnerships for federal income tax purposes. The anti-abuse rules allow the IRS to recharacterize something the taxpayer is treating as a partnership as something other than a partnership. The third rule allows simple partnerships that resemble

---

[1] Reg. §§ 301.7701-1, -2, and -3.   [3] Reg. § 1.761-2.
[2] Reg. § 1.701-2.

jointly owned investments to elect to treat themselves not as partnerships, but as tenants-in-common for tax purposes.

In addition, there is substantive case law distinguishing a partnership from other business arrangements, such as debtor-creditor or employee-employer relationships.

¶ 102 Classification of Partnerships

The "check-the-box" regulations are so called because the entity is allowed to choose their tax treatment by checking a certain box on Form 8832, Entity Classification Election. The check-the-box regulations allow considerable flexibility in what entity a business chooses for federal income tax purposes, with one exception: a business activity *incorporated* under the law of any state, federal, or foreign jurisdiction must be treated as a corporation for federal income tax purposes. If the shareholders of that corporation prefer a tax treatment similar to a partnership, then they should make an S election. However, the fact that the business is incorporated under state law will make it impossible for it to choose to be treated as a partnership for federal income tax purposes.

For unincorporated entities the check-the-box regulations allow much more flexibility. While the default classification of unincorporated entities is usually to be treated as a partnership, a jointly owned, *unincorporated*, profit-motivated domestic business entity (such as a limited liability company or partnership) may elect to be a corporation for tax purposes.

> **Example 1-1:** Clara and Ernie Majors are married and own a hardware store. Ernie operates the hardware store. He reports the tax results on Schedule C, Form 1040. The Majors would like to form an S corporation for federal income tax purposes, but they don't want the trouble and expense of incorporating and following the other corporate formalities. Clara and Ernie enter into a partnership, contributing the hardware business and all related assets to the partnership. The partnership files Form 8832, indicating that it elects to be a corporation for federal income tax purposes. It then files Form 2553, Election by a Small Business Corporation, and thereby elects to be treated as an S corporation for tax purposes. By electing to be classified as an S corporation, pass-through income (in excess of reasonable compensation) will not be subject to the self-employment or Medicare taxes.

If an eligible unincorporated organization does not elect to be a corporation, then it is by default a partnership for tax purposes. As a partnership, the organization will be required to file a Form 1065, U.S. Return of Partnership Income, each year by the fifteenth day of the fourth month after the close of the taxable year. For calendar year partnerships this means that the Form 1065 must be filed by April 15 of the following year.[4] A partnership is allowed an automatic 5-month extension of the time allowed for filing Form 1065. The extension application must be made on Form 7004 and it must be filed by the unextended due date of the Form 1065, but it does not have to contain a reason for the requested extension.[5]

---

[4] Code Sec. 6072(a); Reg § 1.6031(a)-1(e)(2).   [5] Reg. § 1.6081-2T.

A single member unincorporated entity is treated as a "disregarded entity" unless it elects to be a corporation. It cannot be treated as a partnership. For example, a single member LLC owned by an individual will be treated as a sole proprietorship unless the individual elects to be treated as a corporation. Its business income and expenses will be reported on the individual's Schedule C, Form 1040, and its rental income or loss will be reported on the individual's Schedule E, Form 1040. A corporation which owns a single member LLC would report its results as if it were a branch if it didn't elect to treat the LLC as a separate corporate subsidiary.

301.7701-3 Regulations
(Effective for Entities Formed on or After January 1, 1997)[6]

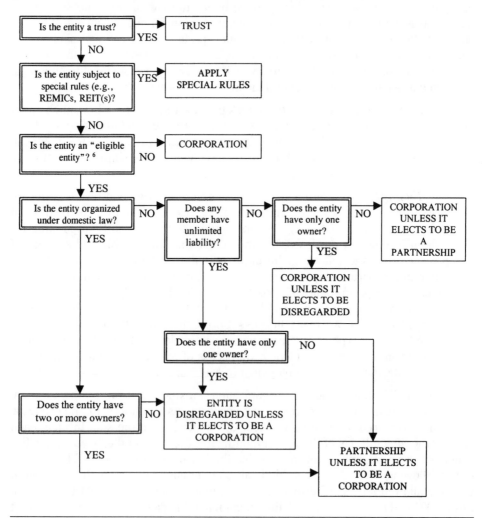

---

[6] An "eligible entity" is any organization not deemed a corporation per Reg. § 301.7701-2(b)(1), (3), (4), (5), (6), (7), or (8).

For entities in existence prior to January 1, 1997, their previously claimed classification will generally be respected for periods prior to that date if it was reasonable under the prior rules.[7]

¶ 103 Advantages and Disadvantages of Operating as a Partnership

Flow-through taxation. Partnerships are a very popular form of business entity, especially from a tax perspective. The primary advantage of operating as a partnership for tax purposes is that although the partnership must file a tax return, a partnership is not taxable; the income from the partnership flows through to the partners and is recognized by them in the same character as it was recognized by the partnership (as ordinary income or capital gain, for example). This can have two positive effects. First, the income of the partnership is only taxed once at the partner level, unlike the double taxation that corporate shareholders must suffer. Second, if the partnership has a loss the partner will be able to deduct their share of the loss (subject to basis, at-risk, and passive loss limitations), whereas a shareholder in a regular C corporation can't deduct their share of a corporate loss. It should be noted, however, that since an S corporation is also a flow-through entity an S corporation shareholder would be able to deduct their share of an S corporation loss. It should also be noted again that an entity does not have to be a partnership to be taxed as one. LLCs are commonly taxed as partnerships, as are specific types of partnerships such as LLPs and LLLPs.

Property distributions. Another often overlooked tax advantage of operating as a partnership is that it can be much less expensive to get assets (especially appreciated non-cash assets) out of a partnership than it is to get them out of a corporation. Generally, distributions of property from a partnership are tax-free to both the partnership and the partner, although distributions of cash can result in gain to a partner. Distributions of property from a corporation, however, are dividend income to the shareholder, and will result in taxable gain to the corporation if the assets distributed are appreciated.

Tax-free formation. It can also be less expensive from a tax perspective to form a partnership than it is to form a corporation. The requirements of Code Sec. 351 must be met in order for the formation of a corporation (whether it is taxed as a C corporation or an S corporation) to be tax-free. This means generally that property must be contributed, stock must be received, and 80-percent control must be owned by the contributors after the contribution. No such requirements exist for partnerships. Contributions of property to partnerships are generally tax-free unless the net liabilities the partner is relieved of due to the contribution exceed the partner's basis in their partnership interest.

Special allocations. A partnership also has the advantage of being able to specially allocate items of income or deduction to different partners. All of the depreciation on a building can be allocated to just one partner, for example. Although there are detailed rules limiting the circumstances under which this can

---

[7] Reg. § 301.7701-3 (h) (2).

be done and the amounts that can be specially allocated, special allocations are commonly used to make investment in a partnership more attractive to high-tax-bracket partners. Shareholders in corporations, whether they are C corporations or S corporations, can't be specially allocated items of income or deduction.

Unlimited liability. Partnerships usually have the disadvantage of not shielding the general partners from the liabilities of the partnership. This is a major disadvantage for the general partners, and is one reason why so many businesses are now operated as LLCs. LLCs generally are taxed as partnerships, but their owners are shielded from the liabilities of the entity.

Self-employment income. A disadvantage of being taxed as a partnership is that any trade or business income of the partnership is taxed to the general partners as self-employment income, subject to the self-employment tax. Guaranteed payments for services provided by limited partners are also treated as self-employment income. Income of a corporation is not self-employment income to the shareholders, although wages paid to the shareholders will be subject to FICA taxes.

Other advantages of the partnership form:

a. Easy to form – no filing with state or even paperwork is necessary (although a written agreement is strongly advised, and states vary in terms of their filing requirements for any business).

b. Liabilities of a partnership increase a partner's basis.

Other disadvantages of the partnership form:

a. Can be more difficult to transfer ownership.

b. Can be more difficult to raise capital.

c. As indicated above, a partner's deduction of losses from a partnership are limited by basis, at-risk amounts, and the passive activity loss rules.

d. The fringe benefit exclusion is generally not allowed because a partner is not an "employee" (health plan premiums are not excludable, and payments are not excludable—but premiums are deductible if there is self-employment income. Other examples are group term life insurance premiums and meals and lodging). On the other hand, a partner is specifically treated as an "employee" for the purposes of many fringe benefits (education assistance, child care, retirement plans, and others)

¶ 104 Tax Issues Involving Classification of LLCs as Partnerships

Some of the quirks of applying partnership tax rules to nonpartnerships have been clearly addressed by statute or regulations while others have not. Of the addressed issues, some of the older provisions have laid out clear rules which probably would be different if the drafters were considering LLC implications. Some of the newer rules have explicitly addressed their LLC implications, but this is still a developing area. This section outlines some of the more commonly encountered problems in applying the partnership tax rules to LLCs. Additional

¶104

issues which may arise in other contexts are discussed throughout the book at points where the application of partnership tax rules to LLCs is unclear. If there is no separate discussion, there is no recognized issue related to application of a partnership tax rule to an LLC.

The federal income tax regulations require most jointly-owned unincorporated domestic business entities, such as LLCs, to be treated as partnerships unless they elect corporate status.[8] Applying the partnership tax rules to an entity which is not a partnership does not normally present an additional layer of complexity for tax planning and compliance. The tax practitioner simply ignores the entity's nontax status, as an LLC for example, and applies the partnership tax rules to the issue at hand. However, complications can arise in applying statutory and regulatory rules mostly written in the mid-1950s and almost all written before 1990.

These rules were intended to apply to common law partnerships and not to other forms of business. For LLCs this can present problems in interpreting the tax laws in several different areas.

1. *Definition of what is a limited and general partner.* General or limited partners may be treated differently for some partnership tax purposes. In the case of state law partnerships, it has been normally routine to identify who are the general partners and who are the limited partners and apply the appropriate tax rule accordingly. However, in the case of an LLC, no member is legally a limited or general partner. All the members resemble limited partners from a limited liability standpoint, while all members who are managers resemble general partners from an operational standpoint.

2. *Classification of debt as recourse or nonrecourse.* Another problem area involves classifying partnership debt as recourse versus nonrecourse for purposes of allocating the debt among the partners for partnership basis and at-risk purposes. Generally, recourse debt is allocated to the partners who bear the risk of paying the creditors if the partnership fails to pay them. In contrast, nonrecourse debts (in the case of the at-risk rules' "qualified nonrecourse debt") are allocated among all partners, general and limited.[9] In either case, these rules, while relatively straightforward when applied to partnerships, become less clear when applied to non-partnership entities, such as LLCs, that elect to be classified as partnerships for federal income tax purposes.

3. *Passive loss limitation rules.* Code Sec. 469(a)(1)(A) disallows a deduction for net passive activity losses incurred by individuals, trusts, estates, and personal service corporations.[10] A passive activity for this purpose means any non-real estate operator's rental activity and any activity that involves the conduct of any trade or business and in which the taxpayer does not *materially participate.*[11] An individual may deduct up to $25,000 of passive activity losses attributable to all real estate activities with respect to which that individual *actively participated* during the year and satisfies other

---

[8] Reg. §§ 1.301.7701-2 and -3.
[9] Reg. § 1.752-3(a).
[10] Code Sec. 469(d)(1); Temp. Reg. § 1.469-2T(b)(1).
[11] Code Sec. 469(c)(1).

requirements.[12] Generally, an individual is treated as materially participating in an activity for a taxable year if he or she meets one of seven tests.

Except as provided in regulations, no interest as a limited partner in a limited partnership will be treated as an interest in which the taxpayer actively participates.[13] A partnership interest is not treated as a limited partnership interest if the individual is also a general partner at all times during the year.[14] An interest in an LLC certainly falls within the literal definition of a limited partnership interest.[15] Commentators have argued that manager-members should not be treated as limited partners for purposes of the material participation test since they are allowed to participate in management, unlike limited partners.[16] In fact, in *Gregg v. U.S.*[17] the LLC member was treated as a general partner for passive loss purposes because he had the element of control required to be considered a general partner under the applicable state law. In *Thompson v. U.S.*[18] the LLC member was treated as a general partner because the Court maintained that a "limited partnership interest" for Code Sec. 469 purposes meant an interest in an entity that was in fact organized as a limited partnership under applicable state law and held by one who is in fact a limited partner. The Court in *Thompson* also held that, even if the taxpayer were considered to hold a partnership interest, the taxpayer might escape passive treatment under the regulations' exception for general versus limited partners, which was distinguished not on the basis of limited liability characteristics, but on the basis of whether the taxpayer had the element of control required under state law. The Courts came to similar conclusions in *Newell*[19] and *Garnett*.[20]

Proposed regulations. The Service has attempted to begin to deal with this uncertainty in treatment by issuing Prop. Reg. § 1.469-5(e)(3)(i) as follows:

(i) In general. Except as provided in paragraph (e)(3)(ii) of this section, for purposes of section 469(h)(2) and this paragraph (e), an interest in an entity shall be treated as an interest in a limited partnership as a limited partner if—

(A) The entity in which such interest is held is classified as a partnership for Federal income tax purposes under § 301.7701-3; and

(B) The holder of such interest does not have rights to manage the entity at all times during the entity's taxable year under the law of the jurisdiction in which the entity is organized and under the governing agreement.

---

[12] Code Sec. 469(i)(1), (2).

[13] Code Sec. 469(i)(6)(C).

[14] Temp. Reg. § 1.469-5T(e)(3)(ii).

[15] Temp. Reg. § 1.469-5T(e)(3)(i)(B).

[16] Jordan and Kloepfer, *The Limited Liability Company: Beyond Classification*, 69 TAXES 203, 210 (1991).

[17] *Gregg v. U.S.*, 2001-1 USTC ¶ 50,169, (DC OR, 11/29/2000).

[18] *Thompson v. U.S.*, 104 AFTR 2d 2009-5381 (87 Fed. Cl. 728), 07/20/2009.

[19] *Lee E. Newell, et ux. v. Commissioner*, TC Memo 2010-23.

[20] *Paul D. Garnett, et ux. v. Commissioner*, 132 TC 368.

Essentially this Proposed Regulation would allow *managing* LLC members to qualify as being material participants in their LLC.

4. *Tax matters partner.* Tax partnerships, including LLCs treated as partnerships, are subject to the unified audit and litigation procedures contained in Sections 6221–6234, unless they are:

- Electing large partnerships,[21] or
- Small partnerships.[22]

The unified audit and litigation procedures require the partnership to appoint a general partner as its tax matters partner.[23] The tax matters partner is the person the IRS will deal with in connection with the unified procedures. The Internal Revenue Code does not define a general partner. If the term were deemed to mean a partner with personal liability for the organization's liabilities, then in an LLC there would be no one whom the partners may designate.[24] Under Code Sec. 6231(a)(7), the partners may designate only a general partner as the "tax matters partner" for purposes of partnership audits. If there is no general partner, the IRS is authorized to designate the tax matters partner.[25] Final regulations under Code Sec. 6231 governing the designation of tax matters partners were finalized on December 23, 1996, and are effective for all designations of tax matters partners on or after that date. Under the regulations, only member managers of LLCs can be designated as the tax matters partner.[26]

5. *Self-employment taxes.* In general, a partner's share of nonseparately stated income from any trade or business carried on by the partnership will be included in her "net earnings from self-employment."[27] However, a limited partner's share of income from a partnership, other than guaranteed payments for services under Code Sec. 707(c), is not subject to self-employment tax (*i.e.*, the income is excluded from "net earnings from self-employment").[28]

LLC members who are treated as limited partners for purposes of Code Sec. 1402(a)(13) cannot take into account their distributive shares that are not subject to Social Security tax for purposes of calculating their retirement plan contributions. For purposes of qualified retirement plans under Code Sec. 401, the term "employee" includes a "self-employed individual."[29] "Self-employed individual" means an individual who has "earned

---

[21] Code Secs. 771–777.

[22] Code Sec. 6231(a)(1)(B) (ten or fewer partners, each being a natural person or an estate, no partner being a nonresident alien and the partnership makes no special allocations).

[23] Code Sec. 6231(a)(7) and (8).

[24] *See Transpac Drilling Venture v. United States*, CA-FC, 94-1 USTC ¶ 50,067, 16 F3d 383, in which court held that limited partners who were designated as general partners for the "limited purpose only" of being tax matters partners did not qualify. *But see* Rev. Proc. 89-12, 1989-1 CB 798, which defines "general partner" to include

a person with significant management authority relative to the other members.

[25] Code Sec. 6231(a)(7).

[26] Reg. § 301.6231(a)(7)-2(a).

[27] Code Sec. 1402(a); Reg § 1.1402(a)-1(a)(2); Reg § 1.1402(a)-2(d).

[28] Code Sec. 1402(a)(13). IRS Letter Ruling 9110003 (12-4-90) held that strict compliance with the state limited partnership act was required for an inactive member of a partnership with limited management rights to qualify as a "limited partner" for purposes of the Code Sec. 1402(a)(13) exclusion.

[29] IRS Letter Ruling 9432018 (5-16-94).

income."[30] "Earned income" means net earnings from self-employment (as defined in Code Sec. 1402(a)).[31] The deduction for retirement plan contributions by self-employed individuals is based upon earned income.[32]

Initially, the IRS ruled that if an LLC is classified as a partnership under Code Sec. 7701, its active members would be treated as general partners for self-employment tax purposes.[33] The ruling stated that a member "actively engaged" in the LLC's professional service business would not be treated as a limited partner under Code Sec. 1402(a)(13) and the member's distributive share of income from the LLC would therefore be treated as net earnings from self-employment.[34]

Proposed regulations. Two sets of proposed regulations have provided guidance on this issue.[35] The first set of proposed regulations issued on December 29, 1994, have since been withdrawn. Proposed regulations were again issued under Code Sec. 1402 early in 1997;[36] they provide that an individual will generally be treated as a limited partner unless he or she:

1. Has personal liability[37] for the debts of or claims against the partnership by reason of being a partner;

2. Has authority to contract on behalf of the partnership under the statute or law pursuant to which the partnership is organized; or

3. Participates in the partnership's trade or business for more than 500 hours during the taxable year.[38]

If, however, substantially all of the activities of a partnership involve the performance of services in the fields of health, law, engineering, architecture, accounting, actuarial science, or consulting, any individual who provides services as part of that trade or business will not be considered a limited partner.

These proposed regulations allow an individual who is not a limited partner for Code Sec. 1402(a)(13) purposes to nonetheless exclude from net earnings from self-employment a portion of his or her distributive share if the individual holds more than one class of interest in the partnership. The proposed regulations permit an individual that participates in the trade or business of the partnership to bifurcate his or her distributive share by disregarding guaranteed payments for services. In each case, however, such bifurcation of interests is permitted only to the extent the individual's distributive share is identical to the distributive share of partners who qualify as limited partners under the proposed regulation (without regard to the bifurcation rules) and who own a substantial interest in the partnership.

---

[30] *See* Samuel P. Starr, *LLC Members May Be Liable for Tax on Self-Employment and Fringe Benefits*, 1 J. LIMITED LIABILITY COMPANIES 2, 51 (1994).

[31] Code Sec. 401(c)(1)(A).

[32] Code Sec. 401(c)(1)(B).

[33] Code Sec. 401(c)(2)(A).

[34] Code Sec. 404(a)(8).

[35] Prop. Reg. § 1.1402(a)-18.

[36] Prop. Reg. § 1.1401-2(d).

[37] As defined in Reg. § 301.7701-3(b)(2)(ii).

[38] Prop. Reg. § 1.1402(a)-2(h)(2).

Together, these rules exclude from self-employment income amounts that are demonstrably returns on capital invested in the partnership. Section 935 of the Taxpayer Relief Act of 1997[39] prohibits issuance of temporary and final regulations under Code Sec. 1402(a)(13) before July 1, 1998. This period has elapsed, but there is still no official controlling guidance as to which members of an LLC will be treated as limited partners for purposes of the self-employment tax and other earned income issues. Tax practitioner's approaches to this problem have varied widely. One position is that, based upon the definition of a limited partner as per the passive loss rules, all the members are limited partners.[40] Another is the possibility of following the approach provided in one of the two sets of proposed regulations. Finally, there is the possibility that no members are limited partners until the IRS issues regulations which expand the definition of limited partner beyond its literal meaning.

6. *Liquidation payments under Code Sec. 736.* Before the Revenue Reconciliation Act of 1993,[41] payments made in liquidation of the interest of any retiring partner or deceased partner attributable to goodwill and unrealized receivables could be treated as a distributive share or guaranteed payment giving rise to a deduction or its equivalent for the benefit of the remaining partners.[42] That special treatment has been limited to payments made to a general partner in a partnership in which capital is not a material income-producing factor.[43] The House Committee report accompanying the Act makes clear that the special rule was intended to preserve the prior law treatment for personal service businesses (*e.g.,* accountants, lawyers, doctors, architects). In order for these rules to apply to personal service LLCs, the retiring or deceased member would have to be treated as a "general partner."[44] "General partner" is not defined, and it is unclear whether an LLC member will be considered a general partner for purposes of Code Sec. 736(b)(3).

7. *At-risk rules.* Generally, under Code Sec. 465 losses incurred by individuals and certain closely held corporations from an activity are deductible only to the extent of the aggregate amount with respect to which the taxpayer is at risk with respect to that activity.[45] Except in the case of "qualified nonrecourse financing," a taxpayer is at risk with respect to amounts borrowed for use in an activity only to the extent that he or she is personally liable for repayment of such amounts, or has pledged property as security for the debt.[46] If a taxpayer guarantees repayment of an amount borrowed by another person for use in an activity, the guarantee does not increase the taxpayer's amount at risk. Even if the guarantor pays the debt, the amount at risk is not increased until the taxpayer has no remaining legal rights against the primary obligor.[47]

---

[39] P.L. 105-34.

[40] Temp. Reg. § 1.469-5T(e)(3)(B).

[41] P.L. 103-66.

[42] Code Sec. 736(a).

[43] *See* Code Sec. 736(b)(3).

[44] Code Sec. 736(b)(3)(B).

[45] Code Sec. 465(a)(1).

[46] Code Sec. 465(b)(2).

[47] Prop. Reg. § 1.465-6(d).

A taxpayer is considered at risk with respect to his or her share of any qualified nonrecourse financing that is secured by real property used in the activity.[48] Qualified nonrecourse financing is generally nonseller financing with respect to which no person is personally liable for repayment.[49] A partner's share of the partnership's qualified nonrecourse financing is determined under Code Sec. 752.[50]

At-risk basis for recourse liability exists only to the extent that any partner or related person bears the economic risk of loss.[51] Nonrecourse debt which is secured by LLC real property that is restricted to the security may be qualified nonrecourse financing. However, the at-risk rules describe nonrecourse debt as financing with respect to which "no person" (instead of 'no member' or 'related person') is personally liable for repayment.[52] In the case of an LLC, the issue was whether recourse debt for which the LLC itself was personally liable could be treated as nonrecourse debt and, therefore, qualified nonrecourse debt if all the requirements were met.

In 1998, the Treasury Department clarified this issue.[53] The regulations under Code Sec. 465 provide a "tailored" definition of nonrecourse debt for purposes of classification as qualified nonrecourse debt.[54] In the case of a partnership, the debt will be considered nonrecourse if:

- The only person personally liable to repay the financing is the partnership;

- The partnership holds only real estate and incidental property; and

- The lender may proceed against only such property to collect on the financing in a default or default-like situation.[55]

Limited partners will, of course, not be considered at-risk with respect to other recourse debt. This could create an unwelcome surprise for partnerships converting to LLCs when the owner's at-risk amount becomes a negative member since recapture for the negative amount is required.[56]

¶ 105 IRS Reclassification

On December 29, 1994, the Internal Revenue Service issued regulations under Code Sec. 701 providing anti-abuse rules under Subchapter K. The regulations provide that the intent of Subchapter K is to permit taxpayers to conduct business for joint economic profit through a flexible arrangement that accurately reflects the partners' economic arrangement without incurring an entity level tax. The regulations add that implicit in the intent of Subchapter K are the following requirements:

- The partnership must be *bona fide* and each transaction or series of related transactions must be entered into for a substantial business purpose;

---

[48] Code Sec. 465(b)(6).

[49] Code Sec. 465(b)(6)(B)(iii).

[50] Code Sec. 465(b)(6)(C).

[51] Field Service Advice 200025018.

[52] Code Sec. 465(b)(6)(B)(iii).

[53] T.D. 8777, 1998-2 CB 219.

[54] Reg. § 1.465-27(b)(1)(iii).

[55] Reg. § 1.465-27(b)(4). There is a similar rule provided for single-member LLCs which are treated as disregarded entities. Reg. § 1.465-27(b)(5).

[56] Code Sec. 465(e).

- The form of each transaction must be respected under substance over form principles; and

- Except as otherwise provided in the regulations, the consequences to each partner from operations and transactions between the partner and the partnership must accurately reflect the partners' economic agreement and clearly reflect the partner's income.[57]

The IRS can recast a transaction involving a purported partnership as if it were not a partnership if (1) the partnership is formed or availed of with a principal purpose of substantially reducing the present value of the partners' aggregate federal tax liability, and (2) the reduction occurs in a manner inconsistent with the intent of Subchapter K. If both requirements are met, the IRS can:

- Disregard the partnership in whole or in part and treat the partnership activity as owned by one or more partners;

- Treat one or more purported partners as not being partners;

- Adjust the method of accounting of the partnership or a partner to clearly reflect income;

- Reallocate the partnership's income; or

- Otherwise adjust the tax treatment of the partners or the partnership.[58]

¶ 106 Distinguishing Partnerships from Other Relationships

.01 Tenancy in Common Distinguished

Even though a jointly held unincorporated activity is not treated as a corporation under the criteria discussed at ¶ 102, partnership status does not necessarily follow. Co-ownership of property, by itself, need not create a partnership for tax purposes. Co-ownership coupled with an expense-sharing arrangement is also not a partnership. If, however, the co-owners "actively and jointly" pursue a business activity, then a tax partnership is deemed to exist.[59] The taxpayers have some control over whether a jointly owned financial venture is treated as a partnership. If the financial venture amounts to an *actively* conducted business, then it *must* be accounted for as a partnership. If a lower level of activity is presented it can be treated as *either* a partnership or co-tenancy.

Intent. In the absence of an actively conducted business, classification as a partnership for tax purposes is determined by the intent of the owners. If the relevant facts and circumstances indicate an intent to operate as a partnership, then there is a partnership for tax purposes. Relevant factors include: (1) the existence of a partnership agreement; (2) filing partnership tax returns; (3) how title to property is taken; and (4) the owners ability to separately sell their shares of the property.

---

[57] Reg. § 1.701-2(a). Prior to amendment, the regulations also applied to taxes other than income taxes. However, the IRS has announced that the rule will be amended to apply solely to income taxes. Announcement 95-8, 1995-7 IRB 56.

[58] Reg. § 1.701-2(b).

[59] Reg. §§ 1.761-1(a) and 301.7701-1(a)(2). In the case of a husband and wife jointly owning a business, partnership treatment would seem to be required if both operated the business. If only one operates the business, his or her name would appear as the proprietor on Schedule C, Profit or Loss From Business, for Form 1040, U.S. Individual Income Tax Return.

For example, joint investments in raw land, stock, and collectibles can be reported as a partnership or each owner can separately report his or her share of income and expenses, depending upon whether the owners have determined that they intend to create a partnership or they merely intend joint ownership. If the parties wish to make their intentions clear, they should consider a Code Sec. 761 election. This election ensures the arrangement is treated as a tenancy in common in spite of a partnership agreement, filing partnership tax returns, and other factors which otherwise might result in partnership treatment.

Rental—Investment of active business? Jointly owned rental operations pose a frequently encountered special problem. Some rentals resemble passive investments and others are operated as active businesses. For example, a joint venture operating an assisted living facility is actively involved in a business and must file tax returns as a partnership. On the other hand, either co-ownership or partnership treatment is appropriate when there is a long-term investment in raw land held for future appreciation which is net leased for farming or grazing to offset carrying expenses.

Absent a demonstrated intent to conduct activity as partners, a co-ownership arrangement, not a partnership, is deemed to exist when two persons who join together as co-owners of an apartment project negotiate and execute leases, collect rents and other payments from tenants, and only perform those services customary to the maintenance of apartments.[60]

One factor used in determining whether co-owners of property must be treated as partners is whether a co-owner provides significant services, either directly or through an agent. If such services are provided, then a partnership may be deemed to exist. The definition of significant service, for a purpose other than those pertaining to Subchapter K, may be useful here. These normally include all services rendered to a customer that are primarily for that particular customer's convenience, rather than services usually or customarily rendered in connection with the rental property's use.[61] Supplying maid service, for example, would not likely constitute usual or customary service, whereas furnishing heat and light or cleaning public areas are not considered "additional services" rendered to an occupant.

Thus, for example, when valet parking, maid and food service are provided at a retirement facility, co-ownership is likely to constitute a partnership, regardless of the owners' subjective intent. The co-ownership of an apartment complex when such "additional services" are not provided allows the co-owners to avoid Subchapter K status if they wish to do so.

When co-ownership of real or personal property exists and such property is leased out to third parties, the use of a "net lease" helps ensure the avoidance of partnership status. If the owners wish to avoid partnership status, the lessee and not the lessor should be responsible for providing any required "additional services" and the rent reduced accordingly. In all cases, however, the net lease's terms

---

[60] Rev. Rul. 75-374, 1975-2 CB 261.

[61] Temp. Reg. §1.469-1T(e)(3)(ii). This provision governs the distinction between rental deemed passive and rental operations sufficiently active to be deemed nonpassive.

must be considered before the issue of partnership status can be decided. Use of a "net lease" by itself does not necessarily preclude partnership treatment. If the owners wish to report as a partnership, the absence of an actively conducted business does not preclude them from partnership status. It is a one-way street—too much activity precludes partnership status, but too little does not.

.02 Election to Be Excluded from Subchapter K

In general, joint ventures and other unincorporated organizations may be excluded from Subchapter K at the election of the partnership by all the members.[62] However, the organization must be formed:

1. For investment purposes only and not for the active conduct of a business;

2. For the joint production, extraction, or use of property, but not for the purpose of selling services or property produced or extracted; or,

3. By dealers in securities for a short period for the purpose of underwriting, selling, or distributing a particular issue of securities.[63]

Additionally, each member of such organization must be able to adequately determine his or her individual income without the necessity of computing partnership taxable income.

Investment Partnerships. A partnership qualifies as an "investing partnership" if:

- The owners can compute their income without the necessity of computing partnership taxable income;[64]

- The owners own the property as co-owners;

- The venture consists of co-owners who reserve the right to separately acquire or dispose of their interests in any property acquired; and

- The co-owners must not use the jointly held property to actively conduct business or irrevocably authorize a representative to purchase, sell, or exchange the investment property. Each participant can, however, separately delegate such authority for a period of one year or less.[65]

A common example of such an arrangement is an equal partnership making an investment in unimproved land when title is held in the partner's names rather than the partnership's name. A strong argument can be made that, according to the regulatory definition of a partnership (even absent such an election), an "investing partnership" need not be treated as a partnership for income tax purposes because of the lack of an actively conducted business. This would make the election especially redundant when no partnership agreement exists and partnership tax returns are not filed. However, given the uncertain effect accorded by judicial decisions of the parties' intentions and representations to third parties, an election in certain circumstances may be wise even when there is no formal partnership agreement and partnership returns are not filed. Where such returns have been

---

[62] Code Sec. 761(a).

[63] *Id.*

[64] Profits and losses are allocated per capital accounts and no special allocations are present.

[65] Reg. § 1.761-2(a)(2).

voluntarily filed, an election to discontinue partnership status would be prudent from an administrative standpoint. The IRS should be notified that the group does not intend to treat itself as a partnership for tax purposes.

These requirements must be met to be eligible for this safe harbor election not to be treated as a partnership. This will sometimes require modifying the business arrangement among the owners and changing title to the property. Modifications to the agreement among the partners can, for tax purposes, be treated as retroactive to the first day of the partnership's taxable year if made by the unextended due date for the partnership tax return.[66]

Joint Production. Participants in a joint production, extraction, or property-use arrangement must also be co-owners (either in fee, under lease, or through another form of contract granting exclusive operating rights), must reserve the right to separately dispose of their interests, and must not jointly sell services or properties either produced or extracted. Each separate participant, however, may delegate authority to sell his or her share of the produced or extracted properties for a period not greater than the minimum needs of the industry or one year (whichever is less).[67]

How Election Is Made. The election is made by filing a timely partnership return for the first taxable year for which an exclusion from Subchapter K is desired with an attached statement in lieu of the numerical information required by Form 1065, U.S. Partnership Return of Income.[68] If all members desire at the time of the organization's formation that it not be taxed as a partnership, they can instead all sign such an agreement and the participants owning substantially all interests must report tax-related items from the venture on their individual returns.[69] The latter method is commonly used by joint venturers of a passive investment, especially in real estate.

.03 Shared Expenses Distinguished

Generally, a partnership does not exist if a joint undertaking is made for the sole purpose of sharing expenses.[70] When, for example, two or more persons construct a ditch to drain surface water from their properties, partnership status will not result.[71] This is true even though the properties are used in separately conducted businesses. It is joint control over the combined business and profit sharing that results in partnership status for tax purposes.

It is not uncommon for two or more professionals to share office expenses, such as rent, supplies, a secretary's salary (even though the secretary is actually an employee of only one of the professionals), utilities and phone service, and still avoid partnership classification. It is most important that each participant personally continue to serve his or her own clients, maintain separate records and bank accounts, and process separate billings, if applicable, in his or her own name.

---

[66] Code Sec. 761(c).

[67] Reg. § 1.761-2(a)(3).

[68] This includes an extended tax return. *See* Reg. § 1.761-2(b)(2)(i).

[69] *See* Reg. § 1.761-2(b)(2)(ii).

[70] Reg. §§ 1.761-1(a) and 301.7701-1(a)(2).

[71] Reg. § 301.7701-1(a).

Partnership status for income tax purposes would ultimately result if the professionals hold themselves out as partners to third parties, conduct their business under their combined names, or pool their money and share profits. In order to assess the parties' true intent, courts have examined objective evidence such as whether the professionals kept joint books or employed joint employees, and whether they previously filed partnership returns. Whenever such an arrangement is recharacterized as a partnership, a new tax entity arises that results in a computation of taxable income subject to the provisions of Subchapter K.[72]

.04 Employment Relationships Distinguished

When two or more persons actively conduct a trade or business with an intention to share profits, but one party lacks a proprietary interest, an employment relationship and not a partnership is likely to exist. Although some elements of a partnership can also be found in many employment relationships (such as profit sharing, shared management control, or jointly provided services and/or capital), an employment arrangement is not a partnership for federal income tax purposes.

Some courts have focused on the degree of managerial control vested with a person in determining whether he or she is a partner or an employee.[73] These decisions give weight to the parties' prior activities indicating whether a partnership was or was not intended. However, even if substantial managerial discretion is vested in a person, he or she may nevertheless be an employee, agent, or independent contractor for tax purposes if the person has no substantial interest in the venture's capital and if the person has no real liability for a proportionate share of the venture's losses.[74]

Generally, the courts have concluded that when one party (usually the provider of capital) has the power to terminate the arrangement and keep the business, an employment relationship exists.[75] Moreover, whenever a provider of services is compensated by a profit-sharing arrangement, at least one of the other partnership elements (such as sharing of losses, capital interest, or mutual control) must not be present in order for that individual to avoid partner status.[76] Though two parties may share profits, for example, and execute a "partnership agreement" while holding themselves out as "partners," no partnership relationship exists if the provider of services has no vested interest in the venture capital.[77] Additional evidence judicially considered in determining partner or employee status include:[78]

---

[72] Reg. § 301-7701-1(a)(2).

[73] *E.C. James v. Commr.*, 16 TC 930, Dec. 18,253 (1951), aff'd per curiam, 52-2 USTC ¶ 9378, 197 F2d 813; *Est. of R.D. McDaniel v. Commr.*, 20 TCM 1551, Dec. 25,111(M), TC Memo. 1961-302; *J.J. Finch v. Commr.*, 14 TCM 692, Dec. 21,109(M), TC Memo. 1955-179.

[74] *P.E. Dorman v. U.S.*, CA-9, 61-2 USTC ¶ 9773, 296 F2d 27; *Est. of C.M. Smith v. Commr.*, CA-8, 63-1 USTC ¶ 9268, 313 F2d 724; *C.L. Pounds v. U.S.*, CA-5, 67-1 USTC ¶ 9191, 372 F2d 342.

[75] See *I.L. Rosenburg v. Commr.*, 15 TC 1, Dec. 17,759 (1950); *R.O. Wheeler v. Commr.*, 37 TCM 883, Dec. 35,198(M), TC Memo. 1978-208; Rev. Rul. 75-43, 1975-1 CB 383.

[76] *See Est. of C.M. Smith v. Commr.*, CA-8, 63-1 USTC ¶ 9268, 313 F2d 724; *R.W. Ewing v. Commr.*, 17 TCM 626, Dec. 23,042(M), TC Memo. 1958-115; *P.E. Dorman v. Commr.*, CA-9, 61-2 USTC ¶ 9773, 296 F2d 27; *R.O. Wheeler v. Commr.*, 37 TCM 883, Dec. 35,198(M), TC Memo. 1978-208; *Est. of H. Kahn v. Commr.*, CA-2, 74-2 USTC ¶ 9524, 499 F2d 1186.

[77] *P.E. Dorman v. U.S.*, CA-9, 61-2 USTC ¶ 9773, 296 F2d 27.

[78] *Commr. v. W.O. Culbertson, Sr.*, SCt, 49-1 USTC ¶ 9323, 337 US 733, 69 SCt 1210; *Commr. v. F.E. Tower*, SCt, 46-1 USTC ¶ 9189, 327 US 280, 66 SCt 532.

1. The agreement between the parties and execution thereof;
2. The manner in which the principal parties represent themselves to third parties;
3. Capital contributed or other capital interest held by each participant;
4. The manner in which the participants kept the books of account;
5. The sharing of losses (rather than profits);
6. Mutual control over the business activities;
7. Restrictions placed on each participant; and
8. Whether or not partnership returns were filed.

.05 Creditor-Debtor Relationships Distinguished

Factors likely to influence recognition of a valid debtor-creditor relationship include:

1. Legally required repayments made with interest, which are relatively certain, suggest debt is present; in contrast, equity contributions are subject to the risks of business activity;[79]
2. The existence of a written agreement or evidence of indebtedness;[80]
3. Whether a prudent third-party lender would make the same loan to a "debtor" under similar circumstances;[81]
4. The extent of the role of the "creditor" in management;
5. The possibility of an underlying intent to profit from the activity other than by merely receiving interest;
6. The testimony from outside parties with regard to any intention to act as creditor and debtor.

Although the practice of issuing equity participation loans has traditionally been used as one method of financing real estate acquisitions, it has also been used in other lending arrangements. In equity participation loans, lenders seek compensation by sharing in the profits of an undertaking they finance. This "equity kicker" is typically used for the purpose of making the loan a feasible undertaking for both the lender (possible additional interest) and the borrower (below-market fixed financing).[82] The borrower should consider how much control to give the lender. If the lender can exercise excessive control, then the lending arrangement may be recharacterized as a partnership.

.06 Lessor-Lessee Relationships Distinguished

Lessor-lessee relationships pose problems similar to that of creditor-debtor arrangements; if the lessor retains too much control over the operation of an active trade or business, a partnership is likely to arise. This is especially true when a lessor has management authority, such as the right to approve business decisions.[83]

---

[79] See E.C. Hartman v. Commr., 17 TCM 1020, Dec. 23,271(M), TC Memo. 1958-206.

[80] See E. Mayer v. Commr., 13 TCM 391, Dec. 20,281(M), TC Memo. 1954-14.

[81] See Astoria Marine Construction Co. v. Commr., 4 TCM 278 Dec. 14,438(M), TC Memo. 1945.

[82] The profit share is treated as interest if a true debtor-creditor relationship exists.

[83] See D.G. Haley v. Commr., CA-5, 53-1 USTC ¶ 9350, 203 F2d 815, rev'g and rem'g 16 TC 1509, Dec. 18,408 (1951), Acq., 1952-1 CB 2.

However, merely sharing in gross receipts or profits derived from leased property in accordance with a leasing agreement will not ordinarily create a partnership for tax purposes.[84] A lessor will run the risk of being deemed a partner, however, in a situation when profits which are to be shared are retained by a lessee and not distributed until requested by the lessor. This relationship may become particularly susceptible to scrutiny when the lessor uses the cash method of accounting and the lessee uses the accrual method. In addition, if the landlord shares a risk of loss from the operation of the tenant's business other than nonpayment of rent, the arrangement suggests a partnership agreement.[85]

---

[84] *See* Reg. §§ 301.7701-3(a) and 1.761-1(a).

[85] *But see Myra Foundation*, CA-8, 67-2 USTC ¶ 9617, 382 F2d 107.

¶106.06

Chapter 2

Partnership Formation and Computation of Partner Basis

¶ 201 Introduction

When property is transferred to a partnership in exchange for a partnership interest, Code Sec. 721 and related provisions generally provide that any gain or loss on the transfer is not recognized. The application of these nonrecognition rules is discussed in this chapter.

¶ 202 General Rule: Contribution of Property Is Treated as a Tax-Free Exchange of Property for a Partnership Interest

Code Sec. 721 provides that if property is contributed to a partnership in exchange for an interest in that partnership, gain or loss is not recognized. This is the result regardless of whether the contribution is made to the partnership upon formation or at a later date. Also, unlike contributions to corporations (where 80-percent control is required after the contribution to get tax-free treatment), control by the contributors is not an issue.

> **S Corporation Observation:** Although the tax treatment of S corporations is like that of partnerships in many ways, contributions to an S corporation in exchange for stock are taxable unless shareholders owning 80 percent or more of the outstanding stock make contributions to the S corporation in the same transaction.[1]

.01 Basis of Partner's Partnership Interest and Partnership's Property

In keeping with the general pattern of nonrecognition provisions, Code Sec. 722 requires that the partner take an "exchanged basis" in the partnership interest,

---

[1] Code Sec. 351.

equal to the combined bases of the contributed properties.[2] As one would expect in an arms-length transaction, the value of the partnership interest received will usually approximate the contributed properties' combined values. If the partnership interest is later sold for its fair market value, the partner will then theoretically recognize gain or loss in approximately the amount not taxed on the original exchange.

Under Code Sec. 723, the partnership takes a "transferred basis" in the contributed property equal to the contributing partner's basis.[3] If the partnership later sells the property and recognizes the deferred gain or loss, under Code Sec. 704(c) the original gain or loss, to the extent recognized by the partnership, will be allocated to the partner who originally contributed the property. The recognition of this deferred gain or loss by the contributing partner will increase or decrease, respectively, his or her basis in the partnership interest by an equal amount.[4] Therefore, if the contributing partner sells his partnership interest after the partnership sells the contributed property, the gain or loss recognized on the sale of the partnership interest will not reflect the gain or loss built into the contributed property.

> *Example 2-1:* Cynthia contributes two parcels of land to a partnership in exchange for a 25-percent interest in the partnership. Parcel A has a fair market value of $100,000 and a basis to Cynthia of $40,000. Parcel B has a fair market value of $150,000 and a basis to Cynthia of $200,000. Cynthia's initial basis in her partnership interest is the sum of the bases of the contributed properties, $40,000 + $200,000 = $240,000. The bases of the parcels of land to the partnership will be the same as they were in Cynthia's hands, $40,000 and $200,000 for Parcels A and B, respectively. If Parcel A is later sold for $120,000, the partnership will recognize a gain of $120,000 – $40,000 = $80,000. Cynthia's precontribution gain of $60,000 ($100,000 – $40,000) will be completely allocated to her under Code Sec. 704(c). The additional $20,000 of gain recognized on the sale will be allocated according to the profit sharing ratios of the partners, so Cynthia will be allocated 25 percent of it, or $5,000. Her total recognized gain from the partnership's sale of the property would be $65,000. Her basis in her partnership interest will be increased by this $65,000 of gain recognized by her. If Parcel A is sold for only $90,000, the partnership will recognize only $50,000 ($90,000 – $40,000) of gain, and Cynthia will be allocated all of it.
>
> The same rules apply for losses. If the partnership sells Parcel B for $110,000, the partnership will recognize a loss of $90,000, and Cynthia's share will be the $50,000 precontribution loss plus $10,000 (her 25-percent share of the $40,000 remainder of the loss).

This system is designed to ensure that gain or loss deferred under Code Sec. 721 upon the contribution of property to the partnership is ultimately recognized by

---

[2] Code Sec. 7701(a)(44).

[3] Code Sec. 7701(a)(43).

[4] In the case of a C corporation there is always a double taxation of any appreciation. This result will occur in the context of partnership taxation only where the partner sells his or her partnership interest before the partnership sells the property and there is no Code Sec. 754 election in effect.

the contributor-partner, either when the partnership disposes of the contributed property or when the partner disposes of the partnership interest, but not both. The partnership must take care, however, to insure that this gain is not recognized twice. For example, if the partner sells his or her interest in the partnership before the partnership disposes of the contributed property, he or she will, in effect, recognize the built-in gain or loss at that time. If the partnership does not take preventative action by making a Code Sec. 754 election, it will recognize the same gain or loss again when it subsequently disposes of the contributed property.[5] The Code Sec. 754 election allows the partnership to adjust its basis in its assets (under Code Sec. 743(b)) to reflect the gain or loss recognized by the contributor-partner on the sale of his or her partnership interest.

> *Example 2-2:* Suppose that Wayne contributed Parcel M (FMV = $100,000, basis = $40,000) to a partnership in exchange for a 25-percent interest in the partnership, and he later sells his partnership interest for $110,000. If his basis in his partnership interest is still $40,000, he will have a gain of $70,000 on the sale of the partnership interest. This gain, in an economic sense, can be thought of as coming from the precontribution appreciation of Parcel M and Wayne's share of the postcontribution appreciation in all of the partnership assets. However, if the partnership later sells Parcel M for $100,000, the $60,000 of precontribution gain in Parcel M will have been recognized twice, once when Wayne sold the partnership interest, and once when Parcel M was sold. To avoid this problem, if a Code Sec. 754 election is in effect, the basis of Parcel M is stepped up by $60,000 (assuming its FMV is still $100,000) on Wayne's sale of the partnership interest.

The objective of the partnership taxation rules is that income or loss generated at the entity level is to be taxed only once and at the partner level. Some of the simplest of these rules are the Code Sec. 705 basis adjustments. A partner's basis in his or her interest is increased by the partner's share of taxed income so that when the partner sells his or her interest or the partnership distributes the previously taxed income the partner is not taxed again. The partner's partnership interest basis is also increased by his or her share of tax exempt income so that the accumulated tax exempt income (which will increase the underlying assets, and thus the value, of the partnership interest) is not taxed when the interest is sold or the partnership makes distributions to him or her. Likewise, nondeductible non-capitalized expenditures (for example, fines or most political contributions) reduce the basis of the partnership interest. The spent funds have reduced the value of all of the partners' partnership interests. If the partnership interests' bases were not also reduced, the expenditure would become indirectly deductible because it would increase the loss (or reduce the gain) on the sale of the interests. Lastly, deductible losses or expenses reduce the basis in a partnership interest because otherwise a second loss would arise on the sale of the interest. These basic partner-level adjustments ensure that income and loss are taken into account only once, tax

---

[5] This gain or loss will be allocated to the contributing partner's successor-in-interest (the partner who purchased his or her interest) under Code Sec. 704(c).

exempt interest remains untaxed, and nondeductible expenditures remain undeducted.

> *Example 2-3:* Patrice has a 30-percent interest in a partnership that has ordinary income of $60,000 and tax-exempt interest of $10,000 during the year. If her basis in the partnership interest at the beginning of the year was $200,000, her basis at the end of the year would be $221,000 ($200,000 + .3($60,000 + $10,000)). During the next year the partnership has a $70,000 loss and a $20,000 nondeductible expense. At the end of that year her basis in the partnership interest would be $194,000 [$221,000 − .3($70,000 + $20,000)].

> *S Corporation Observation:* It is commonly said that S corporations are corporations taxed like partnerships. This statement is true only as an approximate general comparison with a C corporation, but this statement is literally the situation with respect to basis adjustments to the shareholder's stock for the S corporation's income or loss. The S corporation rules are simply a cross reference to the partnership rules.[6]

At a partnership's formation, the total of the partnership's basis in its properties (generally referred to as "the inside basis") will equal the total of the partners' bases in their partnership interests (generally referred to as "the outside basis"). This is because each partner's basis in his or her partnership interest is equal to the partnership's basis in the assets a partner contributed. Also, the partnership's basis in the assets is carried over from and equal to the partners' former basis in the assets. Therefore, both the aggregate basis of the partnership interests to the partners and the aggregate basis of the assets to the partnership are derived from the same source and are equal.

Many events can cause the inside/outside basis equality to terminate. An example is the sale of a partnership interest when, absent a Code Sec. 754 election by the partnership, the partnership's total basis in all its assets (the inside basis) remains unchanged but the aggregate outside basis is changed by the difference between the new and old partner's bases in the partnership interest. This change will usually equal the seller's gain or loss on the sale. However, if there is a Code Sec. 754 election in effect, the equality between inside and outside basis normally continues even though there is a sale (or liquidation) of one of the interests in the partnership.

> *Example 2-4:* Suppose that Juan contributed Parcel Z (FMV = $200,000, basis = $50,000) to a partnership in exchange for a 25-percent interest in the partnership, and he later sells his partnership interest for $200,000. If his basis in his partnership interest is still $50,000, he will have a gain of $150,000 on the sale of the partnership interest. The outside basis of the purchaser of Juan's interest will be $200,000, which is an increase of $150,000 over Juan's outside basis. Without a Code Sec. 754 election, the inside bases of all of the assets will remain the same, and the sale of Juan's interest will have created a difference between the partnership's outside and inside bases. If a Code Sec. 754 election is in effect the basis of Parcel Z is stepped up by $150,000 (assuming its FMV is

---

[6] Code Sec. 1367(a).

still $200,000) on Juan's sale of the partnership interest, and the inside and outside bases will remain equal.

Example 2-5: *Inside/outside basis continuing equality.* Upon formation of a partnership, the partners make the following contributions:

Partner	*Asset*	*FMV*	*Tax Basis*	*Built-In Gain (Loss)*
Kathleen	Cash	$100	$100	$ 0
Heather	Blackacre	200	300	(100)
Anne	Whiteacre	300	150	150
		$600	$550	$50

The partnership has a total initial basis in these assets of $550. After the contribution, the partnership's books of account used in computing taxable income are initially as follows:

Assets	*Tax (Inside) Basis*
Cash	$100
Blackacre	300
Whiteacre	150
	$550

Partners' Tax Bases	*Outside Basis* *
Kathleen	$100
Heather	300
Anne	150
	$550

*If the partnerships had liabilities, each partner's outside basis would be increased by their share of the liabilities.

The partners' outside bases can be incorrectly confused with capital accounts kept according to financial accounting standards. The latter accounts are frequently referred to as "book capital accounts." The partnership's financial accounting books, including book capital accounts, are used in calculating its economic performance. These accounts have initial entries reflecting the *fair market value* of contributions. This allows the partnership to credit each partner with the value of his or her contribution on its financial accounting books. It also requires the partnership to account to the partners for the *value* of the contributions received.

The partnership's initial "book accounting" balance sheet appears as follows:

Assets	Book Value
Cash	$100
Blackacre	200
Whiteacre	300
	$600

Capital Accounts	
Kathleen	$100
Heather	200
Anne	300
	$600

Note that assets are recorded at different amounts for book and tax purposes, and "book" capital accounts will be different from the partners' outside bases, as follows:

Comparison of Outside Basis and
Book Capital Accounts

Partner	Book Capital Account	Outside Basis
Kathleen	$100	$100
Heather	200	300
Anne	300	150
	$600	$550

During the first year, the partnership has the following items of cash receipts and expenses which arise from the only partnership activities and there are no other items of income or expense:

Gross Receipts	$900
Expenses	(600)
Net Income	$300

Assuming that the partnership agreement calls for an equal division of partnership profits, the book accounting balance sheet at the end of the first year appears as follows:

Assets	*Book Value*
Cash	$400
Blackacre	200
Whiteacre	300
	$900

Capital Accounts	
Kathleen	$200
Heather	300
Anne	400
	$900

If the partnership is liquidated on the first day of year two and its assets have market values equaling their book values, each partner can expect to receive cash or property with a value equaling his or her ending book capital account.

The year-end inside and outside bases appear as follows:

Assets	*Tax (Inside) Basis*
Cash	$400
Blackacre	300
Whiteacre	150
	$850

Partners' Tax Bases	*Outside Basis*
Kathleen	$200
Heather	400
Anne	250
	$850

In the examples above the aggregate tax basis of the assets ($550) started out equal to the aggregate bases of the partnership interests. This equality is continued after the first year of income. Three hundred dollars of net income increases both aggregate inside and outside basis to $850.

> **Example 2-6:** *Inside/outside basis inequality after sale of a partnership interest.* If in the above example Anne sells her partnership interest at the end of Year 1 to Dale for its value of $400, Anne has $150 in gain and Dale has a basis in the interest of $400.

Assets	Tax (Inside) Basis
Cash..	$400
Blackacre.....................................	300
Whiteacre	150
	$850

Partners' Tax Bases	Outside Basis
Kathleen	$200
Heather	400
Dale..	400
	$1,000

Anne's $150 gain from the sale of her partnership interest represents only her share of the partnership's untaxed net appreciation in Whiteacre and Blackacre. Anne's $100 share of the partnership's $300 first year income is not taxed again at the time of the sale because Anne's $100 partnership basis increase offsets $100 of sales price.

After Anne's sale of her interest to Dale, the ABD partnership's aggregate inside basis of $850 is $150 less than the aggregate outside basis of $1,000. This disparity can cause the net tax results of its operations to exceed what would be the result if the partnership were credited with a full $1,000 basis in its assets.

If the partnership makes a Code Sec. 754 election, aggregate inside and outside basis will become equal and the partnership's taxable income will reflect the true taxable income of the partners. If a Code Sec. 754 election is not made, the partnership's net income for tax purposes will not reflect the partners' true tax investment in the assets. However, in the absence of a Code Sec. 754 election, Code Sec. 704(c)'s rules will, under some circumstances, produce a result similar to a Code Sec. 754 election for an incoming partner by requiring offsetting adjustments for the continuing partners.

Example 2-7: *Effect on income allocation of built-in gain upon entry of a new partner by way of a cash contribution.* The PLS Partnership, which has been in operation for a few years, was capitalized with cash contributions by Pam, Larry and Simon. Its current balance sheet is as follows:

Assets	Tax (Inside) Basis	FMV
Cash	$350	$350
Blackacre	70	250
Whiteacre	150	300
	$570	$900

Assets	Tax (Inside) Basis	FMV
Partners' Tax Bases		**Outside Basis**
Pam		$190
Larry		190
Simon..		190
		$570

Aggregate inside and outside basis are both $570.

Allan is admitted as an equal partner for a contribution of $300. Whether or not there is a Code Sec. 754 election in effect, the resulting partnership balance sheet is as follows:

Assets	Tax (Inside) Basis	FMV
Cash	$650	$650
Blackacre	70	250
Whiteacre	150	300
	$870	*$1,200*

Partners' Tax Bases	Outside Basis
Pam	$190
Larry	190
Simon..	190
Allan...	300
	$870

The entry of Allan as a new partner through a cash contribution has not affected the equality between inside and outside basis. However, if Whiteacre is sold for $300, the partnership has taxable gain of $150. A Code Sec. 743(b) adjustment is available only on the entry of a new partner by purchase or inheritance. Under Code Sec. 704(b), the partnership must allocate $150 to the continuing partners and zero to Allan (a so-called "reverse Code Sec. 704(c)" allocation).[7]

S Corporation Observation: When there is a purchase of stock in an S corporation or entry of a new shareholder through a contribution to the corporation, there is no mechanism to adjust the S corporation's basis in its assets or allocate its income to reflect the purchase price. There is also no Code Sec. 704(c) type income allocation method which taxes the built-in gain of the assets to the continuing shareholders and not the new shareholder.

Substantial Built-in Loss. If the assets of a partnership have a substantial built-in loss (greater than $250,000), the partnership will essentially be treated as if a Code Sec. 754 election is in effect if an interest in the partnership is sold.[8]

---

[7] Reg. § 1.704-1(b)(4)(i) and (b)(5), Ex. 14 and 18.   [8] Code Sec. 743(d)(1).

.02 Holding Period of a Partner's Partnership Interest and a Partnership's Property

A partner must add ("tack") the holding period of contributed capital and Code Sec. 1231 assets to the holding period of his or her partnership interest received in exchange for contributing such assets.[9] A partnership interest received for contributions of other property starts the day after it is received. The partnership interest will, therefore, have a fragmented holding period when a combination of assets is contributed. The fraction of the partnership interest any particular holding period relates to is determined by the relative fair market value of the asset the holding period was associated with.[10] The partnership includes in its holding period the contributor's holding period for all types of contributed assets.

> **Example 2-8:** Jesse contributed $10,000 cash, land worth $15,000 (basis = $10,000, held more than a year), and inventory worth $15,000 (basis = $16,000) to a partnership in exchange for a 25% partnership interest. 37.5% (15/40) of Jesse's partnership interest will have a carryover holding period from the land, and the other 62.5% of the holding period will begin the day after the contribution.

¶ 203 Depreciation Methods

The general rule under Code Sec. 721 is that no gain or loss is recognized on property transferred to a partnership in exchange for a partnership interest. When depreciable property is contributed in a tax-free exchange, the partnership is treated as if it stepped into the transferor partner's shoes. The partnership must use the transferor's depreciation method and remaining depreciable life.

If a partner recognizes gain on a contribution of encumbered property to a partnership because of net debt relief in excess of the basis of the contributed property, absent a Code Sec. 754 election in effect for the year of contribution, the partnership's basis in the property is the partner's basis. There is no basis increase allowed to the partnership for the gain recognized by the partner. This is true even though, in effect, the partnership is purchasing a portion of the asset through assumption of the partner's debt.

> **Observation:** If the partners agree that the basis to the partnership should reflect the debt, they should consider a sale to the partnership.

If there is a Code Sec. 754 election in effect to the extent that a partner's net debt relief causes gain to be recognized on the contribution, and the property's basis in the partnership's hands exceeds its basis in the transferor's hands, the increase in basis is treated by the partnership as a separate asset placed in service on the date of contribution.

> **Example 2-9:** Carla Smith contributed depreciable residential real property purchased in 1990 to the QRS partnership in exchange for a 10-percent interest therein. Due to excessive debt, she recognized a $50,000 gain on the transfer (gain on the contribution of encumbered property is covered in the

---

[9] Code Sec. 1223(1).   [10] Reg. § 1.1223-3(b)(1).

next section). The original cost of the property, acquired in January 1990, was $300,000. Carla assigned $25,000 of this cost to the land, and $275,000 to the building. She transferred the property to the partnership on May 1, 2000. Since the property is 27.5-year property, Carla's depreciation deductions have been $10,000 per year (with the exception of 1990 in which she was allowed only 11.5/12 of this amount). The partnership will take a carryover basis in the property and will continue to depreciate it over the remaining 17.5 years of its depreciable life. For 2000, Carla will claim 4/12 of the deduction ($3,333), and the partnership will claim 8/12 ($6,667). If the partnership has a Code Sec. 754 election in effect, and this is the partnership's only capital or Code Sec. 1231 asset, it will increase its basis in this property by $50,000 (the amount of gain recognized by Carla on the transfer). This increase will be treated as newly acquired property (acquired May 1, 2000) and will be depreciated, straight-line, over 27.5 years beginning on that date.

When the partnership eventually sells the contributed property, it may be required to recapture depreciation deductions.[11] To the extent the gain on a subsequent sale represents the difference between the fair market value of the Code Sec. 1245 property and the adjusted tax basis at the time of contribution, that gain (including the recapture) will be allocated to the contributing partner under Code Sec. 704(c).

¶ 204 Contributions of Encumbered Property

The results to the partners and the partnership itself described above are affected if the contributed property is encumbered by liabilities. In order to determine the effect on the partners, both the contributing partner and the other partners should treat the contribution of encumbered property as consisting of two separate successive steps:

1. First, the existence of the debt is ignored and the results of the contribution are analyzed as described above—the effect to the contributing partner is an increased basis for his or her partnership interest in the amount of the contributed property's basis. This will have no effect on the outside bases of the other partners.

2. Second, the debt is then taken into account. Each partner has a deemed cash contribution or distribution depending upon whether the total of the liabilities transferred to the partnership results in a net increase or a decrease in his or her share of the liabilities owed by the partnership.[12] Partners with deemed cash contributions will increase their basis by this deemed amount,[13] and partners with deemed cash distributions will reduce their basis by the amount of this deemed distribution.[14] If any partner has a deemed distribution in excess of his or her basis, as determined in step (1) above, such excess is reported as gain from the sale of a partnership

---

[11] Reg. §§ 1.1245-2(c)(2) and 1.1250-3(c)(3).

[12] *See* Code Sec. 752.

[13] *See* Code Sec. 722.

[14] Code Secs. 705(a) and 733.

interest.[15] This gain is capital gain in most instances. However, Code Sec. 751(b) may apply and result in part or all of the gain being recognized as ordinary income.

When encumbered property is contributed to a partnership and the partnership agrees to become primarily liable for paying the debt, the contributing partner's nonpartnership-related liabilities for which he or she is directly responsible decrease by the amount of such debt. This debt relief is treated as a cash distribution from the partnership. In taking over this liability, however, the partnership has a simultaneous increase in its total indebtedness by the same amount. When a partnership's total debt increases, then each partner is treated as if each made a cash contribution to the partnership to the extent of his or her share of that new debt.

Example 2-10: *C* is invited to join the AB equal general partnership. Before *C* is admitted, the partnership's balance sheets are as follows:

AB Partnership

Assets	Tax Basis	FMV
Cash	$500	$500
Stock	50	50
Greenacre	550	550
	$1,100	$1,100
Liabilities	$ 0	$ 0
Capital		
A	$550	$550
B	550	550
	$1,100	$1,100

A and *B* each have a tax basis in their partnership interests of $550. *C* contributes Purpleacre to the partnership, which has a tax basis and value of $850, and is made an equal one-third partner in capital, profits, and losses. The property is encumbered by a recourse indebtedness of $300, which the partnership assumes. When analyzing the tax consequences of this contribution of encumbered property, the first step is to account for the property contribution as if there were no debt relief. The results are as follows:

---

[15] Code Sec. 731(a).

¶204

ABC Partnership

Assets	Tax Basis	FMV
Cash	$500	$500
Stock	50	50
Greenacre	550	550
Purpleacre	850	850
	$1,950	$1,950
Liabilities	$ 0	$ 0
Capital		
A	$550	$550
B	550	550
C	850	850
	$1,950	$1,950

A and B continue to have a $550 basis in their partnership interests and C's partnership interest basis is $850. The debt is then taken into account in the second step as follows:

ABC Partnership

Assets	Tax Basis	FMV
Cash	$500	$500
Stock	50	50
Greenacre	550	550
Purpleacre	850	850
	$1,950	$1,950
Liabilities	$300	$300
Capital		
A	$550	$550
B	550	550
C	550	550
	$1,950	$1,950

A and B are each treated as if they made a $100 cash contribution and their bases are each increased from $550 to $650 (note that this is equal to their tax capital accounts plus one-third of the debt). *C* is treated as if he received a $300 cash distribution and made a $100 cash contribution, for a net cash distribution of $200 and his basis in his partnership interest is reduced from $850 to $650. Also, his capital account now reflects the $550 net book value of his contribution.

Computing the amount of the contributing partner's deemed cash distribution is relatively straightforward. It is the gross amount of debt shifted from the partner to the partnership. It is immaterial whether the contributing partner remains personally liable for repayment on the partnership's default or whether the partnership itself becomes personally liable. Secured debt is treated as the obligation of the securing property's owner.[16]

Computing the offsetting deemed cash contribution is more involved. An increase in a partner's share of partnership liabilities is treated as a cash contribution. This requires a comparison of the partner's share of partnership liabilities before the partnership acquired the new indebtedness to his or her share afterward. Naturally, if the contributing partner was not a member of the partnership before the contribution of the encumbered property, his or her share of the partnership's debt is zero immediately before the contribution. Partnership recourse and nonrecourse liabilities are allocated among the partners according to separate sets of rules.

> **Form 1065 Tip:** It is often not clear to beginning practitioners, but the preparer of the partnership's tax return does not have the responsibility to compute partner level gain caused by contribution of encumbered property. The contributing partner is responsible for that. The preparer of the partnership's tax return does have the responsibility to determine each partner's share of partnership debt. The contributing partner may use that information, as disclosed on the partnership's K-1s, to find his or her net debt relief (which is treated as a deemed money distribution).

> To do this, the partner contributing the encumbered asset may simply compare his or her share of partnership debt as reported on the K-1 for the year-end immediately prior to the contribution to the share of debt for the year-end of the property contribution. If the partner was not a partner in the previous year, his or her share of debt was zero. If there is an increase, it is a deemed money contribution. This deemed money contribution is offset against the partner's debt taken over by the partnership and any net debt relief is a deemed money distribution. If this deemed money distribution exceeds his basis in the partnership interest, the excess is gain.

When a partner contributes property to a partnership with liabilities sufficiently in excess of basis to trigger gain for the contributor, accounting aberrations arise:

> **Example 2-11:** The ABC equal partnership was originally funded with cash contributions from *A*, *B* and *C*. It holds debt-financed long-term invest-

---

[16] Code Sec. 752(c).

ments in real estate. The partners each have a $400 basis in their partnership interests. Its balance sheets are as follows:

ABC Partnership

Assets	Tax Basis	FMV
Cash	$400	$400
Blackacre	600	700
Whiteacre	200	400
	$1,200	$1,500

Liabilities		
(recourse)	$600	$600
A	$200	$300
B	200	300
C	200	300
	$1,200	$1,500

D is admitted to the partnership as a one-fourth equal partner in exchange for a contribution of investment property, Greenacre, with a value of $1,500, a basis of $300, and encumbered by a recourse debt of $1,200, which the partnership assumes. D's results are as follows:

Step 1:

D's basis in his partnership interest under Code Sec. 722.		$300

Step 2:

D's deemed cash distribution	($1,200)	
D's deemed cash contribution	450	
Net deemed cash distribution		(750)
D's basis for his partnership interest		$ 0
D's gain		$450

A, B, and C shares of partnership debt have increased from $200 each to $450 each, increasing their bases in the partnership interests by $250.

The ABCD partnership's balance sheets are as follows:

ABCD Partnership

Assets	Tax Basis	FMV
Cash	$400	$400
Blackacre	600	700
Whiteacre	200	400
Greenacre	300	1,500
	$1,500	$3,000
Liabilities	$1,800	$1,800
Capital		
A	$200	$300
B	200	300
C	200	300
D	(900)	300
	$1,500	$3,000

The aggregate basis of the ABCD partnership for its assets (inside basis) is $1,500. The aggregate basis of the partners in their partnership interests is $1,950 (3 × $650 + $0). This is a disparity of $450. When there is such a disparity, the aggregate outside basis is the partner's true tax investment in the partnership's assets. Generally, a Code Sec. 754 adjustment is available when such a disparity occurs. The Code Sec. 754 adjustment will eliminate the disparity. Here, if a Code Sec. 754 election was in effect, the partnership would be allowed to increase its basis in Blackacre, Whiteacre, and Greenacre by a total of $450 under Code Sec. 734(b)(1)(A).

Partner D has a $900 negative balance in his tax capital account. This reflects the excess of the debt encumbering the property he contributed over the tax basis of such property. When added to his share of the partnership's debt, $450, his tax basis in the partnership interest appears to be $(450). Note that this is the amount of gain recognized by D on contribution of the property to the partnership.[17] Partner D's basis in his partnership interest is, however, zero ($300 basis in property contributed − $1,200 net debt relief + $450 gain). This is another example of a situation in which aggregate outside basis will not equal aggregate inside basis after the transaction.

---

[17] Note that if the partnership had a Code Sec. 754 election in effect, it would increase both D's tax capital account and its tax basis in its assets by $450. This would result in a deficit of only $(450) in D's tax capital account; when added to his share of debt, it would yield his correct tax basis in the partnership interest of zero.

S Corporation Observation: Code Sec. 357 governs the contribution of encumbered property to an S corporation. The rules of Code Sec. 357(c) treat debt relief in excess of the basis of contributed property as gain. Unlike the partnership rules discussed above, the shareholder is not allowed to offset debt relief with any share of corporate debt. As a result, if four shareholders each contributed an asset with a zero basis subject to $100 of recourse debt, each has $100 of gain under Code Sec. 357(c). If they had contributed the same assets to an equal, general partnership and their shares of the $400 partnership debt were $100 each, there would be no *net* relief and no deemed money contribution or distribution and therefore no gain.

¶ 205 Effect of Partnership Operations on Basis

A partner is required each year to adjust his or her basis in the partnership interest for the partner's distributive share of the partnership's income or loss.[18] These adjustments are required because of the principle (inherent in flow-through entities) that income and deductions are to be taxed only once.

.01 Income and Loss—Taxable and Tax-Exempt

The basis of a partnership interest is increased by both the taxable and tax-exempt income allocated to the partner. This increase or decrease in basis is the same whether the income or deduction is separately or nonseparately stated. Without this basis increase, this previously taxed income would theoretically increase the value of the partnership, and could in essence be taxed a second time as gain from the sale of the partnership interest when it is eventually sold. Similarly, a basis increase for a partner's share of tax-exempt income is necessary to avoid having the tax-exempt income result in increased gain (or reduced loss) on the sale of the partnership interest. If increased gain or reduced loss were allowed to result from tax-exempt income, the income would effectively no longer be tax-exempt.

The same considerations require the partner to reduce his or her adjusted basis for his or her share of the partnership's losses. If the partner's basis in his or her interest is not reduced for the partner's share of partnership losses, he or she will be allowed a second loss, or at least a reduced gain, on the sale of the partnership (since the partnership assets, and presumably the sale price, would be reduced by the amount of the losses). Similarly, a basis decrease for a partner's share of non-deductible expenses is necessary to avoid having the non-deductible expenses result in increased loss (or reduced gain) on the sale of the partnership interest. If increased loss or reduced gain were allowed to result from tax-exempt income, the income would effectively no longer be tax-exempt.

Under Code Sec. 705(a)(3), a partner's basis in their partnership interest will also be increased for their share of the excess of depletion over the basis of the property subject to depletion. On the other hand, under Reg § 1.199-5(b)(1)(i), a partner's basis will not be affected by the production activities deduction they are allowed to take as a result of partnership activities. The actual activities of the partnership that result in the deduction (domestic production gross receipts,

---

[18] Code Sec. 705(a).

wages, etc.) will have an effect on the partner's basis, but the production activities deduction itself will not.

.02 Contributions and Distributions

Contributions and distributions result in increases and decreases in basis, respectively, so that the changed after tax investment will not result in taxable income or loss if the partnership interest is sold. For example, if money is contributed, the value of the partnership interest is increased by a like amount. If a corresponding basis increase were not made, a subsequent sale of the partnership interest would produce gain as a result of the contribution. It should be noted that changes in a partner's share of liabilities are treated as cash contributions (for increases in their share of liabilities) and cash distributions (for decreases). Such changes will affect the basis of the partner's interest even though the partner might be completely unaware that they are occurring.

> *Comment:* In all cases when downward adjustments to basis are required, the statute expressly provides that basis is not to be reduced below zero. A basis in a partnership interest *never* has a value below zero. While a negative *capital account* is very common, a negative basis is impossible.

The above-described adjustments to the basis of a partnership interest are intended to ensure that (1) a partner's share of taxable income and deductions is taken into account only once, (2) nondeductible expenditures and tax-exempt income remain characterized as such, and (3) distributions of previous contributions and previously taxed income are not taxed. The necessary adjustments can be obtained from the partnership's Form 1065, are relatively simple to perform, and if they are made on a yearly basis, a partner's basis in his or her interest is normally easy to maintain. Each year's adjustments can be made to the previous year's ending basis. Thus, a partner's basis reflects the cumulative effect of all prior required adjustments.

Unfortunately, while the *adjustments* necessary to keep track of a partner's cumulative basis over time can be obtained from the entire series of the partnership's Forms 1065, the value of the basis itself generally cannot be obtained from one year's Form 1065. This is because, while each partner's beginning capital account is disclosed, no partner's beginning basis is disclosed on the Form 1065. In fact, various factors might make it very difficult, and in some cases impossible, for the partnership to keep track of the partner's bases in their partnership interest. When a partnership interest is sold, for example, the partnership might not know the sales price, and therefore might be unaware of the purchaser's beginning basis. In addition, the partners make some elections that affect their basis in the partnership, such as for depletion or intangible drilling costs, at the partner level, and the partnership would have no way of knowing, (or even any interest in finding out) how each partner elected to treat those items. Unfortunately, in a situation when necessary adjustments from one or more years are unavailable, the historical, year-to-year method of maintaining basis can't be used. When the chain of adjustments is broken, another approach is necessary.

Code Sec. 705(b) provides an alternative rule for determining a partner's basis in his or her partnership interest if it is impractical or impossible to apply the foregoing rules, or if the Commissioner reasonably concludes that the result under the alternative rule will not produce a substantially different result.[19] The alternative rule initially consists of determining the partner's basis by reference to the adjusted basis of his or her *pro rata* share of the partnership property. After making certain necessary adjustments,[20] this is the partner's basis for his or her partnership interest. The regulations add that a partner may also determine his or her basis by making certain adjustments to the sum of his or her tax basis capital account and share of the partnership's liabilities.[21] As a general observation on the usefulness of these alternative methods of finding the basis of a partner's interest, note that while they at first appear an attractive theoretical option, they are in practice difficult to use in anything other than a very simple setting. The necessary adjustments can become unmanageable and a tax-basis capital account difficult to compute. See ¶ 1103 for a complete discussion.

> **Example 2-12:** The ABCD equal partnership was originally funded with contributions from *A*, *B*, *C*, and *D*. *A* made a contribution of property with a basis of $60,000, fair market value of $100,000, and subject to a liability of $20,000. The $20,000 liability is the only liability of the partnership, and during the first year the partnership pays off $12,000 of it. In the first year the partnership has $200,000 of business income, $20,000 of long term capital gains, $5,000 of tax-exempt interest, and makes a charitable contribution of $16,000. In addition, the partnership makes a campaign contribution of $1,000 to a candidate for federal office. *A*'s beginning basis will be $60,000 – ($20,000 – $5,000) net debt relief = $45,000.

A's basis at the end of the first year will be:

Beginning basis	$45,000
Share of:	
Ordinary business income	50,000
Long term capital gains	5,000
Tax-exempt interest	1,250
Charitable contribution	(4,000)
Nondeductible campaign contribution	(250)
Decrease in debt	(3,000)
Ending basis	$94,000

¶ 206 Contributions Requiring Special Consideration

As discussed above, Code Sec. 721 provides an exception to the general rule that, when there is an exchange of property, the realized gain or loss resulting from

---

[19] Reg. § 1.705-1(b).

[20] Necessitated, for example, by contributions of appreciated or depreciated property, partnership interest transfers, and property distributions. Reg. § 1.705-1(b).

[21] Reg. § 1.705-1(b), Ex. 3.

the difference between the value of property received and the basis of the property transferred must be reported in the year of the exchange. If Code Sec. 721 applies, the taxation of this realized gain or loss is deferred. Code Sec. 721 also has limited exceptions. When they apply, gain or loss is recognized in the year of contribution. This section discusses some of these exceptions. It also covers contributions that may initially appear to be excluded from the nonrecognition provisions of Code Sec. 721, but in fact qualify for nonrecognition.

.01 Property Subject to Depreciation Recapture

The depreciation recapture provisions generally require that when recapture property is transferred the potential recapture amount is taxed.[22] These sections specifically state that they generally override any other conflicting Internal Revenue Code provision.[23] Therefore, to avoid recapture on a disposition of recapture property, either Code Sec. 1245 or 1250 must specifically make exception for the transfer from the recapture requirement. The applicable provisions do provide that a contribution of recapture property to a partnership will not itself trigger recapture.[24] The partnership succeeds to the potential for recapture. However, if gain is incurred at the time of the transfer (*e.g.*, under Code Sec. 731(a) or 707), some of or all the gain is characterized as depreciation recapture.[25]

Code Sec. 1245 gain on contribution. Generally, capital gain is triggered by Code Sec. 731(a) upon receipt of a deemed cash distribution in excess of the partner's basis in contributed property (including deemed cash contributions under Code Sec. 752(a)).[26] However, if recapture property is involved, at least part of the gain may be recharacterized as ordinary income. The amount realized (hypothetical distribution of cash) is divided between Code Sec. 1245 and non-Sec. 1245 property based on the fair market value of recapture property versus other property contributed. If half the value of the contributed property is recapture property, half the amount realized is allocated to the Code Sec. 1245 property, and the Code Sec. 1245 recapture is calculated accordingly.[27] This provision gives no consideration to whether the liabilities giving rise to the gain recognition are associated with either the recapture or nonrecapture property.[28]

> **Example 2-13:** Taxpayer A contributes land (FMV = $150,000, basis = $20,000) and machinery (FMV = $50,000, original cost = $60,000, accumulated depreciation = $20,000) to the equal ABC Partnership in return for a 1/3 interest. A liability of $150,000 is associated with the land. A will have net debt relief of $100,000 (150,000 – $50,000), for an overall gain of $40,000 (100,000 – ($20,000 + $40,000)). One-fourth ($50,000/$200,000) of the deemed "cash distribution" (net debt relief) will be allocated to the Code Sec. 1245 property, so the deemed cash distribution allocated to the Code Sec. 1245 property will be $25,000 ($100,000 × 1/4). Recapture would be $10,000, the lesser of (1) the

---

[22] Code Secs. 1245(a) and 1250(a).

[23] Code Secs. 1245(d) and 1250(i).

[24] Code Secs. 1245(b)(3) and 1250(d)(3).

[25] Code Sec. 731(a) triggers gain on the contribution of property to the partnership when encumbered property is

contributed and the partner's net debt relief exceeds the contributed property's basis.

[26] Reg. § 1.731-1(a)(3).

[27] Reg. §§ 1.1245-4(c)(1), 1.1245-4(c)(4) Ex. 3, and 1.1250-3(c)(1).

[28] Reg. § 1.1245-4(c).

deemed cash payment, (2) accumulated depreciation, or (3) the unrecognized gain from the Code Sec. 1245 property. The other $30,000 of the gain would be capital gain.

Partnership recognizes Code Sec. 1245 gain. The depreciable property's basis and the depreciation method and recovery period carries over to the new partnership, and the partnership is subject to potential depreciation recapture.[29] When the partnership eventually sells the contributed property, it may be required to recapture depreciation deductions previously claimed either before or after the contribution of such property to the partnership.[30] To the extent the gain on a subsequent sale represents the difference between the fair market value of the Code Sec. 1245 property and the adjusted tax basis at the time of contribution, that gain including the recapture will be allocated to the contributing partner under Code Sec. 704(c).[31]

.02 Accounts Receivable

Accounts receivable of either a cash- or accrual-basis taxpayer are property and may be transferred free of taxation pursuant to Code Sec. 721.[32] The contributor's basis in the accounts receivable will become the partnership's transferred basis in the receivables, and the contributor's adjusted basis in the partnership interest will be derived from this same amount. The partnership will report income if its collections of these receivables exceed their transferred basis. The partnership must allocate this income to the contributor to the extent the value of the accounts receivable exceed their basis at the time of contribution.[33] Any excess of collections over the value of the accounts receivable at the date of contribution may be allocated according to the partnership agreement. However, any income from the accounts receivable allocated to other partners must be reflected in their capital accounts and ultimately distributed to them.

> **Observation:** The contributor need not report all the income from the receivables. Their value at contribution will often be less than their face amount. The partnership agreement can allocate any amount collected above the initial value of the receivables to any partner. This, however, will increase his or her capital account and share of the partnership's assets.

.03 Third-Party Notes Being Reported on the Installment Method

Dispositions of notes being reported on the installment method normally trigger recognition of gain to the holder.[34] Installment obligations, however, are property within the meaning of Code Sec. 721. Therefore, the partner is not required to treat the contribution of such notes to the partnership as a disposition. The partnership will continue to report the gross profit on the installment method.[35] However, to the extent the value of the note exceeds its tax basis at the time of

---

[29] Prop. Reg. § 1.168-5.

[30] Reg. §§ 1.1245-2(c)(2) and 1.1250-3(c)(3).

[31] Reg. § 1.1245-1(e).

[32] See Rev. Rul. 80-198, 1980-2 CB 133. This revenue ruling, like most authority in this area, involves a contribution to a corporation but, due to the similarities the partnership provisions share with the corporate provi-

sions, most practitioners assume that a partnership contribution will receive the same treatment. See also IRS Letter Ruling 8251114 (9-23-82).

[33] Code Sec. 704(c).

[34] Code Sec. 453B.

[35] Reg. §§ 1.721-1(a) and 1.453-9(c)(2).

contribution, gross profit subsequently recognized by the partnership on receipt of payments on the note must be allocated to the contributor.[36] The remainder of the gross profit can be allocated according to the partnership agreement.

.04 Third-Party Notes Not Being Reported on the Installment Method

When a cash-basis taxpayer receives a note that is not being reported on the installment method, the note must be taken into income at its fair market value on the date received. An accrual-basis taxpayer takes the same note into account at its face amount. In either case, the amount reported as income becomes the note's basis and is recovered as payments are received. The later contribution of such note to a partnership, in exchange for a partnership interest, is not a taxable event. The note's remaining basis will become both part of the contributor's basis in his or her partnership interest and the partnership's basis in the note. If the subsequent collections on the note exceed its transferred basis, then the partnership will incur taxable income. This income must be allocated to the contributor to the extent that the note's value exceeded its basis at the time of its contribution to the partnership.

> **S Corporation Observation:** Because there is no Code Sec. 704(c) counterpart in the S corporation rules, a contribution of accounts receivable, notes receivable, or other appreciated assets will result in all the shareholders reporting a portion of the pre-contribution built-in gain inherent in the contributed property. On the other hand, a contribution of depreciated assets allows all the shareholders to share in the pre-contribution built-in loss.

.05 Partner's Personal Obligations

The prevailing view has been that a partner's contribution of his or her own personal obligation produces neither additional basis in his or her partnership interest nor an increased capital account.[37] The regulations specifically provide that for book capital accounting purposes this is true whether or not it is secured by property or a letter of credit. The obligation is treated as a promise to provide funds in the future. It does not constitute a current contribution of property or money within the meaning of Code Sec. 721.[38]

A controversial Ninth Circuit Court of Appeals case could possibly cast some doubts about the view that no basis arises from a contribution of a partner's own note to a partnership.[39] The case specifically involved a contribution of property with liabilities in excess of basis to a corporation. The Commissioner issued a deficiency notice based on Code Sec. 357(c), which in the corporate context requires the contributing shareholder to report gain to the extent of the excess of the liabilities assumed by the corporation over the basis of the assets contributed by the shareholder. However, the shareholder had also contributed his own note to

---

[36] Code Sec. 704(c).

[37] Leonard O. Oden, TC Memo 1981-184; Linda N. Borrell, TC Memo 1989-251.

[38] The regulations specifically provide that the partner will receive an increase in his or her capital account only when the partner pays the note or the note is sold. Reg. § 1.704-1(b)(2)(iv)(d)(2). If a personal note did constitute property for purposes of Code Sec. 721, the prevailing view is that the result would be similar because the note

would have a zero basis in the hands of the maker. If the regulation's approach to a partner's contribution of his or her own note to a partnership is followed for basis and gain or loss purposes, a partner has a zero basis in the note and this will carry over to the partnership upon contribution. The Partner's basis in his or her partnership interest will be increased by the same amount—zero.

[39] D.J. Peracchi v. Commr., CA-9, 98-1 USTC ¶ 50,374, 143 F3d 487.

the corporation for which he claimed he had a fair market value basis. This would have avoided the application of Code Sec. 357(c). The court held for the taxpayer but *in dicta* indicated that its holding would not apply to S corporations and partnerships.

.06 Personal-Use Property

A partner's contribution of property which, before the contribution, was not considered investment or business property also receives nonrecognition treatment.

Partnership's basis. When property formerly used by the partner for personal purposes is converted to business or investment use by the partnership, the partnership takes the lower of the property's fair market value at the time of contribution, or the contributing partner's adjusted basis, as its basis for computing depreciation.[40] Although there is no authority directly on point, the partnership's basis for loss computations related to the property should be the lower of fair market value or the partner's basis at the time of contribution. For gain computations, the partnership would use the partner's basis plus or minus the basis adjustments attributable to the partnership ownership. There may be situations where using the gain basis produces a loss and the loss basis produces a gain. In such cases, the partnership will report neither gain nor loss.

Partner's basis. Although there is no authority directly on point concerning the partner's computation of loss on the sale of his or her partnership interest, the partner's basis in his or her partnership interest should likewise not include the amount by which the contributed property's basis exceeded its value at the time of contribution. For purposes of limiting a partner's deductible share of partnership loss to the adjusted basis of his or her partnership interest,[41] the exchanged basis should be limited to fair market value. With respect to the computation of gain, both the partner's basis in his or her interest and the partnership's basis in its assets include the contributor's entire basis. For purposes of computing gain on receipt of money distributions in excess of a partner's basis in his or her partnership interest,[42] the exchanged basis should be a carryover basis without reference to the contributed property's fair market value.

.07 Investment Partnerships

While Code Sec. 721(a) provides the general rule that no gain or loss is recognized on the contribution of property to a partnership, an exception found in Code Sec. 721(b) provides that contributions to investment partnerships are ineligible for nonrecognition treatment. The intent of Code Sec. 721(b) is to tax partnership contributions that are intended to achieve (or have the effect of achieving) investment diversification for the contributing partners.[43] The partnership rule runs parallel to a similar rule for corporations.[44]

---

[40] *L.Y.S. Au v. Commr.*, 40 TC 264, Dec. 26,110 (1964), aff'd per curiam, CA-9, 64-1 USTC ¶ 9447, 330 F2d 1008.

[41] Code Sec. 704(d).

[42] Code Sec. 731(a).

[43] S. Rep. No. 938, 94th Cong., 2d Sess., pt 2, at 43, 44 (1976).

[44] Code Sec. 351(e).

Asset ownership test. A partnership (general, limited, or an LLC) is not classified as an "investment company partnership" unless nonidentical assets are contributed, and after the contributions, more than 80 percent of the value of the assets is held for investment and consists of (among other possible investments):

- Money (if to be used for investing purposes);
- Stocks and other equity interests in a corporation;
- Evidences of indebtedness;
- Options, forward or future contracts; or
- Other assets considered investments under Code Sec. 351(e)(1).[45]

Diversification test. There also must be meaningful diversification for the investment company rule to come into play. In IRS Letter Ruling 9608026,[46] a limited partnership among related parties was formed. One partner contributed publicly traded securities with significant value, while the others contributed cash worth less than one percent of the total value of the contributions. The partner contributing the securities did not diversify his portfolio, because he was the only significant contributor. Since diversification cannot be achieved without at least two significant contributors, Code Sec. 721(b) did not apply.[47]

Note that if all contributing partners contribute diversified portfolios of stock and securities, Code Sec. 721(b) should *not* apply. This is because diversification is already present *before* the contributions. Accordingly, the act of contributing a diversified portfolio of investment assets to a partnership does not result in diversification for the contributing partners.[48]

Gain but not loss. If appreciated property is contributed to an investment company partnership, the gain is recognized by the partner upon contribution. However, the general nonrecognition rule still applies to property which has declined in value. The character of any gain recognized under this rule is determined by reference to the character and holding period of such property in the partner's hands just prior to the contribution.

> *Example 2-14:* Sam Talangbayan owns TGM Company common stock (traded on the NYSE). He paid $10,000 for the stock, which is currently valued at $50,000. Tom Mitchell owns MGT Company preferred stock and convertible debentures (traded on the NASDAQ). He paid $25,000 for the convertible debentures and $10,000 for the preferred stock. The stock and debentures have a $50,000 combined value. Sam and Tom decide to diversify their investment risks associated with these investments, so they each contribute their securities to TGMGT Partners (an equal general partnership).
>
> Because TGMGT is an investment company, upon contribution Sam must recognize gain of $40,000 and Tom must recognize gain of $15,000. Sam's initial basis in his partnership interest is $50,000, as is Tom's.[49] The partner-

---

[45] Code Sec. 721(b); Reg. § 1.351-1(c)(1).
[46] IRS Letter Ruling 9608026 (11-21-95).
[47] *See also* Reg. § 1.351-1(c)(5).

[48] Reg. § 1.351-1(c)(6).
[49] Code Sec. 722.

ship's basis in the securities is equal to their fair market value on the contribution date, and the partnership's holding period begins on that date.[50]

.08 Suspended Losses

Property contributed to a partnership may have related losses that were not deductible by the contributing partner because of statutory limitations. For example, the losses could have been suspended because of the Code Sec. 465 at-risk rules or the Code Sec. 469 passive activity rules. Any losses suspended by Code Secs. 465 or 469 prior to the contribution of the related activity remain with the contributing partner and are not transferred to the partnership.[51] If the activity produces income in the partnership's hands, it will be either passive income or "income from a former passive activity" which can be offset by any of the activity's unused passive activity deductions from a prior year.[52] All income generated by the activity on the partnership's hands results in an additional at-risk amount.

---

[50] Code Sec. 723.
[51] Prop. Reg. § 1.465-67(b); Code Sec. 469(g).
[52] Code Sec. 469(f).

Chapter 3

Receipt of a Partnership Interest for Services

¶ 301   Introduction
¶ 302   Capital Interest Received
¶ 303   Profit Interest Received
¶ 304   Proposed Regulations

¶ 301 Introduction

The nonrecognition provisions that apply to the receipt of a partnership interest in exchange for a property contribution do not apply to one who receives a partnership interest in exchange for services. The rules governing both the service partner's and the partnership's results are relatively well defined to the extent that the service partner gets an interest in the partnership's capital. The law governing the receipt of a future profits interest is less clear cut.[1]

A partner is treated as receiving a partnership interest in capital if upon its receipt he or she would have "an interest that would give the holder a share of the proceeds if the partnership's assets were sold at fair market value and the proceeds were distributed in a complete liquidation of the partnership."[2] A profits interest is a share in the results of future operating results and future appreciation in the partnership's assets.

Upon receipt of an interest in partnership capital in exchange for services, the service partner must recognize income equal to the fair market value of the partnership interest received. Note that fair market value is usually not the same as the amount credited to the partner's tax basis capital account in the partnership's books. Also note that valuation discounts for lack of control and marketability should be considered.

> **Observation:** Practitioners have often observed that the IRS position may overstate the value of the partnership interest. This is because for a partner there are restrictions on control over his or her share of the assets and the partner's partnership interest is less marketable than simply having separate

---

[1] The Treasury Department has provided some guidance in this area with Prop. Reg. § 1.721-1(b) and Prop. Reg. § 1.83-3(l), explained in Notice 2005-43, 2005-24 IRB 1221. These Proposed Regulations are discussed later in this chapter, but will not be effective until their finalization and publication in the Federal Register. As of this writing they have not yet been finalized.

[2] Rev. Proc. 93-27, 1993-2 CB 43.

ownership of property having a value equal to his or her share of the cash value of the assets.

¶ 302 Capital Interest Received

.01 Results to Service Partner

An interest in capital that vests in the service partner immediately is valued and treated as personal service income on the date of receipt.[3] For this purpose, an interest is vested if it either is transferable or it is not subject to a substantial risk of forfeiture. If the partnership interest received by the service partner does not vest immediately, but rather is contingent, for example, upon the occurrence of future events (*e.g.*, fully leasing a vacant office building, the partnership reaching a specified level of profitability, etc.) and is not transferable until that date, then the service partner recognizes no income with regard to receipt of the partnership interest until it is vested. At that time, the service partner will recognize compensation income equal to the value of the partnership interest received, as measured at the vesting date.

The service partner may elect, under Code Sec. 83(b), to ignore the contingency associated with receipt of the partnership interest and include the partnership interest in income when initially received and measured at its initial value. Partners making this election cannot take into account the risk of forfeiture or lack of transferability in valuing the interest. Moreover, if the interest is subsequently forfeited, no deduction for the loss will be allowed to such partners even though they have basis in the now forfeited interest[4] (in an amount equal to the amount previously included in income).

Example 3-1: On January 1 of Year 1, Kali is granted an equal one-fourth interest in the ABCD partnership for her agreement to find tenants for the partnership's newly constructed office building. This interest is subject to the condition that it is forfeited back to the partnership in the event that the building is not at least 50% leased as of January 1 of Year 2 and 75% leased as of August 17 of Year 2.

Such a partnership interest would be considered subject to a substantial risk of forfeiture. Unless the service partner elects, within 30 days of receiving the interest, to value and report the interest as income in the year received rather than when it is vested, the interest is not taxable until the risk of forfeiture lapses.[5]

There are two benefits of electing to be taxed in the year of receipt:

- The recipient avoids recognizing subsequent appreciation in the partnership interest as compensation income when the interest becomes vested, and

- Any amounts received as partnership distributions are not recharacterized as compensation (because the service partner is recognized as a partner).[6]

---

[3] Code Sec. 83(a).
[4] Code Sec. 83(b)(1).

[5] Reg. § 1.83-2(b).
[6] The service partner is also treated as a partner for purposes of allocating partnership income and loss.

The Code Sec. 83(b) election is especially beneficial when the initial value of the partnership interest received by the service partner is relatively low or when the difference between that value and the amount paid, if any, for that interest (in addition to services provided) is relatively small. In either case, little income will be recognized at the time the Code Sec. 83(b) election is made, and if the partnership interest subsequently appreciates, the appreciation will not be taxed to the partner as compensation.

Example 3-2: Eddie Horton received a five-percent interest in MidCity Associates, a partnership formed to construct and manage an office tower. The interest is contingent upon Eddie's ability to find tenants for the newly constructed office tower. Construction of the building was recently completed at a total cost of $1.2 million. The partnership's debts total $1,000,000. Thus, if Eddie makes the election under Code Sec. 83(b) to recognize income from the transaction now, he will report at most $10,000 as compensation. This amount may be further reduced by lack of marketability or lack of control discounts. Any gains subsequently recognized upon disposition of the interest would then be taxed as capital gain.

A Code Sec. 83(b) election must, as stated, be made no later than 30 days after the date on which the property is transferred and may be made prior to the transfer.[7] The written election must be separately filed with the Internal Revenue Service Center office where the service provider regularly files income tax returns. The service provider must also attach a copy of the election to his or her income tax return for the year of the transfer[8] and must furnish a copy to the person for whom services are performed.[9]

Until the interest vests, the regulations provide for a curious result when the Code Sec. 83(b) election is not made: the service partner is not considered a partner for tax purposes.[10] It is unclear how to give effect to this regulatory pronouncement and no specific official guidance has been offered. One choice would be to interpret the regulations literally and simply ignore the service partner's membership in the partnership, and, to the extent cash and property are paid to him, he or she would be treated as an employee or independent contractor. The payment would not be subject to the special rules applying to partnership payments to partners under Code Sec. 707(a) and Code Sec. 707(c). Payments would be deducted by the partnership and would be personal services income to the partner. They would not be considered distributions of distributive shares of income. Another approach, apparently more popular but with less regulatory support, is to simply ignore this provision and treat a forfeitable partnership interest the same as any other vested partnership interest.

It is presently unclear how to give effect to the regulations, and except for the Proposed Regulations explained in Notice 2005-43, the IRS has offered no guidance.

Most practitioners who wish to choose a settled means of dealing with these situations elect Code Sec. 83(b) and include the value of the interest in income in

---

[7] Reg. § 1.83-2(b).
[8] Reg. § 1.83-2(c).

[9] Reg. § 1.83-2(d).
[10] Reg. § 1.83-1(a)(1).

the year received. The regulations clearly provide that the service partner is then treated as a partner for tax purposes.

.02 Results to Partnership

When the interest is vested, the partnership is treated as if it transferred a partitioned tenancy-in-common interest in its property to the service partner as compensation for his or her past or future services. It is entitled to a deduction for the value of the capital interest paid to the service partner unless a cash payment to an independent party for such services would be nondeductible. This deduction is allocable to the continuing partners other than the service partner in proportion to their respective indirect interests in the partnership property transferred. The total deduction allowed to the partnership is equal to the value of the property deemed transferred to the service partner.[11] Therefore, each continuing partner's deduction will equal the reduction in his or her interest in the liquidated value of the partnership. The service partner's income will equal his or her increased interest in the liquidated value of the partnership.[12]

Since the partnership is treated as if it transferred an undivided tenancy-in-common interest in its own property to the partner in exchange for services, it must realize gain or loss on the portion of its property used to pay for the services. This gain or loss is allocated to the same partners who are allocated the deduction because they are the partners who used their share of appreciated or depreciated property to pay for services.

The situation can be viewed as if the partnership paid an undivided interest in the partnership's property to the service partner who, therefore, takes it with a basis equal to its fair market value. He or she, in turn, is treated as having contributed such property back to the partnership in exchange for a partnership interest. The partnership therefore takes as its transferred basis for this portion of the property its fair market value. The net effect to the basis of the partnership's property is that it is changed by the gain or loss realized by the partnership. The portion of the partnership's property treated as paid to the service partner is stepped up or down in basis for the amount of gain or loss recognized by the partnership. This portion of the partnership's property will have a basis equal to its value. The benefit or burden of this step up or down in basis should be, and probably is, required to be allocated to the service partner in accordance with Code Sec. 704(c) considerations.

> **Example 3-3:** The ABC partnership was formed by cash contributions and has been holding undeveloped investment realty for long-term appreciation. Its balance sheet is as follows:

---

[11] Often admission of a new partner is accounted for by reallocating the existing capital account values among the new and existing partners. However, when this accounting procedure is used, each partner's tax deduction will equal his or her capital account reduction only if the partnership balance sheet, including the partners' capital accounts, is stated in terms of the asset's current values excepting goodwill. A service partner's receipt of an interest in goodwill represents only a share of the current estimate of future profitability and is treated as a receipt of an interest in future partnership profits and is described at ¶ 303.

[12] The partnership must comply with Form 1099 or W-2 reporting requirements to qualify for the deduction to avoid withholding. *See* Reg. § 1.83-6(a)(2).

¶302.02

ABC Partnership

Assets	Tax Basis	FMV
Real Estate	$90,000	$120,000
Liabilities	$ 0	$ 0
Capital		
A	$30,000	$40,000
B	30,000	40,000
C	30,000	40,000
	$90,000	*$120,000*

Kali, a real estate developer, is admitted as an equal unrestricted one-fourth partner for his promise to produce a feasibility study related to subdividing and marketing the partnership's property. Assuming no discounts for lack of control and marketability, Kali has personal service income of $30,000 and a basis in her partnership interest of $30,000.[13] Assuming Code Sec. 263A does not require capitalizing such a payment, the partnership has a $30,000 deduction.[14] This deduction should be allocated to A, B, and C only because it arose before Kali became a partner.[15] The partnership has capital gain of $7,500.[16] This gain is also allocated only to A, B, and C for the same reason that the $30,000 deduction is allocated to them alone. It is the continuing partners who have used their share of the value of the assets to pay A. They should be allowed the deduction and be required to report gain from using the share of their appreciated assets to pay Kali. The resulting partnership balance sheet is as follows:

ABCK Partnership

Assets	Tax Basis	FMV
Real Estate	$97,500*	$120,000
Liabilities	$ 0	$ 0
Capital		
A**	$22,500	$30,000
B	22,500	30,000
C	22,500	30,000
Kali***	30,000	30,000
	$97,500	*$120,000*

*The real estate's basis is three-fourths of the ABC partnership's basis of $90,000, or $67,500 plus Kali's $30,000 cost basis in the real estate.

---

[13] One-fourth total value of the partnership (1/4 × $120,000 = $30,000).

[14] The partnership is treated as paying Kali with property. The property paid to Kali for her services has a value of $30,000 (1/4 × $120,000).

[15] Code Sec. 706(d). There is a possibility that the deduction arose as Kali became a partner and not before.

However, it must be emphasized that A, B and C are bearing the economic burden of the shift of a portion of the property's value to Kali. They may want the deduction.

[16] The partnership is treated as selling one-fourth of the real estate with a value of $30,000 and a basis of $22,500.

** *A, B,* and *C*'s capital accounts, values, and basis in their interests are reduced by one-fourth. This is the portion of their interest in the partnership transferred to Kali. This is their original capital account of $30,000 less their $10,000 share of the deduction plus their $2,500 share of income.

***Kali's capital account of $30,000 represents her share of the basis of the real estate. Kali is treated as having received one-fourth share worth $30,000 as payment for services and then contributing it to the partnership. This results in a capital account and basis of $30,000.

If the partnership later sells the real estate for its fair market value of $120,000, the gain of $22,500 ($120,000 – $97,500) will be allocated equally ($7,500 each) between A, B, and C. Kali's "share" of the basis of the property is $30,000, and his share of the sales price is $30,000, so he would recognize no gain or loss. If the sales price of the real estate was $130,000, A, B, and C would each recognize $10,000 of gain [($130,000/4) – ((97,500 – $30,000)/3)], and Kali would recognize $2,500 of gain. If the sales price was $110,000, A, B, and C would each recognize $5,000 of gain [($110,000/4) – ((97,500 – $30,000)/3)], and Kali would recognize $2,500 of loss [($110,000/4) – $30,000].

¶ 303 Profit Interest Received

Unless one chooses to rely on the Proposed Regulations, the rules governing a profit interest allowed to a partner in exchange for services are less clear cut than the rules governing a capital interest allowed in exchange for services. The general framework has been established, but the details of application remain unsettled.

Before 1971, tax practitioners were understandably confident that a profits interest allocated to a partner, in exchange for a promise of future services or in payment for past services, would be taken into account in later years when the partnership realized that partner's share of income or loss. The reasons underlying this mistaken confidence were simple. First, valuing an expected interest in future results is usually impossible. Second, even if a profits interest could be valued and this amount reported when the right to share in future profits was established, what could be done in the year that share of income materialized? If the service partner was required to again include his or her share of the income, the partner would have reported the same income twice, first as an estimated amount and second when the actual amounts became known.[17] Also, what if the estimated value did not materialize? The partner will have reported ordinary income in an early year followed by a capital loss in later years. Unfortunately, bad facts and administrative shortsightedness have resulted in bad law. Consequently, the government's right to tax a profits interest to the recipient in the year the right becomes part of the partnership agreement has been established.[18]

---

[17] Because the service partner will increase his or her basis in the partnership interest by the income reported on both occasions, his or her future taxable income will potentially be reduced by the amount of the over-reporting. Eventually, therefore, when the partner receives the benefit of this increased basis, the temporary over-reporting will have reversed itself.

[18] *S. Diamond v. Commr.*, 56 TC 530, Dec. 30,838 (1971), aff'd, CA-7, 74-1 USTC ¶ 9306, 492 F2d 286, 290.

Case law provides the most important potential limitation to the IRS's authority to require reporting the receipt of the profits interest itself as personal services income. The profits interest must be taken into account in the year in which it is created when it has a "determinable market value." The leading decision in this area observes that "[s]urely in many if not the typical situation it will have only speculative value, if any."[19] Due to the obvious problems with reasonably valuing the profits interest through forecasts of future operations, the IRS has taken another approach. The IRS has ruled that the receipt of the right is not taxable if:

1. The partnership does not have a substantially certain stream of income;

2. The interest is held two years; and

3. The partnership interest is not publicly traded.[20]

The occurrence of the event that causes the interest to become substantially vested also will not be taxable if the above three requirements are met and the following three are also met:

1. The partnership and the service provider treat the service provider as a partner from the date the interest is granted, and the service provider recognizes his or her distributive share of partnership income, gain, loss, deduction, and credit in computing income tax liability for the entire period during which the service provider has the interest;

2. Neither the partnership nor any of the partners take any deductions for the value of the interest, either upon the grant of the interest or at the time that the interest becomes substantially vested; and

3. The other conditions stated in Rev. Proc. 93-27 are satisfied.[21]

Although the IRS's position certainly reduces the frequency with which taxpayers will need to resolve the issue before taking a reporting position, it doesn't eliminate it. For example, service partners who receive a profits interest in a partnership which owns property subject to a net lease or service partners who sell their interests within two years will still have to show that the interest had no ascertainable value when received to avoid reporting ordinary income in the year the partnership interest was received rather than capital gains when it was sold.

In addition to the problem, discussed in the previous section, of whether one who has a nonvested profits interest is a partner for tax purposes, other practical results remain uncertain which are not cured by a Code Sec. 83(b) election.[22] If the expected profits interest is taxed before it has materialized, is it taxed again when it

---

[19] *Id. See D.B. St. John v. U.S.*, DC Ill., 84-1 USTC ¶ 9158. By using a liquidation value approach, the court held the ascertainable value to be zero. *See also Campbell v. Commr.*, CA-8, 91-2 USTC ¶ 50,420, 943 F2d 815, rev'g 59 TCM 236, Dec. 46,493(M), TC Memo. 1990-162.

[20] Rev. Proc. 93-27, 1993-2 CB 343. *See also* GCM 36346 (1975).

[21] Rev. Proc. 2001-43, 2001-2 CB 191.

[22] *See* discussion at ¶ 302.01 regarding Reg. § 1.83-2(b) and partners' receipt of capital interest.

is earned? Additionally, can the partnership take a deduction for the value of the profits interest transferred to the partner?

¶ 304 Proposed Regulations

When finalized, a set of proposed regulations under Code Sections 83, 704, 706, and 721 would supply some needed guidance in the situations where partnership interests are exchanged for services.

.01 Results to Service Partner

Under the proposed rules, if a partnership interest is transferred in connection with the performance of services, the fair market value of the interest will be treated as a guaranteed payment to the recipient service partner. It will immediately be included in her income if the partnership interest is vested.[23] On the other hand, if the partnership interest is not vested, then the recipient of the partnership interest is not treated as a partner (and will not generally recognize items of partnership income or loss) unless the recipient makes an election to immediately be taxed on the value of the interest under section 83(b).[24] Even if the section 83(b) election has been made, the holder of a nonvested interest may be allocated partnership income, gain, loss, deduction, or credit that might later be forfeited (if vesting does not occur). For this reason, allocations of partnership items that occur while the interest is not vested cannot have economic effect, and the partner will not generally recognize these partnership items.[25] However, these allocations will be deemed to have economic effect, and will be respected, if (1) the partnership agreement provides for "forfeiture allocations" among the partners to attempt to reverse the forfeited allocations, and (2) all other material allocations are recognized under Code Sec. 704(b).[26]

> **Example 3-4:** Refer back to the facts of Example 3-3. Under the proposed regulations, Kali would recognize a guaranteed payment of $30,000 and would have a basis in her partnership interest of $30,000. Kali would immediately start recognizing allocations of partnership income and loss.
>
> If Kali's partnership interest were not to be substantially vested for five years, Kali can make an election under Code Sec. 83(b) to recognize the interest (as a guaranteed payment) immediately, presumably at its fair market value of $30,000. In that case, if the partnership agreement meets certain requirements (including providing for re-allocations of income in the event of forfeiture) Kali will recognize her share of the partnership's income and loss items in all years before and after vesting. If those requirements aren't met, she is not considered a partner until vesting, and will not recognize any partnership items until then.
>
> If she does not make the election under Code Sec. 83(b), she will recognize the end-of-year-five value of her partnership interest as a guaranteed payment at the end of year five, assuming the interest actually vests then. She

---

[23] Prop. Reg. § 1.721-1(b)(4).
[24] Prop. Reg. § 1.761-1(b).

[25] Prop. Reg. § 1.704-1(a). *See* Chapter 9 for an explanation of economic effect.
[26] Prop. Reg. § 1.704-1(b).

will not be considered a partner until then, and will not recognize any partnership items until then.

.02 Results to Partnership

Under the proposed regulations Code Sec. 721 does not apply to the transfer of a partnership interest in exchange for services. Such exchanges will instead be considered a transfer of property to which Code Sec. 83 applies,[27] whether a profits interest or a capital interest is exchanged. Under Code Sec. 83, no gain or loss (on, for example, the underlying partnership property) will generally be recognized by the partnership in such an exchange when the compensatory partnership interest is either transferred (or substantially vested) or forfeited.[28] In fact, the partnership will treat the partnership interest transferred (for services rendered) as a guaranteed payment for services under Code Sec. 707(c). Like any other guaranteed payment for services, the partnership (1) will be allowed a deduction for the value of the partnership interest transferred, unless the nature of the services is such that their payment would be capitalized, and (2) will be required to recognize income if the partnership interest is forfeited.[29] The partnership will be able to deduct the guaranteed payment in the partnership tax year in which or with which ends the taxable year of the service provider in which he included the guaranteed payment in income.[30]

> **Example 3-5:** Refer back to the facts of Example 3-4. If the partnership interest is immediately vested, the ABC Partnership would immediately have a deduction of $30,000 for the guaranteed payment (assuming it does not have to be capitalized under Code Sec. 263A or any other section), or $10,000 each for A, B, and C. ABC would not recognize any gain or loss from the hypothetical exchange of part of its assets for the services. If the partnership interest is not vested, the ABC partnership will be able to deduct the guaranteed payment in the partnership tax year in which or with which ended Kali's taxable year in which she included the guaranteed payment in income.

.03 Value of the Partnership Interest

Under the proposed regulations the service partner can generally use one of two alternative treatments for determining the value of the compensatory partnership interest. The service partner can use the estimated "willing-buyer-willing-seller" fair market value of the partnership interest, taking into account business prospects, lack of marketability, and the other items that generally go into the estimation of fair market value. Alternatively, the proposed regulations allow the service partner to elect to use a "safe harbor" liquidation value of the partnership interest as the value of the interest.[31] The safe harbor liquidation value is the amount of cash that the service partner would receive if, immediately after the transfer, the partnership sold all of its assets (including goodwill, going concern

---

[27] Prop. Reg. § 1.721-1(b)(1).

[28] Prop. Reg. § 1.721-1(b)(2). However, the rule providing for nonrecognition of gain or loss does not apply to the transfer of an interest in an entity (such as a sole proprietorship) that becomes a partnership as a result of the transfer or substantial vesting of the interest. Pream-

ble to Prop Regs. 5/24/2005. Fed. Reg. Vol. 70, No. 99, p. 29675.

[29] Reg. § 1.83-6(c).

[30] Code Sec. 83(h).

[31] Prop. Reg. § 1.83-3(l).

value, and any other intangibles associated with the partnership's operations) for cash equal to the fair market value of those assets, and then liquidated.[32] Since the liquidation value of a profits interest is zero, any profits interest received as compensation by a service partner will not be taxable if the safe harbor valuation is allowed and is elected.

In order to be eligible for the safe harbor election, the partnership must not be (a) related to a substantially certain and predictable stream of income from partnership assets, such as income from high-quality debt securities or a high-quality net lease, (b) transferred in anticipation of a subsequent disposition, or (c) an interest in a publicly traded partnership. With respect to (b), if the partnership interest is sold or disposed of within two years of the date of receipt of the partnership interest (other than a sale or disposition by reason of death or disability of the service provider) there is a rebuttable presumption that the partnership interest was transferred in anticipation of a subsequent disposition.[33]

Under the safe harbor provisions, the service provider will recognize compensation income at the time of the transfer of a vested partnership interest in an amount equal to the liquidation value of the interest, less any amount paid for the interest. If the service provider receives a nonvested safe harbor partnership interest, does not make an election under Code Sec. 83(b), and holds the interest until it vests, the service provider will recognize compensation income in an amount equal to the liquidation value of the interest when the interest vests, less any amount paid for the interest. If the service provider receives a nonvested safe harbor partnership interest and makes an election under Code Sec. 83(b), the service provider will recognize compensation income on the date of transfer equal to the liquidation value of the interest, determined as if the interest were substantially vested, less any amount paid for the interest.[34]

If the safe harbor is elected, the partnership generally will be entitled to a deduction equal to the amount included as compensation by the service provider. The deduction generally will be allowed for the taxable year of the partnership in which or with which ends the taxable year of the service provider in which the amount is included in the service provider's gross income as compensation.[35]

> *Example 3-6:* Leona receives a partnership interest in exchange for services performed for the XYZ Partnership. Leona and the partnership fulfill the requirements necessary to make the safe harbor election. If the partnership interest is strictly a profits interest, Leona will not have to recognize any income, since she would get nothing upon a current liquidation of the partnership. The partnership also does not get a deduction, although Leona will henceforth be allocated her share of the partnership profits, and the other partners will not have to recognize that amount. Her basis in her partnership interest would begin at zero.
>
> Assume that the partnership interest is a vested capital interest, and an immediate liquidation would result in Leona receiving $50,000 cash. Under

---

[32] Notice 2005-43, 2005-24 IRB 1221, Sec. 4.02.
[33] Notice 2005-43, 2005-24 IRB 1221, Sec. 3.02.

[34] Notice 2005-43, 2005-24 IRB 1221, Sec. 5.01.
[35] Notice 2005-43, 2005-24 IRB 1221, Sec. 5.02.

those circumstances Leona will have to recognize $50,000 as compensation immediately, the partnership will have an equivalent deduction, and Leona's basis in the interest will begin at $50,000. The same result would occur if the capital interest is nonvested but Leona makes a Code Sec. 83(b) election. If the capital interest is nonvested and Leona does not make a Code Sec. 83(b) election, she will not recognize any compensation income until the interest vests, and the amount she will recognize then will be the liquidation value computed at that time, not $50,000.

Chapter 4

Calculation of Partnership Income

¶ 401 Introduction

Generally, in computing its taxable income, the partnership takes into account the same items of income and deduction during the year as does an individual. The partnership, however, must separately state the net amounts of certain items of income and deductions enumerated in Code Sec. 702(a). These separately stated amounts are items that could be subject to special limitations or treatment when recognized by the partners. Any special treatment for a certain type of income, deduction, or credit is generally applied at the partner level and is computed based on the partner's overall tax situation, including income, deductions, and credits from other sources. Code Sec. 702(a) requires that the partnership separately state its net amounts from the following sources:

1. Long-term capital gains and losses.

2. Short-term capital gains and losses.

3. Code Sec. 1231 gains and losses.

4. Charitable contributions.

5. Dividends that are taxed as net capital gains or are eligible for the dividends received deduction.[1]

6. Income taxes paid to foreign countries.

7. Other items required by the regulations.

---

[1] Code Sec. 243.

Examples of items the regulations add are the following:

1. Recoveries of bad debts and taxes.
2. Gains from wagering.
3. Nonbusiness expenses.
4. Medical and dental expenses.
5. Items specially allocated.
6. Any amount that, if separately taken into account by any partner, would result in an income tax liability for that partner different from that which would result if that partner did not take the item separately into account.[2]

Administrative pronouncements and case law add other types of income and deductions that must be separately stated. In preparing the partnership's tax return, these separately stated items are listed on Schedule K of the partnership tax return (Form 1065, U.S. Partnership Return of Income). The remaining amounts of income and deduction that are not separately stated are taken into account by simply netting them on line one of Form 1065, Schedule K.

Example 4-1: The equal AB partnership has the following items of income and deductions for its taxable year:

Gross rents		$250,000
Depreciation	$100,000	
Maintenance expenses	40,000	
Property taxes	10,000	
Insurance	5,000	
Property management fees	30,000	
		(185,000)
Net rental income		*$65,000*
Gains from selling investment land		40,000
Partnership's business or investment income		*$105,000*
Charitable deductions		$10,000

The partnership's business or investment income is $105,000, but this net amount never appears on its tax return. The partnership must separately state its net rental income of $65,000 because this is per se passive income from nonreal estate operations.[3] and each partner's passive losses from other sources are deductible only to the extent of his total passive income from all sources. The capital gains of $40,000 must also be separately stated because a partner's capital losses are deductible only to the extent of his capital gains from all sources (plus $3,000 for individuals). The partnership's charitable contributions are not deductible by the partnership but must be stated separately because each individual partner can deduct these amounts only if his total charitable contributions do not exceed the percentages of adjusted gross income specified in Code Sec. 170.

---

[2] Reg. § 1.702-1(a)(8)(i), (ii).   [3] Code Sec. 469(c)(7).

S Corporation Observation: An S corporation calculates and presents its taxable income in the same manner as does a partnership.[4]

¶ 402 Both Entity and Aggregate Rules Apply

The computation and treatment of partnership taxable income at times treats the partnership as an entity separate from its owners and at times treats the partnership as a joint ownership through a tenancy-in-common of individuals. For example, there is no income tax imposed on the partnership, but the income of the partnership is taxed to the partners. In this case the partnership is treated as an aggregate of a group of individual partners. However, the combined net income for the partnership is computed and reported by the partnership on Form 1065, and in this respect the partnership is treated as an entity separate from the partners.

Partnerships are treated as entities for purposes of making most elections (such as choice of accounting methods) that affect the computation of pass-through items, and for certain procedural purposes.[5] Partnerships are treated similar to tenants-in-common or as an aggregation of individual owners for other purposes. For example, the Code Sec. 469 passive loss limits and the Code Sec. 465 at-risk limits apply at the partner level. In some situations, there is a choice whether to use an entity rule or an aggregate rule. For example, a purchaser of a partnership interest has a new cost basis in his or her interest, but not a cost basis in his or her share of the assets. This rule has an entity approach. However, the partner receives a cost basis in his or her share of the assets if a Code Sec. 754 election is in effect. This is in essence an election to use an aggregate approach.

Another example of treating a partnership as an aggregate is that each partner's gross income includes his or her share of the partnership's gross income.[6] The regulations and instructions for Form 1065 do not specifically provide for gross income to be separately stated. However, examples of its importance to partners include:

- Requirement to file a tax return.[7]
- Application of six-year statute of limitations for omitting more than 25 percent of gross income.[8]
- Tax imposed on S corporations (who are partners in a partnership) with excess investment income and termination of such a corporation's S election.[9]

Other examples of an "aggregate" approach to partnership taxation include:

- Partners are required to report their shares of partnership profit or loss regardless of whether the partnership makes a distribution to them or they pay money to the partnership.[10]
- The character of the income, gain, loss, deduction or credit at the partnership level is passed through to the partners.[11]

---

[4] Code Sec. 1366(a).
[5] *See* Code Secs. 703(b), 6221 and following.
[6] Code Sec. 702(c).
[7] Code Sec. 6012(a).

[8] Code Sec. 6501(e).
[9] Code Secs. 1375 and 1362(d)(3).
[10] Code Secs. 702(a) and 704.
[11] Code Sec. 702(a) and (b).

- Co-inventors of a patent will still be considered "holders" of the patent under Code Sec. 1235 after they form a partnership (or LLC) and transfer the patent to the partnership (or LLC).[12]

- Some elections are made at the partner level:[13]

  1. The Code Sec. 901 election;

  2. Election to deduct certain mining exploration expenditures;[14]

  3. Election related to cancellation of indebtedness income;[15] and

  4. Elections related to nonresident and foreign corporation investments on United States rental realty.[16]

Other examples of an "entity" approach to partnership taxation include:

- An S corporation shareholder may deduct his or her share of losses only to the extent of his or her basis in the stock and the basis he or she has in loans made to the corporation.[17] Loans made by a partnership to an S corporation owned by the partners are not considered as loans by its partners to the S corporation.[18]

- Partnership income is computed at the entity level;[19]

- The partnership files a tax return reporting its taxable income;[20]

- The partnership has its own accounting method;[21]

- The partnership has its own taxable year;[22] and

- The partnership makes most of the elections affecting the computation of its taxable income. A partial list of the elections made at the partnership level follows:

  1. Depreciation elections;[23]

  2. Inventory method;[24]

  3. Election to rollover involuntary conversion gains;[25]

  4. Election to expense a limited amount of depreciable basis in year of acquisition;[26]

  5. Election not to use the installment method for reporting installment sales;[27]

  6. Election to amortize organizational expenses;[28]

---

[12] PLR 200506008, PLR 200506009, PLR 200506019.

[13] Code Sec. 703(b).

[14] Code Sec. 617.

[15] Code Sec. 108(b)(5) and (c)(3).

[16] Code Secs. 871(d)(1) and 882(d)(1).

[17] Code Sec. 1366(d) and (d)(1)(B).

[18] *E.J. Frankel v. Commr.*, 61 TC 343, Dec. 32,250 (1973).

[19] Code Sec. 703(a).

[20] Code Sec. 6031.

[21] Code Sec. 703(b).

[22] Code Sec. 706.

[23] Prop. Reg. § 1.168-5(e)(7).

[24] Code Sec. 472.

[25] Code Sec. 1033.

[26] Code Sec. 179.

[27] Code Sec. 453.

[28] Code Sec. 709.

7. Election to adjust the basis of partnership assets following certain distributions (Code Sec. 734(b)) or transfers of interests in the partnership (Code Sec. 743(b));[29] and

8. Election to apply self-charged interest deduction rule.[30]

.01 Involuntary Conversions

The entity-level application of Code Sec. 1033 to involuntary conversions is an example of the surprising and sometimes unfair results which can occur when the partnership is treated as a separate entity and the actions of the partners are disregarded. If gain is realized when partnership property is involuntarily converted, the partnership itself (rather than the partners) must reinvest in similar or related property to be able to use the nonrecognition provision of Code Sec. 1033.[31]

Example 4-2: The ABCD partnership has an insured building with a value of $100,000 and zero adjusted basis. It is completely destroyed by fire. The insurer pays the partnership $100,000 resulting in a $100,000 realized involuntary conversion gain. If the partnership liquidates and each partner reinvests its share of the proceeds in property which would qualify under Code Sec. 1033 for nonrecognition, the entire gain is still taxed. If the ABCD partnership is not liquidated and the partnership reinvests $100,000 in qualified property, no gain is recognized.

If an individual suffering an involuntary conversion purchases an interest in a partnership which owns qualifying property, the purchase fails to qualify for Code Sec. 1033 treatment.[32] If the individual already owned a partnership interest in a different partnership and that partnership invested in qualifying property, there would be no deferral under Code Sec. 1033.

If the condemned property is encumbered, the IRS has ruled that a partner must recognize gain under Code Sec. 731 if there is a reduction in partnership debt which causes a reduction of a partner's share of that debt to exceed his or her partnership interest basis, even though the partnership satisfies Code Sec. 1033's requirements.[33]

Example 4-3: The equal AB partnership's insured building with a value of $100,000 and basis of zero is subject to a debt of $100,000 and is completely destroyed by fire in Year 1. Prior to the fire, each partner's basis in his interest is zero. The insurer pays $100,000 in insurance proceeds to the lender in Year 1 and in the next taxable year the partnership purchases qualifying replacement property with a value of $100,000 subject to a debt of $100,000. The IRS has ruled that A and B each have a deemed money distribution of $50,000 on the last day of the partnership taxable year in which the debt was paid in Year 1. Under these facts, because each partner's basis is zero, each has a gain of

---

[29] Code Sec. 754.

[30] Prop. Reg. § 1.469(7)(f).

[31] *T.K. McManus v. Commr.*, 65 TC 197, Dec. 33,483 (1975), aff'd, CA-9, 78-2 USTC ¶ 9748, 583 F2d 443; *M. Demirjian v. Commr.*, CA-3, 72-1 USTC ¶ 9281, 457 F2d 1; IRS Letter Ruling 8015044.

[32] *M.H.S. Co., Inc. v. Commr.*, 35 TCM 733, Dec. 33,843(M), TC Memo. 1976-165, aff'd, CA-6, 78-1 USTC ¶ 9442, 575 F2d 1177.

[33] Rev. Rul. 81-242, 1981-2 CB 147; Rev. Rul. 94-4, 1994-1 CB 196.

$50,000. If the partnership had borrowed $100,000 for any purpose by the close of the tax year in which the insurance company paid the lender, there would have been no gain.

.02 Code Sec. 1244 Stock

The application of Code Sec. 1244 is another example of an entity approach to partnership taxation. Code Sec. 1244 allows the owner of qualifying stock a limited amount of ordinary loss when the stock is worthless or is sold at a loss. A partnership qualifies for the ordinary loss treatment if it satisfies the requirements of Code Sec. 1244.[34] However, if the partnership distributes the stock to its partners, they do not qualify for an ordinary loss because Code Sec. 1244 treatment applies only to original holders of the stock. Therefore, even though they are the original owners from an aggregate view of partnership taxation, Code Sec. 1244 adopts an entity view and the partnership itself, not the partners, are the original owners.[35]

.03 Prepaid Expenses

Prepaid expenses are deductible only if after taking the deduction into account income is clearly reflected.[36] If a partnership prepays expenses, the distortion of income test is applied at the partnership level[37] and probably also at the partner level.[38]

¶ 403 Calculation of the Amount of the Partnership's Taxable Income

With a few exceptions, a partnership's taxable income is computed by taking into account the same items of income, gain, loss, deduction, and credit as required of an individual.[39] The characterization and timing rules are also, with a few exceptions, based upon the rules applied to individuals rather than corporations.[40] For example, because a partnership's taxable income is to be computed as if it were an individual, a partnership is entitled to treat losses realized on the disposition of small business corporation stock as defined in Code Sec. 1244 as ordinary losses.[41]

> **S Corporation Observation:** The Tax Court has held[42] that an S corporation is not entitled to an ordinary deduction under Code Sec. 1244 for losses incurred on the worthlessness or sale of otherwise qualified small business corporation stock under Code Sec. 1244.

Many items fall under a category of exceptions found in Code Sec. 703(a) that prevent a partnership from taking some of the same deductions as an individual.

---

[34] Code Sec. 1244 treatment is not available to S corporations. *V.D. Rath v. Commr.*, 101 TC 196, Dec. 49,266 (1993); IRS Letter Ruling 9130003.

[35] Reg. § 1.1244(a)-1(b)(2); *J. Prizant v. Commr.*, 30 TCM 817, Dec. 30,923, TC Memo. 1971-196.

[36] Code Sec. 446(b).

[37] *B. Resnick v. Commr.*, 66 TC 74, Dec. 33,761 (1976), aff'd, CA-7, 77-1 USTC ¶ 9451, 555 F2d 634.

[38] *R.E. Clement v. U.S.*, CtCls, 78-2 USTC ¶ 9566, 580 F2d 422, 217 CtCls 495; *J.R. Parks v. U.S.*, DC Tex., 77-1 USTC ¶ 9404, 434 FSupp 206.

[39] Code Sec. 703(a); Reg. § 1.703-1(a)(1).

[40] Trusts, estates, and S corporations also adopt as a starting point the rules provided for individuals. Code Secs. 641(b) and 1363(b).

[41] *V.D. Rath v. Commr.*, 101 TC 196, Dec. 49,266 (1993). However, if the stock is distributed to the partners, they are not entitled to an ordinary loss. Reg. § 1.1244(a)-1(b)(2); *J. Prizant v. Commr.*, 30 TCM 817, Dec. 30,923(M), TC Memo. 1971-196.

[42] *V.D. Rath v. Commr.*, 101 TC 196, Dec. 49,266 (1993).

Code Sec. 703(a) provides, for example, that a partnership is not allowed a deduction for:

1. Personal exemptions;

2. Taxes paid or accrued to foreign countries;

3. Charitable contributions;

4. Net operating loss carryovers;

5. Additional itemized deductions provided in Code Secs. 211 and following; and

6. Depletion with respect to oil and gas wells.

The disallowance of personal exemptions and net operating loss carryovers or carrybacks prevents a double deduction for these amounts. The partners and the partnership do not both get personal exemptions or their equivalents. The partnership's negative taxable income passes through to its partners and is part of any net operating loss that it may cause to a partner. There is no second carryover of net operating losses at the partnership level.

In addition to these statutory disallowances, the regulations prevent the partnership from taking a deduction for a capital loss carryover.[43] The reason for the disallowance is the same as the reason for denying net operating loss deductions—to prevent two deductions for the same loss—one at the partnership level and the other at the partner level.

It is sometimes difficult to classify items of income or expense as partnership or partner items. When there is doubt about whether a partner or a partnership is the earner of the income, the general rule is that income is reported by the partnership if it is reasonably associated with the partnership's business activity.[44] Income from property is taxed to the beneficial owner and not necessarily the record owner.[45]

It is common for a partnership agreement to require partners to assign certain types of outside service income to the partnership. The IRS has ruled[46] and the Tax Court has held[47] that the partner must report the income himself even if the income is from services similar to services rendered by the partnership. If service income is properly reportable by a partner but turned over to the partnership, and the service partner's share of the income is less than the amount taxed to him, a partner level deduction may be in order.[48]

The general rule is that the partnership must deduct its expenses even though they are paid by a partner.[49] If, however, the partner is personally responsible for the expense and not entitled to reimbursement, the partner appears to be entitled

---

[43] Reg. § 1.703-1(a)(2)(vii).

[44] *S.B. Schneer v. Commr.*, 97 TC 643, Dec. 47,803 (1991).

[45] Rev. Rul. 55-39, 1955-1 CB 403; Rev. Rul. 54-84, 1954-1 CB 284.

[46] Rev. Rul. 64-90, 1964-1 CB 226; Rev. Rul. 80-338, 1980-2 CB 30; IRS Letter Ruling 9514008 (1-4-95).

[47] *W.B. Mayes v. Commr.*, 21 TC 286, Dec. 19,994 (1953).

[48] *See* Rev. Rul. 64-90, 1964-1 CB 226.

[49] *H.K. Stevens v. Commr.*, 46 TC 492, Dec. 28,026 (1966), aff'd per curiam, CA-6, 68-1 USTC ¶ 9174, 388 F2d 298; IRS Technical Advice Memorandum 8442001 (5-14-84).

to the deduction. The relevant authority for this position treats the partner as if he or she were engaged in the partnership's activities directly.[50]

By using a special allocation of a deduction, the partnership and partners may in effect shift a partnership deduction to a partner. For instance, if the partnership makes a deductible guaranteed payment subject to Code Sec. 707(c) to the partner and specially allocates such deduction to the payee partner, there is no net income to the partner. The partner then is entitled to a deduction for his or her "unreimbursable" partnership expense.[51] As long as the expenses are the type that the partner is expected to pay without reimbursement, the partner can deduct the expenses on Schedule E.[52] Unreimbursed expenses would include unreimbursed home office deductions under Code Sec. 280A.[53]

¶ 404 Payments to a Partner

With proper planning, payments to a partner for services (salary, wages, commissions), the use of property (rent, royalties), or the use of capital (interest) may be deductible by the partnership or simply treated as a method of income allocation. If payments are made to a partner acting in a nonpartner capacity, the treatment of the payment is governed by Code Sec. 707(a). If payments are made to a partner acting as a partner, but without regard to partnership profits, they are guaranteed payments governed by Code Sec. 707(c). Code Sec. 707(a) and (c) payments are part of the partnership's aggregated nonseparately stated taxable income calculation unless they are specially allocated. If payments made to a partner acting as a partner are dependent on the level of partnership profits, the payments are first treated as a special allocation of income to that partner under Code Sec. 704 and then as a distribution of that income under Code Sec. 731.

A partnership generally classifies its payments to a partner into one of three categories:

- Code Sec. 707(a) payments;
- Code Sec. 707(c) (so-called "guaranteed") payments; or
- A distributive share of the partnership's income.

As a general rule, Code Sec. 707(a) tends to treat the payment as if it were made to a nonpartner. At the other extreme, payments which are not classified as Code Sec. 707(a) or (c) payments are ignored as "payments" and are considered distributive shares of the partnership's income coupled with a distribution. Code Sec. 707(c) guaranteed payments are treated as distributive shares for some purposes and are treated as payments to nonpartners for other purposes. The following chart summarizes the continuum of comparative attributes and treatment of these payments.

---

[50] IRS Technical Advice Memorandum 9316003 (12-23-92). If the partnership agreement or partnership practice requires a partner to bear the burden of partnership business expenses, he is entitled to a Section 162 deduction. The partner cannot deduct expenses for which he was entitled to, but failed to seek reimbursement. *F.S. Klein v. Commr.*, 25 TC 1045, Dec. 21,573 (1956).

[51] *See* IRS Technical Advice Memorandum 9330001 (4-1-93).

[52] Per the Schedule E instructions, these expenses are reported on a separate line in the same manner as partner-level interest expense incurred in debt traced to the purchase of a partnership interest.

[53] Rev. Rul. 94-24, 1994-1 CB 87.

Nonpartner-type activity; Payment to partner reflects fair market value compensation; not partnership income.	Partner-type activity; Payment reflects fair market value compensation, not partnership income.	Partner-type activity; Payment is share of partnership income not necessarily fair market value compensation.
Code Sec. 707(a) Payment	***Code Sec. 707(c) Payment***	***Code Sec. 704(a) Allocation with a Code Sec. 731 Distribution***
Partnership deduction if not capitalized under Code Sec. 263—but not before the day the partner must include payment in income.	Partnership deduction based solely on its accounting method if not capitalized under Code Sec. 263.	No partnership deduction but reduction in other partners' income simultaneous with payee's partner's income.
Partnership deduction and partner income are simultaneous; partner's income is ordinary—he receives a Form 1099 if applicable.	Partnership deduction and partner's income simultaneous; partner's income is ordinary and the partner income is reported on his or her K-1.	Income's character flows from partnership level.

If a payment is deductible in computing the partnership's taxable income, the timing of the deduction will vary depending upon whether or not the partner is paid for fulfilling his or her duty as a partner in contrast to acting in a nonpartner capacity. A nondeductible payment to a partner which is treated as a distributive share of income (*e.g.*, under Code Secs. 704(a)/731) will, in many respects, result in the functional equivalent of a deduction from the viewpoint of the other partners since it reduces the amount of income they will have to recognize. Often correctly classifying these various payments to ensure their proper tax treatment is inordinately complex in comparison to the differences in tax effect ultimately accorded to such classification.

LLC Observation: Although a limited liability company (LLC) resembles a corporation in many non-income tax respects, an LLC member is not treated as an employee for tax purposes unless there is a special treatment specified by the Internal Revenue Code. Even though the LLC member would generally be a common law employee, the LLC does not treat Code Sec. 707(a) or (c) payments for services as payroll. For example, the LLC does not issue an annual Form W-2 to partners, nor does it withhold any taxes or make Social Security tax payments on behalf of partners.

S Corporation Observation: S corporation payments to shareholders for services fall into three categories. They are treated as payments to employees if the shareholder is an employee under the general common law rules. They are treated as paid to an independent contractor if the shareholder's work does not create an employer/employee relationship. The payments are distributions

¶404

if they are paid on account of stock ownership, including payments received by the shareholder in excess of what would be deemed "reasonable compensation" for services rendered. As such they are nontaxable to the shareholder to the extent of his or her stock basis; once basis is fully recovered, any remainder is generally treated as capital gain.

.01 Payments to Partners as Compensation for Services or Property Not Required as a Condition of Partner Status

Definition. If a partner engages in transactions with the partnership in a capacity other than as a partner, the partner is treated as if he or she were not a member of the partnership with respect to that transaction. Such transactions include loans of money or property, property rentals, sales of property, and providing certain services.[54] Payments made to partners for the use of the partner's money or property, or for "support" services, are normally deductible by the partnership. They are known generally as Code Sec. 707(a) payments. For example, the tax results of a partnership payment for leasing a partner's property are typically clear. The partnership deducts rent and the partnership reports rent. If a partnership borrows money from a partner, it deducts and the partner reports interest.

The definition of support services is not precise, but generally it includes services not required of the partner by the partnership agreement or because of his or her partner status. They are usually services that are not central to the partnership's main function.[55] If the partnership agreement requires certain services to be rendered by a partner as a condition of his or her partner status, amounts paid to the partner which are not dependent on partnership income would normally be classified as guaranteed payments under Code Sec. 707(c) rather than Code Sec. 707(a) payments.

However, if an analysis of the surrounding facts and circumstances shows that there was no business purpose or effect for that portion of the partnership agreement and there was a tax avoidance motive and effect, the provision would be ignored. If the partnership agreement is silent as to who should perform certain services, but there is a contract between the partnership and a partner that allows the partner to perform certain services for a limited time period, this would be strong evidence that the partner is performing nonpartner activities and the payment is a Code Sec. 707(a) payment. It is the contract of employment, not his or her partner status, that both allows and requires that the partner perform the services. If the partner fails to adequately perform his or her duties, the partner will lose his or her employment but not his or her partnership interest.

For example, payments received by a general partner for managing the partnership's office buildings, which are its major assets, would not normally be considered Code Sec. 707(a) payments if these services are required by the partnership agreement. The general partner's profit-sharing arrangement, or guar-

---

[54] Reg. § 1.707-1(a).

[55] Technically, the statutory issue is whether the facts and circumstances indicate that the partner is "acting in his capacity as a partner."

anteed payment, compensates him or her for these expected services. However, payments to a limited partner for providing bookkeeping services for the partnership would qualify as Code Sec. 707(a) payments, if the partnership agreement did not require the services of the limited partner. An important characteristic of Code Sec. 707(a) payments is that they are normally determined by reference to the value of the services or property provided rather than the partnership's profits or losses.

Timing of income and deduction for a Code Sec. 707(a) payment. The rules with respect to the timing of the deduction of a Code Sec. 707(a) payment are meant to prevent a tax deferral resulting from the deduction of the payment (by the partnership) occurring in a year prior to the recognition of income from the payment (by the partner). For the partnership to claim the deduction for a Code Sec. 707(a) payment, two requirements must first be satisfied:

- First, the amount must be currently deductible under the partnership's method of accounting. For example, a cash method partnership must have paid the amount to the partner. An accrual method partnership must have satisfied the "all events" and "economic performance" tests for deductibility.[56]

- Second, under Code Sec. 267, the partnership generally cannot claim a deduction for a payment to a partner until the day the partner must report the payment as income. For example, an accrual method partnership cannot claim a deduction in the current year for a payment which is to be made to a cash method partner in the following year.

The above two requirements mean that Code Sec. 707(a) payments are deductible by a partnership that has an accounting method different from that of the partner on the later of these two days: (1) the day on which such an amount is deductible according to the partnership's normal accounting method, or (2) the day the partner must include such payment in gross income.[57]

Normally, the partner's taxable income and the partnership's deduction will occur at the same time. That time is dictated by the day the partner is required to include the amount as income under his or her normal accounting method whether the partnership is using a cash or accrual basis tax accounting method.

Example 4-4: Partner *A*, who is a calendar-year, cash-method taxpayer, performs noncapitalized Code Sec. 707(a)-type services for the ABC partnership, a calendar-year, accrual-basis partnership in Year 1. *A* receives payment in Year 2. Partner *A* must include this income in his Year 2 individual tax return whether or not the partnership is required to capitalize the expenditure. The partnership may not deduct the amount until Year 2.

---

[56] Code Sec. 461(h).

[57] Code Sec. 267(a) and (e). The partnership always uses a Form 1099 to report these payments to the service partner. Form W-2 is not used even though the partner might be a common law employee, and therefore no withholding of income or payroll tax is required. This treatment can apply even if the payment is made to a party related to a partner, and not to the partner themselves. In such circumstances, the payment shall be considered as occurring between the other person (related to the partner) and the members of the partnership separately. Only the fraction of the payment equal to the related partner's ownership interest will be affected. Reg. § 1.267(b)-1(b)(1).

Example 4-5: Partner *A*, who is a calendar-year, accrual-method tax-payer, performs noncapitalized Code Sec. 707(a)-type services for the ABC partnership, a calendar-year, *cash*-basis partnership, in Year 1. The partnership pays *A* in Year 2. Partner *A* has income in Year 1 whether or not the partnership is required to capitalize the expenditure. ABC deducts the expenditure in Year 2 if capitalization is not required. This is the only situation when *A*'s income and the partnership's deduction will not be recognized simultaneously.

Example 4-6: The same facts as Examples 4-4 and 4-5, except both the partnership and partner are cash-method taxpayers. *A* has income and ABC has a deduction in Year 2.

Example 4-7: The same facts as Examples 4-4 and 4-5, except both are using the accrual-method of accounting. *A* has income and ABC has a deduction in Year 1.

.02 Guaranteed Payments

Definition. "Guaranteed payments" are those payments made to a partner for acting in his or her capacity as a partner when the amount is determined independent of the partnership's operating results. These amounts are also known as "Section 707(c) payments" and can represent either payment for services rendered or payments for use of the partner's capital. The primary reason for making a Code Sec. 707(c) payment is the same as the reason for granting a partner a profits interest—he or she is providing essential services or capital to the partnership. However, in contrast to the normal consideration for these "partner activities," the amount of the payment is determined by reference to the value of the services or property provided rather than by reference to partnership profits. The use of "guaranteed payments" allows more flexibility to the partnership in recognizing the varying contributions of services and capital provided by different partners toward producing the partnership's overall profitability.

Example 4-8: The ABC partnership is owned by a group of CPAs who do both tax and audit services. *A*, *B*, and *C* are the founding senior partners who are well known and active in the business community. They are chiefly responsible for acquiring and retaining new clients. The junior partners perform and supervise most of the work. The partnership wishes to have an income sharing arrangement which both compensates the partners for time spent doing client work and recognizes other considerations. They agree upon a guaranteed Code Sec. 707(c) hourly payment for client-chargeable time spent and an equal division of profits for the partnership's income in excess of this amount.

Example 4-9: The ABC limited partnership holds unimproved unused land for long-term investment and future development. The success of this venture depends heavily on both capital and development activity. The partners agree that the limited partners should receive a compounded cumulative Code Sec. 707(c) guaranteed payment for capital equal to the percentage increase in the Consumer Price Index plus 3% times their yearly ending capital accounts as a return on their invested capital. Partnership profits in excess of this amount will be allocated 50% to the service partners and the remainder to the limited partners in proportion to their ending capital accounts.

Guaranteed payments for use of a partner's capital are similar to interest payments, but the partnership has no duty to repay the principal at a specified date as required in the case of an actual debt. These amounts are paid to partners in consideration for their continued *investment* in the partnership.

In the case of payments for services, the partnership agreement must require these activities or they must otherwise be considered central to the partnership's main activity. If the partner has both the right and duty to perform the services under the partnership agreement as opposed to a separate contract between the partner and partnership, it is a guaranteed payment under Code Sec. 707(c) unless there is strong evidence to the contrary. For example, a fixed payment received by a general partner for supervising the partnership as required by the partnership agreement would normally qualify as a guaranteed payment. In contrast, payments received by a limited partner for performing an isolated consulting task would not qualify unless there were additional factors strongly evidencing that it was his or her duty as a partner to consult with the partnership. The latter payment should be considered a Code Sec. 707(a) payment as described earlier.

The literal language of Code Sec. 707(c) refers to a guaranteed payment as a payment "determined without regard to the income of the partnership." However, payments measured by reference to *gross receipts* have also been held ineligible for Code Sec. 707(c) treatment.[58] The IRS has ruled that despite these decisions the taxpayer may treat payments dependent upon gross *rentals* as guaranteed payments if they otherwise qualify for such treatment.[59]

Timing of income and deduction of a guaranteed payment. Like a Code Sec. 707(a) payment, the partnership is entitled to a deduction if a cash payment to an independent party would have been deductible. Timing of the deduction to the partnership is governed by the partnership's accounting method alone. The partnership is allowed to deduct this amount only from its ordinary income, and the partner, in turn, characterizes the income as ordinary.[60] The partner must include the agreed upon payment as income on the last day of the partnership's year in which the partnership takes the payment into account. This date is determined by the partnership's method of accounting and is independent of the partner's tax accounting method.[61]

Guaranteed payments are considered Code Sec. 162 trade or business expenses but are subject to capitalization under the general rule of Code Sec. 263.[62] If the guaranteed payment is not capitalized by the partnership, the partnership will have an ordinary deduction. In all cases a guaranteed payment results in ordinary

---

[58] *E.T. Pratt v. Commr.*, 64 TC 203, Dec. 33,189 (1975), aff'd, CA-5, 77-1 USTC ¶ 9347, 550 F2d 1023.

[59] Rev. Rul. 81-300, 1981-2 CB 143; *see also* S. Rept. No. 169, 98th Cong., 2d Sess. 230 (1984).

[60] The partnership does not use a Form 1099 or W-2 to report Section 707(c) payments to the partner. Because

Section 707(c) payments are an income share, they are reported on the partner's K-1.

[61] Reg. § 1.707-1(c).

[62] Code Sec. 707(c). Both Section 707(a) payments and distributive shares of income can also be subject to capitalization under Section 263.

income to the partner. The net result is often very similar to treating the guaranteed payment as a distributive share of the partnership's ordinary income. However, in the case of the Code Sec. 707(c) payment, the timing of the partner's income is governed by the year the partnership takes the deduction. In the case of the 707(a) payment, the reverse is true. The timing of the partnership's 707(a) deduction is deferred until the partner must include the payment as income.[63]

There is no direct authority governing the results if a partnership pays the guaranteed amount with appreciated or depreciated property. Code Sec. 707(c) provides that the amount is treated as paid to a nonpartner for purposes of Code Secs. 61 and 162 only—for other purposes it is an income share and a distribution.[64]

> *Example 4-10:* Partner *A*, who is a calendar-year, cash-method partner, performs noncapitalized Code Sec. 707(c)-type services for the ABC partnership, a calendar year accrual-basis partnership, in Year 1. The partnership makes the payment in Year 2. ABC will deduct the amount in Year 1. Partner *A* must include the amount of the guaranteed payment in Year 1 taxable income whether or not the partnership is required to capitalize the expenditure.

> *Example 4-11:* Partner *A*, who is a calendar-year, accrual-method partner, performs noncapitalized Code Sec. 707(c)-type services for the calendar-year, cash-basis ABC partnership in Year 1. The partnership makes the payment in Year 2. ABC will deduct the payment in Year 2. Therefore, *A* will include the payment in Year 2 taxable income whether or not the partnership is required to capitalize the expenditure.

> *Example 4-12:* The same facts as Examples 4-10 and 4-11 above, except that both the partnership and the partner use the cash-accounting method. The partnership deducts the payment in Year 2 and, therefore, the partner must include this amount as income for Year 2.

> *Example 4-13:* The same facts as Examples 4-10 and 4-11 above, except that both the partnership and the partner use the accrual-accounting method. The partnership deducts the payment in Year 1 and, therefore, the partner has income in Year 1.

A Code Sec. 707(c) guaranteed payment generally will not affect the computation of a partner's distributive share of partnership income other than ordinary income. However, complications arise when the partner is entitled to the greater of a specified guaranteed salary payment or a fixed percentage of partnership income computed before the guaranteed payment is taken into account. In that case, the guaranteed payment under Code Sec. 707(c) will be the excess of the fixed minimum dollar amount over the amount the partner would have been allocated based on his or her profit/loss sharing ratios (their distributive share).

> *Example 4-14:* The ABC cash method partnership (a law firm) agreement provides that *A* is to receive one-third of the ordinary income of the partnership, as determined before any guaranteed payment is taken into

---

[63] Code Sec. 267(e)(1).

[64] *U.S. v. T.C. Davis,* SCt, 62-2 USTC ¶ 9509, 370 US 65, 82 SCt 1190.

¶404.02

account, but not less that $21,000. In addition, he is to receive one-third of the losses after taking into account the guaranteed payment. Capital gains and losses are to be shared equally. The ordinary income of the partnership is $90,000, long term capital gains (LTCG) are $30,000, and short-term capital gains (STCG) are $9,000. *A* is entitled to $30,000 (1/3 of $90,000) as his distributive share of partnership ordinary income. No part of this sum constitutes a guaranteed payment since the distributive share is more than the $21,000 minimum amount.[65] *A* would also include his share of LTCG ($10,000) and STCG ($3,000) in his distributive share.

Example 4-15: Assume the same facts as in Example 4-14, except the partnership's ordinary income is only $30,000. *A*'s distributive share of partnership ordinary income is $10,000 (1/3 of $30,000). Since the partnership agreement entitles *A* to not less than $21,000 of ordinary income, the remaining $11,000 is payable to *A* as a guaranteed payment.[66]

	A	*B*	*C*
Guaranteed Payment	$11,000	$ 0	$ 0
Distributive Share of Income	10,000	4,500	4,500
Total Income Reported by Partner	*$21,000*	*$4,500*	*$4,500*

This example effectively allocates the $11,000 deduction for the guaranteed payment equally between *A*, *B*, and *C*, since all deductions of the partnership are shared equally by the partners. There is no express prohibition which would deny the ABC partnership from specially allocating the deduction. However, allocating the $11,000 deduction to *A* would economically eliminate his guaranteed minimum and allocating the deduction to *B* and *C* would effectively increase *A*'s net share to more than $21,000.

Example 4-16: Assume the same facts as in Example 4-14, except the partnership's ordinary income is only $12,000. Relying on the regulations, *A* would have a distributive share of $4,000 (1/3 of $12,000) and a guaranteed payment of $17,000 ($21,000 – $4,000).[67] However, after taking the guaranteed payment into account, the partnership suffers a loss of $5,000 ($12,000 – $17,000) and thus there are not partnership profits from which to allocate a share to *A*.

Profits	$12,000
Code Sec. 707(c)	(17,000)
Code Sec. 702(a)(8) partnership taxable income	*$(5,000)*

It has been suggested that the regulation does not go far enough and that the solution may be to treat the entire payment to the partner as a guaranteed payment whenever the partnership's income before deducting the guaranteed payment is less than the guaranteed payment. Losses then can be ratably

[65] Reg. § 1.707-1(c), Ex. 2.
[66] *Id.*
[67] *Id.*

shared among the partners.[68] Using this approach, *A* would have a guaranteed payment of $21,000 and a distributive share of partnership loss in the amount of $3,000 (1/3 of the $9,000 loss after subtracting the $21,000 guaranteed payment from the $12,000 of partnership income).

Profits before guaranteed payment	$12,000
Code Sec. 707(c)	(21,000)
Partnership taxable income—$(3,000) to each of *A, B,* and *C**	*$(9,000)*

*Another approach that could be provided for in the partnership agreement is that *A* shares only in additional loss items—those not attributable to his guaranteed payment. Thus, the $9,000 loss should be shared only by *B* and *C* ($4,500 each). The partnership agreement should be made clear on this point. A method of arriving at this result is to take the Section 702(a)(8) loss of $5,000, after determining that a $17,000 guaranteed payment is required, and giving *A* a priority positive distributive share of $4,000 of gross receipts which increases the total loss to $9,000, which is shared by *B* and *C* equally.

The computation of the income allocations in these situations can be a little more complicated if the partner is to receive a certain fraction of all of the income (not just the ordinary income) of the partnership, subject to a minimum amount. Under these circumstances, the guaranteed payment is the minimum amount less the partner's total distributive share of all partnership income. The guaranteed payment must then be subtracted from the partnership ordinary income, and the remaining ordinary income and other income of the partnership will be allocated among the partners based on the fraction of total remaining income that each partner is due to receive.

> **Example 4-17:** *F* and *G* are partners in FG, a two-man partnership. The partnership agreement provides that *F* is to receive 30 percent of the partnership income, but not less than $100,000. The partnership agreement makes no provision for sharing capital gains. For the taxable year the partnership income before taking into account any guaranteed payment is $200,000, and consists of $128,000 of ordinary income and $72,000 of capital gains. *F*'s guaranteed payment is $100,000 less *F*'s $60,000 distributive share (30 percent of partnership income of $200,000), or $40,000. The total partnership income for the taxable year, after deduction of the guaranteed payment, is $200,000 – $40,000 = $160,000. Of this amount, *F*'s distributive share, as determined above, is $60,000. *G*'s distributive share is therefore $160,000 – $60,000 = $100,000. Based on these amounts, the effective income sharing ratio for the year is 6/16 for *F* and 10/16 for *G*. This means that the partnership capital gains as well as the partnership ordinary income are to be shared in the ratio of 6/16 for *F* and 10/16 for *G*. Accordingly, the ordinary income of the partnership will be $128,000 – $40,000 (guaranteed payment) = $88,000, and the amounts of

---

[68] McKee, Nelson, & Whitmire, *Federal Taxation of Partnerships and Partners,* ¶ 13.03[3] (1997).

ordinary income and capital gains to be reported by the partners are as follows:[69]

	F	**G**	**Total**
Ordinary income	$33,000 (6/16)	$55,000 (10/16)	$88,000
Guaranteed payment	$40,000		
Total ordinary income	$73,000	$55,000	$128,000
Capital gains	$27,000 (6/16)	$45,000 (10/16)	$72,000
Total	$100,000	$100,000	$200,000

A guaranteed payment is:

- Not a share of profits for purposes of identifying the partnership's required taxable year.[70]

- Not a share of profits for the special rules on the taxation of sales between a partnership and its partners.[71]

- Not a share of profits for purposes of the partnership's technical termination upon the sale of interests in that partnership.[72]

- Not subject to income or payroll tax (FICA and FUTA) withholding.[73]

- Subject to the tax on self-employment income unless the partnership is not engaged in a trade or business[74] or the payment is a guaranteed payment for the use of capital paid to a limited partner.

- Earned income for purposes of contributions to a qualified deferred compensation plan.

- Nonpassive interest income for purposes of the Code Sec. 469 passive loss rules if paid for the use of capital.[75]

- Nonpassive compensation income for purposes of the Code Sec. 469 passive loss rules if paid for services.[76]

---

[69] Rev. Rul. 69-180, 1969-1 CB 183.

[70] Code Sec. 706(b)(1)(B); Reg. § 1.707-1(c).

[71] Code Sec. 708(b); Reg. § 1.707-1(c).

[72] Code Sec. 708(b); Reg. § 1.707-1(c).

[73] Reg. § 1.707-1(c); see Rev. Rul. 69-184, 1969-1 CB 256.

[74] A guaranteed payment is net income from self-employment *only* if the partnership is engaged in a trade or business. Reg. § 1.1402(a)-1(b). For this purpose, a partnership engaged in the business of renting real estate appears to be considered engaged in a trade or business (see Reg. § 1.1402(c)-1) even though real estate rental income is generally excluded from the definition of net income from self-employment. Code Sec. 1402(a)(1); Reg. § 1.1402(a)-4. Therefore, a partner receiving a guaranteed payment from a partnership engaged in the business of renting real estate may have net income from self-employment, even though he would not have net income from

self-employment if he engaged in the same activity as an individual. However, the IRS has ruled that a one-fourth partner in a partnership owning an office building, who performs services for the partnership and receives as remuneration "a specified amount each week from the gross rents collected," is not subject to the self-employment tax on either his distributive share or the weekly amount. Rev. Rul. 64-220, 1964-2 CB 335. The Worksheet for Figuring Net Earnings (Loss) From Self-Employment treats a dealer in real estate's rental income as self-employment income if it is received in the course of a trade or business as a real estate dealer, but the worksheet treats all Section 707(c) guaranteed payments other than guaranteed payments made to limited partners for use of capital as self-employment income.

[75] Reg. § 1.469-2(e)(2)(ii).

[76] *Id.*

Observation: If the payee partner does not materially participate in the partnership's activity or if the partnership's activity is per se passive then this essentially self-charged amount may increase a pass-through passive loss which cannot be offset with the guaranteed payment. Although the self-charged character of these payments arguably qualifies for the "self-charged interest" rules of Proposed Reg. § 1.469-7 if the guaranteed payment is for capital, the self-charged aspect will probably be ignored if the payment is for services.

According to the IRS,[77] premiums a partnership pays for accident and health insurance coverage on behalf of its partners are deemed guaranteed payments for services to the partners—provided the premium payments are paid for services rendered as a partner, and the payments are determined without regard to partnership income. As guaranteed payments, the premiums are deductible by the partnership and included in the recipient partners' gross income. While the partner cannot exclude the premiums from income, the partner can deduct a percentage of the cost of the premiums on his or her individual income tax return in arriving at adjusted gross income (Line 26, Form 1040) under Code Sec. 162(1)—assuming the Code Sec. 162(1) requirements are met.

As noted above, guaranteed payments constitute ordinary income to the recipient, but are not salary or wages for employment tax purposes.[78] Since the payments are not wages, they are not subject to income tax withholding or Social Security withholding requirements.[79]

Because guaranteed payments, from the partnership's point of view, are treated as payments to nonpartners, they have no net direct impact on the recipient partner's tax basis and Code Sec. 704(b) book capital account.[80] Partnership income is reduced by the guaranteed payments and each partner's share of the deduction reduces his or her basis in the partnership interest and is reflected in his or her capital account. Neither the income nor the payment flows through the partnership's or recipient partner's Schedule K-1 capital account reconciliation.[81]

Obviously, if a payment is *not* a guaranteed payment, the distribution and related allocation of income will decrease and increase, respectively, the partner's tax basis in his or her partnership interest—and the amounts will flow through the partner's Schedule K-1 capital account reconciliation. The guaranteed payments do appear in Schedule M-1 in reconciling the partnership's taxable Net Income (Loss) with its Code Sec. 704(b) or other book accounting income (loss). The guaranteed payment is part of the partnership's tax net income, but not part of the partnership's book income. The Code Sec. 707(c) payment is not considered a distribution for purposes of "Analysis of Partners' Capital Account" on Schedule K-1, Item J.

Guaranteed payments for capital—Are they just ordinary income or are they interest? The authority on the specific character of guaranteed payments is contradictory. For example, Code Sec. 707(c) only refers to Code Sec. 162, rather

---

[77] Rev. Rul. 91-26, 1991-1 CB 184.

[78] FICA and FUTA; Rev. Rul. 69-184, 1969-1 CB 256.

[79] Code Sec. 3402.

[80] The portion, if any, of the partnership's deduction allocable to the recipient partner will affect his capital account. Reg. § 1.704-1(b)(2)(iv)(o).

[81] Item J, Schedule K-1, and Schedule M-2, Form 1065.

than Code Sec. 163, when discussing the deductibility of guaranteed payments for capital. This would seem to indicate that guaranteed payments are in the nature of ordinary deductions to the partnership. On the other hand, the passive activity regulations characterize guaranteed payments for services and capital as nonpassive income.[82] These regulations treat a guaranteed payment for services as wages and a guaranteed payment for capital "as the payment of interest."[83] This provision implies that *both* the partnership and partner treat a guaranteed payment for use of capital as interest.[84] Interest income is considered to be portfolio income and therefore is not passive income. A Code Sec. 707(c) guaranteed payment for capital is also considered to be investment income for purposes of the limitations relating to deducting investment interest.[85] Guaranteed payments for capital are also treated as interest for purposes of capitalizing construction period interest.[86]

The Instructions for Form 1065, U.S. Partnership Return of Income, refer to a guaranteed payment for capital as "interest."[87] This is true even though the guaranteed payment is not paid for the use of money the partnership owes to a creditor. However, the instructions say such amounts should not be shown as interest expense on the Form 1065 but as a guaranteed payment on line 10 of page one. Judging from the instructions to Form 1065, the IRS appears in most situations to want the partnership to treat a guaranteed payment for capital as ordinary expense or ordinary income (rather than interest expense or interest income) since there is no explicit instruction to do otherwise. However, this treatment would appear to contradict the passive activity and investment interest expense limitation authority mentioned above.

The correct treatment to be accorded a guaranteed payment for the use of capital as interest, self-employment income, or other income is dependent upon the issue at hand. If the partnership prefers that such payments be treated as interest for all tax purposes, the partners should consider loaning capital to the partnership and receiving interest.[88] The interest payment will be a Code Sec. 707(a) payment and subject to the timing provisions of Code Sec. 267, and the partnership will not be entitled to a deduction until the day the partner must report the interest income.

.03 Payments Not Governed by Code Sec. 707(a) or (c)

If a payment cannot be classified as falling within the definition of either Code Sec. 707(a) or (c), then it will be treated as part of the partnership's agreement regarding the distribution of profits. For example, a payment made for services required by the partnership agreement that are normally performed by a partner and that are based on a percentage of partnership net income will be deemed a distributive share of partnership income. The partnership is not allowed a deduc-

---

[82] Whether the payment is for services or capital, the partner's income is not passive, but the deduction may increase the passive loss (or decrease the passive income) of the partners who do not materially participate.

[83] Reg. § 1.469-2(e)(2).

[84] It is unclear whether the self-charged interest rules will apply because there is no lending transaction.

[85] Code Sec. 163(d)(5) defines an investment as "property which produces income of a type described in Sec-

tion 469(e)(1)." Code Sec. 469(e)(1) includes interest, and Reg. § 1.469-2(e)(2) specifically says a guaranteed payment for capital is interest.

[86] Reg. § 1.263-9(c)(2)(iii).

[87] *See also* GCM 36702 (April 12, 1976).

[88] Naturally, this will change the economic arrangement. The partnership owes a partner debt whether or not the money is lost. A capital account is reduced by a partner's share of loss.

tion for such a payment, but the ultimate effect is very similar to that of a Code Sec. 707(c) payment. The service partner's income is included in the year in which the partnership year ends, and the other partners' shares of the partnership's taxable income are reduced by this amount in the same year. The allocation reduces the other partners' shares of income even though a salary payment for the same type of service would have been capitalized.[89]

Code Sec. 707(c) payments for services, however, are always reported as ordinary income by the partner and are always treated as a deduction from ordinary income by the partnership. In contrast, if the payment is treated as a distributive share of partnership income, then the partner will be treated as having received a *pro rata* share of each type of partnership income. Finally, the partner's basis is increased by his or her share of the partnership's income and then decreased by the actual payment. The payment is treated as a distribution of income previously credited to his or her capital account.

> *Example 4-18:* Cynthia Bond is a partner in the equal ABC Partnership who uses the cash method of accounting and reports her taxable income on the calendar year. She performs services in Year 1 for ABC, which employs the cash method of accounting and calendar year as well. The partnership agreement provides that Cynthia is to receive 25 percent of the partnership's net nonseparately stated income in Year 1 as payment for special services of managing the partnership's activities as required by the agreement. The remaining net income is divided equally between Cynthia, Brad Olson and Andy Napolitano, the other partners. The partnership has $400 of ordinary income in Year 1 and makes no payments. ABC makes a $100 payment to Cynthia in Year 2 for her services in Year 1. An analysis of the payment's purpose and the method of its calculation indicates that it is governed by neither Code Sec. 707(a) nor (c). The result is as follows:

Partnership Results—Year 1

Partnership gross income	$400
Deductions	0
Partnership taxable income	*$400*
Special allocation to Cynthia*	(100)
Amount divided equally	*$300*

> *Required by Code Sec. 702 to be separately stated. Reg. § 1.702-1(a)(9).

---

[89] Code Sec. 707(a)(2)(A) provides that if an allocation of income for services and a distribution, when viewed together, are property characterized as a transaction occurring between the partnership and a partner acting other than in his capacity as a member of the partnership, then the allocation and distribution are treated as a Section 707(a) payment. However, there are no regulations, rulings, cases, or other guidance concerning when and how this provision applies.

Partners' Taxable Income—Year 1

	Andy	Brad	Cynthia
Special allocation to Cynthia.	$ 0	$ 0	$100
Share of partnership income not specially allocated.	100	100	100
Total.	*$100*	*$100*	*$200*

Assuming that the results of operations in Year 2 are the same as in Year 1, but because Cynthia renders no special services in Year 2, the partnership makes no special allocation to her, the results are as follows:

Partnership Results—Year 2

Partnership gross income	$400
Deductions.	0
Partnership taxable income	*$400*
Special allocation to Cynthia	0
Partnership income divided equally	*$400*

Partners' Taxable Income—Year 2

	Andy	Brad	Cynthia
Special allocation	$ 0	$ 0	$ 0
Share of partnership income not specially allocated.	133	133	133
Total	*$133*	*$133*	*$133*

The $100 payment to Cynthia in Year 2 is a distribution and results in gain only if it exceeds her basis.

Example 4-19: Assume the same facts as Example 4-18, but the payment qualifies as a Code Sec. 707(c) payment. Since the partnership is a cash method taxpayer, it deducts the payment in Year 2. Year 1 results are as follows:

Partnership Results—Year 1

Partnership gross income	$400
Deductions.	0
Partnership taxable income	*$400*
Special allocation to Cynthia	0
Amount divided equally	*$400*

Partners' Taxable Income—Year 1

	Andy	Brad	Cynthia
Special allocation to Cynthia..........	$0	$0	$0
Share of partnership income not specially allocated........................	133	133	133
Total............................	*$133*	*$133*	*$133*

Assuming that the results of operations in Year 2 are the same as Year 1, the results are as follows:

Partnership Results—Year 2

Partnership gross income	$400
Deductions......................................	(100)
Partnership taxable income	*$300*
Special allocation to Cynthia	0
Partnership income divided equally	*$300*
Cynthia's ordinary income from the guaranteed payment ...	$100

The $100 payment to Cynthia in Year 2 is treated as a distribution and results in gain only if it exceeds her basis in her partnership interest.

Partners' Taxable Income—Year 2

	Andy	Brad	Cynthia
Special allocation	$0	$0	$0
Share of partnership income	100	100	100
Guaranteed payment	0	0	100
Total............................	*$100*	*$100*	*$200*

Two-Year Summary—Special Allocation vs. Guaranteed Payment

	Special Allocation			Guaranteed Payment		
	Andy	Brad	Cynthia	Andy	Brad	Cynthia
Year 1						
Guaranteed payment	$0	$0	$0	$0	$0	$0
Special Allocation	0	0	100	0	0	0
Share of income not specially allocated	100	100	100	133	133	133
Year 2						
Guaranteed payment	0	0	0	0	0	100
Special allocation	0	0	0	0	0	0

	Special Allocation			Guaranteed Payment		
	Andy	Brad	Cynthia	Andy	Brad	Cynthia
Share of income not specially allocated	133	133	133	100	100	100
Total	$233	$233	$333	$233	$233	$333

The ultimate effect is to reduce Brad and Andy's taxable income, regardless of whether it is classified as a Code Sec. 704/731 income allocation and payment, as in Example 4-17, or a Code Sec. 707(c) payment, as in this example. The classification may, however, alter the timing of when the effects take place. Naturally, the character of income reported by Cynthia and the other partners can also be affected by the classification.

If the payment was classified as a Code Sec. 707(a) payment, the results under the example's assumptions would be the same as those for the Code Sec. 707(c) example, except the payment would be labeled a payment for services rather than a guaranteed payment.

.04 Summary: Is This "Much Ado About Very Little"?

In short—the answer is *usually yes.* In the case of all three classifications, the payee's income and the other partners' reductions in shares of partnership income usually occur simultaneously. This eliminates the group's ability to generate a partnership deduction without a partner having offsetting income. In the case of a Code Sec. 707(a) payment, the partnership generally deducts the payment when the partner reports the income under his or her accounting method. Otherwise, when the payment is a guaranteed payment or a distributive share of income, the payee partner has income at the time his or her payment is subtracted from the other partners' shares of the partnership's taxable income under the partnership's accounting method.

The timing of the partnership's deduction and the partner's income will be the same regardless of which of the three categories the payment falls into if:

1. Both the partnership and the partner are using the cash method of accounting;

2. They both use the calendar year as their taxable year; and

3. The payment is made to the partner during the same year the services or capital is provided by the partner to the partnership.

Similarly, if both the partnership and partner are accrual-method taxpayers using the same taxable year, classification of the payment will not alter the timing regardless of when payment is made. In other cases, the partnership's deduction may be deferred beyond the year in which it normally would be allowed or the partner may have reportable income before he or she is paid. Finally, the income and deduction are always ordinary in the case of Code Sec. 707(a) and (c) payments. However, if the payment does not fit either of these categories and is treated as a share of partnership income, some portion could be, for example, capital gains or Code Sec. 1231 gains. In years in which capital gains are taxed at the same effective rate as ordinary income, this distinction should make little difference in the partners' tax liabilities.

Although in a majority of the situations the correct classification of a payment to a partner will have little if any effect on the partner's tax liability, there are circumstances when there can be an important difference to both the payee partner and the partnership.

> *Example 4-20:* The ABC limited partnership is an accrual method, calendar-year owner and operator of commercial real property. Partner *A* receives 5% of net rental income as payment for his services. It is payable on March 30 of the partnership's following year. If the partnership agreement requires that he perform these duties and receive compensation as an obligation of being a general partner, any payment is a Code Sec. 707(c) payment. *A* must report the guaranteed payment in the year the partnership accrues the expense. Any part of the expense the partnership accrues during the year is taxable to *A* even though he is not paid until March 30 of the following year.

> *Example 4-21:* Assume the same facts as Example 4-20 except that the partnership agreement makes no reference to *A*'s duties as a property manager or payment for such duties. Instead there is a separate five-year contract with *A* to manage the partnership properties with compensation equal to 5% of the net rental income. The payment is a Code Sec. 707(a) payment. If *A* is a cash basis taxpayer, he includes the payment in income on March 30 and the partnership may not deduct the payment until its taxable year which includes March 30.

> *Observation:* Any cash method partner who receives a K-1 from a partnership showing a Code Sec. 707(c) guaranteed payment for a year in which the partner has not received an actual cash payment should review the partnership agreement. If the partnership agreement has not provided for an employment relationship, the payment might be misclassified. If there is a contract outside of the partnership agreement, the payment is probably a Code Sec. 707(a) payment. This means the partner need not report the payment until he or she is paid and the partnership can't deduct the payment until the partner is paid.[90]

¶ 405 Taxable Year

.01 General Rules

Each partner must include in his or her annual taxable income his or her distributive share of the partnership's income and guaranteed payments *for the taxable year of the partnership that ends with or within his or her own tax year.*[91] Therefore, in determining the amount of income from a partnership that a partnership will include for a particular tax year, the critical date is the date of the partnership taxable year end. This rule, standing alone, provides the partner with

---

[90] Form 8088, Missing Information Necessary to Complete Adjustment Request, should be filed notifying the IRS that the partner's tax position is inconsistent with the partnership's tax position.

[91] Code Sec. 706(a).

an opportunity to defer up to 11 months of income earned by the partnership (the maximum 11 months from the partnership year end to the partner's next year end) from taxation until the next year.

   Example 4-22: Fred Dreer, a calendar year partner of a January 31 year-end partnership, will include his share of the partnership's income earned from February 1 of the prior calendar year in his computation of the current year's tax liability. This is a deferral of 11 months (from February 1 to December 31 of the prior year) of the prior year's taxable income until the next year.

   Code Sec. 706(b)(1) imposes limitations on the use of this deferral opportunity. A partnership is allowed to adopt a "business purpose" taxable year if they can show that they have a natural business year or if they meet other requirements that show that they should be allowed to use a taxable year other than one specifically defined by statute.

   In the absence of a business purpose taxable year, the partnership must adopt as its "required year:"

1. The taxable year of its partners who have an aggregate interest in partnership profits and capital of greater than 50 percent;[92]

2. The taxable year of all its principal partners, if a year described in 1, above, does not exist;[93] or

3. The calendar year or such other period as the Secretary may prescribe in Regulations (generally the year with the least aggregate deferral of taxable income), if a year described in (1) or (2), above, does not exist.[94]

   Finally, if the partnership wishes to adopt a year other than a required year as determined by the partners' year-ends or its business purpose year-end as determined by the timing of the partnership's gross receipts, it can adopt a year allowed by Code Sec. 444 if it makes the required payments and satisfies Code Sec. 444's additional rules.

   S Corporation Observation: An S corporation must use a calendar year unless it has a business purpose for a fiscal year, makes a Code Sec. 444 election, or elects to use a 52-53-week taxable year that ends with reference to its required taxable year or a taxable year elected under Code Sec. 444.[95] The presence of a business purpose is determined under the same rules as partnerships.[96]

---

[92] Code Sec. 706(b)(1)(B)(i). A majority interest tax year is the tax year of one or more partners having (on that day) a total interest in partnership profits and capital of more than 50%. Generally, the testing day is the first day of the partnership's tax year. A partnership that changes to a majority interest tax year will not be required to change to another tax year for either of the two tax years following the year of change. Code Sec. 706(b)(4).

[93] Code Sec. 706(b)(1)(B)(ii). A principal partner is one who has an interest of 5 percent or more in the partnership's profits or capital.

[94] Code Sec. 706(b)(1)(B)(iii). The Secretary has provided for the year which produces the least deferral of income.

[95] Reg. § 1.1378-1(a).

[96] Code Sec. 1378; Rev. Proc. 2002-39, 2002-22 IRB 1046.

.02 Majority Interest Required Taxable Year

Under this option, a partnership must have the same tax year as that of its majority partners. The majority partners are those partners having the same tax year and whose combined interest in partnership capital and profits is greater than 50 percent. The ownership of certain foreign partners and a partner who is tax exempt is disregarded in determining the majority interest.[97] The majority interest is established on the first day of the partnership's taxable year; but the Secretary of Treasury may allow the partnership to test for majority interest on some other date.[98] However, before an alternate date will be allowed, the partnership must show that the date is representative of the current ownership interest of the partnership. If a partnership is required to change its tax year to that of its majority partners, it is not required to change again for either of the two years following the year of the change.[99]

> **Example 4-23:** The ABC Partnership was formed by Mary Alar and Graham Bowman who report their income on a calendar year and who each own 25 percent of partnership capital and profits. The other 50 percent is owned by a Cann Corporation which reports its income on a fiscal year ending on June 30. There is no combination of partners with the same taxable year-end with a majority interest (greater than 50 percent) in the partnership, and there are therefore no majority partners.

> **Example 4-24:** Assume the same facts as in Example 4-23, except that Cann Corporation owns only 49 percent of partnership capital and profits. Mary and Graham own 51 percent. The two individual partners are now majority partners and the partnership must use a calendar year.

.03 Principal Partner Required Taxable Year

If there is no business purpose year-end and no one year-end that a majority of the partners share, the partnership must adopt the same tax year as that of all its principal partners. A principal partner is one who owns at least five percent of partnership capital or profits. If there is no tax year that every one of the principal partners use, the partnership must adopt a year that results in the least amount of deferred income to the partners.[100]

If a partnership has both majority partners and one or more principal partners, the partnership must adopt the tax year of the majority partners.

> **Example 4-25:** The ABC Partnership is a limited partnership with 30 individual limited partners and a corporate general partner. Each limited partner owns a 3-percent interest in partnership capital and profits. The corporate general partner owns the remaining 10-percent interest in capital and profits. Twenty-five of the 30 individual limited partners (representing 75 percent of the capital and profits interest in the partnership) have calendar year-ends. The other five have fiscal year-ends ending September 30. The corporate general partner, who is the only principal partner, has a fiscal year

---

[97] Reg. § 1.706-1(b)(5), (6).
[98] Code Sec. 706(b)(4)(A).

[99] Code Sec. 706(b)(4)(B).
[100] Reg. § 1.706-1(b)(2)(i)(C).

ending on June 30. The partnership must adopt the calendar year used by the majority interest partners (the 25 owning 75 percent) rather than the June 30 year-end used by its principal partner.

.04 Year of Least Aggregate Deferral

If there is no year-end that can satisfy the majority interest test and the principal partner test, the partnership must select a year-end (from among the partners' year-ends) resulting in the least aggregate deferral of income to the partners. The partnership does not have the option of choosing between a calendar year or the year of least aggregate deferral of income.[101] In determining the appropriate year-end under this rule, both the year-end and the profits interest of each partner must be taken into account.[102]

The determination of the least aggregate deferral of income is made by multiplying each partner's profits interest for the year by the number of months of deferral that would arise through the selection of the proposed tax year.[103] Months of deferral for this purpose are determined by counting the months from the proposed partnership year-end to the partners' individual year-ends. The partners' individual year-ends are determined using the information available at the beginning of the current tax year (unless the partners have made voluntary changes in their year-ends).[104]

After testing each proposed tax year (using each partner's different tax year-end), the tax year that produces the least aggregate deferral of income is the "required year." If more than one partner's year-end produces the same aggregate deferral, the partnership can use either partner's year-end as its required year-end. If one of the qualifying taxable years is also the partnership's existing taxable year, the partnership must use its existing taxable year.[105] However, once the year-end is chosen, the partnership cannot change to another year-end of equal deferral.[106] The majority interest rule and the principal partners rule look at partners' interests in capital and/or profits. The least aggregate deferral rule looks only at the partners' interests in profits.

A special *de minimis* rule provides that if the tax year with the least aggregate deferral produces an aggregate deferral whose difference from the aggregate deferral of the partnership's existing tax year is less than 0.5, the existing tax year will be treated as the tax year with the least aggregate deferral. Thus, no change in tax year is necessary or permitted under these circumstances.[107]

Partnerships subject to the least aggregate deferral rule must determine the tax year-end with the least aggregate deferral for every year in which the partners' profits interests or year-ends change.

---

[101] Reg. § 1.706-1(b)(2)(i)(C).

[102] However, any tax-exempt partner who had no taxable income from the partnership in the preceding year is disregarded. Likewise, a tax-exempt entity that was not a partner in the preceding year is also disregarded if the partner will have no taxable income from the partnership in the current year. Reg. § 1.706-1(b)(5).

[103] Reg. § 1.706-1(b)(3)(i).

[104] IRS Letter Ruling 8907042 (11-23-88).

[105] Reg. § 1.706-1(b)(3)(i).

[106] *Id.*

[107] Reg. § 1.706-1(b)(3)(iii).

Example 4-26: The SD Partnership has two equal partners, Sam Burns and Danny Ferrer, and reports its income on a fiscal year ending June 30. Sam reports his income on a fiscal year ending June 30 and Danny reports his income on a fiscal year ending July 31. For the taxable year beginning July 1, the partnership will be required to retain its fiscal year since a year ending June 30 results in the least aggregate deferral of income to the partners. This determination is made as follows:

Year End	Int.	Mos. Def.	Int. Def.
June 30 Fiscal Year			
Sam 6/30	50%	0	0
Danny 7/31	50%	1	.5
Aggregate Deferral			.5
July 31 Fiscal Year			
Sam 6/30	50%	11	5.5
Danny 7/31	50%	0	0
Aggregate Deferral			5.5

The partnership must choose June 30th as its fiscal year. It cannot choose a calendar year.

Example 4-27: Corporations A, B, C, and D operate a partnership. A has an April 30 year-end, B has a July 31 year-end, C has a November 30 year-end, and D has a December 31 year-end. A, B, and C each own 30% of the partnership; D owns 10%. The determination of which year-end the partnership must use is made as follows:

Partner	Partner's Year-end	Profits Interest	Months Deferred	Deferral
A's April 30 Year-end				
A	4/30	.3	0	.0
B	7/31	.3	3	.9
C	11/30	.3	7	2.1
D	12/31	.1	8	.8
Aggregate Deferral				3.8
B's July 31 Year-end				
A	4/30	.3	9	2.7
B	7/31	.3	0	.0
C	11/30	.3	4	1.2
D	12/31	.1	5	.5
Aggregate Deferral				4.4

Partner	Partner's Year-end	Profits Interest	Months Deferred	Deferral
C's Nov. 30 Year-end				
A	4/30	.3	5	1.5
B	7/31	.3	8	2.4
C	11/30	.3	0	.0
D	12/31	.1	1	.1
Aggregate Deferral				4.0
D's Dec. 31 Year-end				
A	4/30	.3	4	1.2
B	7/31	.3	7	2.1
C	11/30	.3	11	3.3
D	12/31	.1	0	.0
Aggregate Deferral				6.6

Since the April 30 year-end yields the least aggregate deferral of income, the partnership must select an April 30 year-end for its "required year."

.05 Changes in Required Taxable Years

The partnership's "required year" can change for three reasons:

1. The partners holding majority interests change (or their year-ends change);[108]

2. The principal partners change; or

3. The year-end with the least aggregate deferral changes.[109]

A change in the partnership's "required year" is treated as automatically approved by the IRS.[110] For "required year" changes, there is no four-year spread relief from "income bunching" that occurs because of short period returns. Annualization of the short period income is not required.[111] Unless the partnership has obtained approval for its natural business year, a change in a partner's year-end will often force the partnership to change its year-end.

A partnership that wants to adopt, change, or retain its annual accounting period must complete and file a current Form 1128 with the Director, IRS Center, Attention: ENTITY CONTROL, where the taxpayer files its federal income tax return. No copies of Form 1128 are required to be sent to the national office. In addition, the partnership must attach a copy of the Form 1128 to the partnership's Form 1065 for the first year the change is effective.[112]

---

[108] A consistency rule may avoid the need to change in some cases.

[109] There is a consistency rule and a *de minimis* rule that may avoid the need to change in some cases.

[110] Rev. Proc. 2002-38, 2002-1 C.B. 1037.

[111] Reg. § 1.706-1(b)(8)(i)(B).

[112] Rev. Proc. 2002-38, Sec. 7.02(1), 2002-22 IRB 1037.

If a partnership using the majority interest rule must change its year under that rule, it will not be required to change again for two years following the year of change.[113] However, if the partnership's year-end is required by the principal partner rule, and the year-end of its principal partners change requiring a change in the partnership's year-end, the two year retention of the old year is not allowed.

Partnerships that have a taxable year dictated by the least aggregate deferral of income rule must change years under these rules on an ongoing basis unless the change would produce an aggregate deferral whose difference from the aggregate deferral of the prior year is less than 0.5.[114]

.06 Business Purpose Taxable Year—The Natural Business Year

To establish a business purpose for a taxable year, the taxpayer must show one of the following:

1. They have a natural business year,

2. They have facts and circumstances that support the use of a business purpose taxable year, or

3. They have a non-tax reason to support a business purpose taxable year, and agree to certain additional terms, conditions, and adjustments that have the effect of neutralizing the tax effects of any resulting substantial distortion of income.[115]

If the taxpayer's gross receipts from sales and services for the short period and the three immediately preceding taxable years indicate that the taxpayer has a peak and a non-peak period of business, the taxpayer's natural business year is deemed to end at, or soon after, the close of the highest peak period of business. For these purposes 1 month will be deemed to be "soon after" the close of the highest peak period of business. For example, suppose that a partnership operates a retail business and the highest peak of the partnership's annual business cycle occurs in December each year. In January a significant amount of the merchandise that was purchased by the partnership's customers in December is either returned or exchanged. The partnership's natural business year is deemed to end at December 31 or soon after (January 31), the close of the highest peak period of business in December.[116]

A partnership's natural business year can also be determined under the "25-percent gross receipts test." In fact, a partnership year determined under the 25-percent gross receipts test will be automatically accepted by the IRS.[117] Under this method, a partnership's natural business year is determined by applying a mechanical 25-percent gross receipts test to each year over the most recent three-year period. To pass the test, gross receipts from sales and services for the last two months of each of the three 12-month periods must exceed 25 percent of the total gross receipts for each respective 12-month period. If the partnership qualifies for more than one natural business year under the 25-percent gross receipts test, the

---

[113] Code Sec. 706(b)(4)(B).

[114] Reg. § 1.706-1(b)(3)(iii).

[115] Rev. Proc. 2002-39, Sec. 5.02, 2002-22 IRB 1046.

[116] Rev. Proc. 2002-39, Sec. 5.03(1)(c), 2002-22 IRB 1046.

[117] Rev. Proc. 2002-38, 2002-1 CB 1037.

year-end producing the highest three-year average percentage of gross receipts for the final two months is the partnership's natural business year.[118]

For purposes of this test, the period covered by the "three most recent years" is the three-year period ending with the last month for the requested new tax year-end and before the filing of the request for a year-end change. For example, if a partnership wants to adopt or change to an August 31 year-end in 2010, the three "most recent years" are the three years ending on August 31, 2010.[119]

> **Example 4-28:** The ABC Partnership, which is newly formed but operates a business which has been in existence many years, wants to adopt an August 31 year-end. The gross receipts for the three most recent years for the 12-month period ending August 31 and a two-month period ending August 31 are:
>
> | | | *12-Month* | *2-Month* |
> |---|---|---|---|
> | Year 1— | 9/1/2007 to 8/31/2008 | $270,000 | |
> | | 7/1/2008 to 8/31/2008 | | $73,000 |
> | Year 2— | 9/1/2008 to 8/31/2009 | 310,000 | |
> | | 7/1/2009 to 8/31/2009 | | 80,000 |
> | Year 3— | 9/1/2009 to 8/31/2010 | 340,000 | |
> | | 7/1/2010 to 8/31/2010 | | 86,000 |
>
> Since more than 25% of the gross receipts (27%, 25.81%, and 25.29% respectively) occurred in the last two months for all three prior years, the partnership's natural business year ends in August. The August 31 year-end can be adopted by filing Form 1128, Application to Adopt, Change or Retain a Tax Year, with the IRS by the due date, including extensions, of the partnership's tax return for the first year the new year end is effective.[120] If the change is approved, a short period return is required for the short year ending August 31.

In addition to the approval granted to a partnership requesting a taxable year conforming to a year meeting the 25-percent test, the partnership may request approval of a natural business year characterized by a general facts and circumstances analysis. However, the IRS anticipates that approval of a natural business year under this facts and circumstances test will be granted *only in rare and unusual circumstances*. The following factors will not ordinarily be sufficient to establish that the business purpose requirement for a particular taxable year has been met:

1. The use of a particular year for regulatory or financial accounting purposes;

2. Hiring patterns—for example, a firm that typically hires staff during certain times of the year;

---

[118] Rev. Proc. 2002-39, 2002-1 C.B. 1046.
[119] *Id.*, 5.03(3)(a).
[120] *Id.*, 6.01.

3. The use of a particular year for administrative purposes, such as the admission or retirement of partners, promotion of staff, and compensation or retirement arrangements with staff or partners; and

4. The fact that a particular business involves the use of price lists, model years, or other items that change on an annual basis.[121]

Newly formed partnerships attempting to obtain approval of other than a required tax year on the basis of a business purpose can make a backup Code Sec. 444 election.[122] The backup election, which will become effective if the requested business purpose year-end is denied, is made by filing Form 8716, Election to Have a Tax Year Other Than a Required Tax Year, and typing or printing "BACKUP ELECTION" on the top of the form. However, if the Form 8716 is filed on or after the date the Form 1128 is filed, Form 8716 must have printed or typed across the top "FORM 1128 BACKUP ELECTION."[123]

.07 Adopting a Taxable Year Other Than a "Required Year" or "Natural Business" Year-End

The combination of the allowable required years and the narrow definition of a business purpose year has resulted in the overwhelming majority of partnerships controlled by individual partners being forced to use a calendar year.

In order to provide some relief to many forced conversions to calendar years, Congress enacted a procedure whereby S corporations, personal service corporations, and partnerships could adopt or retain otherwise unpermitted fiscal years.[124] Under Code Sec. 444, such entities are entitled to a one-time election to select a taxable year other than one the Internal Revenue Code requires.[125] Newly formed partnerships that would otherwise be obligated to use a required year may elect a fiscal year having a deferral period of three months or less.[126] If no election is made, the partnership must use the taxable year the Code requires.

However, an election under Code Sec. 444 is not without cost. Each year that an election under Code Sec. 444 is in effect, partnerships must make a "required payment," which is an amount that crudely approximates the tax deferral arising from the fiscal year.[127] Since each year's required payment is adjusted to account for

---

[121] Rev. Proc. 2002-39, 2002-1 C.B. 1046, 5.02(1)(b).

[122] Temp. Reg. § 1.444-3T(b)(4).

[123] If the requested year is denied, a backup election is activated by filing Form 8752, Required Payment or Refund Under Section 7519, and making the required payment. The form must be filed and the required payment made by the later of (1) the normal due date of the required payment, or (2) 60 days from the date the IRS denies the business purpose year-end request. In filing the Form 8752 to activate the backup election, the partnership must type or print "ACTIVATING BACKUP ELECTION" on the top of the form. Temp. Reg. § 1.444-3T has additional guidance on backup elections.

[124] The Omnibus Budget Reconciliation Act of 1987, P.L. 100-203, Act § 10206.

[125] Code Sec. 444(a). The election is made by the entity. Code Sec. 444(d)(1).

[126] Code Sec. 444(b)(1). An entity that came into existence before 1986 could elect to retain the taxable year it

used for its last taxable year beginning in 1986. Code Sec. 444(b)(3). The election must have been made for the first tax year beginning after 1986, and must have been made by July 26, 1988. The Omnibus Budget Reconciliation Act of 1987, P.L. 100-203, Act §§ 10206(d) and 444(b)(2). Alternatively, existing partnerships could change to a new taxable year that provides for a deferral period that does not exceed the lesser of three months or the deferral period of the year that was being changed. A deferral period consists of the number of months between the close of a taxable year elected and the close of the taxable year that would otherwise be required. Code Sec. 444(b)(4).

[127] Code Secs. 444(c)(1) and 7519. No payment is required unless the required payment exceeds $500. Code Sec. 7519(a)(2). A partnership that establishes a business purpose for its adoption of a fiscal year is not subject to the required payment rules.

¶405.07

the required payment of the prior year,[128] the taxpayer is, in effect, required to maintain a noninterest-bearing account with the IRS.

S Corporation Observation: The Code Sec. 444 rules applying to partnerships are virtually identical to those that apply to S corporations.

A partnership that has made the Code Sec. 444 election must file Form 8752, Required Payment or Refund Under Section 7519, with which any required payment is forwarded or refund requested.[129] A payment must be made if the amount remaining on deposit is less than the required amount. A refund is available if it exceeds this amount. If, for example, a calendar year is the partnership's required year, the required deposit amount is calculated by first determining that portion of the partnership's desired taxable year which elapses before the beginning of the calendar year and then dividing this number of months by twelve. This is the deferral ratio.

Example 4-29: A fiscal year ending September 30 results in three months of the income earned during a calendar year being taxable to the partners in the next calendar year. This is a 25% deferral ratio.

The total amount that is required to be on deposit is based upon the taxable income of the previous fiscal year, the "net base-year income." The amount of the deposit is calculated by applying the highest individual tax rate plus one percent to the amount of taxable income deemed deferred during the last year. This deemed deferred income is determined by multiplying the deferral ratio by the "net base-year income."[130] This amount of income is in effect the average income deferred in the previous taxable year.

Example 4-30: New partnership FGH elects a September 30 year-end under Code Sec. 444; there is no required payment because there is no net base-year income.[131] If, however, in the partnership's second taxable year ending on September 30 it has taxable income equaling $100,000, the deferred income is $25,000[132] and the required payment is $10,150.[133] If, in the third year, the taxable income is $200,000, the required payment is an *additional* $10,150.[134]

Due to the fact that the base period's taxable income can be reduced through deductible payments to partners made after the deferral period, a special provision prevents these amounts from reducing base-year income unless they have been paid in the deferral period.[135]

---

[128] *See* Code Sec. 7519(b).

[129] The due date is May 15 of the calendar year which follows the calendar year in which the applicable year begins. Temp. Reg. § 1.7519-2T(a)(4)(ii).

[130] Both the tax rate and the percent of deferred taxable income taken into account are subject to a phase-in through 1989 for some entities in existence in 1986. Code Sec. 7519(d)(4).

[131] Temp. Reg. § 1.7519-1T(b)(4).

[132] 25% × $100,000.

[133] (39.6% + 1%) × $25,000.

[134] [29% × (25% × $200,000)] − $10,150 = $10,150; or $20,300, less the prior year's required payment of $10,150.

[135] Taxable income is first grossed up by the deferral period's allocable share of such payments and then reduced by the payments actually made during the deferral period. Code Sec. 7519(d)(1)(B).

.08 52-53-Week Taxable Year

In order to reduce the compliance burden of partnerships that keep their books on a 52-53-week fiscal year, a 52-53-week taxable year is allowed. A partnership is eligible to elect a 52-53-week taxable year if the partnership uses a 52-53-week fiscal year, and the year would otherwise satisfy the requirements of Code Sec. 441 and the related regulations. For example, a taxpayer that is required to use a calendar year under Reg. § 1.441-1(b)(2)(i)(D) is not eligible.[136]

The 52-53-week year must always end on the same day of the week, and must always end on either (1) the date on which that day of the week last occurs in the calendar month, or (2) the date on which that day of the week falls which is nearest to the last day of the calendar month.

> **Example 4-31:** If a partnership elects a taxable year ending always on the last Friday in November, then for the year 2010, the taxable year would end on November 26, 2010. On the other hand, if the partnership had elected a taxable year ending always on the Friday nearest to the end of November, then for the year 2010, the taxable year would end on December 3, 2010.[137]

If both a partnership and a partner use a taxable year ending with reference to the same month, the partner could potentially get a deferral of their share of the partnership's income. For example, if the partnership's taxable year always ends on November 30, but the partner's taxable year always ends on the last Friday in November, then the partner would often get a deferral of the partnership income.

To keep partners from getting this deferral, the regulations provide a special rule to follow when a partnership or a partner, or both, use a 52-53-week taxable year and the taxable year of the partnership and the partner end with reference to the same calendar month. Under these circumstances, for purposes of determining the taxable year in which items from the partnership are taken into account by the partner, the partner's taxable year is deemed to end on the last day of the partnership's taxable year.[138]

A newly formed partnership may adopt a 52-53-week taxable year without the approval of the Commissioner if the year ends with reference to either the taxpayer's required taxable year (as defined in Reg. § 1.441-1(b)(2)) or the taxable year elected under Code Sec. 444.[139] In order to adopt a 52-53-week taxable year, a partnership must file with its Form 1065 for its first taxable year a statement indicating (1) the calendar month with reference to which the 52-53-week taxable year ends, (2) the day of the week on which the taxable year will end, and (3) whether the taxable year will always end on the last occurrence of that day of the week in the calendar month, or the occurrence of the day of the week that is nearest to the last day of the calendar month.[140]

---

[136] Reg. § 1.441-2(a)(3).
[137] Reg. § 1.441-2(a)(4).
[138] Reg. § 1.441-2(e).

[139] Reg. § 1.441-2(b)(1)(i).
[140] Reg. § 1.441-2(b)(1)(ii).

¶ 406 Accounting Method

In general, partnerships, particularly large partnerships, must use the accrual method of accounting. However, some significant exceptions have been carved out. For example, under Rev. Proc. 2001-10,[141] the IRS will allow a qualifying taxpayer with $1 million or less in average annual gross receipts to use the cash method to account for inventories and the buying and selling of merchandise.

Under Code Sec. 448, partnerships that either (1) have a C corporation as a partner or (2) are tax shelters, are not allowed to use the cash basis accounting method even when it otherwise properly reflects income.[142] This rule does not apply to partnerships with a corporate partner if the partnership meets the $5,000,000 three-year average gross receipts test for all preceding years.[143] A partnership meets the $5,000,000 gross receipts test for a particular year if the partnership's average gross receipts for that year and the preceding two years do not exceed $5,000,000.[144] If a partnership has not been in existence three years, the test period includes the number of years the partnership has been in existence. Partnerships must annualize gross receipts from short tax years before making this computation. Gross receipts are computed using the partnership's tax accounting methods for the year the receipts were recognized, and include total sales of goods or services, investment income (including tax-exempt income), and gains from the sale of assets (the asset's gross sales price is reduced by its basis).[145]

Example 4-32: The ABC Partnership began business on 1/1/2007 and had the following gross receipts in the designated years:

		3-year Average
2007	$3,000,000	$3,000,000
2008	$3,000,000	$3,000,000
2009	$6,000,000	$4,000,000
2010	$3,000,000	$4,000,000
2011	$9,000,000	$6,000,000

Partner *B* is a C corporation. ABC meets the gross receipts test in 2007 through 2010, so ABC could use the cash basis in 2007 through 2011. Because the $5,000,000 gross receipts test is not met in 2011, in 2012 and all later years the partnership would not be allowed to use the cash method.

A C corporation for this purpose is any corporation that is not an S corporation or a "qualified personal service corporation."[146] Thus, a C corporation for this purpose includes a regulated investment company, a real estate investment trust, a

---

[141] Rev. Proc. 2001-10, 2001-1 CB 272.

[142] Code Sec. 448(a). Effective for taxable years beginning after December 31, 1986.

[143] Code Sec. 448(c).

[144] Temp. Reg. § 1.448-1T(f)(1).

[145] Temp. Reg. § 1.448-1T(f)(2)(iv).

[146] Code Sec. 448(b)(2). A "qualified personal service corporation" is defined in Code Sec. 448(d)(2) as a corpo-

ration in which substantially all the activities consist of performing services in certain specified fields, and which is owned by employees performing those services for the corporation or by certain related persons. The permitted fields of activity are health, law, engineering, architecture, accounting, actuarial science, the performing arts, and consulting. Excluded are services where compensation is contingent on the consummation of a transaction, such as sales or brokerage services.

trust having unrelated business income, and a corporation exempt from tax under Code Sec. 501(a) to the extent it has unrelated business income. A tiered arrangement with a C corporation partner in an upper-tier partnership results in the reclassification of all the lower-tier partnerships as partnerships with a C corporation partner.[147]

> **Example 4-33:** The ABC Partnership has four partners. Three are individuals, and the fourth is the XYZ Partnership. Their average gross receipts exceed $5,000,000. XYZ has three partners—two individuals and a C corporation. Since XYZ has a C corporation partner, and it also owns an interest in ABC, the ABC Partnership is treated as having a C corporation partner and is precluded from using the cash method.

Under Rev. Proc. 2002-28,[148] a partnership (except a partnership with a C corporation partner, unless the partnership meets the $5,000,000 gross receipts test, above) that meets a $10,000,000 gross receipts test for all prior years will be allowed to use the cash basis. To meet the $10,000,000 gross receipts test for a particular year, the partnership's average gross receipts for that year and the preceding two years must not exceed $10,000,000.

Tax shelters are prohibited from using the cash method without exception.[149] For this purpose, a tax shelter is defined as:

1. An enterprise in which interests have been offered for sale in any offering required to be registered under state or federal law;[150]

2. All partnerships in which limited entrepreneurs are allocated more than 35 percent of the losses for the taxable year;[151] or

3. Any arrangement that has as its principal purpose the avoidance or evasion of the federal income tax.[152]

> **LLC Observation:** The recent popularity of Limited Liability Companies (LLCs) has raised the question of whether LLCs can use the cash method of accounting. An LLC classified as a partnership for tax purposes can use the cash method when it meets the other tests (*i.e.*, the LLC has no C corporation as a member and is not a tax shelter). However, a blanket assumption that all LLCs can use the cash method is not appropriate, particularly where the LLC will experience tax losses. In Private Letter Rulings, the IRS has permitted certain LLCs to use the cash method.[153] The question is whether the LLC members are limited entrepreneurs for purposes of the 35-percent rule. In each of the letter rulings issued, the LLC was a service entity, and all but one of the LLCs practiced law or accounting. Furthermore, each LLC represented in its ruling request that all members would be active participants in the

---

[147] Temp. Reg. § 1.448-1T(a)(3).

[148] Rev. Proc. 2002-28, 2002-18 IRB 815.

[149] Code Sec. 448(a)(3).

[150] Code Sec. 461(i)(3)(A). This definition also encompasses any "offering" subject to a notice or filing requirement with any state or federal agency. This definition includes all entities—not only those formed with tax avoidance as a motive. Nevertheless, these entities can-

not use the cash method of accounting. Temp. Reg. § 1.448-1T(b)(2).

[151] Code Secs. 461(i)(3)(B) and 1256(e)(3)(B). *See* Reg. § 1.448-1T. A partnership may be required to change its method of accounting in a loss year.

[152] Code Secs. 461(i)(3)(C) and 6661(b)(2)(C)(ii).

[153] IRS Letter Rulings 9321047 (2-25-93), 9328005 (12-21-92), 9350013 (9-15-93), and 9412030 (12-22-93).

business. It appears this representation was critical to the IRS's determination that the members were not "limited entrepreneurs," thereby avoiding classification as a syndicate. How the IRS would rule if a nonservice LLC were involved or if all members did not actively participate in the business remains unclear. This is still a developing area of the tax law.

The following table summarizes these rules:

Average Three-year Gross Receipts (AGR)	Partnership Requirements	Use Cash Basis?
AGR > $10,000,000	Any partnership	No
$10,000,000 ≥ AGR > $5,000,000	Partnership with C corporation partner	No
$10,000,000 ≥ AGR > $5,000,000	Partnership *without* C corporation partner	Yes
AGR ≤ $5,000,000	Any partnership	Yes

¶ 407 Organization and Syndication Expenses—Code Sec. 709

A partnership's deduction for expenses incurred prior to commencing operations confronts two obstacles:

1. There is no partnership trade or business and therefore a Code Sec. 162 expense is not allowed; and

2. A majority of the expenditure will benefit a future taxable year and therefore is potentially a capital expenditure under Code Sec. 263.

Organization, syndication, business investigation and start-up expenditures are four examples of these expenses which are commonly encountered in a partnership context. The rules governing the tax treatment of these expenditures are discussed in this chapter.

.01 Organization Expenses

Under Code Sec. 709(b), up to $5,000 of organizational expenses incurred may be deducted in the taxable year in which the trade or business begins. This $5,000 amount is reduced (but not below zero) by the amount that all organizational expenses exceed $50,000. Any additional organizational expenses are amortizable over the 180-month period that begins with the inception of the trade or business.[154] Under Reg. § 1.709-1 a Code Sec. 709 deduction election is automatically deemed made for the taxable year in which the partnership begins business. Taxpayers can choose to forego the deemed deduction election by clearly electing capitalization treatment on a timely filed return.

Definition of organization expenses. Code Sec. 709(b)(2) defines organizational expenses as expenditures which are:

---

[154] Code Sec. 709(b)(1), as amended by the American Jobs Creation Act of 2004; Committee Report on the American Jobs Creation Act of 2004, Sec. 902.

1. Incident to the creation of the partnership;

2. Chargeable to a capital account; and

3. Are of a character which, if expended incident to the creation of a partnership having an ascertainable life, would be amortized over such life.

These expenditures must be for the creation of the partnership and not syndication costs incurred in selling the partnership interests or business start-up costs or investigatory costs. Partnership organizational expenses are capitalized expenses incurred on the partnership's formation.[155] Examples of these costs include:

1. Legal fees incurred in drafting the partnership agreement;

2. Filing fees for registering the partnership with the state and local authorities; and

3. Accounting fees for services incident to the organization of the partnership.

For example, setting up the partnership's accounting system.

The distinction between organizational expenses and syndication costs is important because organizational expenses can be amortized but syndication costs cannot. Investigatory expenses and start-up costs are not amortized under Code Sec. 709(b), but are amortized under Code Sec. 195 (as discussed at ¶ 408).

Eligible organization expenses. Organizational expenditures eligible for the deduction and amortization election are limited to expenditures incurred during the period that begins within a reasonable time before the partnership began business and ends with the original due date, not including extensions, of the tax return for the year in which the partnership begins business operations.[156] Organizational expenses incurred outside this time period (such as costs incurred after the due date of the tax return for the year in which the business began) are required to be capitalized as nondeductible and nonamortizable partnership expenditures.

If the partnership uses the cash method of accounting, no amortization or deduction is allowed for organizational expenses incurred until it is paid. However, in the year when the expense is paid, the partnership is allowed to add the prior year amortization deduction that would have been allowed had the expense been paid in the year incurred to the amortization deduction claimed in the year of payment.[157] The wording of Reg. § 1.709-1(b)(1) indicates that the $5,000 deduction would also be allowed in the year of payment, if later than the year it is incurred. The result is that the total deduction and amortized expense for the partnership is unaffected by whether or not it uses cash or accrual basis accounting. The accounting method only affects the timing of the amortization deduction.

The time period in which the expenditures must be incurred in order to qualify as "incident to the creation" of the partnership includes a "reasonable time" before the partnership begins business. The end of the period is the date (without extension) for the filing of the partnership return for the taxable year in which the partnership begins business. The beginning of this time period is somewhat

---

[155] Code Sec. 709(b).
[156] Reg. § 1.709-2(a).

[157] Reg. § 1.709-1(b).

ambiguous. There is no authority or guidance as to what is a reasonable time before the partnership begins business. The end of the period is precisely defined, but it can be unreasonable. It is easy to imagine organizational expenses which can be incurred much later than the due date for filing the first partnership tax return. For example, a partnership which converts to a limited partnership or a partnership that converts to an LLC will incur organizational expenses incident to such a "reorganization;" clearly, these will be incurred well after the filing date for the original partnership's initial return.

The amortization deduction. The amortization period starts in the month the partnership begins business. The date on which the partnership begins business is therefore important for three reasons:

1. First, the reasonable time before the partnership begins business starts the period during which eligible organizational expenses must be incurred.

2. Second, the due date for the tax return which includes this date is the last date on which organizational expenditures can be incurred.

3. Third, it is the month in which the partnership is first allowed to amortize the organizational expenditures.

For purposes of amortizing organizational expenses, the partnership is considered to begin business in the month in which it was in the state of readiness to do the business for which it was organized. The acquisition of operating assets necessary to conduct the contemplated business is a primary factor in determining when the partnership's business begins. Mere administrative actions, such as signing the partnership agreement or registering to do business in the state, do not constitute the beginning of business for this purpose.

The regulations deal with the beginning of business as follows:

> The determination of the date a partnership begins business for purposes of section 709 presents a question of fact that must be determined in each case in light of all the circumstances of the particular case. Ordinarily, a partnership begins business when it starts the business operation for which it was organized. The mere signing of a partnership agreement is not alone sufficient to show the beginning of business. If the activities of the partnership have advanced to the extent necessary to establish the nature of its business operations, it will be deemed to have begun business. Accordingly, the acquisition of operating assets which are necessary to the type of business contemplated may constitute beginning business for these purposes. The term "operating assets," as used herein, means assets that are in a state of readiness to be placed in service within a reasonable period following their acquisition.[158]

Part VI of Form 4562, Depreciation and Amortization, is used to report the amortizable tax basis of the partnership's qualifying organizational expenses, the amortization period, and the allowable amortization expense for a particular year. The Code Section cited as authority for the deduction on Form 4562 is Code Sec. 709(b). Form 4562 is required to be attached to Form 1065, U.S. Partnership Return of Income. The deduction for amortization expense, however, is carried from Form

---

[158] Reg. § 1.709-2(c).

4562 into the main body of the Form 1065. If, for example, the partnership is involved in trade or business, the deduction is claimed on the other deductions line on page one of Form 1065. If the partnership is involved in multiple activities, the deduction should be allocated between the activities using a reasonable method of allocation. For example, it may be allocated based upon the fair market values of the respective assets in the different activities.

    LLC Observation: A partnership which converts to a limited liability company is not terminated. Therefore, for tax purposes a new partnership is not created. It is likely that the IRS will contend that these expenses may not be amortized under Code Sec. 709(b)(2)(A) if they are incurred after the due date of the continuing partnership's initial tax return. Case law prior to the enactment of Code Sec. 709 by the Tax Reform Act of 1976[159] treated these expenses as nondeductible capital expenditures.[160] The IRS can be expected to take the position that the tax consequences of conversion are governed by these decisions.

.02 Syndication Costs

    Code Sec. 709(a) denies any deduction for amounts paid and incurred "to promote the sale of (or to sell) an interest in such partnership." The selling expenses are commonly referred to as syndication expenses. Unlike organizational expenses, the regulations specifically provide that the deduction and amortization election under Code Sec. 709(b) is not available for syndication expenses.[161] Syndication expenses include all those connected with the issuing and marketing of interests in the partnership. Examples of syndication expenses are:[162]

1. Brokerage fees;

2. Registration fees;

3. Legal fees of an underwriter, place management, an issuer for securities advice and for advice pertaining to the adequacy of tax disclosure in the prospectus;

4. Accounting fees for preparation of representations to be included in the offering materials; and

5. Printing costs of the prospectus, placement memorandum, and other selling and promotional material.

Legal or accounting expenses involving tax matters may be incurred by a partnership in the process of being formed. Depending upon the facts and circumstances, such expenses may be:

- Currently deductible ordinary and necessary business expenses;

- Costs of organizing the partnership that are not deductible under Code Sec. 709, but amortizable under Code Sec. 709(b)(1); or

- Nondeductible syndication expenses.

---

[159] P.L. 94-455

[160] *A. Wolkowitz v. Commr.*, 8 TCM 754, Dec. 17,168(M) (1949); *Meldrum & Fewsmith, Inc. v. Commr.*, 20 TC 790, Dec. 19,801 (1953); *M.E. Wildman v. Commr.*, 78 TC 943, Dec. 39,093 (1982).

[161] Rev. Rul. 89-11, 1989-1 CB 179. Even if the syndication effort is abandoned, the IRS's position is that the accrued syndication costs are not deductible.

[162] Reg. § 1.709-2(b).

¶407.02

An example of currently deductible legal expense is the cost of the tax opinion incurred at the formation of a partnership relating to the Code Sec. 704(c) implications arising because the partners have already contributed appreciated property. Also, the partnership's payment for a tax opinion related to the application to the partnership of the at-risk rules under Code Sec. 465 would be currently deductible. Legal costs arising from planning for the contribution to the partnership of property, the agreed value of which differs from its adjusted basis in the hands of the contributor, may be required to be capitalized as either organization or syndication expenses. Costs of preparing the partnership agreement related to such contributions would be organization expenses. Costs related to selling the partnership interests would be syndication expenses.[163]

¶ 408 Investigation, Acquisition, and Start-Up Expenses— Code Secs. 195 and 263

Prior to the 1980 enactment of Code Sec. 195,[164] expenses incurred prior to a taxpayer's carrying on a trade or business were held to be nondeductible under Code Secs. 162 and 212.[165]

Code Sec. 195 was directed at two distinct failures arising in the application of Code Secs. 162, 212, and 167 to start-ups. First, these provisions permitted a deduction only in the context of a "trade or business" type activity and this was interpreted to preclude a deduction until such activity commenced. Second, to the extent that amounts could not be identified with the acquisition of specific assets having determinable useful lives, recovery was postponed until the trade or business terminated, or was sold or exchanged in a taxable transaction. As the House Ways and Means Committee noted:

> Under present law, costs incurred prior to the commencement of a business normally are not deductible because they are not incurred in carrying on a trade or business. The start-up or pre-operating costs must be capitalized and often can not be depreciated or amortized because no ascertainable life can be established for these costs. However, the capitalized costs may be covered for purposes of measuring gain or loss on the disposition of the business.[166]

There are two categories of Code Sec. 195 expenses:

1. Investigation expenses; and

2. Pre-opening/start-up expenses.

Up to $5,000 of these expenses may be deducted in the taxable year in which the trade or business begins. However, the $5,000 amount is reduced (but not

---

[163] *R.C. Honodel v. Commr.*, CA-9, 84-1 USTC ¶ 9133, 722 F2d 1462.

[164] P.L. 98-605.

[165] *F.B. Polachek v. Commr.*, 22 TC 858, Dec. 20,453 (1954), and Code Sec. 162; *Richmond Television Corp. v. U.S.*, CA-4, SCt, 65-2 USTC ¶ 9724, 382 US 68, 86 SCt 233; and Code Sec. 162; *A.A. Aboussie v. U.S.*, CA-8, 85-2 USTC ¶ 9860, 779 F2d 424, and Code Sec. 162; *J.K. Johnson v. Commr.*, CA-6, 86-2 USTC ¶ 9534, 794 F2d 1157; *M.H.*

Fishman v. Commr., CA-7, 88-1 USTC ¶ 9137, 837 F2d 309, and Code Sec. 212; *G.S. Sorrell, Jr. v. Commr.*, CA-11, 89-2 USTC ¶ 9521, 882 F2d 484, and Code Sec. 212. The capitalization and amortization rules for start-up expenses also apply to Code Sec. 212 activities, but only if the activity is engaged in anticipation of such activity becoming an active trade or business. Code Sec. 195(c)(1)(A)(iii).

[166] H. Rep. No. 96-1278 at 3, 1980-2 CB 709.

below zero) by the amount that all Code Sec. 195 expenses exceed $50,000. Any additional organizational expenses are amortizable over the 180-month period that begins with the commencement of the trade or business.[167] Prior to October 23, 2004, partnerships could elect to amortize Code Sec. 195 expenses over a period of not less than 60 months, beginning with the month in which the partnership commenced its trade or business.

.01 Investigation Expenses

The first question in determining the treatment of an investigation expenditure is whether the expenses in question are incurred to expand the present business or are costs incurred in entering into a new business. Expenses incurred in expanding a taxpayer's current business are deductible currently as trade or business expenses.

Costs of investigating "new business." Assuming that the partnership is entering into a new business and not expanding an old business, the question is what expenses are allowed to be capitalized under Code Sec. 195 and deducted or amortized, and what expenses must be capitalized as acquisition expenses of the business assets and must be depreciated over the assets' useful lives. The House Ways and Means Committee described Code Sec. 195 start-up costs as, "[u]nder the provision, eligible expenses consist of investigatory costs incurred in reviewing a prospective business prior to a final decision to enter that business."[168]

The IRS describes investigatory expenditures as follows:

> Expenditures incurred in the course of a general search for, or investigation of, an active trade or business in order to determine *whether* to enter a new business and *which* new business to enter (other than costs incurred to acquire capital assets that are used in the search or investigation) qualify as investigatory costs that are eligible for amortization as start-up expenditures under § 195. However, expenditures incurred in an attempt to acquire specific businesses do not qualify as start-up expenditures because they are acquisition costs under § 263. The nature of the cost must be analyzed based on all the facts and circumstances of the transaction to determine whether it is an investigatory cost incurred to facilitate the *whether* and *which* decisions, or an acquisition cost incurred to facilitate consummation of an acquisition.[169]

The IRS also stated that:

> we believe the reference to a final decision describes the point at which a taxpayer makes its own decision whether to acquire a specific business, and subsequently incurs costs in an effort to consummate the acquisition. At that point the general and preliminary investigation ceases and the taxpayer initiates its acquisition process. Costs incurred in connection with this process must be capitalized.[170]

It is settled that during the acquisition process there will be a point in time when expenses cease being capitalized and deducted or amortized under Code Sec.

---

[167] Code Sec. 195(b), as amended by the American Jobs Creation Act of 2004; Committee Report on the American Jobs Creation Act of 2004, Sec. 902.

[168] H. Rep. No. 96-1278 at 10, 1980-2 CB 712. Of course, if the business never begins, Code Sec. 195 never comes into play. *See, e.g., R.I. Koenig v. Commr.*, 75 TCM 2484, Dec. 52,743(M), TC Memo. 1998-215.

[169] Rev. Rul. 99-23, 1999-1 CB 998.

[170] IRS Technical Advice Memorandum 199901004 (9-28-98).

195 and start being capitalized under Code Sec. 263 as cost of acquiring the business itself. According to a pre-Code Sec. 195 ruling:

> a taxpayer will be considered to have entered into a transaction for profit if, based upon all the facts and circumstances, the taxpayer has gone beyond the general investigatory search . . . to focus on the acquisition of a specific business or investment . . . Expenses incurred in the course of a general search for a preliminary investigation of a business or investment involve expenses related to the decision of whether to enter a transaction and which transaction to enter . . . Once the taxpayer has focused on the acquisition of a specific business or investment, expenses that are related to acquire such business or investment are capital in nature [.][171]

In the case of an investigatory expense incurred in acquisition of a partnership interest by a partner, the amortization deduction is taken by the partner.

Business expansion expenses. As noted above, start-up expenses do not include the costs involved in expanding an existing business. These amounts are currently deductible under Code Sec. 162. However, even in the case of an expansion of an existing business, if the expenses are incurred in connection with the acquisition of assets, Code Sec. 263 requires capitalization in the cost basis of those assets. In the case of a partnership, the test of whether there is an existing business which is being expanded is applied at the partnership level.[172] For example, if two individuals who are already engaged in a hardware business join together in a partnership to jointly open up a new store and incur expansion expenses in seeking a new location for the hardware business, the partnership would be considered to be in a new trade or business even though from the partners' standpoint this could be considered a mere expansion of the existing hardware business. The partnership itself was not in the business before and now it is.

There is also a question of fact whether a partnership with an established ongoing business is expanding the existing business or is entering a new business. Factors which could imply expansion of the business would be geographically extending the business or vertical integration. Factors indicating a new trade or business might include involvement in marketing products that differ significantly from the products currently being marketed or marketing the same products to new and different customers. For example, a distributor of flowers who is currently working in the wholesale market who opens up a retail shop might be considered to be entering into a new business.

.02 Pre-opening Start-Up Expenses

As mentioned, there are two classes of Code Sec. 195 expenses. In addition to investigatory costs discussed above, there are also start-up costs. Start-up costs are incurred after the decision has been made to establish a particular business and before the time a new business begins. Examples include:

- Advertising;
- Wages paid to employees who are being trained and to instructors;

---

[171] Rev. Rul. 77-254, 1977-2 CB 63.

[172] *Madison Gas and Electric Co. v. Commr.*, CA-7, 80-2 USTC ¶ 9754, 633 F2d 512, aff'g 72 TC 521, Dec. 36,142

(1979); *R.C. Goodwin v. Commr.*, 75 TC 424, Dec. 37,502 (1980), aff'd without published opinion, CA-9, 691 F2d 490.

- Travel and other expenses incurred in lining up prospective distributors, suppliers or customers; and

- Salaries or fees paid or incurred for executives, consultants, and/or similar professional services.

These expenses are sometimes referred to as "pre-opening expenses." Code Sec. 195 applies only to expenses which have a trade or business requirement as a prerequisite to deductibility and are not capitalized under another provision of the Internal Revenue Code. For example, marketing expenses and the cost of training employees are deductible under Code Sec. 162 if the partnership is already engaged in the trade or business to which they relate. *Richmond Television Corporation v. United States* involved a corporation formed to construct and operate a television station and is a good example of start-up expenditures.[173] During the three years the application to the Federal Communications Commission for a permit to engage in that activity was pending, the taxpayer conducted a training program to train staff available once the permit was granted. The training expenses incurred between the decision to establish a business and the actual beginning of the business operations were disallowed as a deduction because the taxpayer was not "carrying on" a trade or business when the expenses were incurred.[174] But, if such expenses are now incurred before business begins, they are subject to the provisions of Code Sec. 195.

Expenses which are deductible in the absence of an existing business are deductible without reference to Code Sec. 195's requirements. Code Sec. 195 does not apply to interest and taxes deductible under Code Secs. 163 and 164 because they are deductible whether or not there is a related trade or business. They are not Code Sec. 195 expenses even though a deduction for these expenses may be disallowed under another provision of the Internal Revenue Code. For example, they may be required to be capitalized under Code Sec. 263, even though the partnership is engaged in active trade or business.[175] Interest capitalized under Code Sec. 263A is not amortized under Code Sec. 195.

Start-up period. For purposes of Code Sec. 195, the start-up period begins with the end of the investigatory phase of whether to enter the business or which business to enter and it ends when the associated trade or business is actively conducted. The start-up period ends and amortization begins at the point when the partnership is engaged in an *active* trade or business. The question of when a taxpayer is actively engaged in a trade or business is a facts and circumstances determination. Generally, taxpayers are considered to be actively engaged in a trade or business when they actually begin earning revenue from that trade or business. In contrast, a taxpayer may begin depreciating an asset when it is in a state of readiness to be used in that business, as he or she is considered to have placed the asset in service in a trade or business. Similar rules apply under Code

---

[173] *Richmond Television Corp. v. U.S.*, SCt, 65-2 USTC ¶ 9724, 382 US 68, 86 SCt 233.

[174] Expenditures had to be capitalized and could have been amortized if the asset acquired had a limited life.

The year involved was before the enactment of Code Sec. 195.

[175] However, interest and taxes may be required to be capitalized under some other Code sections, such as Code Sec. 263A.

Sec. 709, which allows the taxpayer to begin amortizing organizational expenses when the partnership is ready to begin conducting business; under that section, the trade or business is deemed to begin when the partnership is in a position to begin doing business. However, Code Sec. 195 requires an active trade or business.

.03 Unamortized Investigation and Start-Up Expenses

Like organizational costs not fully amortized when the partnership liquidates, unamortized start-up expenses can be deducted as an ordinary loss under Code Sec. 165 if the trade or business is completely disposed of before such costs have been fully amortized.[176] It is possible that an in-kind distribution of trade or business operating assets to one or more of the partners in liquidation of their partnership interests should be considered a complete disposition of the trade or business for these purposes. The rules provide for a deduction of the unamortized expenses only if the taxpayer *completely* disposes of the trade or business generating the expenditures before the end of the amortization period.

.04 Code Sec. 195 Procedure

The election. Although an affirmative election to expense or amortize Code Sec. 195 expenses used to be required, that is no longer the case. Under Reg. § 1.195-1, a taxpayer is deemed to have made an election under Code Sec. 195(b) to amortize start-up expenditures for the taxable year in which the active trade or business to which the expenditures relate begins. A taxpayer may choose to forgo the deemed election by clearly electing to capitalize its start-up expenditures on a timely filed federal income tax return (including extensions) for the taxable year in which the active trade or business to which the expenditures relate begins. The election either to amortize start-up expenditures under Code Sec. 195(b) or to capitalize start-up expenditures is irrevocable and applies to all start-up expenditures that are related to the active trade or business.

Tax return presentation. Start-up expenses are included within the definition of "amortizable property" in the instructions to Form 4562, Depreciation and Amortization. The required information is entered in Part VI, Capital Amortization, of Form 4562, and from there the current year's deduction for rental trade or business activity flows through the "Other Deductions" line on page 1 of Form 1065 (not the "Depreciation" line). Therefore, the current year's deduction for start-up expenses is included in the computation of the partnership's ordinary income or loss for operations.

---

[176] Code Sec. 195(b)(2).

SUMMARY TABLE FOR TAX TREATMENT OF
PRE-OPENING EXPENSES

	Organizational Expenses	*Syndication Costs*	*Investigation and Start-up Expenses*
Proper year to make election.	In tax year business begins.	Not applicable.	In any tax year up to the year the active trade or business begins.
Proper time to begin deduction and/or amortization.	In month partnership begins business.	Not applicable.	In month *active* conduct of business operation begins.
Treatment if partnership liquidates.	If election applies, partnership takes ordinary loss deduction under Code Sec. 165. If election does not apply, partnership has no loss but the partners have increased loss or reduced gain on liquidation.	Capitalized amount will reduce partner's capital gain or increase capital loss on liquidation of his or her interest.	If election applies, partnership takes ordinary loss deduction under Code Sec. 165. If election does not apply, partnership has no loss but the partners have increased loss or reduced gain on liquidation.
Treatment of capitalized amounts for which election is not available or no election applies.	Permanently capitalized. No tax benefit until partner sells interest or partnership liquidates. At that time, capitalized amount will reduce partner's capital gain or increase capital loss.	Permanently capitalized. No tax benefit until partner sells interest or partnership liquidates. At that time, capitalized amount will reduce partner's capital gain or increase capital loss.	Permanently capitalized. No tax benefit until partner sells interest or partnership liquidates. At that time, capitalized amount will reduce partner's capital gain or increase capital loss.

¶408.04

Chapter 5

Character and Presentation of Partnership Income

¶ 501 Introduction

A partnership is not a separate tax-paying entity. Rather, the partnership's income (or loss) is passed through to its partners, who then compute their tax liabilities based on the rates in Code Sec. 1.[1]

Generally, as discussed in Chapter 4, a partnership computes its taxable income in the same manner as do individuals.[2] Once computed, the partnership's items of income, loss, deduction, or credit are passed through to partners for inclusion in their taxable income for their tax year in which the taxable year of the partnership ends.[3] Items that may have potentially varying tax consequences to particular partners must be separately stated;[4] all other items are aggregated and passed through as a net lump sum.[5] These items are allocated among the partners in accordance with the partnership agreement.[6] The partnership's pass-through items retain the character they possessed at the partnership level; for example, tax-exempt interest earned by the partnership is treated as tax-exempt interest in the hands of the partners.[7]

> ***S Corporation Observation:*** In contrast to the flexibility extended to partners, who can make disproportionate or special allocations of tax items if

---

[1] Code Sec. 703(a).

[2] *Id.*

[3] Code Sec. 706(a).

[4] Code Sec. 703(a)(2).

[5] Code Sec. 702(a)(1) and (8).

[6] Code Sec. 704(a). In contrast, the *pro rata* share of a shareholder of an S corporation is determined by allocating an equal portion of each item to each day of the

corporation's taxable year, and then dividing that amount by the shares outstanding on the day. Code Sec. 1377(a)(1). As in the case of partnerships, the IRS has the authority to make adjustments to the amounts passed through where such is necessary to reflect the value of services or capital provided by a family member of one or more shareholders. Code Secs. 704(e) and 1366(e).

[7] Code Sec. 702(b).

such allocations have "substantial economic effect," special allocations of tax items among the S corporation shareholders are not allowed.[8]

The character of a tax item realized by a partnership "shall be determined as if such item were realized directly from the source from which realized by the partnership, or incurred in the same manner as incurred by the partnership."[9] Although this language has been the subject of academic discussion, the generally accepted view is that the character of the item is determined by reference to partnership-level factors.[10]

> **Example 5-1:** A real estate dealer who trades in apartment buildings is a limited partner in a partnership that owns an apartment building it has managed for 20 years. The partnership sells the building under circumstances such that its gain is considered Code Sec. 1231 gain. Each partner's share, including the real estate dealer's, is taxed as Code Sec. 1231 gain.

Generally, a partner increases his or her basis by the amount of taxable and tax-exempt income passed through, and decreases his or her basis (but not below zero) by items of loss and deduction and any expenses of the partnership that were not deductible in computing its taxable income and which were not properly chargeable to capital account (for example, life insurance premiums paid to insure the lives of the partners).[11]

¶ 502 Presentation of a Partnership's Taxable Income

Although a partnership accounts for roughly the same items of income and deduction as an individual, the format in which it reports this information is quite different. An individual first subtracts from his or her gross income the sum of his or her "above the line" deductions. This subtotal is the individual's "adjusted gross income."[12] An individual next reduces adjusted gross income by the sum of any "itemized deductions."[13] The resulting *single* number is taxable income.[14] A partnership reports the results of the taxable year's operations differently. It separately lists the net amount of any item of income, loss, or deduction that could affect the various partners differently.[15] For example, tax-exempt interest income and other

---

[8] S corporations can in effect "specially allocate" amounts of income among their owner-employees only through salary adjustments. Amounts of income allocated among shareholders can also be altered through changes in stock ownership. The shareholders must, however, transfer their stock during the year for the allocation to be effective because the S corporation's income is allocated among the shareholders based upon the number of days they have owned the shares. In contrast, partnership income is allocated according to the partnership agreement, including amendments made by the due date of the tax return. It is possible, therefore, for the partners to wait until the tax year is complete before deciding how to allocate the partnership's income among themselves. In the case of an S corporation, unlike a partnership, it is impossible to allocate a particular item of income or deduction. Depreciation, for example, is required to be shared by all the shareholders based upon their stock ownership.

[9] Code Sec. 702(b).

[10] *U.S. v. J.A. Basye*, SCt, 73-1 USTC ¶ 9250, 410 US 441, 93 SCt 1080. The opposite interpretation is that a partner treat partnership items as if he or she generated them directly. For example, a partner who was a dealer in land would treat the partnership's land sale as if it were his or her sale, ordinary income being the likely result. The entity-level partnership characterization rule is described in Rev. Rul. 67-188, 1967-1 CB 216. *See also E.G. Barham v. U.S.*, DC Ga., 69-1 USTC ¶ 9356, 301 FSupp 43.

[11] Code Sec. 705.

[12] Code Sec. 62. An individual income tax return (Form 1040) will take these deductions into account on page one or its supporting schedules.

[13] Itemized deductions are all deductions not enumerated in Code Sec. 62.

[14] Code Sec. 63.

[15] The net amount of each item is shown on a separate line of Schedule K (Form 1065, U.S. Partnership Return of Income).

tax exempt income are each separately stated. The net amount of each type of nondeductible expenditure is separately listed.[16] Any item of a partnership's income or deduction which is specially allocated to a particular partner is separately stated even though absent the special allocation it need not have been separately stated. The remainder of the partnership's items of income, loss, and deduction are simply aggregated as one net number.[17] Unlike an individual, a partnership's taxable income is not reduced to one number.[18] This section discusses which items of partnership income and deduction must be separately stated.

¶ 503 Separately Stated Items

The law provides only that a partnership must separate its items of income, loss, and deduction that could, by their nature, affect the various partners differently.[19] But it is also necessary to inform the partners of their shares of nontaxable income and expenditures that are not deductible by the partnership. Normally, the partnership tax return preparer will probably not separately report to the partners each item that might conceivably constitute a separately stated item of income, loss, and deduction. It is therefore not unlikely that partners may need to request additional information in order to prepare their returns.

A partnership is denied certain deductions.[20] In most cases the result is clear. The partnership acts in a manner similar to that of a nominee. It reports the amount and nature of the nondeductible expenditure to the partners, and its intermediary status is ignored. The partners are simply treated as if they had paid the amounts directly.[21] Because the partners' bases are reduced by nondeductible expenditures, these payments are often dealt with as if the partnership first distributed these amounts and then the partners made the payments themselves.[22]

---

[16] These items are reported separately on Schedule K. Each partner will decrease his or her partnership interest adjusted basis for his or her share of nondeductible expenditures and increase his or her partnership interest adjusted basis for tax-exempt income.

[17] This net number is calculated on page one of the Form 1065 and is the first entry on Schedule K.

[18] When it is necessary for a partner to know his or her gross income from all sources such gross income includes the partner's *pro rata* share of the partnership's gross income. Code Sec. 702(c). This amount is not normally part of the information provided with the partner's K-1.

[19] Code Sec. 702(a)(1)-(8).

[20] Code Sec. 703(a)(2).

[21] The partners are required to reduce partnership interest adjusted basis by their share of the expenditure. Code Sec. 705(a)(2)(B). This is because the partnership no longer has the money and its ownership interests are therefore less valuable. If a partnership interest adjusted basis reduction were not required the partner would have a loss or reduced gain on the sale of his or her ownership interests and this would result in a second tax benefit for the same expenditure. The result is very similar to treating the partnership as having distributed the nondeductible amount to the partner who paid it to the ultimate payee. The partnership interest's basis should, however, be reduced only once, not for both the nondeductible expenditure and the deemed distribution.

[22] The partners will be required to reduce their bases in their partnership interests by their allocable shares of nondeductible expenditures. Code Sec. 705(a)(2)(B). Absent this basis adjustment the partners would receive a tax benefit for expenditures that should be denied at both the partner and partnership level. For example, neither the partnership nor partner should be entitled to deduct expenses incurred to produce tax-exempt income. If a partnership's funds have been spent providing life insurance the interests in the partnership have been reduced in value by the amount of the expenditures. If the partner's basis in their interests is not reduced by the expenditure, subsequent sale of the partnership interest will generate additional loss or a reduced amount of gain in the amount of the expenditure. For amounts that are deductible by the partner but not by the partnership, absent a basis reduction to the partnership interests, a double tax benefit will be generated by items passed through to the partner and deducted by him or her. Investment expenses other than interest are an example of a possible double deduction if no basis adjustment is made. Code Sec. 212 allows an individual to deduct such expenditures, but a partnership is disallowed Code Sec. 212 expenses. A deduction that is allowed to an individual by Code Sec. 212 is specifically disallowed to a partnership. The tax return for a partnership requires that these expenses be separately stated. (Schedule K, Form 1065.) The individual partner deducts these amounts along with his or her other itemized deductions. If he or she is not required to reduce his or her ownership interest's basis

There is a slim technical distinction between a partnership's nondeductible separately stated item of expenditure and a separately stated deductible partnership expenditure. The ultimate result is normally the same whether the item is a separately stated partnership deduction or a separately stated nondeductible amount. There is only one narrow practical distinction between nondeductible expenditures that are separately stated and deductible expenditures that are separately stated. The possible difference exists in the application of the basis limitation on the deductibility of losses. A partner's "distributive share of partnership loss (including capital loss) shall be allowed only to the extent of the adjusted basis of such partner's interest in the partnership."[23] A literal interpretation of the basis limitation rules would conclude that the partner of a partnership is not subject to those rules for his share of the partnership's nondeductible expenditures.[24]

.01 Rental Real Estate Activities

Income and expenses attributable to these activities flow through to the partners as real estate rental activity. Passive losses incurred in rental real estate activities are subject to a special $25,000 deduction allowance in excess of passive income at the general partner level depending upon the level of the partner's adjusted gross income and whether he or she "actively participates" in the rental activity.[25] Also, taxpayers in a real property business who materially participate in any real estate rental activity treat income or loss from that activity as nonpassive.[26]

The partnership has the obligation to define the boundaries of its various activities. The partner then may group activities conducted directly and through other Code Sec. 469 entities with the activities of the partnership. Once the partnership has set the boundaries of its activities, the partner may not treat portions of the partnership's activities as separate activities. He or she may only combine his or her share of the partnership defined activity with other activities to form an activity with wider borders than the partnership's.[27]

.02 Rental Activities Other Than Real Estate

Income and expenses attributable to non-real estate rental activities generally flow through to the partners as passive without the special $25,000 allowance or the active income treatment available to real estate operators described in the previous paragraph. The partnership also has the obligation to define the boundaries of these various activities.[28]

.03 Compensation Paid to Service Partners

Partnership payments to a partner for independent contractor type services which are subject to Code Sec. 707(a) are not subject to withholding. The related

---

(Footnote Continued)

by the expenditure, the ownership interest's sale at its reduced value caused by the expenditure will generate a loss or a reduced amount of gain reflecting such expenditures as an additional tax benefit.

[23] Code Sec. 704(d).

[24] Conversely, if expenditures disallowed at the partnership level are deductible by the partner only to the extent of his or her basis, the carryover rules of Code

Sec. 704(d) should provide an unlimited carryover even though they are not components of a net operating loss within the meaning of Code Sec. 172.

[25] Code Sec. 469(i).

[26] Code Sec. 469(c)(7).

[27] Reg. § 1.469-4(d)(5)(i).

[28] Id.

deduction is not separately stated unless it is specially allocated. The payment to the partner is reported on a Form 1099 and not the partner's K-1 or Form W-2. A partner who receives payments from the partnership for required partner/employee type services rendered which are determined without regard to partnership profits (these are guaranteed payments under Code Sec. 707(c)) is not regarded as an employee of the partnership for purposes of withholding. The partnership's deduction for guaranteed payments is not separately stated unless it is specially allocated. The partnership's total guaranteed payments are deducted on Form 1065, line 10. Unlike Code Sec. 707(a) payments, Code Sec. 707(c) payments made to a partner are not reported on Form 1099, but rather appear as a separately stated amount on Schedule K-1, box 4. For more detail related to the deductibility timing, character, and other treatment of payments to partners, see ¶ 404. Compensation paid to any employee other than a partner is subject to withholding for income tax purposes and is also subject to withholding for FICA[29] and FUTA[30] purposes. Liability is imposed under such provisions with respect to "wages." The term "wages" is defined by Code Secs. 3121(a) and 3306(b) as "all remuneration for employment." The definition of wages for purposes of withholding is similar.

> **LLC Observation:** Although for nontax purposes LLCs resemble corporations, for federal income tax purposes they are generally treated as partnerships (since their members generally elect to be treated that way, and that is usually the default treatment). The rules described immediately above apply in the same manner to LLCs and LLPs. Unlike publicly traded corporations, LLCs, LLPs, and other partnerships are not subject to the $1,000,000 compensation deduction limitation of Code Sec. 162(m). This is so even if a publicly traded corporation is a partner in a partnership, and the partnership and the corporation have common employees.[31]

.04 Interest and Royalty Income

The partnership separately states its total interest and royalty income on Form 1065, Schedule K, on lines 5 and 7, respectively. Each partner's share of the partnership interest and royalty income is shown on Schedule K-1, boxes 5 and 7.

.05 Dividends

The deduction allowed under Code Sec. 243 to corporations for a percentage of the dividends received from other corporations is not allowed to a partnership because its taxable income is computed as if it were an individual. Corporate partners will separately determine their eligibility for this deduction. The corporate partner will not be required to reduce basis for this amount. The partnership separately states its ordinary dividend income[32] on Form 1065, Schedule K, line 6a, "Ordinary dividends." Each partner's share of ordinary dividends is shown on Schedule K-1, box 6a, "Ordinary dividends." The amount for "Ordinary dividends" will generally include the amount of "Qualified dividends" disclosed on line 6b and in box 6b of the Schedule K and K-1, respectively.

---

[29] Code Sec. 3101, et seq.
[30] Code Sec. 3301, et seq.

[31] IRS Letter Ruling 200614002.
[32] Code Sec. 702(5).

For purposes of determining the tax on long-term capital gains, "qualified dividend income" is added to net capital gain and adjusted net capital gain.[33] However, in computing the tax on dividends, the qualified dividend income cannot be offset by any capital losses.[34] The net effect of these rules is to tax qualified dividend income at either a 0, 15, or 20 percent rate, depending on what the taxpayer's marginal tax rate is. If the taxpayer's marginal tax rate on taxable income is 15 percent or below, the tax rate on qualified dividend income is 0 percent. If the taxpayer's marginal tax rate on taxable income is above 15 percent, qualified dividend income will generally be taxed at 15 percent, but if the taxpayer's marginal rate on taxable income is 39.6%, their tax rate on dividend income is 20%.[35] "Qualified dividend income" consists of dividends received from domestic and qualified foreign corporations, but only if the taxpayer held the stock for at least 61 days of the 121-day period beginning 60 days before the ex-dividend date.[36] The partnership separately states its qualified dividend income on Form 1065, Schedule K, line 6b, "Qualified dividends." Each partner's share of qualified dividend income is shown on Schedule K-1, box 6b, "Qualified dividends."

.06 Capital Gains and Losses

Short and long-term capital gains and losses are each separately netted and stated as two net amounts.[37] The reporting procedure for partnership capital gains and losses and other portfolio income and expenses is discussed at ¶ 503.08.

.07 Code Sec. 1231 Gains and Losses

The partnership's net Code Sec. 1231 gain or loss is separately stated on Form 1065, Schedule K, line 10, "Net section 1231 gain (loss)." The partnership's net Code Sec. 1231 gain or loss from rental activity should be specified. Each partner is allowed to treat his or her net share of the partnership's Code Sec. 1231 gains and losses as if they were a direct result of his or her sales activity. The Code Sec. 1231 character is determined at the partnership level but each partner combines his or her net share of the partnership's Code Sec. 1231 gains and losses with such gains and losses from all other sources.[38] Gain characterized as ordinary income under recapture provisions[39] which is not required to be specially allocated is not separately stated and is therefore netted with the other nonseparately stated items on page one of Form 1065. The partnership's total ordinary nonrental income from this source is entered on Form 1065, line 6, "Net gain (loss) from Form 4797, part II, line 17."[40] Recapture income from rental activities is part of the net income or loss from rental activity. Code Sec. 1231 requires a preliminary netting of gains and losses from thefts and casualties of trade and business assets.[41] If this preliminary netting results in a loss, each loss is treated as an ordinary loss and it is not part of

---

[33] Code Secs. 1(h)(3)(B) and 1(h)(11)(A).

[34] Code Sec. 1(h)(3).

[35] Code Sec. 1(h).

[36] Code Sec. 1(h)(11)(B).

[37] These net amounts are calculated on the partnership's Schedule D (Form 1065) and flow through to the *partner's* Schedule D.

[38] This is reported on the *partner's* Form 4797, Sales of Business Property.

[39] The most commonly encountered examples are the depreciation recapture provisions of Code Secs. 1245 and 1250. Reg. § 1.1245-1(e)(2), for example, requires the recapture to be allocated to the partnership interest which received the depreciation deduction.

[40] The partnership's information concerning the recapture of Code Sec. 179 expense is entered on Form K-1, box 20, but the income goes on Form 1065, line 6.

[41] Code Sec. 1231(a)(4)(C).

¶503.06

the general Code Sec. 1231 netting process. A partnership which has casualty and theft gains and losses should report two net Code Sec. 1231 amounts—the net gain or loss from casualties and thefts and the net of the remaining Code Sec. 1231 transactions. The partnership net income or loss from involuntary conversions due to casualties or thefts are shown on Form 1065, Schedule K, line 11, and on Schedule K-1, box 11.

.08 Portfolio (Investment) Income and Related Deductions Other Than the Interest Deduction

Items that qualify as portfolio income or deductions are not taken into account in computing passive income and loss.[42] The partner takes his or her share of these partnership items into account with such items from other sources for purposes of the investment interest limitations.[43] Types of income in this category include: interest, dividends, royalty and annuity income not derived in the ordinary course of business, and gain from disposition of property producing such income. Expenses other than interest directly related to producing portfolio (investment) income and losses incurred on the disposition of portfolio (investment) assets are the only deductions in this category.[44]

Portfolio (investment) expense other than interest expense is a common example of an expenditure that is not deductible by the partnership but is separately stated.[45] Form 1065, Schedule K, requires the partnership to separately state dividend and royalty income on Form 1065, Schedule K, lines 6 and 7. "Qualified" dividends are entered on line 6b of Schedule K and box 6b of Schedule K-1, and all taxable ordinary dividends are entered on line 6a and in box 6a, respectively, of Schedules K and K-1. Net short-term capital gains and losses are entered on line 8 of Schedule K and in box 8 of Schedule K-1. Net long-term capital gains and losses are entered on line 9a and box 9a, respectively, of Schedules K and K-1.

Unrecaptured section 1250 gains and collectibles gains are entered on lines 9c and 9b, respectively, of Schedule K. The partnership's total remaining gross portfolio income is entered on line 11 of Schedule K. The partnership must attach a schedule showing the composition of the income entered on line 11. The partnership enters portfolio income (except for other portfolio gains and losses) which is also investment income on line 20a of Schedule K. All Code Sec. 212 expenses directly related to producing portfolio income are entered on Schedule K, line 13d. The partnership must attach a schedule showing the composition of the Code Sec. 212 portfolio expenses entered on Schedule K, line 13d. The partnership enters the portion of portfolio expense which is also investment expense on Form 1065, Schedule K, line 20b. Investment expenses that are portfolio expenses are also included on Schedule K, line 13d.

---

[42] Code Sec. 469(e)(1)(A). Working capital is considered a portfolio (investment) asset. Code Sec. 469(e)(1)(B).

[43] Code Sec. 163(d).

[44] Code Sec. 163(d)(4)(C) and (5)(B).

[45] Code Sec. 67(c).

.09 Code Sec. 212—Expenses for the Production of Income

These amounts are not classified as a partnership deduction but they are separately stated and passed through to the partners as is discussed in ¶ 503.08 and ¶ 503.28.

.10 Code Sec. 179 Expense

When lawmakers are trying to stimulate the economy, they seem to like to tinker with the Code Sec. 179 deduction, so any amounts listed below might have changed, and should be verified using the latest tax sources. As of this writing, a taxpayer is entitled to deduct up to $500,000 ($25,000, adjusted for inflation, in tax years beginning after 2013) of amounts paid during any taxable year beginning before 2014 for tangible personal property used in a trade or business. The $500,000 maximum is reduced by the excess of (1) qualifying property placed in service over (2) $2,000,000.[46] For tax years beginning after 2013, the deduction limit and phase-out floor are scheduled to go back to $25,000 and $200,000.[47]

The $500,000 deduction limit and $2,000,000 phase-out floor apply at both the partnership and partner levels.[48] This limitation means that a partnership's total Code Sec. 179 deduction cannot exceed $500,000 and that a partner's individual Code Sec. 179 deduction (taking into account his or her share of the Code Sec. 179 deduction from the partnership and Code Sec. 179 deductions from his or her other activities) may not exceed $500,000.

In addition to the $500,000 limit there is an active trade or business income limitation. The Code Sec. 179 deduction cannot create an overall trade or business loss at either the partnership level or the partner level.[49] Neither the partner's nor the partnership's Code Sec. 179 deduction can exceed its net active trade or business taxable income from all sources.[50] The limits are applied first at the partnership level and amounts in excess of only the active trade or business income limit are carried over at the partnership level.[51] There is no carryover provision for amounts exceeding the $500,000 limit.[52]

> *Observation:* An allocation of a Code Sec. 179 expense from a partnership to a partner who exceeds the $500,000 limit is in effect an income allocation. This is because even though the deduction is disallowed, partnership interest adjusted basis is reduced which causes more gain or less loss on sale of the interest.

The partnership must, however, reduce its basis in its qualifying assets (for which the election was made) by the entire expense elected.[53] The partnership selects the properties and the apportionment of cost that is subject to any carry-

---

[46] Code Sec. 179(b)(2).

[47] Code Sec. 179(b)(1), (2), and (7).

[48] Code Sec. 179(d)(8).

[49] Code Sec. 179(b)(3).

[50] For this purpose, net taxable income excludes any suspended deduction or net operating loss carryover but includes Code Sec. 1231 gains (or losses) from sales and interest from working capital. Reg. § 1.179-2(c)(1). Active income requires meaningful participation in management or operations in a Code Sec. 162 activity. Reg. § 1.179-2(c)(6)(i). A passive investor's income does not qualify. Reg. § 1.179-2(c)(6)(ii). Rental activity other than a net-lease arrangement seems to satisfy this test. Reg. § 1.179-1(h)(2), Ex.

[51] Code Sec. 179(b)(3); Reg. § 1.179-2(c)(2).

[52] Reg. § 1.179-3(b)(1).

[53] Reg. §§ 1.179-1(f)(2) and -3(g)(2).

over.[54] If the partnership disposes of Code Sec. 179 property while there is a related carryover it is added to the property's basis.[55] Code Sec. 179 deductions that have survived the gamut of the partnership-level limits are tested with the same limits and carryover rules at the partner level. The partner's basis in the partnership interest is reduced by the full amount allocated from the partnership whether or not the partner can deduct or carryover the amount allocated.[56] If the partner disposes of his or her interest while there is a related carryover it is added to his or her basis in the partnership interest.[57] The partnership enters its total Code Sec. 179 deduction on Form 1065, Schedule K, line 12, "Section 179 deduction." Each partner's share of the Code Sec. 179 expense is shown on Schedule K-1, box 12, "Section 179 deduction."

.11 Charitable Contribution Deduction

A partnership is not officially entitled to deduct a contribution to a charitable organization.[58] The partnership, however, must separately state its total net contributions to each separate category of charity as defined by Code Sec. 170. It must also identify the type of property contributed because the information could affect a shareholder's individual income tax calculation.[59] Each partner then combines the contributions passed through from the partnership and other pass-through entities with any of the year's other charitable contribution pass-throughs and his or her direct contributions to compute the year's allowed charitable contribution deduction. The partner is treated as having received a money distribution for whatever share of the contribution was paid on his or her behalf. The partner's capital account and basis in his or her interest are reduced by this amount. The partnership enters the total amount of these payments on Form 1065, Schedule K, line 13a, "Contributions." Each partner's share of this amount is shown on Schedule K-1, box 13, "Other deductions," with codes A through G to indicate the limitation category the contribution should be placed in. The partnership must provide a copy of its Form 8283, Noncash Charitable Contribution, to every partner if the value of an item or a group of similar items exceeds $5,000, even if the amount allocated to each partner is $5,000 or less.

.12 Self-Employment Income

Each general partner has self-employment income for his or her share of the partnership's trade or business income. However, a limited partner's distributive share is not treated as net earnings from self-employment.[60] But guaranteed payments to limited partners for services rendered do constitute earned income for purposes of the self-employment tax. A partner includes his or her share of self-employment income in his or her year with or within which the partnership's year

---

[54] Reg. § 1.179-3(e).

[55] Reg. § 1.179-3(g)(3).

[56] Reg. § 1.179-3(h)(1).

[57] Reg. § 1.179-3(h)(2). There is no partner-level carryover for Code Sec. 179 expenses exceeding the $500,000 limit.

[58] Code Sec. 703(a)(2)(C). Even though charitable contributions are not deductible by a partnership, Schedule K specifically lists it among its separately stated amounts.

The partnership informational tax return treats a charitable contribution as if it were a separately stated partnership deduction.

[59] An individual's deduction for gifts to charities is limited to various percentages of his or her adjusted gross income. The specific percentage is governed by the type of charity and also whether cash or property is gifted. Code Sec. 170(b) and (e).

[60] Code Sec. 1402(a)(13).

ends.[61] If a partner dies, his or her self-employment income includes only the portion of the year ending on the first day of the month following his or her death.[62] There is net income from self-employment *only* if the partnership is engaged in a trade or business.[63] For this purpose, a partnership engaged in the business of renting real estate appears to be considered engaged in a trade or business.[64]

The Worksheet for Figuring Net Earnings (Loss) From Self-Employment treats the taxpayer's rental income as self-employment income only if it is received in the course of the taxpayer's trade or business as a real estate dealer. The partnership enters its total self-employment income on Form 1065, Schedule K, line 14a. It represents the amount of partnership income reported elsewhere in the tax return which should be classified as earned income; thus, the amount reported on this line is *not* treated as additional income by the partners. Each partner's share of the self-employment income is shown on Schedule K-1, box 14.

LLPs and LLCs. Code Sec. 1402(a)(13) generally excludes a limited partner's share of partnership income from Social Security taxation. However, limited partners are subject to Social Security taxation for payments by the partnership to them for services. There is currently no definitive guidance as to who among members of an LLC or LLP is a limited partner for Code Sec. 1402(a)(13) purposes. However, proposed regulations treat a partner in a tax partnership as a limited partner unless he or she (1) has personal liability for the debts of the entity, (2) has the authority to contract on behalf of the entity, or (3) participates more than 500 hours in the partnership during the year.[65] With respect to LLPs, IRS Letter Ruling 200403056 addresses the issue of whether certain retirement payments to the partner of a professional LLP are self-employment income, and rules that they are not if they meet the requirements of Code Sec. 1402(a)(10). The letter ruling does not, however, identify the characteristics that would indicate that a partner in an LLP is a limited partner.

.13 Deduction for Foreign Taxes and Taxes of U.S. Possessions Allowed Under Code Secs. 164(a) and 901

Technically, this expenditure is not deductible by a partnership.[66] These taxes paid by a partnership pass through to its partners who then elect to either deduct the taxes or take a foreign tax credit.[67] It is treated as if the partnership distributed the funds to pay the taxes and the partners paid the tax. The partner's share of foreign income, deduction, foreign taxes and other information is entered on the partnership's Form 1065, Schedule K, lines 16a-n, "Foreign Transactions," and reported to the partner on Schedule K-1, box 16, "Foreign Transactions."

---

[61] Reg. § 1.1402(a)-2(e).

[62] Code Sec. 1402(f).

[63] Reg. § 1.1402(a)-1(b).

[64] Code Sec. 1402(a)(1); Reg. § 1.1402(a)-4; *see* Reg. § 1.1402(c)-(1), even though real estate rental income is generally excluded from the definition of net income from self-employment.

[65] Prop. Reg. § 1.1402(a)-2(h)(2)(iii).

[66] Code Sec. 703(a).

[67] These are nondeductible expenditures and therefore the basis of the partnership interests are reduced. The partners' capital accounts are also reduced for their shares of the taxes.

¶503.13

.14 Alternative Minimum Tax Information

Individuals and some corporations are subject to the alternative minimum tax (AMT).[68] The base for the AMT is alternative minimum taxable income (AMTI), which is generally equal to taxable income modified by adjustments[69] and preferences.[70] When the AMT exceeds the taxpayer's regular tax liability, the excess is an additional tax. When the reverse is true, a credit is available if the difference is due to a timing adjustment which either accelerated income or deferred deductions and caused an AMT liability in an earlier year.

Timing adjustments are amounts of income or deductions which are reported in different years for AMT and regular tax purposes. For example, depreciable basis is generally recovered faster for regular tax than AMT. In earlier years, AMTI will exceed regular taxable income; in later years the reverse is true. Timing adjustments include:

- Depreciation deductions.[71]
- Mining and development costs.[72]
- Long-term contract income.[73]
- AMT net operating loss deduction.[74]
- Amortization of pollution control facilities.[75]

The partnership should report separately to each partner his or her share of AMT income, gain and deduction for each separately stated regular tax amount affected. The partnership will generally use the 150 percent declining balance method of depreciation, so if MACRS 200 percent declining balance depreciation is used for regular tax purposes, there will be a depreciation adjustment. Any difference in AMTI and regular taxable income generated by the partnership should result in a different basis in the partnership interest for regular tax and AMT purposes. Therefore, if the partner sells his or her partnership interest which has an AMT/regular tax basis difference, the partner will have this difference reflected in the gain or loss computed for AMT and regular tax purposes.[76]

The partnership enters the total difference between the amount of depreciation for AMT purposes and regular tax purposes as a positive or negative number on Form 1065, Schedule K, line 17a, "Post-1986 depreciation adjustment." Each partner's share of this adjustment is shown on Schedule K-1, box 17. Positive adjustments are added to the partner's share of partnership income for AMT purposes. The reverse is done with negative adjustments. The net difference in any gains or losses from the disposition of property because of different bases for AMT and regular tax are reported on the partnership's Form 1065, Schedule K, line 17b, "Adjusted gain or loss." Each partner's share of the net difference from gains and losses from the disposition of property for AMT and regular tax are shown on

---

[68] Code Sec. 55.

[69] Code Sec. 56.

[70] Code Sec. 57.

[71] Code Sec. 56(a)(1).

[72] Code Sec. 56(a)(2).

[73] Code Sec. 56(a)(3).

[74] Code Sec. 56(a)(4).

[75] Code Sec. 56(a)(5).

[76] It is possible that the IRS will object to this analysis. It may take the approach that Code Sec. 56(a)(6) allows AMT basis only for property directly subject to AMT depreciation.

Schedule K-1, box 17, "Alternative minimum tax (AMT) items." The partnership's total tax preferences and adjustments, other than depreciation and gain and loss adjustments, are entered on Form 1065, Schedule K, line 17f, "Other AMT items (attach statement)." The partnership must attach a schedule showing each partner's share of these items. Each partner's Schedule K-1 shows his or her share of each of these items on Schedule K-1, box 17, "Alternative minimum tax (AMT) items." The partnership should attach a schedule showing the composition of these items.

.15 Code Sec. 611—Oil and Gas Well Depletion

A partnership cannot take a deduction for oil and gas depletion. Instead, oil and gas depletion is passed through and computed at the partner level.[77] Partnership oil and gas depletion information needed by each partner to compute their depletion amount should be disclosed on line 20c and in box 20 (code T) of the Schedule K and K-1, respectively.

.16 Income Attributable to Domestic Production Activities

Code Sec. 199 allows a deduction of nine percent (beginning in 2010) of a taxpayer's income from domestic production activities. The deduction is calculated by multiplying nine percent by the lesser of (1) the qualified domestic production activities income of the taxpayer for the taxable year, or (2) taxable income for the taxable year (or adjusted gross income, if the taxpayer is an individual).[78] However, the amount of the deduction for any taxable year cannot exceed 50 percent of the W-2 wages of the taxpayer for the taxable year.[79]

In general, domestic production activities under Code Sec. 199 include any lease, rental, license, sale, exchange, or other disposition of tangible personal property which was manufactured, produced, grown, or extracted by the taxpayer in whole or in significant part within the United States. Also allowed as domestic production activities are film, electricity, natural gas, or potable water produced by the taxpayer in the United States, construction performed in the United States, and engineering or architectural services performed in the United States for construction projects in the United States.[80]

In the case of partnerships or S corporations, Code Sec. 199 will be applied at the partner or shareholder level. As a result, each partner must compute its deduction separately. Each partner is allocated its share of items allocated or attributable to the partnership's qualified production activities, along with any other items of income, gain, loss, deduction or credit of the partnership. To determine its Code Sec. 199 deduction for the taxable year, a partner will aggregate its share of the qualified production activity items allocated to it from the partnership and those items of the partner that are attributable to sources other than the partnership. A partnership may specially allocate items of income, gain, loss, or deduction attributable to the partnership's qualified production activities as long as the allocations have substantial economic effect.[81] For purposes of the W-2 wage limitation, each

---

[77] Code Sec. 613A(c)(7)(D).
[78] Code Sec. 199(a)(1), (d)(2).
[79] Code Sec. 199(b)(1).

[80] Code Sec. 199(c)(4).
[81] Notice 2005-14, Sec. 4.06(1)(a)(i), 2005-7 IRB 498.

partner will be treated as having W-2 wages for the taxable year equal to that partner's allocable share of the W-2 wages of the partnership.[82] Partnership production activities deduction information needed by each partner to compute its production activities deduction should be disclosed on line 13d and in box 13 (codes T, U, and V) of the Schedules K and K-1, respectively.

Because the sale of an interest in a pass-thru entity does not reflect the realization of QPAI by that entity, QPAI generally does not include gain or loss recognized on the sale, exchange or other disposition of an interest in the entity. However, if Code Sec. 751(a) or (b) applies, gain or loss allocated to assets of the partnership the sale, exchange, or other disposition of which would give rise to an item of QPAI is taken into account in computing the partner's Code Sec. 199 deduction.[83]

The deduction, with one adjustment, is allowed in computing alternative minimum taxable income.[84] However, the deduction is not allowed in computing income from self-employment.[85]

.17 Interest Deductions

Business, rental, and investment interest. The partnership's deductible interest expense must be traced to its various activities.[86] Interest paid for borrowed funds is traced to the partnership's purchase of, or investment in, its various activities. The potential activities to which the debt is traced under these regulations include:

1. Real estate rental activities;
2. Nonreal estate rental activities;
3. Trade or business activities in which it does not materially participate;
4. Trade or business activities in which it does materially participate;
5. Trade or business activities in which it does materially participate but formally did not materially participate[87] ; and
6. Its investments in portfolio assets.

With the exception of interest expense on debt traced to investments (portfolio assets), the interest expense related to each of the above activities must be aggregated with the other related expenses and netted against income from the activity.[88] The net result for each activity after taking into account the interest and other expenses related to that activity is separately stated.[89]

---

[82] Code Sec. 199(d)(1)(A)(iii). For tax years beginning before May 18, 2006, the partner's share of W-2 wages from the partnership was limited to the lesser of (1) its allocable share of the W-2 wages of the partnership for the taxable year or (2) two times the specified percentage (3, 6, or 9 percent) of the partner's allocable qualified production activities income from the partnership. Code Sec. 199(d)(1)(A)(iii) before amend by Sec. 514(b)(1), PL 109-222, 5/17/2006.

[83] Notice 2005-14, Sec. 4.06(2), 2005-7 IRB 498.

[84] Code Sec. 199(d)(6).

[85] Code Sec. 1402(a)(16).

[86] The interest allocation rules contained in Temp. Reg. § 1.163-8T apply to individuals, partnerships, and S corporations.

[87] A former passive activity. Code Sec. 468(f).

[88] Interest traced to investments (portfolio assets), other expenses directly connected with producing investment income (portfolio income), and investment income (portfolio income) are separately stated as three distinct totals.

[89] The boundaries of the partnership's various activities are defined by the partnership. Reg. § 1.469-4(d)(5). The partner then may group activities conducted directly and through entities. Reg. § 1.469-4(d)(5)(i).

Interest on partnership debt which is traced to purchasing portfolio assets is separately stated on the partnership's Form 1065, Schedule K, line 13b, "Investment interest expense" and not on line 13d, which includes deductions related to portfolio income. The interest on partnership debt traced to purchasing investment assets which are not portfolio assets is separately reported on Form 1065, Schedule K, line 13d, "Other Deductions." Line 13d may be used when the partnership has interest traced to working interests in oil and gas property.[90] Each partner's share of partnership interest expense traced to purchasing portfolio assets is shown on Schedule K-1, box 13, code H.

Construction interest. Interest on debt incurred or continued for construction is capitalized as part of the constructed asset's cost during the construction period. This includes both interest on debt directly traced to construction and debt assigned to construction under the "avoided-cost" allocation system enacted by The Tax Reform Act of 1986.[91] The avoided-cost system is used to temporarily assign nonconstruction related debt to construction during the construction period. This is debt which, prior to commencement of construction, had been traced to other activities under the tracing rules.[92] Theoretically, if the partnership could have repaid a debt (and therefore not incurred the interest expense) instead of making construction payments, the interest must be capitalized under the avoided-cost method.

With respect to partnerships, interest capitalization requirements are applied first at the partnership level and then at the partner level.[93] The partnership subtracts from its accumulated construction expenditures its debt directly traced to construction. Construction expenditures in excess of debt directly traced to construction (excess construction costs) are considered to have been provided by the partnership's remaining debt under the avoided-cost method. If such construction expenditures exceed the partnership's remaining debt any excess is treated as received from any partner borrowing. When construction costs exceed all partnership debt, the partners are subject to the interest capitalization rules as if they had paid any construction expenditures in excess of the partnership's debt with partner-level borrowing.[94]

The partnership reports each partner's share of the excess of construction costs over the partnership's debt allocated to construction costs on the Partner's K-1, other information, box 20 (code R), with a description. Each partner is required to capitalize interest on debt previously traced to other activities during the construction period in an amount equal to his or her share of the partnership's construction costs in excess of his or her share of the partnership's debt. The partner is to maintain a "deferred asset" consisting solely of the capitalized interest attributable to his or her portion of the partnership's construction expenditures in excess of its debt.[95] The deferred asset is accounted for in the same manner as the

---

[90] Code Secs. 163(d)(5)(A)(ii) and 469(c)(3).

[91] P.L. 99-514; Code Sec. 262A(f).

[92] Debt traced to personal use, qualified residence debt, and debt incurred or continued to produce tax-exempt income is not reassigned to construction. Reg. § 1.263A-9(a)(4).

[93] Code Sec. 263A(f)(2)(C).

[94] Notice 88-99, 1988-2 CB 422.

[95] *De minimis* rules provide that the partner may ignore the partnership's activities if: (1) he or she owns 20% or less of the partnership interests; and (2) the partner's

¶503.17

partnership accounts for the constructed asset. The partner is allowed to treat any remaining capitalized cost as partnership interest adjusted basis if he or she disposes of his or her partnership interest.[96] The complexities of the partner-level deferred asset treatment may often be avoided by an election to capitalize otherwise deductible expenditures at the partnership level.[97]

Tax-exempt income and related expenses including interest on debt borrowed to produce tax-exempt income. Interest on debt incurred or continued for the purchase or carrying of obligations producing tax-exempt income is disallowed.[98] Expenses other than interest allocable to producing tax exempt income are disallowed.[99] The interest expense disallowed, the related tax-exempt income, and any other expense allocable to producing tax-exempt income are separately stated.

The partnership's total tax-exempt interest is entered on Form 1065, Schedule K, line 18a, "Tax-exempt interest income." Each partner's share of the partnership's tax-exempt interest income is shown on Schedule K-1, box 18 (code A). The partnership total tax-exempt income other than interest is entered on Form 1065 Schedule K, line 18b, "Other tax exempt income." Each partner's share of the partnership tax-exempt income other than interest is shown in Schedule K-1, box 18. The partnership's total expenses allocable to tax exempt income other than the interest expense are entered on Form 1065, Schedule K, line 18c, "Nondeductible expenses." Each partner's share of the partnership total expense allocable to producing tax-exempt income other than the interest expense is shown on Schedule K-1, box 18. Absent a "direct relationship," very little authority addresses the issue of whether interest paid or incurred by a partnership and passed through to a partner could be attributed to tax-exempt obligations held by the partner, or whether tax-exempt obligations held by the partnership could be treated as purchased or carried by a partner incurring interest expense on individual debt.[100]

Interest on distributed debt. It is not uncommon for a partnership to borrow funds to make distributions to partners. When a partnership applies the tracing rules to outstanding debt it may be traceable to a distribution to the partners. Under the interest tracing rules, if debt incurred by a partnership is traced to a distribution, the partnership itself cannot determine the character of the interest expense.

(Footnote Continued)

share of the construction expenditures in excess of its debt are $250,000 or less. Notice 88-99, 1988-2 CB 422.

[96] Under the avoided-cost method of debt allocation, a partner who incurs construction expenditures is also required to capitalize interest on debt directly traced to construction as well as interest on debt not traced to construction to the extent that construction expenditures exceed debt directly traced to construction. For this purpose the partner's share of the partnership's debt is considered to be his or her debt. The result is that he or she may be required to capitalize some or all of his or her share of the partnership's interest expense. In practice this may require the partner to request that the partnership separately state interest normally included in determining the net results of its various activities.

When a partner owning 20% or less of the partnership interests is engaged in construction and receives

pass-through interest expense of less than $25,000, the interest capitalization rules will not apply to the interest expense passed through from the partnership. Notice 88-99, 1988-2 CB 422.

[97] *See* Notice 88-99, 1988-2 CB 422.

[98] Code Sec. 265(a)(2).

[99] Code Sec. 265(a)(1).

[100] *B.P. McDonough,* 36 TCM 213, Dec. 34,277(M), TC Memo. 1977-50, aff'd, CA-4, 78-2 USTC ¶ 9490, 577 F2d 234. Tax-exempt interest income and interest expense of partners and partnership is aggregated for Code Sec. 265(2) purposes. *See also O. Phipps v. U.S.,* CtCls, 75-1 USTC ¶ 9399, 206 CtCls 583, 515 F2d 1099. Tracing debt from its source to its use is done in accordance with case law rather than the tracing regulations. *See generally* Rev. Proc. 72-18, 1972-1 CB 740.

Instead, the partners must characterize a portion of interest expense flowed through to them based on their use of the distributed funds unless the partnership chooses the alternative treatment.[101] The partnership enters the total interest paid or incurred on funds borrowed traced to a distribution to the partners on Form 1065, Schedule K, line 13d, "Other deductions."[102] The partnership's alternative is to allocate the debt proceeds among the entity's other expenditures during the taxable year to the extent that debt proceeds have not otherwise been allocated to such expenditures. There is no special election to use this alternate allocation method. The interest expense allocated to the partnership's activities is reported on Form 1065 and flows through to the individual partner's K-1 in box 13.

Interest on debt used to retire a partner. There is no formal guidance concerning the allocation of debt used to finance the retirement of a partner. The ultimate result of a debt-financed retirement is that the continuing partners have indirectly borrowed to purchase an increased ownership interest in the partnership. If the interest expense treatment is forced into the Code Sec. 736 pattern, the interest on borrowed money that is distributed to the partner and classified as Code Sec. 736(b) payments should be treated as interest on distributed borrowed money. However, the retiring partner would not get an allocation of any share of the interest deduction and the continuing partners should not have their treatment of the interest dependent upon the retiring partner's use of the funds.

The partnership is allowed an election to treat the funds as if they had been spent on partnership activities.[103] Interest paid for the use of borrowed money that is paid to the retired partner and classified as a Code Sec. 736(a)(1) "distributive share" of income cannot be classified under the normal rules. This payment is neither a partnership distribution nor an expense. It is an income share under Code Sec. 736(a). The tracing rules do not classify debt traced to a share of income as a use of borrowed money. Interest on indebtedness traced to a Code Sec. 736(a)(2) "guaranteed payment" possibly could be considered as debt incurred to pay a Code Sec. 162 expense.[104] If so, it would be a nonseparately stated interest expense traced to the partnership's business.

However, whether the payments are Code Sec. 736(a) or (b) payments, they are being made to acquire the retiring partners' share of the partnership assets. It would be reasonable to treat the debt as traced to purchasing the retired partner's interest in the partnership assets. The continuing partners would treat this indirect purchase of the underlying assets the same as a direct purchase of his or her partnership interest.[105] The remaining partners should be entitled to treat the

---

[101] Notice 88-20, 1988-1 CB 487. The total interest expense should be entered on the partnership's Form 1065, Schedule K, line 11 [now line 13e], "Other Deductions." Each partner's share of the interest expense should be included on line 11 [now line 13e] on Schedule K for "Other Deductions." A schedule should also be attached to the K-1 listing all distributions to the shareholder to which debt proceeds are traced indicating the amount of the debt proceeds and interest expense allocated to each distribution. *See also* Notice 89-35, 1989-1 CB 675.

[102] If the partner who received the distribution transfers his or her partnership interest, an interesting but unanswered question arises. Should the buyer be required to ascertain the seller's treatment and continue it, or can this be looked at as if it were a leveraged or bootstrapped acquisition? If the latter alternative is correct the new owner's share of the debt is treated as if it were incurred on debt traced to the purchase of the partnership's assets. Notice 89-35, 1989-1 CB 675.

[103] Notice 88-20, 1988-1 CB 487, and Notice 89-35, 1989-1 CB 675.

[104] Reg. § 1.707-1(c).

[105] Notice 89-35, 1989-1 CB 675.

interest as paid on indebtedness incurred to purchase the retiring partner's share of unrealized receivables, goodwill, and other property. What is clear is that interest on borrowed funds traced to payments to retire a partner are not covered by official guidance.[106]

Partnership interest paid on debt owed to a partner—Self-charged interest. When a partner lends money to the partnership, the partner both receives interest income and is allocated a share of the partnership's interest deduction. Absent a special rule, and assuming the loan proceeds are used in the partnership's activities classified as passive for the lending partner, the interest income would be portfolio interest income and the interest expense would be a passive deduction. Accordingly, the interest expense would not be available to offset the interest income. If the partner borrows from a third party to make the loan to the partnership, however, the interest expense on the third-party loan would be a portfolio deduction, which would offset the portfolio income paid by the partnership.[107]

Congress did not intend for these types of lending transactions to cause these unfavorable results.[108] The Conference Committee Report to The Tax Reform Act of 1986 refers specifically to loans between a pass-through entity and its owners.[109]

> Under certain circumstances, the interest may essentially be "self-charged," and thus lack economic significance . . . Under these circumstances, it is not appropriate to treat the transaction as giving rise both to portfolio interest income and to passive interest expense. Rather, to the extent that a taxpayer receives interest income with respect to a loan to a pass-through entity in which he or she has an ownership interest, such income should be allowed to offset the interest expense passed through to the taxpayer from the activity for the same taxable year.

With respect to loans from the partner to the partnership, in general, certain owner/lender self-charged interest income is recharacterized as passive income, thus allowing the use of self-charged interest expense to offset self-charged interest income.[110] The recharacterization rules apply to both interest received from direct partner loans to the partnership and indirect loans when an S corporation shareholder lends money to a partnership in which the S corporation is a partner and the lending shareholder has a direct or indirect "qualifying interest" (a 10 percent

---

[106] If funding for the ex-partner's liquidating distributions were provided by the retiring partner accepting an interest-bearing note from the partnership, the "interest" payments are not considered interest. They are considered part of the money distributed under Code Sec. 736.

[107] A similar problem is created when a loan in the opposite direction is made. When a partnership lends money to its partner, the partner both incurs an interest deduction and is allocated a share of the partnership's interest income. Absent a special rule, and assuming the partner invests the loan proceeds in a passive activity, his or her share of the partnership interest income would be portfolio income and the interest expense would be a passive deduction even if the partnership's other income items were passive to the partner. Accordingly, the interest expense would not be available to offset the interest income. If instead the partner invests the loan proceeds in a portfolio investment, or if the partnership borrows

from a third party to make the loan to the partner, the interest expense on the third-party loan would be a portfolio deduction, which would offset the portfolio income.

[108] Inequitable results of a similar nature are apparently acceptable. For example, if a partnership conducts a passive activity and pays one of its partners a fee for services, the partner would have compensation income and could have a passive activity loss attributable to the partnership's passive activities. The self-charged interest rules do not permit the salary to be offset by the passive activity loss.

[109] H.R. Rep. No. 841, 99th Cong., 2d Sess. II-146-II-147 (1986) (Conference Report to P.L. 99-514); *See also* Staff of the Joint Committee on Taxation, *General Explanation of the Tax Reform Act of 1986* (Blue Book), at p. 233, n. 26 (similar rule for loans from the entity to its owners) and S. Rep. No. 841, 99th Cong., 2d Sess. II-146 to 147 (1986).

[110] Reg. § 1.469-7.

¶503.17

ownership interest). When the recharacterization rules apply, the "applicable percentage" of the partner's interest income from interest paid by the borrowing partnership is recharacterized as passive income from the pass-through entity's activity. In addition, the "applicable percentage" of the partner's related interest expenses is treated as a passive activity deduction.[111] The partner's applicable percentage is determined by dividing the partner's share of the self-charged interest deductions that constitute passive activity deductions by the greater of (1) the partner's share of total self-charged interest deductions (regardless of whether these deductions are treated as passive activity deductions), or (2) the partner's income from interest charged to the partnership.[112] The partnership should include each partner's share of the partnership's self-charged interest expense on Schedule K-1, box 20, "Other information."

The recharacterization rules in the regulations do not apply if the partnership (rather than the partner) elects not to have self-charged treatment apply.[113] The election is made for a taxable year by attaching a written statement to the partnership's return or amended return for the taxable year. It applies to all loan transactions between the pass-through entity and its direct or indirect owners for all subsequent taxable years that end before the date on which the election is revoked.[114] The election can not be revoked without the consent of the IRS.[115]

With respect to loans from the partnership to a partner, if certain requirements are satisfied, a partner's "applicable percentage" of self-charged interest income of the partnership attributable to loans made by the partnership to its partners is recharacterized as passive activity gross income. The applicable percentage of the partner's share of related interest expenses is treated as a passive activity deduction.[116] The self-charged interest rules relating to loans from a partnership are applicable only if:

1. The partnership has interest income arising from loans made to its partners ("self-charged interest income");

2. A partner owns a direct or qualifying indirect interest[117] in the partnership sometime during the partnership's taxable year and has deductions for interest paid to the partnership; and

3. The partner's deduction for interest charged by the partnership is included in his or her passive activity deductions.[118]

A partner's applicable percentage is equal to his or her passive activity deductions for interest charged by the partnership, divided by the greater of (1) the partner's deduction for all interest that the partnership charges the partner (regard-

---

[111] Reg. § 1.469-7(c)(2).

[112] Reg. § 1.469-7(c)(3).

[113] Reg. § 1.469-7(g)(1). The self-charged interest rules may be undesirable because (1) of the administrative burden associated with the application of the rules; (2) in certain circumstances the application of the rules produces no benefit; or (3) the recharacterization of the interest income may have adverse consequences for certain partners. The partnership-level nature of the election out could cause serious conflicts among the partners of a partnership—*e.g.*, if one partner has investment interest carryovers under Code Sec. 163(d) and the other partners do not.

[114] Reg. § 1.469-7(g)(2) and (3).

[115] Reg. § 1.469-7(g)(4).

[116] Reg. § 1.469-7(d)(2).

[117] Reg. § 1.469-7(c)(1).

[118] Reg. § 1.469-7(c)(1)(iii).

¶503.17

less of whether the deductions are treated as passive activity deductions), or (2) the partner's share of the partnership's self-charged interest income.[119] The partnership should include each partner's share of self-charged interest income on Schedule K-1, box 20, "Other Information."

.18 Recovery of Previously Deducted Amounts

Partnership recoveries of amounts deducted in prior years must be separately stated.[120] The separately stated amount is tested for exclusion at the partner level under Code Sec. 111.[121] The partnership enters its total recoveries of previously deducted amounts on Form 1065, Schedule K, line 11, "Other income (loss)." Each partner's share of this amount is shown on Schedule K-1, box 11, "Other income (loss)." This amount is reported by a partner who is an individual on Form 1040, line 21, only to the extent it reduced taxable income in a prior year.

.19 Cancelled Debt Income

In general, a partnership's cancellation of indebtedness income (COD) is reported as separately stated ordinary gross income. The partnership enters its total COD on Form 1065, Schedule K, line 11, "Other Income." Each partner's share of the partnership COD is reported on Schedule K-1, box 11 (code E, or code F for cancelled debt income deferred under Code Sec. 108(i)), "Other income." It is ordinary income derived from the activity to which the debt is traced under the tracing rules.[122]

Sources of cancelled debt income. The following are examples of situations when, absent special circumstances making an exclusion from gross income available, a partnership may incur cancellation of indebtedness income:

1. A reduction in the principal amount of its liability.

2. A material modification of the debt. For example, a reduction in the interest rate on outstanding debt. A change in the interest rate may be a material modification in the existing debt requiring the partnership to treat the original debt as if it had been refinanced with the new debt. When new debt is issued in satisfaction of existing debt the partnership is treated as if it paid the existing debt with an amount of money equal to the "issue price" of the new debt instrument.[123] Therefore, the issuance of the new debt will generate discharge of indebtedness income if the issue price is less than the balance of the old debt.[124] However, new debt with an interest rate at least equal to the applicable federal rate will not result in debt discharge income.

---

[119] Reg. § 1.469-7(c)(3).

[120] Reg. § 1.702-1(a)(8)(i).

[121] *See T.A. Frederick v. Commr.*, 101 TC 35, Dec. 49,165 (1993) (S corporation case).

[122] Temp. Reg. § 1.163-8T. Thus, if the debt proceeds had been traced to the partnership's trade or business activity it would be reported as "Other income" one page one of Form 1065.

[123] Issue price is defined in Code Sec. 1274 as the present value of all payments to be made with respect to the obligation (stated interest and principal) at a discount factor equal to the "applicable federal rate." The applicable federal rate is published through monthly revenue rulings.

[124] Code Sec. 108(e)(11); Reg. § 1.1001-3(a). Added to Code Sec. 108(e) by Act § 11325(a)(1) of P.L. 101-508 (The Omnibus Budget Reconciliation Act of 1990), generally applies to debt instruments issued after October 9, 1990.

3. When a person related to the debtor directly or indirectly acquires debt from a person who is not related to the debtor, debt discharge income may result.[125] The amount of the income equals the excess of the face amount of the debt over its value.[126]

In a number of circumstances, however, the Internal Revenue Code provides specific exceptions to the general rule that cancellation of indebtedness triggers income to the debtor.[127] Income realized from the forgiveness of indebtedness is excluded:

1. If the discharge occurs in a Title 11 case;[128]

2. To the extent the debtor remains insolvent;[129]

3. If the debt was incurred incident to the purchase of property and the seller/creditor reduces the amount of the debt when the debtor is solvent;[130]

4. If it is a discharge of qualified farm debt of a solvent farmer;[131]

5. Payment of the debt would have been deductible;[132]

6. The debt is "qualified real property business indebtedness;" or

7. The debt is "qualified principal residence indebtedness."

Foreclosures, etc., and cancelled debt income. When debt is secured by the partnership property and the partnership transfers that property to the lender as part of the cancellation, the exclusion provisions for *cancelled debt* may be partially or completely inapplicable. This is the result whether the property is transferred in a foreclosure, a voluntary transfer to the secured creditor (a deed in lieu), or an indirect transfer to the secured creditor by way of an abandonment.[133]

---

[125] Code Secs. 267(b) and 707(b)(1) define a related party for this purpose.

[126] Code Sec. 108(e)(4). An indirect related party acquisition includes when an unrelated person acquires the debt in anticipation of becoming related. Reg. § 1.108-2(c).

[127] Code Sec. 108. In addition to the statutory exclusions from gross income provided for cancelled debt there are a number of judicial decisions which may expand the possibilities for not reporting cancelled debt income. These decisions generally predate the Bankruptcy Tax Act of 1980 (P.L. 96-589) and their viability is not certain. *See* Code Sec. 108(e)(1).

[128] Code Sec. 108(a)(1)(A) and (d)(2). Title 11 of the United States Code federal bankruptcy proceedings. A debtor who is in a bankruptcy proceeding is entitled to the statutory bankruptcy exclusions even if he or she is solvent immediately after the debt discharge within Code Sec. 108's definition.

[129] Code Sec. 108(a)(1)(B) and (3). Insolvency is defined as the excess of liabilities over the fair market value of assets. A debtor who is not in bankruptcy is entitled to this statutory exclusion only to the extent the discharge does not cause the fair market value of his or her assets to exceed his or her remaining debt. There is some question as to how goodwill and an individual's "exempt assets" are accounted for. Exempt assets are those which the bankrupt individual is allowed to keep after a bankruptcy. *See* Code Sec. 522 of the Bankruptcy Code. The cases of *R.S. Cole v. Commr.*, 42 BTA 1110, Dec. 11,364 (1940); *Fifth Avenue-14th Street Corp. v. Commr.*, CA-2, 45-1 USTC ¶ 9115, 147 F2d 453; *Est. of B.M. Marcus v. Commr.*, 34 TCM 38, Dec. 33,012(M), TC Memo. 1975-9; and *C.L. Hunt v. Commr.*, 57 TCM 919, Dec. 45,833(M), TC Memo. 1989-335, have all held that exempt assets are not taken into account in determining the fair market value of the debtor's assets after the debt discharge for purposes of the insolvency exception. The judicial reasoning is that the debt discharge does not free up these assets because they are assets the debtor can keep even if the debts are not discharged. The IRS's position is that exempt assets are included in the solvency determination. IRS Technical Advice Memorandum 199935002 (5-3-99); IRS Letter Ruling 199932013 (5-4-99).

[130] Code Sec. 108(e)(5). The property is treated as if it were purchased for the reduced price.

[131] Code Sec. 108(g).

[132] Code Sec. 108(e)(2).

[133] Reg. § 1.1001-2(c), Ex. 8; Rev. Rul. 90-16, 1990-1 CB 12; *M.L. Middleton v. Commr.*, 77 TC 310, Dec. 38,124 (1981), aff'd per curiam, CA-11, 82-2 USTC ¶ 9713, 693 F2d 124 (abandonment); *J.W. Yarbro v. Commr.*, CA-5, 84-2 USTC ¶ 9691, 737 F2d 479, cert. denied, 489 US 1189, 105 SCt 959 (abandonment); and Rev. Rul. 76-111, 1976-1 CB 215.

The entire amount of a nonrecourse debt cancelled in connection with the property's transfer is treated as amount realized for its sale. Therefore, no cancellation of debt income is generated when property subject to a nonrecourse debt is transferred in whole or partial satisfaction of the debt. The transfer of property by a debtor in partial or whole satisfaction of a recourse debt is treated as payment of the debt to the extent of the property's value. Gain or loss, but not cancellation of debt income, is realized on the difference between the property's value and its adjusted basis.[134] Any excess of the debt over the fair market value of the transferred property generates cancellation of debt income if and when the debt becomes uncollectible. Gain generated by a partnership's transfer of its encumbered assets to its creditors will be taxable to the partners whether or not the partnership or the partner is insolvent or bankrupt. Seldom can this gain be offset with an ordinary loss from the abandonment of a worthless partnership interest. The gain generates basis in the partnership interest which could, possibly, generate more worthless partnership interest loss. However, the deemed money distribution resulting from the liquidated partnership's debt under Code Sec. 752(b) would probably result in the liquidation being treated as capital gain or loss on a liquidating distribution rather than an abandonment of a worthless partnership interest. Any basis not recovered through the deemed money distribution would be a capital loss.[135]

Assuming the gain and debt are allocated in the same manner, the basis increase resulting from the gain will be offset by the deemed cash distribution associated with the reduction in the partner's share of partnership debt. Even though the income from the foreclosure may be offset by a loss on dissolution of the partnership interest, a net tax liability can be generated when the pass-through gain is ordinary and the loss is capital or if the income is passed through in a year prior to the loss on the worthless partnership interest.

> **Example 5-2:** *Partnership debt is recourse.* The equal ABC partnership has the following balance sheet:

ABC Partnership

Assets	*Tax Basis*	*FMV*
Blackacre	$30,000	$60,000
Liabilities		
(recourse)	$90,000	$90,000
Capital		
A	$(20,000)	$(10,000)
B	(20,000)	(10,000)
C	(20,000)	(10,000)
	$(60,000)	*$(30,000)*

---

[134] Rev. Rul. 90-16, 1990-1 CB 12.   [135] Code Secs. 731(a) and 741.

¶503.19

ABC partnership deeds Blackacre to the lender in lieu of a foreclosure and the remaining debt is cancelled. The results to the ABC partnership are as follows:

	Deemed Sale	Cancelled Debt Income
Deemed Sales Price	$60,000	$30,000
Adjusted Basis	(30,000)	
Gain	*$30,000*	

The ABC partnership separately reports the $10,000 gain and $10,000 cancelled debt income for each partner.

Each partner's result is as follows:

Beginning partnership interest basis	$10,000
Increase for gain	10,000
Increase for cancelled debt income	10,000
Subtotal	*$30,000*
Reduction in debt share deemed distribution	(30,000)
Ending basis	$ 0
Gain/Loss	$ 0

Observation: Each partner's basis in his or her partnership interest is increased by the cancelled debt income whether or not it is excluded from the partner's income under Code Sec. 108.[136]

Example 5-3: Partnership debt is nonrecourse. If the debt had been nonrecourse, the results would have been as follows:

	Deemed Sale	Cancelled Debt Income
Deemed Sales Price	$90,000	$ 0
Adjusted Basis	(30,000)	
Gain	*$60,000*	

The ABC partnership separately states $20,000 gain for each partner and the result is as follows:

Beginning partnership interest basis	$10,000
Increase for gain	20,000
Increase for cancelled debt income	0
Subtotal	*$30,000*
Reduction in debt share deemed distribution	(30,000)

---

[136] Code Sec. 705(a)(1)(A) and (B).

Ending basis . . . . $ 0

Gain/Loss . . . . $ 0

Example 5-4: Assume the same facts as in Example 5-2, except that the ABC partnership allocated the cancelled debt income (COD) differently than the partners shared in debt under Code Sec. 752 and that the allocation has substantial economic effect or its equivalent under Code Sec. 704(b). Assume the COD is allocated 50% to *A* and the remainder equally to *B* and *C*. The result would have been as follows:

	A	*B*	*C*
Beginning partnership interest basis . .	$10,000	$10,000	$10,000
Increase for gain	10,000	10,000	10,000
Increase for cancelled debt income . . .	15,000	7,500	7,500
Subtotal	*$35,000*	*$27,500*	*$27,500*
Reduction in debt share deemed distribution	(30,000)	(30,000)	(30,000)
Ending basis	*$5,000*	$ *0*	$ *0*
Gain	$ 0	$2,500	$2,500

A's unrecovered basis will be a capital loss if the partnership is terminated as part of the transaction. Partners *B* and *C* each have a capital gain of $2,500.

The insolvency/bankruptcy exclusion of cancelled debt income. Tax attributes must be reduced if cancelled debt is excluded from gross income by the statutory provisions for bankrupt or insolvent persons.[137] In the context of a partnership debt it is the partner's insolvency or bankruptcy that qualifies each partner for an exclusion, and tax attributes are reduced at the partner level.[138] The partnership's insolvency or bankruptcy is irrelevant. When a partner, but not the partnership, files bankruptcy and the partner's liability for his or her share of partnership debt is discharged, but the partnership remains liable for the entire debt, there is a deemed cash distribution to the bankrupt partner (and a deemed cash contribution by those partners whose responsibility for repayment of the debt has increased).[139] If this deemed distribution exceeds the partner's basis, there is gain for the excess.[140] The holder of the partnership interest at year end must report the gain.[141]

S Corporation Observation: In the case of an S corporation, the exclusion is available if the S corporation is insolvent without regard to the solvency of the shareholders.[142]

LLC Observation: For nontax purposes, an LLC provides protection from creditors that is comparable to a shareholder's protection from the creditors of

---

[137] The attribute reductions are made after a determination of the debtor's tax liability for the years of discharge. Code Sec. 108(b)(4)(A).

[138] Code Sec. 108(d)(6).

[139] Code Sec. 752(b).

[140] Code Sec. 731(a).

[141] IRS Letter Ruling 9619002 (1-31-96).

[142] Code Sec. 108(d)(7)(A).

the corporation. From an income tax standpoint, if the LLC is treated as a partnership, its solvent/nonbankrupt members will incur taxable income when the creditors are not paid. Although a tax liability for not paying the debts is certainly less expensive than paying the debts, the members should be aware of the tax consequences. They will not normally be walking away from the activity free of all financial obligations.

With one exception, tax attributes must be reduced in the following order:

1. *Net operating losses.* A partner's net operating losses (NOLs) for the taxable year of the discharge are reduced first and then carryovers to that year are reduced in the order in which they arose.[143]

2. *General business credit.* A partner's tax credit carryovers are reduced in the same order in which they were taken into account. For credits earned in years beginning after December 31, 1986, the credits are reduced by 33-1/3 percent of the dollar amount of cancelled debt.

3. *Minimum tax credit.* Credit available on the first day of the next taxable year.[144]

4. *Capital loss carryovers.* A partner's net capital losses for the taxable year of the discharge are reduced first and then carryovers to that year are reduced in the order they arose.[145]

5. *Basis reduction.* The debtor's property basis is reduced according to the provisions of Code Sec. 1017. The order of the basis reduction of assets is prescribed by the regulations.[146] No basis reduction is required for property exempted from the bankruptcy proceedings by Code Sec. 522 of Title 11 of the United States Code.[147] The basis adjustments are treated as depreciation for purposes of Code Sec. 1245 and as "additional depreciation" (accelerated) for purposes of Code Sec. 1250, whether or not the property is Code Sec. 1245 or Code Sec. 1250 property.[148]

6. *Passive activity loss and credit carryovers.*

7. *Foreign tax credit carryovers.* Any carryover to or from the taxable year of discharge allowed under Code Sec. 33. For credits earned in years beginning after December 31, 1986, the credits are reduced by 33-1/3 percent of the dollar amount of cancelled debt.

The reduction in each category of carryovers is made in the order of taxable years in which the items would be used, with the order determined as if the debt discharge amount were not excluded from income. The reductions are made after the computation of the current year's tax.[149]

---

[143] Code Sec. 108(b)(2)(A) and (4)(B).

[144] Code Sec. 108(b)(2)(C).

[145] Code Sec. 108(b)(2)(A) and (4)(B).

[146] Reg. §1.1017-1. (1) Real property used in the trade or business or held for investment that secured the discharged debt immediately before the discharge; (2) property (other than inventory, notes and accounts receivable) used in the trade or business; (3) any other property (other than inventory, notes and accounts re-

ceivable) used in the trade or business; (4) inventory, notes and accounts receivable used in the trade or business; (5) property held for the production of income; (6) other property.

[147] Code Sec. 1017(c)(1).

[148] Code Sec. 1017(d).

[149] Code Sec. 108(b)(4)(A). The tax attributes are available for the calculation of the tax liability for the taxable year of discharge. In all cases, the reductions are made as

Bankrupt and insolvent persons, including partners, can avoid the statutory order of attribute reduction only by making an election to first reduce the basis of depreciable assets to zero and then resume the statutory order of attribute reduction for any remaining cancelled debt excluded from income by the insolvency and bankruptcy provisions. The partner can elect to apply any portion of the required attribute reduction to reduce the basis of the depreciable property before resuming the statutory order.[150] A partner's partnership interest is considered depreciable property to the extent of his or her share of the partnership's depreciable property.[151]

> **Observation:** Although reducing the basis of depreciable property for excluded cancelled debt income before following the statutory tax attribute reduction pattern is elective, it is an election which is generally made.

The regulations provide guidance for treating partnership interests as depreciable property if an election is made not to use the general attribute reduction rules. As a general rule, a partner can independently determine whether to request that the partnership reduce his or her share of depreciable basis in partnership property enabling him or her to treat the partnership interest as depreciable property (or depreciable real property in the case of qualified real property business indebtedness). However, a partner must request consent if the partner owns (directly or indirectly) more than 50 percent of the partnership's capital and profits interest or if the partner receives a distributive share of cancellation of indebtedness income from the partnership. The partner's request must be made before the due date (including extensions) for filing his or her federal income tax return for the tax year in which he or she has the cancellation of indebtedness income.[152]

The partnership generally is free to grant or deny its consent. The partnership, however, is required to grant consent if requests are made by partners owning (directly or indirectly) an aggregate of more than 80 percent of the partnership capital and profits or five or fewer partners owning (directly or indirectly) an aggregate of more than 50 percent of the capital and profits interests.[153] A partnership that consents to a basis reduction must include a consent statement with its Form 1065 for the tax year following the year that ends with or within the tax year the taxpayer excludes the COD income. The partnership must also provide a copy of that statement to the affected partner(s) on or before the due date of the taxpayer's return (including extensions) for the tax year in which the taxpayer partnership and the amount of (1) the reduction to the partner's proportionate interest in the adjusted basis of the partner's depreciable property, or (2) depreciable real property, whichever is applicable.[154] For taxable years beginning before January 1, 2003, this statement should also be attached to the partner's timely filed

---

(Footnote Continued)

of the first day of the succeeding year. Thus, gain or loss on property sold during the discharge year is not affected by any basis reduction. Property acquired any time during the discharge year and held on the first day of the next year is eligible for basis reduction.

[150] Code Sec. 108(b)(5). An election is available to treat real property held for sale to customers (dealer property) as depreciable property. Code Sec. 1017(b)(3)(E).

[151] But the partnership is required to reduce the basis of its depreciable property by the same amount. Code Sec. 1017(b)(3)(C).

[152] Reg. § 1.1017-1(g)(2)(ii)(A).

[153] Reg. § 1.1017-1(g)(2)(ii)(c).

[154] Reg. § 1.1017-1(g)(2)(iii).

(including extensions) tax return for the year in which the income is excluded under Code Sec. 108(a). For later years, the statement should be retained and be available for inspection.[155]

Form 982, Reduction of Tax Attributes Due to Discharge of Indebtedness (and Section 1082 Basis Adjustment), must be filed and signed by the partner whenever debt discharge income is excluded from gross income. The special basis reduction elections are also made on Form 982.

In applying the partner-level tax attribute reduction rules, a partnership interest is treated as depreciable property to the extent of the partner's interest in the partnership's depreciable property.[156] The basis reduction in the depreciable partnership property is an adjustment to the basis of partnership property only with respect to the electing partner. No adjustment is made to the common basis of partnership property. For purposes of income, deduction, gain, loss and distribution, the partner will have a special basis for those partnership properties for which the basis was adjusted under Code Sec. 1017. The recovery of adjustments to the basis of the partnership property for the partner making this election is recovered in the manner described in Reg. § 1.743-1.[157] In effect, the partnership records a negative basis which is amortized as an offset to depreciation specially allocated to the electing partner or as additional gain on the property's disposition which may be reported partially as ordinary income.[158] Adjustments to the basis of partnership property are treated in the same manner and have the same effect as an adjustment to the basis of partnership property under Code Sec. 743.[159]

As mentioned, eligibility for Title 11 and insolvency exclusions provided for debt discharge income is tested at the partner level.[160] The solvency or bankruptcy of the partnership is irrelevant to the exclusion of the forgiveness of indebtedness income at the partner level.[161] Tax attribute reduction is likewise applied at the partner level.[162] If a partner is bankrupt or insolvent and does not recognize cancellation of indebtedness income, the partner may make the election to reduce his or her basis in depreciable property before reducing other tax attributes.[163] No new taxable entity is created when a partnership files a bankruptcy petition.[164] This tax provision should not be confused with the bankruptcy provisions, other than income tax, providing that a new entity, the bankruptcy estate, is created for the administration of the bankruptcy rules. The partnership continues to file a Form 1065 according to its normal taxable year.[165] If a partner who is an individual is bankrupt, a new taxable estate is created.[166] His or her partnership interest is treated as owned by the estate but there is deemed not to be a transfer of his or her

---

[155] Temp. Reg. § 1.1017-1T(g)(2)(iii)(B).

[156] Code Sec. 1017(b)(3)(C).

[157] Reg. § 1.1017-1(g)(2)(v)(B).

[158] Code Sec. 1017(d). S. Rep. No. 1035, 96th Cong., 2d Sess. (1980), at 14.

[159] Reg. § 1.1017-1(g)(2)(v)(C).

[160] Code Sec. 108(d)(6).

[161] If cancelled debt is not eligible for exclusion at the partner level its partners are responsible for the tax liability generated by the debt discharge.

[162] Code Sec. 108(d)(6).

[163] Code Sec. 108(d)(7). *See* Form 982, Reduction of Tax Attributes Due to Discharge of Indebtedness.

[164] Code Sec. 1399. A separate taxable estate is created for an individual bankruptcy proceeding but not for corporations or partnerships.

[165] The trustee of the partnership's Chapter 7 bankruptcy estate is responsible for filing returns due after the petition is filed.

[166] Code Sec. 1398(a).

¶503.19

interest.[167] Therefore, there is no possibility that the partnership will terminate under Code Sec. 708(b)(1)(B), and all income is taxed to the estate.

Qualified real property business indebtedness exclusion of cancelled debt income. Taxpayers other than C corporations may elect to exclude from gross income certain discharge of qualified real property business indebtedness if they are not bankrupt and not insolvent.[168] The amount so excluded cannot exceed the basis of certain depreciable real property of the taxpayer and is treated as a reduction in the basis of that property.

Qualified real property business indebtedness is indebtedness that:

1. Is incurred or assumed in connection with real property used in a trade or business;

2. Is secured by that real property; and

3. With respect to which the taxpayer has made an election under this provision.[169]

Indebtedness incurred or assumed on or after January 1, 1993, is not qualified real property business indebtedness unless it is either:

1. Debt incurred to refinance qualified real property business debt incurred or assumed before that date (but only to the extent the amount of such debt does not exceed the amount of debt being refinanced), or

2. Qualified acquisition indebtedness.[170]

Qualified real property business indebtedness does not include qualified farm indebtedness.

Qualified acquisition indebtedness is debt incurred to acquire, construct, or substantially improve real property that is secured by such debt, and debt resulting from the refinancing of qualified acquisition debt, to the extent the amount of such debt does not exceed the amount of debt being refinanced.[171]

The amount excluded under the provision with respect to the discharge of any qualified real property business indebtedness may not exceed the excess of (1) the outstanding principal amount of such debt (immediately before the discharge), over (2) the fair market value (immediately before the discharge) of the business real property serving as security for the debt. For this purpose, the fair market value of the property is reduced by the outstanding principal amount of any other qualified real property indebtedness secured by the property immediately before the discharge.

> *Example 5-5:* Assume that Individual *J* owns a building worth $150,000, used in his trade or business, that is subject to a first mortgage securing a debt of *J*'s of $110,000 and a second mortgage securing a second debt of *J*'s of $90,000. *J* is neither bankrupt nor insolvent and neither debt is qualified farm indebtedness. *J* negotiates with his second mortgagee to reduce the second

---

[167] Code Sec. 1398(f).
[168] Code Sec. 108(a)(2).
[169] Code Sec. 108(c)(3).

[170] Code Sec. 108(c)(3).
[171] Code Sec. 108(c)(3).

mortgage debt to $30,000, resulting in discharge of indebtedness income in the amount of $60,000. Assuming that *J* has sufficient basis in business real property to absorb the reduction (see below), *J* can elect to exclude $50,000 of that discharge from gross income. This is because the principal amount of the discharged debt immediately before the discharge (*i.e.*, $90,000) exceeds the fair market value of the property securing it by $50,000 (*i.e.*, $150,000 of free and clear value less $110,000 of other qualified business real property debt or $40,000). The remaining $10,000 of discharge is included in gross income.

The amount excluded under this provision may not exceed the aggregate adjusted bases (determined as of the first day of the next taxable year or, if earlier, the date of disposition) of depreciable real property held by the taxpayer immediately before the discharge, determined after any reductions under subsections (b) and (g) of Code Sec. 108. Depreciable real property acquired in contemplation of the discharge is treated as not held by the taxpayer immediately before the discharge.[172]

The amount of debt discharge excluded under the provision reduces the depreciable realty's basis, following the rules of Code Sec. 1017. See the discussion earlier in this section.

The deemed distribution[173] arising from the reduction in a partner's share of partnership liabilities attributable to the discharge of partnership debt is treated as follows. The allocation of an amount of excluded debt discharge income to a partner results in that partner's basis in the partnership being increased by such amount.[174] The reduction in a partner's share of partnership liabilities caused by the debt discharge also results in a deemed distribution,[175] which in turn results in a reduction[176] of the partner's basis in his or her partnership interest. This basis reduction is separate from any reduction in basis of the partner's interest under the provision—*i.e.*, the basis reduction that occurs as a result of treating the partnership interest as depreciable real property to the extent of the partner's proportionate interest in the depreciable real property held by the partnership (provided the partnership makes a corresponding reduction in the basis of depreciable partnership real property with respect to that partner).

> ***S Corporation Observation:*** In applying these rules to income from the discharge of indebtedness of an S corporation, the election is made by the S corporation,[177] and the exclusion and basis reduction are both made at the S corporation level.[178] The shareholders' stock basis is not adjusted by the amount of debt discharge income that is excluded at the corporate level. As a result of these rules, if an amount is excluded from the income of an S corporation under this provision, the income flowing through to the shareholders will be reduced (compared to what the shareholders' income would have been without the exclusion). Where the reduced basis in the corporation's depreciable property later results in additional income (or a smaller loss) to

---

[172] Code Sec. 108(c)(2)(B).
[173] Code Sec. 752.
[174] Code Sec. 705.
[175] Code Sec. 752.

[176] Code Sec. 733.
[177] Code Sec. 1363(c).
[178] Code Sec. 108(d)(7).

the corporation because of reduced depreciation or additional gain (or smaller loss) on disposition of the property, the additional income (or smaller loss) will flow through to the shareholders at that time, and will then result in a larger increase (or smaller reduction) in the shareholder's basis than if this provision were not available. Thus, these rules simply defer recognition of income by the shareholders.

If depreciable real property, the basis of which was reduced under these rules, is disposed of, then for purposes of determining the amount of recapture under Code Sec. 1250: (1) any such basis reduction is treated as a deduction allowed for depreciation, and (2) the determination of what would have been the depreciation adjustment under the straight line method is made as if there had been no such reduction. Thus, the amount of the basis reduction that is recaptured as ordinary income is reduced over the time the taxpayer continues to hold the property, as the taxpayer forgoes depreciation deductions due to the basis reduction.[179]

.20 Code Sec. 172—Net Operating Deduction, and Code Sec. 1212— Capital Loss Carrybacks and Carryovers

These amounts are not carried over or back by the partnership.[180] A partnership's inability to carry net operating losses forward generally does not affect its partners. If the loss clears the basis, at risk, and passive loss rules, and the partner does not have sufficient current income to absorb the loss, he or she is allowed to individually carry the unused losses forward or back.[181]

.21 Deduction for Personal Exemptions

Although a partnership typically computes its deductions in the same manner as an individual, it is not entitled to a deduction for a personal exemption. There is no partnership expenditure and no reduction in the basis of the partnership interests, and the item is simply disregarded.

.22 Code Sec. 213—Medical Expenses

A partnership is not allowed a deduction for expenditures for medical expenses as a *medical expense*. If a partnership pays medical costs for the benefit of its nonpartner employees it is able to deduct the payments as additional compensation. If it pays these amounts for the benefit of a service partner under a Code Sec. 104 self-insured health plan or Code Sec. 105 insured health plan, the IRS's position is that they are deemed Code Sec. 707(c) guaranteed payments.[182] If the medical payments are for the benefit of a nonservice partner or if the IRS's position is not followed, such payments are treated as money distributions to the affected partner. The partner's basis and capital account are reduced accordingly and the partner is

---

[179] The provision is effective with respect to discharges after December 31, 1992, in taxable years ending after that date.

[180] Code Sec. 703(a); Reg. § 1.703-1(a)(2)(vii). The partnership loss reduces the partners' basis in their interest whether or not it is disallowed by the at-risk rules (Code Sec. 465) or the passive loss rules (Code Sec. 469).

[181] Code Sec. 172. If the losses are disallowed at the partner level because they are suspended under the basis, at-risk, or passive limitations, the losses are not available to a partner for net operating loss carryback but are carried over for an unlimited time until the partner has sufficient basis, at-risk amount, or passive income.

[182] The compensation to a service partner would be treated as a Code Sec. 707(c) payment. Rev. Rul. 91-26, 1991-1 CB 184.

entitled to any applicable deduction as if he or she paid the expense directly. See the detailed discussion of fringe benefits at ¶ 503.27.

.23 Code Sec. 215—Alimony

A partnership is not allowed an alimony deduction. If a partnership pays alimony for the benefit of its employees or its service partners, it may be able to deduct the payments as additional compensation or treat them as a money distribution.[183] If these amounts are paid on behalf of a partner who does not perform services, the payment is treated as a distribution to such partner. The partners' basis in his or her partnership interest and capital account are reduced by the alimony payment.

.24 Code Sec. 217—Moving Expenses

A partnership is not allowed a moving expense deduction. If a partnership pays these amounts for the benefit of its nonpartner employers it is additional compensation. If it pays these amounts to its service partners, it may be able to deduct the payments as Code Sec. 707(a) or (c) guaranteed payments.[184] If these amounts are paid on behalf of a partner who does not perform services, the payments are treated simply as distributions. The partner for whom the partnership paid the expenses is treated as receiving a distribution equal to the expenses paid. His or her capital account and basis in his or her partnership interest are reduced by this amount.

.25 Code Sec. 219—Retirement Savings

A partnership is not allowed a deduction for contributions to a plan for its benefit. If a partnership contributes amounts for the benefit of its service partners, it may be able to deduct the payments as Code Sec. 707(a) or (c) guaranteed payments.[185] If these amounts are paid on behalf of a partner who does not perform services, the payment is treated as a distribution.

.26 Trust or Estate Partner

All depreciation deductions must be separately stated if a trust or estate is a partner.[186]

.27 Fringe Benefits

Employee fringe benefits generally consist of property or services provided directly or indirectly to or for an employee as a salary or wage supplement. One of the advantages of a C corporation is that it permits an owner/employee of the business to participate in certain fringe benefits provided for employees and receive the same favorable tax benefits. The value of many of these benefits is excluded from the employee's income by specific statutory provisions but the corporation is entitled to deduct the cost. Two major questions related to this subject are:

1. What are fringe benefits?

2. How do partnerships treat fringe benefits?

---

[183] Rev. Rul. 91-26, 1991-1 CB 184.

[184] Id.

[185] Id.

[186] Rev. Rul. 74-71, 1974-1 CB 158.

¶503.23

There is no inclusive definition of "employee fringe benefit." Subchapter K of the Internal Revenue Code, dealing with the tax treatment of partners and partnerships, contains no direct reference to "employee fringe benefits." The general rule is that partners do not qualify for the exclusions afforded certain employee fringe benefits due to the absence of an employer-employee relationship.[187] Absent an official definition of a fringe benefit in the partnership provisions, other sections of the Code must be examined to arrive at a definition of "employee fringe benefits." Such an examination reveals that although there is no statutory definition, the legislative history of Code Sec. 1372 does list five employee benefits that Congress considers to be fringe benefits.[188]

1. The former $5,000 death benefit exclusion set forth in former Code Sec. 101(b).

2. The exclusion from income of amounts received by the taxpayer from an accident and health plan as set forth in Code Sec. 105(b), (c) and (d).[189]

3. The exclusion from income of amounts paid by an employer to an accident and health plan as provided in Code Sec. 106.

4. The exclusion of the cost of up to $50,000 in group term life insurance on an employee's life provided by Code Sec. 79.[190]

5. The exclusion from income of meals or lodging furnished for the convenience of the employer set forth in Code Sec. 119.

There are a number of benefits that partnerships and a C corporations can make available to their partners or shareholders, which might be considered fringe benefits for this purpose, that are deductible by the partnership or C corporation but not taxable to the partners or shareholders. These employee benefits are available to partner/partnership arrangements because the applicable code provision treats the partner as an employee.[191] These employee benefits include:

1. Group legal services plans.[192]

2. Employer-provided educational assistance.[193]

3. Child and dependent care assistance.[194]

4. No-additional-cost services.[195]

---

[187] *See* the legislative history of Code Sec. 707(c).

[188] H.R. Rep. No. 826, 97th Cong., 2d Sess. (1982), note 2 at 21 S. Rep. No. 640. 97th Cong., 2d Sess. (1982), note 2 at 22. It should be noted that the list includes only items that are statutorily excluded from the employee's income.

[189] Code Sec. 105(g).

[190] Reg. § 1.79-0.

[191] For purposes of qualified retirement plans, Code Sec. 401(c)(1) treats self-employed individuals with earned income, including partners, as employees. Code Sec. 401(c)(2) defines earned income by reference to Social Security taxes imposed by Code Sec. 1401. This definition of an employee is incorporated by reference in several employee fringe benefit provisions.

[192] Code Sec. 120(d)(1) defines an employee by reference to Code Sec. 401(c)(1). The partnership is consid-

ered an employer of any partner/employee. Code Sec. 120(d)(2).

[193] Code Sec. 127(c)(2) defines an employee by reference to Code Sec. 401(c)(1). The partnership is considered an employer of any partner/employee. Code Sec. 127(c)(3). However, not more than 5% of the cost of these benefits may be provided for the group of greater-than-5% partners. Code Sec. 127(b)(3).

[194] Code Sec. 129(e)(3) defines an employee by reference to Code Sec. 401(c)(1). The partnership is considered an employer of any partner/employee. Code Sec. 129(e)(4). However, not more than 25% of amounts spent for dependent care assistance can be provided for greater-than-5% partners. Code Sec. 129(d)(4).

[195] Code Sec. 132(b). Reg. § 1.132-1(b)(1) provides that "any partner who performs services for the partnership is considered employed by the partnership."

5. Qualified employee discounts.[196]

6. Working conditions fringe benefits.[197]

7. *De minimis* fringe benefits.[198]

8. On-premises athletic facilities.[199]

9. Qualified retirement plans.[200]

There is no definition of an employee under Code Sec. 125 for cafeteria plans. Proposed Regulations[201] include present and former employees as employees but specifically reject the deferred compensation[202] definition. This seems to exclude partners working for the partnership.

In addition, partners are not employees for purposes of the qualified transportation fringe benefit.[203] It is unclear whether or not partners are employees with respect to the qualified moving expense or the qualified retirement service fringe benefits.[204] With respect to qualified retirement service fringe benefits, the related definition of a qualified plan indirectly indicates that a partner would be considered an employee.[205]

The 1982 legislative history also explains Congress' impression of how a partnership treats a fringe benefit for tax purposes.

> Under the bill, the treatment of fringe benefits of any person owning more than 2% of the stock of the corporation will be treated in the same manner as a partner in a partnership. Thus, for example, amounts paid for medical care of a shareholder-employee *will not be deductible by the corporation (by reason of Sections 1363(b)(2) and 703(a)(2)(E))*, will be deductible by that individual only to the extent personal medical expenses will be allowed as an itemized deduction under Section 213. However, similar amounts paid by the corporation on behalf of shareholders owning 2% or less of the corporation may be deducted as a business expense.[206]

The 1982 legislative history created confusion as to how a partnership is to treat fringe benefits. Traditionally, however, payment of fringe benefits for partners have been treated as a nondeductible deemed distribution which reduces the partner's basis in his or her interest and which the partner treats as if the partner paid directly. If there is a deemed money distribution, partnership interest basis has no net change. Assuming that the insured partner's share of income is the same as his share of the insurance expense, it is first increased by the income not offset by the disallowed expense and then reduced by the deemed distribution.

---

[196] Code Sec. 132(c). Reg. § 1.132-1(b)(1) provides that "any partner who performs services for the partnership is considered employed by the partnership."

[197] Code Sec. 132(d). Reg. § 1.132-1(b)(2)(ii) provides that "any partner who performs services for the partnership is considered employed by the partnership."

[198] Code Sec. 132(e). Reg. § 1.132-1(b)(4) defines an employee as any recipient of a fringe benefit.

[199] Code Sec. 132(h)(5). Reg. § 1.132-1(b)(3) provides that "any partner who performs services for the partnership is considered employed by the partnership."

[200] Code Secs. 401-420.

[201] Prop. Reg. § 1.125-1, Q&A 4.

[202] Code Sec. 401(c).

[203] Reg. § 1.132-9, Q. 24.

[204] Code Sec. 132(g), (m).

[205] Code Secs. 132(m)(3), 219(g)(5), 401(a)(1), and 401(c)(1).

[206] Emphasis added. H.R. Rep. No. 826, 97th Cong., 2d Sess., 21 (1982); S. Rep. No. 640, 97th Cong., 2d Sess., 22 (1982). It is likely that the emphasized portion of the text should have been deleted. The conjunction "and" is needed and the explanation of the Subchapter S Revision Act of 1982 (P.L. 97-354) prepared by the Staff of the Joint Committee on Taxation (Sept. 8, 1982) omits this language.

¶503.27

Revenue Ruling 91-26 clarified the IRS's view of the correct treatment of fringe benefits provided to service partners.[207] The fringe benefits are treated as additional compensation to the service partner. Thus, such payments are treated as guaranteed payments under Code Sec. 707(c) which are treated by the service partner as ordinary earned income. Since the service partner is treated as if he or she then paid for the fringe benefits directly, the partner may be entitled to deduct them on his or her personal return (*e.g.*, as self employed medical insurance, medical expenses, etc.).

.28 Code Sec. 212(3)—Tax Return Preparation Expenditures

A partnership must file a return for each taxable year beginning with the year in which it receives income or incurs expenditures allowable as deductions, unless the partnership is excluded from filing because it has no income, deductions, or credits for federal income tax purposes for the year.[208] In addition, a partnership that elects out of the partnership rules of Subchapter K does not have to file a partnership return, except that the partnership must file a return containing the information required by Reg. § 1.761-2(b)(2)(i).[209] Finally, a partnership that derives all of its income from the holding or disposition of tax-exempt obligations or shares in a regulated investment company that pays exempt-interest dividends and that the IRS has excepted from the partnership reporting requirements does not have to file a partnership return.[210]

The partnership return must be filed on or before the fifteenth day of the fourth month following the end of the partnership's taxable year.[211] An automatic five month extension is allowed upon filing Form 7004, Application for Automatic Extension of Time To File Certain Business Income Tax, Information, and Other Returns.[212] The return must be filed in the district in which the partnership has its principal office or place of business within the United States.[213]

The return must be signed by a partner, and any partner's signature is prima facie evidence of his or her authority to sign the return on behalf of the partnership.[214] The return must state (1) the partnership's gross income and allowable deductions; (2) the names and addresses of all partners; and (3) the amount of each partner's distributive share of partnership income, loss, and so forth.[215]

The failure of a partnership to file a timely return subjects it to a penalty unless the partnership can show that the failure was due to reasonable cause. The penalty equals $195, multiplied by the number of persons who were partners in the partnership during any part of its taxable year, multiplied by the number of months (or fraction thereof) during which the failure to file continues (but not in excess of five months). The penalty is assessed against the partnership, and the deficiency procedures in Code Secs. 6211 and 6216 are inapplicable.[216]

---

[207] Rev. Rul. 91-26, 1991-1 CB 184.

[208] Reg. § 1.6031(a)-1(a)(3).

[209] Reg. § 1.6031(a)-1(c)(1)(i).

[210] Reg. § 1.6031(a)-1T(a)(3)(ii).

[211] Reg. § 1.6031-1(e)(2).

[212] Temp. Reg. § 1.6081-2T.

[213] Reg. § 1.6031-1(e)(1).

[214] Code Sec. 6063.

[215] Reg. § 1.6031-1(a)(1).

[216] Code Sec. 6698; *see F.E. Bader v. United States*, ClsCt, 86-1 USTC ¶ 9432, 10 ClsCt 78. In *Christian Laymen in Partnership, Ltd. v. United States*, DC Okla., 90-1 USTC ¶ 50,042, a district court held that the entire Code Sec. 6698 penalty must be paid before a refund suit can be brought. A partial payment (one month of the penalty)

The legislative history of the penalty provisions of Code Sec. 6698 states that the reasonable cause test is intended to protect "small partnerships" (those with ten or fewer partners) from the penalty as long as each partner reports his or her share of partnership income and deductions.[217] The IRS has announced that any domestic partnership with 10 or fewer partners that comes within the exceptions provided in Code Sec. 6231(a)(1)(B) (part of the partnership level audit adjustment procedures[218]) will be considered to have met the reasonable cause test and will not be subject to Code Sec. 6698 if it establishes that all partners timely reported their full shares of all partnership items. If a partnership consisting of ten or fewer partners does not satisfy these requirements, it may show other reasonable cause for failure to file a timely return.

A partnership must furnish to its partners a copy of the information shown on the partnership's return "as may be required by regulations." Temporary Regulations issued in 1988 require the partnership to furnish to each person who was a partner at any time during the taxable year a written statement including the partner's distributive share of partnership income, gain, loss, deduction or credit, and any other information required by the form or accompanying instructions.[219] The statement must be furnished on or before the due date for the partnership return (determined with regard to extensions).[220] The partnership must assume that a nominee (other than a clearing agency) is actually the beneficial owner of the interest if the nominee fails to furnish to the partnership the requisite statement containing information about the beneficial owner.[221]

In the case of an individual, the miscellaneous itemized deductions for any taxable year are allowed only to the extent that the aggregate of such deductions exceeds two percent of adjusted gross income.[222] Itemized deductions include an individual's deduction under Code Sec. 212(3) for amounts paid or incurred "in connection with the determination, collection, or refund of any tax."[223] An individual's share of a pass-through entity's expenditures are disallowed to the extent they would have been disallowed under the itemized deduction rule if he or she paid them directly.[224] The regulations list "tax counsel fees and appraisal fees" as examples of itemized deductions allowed by Code Sec. 212(3)[225] and therefore subject to the restrictions limiting itemized deductions. The regulations also provide an example of a partnership's generic Code Sec. 212 expense being passed through to its partners.[226] Finally, the regulations require that fees incurred for "income tax return preparation or income tax advice" by a nonpublicly offered regulated investment company (RIC), which is another type of pass-through entity,

---

(Footnote Continued)

does not satisfy the "divisible tax" rule. The significance of this holding is magnified because the ordinary deficiency procedures are inapplicable to this penalty. Effectively, the partners must pay the entire penalty asserted before they are entitled to their day in court.

[217] *See* HR Rep. No. 1445, 95th Cong., 2d Sess., 75 (1978).

[218] Rev. Proc. 84-35, 1984-1 CB 509.

[219] Code Sec. 6031(b); Temp. Reg. § 1.6031(b)-1T(a)(1) and (3).

[220] Temp. Reg. § 1.6031(b)-1T(b).

[221] Temp. Reg. § 1.6031(b)-1T(a)(2).

[222] Code Sec. 67(a).

[223] Code Sec. 63(d) defines an itemized deduction. Code Sec. 67 limits them to the excess of 2% of adjusted gross income. Code Sec. 212(3) allows an individual's deduction for his or her income tax related expenditures.

[224] Code Sec. 67(c)(1).

[225] Temp. Reg. § 1.67-1T(a)(1)(iii).

[226] Temp. Reg. § 1.67-2T(b)(2). The example states only that they "are expenses to which section 212 applies."

are to be passed through as itemized deductions. Most practitioners, however, take the position that the costs of preparing a partnership's Form 1065 are not incurred "in connection with the determination, collection, or refund of any tax." They are deducted as the partnership's accounting fees related to its business or its other activities.[227]

The partnership enters its nonseparately stated items of income on Form 1065, lines 1-7, and its nonseparately stated deductions on lines 9-20. The net nonseparately stated income is entered on line 22 and on Form 1065, Schedule K, line 1. Each partner's share of this nonseparately stated income is shown on Schedule K-1, box 1.

.29 Special Allocations

All specially allocated items of ordinary income or loss should be reported on line 11 of Schedule K and in box 11 of Schedule K-1. Reg. § 1.702-1(a)(8)(i) requires the separate reporting of any item subject to a special allocation "under the partnership agreement." Does this apply to the *mandatory* special allocations under Code Sec. 704(c)(1)(A)? Most likely, yes. Recall that Code Sec. 704(c) was amended in 1984[228] to make the previous optional-by-agreement adjustment regarding contributed property a mandatory one. Reg. § 1.702-1(a)(8)(i) predates the 1984 amendment and thus refers to the pre-1984 Code Sec. 704(c) provision. Similarly, any "curative allocations" should be separately reported.

¶ 504 Schedules M-1, M-2, and M-3

.01 Schedules M-1 and M-2

Partnership returns include Schedule M-1 and M-2, in a fashion similar to C corporations.

Schedule M-1, Reconciliation of Income Per Books With Income Per Return:

1. Starts with book income.
2. Adds income items reflected on the partners' K-1s but not on the books (line 2), Guaranteed Payments (line 3), and expenses per books not on the K-1s (line 4).
3. Subtracts income items on the books but not reflected on the K-1s, including tax exempt interest (line 6), and items of deductions on the K-1s not on the books (line 7).
4. Ends with the total of the income and deduction items distributable to the partners on their K-1s (this ties with the net income in the Analysis of Net Income (Loss), p. 5 of Form 1065).

Schedule M-2, Analysis of Partners' Capital Accounts:

1. Starts with the capital account balances at the beginning of the year.
2. Adds capital contributed during year (line 2).

---

[227] *See* Rev. Rul. 92-29, 1992-1 CB 20, in support of this position. It allows expenses in preparing business-related schedules as business deductions.

[228] Deficit Reduction Act of 1984, P.L. 98-369.

3. Adds net income per books (line 3) and other increases (line 4).

4. Subtracts distributions to partners (line 6).

5. Subtracts other decreases (line 7).

6. Equals the capital account balances at the end of the year.

Partners' individual capital accounts are reconciled in item L of Schedule K-1. Prior to the 1991 forms, the amounts of income and deductions on Schedule K-1 could be traced to the capital account reconciliation. Now, however, all the income and deduction effects on the capital accounts are combined and appear in "Current year increase (decrease)" line of item L.

Thus, it is very important that the amount in the "Current year increase (decrease)" line of item L, which is *not* always explained on Schedule K-1, be reported to the partners. It appears that the appropriate place to make such reporting is in the other information item of the K-1. Such items are:

- Variances between book income and K-1 line items of distributable income and deductions (Schedule M-1, lines 2, 4, 6 and 7); and

- Other increases and decreases to the capital account balance.

.02 Schedule M-3

Certain partnerships are required to file Schedule M-3 for any tax year ending on or after December 31, 2006. Specifically, any entity which files Form 1065 or Form 1065-B must complete and file Schedule M-3 in lieu of Schedule M-1 if any of the following is true:

1. The amount of total assets at the end of the tax year is equal to $10 million or more.

2. The amount of adjusted total assets for the year is equal to $10 million or more. The amount of adjusted total assets is total assets at the end of the tax year before capital distributions, losses, and adjustments that reduce total capital.

3. The amount of total receipts for the taxable year is equal to $35 million or more.

4. The partnership has a "reportable entity partner." A reportable entity partner is an entity that (1) owns or is deemed to own a 50 percent or greater interest in the income, loss or capital of the partnership on any day of the tax year, and (2) was required to complete Schedule M-3 on its most recently filed US federal income tax return.

A partnership filing Form 1065 or Form 1065-B that is not required to file Schedule M-3 may voluntarily file Schedule M-3 in place of Schedule M-1. A partnership filing Schedule M-3 is not required to file Schedule M-1.

In Part I of Schedule M-3 certain questions about the partnership's financial statements, such as whether or not Form 10-K was filed by the partnership, and whether the partnership prepared an audited income statement, are required to be answered. In addition, a reconciliation of financial statement net income for the

¶504.02

consolidated financial statement group to income per the income statement for the partnership is also required.

Parts II and III of Schedule M-3 reconcile financial statement net income (loss) for the partnership (per Schedule M-3, Part I, line 11) to income (loss) per the return on Form 1065 (page 5) and Form 1065-B (page 4) Analysis of Net Income (Loss), line 1. Items that must be disclosed include temporary and permanent differences due to tax expenses, hedging transactions, cost of goods sold, depreciation, and oil and gas depletion. Book/tax differences related to income are disclosed in Part II, and book/tax differences with respect to expenses are disclosed in Part III.

¶ 505 Reporting Taxable Income for Large Partnerships/LLCs

Special rules allow electing large partnerships to compute their taxable incomes using a simplified method. Under this method, the Schedule K-1 received by the partners/LLC members is structured much like Form 1099, which investors are accustomed to receiving. The partnership/LLC's income, loss, and credits are to be reported by the partner/member in the following categories:

1. Taxable income or loss from passive loss limitation activities,

2. Taxable income or loss from other activities,

3. Net capital gain (or net capital loss)—

   a. To the extent allocable to passive loss limitation activities, and

   b. To the extent allocable to other activities,

4. Tax-exempt interest,

5. Applicable net AMT adjustment separately computed for—

   a. Passive loss limitation activities, and

   b. Other activities,

6. General credits,

7. Low-income housing credit,

8. Rehabilitation credit,

9. Foreign income taxes,

10. The credit for producing fuel from a nonconventional source, and

11. Other items to the extent that the Secretary determines that the separate treatment of such items is appropriate.[229]

A large partnership/LLC will file Form 1065-B, rather than Form 1065. As implied from the above categories, all capital gains and losses are netted at the partnership/LLC level. Net long-term capital gain (loss) is divided between passive and other activities, and reported separately to the partners/members. In contrast, any excess of net short-term capital gain over net long-term capital loss is consolidated with the partnership's other taxable income and is not separately reported.

---

[229] Code Sec. 772(a).

Similarly, electing large partnerships consolidate general credits and separately report them to partners/members as a single item. Partners and LLC members report their shares as a current year general business credit. Other credits are claimed by the partnership/LLC itself, rather than being passed through to partners or LLC members. For example, the refundable credit for federal tax paid on fuels and the refund or credit for tax paid on undistributed capital gains of a regulated investment company or a real estate investment trust are taken by the partnership and thus are not separately reported to partners. The partnership/LLC also recaptures the investment credit and low-income housing credit.

.01 Eligibility

To be eligible, a partnership or LLC must have had at least 100 partners during the *preceding* taxable year.[230] Thus, a partnership/LLC may not elect to use the simplified rules in its first tax year. In determining the number of partners or LLC members in the prior year, *service* partners are not counted.[231] For this purpose, a service partner is any partner/member who must perform substantial services in connection with the entity's activities, or who has performed such services in past years. Indeed, *service partnerships* or LLCs are not allowed to elect to be treated as large partnerships. A service partnership/LLC is one for which "substantially all" of the partners/members are:

1. Individuals performing substantial services in connection with the entity's activities,

2. Personal service corporations with the owner-employees performing the services,

3. Retired partners/members who had previously performed the services prior to retirement, or

4. Spouses of any of the above.

Commodities partnerships—those whose principle business consists of trading in commodities (other than inventory as defined in Code Sec. 1221(a)(1)) or in commodity options, futures or forwards—are also ineligible to elect large partnership status.

.02 Making the Election

The election to be treated as a large partnership is made by filing Form 1065-B, rather than Form 1065. The election is applicable beginning with the first year in which Form 1065-B is filed, and remains in effect for all future years as long as the partnership or LLC continues to have 100 or more partners or members.

---

[230] Code Sec. 775(a)(1)(A).   [231] Code Sec. 775(b)(1).

PART II

PARTNERSHIP ALLOCATIONS

Chapter 6

Allocation of Partnership Income among the Partners: The Substantial Economic Effect Requirement

¶ 601 Introduction

Although the partnership reports its taxable to the IRS on Form 1065, it pays no tax. Instead, it allocates its income among its partners and they pay the income tax. Note that partners must pay income tax on their allocated shares of partnership income whether or not such income is distributed to them. Such shares of income are often called a partner's "distributive share of partnership income," reflecting the fact that the partners have a claim to such income even if it has not yet been distributed.

The code gives partnerships wide latitude in determining how income is allocated among their partners. Generally speaking, partnerships are allowed to allocate their income among the partners in any way that the partners see fit, subject to the following limitations:

- Code Sec. 704(b) requires that allocations must have "substantial economic effect;"

- Code Sec. 704(c) requires that pre-contribution, or "built-in," gain or loss must be allocated to the partner(s) who contributed the property;

- Code Sec. 704(e) limits the ability of family partnerships to allocate income derived from services provided by one partner to other partner-family members;

- Code Sec. 706(d) prohibits partnerships from allocating income to partners that was earned by the partnership before such partners joined.

This chapter focuses on the first restriction above, the requirement that allocations have substantial economic effect. The requirement that built-in gains be allocated to the contributing partners is the subject of Chapter 7. The rules governing family partnership allocations and retroactive allocations are discussed in Chapter 8.

¶ 602 The Partnership Agreement Is a Legal Contract

Under Code Sec. 704(b), the partnership may allocate any item of taxable income or loss in any manner the partners desire so long as the tax allocation reflects the manner in which the partners are sharing the economics that generated the related tax item. The tax law looks to the partnership agreement to determine how the partners share in the economic benefits or detriments of partnership operations. Since the partnership agreement represents the legal contract between the partners, partners generally must abide by the provisions contained therein unless such provisions are in violation of local or state law. The law therefore looks to the partnership agreement to see how partners have agreed to share the profits and losses generated by partnership operations. The partnership agreement also governs how partnership assets will be divided among the partners in the event of liquidation of the partnership, or of a partner's interest therein. The partnership agreement is considered to retroactively include all changes made by the due date of the partnership tax return (excluding extensions).[1]

Generally speaking, an allocation has economic effect if it affects the amount of money or other assets to which the partner will be entitled upon leaving the partnership. If the partnership agreement does not tie the partner's rights at liquidation to the allocations he or she has received during the time he/she has been a member of the partnership, then those allocations will not have economic effect.

> ***Example 6-1:*** Bill Burke became a 25% partner in the Bowhay partnership by contributing land with a basis of $300,000 and a fair market value of $400,000. The partnership agreement allocates 40% of all income and losses for the first four years to Bill, but if the partnership liquidates, the partnership agreement provides that the liquidation proceeds will be divided equally among the four partners. The 40% allocation of partnership profits and losses is a discretionary allocation under Code Sec. 704(b). However, the allocation will be invalid because it will not be reflected in the distributions that will occur upon liquidation, and thus has no "economic effect."

If the allocation of partnership profits and losses provided for in the partnership agreement has "substantial economic effect," amounts allocated to partners will be valid for income tax purposes.[2] If, however, the allocation of any item lacks "substantial economic effect," such item must be reallocated among the partners in accordance with their economic interests, if any, in the item of income or deduc-

---

[1] Code Sec. 761(c).   [2] Code Sec. 704(a).

tion.[3] Due to the imprecision of this facts-and-circumstances analysis, as well as the Commissioner's presumption of correctness in determining its meaning, it is very important that the allocations provided in the partnership agreement have substantial economic effect or its equivalent if the partners wish to be certain of the validity of their tax allocations.

¶ 603 General Requirements for Substantial Economic Effect

The "substantial economic effect" test is intended to ensure that if a tax deduction allowed for a partnership expense involves a possible economic risk of loss to the partnership itself, then that tax deduction is allocated to the specific partner who is most likely to bear the economic burden of that loss. It is also intended to ensure that taxable income is allocated only to partners most likely to enjoy the economic benefit from the transaction generating the taxable income.

The "substantial economic effect" test has two parts:

1. Does the agreement have "economic effect"?

2. If the agreement has "economic effect," is that economic effect "substantial"?

¶ 604 The First Requirement: "Economic Effect"

The regulations provide that an agreement has "economic effect" if it:

1. has economic effect under the general rule;

2. meets the alternate test for economic effect; or

3. has economic effect equivalence.

These three rules govern the allocation of deductions that arise from contributions and those allowed because of borrowed funds for which one or more partners has personal liability for repayment. These are deductions for which members in the partnership will bear the economic loss associated with the tax deductions if the venture is a failure. These three rules also govern the allocation of taxable income other than reversals of nonrecourse debt deductions.

.01 General Rule

To satisfy the economic effect requirement under the general rule three tests must be satisfied. The partnership agreement (or local law) must provide that:[4]

1. The partners' capital accounts must be "properly maintained" in accordance with the accounting rules contained in the regulations (Code Sec. 704(b) accounting);

2. Liquidating distributions must be made in accordance with those capital accounts; and

3. Partners with a deficit balance in their capital accounts must be required, either by local law or the partnership agreement, to restore such deficit balances to the partnership upon liquidation of their interests (for example, by making a payment to the partnership sufficient to bring the balance in their accounts back to zero).

---

[3] Code Sec. 704(b)(2).   [4] Reg. § 1.704-1(b)(2)(ii)(b).

The third requirement above assures that sufficient funds will be available to the partnership to repay its creditors and to liquidate the interests of those partners with positive capital balances.

Example 6-2: Wayne is a one-third partner in the Andrews Partnership. Although Wayne contributed only one-third of the partnership's capital, he is allocated 50% of the profits and losses of the partnership under the partnership agreement. Assume that the partners' capital accounts are maintained in accordance with Code Sec. 704(b), and any liquidating distributions must be made according to the partners' capital account balances. However, the partnership agreement provides that if Wayne has a negative capital account balance upon liquidation, the other partners will contribute money or property on his behalf to bring it up to zero. Since the third test of the general rule is not met, the 50% allocation does not have economic effect, and will not be recognized for tax purposes.

Example 6-3: Rico, Ariana, and Dan form the equal RAD partnership with cash contributions of $200,000 each. The partnership used the cash to purchase equipment for $600,000. The equipment has a depreciable life of four years, and depreciation is computed using the straight-line method. Under the partnership agreement, all depreciation expense is allocated to Rico. Capital accounts are properly maintained. The partnership agreement also provides that liquidating distributions will be made in accordance with the capital accounts of each partner. Partners are required to restore deficit capital accounts upon liquidation. Income before depreciation is $90,000 each year. Assuming that the fair market value of the equipment is equal to its book value, the partners would receive the following amounts if the partnership were to liquidate at the end of year one:

	Rico	*Ariana*	*Dan*
Contribution	$200,000	$200,000	$200,000
Income	$30,000	$30,000	$30,000
Depreciation (1 yr)	-$150,000		
Capital balance, End of year 1	$80,000	$230,000	$230,000

If the liquidation occurred at the end of year two, each partner would receive the following amount:

	Rico	*Ariana*	*Dan*
Contribution	$200,000	$200,000	$200,000
Income (2 yrs)	$60,000	$60,000	$60,000
Depreciation (2 yrs)	-$300,000		
Capital Balance, end of year 2	-$40,000	$260,000	$260,000
Liquidation amount	$0	$260,000	$260,000

Note that the only way Ariana and Dan will actually receive $260,000 each is if Rico contributes $40,000 to the partnership. Otherwise the partnership assets will only total $480,000 ($600,000 equipment price – $300,000 depreciation + $180,000 income = $480,000), and Ariana and Dan would only receive $240,000 each (assuming the equipment is sold for its adjusted basis at the time of liquidation). If this were the case then Ariana and Dan, not Rico, would bear the economic burden of the last $40,000 of depreciation deduction allocated to Rico.

Capital Account Maintenance Requirements. Since tax basis capital accounts seldom reflect fair market values, the regulations require the creation and maintenance of a separate set of investor capital accounts. These capital accounts are similar to the partnership's tax capital accounts with a few minor differences. They are intended to reflect as accurately as possible the economic relationship between the partners.

The regulations require that capital accounts be increased by:

1. Cash contributions (including increases in the partners' shares of partnership liabilities);[5]

2. The *fair market value* of property contributed to the partnership by the partners (net of liabilities assumed by the partnership); and

3. Allocated items of *book* income and gain as determined under Code Sec. 704(b) and the regulations thereunder, including non-taxable income and gain.

Capital accounts must be decreased by:

1. Distributions of cash from the partnership to a partner (including partner liabilities assumed by the partnership, but not including guaranteed payments made to the partner by the partnership);

2. The *fair market value* of any property distributed to a partner (net of liabilities assumed by the distributee in connection with the distribution);

3. Allocated expenditures that are not deductible in computing partnership income under Code Secs. 702 or 703 and are not properly chargeable to capital (e.g., syndication costs, expenses incurred in generating tax-exempt income, etc.); and

4. Allocated items of *book* loss and deduction as determined under Code Sec. 704(b) and the regulations thereunder, including "simulated" oil and gas depletion.[6]

Note that in accounting for a distribution of appreciated property, the partnership must first record the appreciation in such property (over its book value) as a

---

[5] Reg. § 1.704-1(b)(2)(iv)(c). [6] Reg. § 1.704-1(b)(2)(iv)(b)..

¶604.01

gain in the partners' capital accounts. This will increase the book value to fair market value, which is then subtracted from the distributee-partner's capital account.

Example 6-4: The equal ABCD partnership has the following balance Sheets at December 31:

Assets	Tax Basis	Sec. 704(b) Book Value	FMV
Cash	$100,000	$100,000	$100,000
Accounts Receivable	100,000	100,000	100,000
Property, Plant, & Equipment	150,000	150,000	500,000
Land	50,000	50,000	100,000
Total Assets	$400,000	$400,000	$800,000
Liabilities	$0	$0	$0
Capital, *A*	100,000	100,000	200,000
Capital, *B*	100,000	100,000	200,000
Capital, *C*	100,000	100,000	200,000
Capital, *D*	100,000	100,000	200,000
Total Liabilities and Capital	$400,000	$400,000	$800,000

On that date, the partnership distributes the land to *A*, reducing his interest in the partnership from one-fourth (200,000/800,000) to one-seventh (100,000/700,000). The partnership must first recognize the $50,000 appreciation in value of the land in its Code Sec. 704(b) balance sheet, before writing the land off at fair market value against *A*'s capital account. This book gain will be allocated equally among the partners (because it is deemed realized before *A*'s interest is reduced). Assuming the partnership does *not* opt to revalue its remaining assets, the post-distribution balance sheets would appear as follows:

Assets	Tax Basis	Sec. 704(b) Book Value	FMV
Cash	$100,000	$100,000	$100,000
Accounts Receivable	100,000	100,000	100,000
Property, Plant, & Equipment	150,000	150,000	500,000
Total Assets	$350,000	$350,000	$700,000

Liabilities	$0	$0	$0
Capital, *A*	50,000	12,500	100,000
Capital, *B*	100,000	112,500	200,000
Capital, *C*	100,000	112,500	200,000
Capital, *D*	100,000	112,500	200,000
Total Liabilities and Capital	$350,000	$350,000	$700,000

Each partner's Code Sec. 704(b) capital account will be increased by his or her $12,500 share (25%) of the $50,000 book gain. *A*'s Code Sec. 704(b) capital account will then be reduced by the $100,000 fair value of the land. Note that in accounting for the distribution on the partnership's tax basis balance sheet, no gain is recognized (because the distribution is not taxable); rather, *A*'s capital account is merely reduced by the partnership's *tax basis* in the land. Similarly, on the fair market value balance sheet, no gain is recognized because all assets are already reflected at fair market value.

As noted previously, the partnership has the option to revalue all its assets *on its Code Sec. 704(b) balance sheet* following the distribution to A.[7] If it does so, its Code Sec. 704(b) book balance sheet will look exactly like the FMV balance sheet above. Revaluation is generally preferred if determining the fair value of all the partnership's assets is not too expensive. Since the Code Sec. 704(b) capital accounts reflect the partners' rights to partnership assets at liquidation, it is best if the capital accounts reflect the true value of all the partnership's assets.

In addition to *requiring* that contributed and distributed property be revalued for proper capital account maintenance, the regulations *allow* the partnership to revalue *all* partnership property at any time money or other property is either contributed to, or distributed from, the partnership.[8] Revaluations, which are reflected in the partners' *book* capital accounts only, may reflect the partners' agreement regarding the value of partnership assets or may be based on any other reasonable method.

.02 "Alternate" Test for Economic Effect

If the partnership agreement meets the first and second requirements for economic effect described above, but a partner to whom an allocation is made *is not required to restore his or her deficit capital account balance* or is obligated to restore only a limited dollar amount of such deficit balance, the "alternative" economic effect test can still be met if the *partnership agreement* contains a special capital account adjustment provision and a *"qualified income offset."*[9]

If these requirements are satisfied, an allocation to the partner will be considered to have economic effect to the extent that the allocation *does not cause or increase a deficit balance* in such partner's adjusted capital account (in excess of any

---

[7] The tax basis of the assets will not be affected by the revaluation.

[8] Under Prop. Reg. § 1.704-1(b)(2)(iv)(f)(5), this revaluation would also be allowed when a service provider recognizes income from the receipt of a compensatory partnership interest.

[9] Reg. § 1.704-1(b)(2)(ii)(d)(1).

deficit balance that the partner is obligated to restore) as of the end of the partnership tax year to which such allocation relates.

 Example 6-5: Forrest, Jennie, and Dan each contribute $150,000 cash to newly formed Alphabet Partnership. The partnership purchases equipment for $450,000. The equipment is to be depreciated using the straight line method over five years, and all depreciation is allocated to Forrest. Capital accounts are properly maintained under Code Sec. 704(b). The partnership agreement provides that liquidating distributions will be made in accordance with the partners' capital accounts. However, no partners are required to restore deficit capital accounts upon liquidation, except that Forrest must restore up to $100,000 if he ends up with a deficit balance. Income aside from depreciation is $30,000 each year. The amount of depreciation that will be allocated to each partner in the first three years is as follows:

	Forrest	*Jennie*	*Dan*
Initial Capital Contribution	$150,000	$150,000	$150,000
Income (3 yrs)	$30,000	$30,000	$30,000
Depreciation (3 yrs)	-$270,000		
Ending Capital Balances	-$90,000	$180,000	$180,000

 Thus, the special allocation of depreciation for the first three years will have economic effect because the deficit balance in Forrest's capital account is less than the amount he is obligated to restore. As shown below, however, in year 4 only $20,000 of the $90,000 of depreciation can be allocated to Forrest, because to allocate more would cause his capital account deficit to exceed the amount he is required to restore. This excess part of the allocation will not have economic effect. Jennie and Dan would be allocated $35,000 each of the extra $70,000 of depreciation, and this allocation would have economic effect.

	Forrest	*Jennie*	*Dan*
Beginning Capital	-$90,000	$180,000	$180,000
Income	$10,000	$10,000	$10,000
Depreciation	-$20,000	-$35,000	-$35,000
Ending Capital Account Balances	-$100,000	$155,000	$155,000

Capital account adjustments. In order to prevent a partner's capital account from inadvertently falling below the partner's limited deficit capital account make-up requirement, special adjustments must be made to the capital account. Before evaluating the economic effect of an allocation to a partner, the partner's capital account must first be reduced by:

¶604.02

1. Certain expected allowable depletion deductions;[10]

2. Allocations of loss and deduction that, as of the end of such year, are expected to be made to such partner under Code Sec. 704(e)(2) (family partnership rules), 706(d) ("varying interest") rules, and certain gain or loss deemed to occur under Code Sec. 751;[11] and

3. Distributions that, as of the end of such year, are *"reasonably expected" to be made to such partner* (to the extent that such distributions are expected to exceed offsetting increases to the partner's capital account that are also reasonably expected to be made).[12]

Note that the purpose of adjustment 3 above is to prevent the partnership from delaying a distribution to the year following a loss year, so that the partner will have sufficient capital to absorb a current year loss allocation.

> *Example 6-6:* George Douglas is a partner in Dugout Partnership. At the end of the year, the balance in his capital account on Dugout's Code Sec. 704(b) balance sheet ("book" balance sheet) is $25,000. His tax basis in his partnership interest is $75,000. Assume that the partnership is required under the partnership agreement to distribute $25,000 to George at the beginning of the following year (the partnership is expected to be able to meet its requirement). Further assume that George's share of current year partnership losses is ($25,000). Under the partnership agreement, George is not required to restore negative balances in his capital account. The partnership may not allocate the loss to George (even though at the time of the allocation he has sufficient capital to absorb the loss allocation) because the required distribution is reasonably expected to be made and *prior to the allocation of the loss* George's capital account must be reduced by the amount of the distribution, even though the distribution is to occur in the following year.

Qualified income offset provision. In addition to the prohibition against creation of a deficit in the partner's adjusted capital account, in order for a special allocation to have economic effect under the alternate test, the partnership agreement must contain a "qualified income offset provision." A qualified income offset provision requires that a partner who receives an adjustment, allocation, or distribution that is not "reasonably expected" and results in a deficit capital account balance in excess of the partner's limited deficit capital account make-up requirement will be allocated items of *gross* income and gain in an amount and manner sufficient to eliminate such deficit as quickly as possible.[13]

> *LLC Observation:* An LLC member is not as a general rule responsible under local law for additional capital contributions. Therefore, in the case of an LLC there must generally be an explicit unlimited capital account restoration provision in order for allocations to have economic effect under the general rule.

---

[10] Reg. § 1.704-1(b)(2)(iv)(k).

[11] Reg. § 1.704-1(b)(2)(ii)(d)(5).

[12] Reg. § 1.704-1(b)(2)(ii)(d)(6).

[13] Reg. § 1.704-1(b)(2)(ii)(d)(3).

The first two tests of the general rule ensure that the economic burden of an allocation is adequately estimated and accounted for. The third test requires that the partner that benefited from the allocation also suffers its economic burden. It also ensures that partners who are allocated income enjoy the potential economic benefit from such allocation. The capital accounts are the scoreboard that keeps track of the partners' interests in the book value of the partnership's assets. If there is no agreement to the contrary, limited partners are not responsible for restoring a negative capital account balance to zero upon liquidation of the partnership (or of a partner's interest therein). The first two requirements alone theoretically result in a reduced claim on the book value of the partnership's assets by the partner claiming the deduction, including limited partners. Once the balance in a limited partner's capital account reaches zero, however, he or she theoretically has no further claim on the partnership's assets. Requiring that the limited partner reduce his or her capital account for additional tax deductions allocated to that partner would have no economic effect unless the partner is required to repay the deficit. The general rule, however, takes an all or nothing approach: all three requirements must be satisfied. Even though the absence of a deficit restoration requirement is economically important only if there is a deficit capital balance, the regulations conclude that the general rule is not satisfied unless there is an unlimited deficit capital account restoration requirement that will apply when there is a deficit balance in any partner's capital account.[14]

.03 Economic Effect Equivalence

Where the partnership agreement does not satisfy the requirements of either the general test or the alternate test for economic effect, allocations which produce economic results which are identical to those that would have been produced if the agreement had been in compliance with the stated rules are deemed to have economic effect. For example, assume a partnership agreement is silent with regard to the partners' rights at liquidation, but under state law, liquidating distributions are required to be made in accordance with the balances in the partners' capital accounts, and partners are obligated to make restitution payments to the partnership at liquidation in the event the balance in their capital accounts is negative. In such a case, the economic results to the partners would be the same as those under the prescribed rules, and the partnership allocations will have economic effect.[15]

¶ 605 The Economic Effect of Partnership Allocations Must Be "Substantial"

The drafters of the regulations realized that it would be possible for the partnership agreement to comply with the economic effect tests, but, through timing and/or character allocations, it would still be possible for an allocation to reduce the partners' individual tax burdens without substantially affecting their economic claims against partnership assets. For example, a partnership could allocate capital gain to one partner and ordinary income in the same amount to

---

[14] Reg. § 1.704-1(b)(1)(ii).   [15] Reg. § 1.704-1(b)(2)(ii)(i).

another partner. Both partners' capital accounts would be increased by the same amount, and thus their rights at liquidation would not be affected by the allocations. Such an allocation, although it satisfies the requirements for "economic effect" will not be recognized by the IRS because the economic effect is not "substantial."

With regard to substantiality, the regulations provide that the economic effect of an allocation is not substantial if, at the time the allocation (or allocations) becomes part of the partnership agreement:

1. the after-tax consequences of at least one partner may, in present value terms, be enhanced compared to such consequences if the allocation (or allocations) were not contained in the partnership agreement, and

2. there is a strong likelihood that the after-tax consequences of no partner will, in present value terms, be substantially diminished compared to such consequences if the allocation (or allocations) were not contained in the partnership agreement.[16]

The regulations establish three tests that must be satisfied in order for the economic effect of an allocation to be deemed substantial: (1) the "shifting allocations" test, (2) the "transitory allocations" test, and (3) the "overall tax effects" test. If an allocation fails *any* of these tests, it will be deemed to lack substantiality and will not be recognized by the IRS.

.01 Shifting Allocations Test

A partnership allocation is a shifting allocation, and will not be substantial, if it does not change the overall amount of income or loss allocated to different partners, but allocates items of income or loss in such a way that the character of the items allocated reduces the overall tax liabilities of the partners. Specifically, the economic effect of an allocation is not substantial if, at the time the allocation becomes part of the partnership agreement, there is a strong likelihood that:

1. The effect of the allocation on the partners' capital accounts for the current taxable year will not differ substantially from the changes in the partners' respective capital accounts that would have occurred if the allocations were not followed, and

2. The total tax liability of the partners for the years of the allocations will be less than if the allocations were not contained in the partnership agreement.

Generally, this test addresses situations like that described above in which a partnership may attempt to make "character" allocations in differing amounts between partners. If, at the end of a partnership tax year to which an allocation relates, it turns out that *both* conditions 1 and 2 above did occur, there is a presumption that, at the time the allocation became part of such partnership agreement, there was a strong likelihood that these results would occur. This presumption may be overcome by a showing of facts and circumstances that prove otherwise.[17]

---

[16] Reg. § 1.704-1(b)(2)(iii)(*a*).   [17] Reg. § 1.704-1(b)(2)(iii)(b).

Example 6-7: Anne and Bob are equal partners in the Havmaker Partnership. For the current year, the partnership reported $100,000 of long-term capital gains and $100,000 of ordinary income. Rather than allocating each item of income equally between them, the partnership agreement is modified for this year to allocate the capital gains to Anne and the ordinary income to Bob. Assume that both partners are in the 35% tax bracket, and that neither has a net operating loss or net capital loss carryforward from prior years. In such a case, it is likely that the allocation of the entire capital gain to Anne will reduce her tax liability, while the allocation of the entire ordinary income to Bob will increase his tax (as compared to the situation where the partnership allocated both items equally between the two partners). If the *total* or combined tax liability of the two partners is not reduced, then this special allocation of character will *not* violate the shifting tax consequences test, and the allocation will be recognized by the IRS.

In contrast, assume that Anne has a large capital loss carryover from a prior year and that the purpose of the special character allocation from the partnership is to allow her to use this carryover before it expires. Now, the allocations will reduce Anne's tax liability by more than they will increase Bob's. As a result, the partners' combined tax liability will be lower in the year of the allocations and they will violate the shifting tax consequences test. The allocations will not be recognized for tax purposes and each partner will be required to report $50,000 in capital gain and $50,000 in ordinary income on his or her individual tax return.

.02 Transitory Allocations Test

The shifting allocations test addresses allocations that shift tax costs between partners within the same tax year. The regulations also address situations in which allocations shift tax costs between partners over multiple tax years. For example, in the example above, the partnership might allocate capital gains to Anne in the current year allowing her to utilize her capital loss carryforward before it expires. Rather than offsetting this allocation by shifting ordinary income away from her in the current year, however, the partners agree to allocate a like amount of capital gains to Bob next year. The result: over the *two*-year period, the balances in the partners' capital accounts are the same as they would have been without the special allocations and the combined tax liability of the two partners is reduced (Ann's is reduced and Bob's is unchanged). These are known as transitory allocations, and they lack substantiality.

Transitory allocations are allocations of income or deductions in an earlier year with a planned allocation of reasonably expected offsetting results in later years. As with shifting allocations, the regulations provide that an allocation is not substantial if there is a strong likelihood that:[18]

1. The original allocation will be substantially offset by an offsetting allocation in the current or a future tax year; and

---

[18] Reg. § 1.704-1 (b) (2) (iii) (c).

¶605.02

2. The total tax liability of the partners for the years of the original and offsetting allocations is less than if the allocations were not made.

The regulations add that if conditions 1 and 2 above do in fact occur, the allocations will be presumed to lack substantiality unless the taxpayer can prove that there was not a strong likelihood that the offset would occur at the time of the first allocation.

In addition, the regulations treat an original and offsetting allocation as substantial if at the point of the original allocation there is a strong likelihood that the offsetting allocation will not in "large part" be made within five years after the original allocation.[19]

> *Example 6-8:* Assume the same facts as in Example 6-6. Bob and Anne are equal partners in the Havmaker Partnership, which reports $100,000 of long-term capital gains and $100,000 of ordinary income for the current year. Anne has a capital loss carryover that will expire this year, so the partners amend the partnership agreement to allocate 100% of the partnership's capital gains to Anne this year, with the first $100,000 of future capital gains to be allocated entirely to Bob. Ordinary income is allocated equally between the two partners. A review of the past five years' partnership tax returns indicates that this year was the only year in which the partnership reported income from capital gains. Accordingly, it is unlikely that the offsetting allocation of capital gains to Bob will not occur within the next five years, and the special allocation of capital gains to Anne will have substantial economic effect.

.03 Special Rule for Allocations of Future Gain on Disposition of Partnership Property

The regulations provide a very important exception to the transitory allocations test for planned future allocations of partnership gain on the sale or disposition of partnership property. Reg. § 1.704-1(b)(2)(iii)(c)(2) provides that for purposes of Code Sec. 704(b), the fair market value of partnership property is deemed to be equal to its book value. This presumption is nonrebuttable. The practical effect of this provision is to create a strong presumption that future allocations of gain from the sale or other disposition of partnership property will not be sufficient to offset current allocations of depreciation or other items of income or expense. Because the fair market value of partnership property is deemed to equal its book value both now and in the future, the presumption is that there will be no future gain when the property is sold. Therefore, an allocation of future gain cannot be reasonably anticipated to offset a current year allocation and such future allocations do not violate the transitory allocations test. Partnerships often use this exception to make "balancing" allocations of future gain on the sale of depreciable property to offset special allocations of depreciation expense with respect to that property, allowing liquidating distributions upon dissolution of the partnership to be made to partners in the same ratios as their original capital contributions.

---

[19] Reg. § 1.704-1(b)(2)(iii)(c)(2).

.04 Overall Tax Effects Test

The final test which must be met before the economic effect of an allocation will be deemed substantial is much broader than those previously discussed. In an attempt to catch questionable allocations which avoid the limitations of the more specific provisions against transitory allocations and allocations which merely shift the tax consequences of partnership operations among the partners, the regulations provide an overall tax effects test. Under this test, the economic effect of an allocation will not be substantial if:

1. The allocation may, *in present value terms*, enhance the after-tax *economic* consequences of at least one partner; and

2. There is a strong likelihood that no partner will suffer substantially diminished after-tax *economic* consequences, again in present value terms.[20]

Essentially, these provisions provide that allocations that leave some partners better off after taxes, while leaving no partners worse off after taxes, will not be recognized. As with all the substantiality tests, in applying these rules, the interaction between partnership allocations and the partners' individual tax attributes outside the entity will be taken into account.

---

[20] Reg. § 1.704-1(b)(2)(iii)(a).

DETERMINING THE LEGITIMACY OF PARTNERSHIP DEDUCTIONS

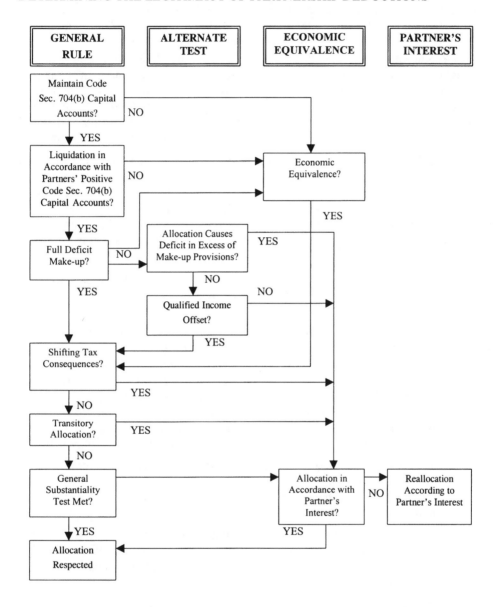

¶ 606 Allocating Partnership "Nonrecourse Deductions"

.01 Overview

The regulations are predicated upon the assumption that allocations of losses and deductions attributable to nonrecourse debts cannot have substantial economic effect. The regulations assume that such deductions can have no economic effect upon the partners because it is the lender who bears the risk that the partnership

will lose the borrowed funds.[21] The regulations instead analyze whether an allocation will be *deemed* to be made in accordance with the partners' *economic interests* in
the partnership. If the requirements of this test are satisfied, the agreement will
have the functional equivalent of "substantial economic effect."[22] While there are
other requirements that must be satisfied, the most fundamental is that the
deductions derived from nonrecourse financing must be allocated in a manner
reasonably consistent with the allocation of other significant items of income or
deductions that have met the economic effect test. In short, the nonrecourse debt
deductions must be allocated in a manner reasonably consistent with other material
items of income or deductions generated by recourse debt or contributed equity.

> *LLC Observation:* Nonrecourse debt is defined as a debt for which "no
> partner or related person bears the economic risk" as defined by the regula-
> tions.[23] In the case of an LLC, the partners are protected from most creditors
> by operation of the state's LLC statute. Therefore, unless a partner assumes an
> economic risk under Reg. § 1.752-2 with respect to an LLC's liabilities all debt
> financed deductions must satisfy the nonrecourse debt deduction rules de-
> scribed in this section.

The allocation of deductions attributable to nonrecourse debt will be *deemed* to
be in accordance with the partners' economic interests if the following conditions
are met:[24]

1. All partnership allocations of equity and recourse deductions have economic effect. This condition is met if either (a) the three mechanical tests
   of economic effect are satisfied (proper maintenance of capital accounts,
   liquidating distributions made in accordance with these properly maintained positive capital accounts, and, upon liquidation of a partner's interest, a deficit capital account make-up requirement), or (b) the alternate test
   is satisfied (the first two of the three mechanical tests are met and
   deduction allocations causing deficit capital accounts are not allowed);

2. The partnership agreement provides for the allocation of nonrecourse
   deductions in a manner that is reasonably consistent with allocations of
   other deductions, from the same source, which do have substantial economic effect;

3. The partnership agreement states that if there is a reduction in the amount
   of partnership "minimum gain," the partners who have been allocated
   deductions attributable to nonrecourse debts must be allocated items of
   income equal to their reduced share of the minimum gain; and

4. All other (other than nonrecourse) material allocations and capital account
   adjustments under the partnership agreement are valid.

.02 Minimum Gain

Naturally, the first question to be answered is: when is a partnership allocating
nonrecourse deductions?

---

[21] Reg. § 1.704-2(b)(1).
[22] *Id.*

[23] Reg. §§ 1.704-2(b)(3) and 1.752-1(a)(2).
[24] Reg. § 1.704-2(e).

¶606.02

In general, deductions incurred by a partnership are considered to be attributable to borrowed funds (recourse and nonrecourse) when the "book" value of the property securing those borrowed funds is less than the secured debt. Where the debt secured by the property is nonrecourse in nature, the presumption that there will be no future gain on disposition of the property does not apply. Instead, the regulations under Code Sec. 1001 provide that the amount realized upon a subsequent disposition of the property will not be less than the outstanding principal balance of the nonrecourse loan.[25] Accordingly, where the book value of the property is less than the principal balance of the nonrecourse loan, it can be reasonably presumed that the partnership will recognize gain on disposition of the property in an amount at least equal to the excess of the debt balance over the book value of the property.[26] Thus, the regulations introduce the concept of partnership "minimum gain." If nonrecourse deductions cause a partner's capital account to fall below zero no more than the difference between the outstanding principal balance of the nonrecourse debt and the book value of the property securing the loan, there will be a guaranteed amount of future income (minimum gain) at least sufficient to restore the capital account to zero. No partner's capital deficit can exceed his or her share of partnership minimum gain (in absolute value) unless the partner is obligated to restore deficit capital balances to zero.

The amount of nonrecourse deductions which are allocated under this rule for a partnership year equals the net increase in "partnership minimum gain."[27] Partnership minimum gain is the total gain which would be realized for all property subject to the nonrecourse debt.[28] Nonrecourse deductions consist first of depreciation, but if they exceed the partnership depreciation they consist of a *pro rata* share of other partnership losses, deductions and other nondeductible noncapitalized expenditures.

> ***Example 6-9:*** *Nonrecourse deductions.* Sam and Tom each contribute $100,000 to form ST Partnership. ST purchases a building for $800,000 using the $200,000 cash as a down payment and financing the remainder with a $600,000 *nonrecourse* note. The note calls for payments of interest only for 15 years, with the entire principal balance to be paid at the end of the 15-year term. The partnership agreement satisfies the first two requirements of the general test of economic effect, but does not require Sam to restore any deficit balance which may accumulate in his capital account. The partnership agreement allocates all annual depreciation deductions wholly to Sam. As illustrated below, the first $100,000 of depreciation can be allocated wholly to Sam.
>
> The partners' capital accounts after the allocation of the first $100,000 in depreciation deductions are as follows:

---

[25] Reg. § 1.1001-2. See in particular Examples 7 and 8.

[26] Abandonment or foreclosure of the property securing the nonrecourse loan is treated as a sale of such property to the nonrecourse lender for the outstanding balance of the debt.

[27] Reg. § 1.704-2(c).

[28] Reg. § 1.704-2(d) and (b)(2).

	Sam	*Tom*
Capital account, beginning	$100,000	$100,000
Depreciation.	(100,000)	0
Capital account, ending	*$0*	*$100,000*

At this point, should the partnership sell the property for its book value ($700,000) and liquidate, the first $600,000 of the sales proceeds would be paid to the nonrecourse creditor, with the remainder being paid to Tom to liquidate his interest in the partnership. Sam has a capital balance of zero and is entitled to receive nothing. Thus, he has borne the burden of the $100,000 decline in the value of the building and is entitled to tax deductions for $100,000 of depreciation expense.

In contrast, no portion of the next $100,000 in depreciation can be allocated to Sam because he is not obligated to restore deficit balances in his capital account, and there is no partnership minimum gain that can be allocated to him (the book value of the property is $700,000, which exceeds the $600,000 outstanding principal balance of the loan). Thus, assuming that the partnership continues to break even before depreciation expense, the next $100,000 of depreciation must be allocated to Tom. At that point, the book value of the property will equal the $600,000 outstanding principal balance of the nonrecourse note. All future depreciation deductions will now increase the partnership's "minimum gain," which can be allocated to Sam to restore a deficit balance in his capital account. Thus, from this point forward, depreciation can once again be allocated wholly to Sam. To illustrate, consider the capital account effects of the next $150,000 in depreciation allocations:

	Sam	*Tom*
Capital account, beginning	$0	$0
Depreciation.	(150,000)	0
Capital account, ending	*$(150,000)*	*$0*

At this point, if the partnership sells the property and liquidates, the selling price will be at least $600,000 (the amount of debt assumed by the buyer in connection with the sale). The book value of the property is now $450,000 (purchase price of $800,000 less depreciation expense of $350,000). Thus, it will recognize *at least* $150,000 in gain which can be allocated to Sam restoring the balance in his capital account to zero. The special allocation of the last $150,000 in depreciation expense to Sam will be deemed to have substantial economic effect under the regulations.

.03 Partnership Agreement Must Contain a "Minimum Gain Chargeback Provision"

As noted above, the regulations allow a partner to be allocated nonrecourse deductions, even if he or she is not required to restore deficit balances in his/her capital account, so long as the deficits do not exceed the amount of partnership minimum gain which can be allocated to the partner in the event of a partnership liquidation. Note, however, that when the partnership makes payments against the

¶606.03

principal balance of its nonrecourse debt, its minimum gain may decrease. In the event the minimum gain decreases to a level such that the deficit balance in a partner's capital account exceeds his or her share of partnership minimum gain, the regulations require that the partner immediately be allocated sufficient income to bring the deficit balance in his or her capital account back into alignment with his or her share of partnership minimum gain.[29] This requirement is known as a "minimum gain chargeback" provision.

Minimum gain can be reduced by the cost of capital improvements made to the property (which increase its tax basis and book value) as well as by payments of debt principal. When the partnership has insufficient income to allocate to a partner to bring his or her capital balance into alignment with his/her share of partnership minimum gain, the unsatisfied chargeback carries forward to succeeding years.[30] The partnership *must* allocate sufficient income to the partner to make up the deficit as soon as possible.

.04 Identifying Nonrecourse Deductions Where the Partnership Has Both Recourse and Nonrecourse Indebtedness

Nonrecourse deductions equal the increase in partnership minimum taxable gain, which in turn is the excess of the total partnership nonrecourse indebtedness over the book value of all property securing such debt. When the property is secured by both recourse and nonrecourse debt, the nonrecourse debt rules apply only when the partnership is deducting amounts due to nonrecourse financing. If there is more than one debt secured by a single property an allocation of the book value is necessary.

Where the debts are of equal priority, the book value is allocated according to their relative amounts. If they are of unequal priority the book value is allocated first to the superior debt, then any excess is allocated to the inferior debt.[31] Thus, where the nonrecourse debt is junior to the recourse debt, nonrecourse deductions will be considered taken after those generated by contributions but before recourse loan deductions. The liability with the least priority under local law is, in effect, considered to be the first source of the deductions generated by debt. This is because in a hypothetical liquidation scenario where the FMV of the secured asset is assumed to equal its book value, the high-priority debt is assumed to be paid off first. This means that the true economic burden of the deduction will show up in the low-priority debt, since that is paid off last, and therefore is much more likely to be the source of required payments by the partners (or gain chargeback, in the case of nonrecourse debt). In order to get an accurate initial measurement of the economic effect of an allocation of a deduction, the deduction is always deemed to come from the low-priority debt first.

> **Example 6-10:** *A* is the general partner of the ABC limited partnership. The partnership agreement allocates income or loss other than depreciation equally. Depreciation is allocated entirely to partner *C*. The partnership purchases improved real estate for $600,000. The terms are:

---

[29] Reg. § 1.704-2(b)(2).

[30] Reg. § 1.704-2(f)(6) and (j)(2)(iii).

[31] Reg. §§ 1.704-2(d)(2)(ii) and 1.752-2.

Cash paid with contributed funds	$200,000
Funds borrowed from third party (Recourse debt secured by realty with a first-trust deed)	100,000
Seller financing (Nonrecourse debt secured by the realty with a subordinated trust deed)	300,000
Book value of property	**$600,000**

In the first year, operating cash expenses are equal to operating income, and there is a net taxable loss of $100,000 due to depreciation. No principal payments are made toward the debts. As the property's year-end basis ($500,000) exceeds the securing debt ($400,000), no minimum gain is created. The tax loss is not a nonrecourse debt deduction. The partnership is bearing the risk of loss and the partnership's allocation of the depreciation deduction must have substantial economic effect or it will be re-allocated according to the facts-and-circumstances test.

In the second year, the operating results are the same. Again, because no minimum gain is created, the partnership is assumed to be incurring losses of its invested equity. The partnership's allocation of the depreciation must have substantial economic effect to avoid a facts-and-circumstances allocation.

In the third year, the operating results are again the same as in the first two years. There is a $100,000 taxable loss. The outstanding debt of $400,000 now exceeds the property's basis of $300,000 by $100,000.

Debt		$400,000
Cost	$600,000	
Depreciation	(300,000)	
Book value		(300,000)
Debt exceeding book value		**$100,000**

Is it the recourse or nonrecourse debt which is responsible for the excess over book value? The regulations allocate book value first to the most superior debt (for example, a first-trust deed), then to other debts in their declining order of priority. The liability with the least priority is allocated book value last.[32] In this example, the third-party recourse debt is superior to the nonrecourse seller financing.

Book value	$300,000
Less amount allocated to superior debt	(100,000)
Book value allocated to inferior nonrecourse debt	200,000
Inferior nonrecourse debt	(300,000)
Nonrecourse debt deduction (minimum gain)	**$100,000**

---

[32] Reg. § 1.704-2(d)(2).

The depreciation deduction will be deemed to have been allocated according to the partners' interests in the partnership if it is allocated in a "manner that is reasonably consistent with allocations, which have substantial economic effect, of some other significant partnership item attributable to the property securing the nonrecourse liabilities of the partnership" and the other requirements for safe harbor nonrecourse debt deduction allocations are satisfied.[33] In this example, if *C* is allocated the depreciation deduction in year three, this nonrecourse debt deduction is consistent with allocations of deductions from the same source that have economic effect, namely depreciation for years one and two.

In the fourth and fifth years, if the results of operations are the same, the partnership's taxable losses are nonrecourse debt deductions. This is because each year the excess of the nonrecourse debt over the book value allocated to it (the minimum gain) grows larger. Book value is decreasing by the amount of the depreciation deduction and, in our example, the nonrecourse debt remains constant.

In the sixth year, if the results of operations continue to remain constant, the loss will not be a nonrecourse debt deduction and its allocation by the partnership must have substantial economic effect. This is because all the nonrecourse debt has been allocated to previous deductions. There is a nonrecourse debt deduction only to the extent of an *increase* in minimum gain. Minimum gain equals the excess of the outstanding nonrecourse debt over the book value allocated to it.

Example 6-11: *C* and *S* form the CS general partnership with equal contributions of $100,000 each. All items of income, deduction, loss, and gain are shared equally except depreciation, which is allocated entirely to *S*. Under the terms of the partnership agreement, *C* has an unlimited obligation to restore deficit balances in her capital account, while *S* is obligated to restore deficit balances in his capital account only up to $100,000.

The first two requirements of economic effect are satisfied and the partnership agreement contains a qualified income offset and a minimum gain chargeback provision. The partnership purchases a building for $1,000,000, using the contributions and $800,000 of borrowed funds. A bank has made a recourse loan of $600,000 which has priority over nonrecourse seller financing of $200,000. Excluding $100,000 of depreciation per year, income equals deductions.

In both Year 1 and Year 2, the allocation of all $100,000 depreciation expense to *S* will have economic effect under the alternate test.[34]

In Year 3, the depreciation deduction creates partnership minimum gain of $100,000. Debt ($800,000) exceeds book value ($1,000,000 cost basis less $300,000 depreciation = $700,000) by $100,000. Nonrecourse deductions are $100,000 because the economic burden of the deduction is borne by the

---

[33] Reg. § 1.704-2(e)(2).   [34] Reg. § 1.704-1(b)(2)(ii)(*d*).

nonrecourse creditor alone. The book value of the partnership property is first allocated to the bank's superior priority debt of $600,000. Therefore, the $100,000 in remaining book value is exceeded by $200,000 of nonrecourse debt. The third year's allocation does not have economic effect. However, because the four requirements of Reg. § 1.704-2 are satisfied, the allocations are deemed to be in accordance with the partners' interests in the partnership. The requirements are satisfied as follows:

1. Equity and recourse deductions have economic effect. This condition is satisfied if either the three mechanical tests of economic effect are satisfied (proper maintenance of capital accounts, liquidating distributions made in accordance with these properly maintained positive capital accounts, and, upon liquidation of a partner's interest, an unlimited deficit capital account make-up requirement), or the alternate test is satisfied (the first two of the three mechanical tests are met and deduction allocations causing deficit capital account in excess of the partner's limited deficit capital account make-up requirement are not allowed);

2. The allocation of nonrecourse deductions is reasonably consistent with allocations of deductions, from the same source, which do have substantial economic effect;

3. The partnership agreement states that if there is a reduction in the amount of minimum taxable gain, the partners who have taken deduction allocations attributable to nonrecourse debt must be allocated items of income equal to their share of the minimum gain; and

4. All other (other than nonrecourse) material allocations and capital account adjustments under the partnership agreement are valid.

¶ 607 Other Issues

.01 Transfer of a Partnership Interest

The Code Sec. 704(b) accounting rules require that the transferee step into the shoes of the transferor following the transfer of a partnership interest.[35] If the partnership has a Code Sec. 754 election in effect for the year of a sale or exchange of a partnership interest, no adjustment is made to the Code Sec. 704(b) "book value" of the partnership assets or to the Code Sec. 704(b) "book" capital account of the transferred interest.[36]

.02 Distributions Causing Code Sec. 734(b) Adjustments

Adjustments to partners' capital accounts are required when Code Sec. 734(b) adjustments to the tax basis of partnership property are required. In a nonliquidating distribution, the partners' capital accounts are adjusted by the total amount of the basis adjustment. The adjustment is allocated around the partners capital accounts since they would share an equal amount of income, gain or loss had the property been sold by the partnership for its recomputed basis. The adjustment is

---

[35] Reg. § 1.704-1(b)(2)(iv)(l).   [36] Reg. § 1.704-1(b)(2)(iv)(m).

presumably allocated among the assets in the same manner the tax allocation is made under Code Sec. 755. In a liquidating distribution, the entire basis adjustment is allocated to the capital account of the liquidated partner. In both a liquidating and nonliquidating distribution, the adjustment is, however, limited to the partnership's ability to allocate it to partnership property.[37]

.03 Nondeductible, Noncapital Expenditures

A partner's capital account is reduced by the partner's share of nondeductible expenditures which are not capitalized. These expenses reduce cash available for distribution. Code Sec. 709 organization and syndication expenses are treated in this manner except to the extent of the amortization expenses.[38]

.04 Guaranteed Payments

Guaranteed payments are treated as an ordinary partnership expense. They reduce capital accounts based upon the partners' profit and loss sharing arrangement.[39]

.05 Adjustments Where Guidance Is Lacking

Partnership transactions where Code Sec. 704(b) accounting is not specified are to be made in a manner which:

1. Maintains the equality between assets and capital accounts plus liabilities;

2. Is consistent with the partners economic arrangement; and

3. Is based on federal tax accounting principles.

.06 Optional Revaluation of All Property and Capital Accounts

On the contribution or distribution of property, the contributed or distributed property itself must be "revalued" to its fair market value for capital account maintenance purposes.

This revaluation is *not* optional. However, there are four situations under the capital account maintenance rules in which an *optional* adjustment may be made to the book value of *all* the partnership's property, and, correspondingly, the capital accounts of all the partners, provided that the revaluation is for substantial non-tax business purposes:

1. Contribution of property (including money) to a partnership in exchange for a partnership interest;

2. Distribution of property (including money) from a partnership in exchange for a partnership interest; and

3. Grant of an interest in the partnership (other than a *de minimis* interest) on or after May 6, 2004, as consideration for the provision of services to or for the benefit of the partnership by an existing or new partner acting in a partner capacity;

---

[37] Reg. § 1.704-1(b)(2)(iv)(m)(4) and (b)(5), Ex. 14(vii).

[38] Reg. § 1.704-1(b)(2)(iv)(i).

[39] Reg. § 1.704-1(b)(2)(iv)(o).

4. Under "generally accepted industry accounting practices" where substantially all of the partnership's property (excluding money) is stock, securities, commodities, options, warrants, futures, or similar instruments that are readily traded on an established securities market.[40]

Revaluation procedures. If the partnership elects to revalue all of its assets, the procedures are as follows:

1. The adjustments are based on the fair market value of the property on the date of adjustment.

2. The property is treated as sold, and "gain" or "loss" is recognized *for book purposes only* by subtracting the book value of the property from the fair market value of the property. There is no current tax recognition.

3. The gain or loss so determined is allocated among the partners on the basis of their economic agreement as provided in the partnership, and reflected in their capital accounts.

4. *Book* depreciation, amortization, and depletion, and book gain or loss for the revalued property, must be calculated as provided in the safe harbor regulations.[41]

5. Allocation of *tax* depreciation, amortization, and depletion, and tax gain or loss must reflect the variation between the tax and book values and amounts under the same principles as apply to treatment of such variations under Code Sec. 704(c).[42] Income and loss concerning receivables and payables must be similarly handled.[43]

Decision to revalue. Much of the decision to revalue partnership assets is based upon accounting considerations. Revaluation generally enhances the usefulness of the partnership's balance sheet. For example, revaluing the partnership's assets when a partner's interest has been liquidated by a cash distribution can avoid the unbalanced books problem caused by his or her ending capital account not being equal to the cash distribution. Revaluation will also cause the assets and capital accounts to more closely track fair market values rather than the residual of cost basis net of depreciation and other book adjustments to carrying values. This is especially useful to users of the balance sheet who understand little of historical cost accounting or have very little idea of the value of their partnership interest.

While the decision to revalue is "optional," the regulations contemplate that in the usual context the election will be made. If the election is not made then the partnership agreement must otherwise provide for effectively the same results as if the election had been made.[44] Otherwise, the regulations caution, there may be other tax ramifications outside of the allocation arena (*e.g.*, gift or compensation).[45]

The decision to revalue or not revalue partnership property, and the decision to use the safe harbor or some other approach under the partners' interests in the partnership rules for handling the book depreciation, amortization, and depletion,

---

[40] Reg. § 1.704-1(b)(2)(iv)(*f*).
[41] As provided in Reg. § 1.704-1(b)(2)(iv)(*g*).
[42] Reg. § 1.704-1(b)(2)(iv)(*f*).

[43] Reg. § 1.704-1(b)(2)(iv)(*g*)(*2*).
[44] Reg. § 1.704-1(b)(5), Ex. 14(iv).
[45] Reg. § 1.704-1(b)(2)(iv)(*f*).

¶607.06

may have significant economic consequences to the partners, and may not be made only "for tax purposes." Partners should be extremely careful in making these decisions.

> *Observation:* If the partnership agreement allocates the entire depreciation deduction to one partner, an increased book value of the depreciable asset will result in a larger book expense. This may result in a reduced share of the partnership's net income.

¶ 608 Summary and Concluding Remarks

The Code Sec. 704(b) regulations are based on a simple premise. Tax allocations will only be recognized for tax purposes if they mirror the allocation of the economic benefits and detriments of partnership operations. The economic effects of partnership operations, in turn, are best measured over time by reference to the cash flows ultimately attributable to the partners. Thus, for a tax allocation to be recognized, it must ultimately affect the cash flows to the partners of the partnership. These cash flows are reflected in the partners' capital accounts—but only if these capital accounts are used to determine how the partnership's net assets are actually distributed among the partners upon liquidation.

Somewhat different rules apply when partnership deductions are supported by nonrecourse debt. Here, no partner bears the economic risk of loss, because no partner is personally responsible for repayment of the partnership's nonrecourse liability. Nonrecourse deductions must be allocated in accordance with the manner in which investors will ultimately share the tax gains (and thus the tax liability) which will eventually be recognized by the partnership as a result of these deductions. Again, these consequences are best reflected in partner capital accounts. Thus, regardless of the nature of the partnership's activities, the consequences to the partners of those activities are ultimately reflected in the partners' capital accounts. The tax law looks to those capital accounts to determine how partnership activities should be reflected on the partners' tax returns. It is therefore imperative that partners, or their advisors, understand capital account accounting.

Chapter 7

Allocation of Income and Deductions from Contributed Property: Code Sec. 704(c)

¶ 701 Introduction

Code Sec. 704(b), requiring allocations to have substantial economic effect, is designed to prevent tax avoidance through the use of economically meaningless allocations of partnership income or loss. Partners can reduce their individual tax liabilities by use of special partnership allocations, but only if those allocations are associated with real economic costs. Code Sec. 704(c), in contrast, *requires* special allocations that do not cause the partner to suffer nontax *economic* costs, in order to prevent the use of partnerships and LLCs as tax avoidance vehicles.

Code Sec. 704(c) applies whenever a partner contributes property to a partnership with a fair market value that differs from its tax basis. When property with a built-in gain or loss is contributed to the partnership, tax gains and losses, and depreciation and depletion with respect to the contributed property, differ from the amounts recorded for "book" purposes under Code Sec. 704(b). To the extent of these differences, the tax consequences of a partnership allocation do not reflect the economic cost or benefit associated with that allocation. Accordingly, Code Sec. 704(b) cannot, by itself, prevent investors from using partnerships to manipulate their tax liabilities when there is a contribution of appreciated or depreciated property.

> **Example 7-1:** A and B enter into a partnership to which A, a taxpayer in the 35% tax bracket, contributes inventory with a $10,000 basis and a $50,000 fair market value in exchange for a 50% interest in capital, profits, and losses. B, a taxpayer in the 15% tax bracket, contributes $50,000 cash in exchange for the remaining 50% interest in the partnership. The partnership subsequently sells the property contributed by A for its $50,000 fair market value. The partnership agreement allocates 50% of all profits to each partner. Thus, in the

absence of Code Sec. 704(c), *A* and *B* would each recognize $20,000 income. *A* would owe $7,000 income tax (35% × $20,000), while *B* would owe $3,000 (15% × $20,000). Not only would *A* shift a portion of his tax burden to *B*, but the total income tax paid on the gain recognized from sale of the inventory would be $4,000 less than if Partner *A*, rather than the partnership, had sold the property.

As first enacted, Code Sec. 704(c) was an elective provision designed to protect the other investors in a partnership when a partner contributed appreciated property. Thus, where a partner contributed depreciable property with a basis less than its fair market value, the partnership could *elect* to allocate tax gain from the subsequent disposition of such property to the contributing partner to the extent of the original difference between value and basis. Similarly, tax depreciation during the period prior to disposition could be allocated away from the contributing partner in a like amount. In this way, the other partners would not be affected by any difference between fair market value (Section 704(b) book value) and tax basis at the date of contribution. Only the contributing partner would receive allocations of tax gain or loss unaccompanied by economic consequence under Code Sec. 704(b).

The Tax Reform Act of 1984 changed Code Sec. 704(c) from an elective provision to a mandatory one. Special allocations are now *required* when property is contributed to a partnership or LLC with a tax basis different from its fair market value.

The purpose of the statute is to ensure that gain or loss inherent in contributed property is allocated to the contributor and to allocate among the noncontributing partners only the gain or loss that accrues after the date of contribution.

Between 1993 and 1995, the IRS issued new regulations under Code Sec. 704(c)(1)(A).[1] The regulations require partnerships and LLCs to take into account built-in gains and losses inherent in contributed properties in making allocations among partner/members. They allow partnerships/LLCs to allocate items of tax depreciation, depletion, gain, or loss with respect to contributed property using any reasonable method, as long as the method is consistently applied. The regulations further identify three reasonable methods: the "traditional" method, the traditional method with curative allocations, and the remedial allocations method. Other reasonable methods are allowable, but the taxpayer must be able to demonstrate that they do not shift the tax burden associated with built-in gains to partners other than the contributing partner.[2]

These rules apply on a property-by-property basis, with limited exceptions. Therefore, in determining whether there is a disparity between adjusted tax basis and fair market value, the built-in gains and losses inherent in items of contributed property cannot be aggregated. The partnership may use different methods with respect to different items of contributed property, but a single reasonable method is applied for each item of contributed property. The overall method or combination of

---

[1] Reg. § 1.704-3, issued 12/21/93, amended 12/27/94, 5/8/97, and 8/19/97.

[2] Reg. § 1.704-3(a)(1).

methods must be reasonable based on the facts and circumstances.[3] For example, it may be unreasonable to use one method for appreciated property and another method for depreciated property. Similarly, it may be unreasonable to use the traditional method for built-in gain property contributed by a partner with a high marginal tax rate while using curative allocations for property contributed by a partner with a low marginal tax rate.[4]

> ***Comment:*** Code Sec. 704(c) and the regulations apply to property contributed to the partnership when there is a built-in gain or loss. Code Sec. 704(c) allocates the built-in gain or loss to the partner who owned the property when the gain or loss arose. When a new partner joins a partnership which holds property with built-in gain or loss, the partnership's built-in gain or loss must be allocated to the partners who owned their partnership interests when the built-in gain or loss arose. These are Code Sec. 704(b) allocations and are generally referred to as "reverse Code Sec. 704(c) allocations."

.01 Anti-abuse Rule

An allocation method (or combination of methods) is not reasonable if the contribution of property (or optional revaluation under Code Sec. 704(b)) and the corresponding allocation of tax items with respect to the property are made with a view to shifting the tax consequences of built-in gain or loss among the partners in a manner that substantially reduces the present value of the partners' aggregate tax liability.[5]

¶ 702 Traditional Method

.01 General

In general, the traditional method requires that when the partnership has income, gain, loss, or deduction attributable to Code Sec. 704(c) property (*i.e.,* property whose book value differs from the contributing partner's adjusted tax basis at the time of contribution), it must make appropriate allocations to the partners to avoid shifting the tax consequences of the built-in gain or loss. Thus, if the partnership sells Code Sec. 704(c) property and recognizes gain or loss, the recognized gain or loss must be allocated first to the contributing partner to the extent of built-in gain or loss inherent in the property at the date of contribution.[6]

For Code Sec. 704(c) property subject to amortization, depletion, depreciation, or other cost recovery, the allocation of these deductions must also take into account built-in gain or loss inherent in the property at the date of contribution. Thus, tax allocations to the noncontributing partners of depreciation with respect to Code Sec. 704(c) property must, to the extent possible, equal book allocations to those partners.[7]

The "traditional method" is the term applied to the historical rules which existed under former Reg. § 1.704-1(c). Built-in gain or loss inherent in contributed property (Code Sec. 704(c) gain or loss) is attributable to the contributing partner

---

[3] Reg. § 1.704-3(a)(2).
[4] *Id.*
[5] Reg. § 1.704-3(a)(10).

[6] Reg. § 1.704-3(b)(1).
[7] *Id.*

(or, on the admission of a new partner with "book-up" or "book-down," to the existing partners). If the contributed property is disposed of in a non-taxable exchange, the property received with a substituted basis becomes Code Sec. 704(c) property. If the contributed property is disposed of in an installment sale, the installment obligation received by the partnership is treated as the section 704(c) property with the same amount of built-in gain as the section 704(c) property disposed of by the partnership (with appropriate adjustments for any gain recognized on the installment sale).[8] Taxable gain or loss on disposition of the property and tax depreciation and other cost-recoveries must be allocated to the *non-contributing* partners so as to reflect their "views" of the property, *i.e.*, the *book* gain, loss, depreciation, etc.

In general, under the traditional method, tax deductions for depreciation, depletion, etc. with respect to contributed property are first allocated to the non-contributing partners to the extent of "book" allocations of these items. Any remainder is then allocated to the contributing partner. In this way, the contributing partner bears the tax burden associated with the built-in gain in the form of lesser depreciation deductions over the remaining life of the party.

> **Example 7-2:** *J*, *D*, and *R* form the equal JDR partnership to develop and manage commercial real estate. *J* contributes depreciable property with a tax basis of $325,000 and a fair value of $450,000. The property has 10 years remaining in its depreciable life and is depreciated using the straight-line method. *D* and *R* each contribute cash of $450,000. The property contributed by *J* is Code Sec. 704(c) property, with a built-in gain of $125,000. Under the "traditional method" as described in the regulations, tax deductions for depreciation with respect to this property will be allocated in the following manner:

	J		*D*		*R*	
	Tax	*Book*	*Tax*	*Book*	*Tax*	*Book*
First, allocate book depreciation equally among the partners		$15,000		$15,000		$15,000
Next, allocate tax depreciation to *D* and *R*, the non-contributing partners in a like amount			15,000		15,000	
Any remaining tax depreciation is then allocated to *J*	2,500					

In the above example, note that *J*'s book capital account is reduced by $15,000 each year to record depreciation expense on the property she contributed. Since her book capital account represents the amount she is entitled to receive at liquidation, each year she is relinquishing a claim to $15,000 of partnership assets.

---

[8] Reg. § 1.704-3(a)(8)(ii).

However, she is only allowed a tax deduction for $2,500. Over the 10 year depreciable life of the property, she will relinquish rights to $150,000 in partnership assets and claim a corresponding tax deduction of only $25,000. The result of these unbalanced allocations is that *J* will bear the tax burden on the $125,000 built-in gain inherent in the property at the rate of $12,500 per year for ten years. *D* and *R*, in contrast, will receive the same deductions they would have received if the property had been purchased for its fair market value rather than being contributed by *J*.

This approach works well so long as there is sufficient tax depreciation to give the non-contributing partners the same deductions for book as they receive for tax. The regulations impose a "ceiling rule," however, under which the allocations to the non-contributing partners of tax depreciation or other deductions with respect to the contributed property cannot exceed the total amount of depreciation, etc. claimed with respect to that property for tax purposes. Thus, where the book depreciation deductions allocated to the noncontributing partners exceed the total tax depreciation deduction, use of the "traditional method" under Code Sec. 704(c) will not fully protect them from bearing a portion of the tax burden on *J*'s built-in gain.

.02 Ceiling Rule Limitation

As noted, under the ceiling rule, total income, gain, loss, or deduction allocated to the partners for a taxable year with respect to a Code Sec. 704(c) property cannot exceed the total partnership income, gain, loss, or deduction with respect to that property for the taxable year. If the partnership has no property with respect to which allocations are limited by the ceiling rule, the traditional method is reasonable when used for all contributed property.[9]

> **Example 7-3:** *A* and *B* form an equal partnership. *A* contributes property with an adjusted basis of $4,000 and a fair market value of $10,000. *B* contributes $10,000 cash. The property is depreciated, for both book and tax purposes, on the straight-line method over the property's remaining recovery period of 10 years.
>
> *A* has an initial built-in gain of $6,000 ($10,000 − $4,000). Book depreciation of $1,000 per year is allocated $500 to both *A* and *B*. If the property had been purchased, *B* also would have received $500 of tax depreciation. Tax depreciation, however, amounts to only $400 and must be totally allocated to *B*. The ceiling rule prevents *B* from being allocated a full $500 of tax depreciation.
>
> The ceiling rule does not just apply to the allocation of depreciation and depletion deductions. It also applies to the allocation of gain or loss on sale or disposition of the property. Indeed, it is possible that the ceiling rule may be triggered when a partnership sells property that has not previously been subject to the ceiling rule. In such cases, if the partnership has been using the traditional method with respect to that property, it will not be allowed to change methods to allocate gain or loss on sale of such property merely

---

[9] *Id.*

because the ceiling rule prevents the allocation of the entire remaining built-in gain to the contributing partner.

Example 7-4: A and B form an equal partnership. A contributes property with an adjusted basis of $5,000 and a fair market value of $10,000. B contributes $10,000 cash. The property is depreciated, for both book and tax purposes, on the straight-line method over the property's remaining recovery period of 10 years.

- A has an initial built-in gain of $5,000 ($10,000 – $5,000).

- Book depreciation of $1,000 per year is allocated $500 to both A and B. Tax depreciation, however, amounts only to $500 and must be allocated entirely to B.

- At the end of year one, the property has a book value of $9,000 and an adjusted basis of $4,500. A's built-in gain has been reduced to the remaining book/tax differential of $4,500 ($9,000 – $4,500).

- If the property is sold at the end of Year 1 for $10,000, the book gain is $1,000, allocated $500 each to A and B. The tax gain, however, is $5,500. This is allocated $5,000 to A (his remaining $4,500 of built-in gain plus his $500 of book gain) and $500 to B.

- If the property is sold at the end of year one for less than $9,000, the entire tax gain, being less than the remaining built-in gain, is allocated to A and none to B. The ceiling rule prevents B from having a tax loss, even though he has a book loss.

For example, assume the property is sold for $7,000. The partnership will recognize a book loss of $2,000, allocated $1,000 each to A and B. For tax purposes, however, the partnership recognizes a gain of $2,500. The ceiling rule will not allow the partnership to allocate any loss to B (because the partnership does not recognize a loss for tax purposes), although she realized a book loss of $1,000. Rather, the entire $2,500 of taxable gain will be allocated to A. Although all the gain is allocated to Partner A, A has effectively shifted the tax burden on $1,000 of the pre-contribution built-in gain to B.

¶ 703 Traditional Method with Curative Allocations

To correct distortions created by the ceiling rule, a partnership may make so-called "curative" allocations to reduce or eliminate disparities between book and tax items of noncontributing partners. A curative allocation is an allocation of income, gain, loss, or deduction for tax purposes that differs from the partnership's allocation of the corresponding book item. For example, if a noncontributing partner is allocated less tax depreciation than book depreciation with respect to an item of Code Sec. 704(c) property because of the ceiling rule, the partnership may make a curative allocation to that partner of tax depreciation from another partnership property to make up the difference, notwithstanding that the corresponding book depreciation is allocated to the contributing partner.[10]

---

[10] Reg. § 1.704-3(c)(1).

If the partnership has insufficient depreciation on other properties, it may make reasonable curative allocations of *other* tax items of income, gain, loss or deduction, provided they are of the same *character* as the item limited by the ceiling rule. Thus, a partnership may allocate ordinary income away from the non-contributing partner (and to the contributing partner) to make up for an inability to allocate sufficient tax depreciation to the non-contributing partner. In such a case, the non-contributing partners will have equal allocations of book and tax income in total, although differences may exist between the book and tax allocations of particular items of income or deduction. Taken as a whole, the allocations of total taxable income will reflect their "view" of the contributed property.

To be reasonable, a curative allocation of income, gain, loss, or deduction must be expected to have substantially the same effect on each partner's tax liability as the tax item limited by the ceiling rule. The expectation must exist at the time the Code Sec. 704(c) property is obligated to be (or is) contributed to the partnership.[11]

If a partnership does not have items sufficient in amount and character to equalize the non-contributing partners' book and tax allocations, the partnership may make the curative allocation in the next succeeding year that it has such sufficient items. However, the curative allocations must be made within a reasonable period of time, and, further, must be provided for in the partnership agreement for the year of contribution or revaluation.

A curative allocation is reasonable only to the extent that it does not exceed the amount necessary to avoid the distortion created by the ceiling rule for the current year and only if the items used have the same effect on the partners as the item affected by the ceiling rule. For example, if depreciation on a contributed asset is affected by the ceiling rule, only items of depreciation from other assets or ordinary income, and not capital gain, may be used as a curative allocation. There is an exception to the similar-in-character rule and yearly effect of the ceiling rule limit. If depreciation on a contributed asset has been limited by the ceiling rule and the asset is sold at a gain (*i.e.*, Code Sec. 1231 gain), it is not unreasonable to make a curative allocation of this gain to the contributing partner that takes into account the accumulated depreciation deficit allocated to the noncontributing partner. This amount exceeding the yearly ceiling rule limit and mismatching of character is available only if properly provided in the partnership agreement in effect for the year of contribution or revaluation.[12]

> ***Example 7-5:*** [13] *A* and *B* form an equal partnership. *A* contributes property with an adjusted basis of $4,000 and a fair market value of $10,000. *B* contributes $10,000 cash. The property is depreciated, for both book and tax purposes, on the straight-line method over the property's remaining recovery period of 10 years. As above, book depreciation will be $1,000 per year, allocated $500 each to *A* and *B*. Tax depreciation, however, is limited to $400 per year, and will be allocated entirely to *B*. If the partnership opts to use the traditional method with curative allocations with respect to the property con-

---

[11] Reg. § 1.704-3(c)(3)(iii)(A).
[12] Reg. § 1.704-3(c)(3)(iii)(B) and (i).

[13] Reg. § 1.704-3(c)(4), Ex. 1.

tributed by *A*, the $100 disparity between the book and tax depreciation allocated to *B* may be eliminated by a curative allocation of $100 of ordinary income to *A*, thereby reducing the ordinary income allocable to *B*. The net tax effect to *B* is now equal to his book position.

While *A* has additional taxable income of $100, and his built-in gain is reduced to $5,400, the difference between his book and tax capital accounts is now equal to the built-in gain.

Assume the property is sold at the end of one year for $7,000, generating a book loss of $2,000, which would be a Code Sec. 1231 loss. In the absence of any other partnership Code Sec. 1231 gains or losses, there must be a curative allocation of another type of gain, loss, income or deduction available to allocate to *B* which has substantially the same effect on his tax liability as his allocation of Code Sec. 1231 book loss. This requirement will be difficult to satisfy because the Code Sec. 1231 loss will first be netted by *B* against Code Sec. 1231 gains (if any). Any excess will be deductible as an ordinary loss. Thus, it is unlikely that the partnership will be able to cure this disparity in the current year unless it has Code Sec. 1231 gain or loss from the sale of another property. It can, however, cure the deficiency in a subsequent year if it has Code Sec. 1231 gain or loss from a later sale of property.

¶ 704 Remedial Allocations Method

The remedial allocations method is similar to the traditional method with curative allocations. The difference is that a "remedial" allocation can be made whether or not the partnership has other items of income or loss available to allocate to the noncontributing partner(s). Remedial allocations are tax allocations of *artificial* income, gain, loss, or deduction used to offset disparities attributable to the ceiling rule under Code Sec. 704(c). These tax allocations are created by the partnership and have no effect on the partnership's book capital accounts.[14]

A partnership may adopt the remedial allocations method to eliminate the disparities caused by the ceiling rule. Under this method, the partnership makes a remedial allocation of income, gain, loss, or deduction to the noncontributing partner equal to the amount of the limitation caused by the ceiling rule and a simultaneous offsetting remedial allocation of deduction, loss, gain, or income to the contributing partner. Remedial allocations are notional tax items created by the partnership solely for Code Sec. 704(c) and reverse Code Sec. 704(c) purposes. They are not a share of the partnership's taxable income or loss. In effect, a partnership using the remedial allocations method creates negative depreciation expense to offset a ceiling rule depreciation limitation with respect to Sec. 704(c) property. The allocation of negative depreciation to the contributing partner has the effect of allocating her ordinary income.

> *Example 7-6:* *A* contributes depreciable property to the AB limited partnership with a tax basis of $3,000, and a fair market value of $10,000. *B* contributes $10,000 cash. Assume that book depreciation for the partnership's

---

[14] Reg. § 1.704-3(d)(1).

first year of operations with respect to the property contributed by *A* is $5,000, and that this depreciation is allocable 50% to each partner. Tax depreciation with respect to this property is $1,500. Finally, assume the partnership breaks even before depreciation expense.

Under Code Sec. 704(c), the first $2,500 of tax depreciation must be allocated to Partner *B*, with any remainder allocable to *A*. Applying the ceiling rule, however, *B* can only be allocated $1,500 of tax depreciation, creating a $1,000 book-tax disparity in *B's* capital accounts. Under the remedial allocations method, this ceiling rule distortion can be eliminated by creating $1,000 in "remedial" depreciation expense, allocable to *B*, and offsetting this allocation by creating $1,000 "remedial" income to be allocated to *A*. The effects on the partners' capital accounts would be as follows:

	A		*B*	
	Book	*Tax*	*Book*	*Tax*
Initial contribution	$ 10,000	$ 3,000	$ 10,000	$ 10,000
Depreciation	(2,500)	0	(2,500)	(1,500)
Remedial depreciation				(1,000)
Remedial income		1,000		
Ending capital balances	$7,500	$4,000	$7,500	$7,500

Similarly, a partnership facing a ceiling rule limitation on the allocation of loss from the sale of Code Sec. 704(c) property allocates an artificial loss to the *non-contributing* partner(s), offset by an allocation of artificial gain to the contributing partner. This is a significant difference from the traditional method with curative allocations. The traditional method with curative allocations requires that if the property is sold at a tax gain (loss), but a book loss (gain), the disparity between the book and tax results *cannot* be cured by allocating a tax loss (gain) to the non-contributing partner unless that tax loss (gain) has been generated by the disposition of another asset which will have substantially the same effect on the partner's tax liability as the property sold.[15]

This is not the case with the remedial allocations method. Under this method, if property is sold at a gain for tax but at a loss for book, the non-contributing partners may be allocated a tax *loss* and the contributing partner an offsetting *larger gain* than the reported tax gain from the sale. In effect, the ceiling rule limitation is simply ignored.

Example 7-7: [16] *A* and *B* form an equal partnership. *A* contributes land with an adjusted basis of $4,000 and a fair market value of $10,000; *B* contributes $10,000 cash. The property is later sold for $9,000, resulting in a capital gain of $5,000 and a book loss of $1,000. If provided for in the partnership agreement, a remedial allocation of a $500 capital loss to *B* with an offsetting

---

[15] Reg. § 1.704-3(c) (3) (iii) (A).   [16] Reg. § 1.704-3(d) (7), Ex. 2.

remedial allocation of a $500 capital gain to *A* may be made, resulting in the following capital accounts:

| | *A* | | *B* | |
	Book	*Tax*	*Book*	*Tax*
Contributions	$ 10,000	$ 4,000	$ 10,000	$ 10,000
Sale of land	(500)	5,000	(500)	0
Remedial allocations		500		(500)
	$9,500	$9,500	$9,500	$9,500

¶ 705 Special Rules

.01 Depreciation Methods

In order to ensure that partnerships or LLCs do not attempt to avoid Code Sec. 704(c) by choosing different accounting methods or different useful lives for book and tax, the regulations under Code Sec. 704(b) require that *book* depreciation and other cost recovery deductions be calculated at the same *rate* used in the tax computations of those items.[17] Thus, where a depreciable asset has three years remaining in its depreciable life for tax purposes, it must be depreciated over three years for book purposes as well. Furthermore, if the percentage rate at which tax depreciation is calculated differs for one or more of the asset's remaining depreciable years, this difference must be reflected in the Code Sec. 704(b) depreciation computation as well.

> *Example 7-8:* *A* contributes five-year depreciable property to a limited liability partnership in January, year 3. The property was purchased in January, year 1 for $20,000. Its value at the date of contribution is $15,000. Its remaining tax basis is $9,600 ($20,000 original cost – $4,000 depreciation in year 1 – $6,400 depreciation in year 2). The property will be depreciated over another four years for tax purposes (remaining three-year useful life + ½ year depreciation in sixth year). Tax depreciation in the partnership's first taxable year will be $3,840 ($20,000 × 19.20%).
>
> Thus, book depreciation under Code Sec. 704(b) will be $6,000 ([3,840/9,600] × 15,000). In the partnership's second year, tax depreciation will be $2,304 ($20,000 × 11.52%). Code Sec. 704(b) book depreciation will be $3,600 ([2,304/9,600] × 15,000).

The above rule is unnecessary when the partnership uses the remedial allocations method. When that method is used, the partnership essentially ignores the ceiling rule; as a result, the use of different depreciation methods for book and tax does not provide the opportunity to avoid application of Code Sec. 704(c). Accordingly, a special rule applies for calculating book depreciation when the remedial allocation method is used. The portion of the book basis up to the tax basis is recovered in the same manner as the tax basis. The remainder of the book basis is

---

[17] Reg. § 1.704-1(b)(2)(iv)(g)(3).

recovered using any available tax method and period for newly purchased property of the type contributed or revalued.[18]

Example 7-9: [19] *A* and *B* form an equal partnership. *A* contributes property with an adjusted basis of $4,000 and a fair market value of $10,000. *B* contributes $10,000 cash. The property has four years remaining on its 10-year recovery period. Under the remedial method, the partnership's book depreciation for each of the first four years equals $1,600 [$1,000 ($4,000 tax basis divided by four years) + $600 ($6,000 excess of book value over basis divided by 10 years)]. *A* and *B* are each allocated 50% of the book depreciation under the partnership agreement. For the first four years, *B* is allocated $800 of tax depreciation and *A* is allocated the remaining $200 of tax depreciation. No remedial allocations are made because the ceiling rule does not result in a book allocation of depreciation to *B* different from the tax allocation. At the end of Year 4, the capital accounts are as follows:

	A		*B*	
	Book	*Tax*	*Book*	*Tax*
Contribution	$10,000	$4,000	$10,000	$10,000
Depreciation	(3,200)	(800)	(3,200)	(3,200)
	$6,800	*$3,200*	*$6,800*	*$6,800*

Beginning in Year 5, the ceiling rule would cause an annual disparity of $300 between *B*'s book and tax capital accounts (tax depreciation is $0, but book depreciation is $600, allocated $300 each to *A* and *B*). Consequently, under the remedial method, the partnership must make remedial allocation of $300 of ordinary deductions (with the same character as depreciation) to *B* and $300 of ordinary income to *A*. At the end of Year 10, the capital accounts are as follows:

	A		*B*	
	Book	*Tax*	*Book*	*Tax*
Balances, End of Year 4	$6,800	$3,200	$6,800	$6,800
Book Depreciation	(1,800)	0	(1,800)	0
Remedial Allocation		1,800		(1,800)
	$5,000	*$5,000*	*$5,000*	*$5,000*

Note that the "traditional method with curative allocations" and the "remedial allocation method" look deceptively similar. They are, however, different as to depreciation:

- In the "traditional method with curative allocations," the partnership must depreciate contributed property for book purposes over the same period

---

[18] Reg. § 1.704-3(d)(2). Note that this rule only applies when the partnership uses the remedial allocations method. If the partnership uses any other method under Code Sec. 704(c), it must depreciate property at the same rate for book purposes as it uses for tax purposes.

[19] Reg. § 1.704-3(d)(7), Ex. 1.

and at the same rate as it uses for tax purposes.[20] As a result, disparities between book and tax depreciation are "cured" over the remaining tax life of the property.

- In the "remedial allocation method," however, the book-tax disparity is "remedied" over the longer tax recovery period for new property.

.02 Small Disparities

A partnership may disregard the mandatory allocations under Code Sec. 704(c), or only allocate gain or loss on the disposition of the property, where the "disparity" between book and tax basis at the date of the contribution of property is "small."[21] The disparity between the book values (FMV) and adjusted bases of all properties contributed by a partner within a single taxable year of the partnership is a "small disparity" if:

- The difference between the book values and adjusted bases of all items of contributed property is not more than 15 percent of their adjusted bases; and

- The total disparity for all such properties does not exceed $20,000.

.03 Aggregation of Properties

For all purposes of Code Sec. 704(c), properties may be *aggregated* and treated as one item of property, as follows:

- All properties, except real estate that are included in the same general asset account under Code Sec. 168.

- Zero basis property other than real property.

- For partnerships that do not use a specific identification method of accounting, each item of inventory, other than securities.

- Other classes of property as published in the Internal Revenue Bulletin or permitted in a letter ruling.

- Special aggregation rules apply to securities partnerships.[22]

.04 Code Sec. 704(b) Revaluations

The regulations require that the principles of Code Sec. 704(c) be applied when partnerships revalue property under Reg. § 1.704-1(b)(2)(iv)(f).[23] Under this provision, partnerships are allowed to revalue all of their assets at fair market value upon the admission of a new partner, the liquidation of all or part of an existing partner's interest, or in connection with the grant of a partnership interest after May 5, 2004, in exchange for services to the partnership. In such cases, all partners whose Code Sec. 704(b) capital accounts are restated are treated as contributors from that point on, and future tax allocations must reflect the differences between the book and tax values of partnership assets resulting from the revaluation.

> **Example 7-10:** *A* and *B* are equal partners in the AB partnership. At January 1, the partnership had the following balance sheets:

---

[20] Reg. § 1.704-1(b)(2)(iv)(g)(3).
[21] Reg. § 1.704-3(e).

[22] Reg. § 1.704-3(e)(3).
[23] Reg. § 1.704-3(a)(6).

Assets	*Book and Tax Basis*	*FMV*
Land	$800,000	$1,000,000

Capital		
Capital, *A*	$400,000	$500,000
Capital, *B*	400,000	500,000
	$800,000	$1,000,000

At that date, the partnership admits new partner *C* as a one-third partner in exchange for a $500,000 cash contribution. To ensure that the partners' book capital accounts reflect the true sharing arrangements between the partners, the partnership elects to "book up" its sole asset (land) to its fair market value of $1,000,000 at the date of *C*'s admission.

This revaluation causes *A*'s and *B*'s book capital accounts to be increased to $500,000 each, so that the new partnership balance sheets are as follows:

Assets	*Tax Basis*	*Book Value*
Cash	$500,000	$500,000
Land	800,000	1,000,000
	$1,300,000	$1,500,000

Capital		
Capital, *A*	$500,000	$500,000
Capital, *B*	400,000	500,000
Capital, *C*	400,000	500,000
	$1,300,000	$1,500,000

For purposes of Code Sec. 704(c), the land is now treated as contributed property (contributed by partners *A* and *B* to "new" partnership ABC). Accordingly, upon a subsequent sale of the property for $1,150,000, partners *A* and *B* will each be required to recognize their $100,000 shares of the built-in gain inherent in the property before *C*'s admission to the partnership, plus their one-third shares ($50,000) of the post-admission gain.

.05 Nontaxable Dispositions

When a partnership or LLC disposes of Code Sec. 704(c) property in a nontaxable exchange (e.g., a like-kind exchange under Code Sec. 1031, contribution to a corporation under Code Sec. 351, etc.), the disposition does *not* trigger recognition of built-in gain or loss under Code Sec. 704(c) using the traditional method. Property received in the exchange, however, becomes Code Sec. 704(c) property so that any built-in gain or loss will be subject to Code Sec. 704(c) when it is subsequently sold (or otherwise disposed of). Also note that any gain or loss recognized on the exchange itself (i.e., upon receipt of boot) is subject to Code Sec. 704(c) to the extent of the built-in gain or loss inherent in the property at the date of the exchange.[24]

Example 7-11: A transfers property with a tax basis of $60,000 to the AB Partnership. At the date of the contribution, the FMV of the property is $100,000. B transfers $100,000 cash. The partnership agreement allocates all items of income, gain, loss or deduction equally to A and B. The partnership opts to use the traditional method to allocate gains and losses under Code Sec. 704(c). Two years later, AB exchanges the property for like-kind property with a fair market value of $100,000. No boot is received in the exchange and AB recognizes no gain. A (the contributing partner) will not recognize any gain under Code Sec. 704(c) on the exchange. The "new" property, however, will be treated as Code Sec. 704(c) property contributed by A. If the property is subsequently sold in a taxable transaction, the first $40,000 of gain recognized must be allocated entirely to A under Code Sec. 704(c).

Example 7-12: Assume the same facts as in Example 7-11, except that AB exchanged the property contributed by A for like-kind property worth $80,000, and $20,000 cash. Under Code Sec. 1031, AB must recognize a $20,000 gain for tax purposes on the exchange (because it received $20,000 boot), and will take a $60,000 basis in the like-kind property received (the same as it had in the property originally contributed by A). Under Code Sec. 704(b), the partnership would not recognize any book gain on the exchange because the original property's book value was equal to its fair market value. The book value of the replacement property would be $80,000 ($100,000 book value of original property less $20,000 cash received in exchange).

This $20,000 taxable gain is allocable entirely to A under to Code Sec. 704(c). Moreover, the like-kind property received is again treated as Code Sec. 704(c) property, but the built-in gain in such property is reduced to $20,000 (FMV of $80,000 less $60,000 basis). Thus, a subsequent sale of the substitute property for $110,000 would result in a $50,000 gain to AB, of which $35,000 would be allocated to A (first $20,000 plus half of remaining $30,000) and $15,000 to B.

---

[24] Reg. § 1.704-3(a)(8).

Chapter 8

Other Limitations on Partnership Allocations

¶ 801   Allocation of Partnership Income and Loss on Transfer or Change in a Partner's Interest in the Partnership

¶ 802   Allocations in Family Partnerships—Code Sec. 704(e)

¶ 803   Depreciation Recapture

¶ 804   Credits

¶ 805   Income Allocation Recharacterized as Payment for Capital Expenditure

---

¶ 801 Allocation of Partnership Income and Loss on Transfer or Change in a Partner's Interest in the Partnership

.01 General

On the transfer of a partnership interest, it is necessary to allocate partnership profit or loss between the transferor partner and the transferee partner. In addition, if a new partner is admitted to the partnership or a partner's interest is increased, reduced or liquidated, it is necessary to allocate the partnership's income by taking into account the partners' varying interests in the partnership during the year. Generally, the taxable year of the partnership as a whole does not close on the transfer of a partner's interest.[1] Nor does the taxable year of the partnership *as a whole* close upon the admission of a new partner, departure of a partner, or change in a partner's interest in the partnership.[2] However, the partnership tax year does close with respect to a partner who terminates his or her entire partnership interest by transfer, death or liquidating distribution.[3] In such cases, the partnership's tax year closes with respect to the departing partner on the date of sale, death or liquidating distribution, and the departing partner's distributive share of partnership income or loss for the short period ending on the disposition date is included in his or her tax return for the taxable year that includes the date of sale.

Ordinarily, this requirement results in the departing partner including a partial year share of the partnership's taxable income in his or her tax return for the year of sale. Where the partnership does not use the calendar year for tax purposes, this

---

[1] Code Sec. 706(c)(1). This is true even though the transfer results in the partnership's technical dissolution under the *nontax* rules of most jurisdictions.

[2] Code Sec. 706(c)(1).

[3] Code Sec. 706(c)(2)(A).

¶801.01

can accelerate the recognition of income by the departing partner into the tax year ending before the partnership's tax year ends. For example, assume a calendar year partner who has an interest in a partnership with a July year end. If the partner sells his partnership interest in December of Year 1, he will have to report a share of his income for the partnership tax year ending July, Year 2. Had he waited to sell his interest until January of Year 2, he could defer recognition of this income for an additional year.

Note that not only does the above rule have the potential to accelerate the recognition by the partner of income, it can also result in the partner having to report more than a year's share of partnership income in a single tax year. Consider the above example in which a calendar year partner sells his or her interest in a partnership with a July year end. Assume, however, that the partner waits until December of Year 2 to sell his partnership interest, rather than selling in December of Year 1. For calendar year 2, the partner will report his share of the partnership's income for the period ending in July, Year 2, *plus* his share of the partnership's income for the five months from August through December. Thus, in this case, the partner will be required to report as many as 17 months of partnership income on his tax return for the year of sale.

If a partner transfers less than his or her entire interest in a partnership or the interest is partially liquidated, the partnership year does *not* close with respect to the selling partner; the selling partner's distributive share of partnership income is includible in his or her taxable year, within which ends the normal partnership year-end. However, the partner is allowed to increase the tax basis of the portion of the interest sold by the appropriate share of partnership income through the date of the sale or partial liquidation.

> **Example 8-1:** *J* was a thirty percent partner in JDR Partners until July 1, when she sold half her interest in the partnership to *Q*. Her tax basis in the partnership interest at the beginning of the year was $10,000. The partnership reported net taxable income for the year of sale of $30,000. Both *J* and the partnership use the calendar year for tax purposes. *J*'s share of the partnership's income for the entire year will be $6,750, computed as follows:
>
> | | |
> |---|---:|
> | Partnership income, January 1–July 1 | $15,000 |
> | *J*'s share (30%) | 4,500 |
> | Partnership income, July 1–December 31 | $15,000 |
> | *J*'s share (15%) | 2,250 |
> | *J*'s total share of partnership income ($4,500 + $2,250) | $6,750 |

J's tax basis in her partnership interest as of July 1 will be $14,500 (beginning basis of $10,000 plus $4,500 share of partnership income through July 1). Her basis in the portion of the interest she sold (50%) will therefore be $7,250.

As illustrated in Example 8-1, the partner must adjust the tax basis of that portion of the interest that is transferred to reflect his or her share of the

¶801.01

partnership's profit or loss up to the date of sale.[4] Even though the income attributable to the portion of the partnership interest transferred is includible in the partner's income at the same time as the income attributable to the retained portion, any gain or loss on the transfer is determined by adding it to the basis of the portion of the partnership interest that is transferred.

A transferring partner's distributive share of partnership income, gain, loss, deduction, and credit is determined by taking into account his or her "varying interest" in the partnership during the year of the sale. The regulations afford the partners a measure of flexibility in making this determination by providing two methods of allocation.[5] The first method provides for an "interim closing" of the partnership books whenever the partners' interests change, whereas the second (which requires "agreement among the partners") provides for the proration of partnership income, gain, loss, deduction, and credit over the entire taxable year of the partnership.[6] In addition, if the partnership liquidates a partner's interest, or if there is a change in a partner's share of partnership profits and losses during the year as a result of a contribution or distribution or otherwise, the partner's share of partnership profits and losses is determined by using the same two methods.[7]

> **Example 8-2:** On December 1 of Year 1, *D* buys *A*'s one-third interest in the ABC partnership. ABC is a calendar-year partnership with total expenses of $360,000 for the year, $240,000 of which were accrued prior to December 1. The remaining $120,000 of the partnership's expenses were incurred in the month of December. The partnership has total income of $360,000, which has been earned equally over the taxable year.
>
> Under the "interim closing" method of allocation, *D*'s distributive share of the partnership's expenses is $40,000 (incurred during December of Year 1 after *D* bought the partnership interest), and *D*'s share of partnership income is $10,000. Accordingly, *D* reports a ($30,000) loss from the partnership.
>
> Under the second method of allocation, *D*'s share of partnership income will be decidedly different. If the partnership chooses a prorated method of allocation, *D*'s share of partnership expenses will be $10,000 (1/3 partner × 1/12 of the year × $360,000), and his share of partnership income is also $10,000 (1/3 partner × 1/12 of the year × $360,000). Accordingly, *D* would report no income or loss from the partnership for Year 1.

Even though the buyer and seller's initial impression is that each will prefer the method of income allocation that will result in the least income, a closer analysis will reveal that the buyer is normally much more concerned with avoiding income than is the seller. For example, if the seller agrees to the method of income allocation that increases his or her share of the year's partnership income, the seller also increases basis in the partnership interest by an equal amount. This increased basis results in a decreased gain on sale of the partnership interest. The offsetting amounts occur in the seller's same taxable year. Typically the seller has

---

[4] Reg. § 1.705-1(a)(1).

[5] Reg. § 1.706-1(c).

[6] Reg. § 1.706-1(c)(2).

[7] S. Rep. No. 938, 94th Cong., 2d Sess. 98 (1976); *Richardson v. Commr.*, 76 TC 512, Dec. 37,801 (1981), aff'd CA-5, 83-1 USTC ¶ 9109, 693 F2d 1189.

¶801.01

no change in the amount of income, but will have less capital gain and more ordinary income. The net result is increased tax for the ordinary income/capital gains rate differential applied to the income shifted to him.

The buyer's increased income share also results in an increased basis for his or her partnership interest. But the buyer reports the income currently while any benefit from the increased basis in the partnership interest will most likely be realized in the distant future. The present value of the tax benefit obtained from the basis adjustment is much less than the seller's. The buyer and seller should consider an increased price that would compensate the seller for any increased tax liability coupled with adopting an income allocation method that minimizes the buyer's share.

> *Observation:* The method of allocating partnership taxable income between the buyer and seller need not be consistent with any method used to fix the price paid for the partnership interest.

.02 Special Rules Limiting Loss Allocations on Transfer or Change in a Partner's Interest

Code Sec. 706(c)(2) was amended in 1976 to make it clear that the statutory prohibition against "retroactive" allocations applies to partners who acquire interests by transfer from other partners as well as those who acquire or increase their interests by making additional contributions to the partnership.[8] Notwithstanding the 1976 amendments, the Congressional objective to prevent retroactive allocations largely went unrealized due to a number of techniques that were developed—paramount among these was the use of the closing of the books method of income allocation in tiered partnership arrangements and cash-basis partnerships.

Tiered partnership structures are created when a parent partnership owns an interest in a subsidiary partnership. Before the statute was revised, when a new partner purchased an interest in the parent partnership, the "interim closing" method of allocation was used and the buyer claimed that, since the parent partnership only realized its share of the subsidiary's income, gain, losses, and deductions on the last day of the subsidiary's taxable year, the incoming partner was entitled to a full distributive share of any losses incurred by the subsidiary. The IRS rejected this approach and took the position that the parent sustained the losses at the same time as the subsidiary partnership and that the subsidiary's losses could, accordingly, not be retroactively allocated.[9] However, Congress felt this area remained open to abuse by taxpayers. Partnerships also sought to make retroactive allocations by adopting the cash method of accounting, utilizing the interim closing-of-the-books method, and deferring the payment of deductible expenses until near the close of the partnership's taxable year.[10]

---

[8] *See* General Explanation of the Tax Reform Act of 1976 (P.L. 94-455), Staff of the Joint Committee on Taxation, 94th Cong. 2d Sess., 91-94 (1976).

[9] Rev. Rul. 77-311, 1977-2 CB 218.

[10] The legislative history of the 1976 amendments to Code Sec. 706 seems to sanction this technique. However, the committee reports on the 1984 amendments to Code Sec. 706 refer to it as an area of abuse.

With the Tax Reform Act of 1984,[11] Congress attempted to combat the above-mentioned abuses by providing, in Code Sec. 706(d), specific rules for the determination of each partner's distributive share of items of income, gain, loss, deduction, or credit of the partnership following a change in any partner's interest during the partnership's taxable year. Code Sec. 706(d)(1) provides as a general rule that each partner's distributive share of the above items is to be determined by using any method prescribed by regulations that takes into account the varying interests of the partners in the partnership during the taxable year.

This general rule is, however, subject to two exceptions specified in Code Sec. 706(d)(2) and (3). Certain "allocable cash-basis items" must be prorated over the period to which they are attributable.[12] In addition, partnerships which are partners in another partnership must consider the income of that partnership as earned *pro rata* over the taxable year.[13]

The first exception applies only to partnerships using the cash method of accounting. The "allocable cash-basis items" that must be prorated are (1) interest, (2) taxes, (3) payment for services or for the use of property, and (4) "any other item of a kind specified in regulations prescribed by the Secretary as being an item with respect to which the application of Code Sec. 706(d)(2) is appropriate to avoid significant misstatements of the income of the partners." Both the House Committee and the Senate Committee interpret significant misstatements of income as retroactive allocations to the partners. Any item within this category is to be assigned to each day in the period to which it is attributable.[14] The amounts so assigned are then apportioned among the partners in proportion to their interests in the partnership at the close of each day.[15] Both the House and the Senate Committee Reports make it clear that the determination of the period to which an expense is attributable for this purpose is to be made in accordance with "economic accrual principles." Thus, in effect, cash method partnerships are placed on the accrual method of accounting, but only for purposes of allocating income and deductions to incoming partners with respect to "allocable cash-basis items" which have been paid by the partnership. The partnership's deduction, however, is allowed only when the item is paid, even though the accrual system is used in determining which partners are entitled to that deduction.

If a payment of an allocable cash basis item is attributable to a year following the year of payment, it is assigned to the last day of the year of payment. All allocable cash-basis items that are attributable to periods before the current taxable year must be allocated entirely to the first day of the year in the case of items allocable to prior years, and entirely to the last day of the year in the case of items allocable to future periods.[16] Any portion of a *deductible* cash-basis item that is assigned in this manner to the first day of any taxable year is allocated among persons who are partners during the prior period to which the portion is attributa-

---

[11] The Tax Reform Act of 1984, P.L. 98-369.

[12] Code Sec. 706(d)(2).

[13] Code Sec. 706(d)(3).

[14] Code Sec. 706(d)(2)(A)(i).

[15] Code Sec. 706(d)(2)(A)(ii).

[16] Code Sec. 706(d)(2)(C).

ble, in accordance with their varying interests in the partnership during such prior period, rather than in accordance with their interest on the first day of the year.[17]

If, however, all or part of a deductible cash-basis item is allocated to persons who are no longer partners on the first day of the taxable year in which the items are taken into account, then such part of the item must be capitalized by the partnership and allocated to the basis of partnership assets under Code Sec. 755.[18]

Capitalized expenditures that are allocated to basis under Code Sec. 755 will presumably be treated as Code Sec. 743(b) adjustments. As such, they will reduce the new partner's shares of partnership income. The effect of the basis adjustment will depend upon whether the regulations allocate the basis adjustments solely to the buying partners or treat them as common basis adjustments.

Example 8-3: The Marrakesh Partnership is a cash-basis, calendar-year partnership in which David, Neil, and Graham are equal partners. David sells his 1/3 interest to Steven on 5/1/Y2. Revenue to the partnership is $6,000 per month, and expenses are $2,400 per month, except for (1) rent expense for the year of $12,000, paid on 2/1/Y2, (2) real estate taxes of $15,000 for the year, paid on 4/1/Y2, and (3) a long term capital gain of $24,000 from the sale of property on 1/15/Y2. Under the interim closing method David would be allocated the following income and expenses in Y2:

Revenue = $6,000 × 1/3 × 4 = $8,000

Expenses = $2,400 × 1/3 × 4 = $3,200

Rent expense = $12,000 × 4/12 × 1/3 = $1,333

Real estate taxes = $15,000 × 4/12 × 1/3 = $1,667

Long term capital gain = $24,000 × 1/3 = $8,000

If the rent expense was for the 12 months from 7/1/Y1 to 6/30/Y2, and the real estate taxes were for the period from 3/1/Y2 to 2/28/Y3, under the interim closing method David's share of the rent expense from year Y1 ($12,000 × 1/3 × 6/12 = $2,000) would be assigned to the first day of Y2, to David. In addition, David would be allocated $12,000 × 1/3 × 4/12 = $1,333 of the rent expense for the Y2 months during which he was a partner. Steven's share of the real estate taxes for year Y3 would be assigned to the last day of year Y2, and Steven's share would be $15,000 × 1/3 × 2/12 = $833. In addition, Steven would be allocated $15,000 × 1/3 × 8/12 = $3,333 for the year Y2 months in which he was a partner.

If David had sold his 1/3 interest to Steven on 1/1/Y2, David would not be a partner on the first day of the year Y2, and would not be allocated any of the rent expense from either year Y1 or year Y2. David's share of the rent expense would not be deductible, but would be added to the basis of partnership assets, presumably for the benefit of Steven.

Code Sec. 706(d)(2) denies the partnership the ability to allocate the specified deductions that were generated prior to the new partner's admittance. These rules

---

[17] Code Sec. 706(d)(2)(D)(i).

[18] Code Sec. 706(d)(2)(D)(ii).

do not prohibit the partnership from allocating a disproportionate share of deductions to the new partners if they were generated after their admission to the partnership. The application of Code Sec. 706(d)(2) to cash-method *income* items is unclear.

While the focus of both the statute and the accompanying legislative history clearly is on cash method *deductions*, the definition of "allocable cash-method items" in Code Sec. 706(d)(2)(B) includes income items as well. Code Sec. 706(d)(2)(B)(iv) includes any "item" specified by regulations and does not, by its terms, limit the regulations to deductible items. In addition, the general rule provided in Code Sec. 706(d)(1) refers to "items" as including both income and deduction.

> *Comment:* The combined expense of closing the books of the partnership and working with the allocable cash basis item rule may encourage more partnerships to use the easier method of prorating items rather than the more precise cut-off method.

If Code Sec. 706(d)(2) is applicable to income items, several questions arise. First, what is the relationship between Code Sec. 706(d)(2) and Code Sec. 751, which provides rules for dealing with shifts in the partners' interests in unrealized receivables? Second, what is a cash-method income item? As an example, does it include installment receivables under Code Secs. 453 and 453A? Third, what are the mechanical rules for assigning an "appropriate portion" of a cash-method income item to each day in the period to which it is attributable? Suppose, for example, that an accounting partnership: (1) accepts an engagement on January 1, receiving a retainer on that day; (2) performs services at various times through the remainder of the year; and (3) renders a statement for its fee (net of the retainer) on January 1 of the following year. To what days is the fee allocable? Is it necessary to account for the services rendered on a daily basis? Are the rules different if the fee eventually charged is result-oriented or is wholly contingent? If an income item is allocated to one who is no longer a partner, what adjustment is made to the partnership assets?

The requirement that partnership items must be determined and allocated to the partners on a *daily* basis can cause significant administrative burdens for partnerships if there are frequent changes in the partners' interests. In connection with the 1976 amendments,[19] the Conference Report suggests that this problem should be addressed by regulations that would allow "interim closing" on the fifteenth and last days of each month, rather than requiring daily closing.[20] Since 1976, in the absence of any new regulations under Code Sec. 706, many partnerships have used considerably more aggressive allocation techniques based on monthly or even quarterly closing. Typically, partnerships using these techniques allocate monthly or quarterly losses to the persons who are partners on the last day of the month or quarter without regard to whether they held their partnership interests for all or only a portion of the month or quarter. The validity of these techniques under the 1976 amendment is, of course, subject to serious question.

---

[19] Tax Reform Act of 1976, P.L. 94-455.   [20] H.R. Rep. No. 861, 98th Cong., 2d Sess. 858 (1984).

The Senate version of Code Sec. 706(d)(2) and (3) would have allowed partnerships to make an annual election to determine the varying interests of the partners by using a monthly convention that treats all changes in the partners' interests in the partnership during any month as occurring on the first day of the month. The Conference Committee to the Deficit Reduction Act of 1984[21] removed this provision from the statute based on its understanding that the Treasury would provide, by regulation, a monthly convention to treat partners entering after the fifteenth day of a month as entering on the first day of the following month, and partners entering during the first 15 days of a month as entering on the first day of the month. During the discussion on the floor of the Senate that preceded approval of the final version of the 1984 Act, Senator Dole, chairman of the Senate Finance Committee, stated that the mid-month convention described in the Conference Report was not intended to restrict the Treasury's discretion to provide a more flexible convention by regulations when no abuse potential is present. He then stated that regulations could provide that, in non-abusive cases, any partner admitted to a partnership during a calendar month could, for purposes of the retroactive rules, be treated as having been admitted on the first day of such month.

Code Sec. 706(d)(3) contains the Congressional response to tiered partnership arrangements aimed at effecting retroactive allocations. It provides that when a parent partnership holds an interest in a subsidiary partnership and during the taxable year there is a change in any partner's interest in the parent partnership, then, except to the extent provided by regulations, the parent partnership's share of any item of income, gain, loss, deduction, or credit of the subsidiary partnership is to be apportioned over that portion of the taxable year during which the parent partnership had an interest in the subsidiary.[22] The effect of this amendment is to place the parent partnership effectively on a consolidated basis of accounting vis-à-vis the subsidiary partnership.

.03 Retroactive Allocations Among Newly Admitted and Continuing Partners

The partnership may not allocate items of income or deduction to a partner if they arose before he or she became a member of the partnership. Code Sec. 706(c)(2) was amended in 1976[23] to make it clear that the prohibition against "retroactive" allocations applies to partners who acquire or increase their interests by contributing property to the partnership as well as those who acquire their interests by transfer from other partners.[24] The legislative history of the 1984 changes in Code Sec. 706 explicitly approves the position of the Tax Court in *Kenneth E. Lipke v. Commissioner*.[25] *Lipke* indicates that retroactive allocations (or

---

[21] P.L. 98-369.

[22] This apparently confirms the IRS's position that losses in this situation are sustained by the parent partnership at the same time they are sustained by the subsidiary partnership. *See* Rev. Rul. 77-311, 1977-2 CB 218.

[23] Tax Reform Act of 1976, P.L. 94-455.

[24] A detailed discussion of allocating income between the new and continuing partners may be found at ¶ 905.

[25] *K.E. Lipke v. Commr.*, 81 TC 689, Dec. 40,528 (1983). *See* General Explanation of the Tax Reform Act of 1976

(P.L. 94-455), Staff of the Joint Committee on Taxation, 94th Cong., 2d Sess., 91-94. Code Sec. 761(c) defines a "partnership agreement" to include any modifications made prior to the due date for filing the partnership return and, under Code Sec. 704(a), a partner's distributive share is determined by the partnership agreement. On the surface, it appears that retroactive allocations to partners who increase or decrease their interest in the partnership's results through contributions or distributions may be possible through an amendment to the agreement. This result was not intended (*see also* Code

reallocations) of partnership income or loss among contemporaneous partners are permissible,[26] provided they are not related to the infusion of new capital into the partnership.[27] This is good news for legal, accounting, and other service partnerships, many of which traditionally have allocated their income after the end of their tax year.

¶ 802 Allocations in Family Partnerships—Code Sec. 704(e)

.01 Allocations Within the Family

Originally, "family" partnerships were an important means of diverting income from parents to their children.[28] In the past they engendered the largest portion of the litigation relating to the taxation of partnerships. The income tax incentive to use a family limited partnership to divert income to family members with lower marginal tax rates has diminished since the enactment of Code Sec. 704(e). In addition to Code Sec. 704(e), there are two major reasons for this change. First, effective in 1987, the tax on unearned income of a child under age 14 is computed at the parent's marginal tax rate.[29] Indeed, the statute allows the parent an election to claim the child's unearned income on the parent's tax return.[30] For purposes of taxing the unearned income of a child under 14 at the parent's highest tax rates, earned income includes wages, salaries, and other compensation for personal services. Therefore, unless the child renders services to or on behalf of the partnership, all the child's distributive share of partnership income will be unearned income.

Second, in prior years, family members could have a wide variation in their highest marginal tax rates. Historically, maximum individual income tax rates have reached as high as 94 percent. Currently the highest bracket is less than half that amount and the tax rates for individuals reach 28 percent at a relatively low level of income. In addition, if a trust holds the partnership interest, the trust is taxed at the highest individual rate on taxable income in excess of a negligible amount.

.02 Principles Underlying Code Sec. 704(e)

Code Sec. 704(e) provides a statutory rule for partnerships which follows two well-established principles of tax law:

1. that income derived from property is to be taxed to the owner of the property,[31] and

---

(Footnote Continued)

Sec. 761(f)), but the legislative history of the Deficit Reduction Act of 1984 (P.L. 98-369) makes it clear that Code Sec. 761(c) still permits retroactive modifications to the partnership agreement that result in shifts of interests among the partners who are members for the entire taxable year, provided those shifts are not attributable to additional capital contributions. See General Explanation of the Revenue Provisions of the Deficit Reduction Act of 1984 (P.L. 98-369), Joint Committee on Taxation, 98th Cong., 2d Sess., 219.

[26] Under Code Secs. 706 and 761.

[27] See Rev. Rul. 77-310, 1977-2 CB 217.

[28] Prior to 1948, in which year income-splitting was authorized for all spouses, family partnerships were uti-

lized primarily to divert income from one spouse to another. Act §301 of the Revenue Act of 1948 (P.L. 471), providing for income-splitting between spouses, obviated the necessity for this device.

[29] Code Sec. 1(g).

[30] Code Sec. 1(g)(7).

[31] E.T. Blair v. Commr., SCt, 37-1 USTC ¶ 9083, 300 US 5, 57 SCt 330. Compare cases dealing with the assignment of merely the income derived from property, C.H. Harrison v. S.H. Schaffner, SCt, 41-1 USTC ¶ 9355, 312 US 579, 61 SCt 759, and G.T. Helvering v. P.R.G. Horst, SCt, 40-2 USTC ¶ 9787, 311 US 112, 61 SCt 144. Compare cases where the donor or property retained control over the income therefrom, Commr. v. J. Sunnen, SCt, 48-1

2. that income derived from services is to be taxed to the person performing the services.[32]

The family-partnership provisions of Code Sec. 704(e) are virtually the same as the amendments to the 1939 Code enacted in 1951 in order to assure that a bona fide owner of a capital interest in a family partnership in which capital is an income-producing factor will be respected as such.[33] They state that a person shall be recognized as a partner for income tax purposes "if he owns a capital interest in a partnership for which capital is a material income-producing factor, whether or not such interest was derived by purchase or gift from any other person."[34] In addition, they state that in a partnership in which capital is a material income-producing factor, a donee partner's distributive share of income under the partnership agreement shall be taxed to him or her except to the extent that such share is determined without allowance of reasonable compensation to the donor for his or her services to the partnership, and, to the extent that such share is attributable to donated capital, it is proportionately greater than the donor's share attributable to his or her capital.[35] For the purpose of these allocation provisions, an interest purchased from a member of the family is treated as a donated interest.[36]

Where capital is a material income-producing factor, the partnership's income must, as mentioned, include a reasonable payment to the donor as compensation for any services rendered for or on behalf of the partnership. When the donor is a

---

(Footnote Continued)

USTC ¶ 9230, 333 US 591, 68 SCt 715, or the property itself *G.T. Helvering v. G.B. Clifford, Jr.*, SCt, 40-1 USTC ¶ 9265, 309 US 331, 60 SCt 554.

[32] *G.T. Helvering v. G.A. Eubank*, SCt, 40-2 USTC ¶ 9788, 311 US 122, 61 SCt 149, rehearing denied, 312 US 713 (1941); *R.H. Lucas v. G.C. Earl*, SCt, 2 USTC ¶ 496, 281 US 111, 50 SCt 241 (1930).

[33] The Revenue Act of 1951 (P.L. 183); Code Sec. 340; S. Rep. No. 1622, 83d Cong., 2d Sess. 384 (1954). In *Commr. v. W.O. Culbertson, Sr.*, SCt, 49-1 USTC ¶ 9323, 337 US 733, 69 SCt 1210, the Supreme Court reaffirmed the principle that income derived from property is taxable to the real owner of the property, and held therefore that a donee of property who invests it in a family partnership and exercises real control over the property and the disposition of the income derived therefrom can qualify as a true partner. However, some later lower court decisions, *see, e.g.*, *H. Feldman v. Commr.*, 14 TC 17, Dec. 17,425 (1950), aff'd, CA-4, 50-1 USTC ¶ 9122, 186 F2d 87; *W.S. Barrett v. Commr.*, 13 TC 539, Dec.17,231 (1949), aff'd, CA-1, 50-2 USTC ¶ 9501, 185 F2d 150, continue to hold that a wife would be recognized as a valid partner in her husband's enterprise only if she invested "capital originating with her" (*see, e.g.*, *G. Graber v. Commr.*, CA-10, 48-2 USTC ¶ 9409, 171 F2d 32, 35; *C.L. Canfield v. Commr.*, CA-6, 48-2 USTC ¶ 9337, 168 F2d 907, 913; *cf. F. Smith v. L. Henslee*, CA-6, 49-1 USTC ¶ 9216, 173 F2d 284), or performed "vital additional services" (*see, e.g.*, *S. Friedman v. Commr.*, 10 TC 1145, Dec. 16,461 (1948); *W.E. Grace v. Commr.*, 10 TC 1, Dec. 16,203 (1948)), although the opinion in the *Culbertson* case said that the Court's earlier opinions in *Commr. v. F.E. Tower*, SCt, 46-1 USTC ¶ 9189, 327 US 280, and *A.L. Lusthaus v. Commr.*, SCt, 46-1 USTC ¶ 9190, 327 US 293, on which the lower courts were relying, were being misinterpreted.

[34] Code Sec. 704(e)(1). The donee partner may be a corporation, all of whose stock is owned by the donor. *C. Turner v. Commr.*, 24 TCM 544, Dec. 27,344(M), TC Memo. 1965-101 (1965), appeal dismissed (CA-9, 1965); compare *L.F. Noonan v. U.S.*, CA-9, 71-2 USTC ¶ 9756, 451 F2d 992, aff'g per curiam 52 TC 907, Dec.29,725 (1969) ("shell" corporation disregarded, and its share of partnership income attributed to sole shareholder). For tax purposes, such a corporation may be treated as a donee partner even if, in form, it is the assignee of the donor's entire interest in the partnership, but is not substituted in his or her place as a partner and is not considered to be a partner under local law. *D.L. Evans v. Commr.*, 50 TC 40, Dec. 29,915 (1970), aff'd, CA-7, 71-2 USTC ¶ 9597, 447 F2d 547.

[35] Code Sec. 704(e)(2).

[36] Code Sec. 704(e)(3). The Internal Revenue Code limits "family" for this purpose to only a spouse, ancestors, lineal descendants, and trusts for the primary benefit of such persons. *G.A. Paul v. Commr.*, 16 TCM 752, Dec. 22,560(M), TC Memo. 1957-170. Note, however, that this limitation applies only to bona fide purchases, and that the allocation rules will apply to the purported purchase of a partnership interest by an individual only *collaterally related* to the seller (or unrelated) if the transfer has "any of the substantial characteristics of a gift." Reg. § 1.704-1(e)(3)(ii)(*b*). If the purchase does not have "the usual characteristics of an arm's-length transaction," it will be bona fide only if it is "genuinely intended to promote the success of the business by security participation of the purchaser in the business or by adding his or her credit to that of the other participants." Reg. § 1.704-1(e)(4)(ii).

¶802.02

partner, the payment is characterized as a Code Sec. 707(a) or 707(c) payment, depending upon the criteria discussed in Chapter 14. If the donor is not a partner, it is not clear whether Code Sec. 704(e) applies. A literal interpretation of the statute implies that the donor must be paid reasonable compensation whether or not the donor remains a partner. If Code Sec. 704(e) does apply to a donor partner who is no longer a partner, the payment is treated as made to an unrelated employee or independent contractor. After the donor's reasonable compensation is taken into account, the partnership is free to allocate its remaining income in any manner it sees fit, subject to one exception. Based upon relative capital accounts, the donee's share of the partnership's income cannot exceed the donor's share. For this purpose, payments to the donee for services are not considered a share of income.[37] As a result, disproportionate distributions will not necessarily be considered a prime factor in determining whether a donee is a partner, but only in determining the extent to which the reallocation of income through the partnership will be recognized for income tax purposes. However, when an incoming donee partner is allocated a disproportionate share of the partnership's income, that part of his or her distributive share which is disproportionate will remain taxable to the donor.[38] What constitutes reasonable compensation paid to the donee is a facts and circumstances question.[39]

Despite the existence of these provisions, the questions of whether, in a particular case, "capital is a material income-producing factor" and whether the services of the donor have been reasonably compensated[40] still can create considerable uncertainty.

> **S Corporation Observation:** Like the family partnership rules of Code Sec. 704(e), Code Sec. 1366(e) permits the IRS to reallocate S corporation income among members of a "family"[41] if one or more of the S corporation's shareholders renders services or furnishes capital without receiving reasonable compensation in exchange for the services or capital. The significant difference between the Subchapter S family reallocation rule and the Sub-

---

[37] Reg. § 1.704-1(e)(3)(i)(b).

[38] *Bayou Verret Land Co. v. Commr.*, CA-5, 71-2 USTC ¶ 9713, 450 F2d 850, aff'g, rem'g and rev'g 52 TC 791, Dec. 29,744 (1969), Acq. (result only, as to a different issue).

[39] *See* Code Sec. 704(e)(2); Reg. § 1.704-1(e)(3)(i)(c). Under prior law, the IRS had contended that it could reallocate income in proportion to capital invested and services rendered. I.T. 3845, 1947-1 CB 66 (declared obsolete, Rev. Rul. 69-43, 1969-1 CB 310); *see also* Mim. 6767, 1952-1 CB 111 (declared obsolete, Rev. Rul. 69-31, 1969-1 CB 307). The courts, however, generally disagreed. *W.B. Woosley v. Commr*, CA-6, 48-1 USTC ¶ 9292, 168 F2d 330; *C.L. Canfield v. Commr.*, CA-6, 48-2 USTC ¶ 9337, 168 F2d 907; *R. Adams v. M.H. Allen*, DC Ga., 51-1 USTC ¶ 9300; *M.E. Trapp v. H.C. Jones*, DC Okla., 50-1 USTC ¶ 9101, 87 FSupp 415, aff'd on this point, CA-10, 51-1 USTC ¶ 9116, 186 F2d 951; *N.B. Drew v. Commr.*, 12 TC 5, Dec. 16,757 (1949), Acq., but cf. *D.L. Jennings v. Commr.*, 10 TC 505, Dec. 16,309 (1948), Acq.; *M. German v. Commr* 2 TC 474, Dec. 13,378 (1943), Acq. The Committee Report to the Revenue Act of 1951 (P.L.

183) states that after making "a reasonable allowance . . . for the services rendered by the partners . . . the balance of the income will be allocated according to the amount of capital which the several partners have invested." H.R. Rep. No. 586, 82d Cong., 1st Sess., 34 (1951). If the standards for determining reasonable compensation for members of a family partnership resemble those applied to stockholder-employees of corporations, considerable partnership income that is actually attributable to personal services, but which is in excess of "reasonable compensation for services," may be deflected to the donee. The Internal Revenue Code also provides that a partner's distributive share of partnership earnings need not be diminished merely because of his or her absence due to military service. Code Sec. 704(e)(2).

[40] *W.L. Peterson v. W.M. Gray*, DC Ky., 59-2 USTC ¶ 9692.

[41] The term "family" is defined by reference to Code Sec. 704(e)(3), which provides that the family of any individual includes "only his spouse, ancestors, and lineal descendants, and any trusts for the primary benefit of such persons."

chapter K family reallocation rule is that the Subchapter S reallocation rule can apply to an undercompensated family member who does not have an ownership interest in the S corporation and who did not transfer any ownership interest to a family member.[42] The reallocation rule of Code Sec. 1366(e) was intended to prevent family members from shifting income among themselves to minimize tax liability.

> **Example 8-4:** Picture Palace, an S corporation, has two equal shareholders, Leopold and Catalina, who are brother and sister. Their father, Fred, renders services to the corporation. In an attempt to shift income to Leopold and Catalina, Fred renders services to the corporation and is paid less than the reasonable value of the services. Under Code Sec. 1366(e), the IRS can apparently increase Fred's gross income to reflect the additional compensation Fred should have received from the corporation and can apparently increase the compensation deductions to Leopold and Catalina, decreasing their income.

If one family member is undercompensated for capital provided to an S corporation, Code Sec. 1366(e)(3) permits the IRS to reallocate items of income. Apparently, Code Sec. 1366(e) permits the IRS to reallocate income in a situation in which a parent provides capital to the corporation but does not receive a sufficient amount of stock in exchange for the property. In those same circumstances, the regulations under the gift tax provisions provide that the parent is treated as making a gift and is potentially liable for gift tax.[43]

.03 Capital as a Material Income-Producing Factor

The regulations state that capital is a material income-producing factor if a substantial portion of the gross income of the business is attributable to capital. Ordinarily, this will be deemed to be the case if the business requires substantial inventories or substantial investment in plant, machinery, or equipment.[44]

The Tax Court, in a case involving the analogous requirements of former Code Sec. 1361, stated that "[c]apital will be deemed to be a material income-producing factor when it 'gives character to a sizable portion of the operations . . .' but if capital is utilized merely in the form of salaries, wages, or office rent it is not a material income-producing factor."[45]

A majority of the Tax Court, with eleven Judges disagreeing, held that capital was not a material income producing factor for purposes of Code Sec. 704(e)(1) in a family limited partnership which borrowed substantial sums necessary for its

---

[42] Code Secs. 704(e) and 1366(e).

[43] *See* Reg. § 25.2511-1(h)(1). Read literally, Code Sec. 1366(e) and the gift-tax regulations may mean that a shareholder who contributes excess capital to an S corporation could have both gift-tax liability and an additional share of income allocated to him. This result seems anomalous. If the gift-tax rules apply, it simply means that a shareholder transferred a share of the contributed property or a share of stock to another family member. Viewed in this manner, the contributions of the shareholders would be proportionate and not trigger application of Code Sec. 1366(e). Alternatively, since the

shareholder providing services is not being adequately compensated, expect the IRS to argue that he or she is subject to income tax as if adequate compensation were received *and* gift tax as if it were subsequently transferred to the other "donee" shareholder(s).

[44] Reg. § 1.704-1(e)(1)(iv). Compare Reg. § 1.1361-2(e)(2); *S.H. Hartman*, 43 TC 105, Dec. 27,022 (1964).

[45] *Fred J. Sperapani*, 42 TC 308, 334 (1964), appeal dismissed (CA-4, 1965); cf. *Payton v. United States*, CA-5, 425 F2d 1324, cert. denied, 400 US 957 (1970).

business of constructing homes.[46] The borrowings were secured by personal guarantees of the family head who, although not directly a partner, was president and principal stockholder of the sole corporate general partner. The Court majority, in attempting to distinguish "borrowed" capital from capital contributed directly to the partnership by its partners, was obviously straining to disallow a purported allocation of 90 percent of the partnership's profits to five limited partner family trusts created with nominal cash contributions. This decision is questionable and a more reasonable alternative on the facts would have been either to disregard the partnership as a sham, as suggested by the concurring Judges, or to have allocated partnership profits in proportion to capital contributions after allocating all borrowed capital to the corporate general partners, as suggested by the dissenting Judges.

A capital investment by a donee partner is not in itself sufficient to validate a family partnership where the investment is unnecessary to the business of the partnership.[47]

.04 Donor's Reasonable Compensation

In determining reasonable compensation, the regulations indicate that among other factors to be considered are the degree of managerial responsibility of each partner, the cost ordinarily necessitated in securing comparable services from a person with no capital interest in the partnership, and, in the case of limited partnerships, the risk to which a general partner's credit is subject.[48]

.05 Donee's Status as the Owner of the Partnership Interest

The Commissioner is still free to question the "reality" of the donee's ownership of his or her interest in the partnership.[49] Where such ownership is derived from a gift, the regulations provide that the execution of legally sufficient deeds under state law is a factor to be taken into account, but is not determinative.[50] The Tax Court has interpreted this to mean that unless there has been compliance with all state law formalities required to evidence a completed gift, no valid gift of a capital interest in the partnership has been consummated for tax purposes.[51] In addition, the donee must be granted an interest in the partnership capital as such,

---

[46] *Carriage Square, Inc. v. Commr.*, 69 TC 119, Dec. 34,710 (1977).

[47] *A. Pogetto v. United States*, CA-9, 62-2 USTC ¶ 9660, 306 F2d 76; *U.S. v. J.R. Ramos*, CA-9, 68-1 USTC ¶ 9337, 393 F2d 618, cert. denied, 393 US 983, 89 SCt 454 (1968); *M.W. Grober v. Commr.*, 31 TCM 1179, Dec. 31,623(M), TC Memo. 1972-240 (nominal capital contributions from donees; 99% of required capital borrowed from corporation controlled by donor). Cf. the present provisions relating to earned income from foreign sources (Code Sec. 911(b)), which were derived from Code Sec. 116(a)(3) of the 1939 Code. *See Graham Flying Service v. Commr.*, 8 TC 557, Dec. 15,674 (1947), aff'd, CA-8, 48-1 USTC ¶ 5921, 167 F2d 91, cert. denied, 335 US 817, 69 SCt 38 (1948); *Gus Grissman Co., Inc. v. Commr.*, 10 TC 499, Dec. 16,308 (1948); *Fairfax Mutual Wood Products Co. v. Commr.*, 5 TC 1279, Dec. 14,881 (1945), Acq.; *L.L. Tweedy v. Commr.*, 47 BTA 341, Dec. 12,588 (1942), appeal dismissed (CA-2, 1945); *I. Garnets v. Commr.*, 26 BTA 384, Dec. 7624 (1932); Mim. 3802, 1930-1 CB 121. Compare

the rulings issued under Section 209 of the Revenue Act of 1917 (P.L. 50) and subsequent similar provisions relating to businesses with no more than nominal capital. *See also* ¶ 1902.01.

[48] Reg. § 1.704-1(e)(3)(i)(c) and (ii)(c).

[49] H.R. Rep. No. 586, 82d Cong., 1st Sess., 331 (1951); *Bayou Verret Land Co v. Commr.*, CA-5, 71-2 USTC ¶ 9713, 450 F2d 850; *J.D. Ballou v. U.S.*, CA-6, 67-1 USTC ¶ 9141, 370 F2d 659, cert. denied, 338 US 911, 87 SCt 2114 (1967); *F. Occhipinti v. Commr.*, 28 TCM 968, Dec. 29,746(M), TC Memo. 1969-190; cf. *M.J. Spiesman, Jr. v. Commr.*, 28 TC 567, Dec. 22,411 (1957), aff'd, CA-9, 58-2 USTC ¶ 411, 260 F2d 940.

[50] Reg. § 1.704-1(e)(2); *see Driscoll v. U.S.*, DC Cal., 69-2 USTC ¶ 9536.

[51] *L.A. Woodbury v. Commr.*, 49 TC 180, Dec. 28,696 (1967); cf. *L.E. Tennyson, Jr. v. U.S.*, DC Ark., 76-1 USTC ¶ 9597 (gift not complete until satisfaction of conditions precedent).

including accretions thereto, which interest must be distributable to him or her upon withdrawal or upon dissolution or liquidation of the partnership.[52] An assignment of the economic rights to a partnership interest should be recognized as a transfer of a partnership interest for purposes of Code Sec. 704(e)(1).[53] The regulations define a "capital interest in a partnership" as "an interest in the assets of the partnership, which is distributable to the owner of the capital interest upon his or her withdrawal from the partnership or upon liquidation of the partnership.[54]

As a result of the Commissioner's right to question the "reality" of the donee's ownership of his or her interest in the partnership, many of the issues involved in pre-1951 cases continue.[55] For example, where the donor retains substantial incidents of ownership, he or she may continue to be recognized as the true owner of the interest purportedly transferred.[56] In this respect, however, the Committee Report on the Revenue Act of 1951[57] states that a distinction should be made between retained powers vested in the donor for his or her own benefit and those exercisable for the benefit of others. The retention of substantial powers by the donor "as a managing partner or in any other fiduciary capacity" will not, according to the Committee, necessarily taint the gift as a sham transaction.[58]

The regulations[59] indicate continued suspicion of family partnerships, particularly those which include minor children.[60] Unless it can be shown that a minor child is competent to manage his or her own property and participate in partnership activities,[61] the child's interest in any family partnership will be recognized only if it is controlled for his or her sole benefit by a judicially supervised fiduciary[62] or is

---

[52] Reg. § 1.704-1(e)(1)(v). If these requirements are satisfied, the assignee of a partner's entire interest in a partnership will be treated for these purposes as a donee partner, even though such assignee is not a substituted partner for purposes of local law. *Evans v. Commr.*, 50 TC 40, Dec. 29,915 (1970), aff'd, CA-7, 71-2 USTC ¶ 9597, 447 F2d 547.

[53] *Evans v. Commr.*, 71-2 USTC ¶ 9597, 447 F2d 547.

[54] Reg. § 1.704-1(e)(1)(v).

[55] Among the previous sources of litigation eliminated by the Internal Revenue Code of 1954 (P.L. 591) were the presence or absence of a business purpose or a tax-avoidance motive. *See, e.g., E.A. Ardolina v. Commr.*, CA-3, 51-1 USTC ¶ 9133, 186 F2d 176 (prior law); *J. Maiatico v. Commr.*, CA-DC, 50-1 USTC ¶ 9343, 183 F2d 836; *S.H. Miller v. Commr.*, CA-6, 50-1 USTC ¶ 9327, 183 F2d 246; *A. Slifka v. Commr.*, CA-2, 50-1 USTC ¶ 9314, 182 F2d 345. *But see* Reg. § 1.704-1(e)(2)(x) (". . . the presence or absence of a tax-avoidance motive is one of many factors to be considered in determining the reality of the ownership of a capital interest acquired by gift"); *J.T. Finlen v. F.J. Healy*, DC Mont., 60-2 USTC ¶ 9688, 187 FSupp 434.

[56] *G.T. Helvering v. G.B. Clifford, Jr.*, SCt, 40-1 USTC ¶ 9265, 309 US 331, 60 SCt 554; *R.G. Hornback v. U.S.*, DC Mo., 69-1 USTC ¶ 9377, 298 FSupp 977. Prior to the Revenue Act of 1951 (P.L. 183), and subsequent to the *Culbertson* (49-1 USTC ¶ 9323) decision, most family-partnership litigation was directed toward determining the reality of the parties' intention to participate in a joint

enterprise. In making this determination, some courts considered the question of "control" over donated capital, and the use to which the partnership income was put. *See, e.g., W.M. Lamb v. F.R. Smith*, CA-3, 50-2 USTC ¶ 9418, 183 F2d 938; *T.M. Stanback v. C.H. Robertson*, CA-4, 50-2 USTC ¶ 9414, 183 F2d 889, cert. denied, 340 US 904, 71 SCt 280. Under the Internal Revenue Code, these factors continue to be of major importance.

[57] P.L. 183.

[58] H.R. Rep. No. 586, 82d Cong., 1st Sess., 33 (1951). The regulations caution, however, that retention of management powers "inconsistent with normal relationships among partners" will negate the reality of any purported gift. Reg. § 1.704-1(e)(2)(ii)(d).

[59] Reg. § 1.704-1(e).

[60] "The use of the child's property or income for support for which a parent is legally responsible will be considered use for the parent's benefit." Reg. § 1.704-1(e)(2)(viii); *C.T. Olson v. U.S.*, DC Cal., 67-1 USTC ¶ 9239, appeal dismissed (CA-9, 1967). Where the wife is the donor of the interest, note Reg. § 1.704-1(e)(3)(ii)(a), Ex. 2.

[61] *J.T. Finlen v. F.J. Healy*, DC Mont., 60-2 USTC ¶ 9688, 187 FSupp 434.

[62] Judicial supervision "includes filing of such accounts and reports as are required by law." Reg. § 1.704-1(e)(2)(viii); *A. Pflugradt v. U.S.*, CA-7, 63-1 USTC ¶ 9112, 310 F2d 412; *M.J. Spiesman, Jr.*, 28 TC 567, Dec. 22,411 (1957), aff'd, CA-9, 58-2 USTC ¶ 9890, 260 F2d 940.

placed in trust. An independent trustee is ordinarily recognized as the true owner of the partnership interest.[63]

The regulations state that if a trustee is made a partner, the trustee-partner will ordinarily be recognized as the owner of the partnership interest which he or she holds for the trust, provided that the trustee-partner is unrelated to and independent of the grantor, participates as a partner and receives distribution of the income distributable to the trust, and that the grantor retains no controls inconsistent with such ownership.[64]

If the trustee is the donor or a person amenable to his or her will, the regulations add scrutiny. The trustee must demonstrate that he or she is acting in the donee's best interest, the trust is visibly part of the partnership's activities, and there is no excess retention of profits.[65] Where the grantor or a person "amenable to his or her will" is trustee, special scrutiny of the trustee's responsibilities as a fiduciary and of his or her activities will follow, with particular attention to whether the trust is recognized as a partner in business dealings and to the use of the trust income for the sole benefit of the trust beneficiaries.[66] Exculpatory clauses for the trustee are frowned upon.[67] In this context, both the extent of the trustee's powers under the terms of the trust instruments and the actual pattern of exercise of these powers by the trustee pursuant to such instruments are relevant.[68]

The donee's right to sell or liquidate his or her interest without financial penalty is another factor relating to "real ownership" which is given considerable emphasis in the regulations.[69] Any restriction on such rights of the donee will be considered by the Treasury as a particularly significant factor indicative of the donor's real ownership and control. This factor is especially troublesome if either the donee is a limited partner[70] or the donor of a general partnership interest has otherwise retained control of business management.[71]

> ***LLC Observation:*** In the context of an LLC, for purposes of Code Sec. 704(e), a donee non-manager member's ownership of the interest will probably

---

[63] Reg. § 1.704-1(e)(2).

[64] Reg. § 1.704-1(e)(2)(vii). *See J. Smith,* 32 TC 1261, Dec. 23,764 (1959), Acq.; *S.H. Hartman v. Commr,* 43 TC 105, Dec. 27,022 (1964); cf. *J.D. Ballou v. U.S.,* CA-6, 67-1 USTC ¶ 9141, 370 F2d 659, cert. denied, 338 US 911, 87 SCt 2114 (1967); *Carriage Square, Inc. v. Commr.,* 69 TC 119, Dec. 34,710(1977).

[65] Reg. § 1.704-1(e)(2)(vii).

[66] *Id.; M. Kuney, Jr. v. W.E. Frank,* CA-9, 62-2 USTC ¶ 9769, 308 F2d 719; *H.S. Reddig,* 30 TC 1382, Dec. 23,195 (1958), appeal dismissed (CA-6, 1960); *A.K. Krause v. Commr.,* 57 TC 890, Dec. 31,322 (1972), aff'd, CA-6, 74-1 USTC ¶ 9470, 497 F2d 1109.

[67] *See Mim.* 6767,1952-1 CB 111 (declared obsolete, Rev. Rul. 69-31, 1969-1 CB 307).

[68] Compare *M.J. Kuney, Jr. v. U.S.,* CA-9, 71-2 USTC ¶ 9646, 448 F2d 22, on remand, DC Wash., 72-1 USTC ¶ 9385, with *M.J. Kuney, Jr. v. W.E. Frank,* CA-9, 62-2 USTC ¶ 9769, 308 F2d 719. In a 1971 decision, the Ninth Circuit held that a taxpayer should be given an opportunity to show that changes in subsequent years (1958-1963) in prior practices (1952-54) of which the

court had been critical in its 1962 decision warranted different determination as to ultimate question of ownership of corpus for tax purposes, despite absence of any amendments to trust instruments limiting powers vested in trustee thereunder; a difference in facts as shown by record thus necessitated remand. On remand, the District Court found that the trustee had not properly acted in a fiduciary capacity, but this finding was reversed by the Ninth Circuit on appeal. *M.J. Kuney, Jr. v. U.S.,* CA-9, 75-2 USTC ¶ 9767, 524 F2d 795.

[69] Reg. § 1.704-1(e)(2)(ii)(b).

[70] Reg. § 1.704-1(e)(2)(ix). Provisions in the partnership agreement restricting the assignability of a limited partner's interest, and permitting withdrawal of a limited partner's contribution only upon the expiration of an extended term, are not, however, unusual in normal limited partnership agreements.

[71] Reg. § 1.704-1(e)(2)(ii)(d). A donee will not be considered free to withdraw his or her interest unless he or she "is independent of the donor and has such maturity and understanding of his rights as to be capable of deciding to exercise, and capable of exercising, his right to withdraw."

¶802.05

be treated as ownership by a limited partner for purposes of Code Sec. 704(e). Therefore, the ownership may be disregarded if he or she has no right to liquidate the interest. Code Sec. 704(e) is a safe harbor. This would still leave the donor and donee free to treat the donee as a member for income tax purposes. However, the IRS is free to disagree.

Of course, if the donee actually participates substantially in formulating the management policies of the business and is otherwise actively engaged in the venture, the evidence of the donee's ownership is greatly strengthened.[72] Actual distribution to the donee of all or most of his or her distributive share of the partnership's income coupled with independent control of the use and enjoyment of such funds is also strong evidence of the donee's real ownership.[73]

.06 Purchasing Family Member's Status as a Partner

The regulations provide that where a partnership interest has been acquired by purchase from a family member, or by or through a loan from such a person, the purchase will be recognized as bona fide if:

- The terms of the purchase are similar to those that would be expected in an arm's length transaction; or

- The purchase is genuinely intended to promote the success of the partnership business.[74]

In addition, the "purchase" qualifies as a transfer by satisfying the rules as to whether a gift is a transfer of a partnership interest.

If payment of the purchase price is made out of partnership earnings, the transaction may be regarded as a gift subject to deferred enjoyment of the income and, therefore, lacking in reality either as a gift or a purchase.[75]

.07 Gifts of Partnership Interest When Partnership Capital Is Not a Material Income-Producing Factor

In those family partnerships in which capital is not a material income-producing factor, the recognition of a donee partner's interest continues to depend upon the previous judicial standards, and it will undoubtedly be difficult to sustain the validity of a donee's interest unless he or she performs some substantial services.[76]

.08 Nonpartner Family Member Performs Services for the Partnership

Code Sec. 704(e) applies only if there is a transfer of a partnership interest. If a partnership is formed and one who is never a member of the partnership is

---

[72] "Such participation presupposes sufficient maturity and experience . . . to deal with the business." Reg. § 1.704-1(e)(2)(iv).

[73] Reg. § 1.704-1(e)(2)(v). Income may be retained by the partnership "for the reasonable needs of the business." Reg. § 1.704-1(e)(2)(ii)(a).

[74] Reg. § 1.704-1(e)(4). See, e.g., F. Occhipinti v. Commr., 28 TCM 968, Dec. 29,746(M), TC Memo. 1969-190; Carriage Square, Inc. v. Commr., 69 TC 119, Dec. 34,710 (1977). The mimeograph relation to pre-1951

family partnerships included a much more stringent test. Mim. 6767, 1952-1 CB 111 (declared obsolete, Rev. Rul. 69-31, 1969-1 CB 307); Code Sec. 191 (purchase from family member treated as a gift).

[75] Reg. § 1.704-1(e)(4)(i).

[76] B.H. Nichols v. Commr, 32 TC 1322, Dec. 23,773 (1959), Acq. (wife performed substantial services). Compare Teitelbaum v. Commr., CA-7, 65-1 USTC ¶ 9440, 346 F2d 266.

employed by the partnership and is paid less than the partnership is paid for the services, net income may be shifted to the partners.

> **Observation:** A variant to the family partnership is a partnership consisting entirely of relatives of the prime earner—a partnership in which the prime earner is never a member at all even though he or she may make substantial contributions to the success of the partnership's business. The family partnership provisions discussed here have no application to such a partnership, and, so long as the partnership's income is actually earned by it, the fact that a related individual, not a member of the partnership, may control the source of the partnership's business is not likely to result in the imputation of partnership income to such individual under Code Sec. 704(e).[77] However, the application of Code Sec. 482 could result in a reallocation of the income from the partnership to a non-practitioner (*e.g.* family member) who is performing services for the partnership.

An interesting illustration of this principle is furnished by the case of *Robert P. Crowley v. Commissioner.*[78] In this case a partnership consisting of the mother as a trustee for each of four minor children was created to engage in the insurance and real estate loan business. The father, who was the chief executive officer and the controlling stockholder of a federal savings and loan association, thereupon directed a substantial number of appraisal and inspection fees, insurance commissions, and abstract and title policy commissions to the partnership through his control of the savings and loan association. The services performed by the partnership to earn these fees and commissions were performed by the eldest son. In addition, the partnership made loans on which it received interest. Most of the funds for these loans were derived from advances made by the parents to the partnership in return for demand promissory notes bearing interest at 2-1/2% per annum. The partnership lent these funds out at 6% per annum.

The Commissioner argued that all the partnership's income was in essence due to the activity of the father and should therefore be taxable to him. A majority of the Tax Court, with four judges dissenting, held that all of the partnership income, other than the income resulting from the loans made by the partnership, should be taxed to the partnership members and not to either of the parents. The majority determined that the partnership's noninterest income was in fact due to the personal services rendered by the eldest son and with respect to the father drew a distinction between "being in a position to control who shall perform the activities which produce the income and being in a position to control either the use of income-producing capital or who shall receive income after it is produced."[79]

The court, however, took a different view of the interest income earned by the partnership from the use of capital loaned by the parents to the partnership. With one judge dissenting, the court determined that the parents had not fully relin-

---

[77] *R.P. Crowley v. Commr.*, 34 TC 333, Dec. 24,198 (1960), Acq.; cf. *Nat Harrison Associates, Inc. v. Commr.*, 42 TC 6011, 621, Dec. 26,858 (1964), appeal dismissed (CA-5, 1964); *Alabama-Geogia Syrup Co. v. Commr.*, 36 TC 747, 767, Dec. 24,957 (1961), Acq. But cf. *Carriage Square, Inc. v. Commr.*, 69 TC 119, Dec. 34,710 (1977).

[78] *R.P. Crowley v. Commr.*, 34 TC 333, Dec. 24,198 (1960), Acq.

[79] *Id.*

quished ownership or control over the capital used by the partnership in the loan business.[80]

.09 Estate Tax Planning with Family Partnerships

Family limited partnerships are currently popular mostly because of the estate and gift tax benefits they can provide. Using the proper planning for transfers of partnership interests, a donor has the potential to transfer partial interests in his or her business which have a discounted value for estate and gift tax purposes because of the recipient partner's lack of control and the lack of marketability of the partnership interest. At the same time the donor can control the business in his or her capacity as a general partner.

The common approach has been for the parent or grandparent to transfer property to a family limited partnership, retain control of the assets through the partnership, and use the argument that the limited partnership interests lacked marketability to limit their value for estate tax purposes.

Unfortunately, these arrangements have been successfully attacked as estate planning tools by the IRS. In general, whether or not the estate-planning aspects of the arrangement will be respected depends on the facts and circumstances of each case, and whether or not there was a bona fide nontax reason for the arrangement.

The focal point of litigation between the IRS and taxpayers with respect to the use of family partnerships in estate planning transactions has been the legitimacy of the partnership. The courts and the IRS have accepted the validity of valuation discounts for lack of marketability and lack of control.[81] Indeed, the validity of such valuation discounts is so widely acknowledged that in 2009, Congress introduced a bill which would expressly prohibit the use of valuation discounts with respect to non-business assets for purposes of the federal estate tax.[82] Although the bill had not been voted upon by the time this chapter was sent to print, the fact that some members of Congress felt compelled to change the statute to disallow valuation discounts in certain circumstances is indicative of the extent to which valuation discounts have become accepted wisdom in the case law.

Thus, while the IRS may attack the magnitude of a taxpayer's proposed valuation discounts in connection with the transfer of an interest in a family partnership to a family member, it will seldom question the validity of the discount itself. Instead, it tends to scrutinize the legitimacy of either the partnership or of the transfer of property into the partnership. Code Sec. 2036 requires that the gross estate will include any transfers where the decedent retained possession, enjoyment, or the right to income from the transferred property. In effect, the law

---

[80] *Id.*

[81] *See* for example, *Mandelbaum v. Commissioner* [Dec. 50,687(M)], T.C. Memo. 1995-255, affd. without published opinion [96-2 USTC ¶ 60,240]91 F.3d 124 (3d Cir. 1996), *Peracchio*, 86 TCM 412, Dec. 55,307(M), TC Memo. 2003-280, *Gross*, 96 TCM 187, Dec. 57,544(M), TC Memo. 2008-221, *C. McCord, Jr.*, 120 TC 358, Dec. 55,149. Rev'd and rem'd CA-5, 2006-2 USTC ¶ 60,530, 461 F3d 614, *Lappo*, 86 TCM 333, Dec. 55,282(M), TC Memo. 2003-258, *E. Dailey Est.*, 84 TCM 633, Dec. 54,506(M), TC

Memo. 2001-263, *W.W. Jones II, Est.*, 116 TC 121, Dec. 54,263, *L.M. McCormick Est.*, 70 TCM 318, Dec. 50,813(M), TC Memo. 1995-371, and *J.R. Moore*, 62 TCM 1128, Dec. 47,723(M), TC Memo. 1991-546, among others.

[82] H.R. 436, "Certain Estate Tax Relief Act of 2009," introduced January 9, 2009. As of the date this chapter was sent to print, the bill had not passed the U.S. House of Representatives.

¶802.09

requires that the decedent completed a bona fide transfer of the property to the partnership. Oftentimes, the IRS will challenge the legitimacy of the decedent's transfer of property to the family partnership. If the decedent retained a substantial amount of control over the property, or if the other partners do not receive any meaningful current benefit from the transfer, then it will oftentimes not be recognized. An alternative approach to questioning the bona fides of the transfer is whether the decedent sold the property to the recipient in a bona fide sale for full and adequate consideration. If the decedent did not receive adequate consideration from the purported sale, the presumption is that the sale was not bona fide, and the decedent may be deemed to have retained control.

In *Estate of Wayne C. Bongard*, (2005) 124 TC No. 8, the gross estate didn't include stock in the decedent's and family trust's closely owned corp., which he transferred to an LLC within three years of death. The court held that the transfer qualified for Code Sec. 2036(a)'s bona fide sale for adequate consideration exception, and did not have to be included in the gross estate. It determined that the LLC was formed for a legitimate and significant nontax business reason, specifically that of positioning the corporation for a liquidity event. On the other hand, the gross estate was held to include class B units in the LLC, which the decedent purportedly transferred to a newly-formed family limited partnership the day after capitalizing the LLC. The transfer didn't qualify for the bona fide sale exception of Code Sec. 2036(a) since the family limited partnership never conducted any business, the transfer was effected for no legitimate reason other than to provide a preferential estate tax vehicle, and the decedent retained a life estate by virtue of an implied agreement giving him continued control or enjoyment of the transferred units.

In *Bigelow*, real rental property transferred from the decedent's revocable trust to a family limited partnership was included in the gross estate under Code Sec. 2036(a). In this case, the court found that decedent retained a lifetime right to the property's rental income and economic benefit via an implied agreement. Evidence of that agreement included facts that the decedent replaced income she lost from the property's transfer with partnership income and used the same to secure her loan obligations, make loan payments, and provide funds for her general support; and no distributions were made to any partner other than trust before she died.

Also, the transfer wasn't a bona fide good faith sale for adequate consideration where it effectively left the decedent insolvent, partnership formalities weren't respected, and there was no real potential for any legitimate non-tax benefit.[83] In another case, the fair market value of the residence that the decedent transferred to a family partnership before her death was includible in her gross estate. The court reasoned that the decedent retained possession and enjoyment within the meaning of Code Sec. 2036(a)(1) because the transfer had been made with the express understanding that she would continue to live in the residence for the remainder of her lifetime. Evidence of her retained interest included: (1) the transfer and related lease agreements were drafted so as to give her the same unlimited and exclusive use and right to enjoy the residence as she held before its transfer, (2) the

---

[83] *Estate of Bigelow, et al.*, (2005) TC Memo 2005-65.

partnership conducted no business and just served as conduit, (3) the transfer was effected when the decedent was aged and infirm, and (4) the decedent's attorney recommended the transaction as a means to minimize estate tax. The fact that lease agreements were in place was disregarded since fair rent was neither demanded nor paid. The argument that the decedent shared the residence and thus needed to pay only partial rent as fair rent was rejected.[84]

In *Strangi*,[85] a Fifth Circuit Court of Appeals case, the Court determined that the estate wasn't entitled to use Code Sec. 2036(a)'s bona fide sales exception to exclude from the gross estate the decedent's retained interest in significant assets transferred to the family limited partnership a few months before his death.

Although adequate and full consideration was given in the form of a proportional partnership interest, the transfer didn't qualify as a bona fide sale in that there was no substantial non-tax business purpose for it. The taxpayer's various attempts to cast the arrangement as designed to avoid potential/speculative litigation by the decedent's former housekeeper, to avoid a will contest, to save on executor fees by persuading the executor to decline service, to establish a joint investment vehicle, or to permit the centralized active management of working assets, were all refuted by evidence that none of those objectives were a realistic or valid rationale for the transfers.

On the other hand, the Fifth Circuit Court of Appeals ruled, in *Kimbell*,[86] that the transfer of assets through a trust and an LLC to a family partnership prior to death was a bona fide sale for adequate and full consideration. The Court of Appeals ruled that the District Court's finding of no adequate/full consideration failed to give appropriate weight to the following facts: the decedent received a proportional partnership interest for her assets, the assets were properly credited to her capital account, and the partners were entitled to a *pro rata* distribution on dissolution. The Court of Appeals further found that the District Court's finding that the transfer wasn't a bona fide sale was based on the erroneous assumption that such a sale could only occur in an arm's length transaction between unrelated persons, and ignored objective proof that the appropriate partnership formalities were followed and that the transfer was an actual transaction entered into for substantial business and nontax reasons.

In *Kimbell*, the Fifth Circuit identified the following practices that should be followed in order for a family limited partnership discount to be valid under the bona fide sale exception:

- The partnership should maintain proper capital accounts in the partnership, properly accounting for contributions, distributions, and allocations of income.

- The partnership agreement should provide that distributions upon liquidation be dependent on the partners' capital account balances.

[84] *Estate of Disbrow*, (2006) TC Memo 2006-34.
[85] *Strangi*, 417 F.3d 468, (8/08/2005, CA-5).
[86] *Kimbell*, 371 F.3d 257 (5/20/2004, CA-5).

- The donor partner should retain significant assets outside the partnership (so that he or she clearly has sufficient means of support without reliance on the assets of the partnership).

- The donor partner should not commingle partnership and personal assets.

- The partnership should keep track of the management duties required and performed by the general partner.

- The partnership and the donor should keep records of and be prepared to substantiate significant nontax reasons for the transfer, such as protection from legal liability, ease of transfer of interests from generation to generation, preservation of property as separate property for the descendants, and providing for the continuity in management, should something happen to one of the parties involved.

LLC Observation: Although an LLC may be treated as a partnership for income tax purposes, for estate planning purposes there may be differences in any discounts in valuation on account of lack of marketability. One factor in valuing this discount is the partner or members' right to liquidate his or her interest. In some jurisdictions, LLC members have rights to liquidate their interests that are superior to those normally available to limited partners. This would result in a lower valuation discount for the interest transferred. For estate and gift tax purposes, the only restrictions which are taken into account in valuing the LLC or partnership interest are those created by local law. Additional restrictions provided in the LLC or partnership agreement are disregarded.[87]

¶ 803 Depreciation Recapture

A partner's share of depreciation recapture income is equal to the lesser of:

1. That partner's share of the total gain realized by the partnership on the disposition of the property generating the recapture income; or

2. That partner's share of the depreciation or amortization claimed by the partnership with respect to the property.[88]

A partner's share of the recapture income with respect to property contributed to the partnership includes depreciation allowed to the partner before the contribution. A transferee of a partnership interest steps into the shoes of the transferor. Finally, a partner's share of the recapture is adjusted for curative or remedial allocations under Reg. § 1.704-3(c) and (d).

¶ 804 Credits

Allocation of a credit must be made in the same manner as losses or deductions arising from the same expenditure.[89]

---

[87] Reg. § 26.2704-2(b).
[88] Reg. § 1.1245-1(e)(2).

[89] Reg. § 1.704-1(b)(4)(ii) and (5), Ex. 11.

¶ 805 Income Allocation Recharacterized as Payment for Capital Expenditure

Some payments a partnership makes are nondeductible and must instead be capitalized. One example is payments for land and legal fees that are incurred in connection with the acquisition of land, which would be capitalized under Code Sec. 263 as part of the land's basis. Such payments can be made to an existing partner or an outside party (see Chapter 14). If the payments are made to an existing partner and are properly categorized as Code Sec. 707(a)(1) or (c) payments, they are capitalized under Code Sec. 263 as though made to an outside party. On the other hand, if a partner is allocated income for services to the partnership, the partner's income allocation is effectively a deduction with respect to the remaining partners. Prior to the Deficit Reduction Act of 1984, the technique used to avoid the capitalization was to structure the payment as a distributive share of partnership income. If the person performing services or "contributing property" was not already a partner, he or she would be made a partner for purposes of the arrangement. If the payment is considered the partner's distributive share of partnership income, the payment simply reduced the income taxed to the other partners— effectively allowing them to deduct the payment and avoid the capitalization requirements of Code Sec. 263.

This approach was used when the tax effect to the service or "contributing" partner was the same whether it was a payment for services or a share of the partnership's income.

Code Sec. 707(a)(2)(A) and (B) state that if a transaction appears to be properly characterized as one between a nonpartner and the partnership, the transaction will be governed by Code Sec. 707(a)(1). The Senate Finance Committee report[90] lists six factors that are important in determining whether the allocation/distribution arrangement is in reality a payment for capitalizable services or property:

1. A partner must bear the risk of failure of the business venture.

2. The duration of the partner's interest in the partnership should not be merely transitory.

3. A short time period between the performance of services or transfer of property and the "allocation and distribution" is viewed as a payment rather than a distributive income share.

4. If under all the facts and circumstances, it appears that the recipient became a partner primarily to obtain tax benefits for himself or for the partnership, which would not have been available had the recipient rendered services to the partnership in a third-party capacity, he or she will be disregarded as a partner.

5. A relatively small size of continuing partnership interest after a major allocation/distribution is viewed as a payment.

---

[90] S. Rep. No. 169, 98th Cong., 2d Sess., 226-30 (1984).

6. If, in the case of a sale disguised as a property contribution, after an income allocation equal to the property's value, the "partner" will no longer be entitled to future allocations and distributions the partnership interest will be disregarded.

The report directs the Secretary to outline other relevant factors in regulations and states:

> In applying these various factors, the Treasury and courts should be careful not to be misled by possibly self-serving assertions in the partnership agreement as to the duties of a partner in his partner capacity, but should instead seek the substance of the transaction.

On September 25, 1992, the IRS finalized the regulations under Code Sec. 707(a)(2)(B) for disguised sales of property, but not under Code Sec. 707(a)(2)(A) for disguised payments for services. Reg. § 1.707-2, "Disguised payments for services," remains "reserved." Until regulations are issued, some guidance may perhaps be gleaned from the general concepts of the disguised sale rules. Under the disguised sale regulations, a transfer of property (excluding money or an obligation to contribute money) by a partner to a partnership and a transfer of money or other consideration by the partnership to the partner is a sale of property only if, based on all the facts and circumstances:

- The transfer of money would not have been made but for the transfer of property; and

- In cases in which the transfers are not made simultaneously, the later transfer is not dependent on the entrepreneurial risks of partnership operations.[91]

Transfers between a partnership and a partner that are made within two years of each other are presumed to be a sale, and transfers made more than two years apart are presumed not to be a sale. Each of these presumptions may be rebutted with facts and circumstances that clearly establish to the contrary.[92] The regulations provide for exceptions for guaranteed payments for capital, reasonable preferred returns, or when operating cash flow distributions applies.[93]

---

[91] Reg. § 1.707-3(b)(1).
[92] Reg. § 1.707-3(c)(1) and (d).

[93] *See* Reg. § 1.707-4.

Chapter 9

Partner's Share of Partnership Debt

¶ 901   Introduction
¶ 902   Partner's Share of Debt Included in Tax Basis
¶ 903   What Is a "Liability" for Purposes of Code Sec. 752?
¶ 904   Classification of Partnership Liabilities as Recourse vs.
         Nonrecourse
¶ 905   Partner's Share of Partnership Recourse Debt
¶ 906   Partner's Share of Partnership Nonrecourse Debt
¶ 907   Reg. § 1.752-7 Liabilities (Contingent Liabilities)

¶ 901   Introduction

In keeping with an aggregate approach to partnership taxation, the partners are allowed to include the partnership's liabilities in the basis of their partnership interests. This chapter discusses the importance of including debt in a partner's basis in his or her partnership interest, what debts are included in basis and how a partner determines his or her share of the debt to be included in the basis of a partnership interest.

¶ 902   Partner's Share of Debt Included in Tax Basis

.01 *Adjustments to Basis for Changes in Partner's Share of Liabilities*

A partner must know his or her share of the partnership's debt to determine his or her basis in the partnership interest. The partnership must disclose on Schedule K-1 each partner's share of:

1. Nonrecourse debt other than that considered qualified nonrecourse debt under Code Sec. 465(b)(6).[1]

2. Qualified nonrecourse financing.

3. Other. This last category will consist of each partner's share of the partnership's recourse debt. Recourse debt is a liability for which any partner or party related to a partner bears the economic risk of loss.[2]

---

[1] The at-risk rules of Code Sec. 465 are discussed in Chapter 10. Generally speaking, nonrecourse debt does not increase a partner's amount at risk under Code Sec. 465 unless the nonrecourse debt is "qualified." Qualified nonrecourse debt is debt secured by real estate which is borrowed from a qualified lender (generally one that is unrelated to the borrower or the seller of the encumbered real estate).

[2] Reg. § 1.752-1(a)(1).

Code Sec. 752 treats an increase or a decrease in a partner's share of partnership liabilities as a deemed money contribution or distribution, respectively. Deemed money contributions increase a partner's basis in his or her interest in the partnership.[3] Deemed distributions decrease a partner's basis in his or her interest, but not below zero; distributions in excess of basis trigger recognition of gain.[4] It is a *change* in the share of the partnership's liabilities which generates the deemed money contribution or distribution. A deemed contribution or distribution will arise only if one or both of the following events occurs:

1. The total partnership debt changes; and/or

2. The method for sharing partnership debt changes.

A partner's share of debt is calculated as of the last day of the partnership year. A partner, therefore, can easily determine whether there has been a deemed money contribution or distribution due to a change in debt share by comparing his or her total share of the partnership debt appearing in Item F of Schedule K-1, Form 1065, at the end of the current year to his share of the debt at the end of the previous year. Thus, the partner's deemed money contribution or distribution is relatively simple to determine at the partner level from review of the partner's K-1 received from the partnership. Allocation of partnership liabilities among the partners is a partnership-level process, and is much more involved as discussed at ¶ 905.

.02 Contributions and Distributions of Encumbered Property

Code Sec. 752 treats a partner who assumes a partnership liability or takes property subject to a partnership liability as contributing money to the partnership. This is the case, for example, when a partnership distributes encumbered property. If the partner assumes the debt or takes the property subject to the debt he or she is treated as having contributed money to the partnership equal to the debt assumed (i.e., the debt encumbering the property).[5] When a partnership assumes a partner's liability or takes property subject to a partner's liability in a contribution, the partner is treated as if he or she received a distribution of cash in an amount equal to the amount of the debt transferred. Of course, the transaction also alters the total amount of partnership debt outstanding as well. The partner must take into account his or her altered share of the partnership's liabilities in order to determine the ultimate consequences of the contribution or distribution.

Contribution of encumbered property. The contribution of encumbered property to a partnership should be analyzed as two separate transactions: (1) the contribution of property by the partner to the partnership, followed by (2) a distribution of cash by the partnership to the partner. Note that the deemed cash distribution in step 2 above is equal to the amount of the liability encumbering the property (and thus assumed by the partnership) *less* the contributing partner's share of the transferred debt.

---

[3] Code Sec. 722.

[4] Code Secs. 733(1) and 731(a)(1). Deemed money distributions as well as actual money distributions can generate ordinary income to the partner even in the absence of a distribution in excess of basis if the partnership holds substantially appreciated inventory as defined by Code Sec. 751(d). *See* Code Sec. 751(b).

[5] Code Sec. 752(c).

Example 9-1: J contributes undeveloped realty to Jaybird Partners in exchange for a 10 percent interest in partnership capital and profits. *J's* tax basis in the property is $500. The property is encumbered by a $300 liability for which the partnership assumes responsibility. Assume the partnership has no other liabilities. *J's* tax basis in her partnership interest will be $230, computed as follows:

1. Tax basis of property contributed by *J* to partnership................................		$500
Liability encumbering property assumed by partnership............................	(300)	
J's share (10%) of partnership liability........	30	
2. Deemed cash distribution to *J*		(270)
J's initial tax basis in partnership interest		$230

Of course, if another partner also contributes encumbered property to the partnership as part of the same transaction (e.g., as might be the case at formation of the partnership), the deemed cash distributed must also be offset by the contributing partner's share of the other debt(s) assumed by the partnership. Similarly, if the partnership has existing debt at the date the encumbered property is transferred to the partnership, the contributing partner's share of this debt must also be considered in measuring the net amount deemed to be distributed to (or contributed by) the contributing partner.

Example 9-2: R and *Q* form a new partnership to invest in real property. *R* contributes property with a tax basis of $750, and a fair market value of $1,200, in exchange for a 50 percent interest in partnership capital and profits. The property is encumbered by a $700 mortgage for which the partnership assumes responsibility. *Q* contributes property with a tax basis of $300 and a fair market value of $600 in exchange for the remaining 50 percent interest in capital and profits. The property contributed by *Q* is encumbered by a $100 liability. Each partner's initial tax basis in his or her partnership interest is calculated as follows:

		R		*Q*
1. Tax basis of property contributed to partnership		$750		$300
Liability encumbering property assumed by partnership	(700)		(100)	
Partner's share of partnership liabilities (50% each)	400		400	
2. Deemed cash contribution by (distribution to) each partner		(300)		300
Partner's initial tax basis in partnership interest		$450		$600

¶902.02

As illustrated in the above example, the contribution of encumbered property to a partnership alters every partner's share of the partnership's liabilities. The changes in debt shares come in two forms. First, of course, the liability encumbering the contributed property increases the partnership's total liabilities, thus increasing each partner's share of those debts. These increases, however, will be partially, or perhaps wholly, offset by the dilutive effect of adding a new partner to the partnership. For example, the admission of a third, equal, partner to a two-person partnership reduces each original partner's interest in the partnership from one-half to one-third. If their shares of partnership liabilities are reduced in the same ratios, admission of the new partner may result in a net reduction in each of the original partner's basis in his or her interest in the partnership.

Example 9-3: L and T are equal partners in the LT Partnership. Each has a tax basis in his 50 percent interest in the partnership of $2,500, consisting of his $1,000 contribution to partnership capital and his $1,500 share of partnership debt. The partnership admits C as an equal one-third partner. In exchange for her one-third interest in partnership capital and profits, C contributes property with a tax basis of $600, but encumbered by a $300 mortgage for which the partnership will assume responsibility. C's admission to the partnership will affect the partners as follows:

	L	*T*	*C*
Initial basis in partnership interest	$2,500	$2,500	-0-
Basis of property contributed	-	-	$600
Debt transferred from C to partnership (treated as distribution to C)	-	-	(300)
Each partner's share of liability transferred from C (treated as contribution)	100	100	100
C's share of partnership's existing liabilities (treated as contribution by C, distribution to L & T)	(500)	(500)	1,000
Each partner's post-admission tax basis in partnership interest	$2,100	$2,100	$1,400
Reconciliation:			
Each partner's contribution to capital of partnership	1,000	1,000	300*
Each partner's share of partnership liabilities (1/3 of $3,300)	1,100	1,100	1,100
Basis in partnership interest	$2,100	$2,100	$1,400

*$600 tax basis of contributed property less $300 liability encumbering property.

Distribution of Encumbered Property. Similar rules apply when a partnership distributes encumbered property to a partner. As with the contribution of encumbered property, a partnership distribution of property encumbered by a liability should be analyzed as two transactions: (1) the distribution of unencumbered property to the partner, accompanied by (2) the contribution by the recipient-partner of money to the partnership. The deemed contribution in step 2 is equal to the amount of the liability encumbering the distributed property. Note that the assumption by the partner of partnership debt is treated as a cash contribution to the partnership. As such, it increases the partner's basis in the partnership interest rather than his or her basis in the distributed property.

Example 9-4: John is a partner in MP Partners. His tax basis in his partnership interest is $50,000, consisting of his $30,000 contribution to partnership capital and his $20,000 (50%) share of partnership debt. In a non-liquidating distribution, John receives property with a tax basis of $45,000. The property is encumbered by the partnership's $40,000 mortgage for which John assumes responsibility. Assume this was the partnership's only debt. John will take a $45,000 tax basis in the distributed property, and will have a $25,000 tax basis in his remaining partnership interest, computed as follows:

Pre-distribution basis in partnership interest	$50,000
Reduction in share of partnership debt (treated as cash distribution by partnership)	(20,000)
Assumption of liability (treated as cash contribution to partnership)	40,000
Basis in property received in distribution (carryover from partnership)	(45,000)
Remaining basis in partnership interest	$25,000

As illustrated in the above example, the deemed contributions and/or distributions of cash associated with the liability transfer are accounted for before the actual distribution of property with which they are associated.[6]

¶ 903 What Is a "Liability" for Purposes of Code Sec. 752?

.01 Debt vs. Equity

Many issues involved in determining the validity of a debt are essentially the same as those involved in determining whether the "lender" is really an equity partner. It is a factual determination. Given the facts of a particular transaction, is it more properly characterized as a debt or something else—such as a contribution to the partnership's equity? The essential question is whether or not the "lender" was participating in the enterprise as (1) an entrepreneur providing risk capital, or (2) a creditor seeking a *return on capital independent of the success or failure of the venture.*[7]

---

[6] Code Sec. 752.

[7] *See, e.g., U.S. v. Title Guarantee & Trust Co.,* CA-6, 43-1 USTC ¶ 9293, 133 F2d 990 (stockholder intends to take corporate risk and chance of profit, creditor does

Debt factors. The following factors are among those that have been used in determining whether a transaction creates a bona fide "debt":

1. Fixed payment date in the not-too-distant future.[8]

2. Loan is secured by property with a value in excess of the loan principal.[9]

3. The extent to which the loan is subordinated to other liabilities of the business.[10]

4. Return on the loan is fixed and not dependent on profit from the enterprise.[11]

5. Borrower is not too thinly capitalized.[12]

6. Control over daily business decisions is a partner characteristic. Excessive powers of this type vested in the "lender" would, along with other factors, add to a finding of partner status.

7. Expectation of repayment and presence of security.[13]

Contingent interest. Although there has been some dissent on the issue (notably the *Farley* decision[14]), the courts have generally disregarded the fact that the lender received some form of contingent interest in the venture's profits as additional interest in ruling on the validity of purported debt instruments.[15]

.02 Additional Code Sec. 752 Requirements

Under the principles of balancing inside and outside basis, a "liability" is any "obligation" that either creates/increases basis in a partnership asset (including cash), is generated as part of a deduction taken into account in computing the taxable income of the obligor, or is an expenditure that is not deductible in computing the obligor's taxable income and is not properly capitalized.[16]

> **Example 9-5:** Based upon the above reasoning, it is the IRS's opinion that a cash-method taxpayer's trade payables do not create basis under Code Sec. 752(a), notwithstanding that the obligation is clear and would be fully "accruable" if the partnership was an accrual basis partnership. Thus, the same

---

(Footnote Continued)

not); *Commr. v. O.P.P. Holding Corp.*, CA-2, 35-1 USTC ¶ 9179, 76 F2d 11 (repayment of shareholder capital contingent; repayment of debt not contingent); *J.W. Hambuechen v. Commr.*, 43 TC 90, Dec. 27,018 (1964); Rev. Rul. 72-350, 1972 CB 394 (convertible "loan" to partnership held to be capital placed at risk in the venture).

[8] *Wood Preserving Corp. of Baltimore, Inc. v. U.S.*, CA-4, 65-2 USTC ¶ 9509, 347 F2d 117.

[9] *Ambassador Apartments, Inc. v. Commr.*, 50 TC 236, Dec. 28,945 (1968), aff'd, CA-2, 69-1 USTC ¶ 9164, 406 F2d 288.

[10] *P.M. Finance Corp. v. Commr.*, CA-3, 62-1 USTC ¶ 9465, 302 F2d 786.

[11] *Farley Realty Corp. v. Commr.*, CA-2, 60-2 USTC ¶ 9525, 279 F2d 701.

[12] *Fin Hay Realty Co. v. U.S.*, CA-3, 68-2 USTC ¶ 9438, 398 F2d 694.

[13] *Gibson Products Co. v. U.S.*, CA-5, 81-1 USTC ¶ 9213, 637 F2d 1041 (note given by partnership not true loan— no expectation of repayment, absence of security).

[14] *Farley Realty Corp. v. Commr.*, CA-2, 60-2 USTC ¶ 9525, 279 F2d 701.

[15] *See e.g.*, *K.D. Dorzback v. N. Collison*, CA-3, 52-1 USTC ¶ 9263, 195 F2d 69; *Wynnefield Heights, Inc. v. Commr.*, 25 TCM 953, Dec. 28,070(M), TC Memo. 1966-185; Rev. Rul. 76-413, 1976-2 CB 214; Rev. Rul. 72-2, 1972-1 CB 19.

[16] *See* former Temp. Reg. § 1.752-1T(g). The final regulations do not contain the same language, but there is no reason to think this indicates a change in the IRS's position.

"obligation" may or may not be a "liability" for Code Sec. 752 purposes depending on the accounting method of the partnership.[17]

In preparing Form 1065, the partnership will in most instances ignore cash basis accounts payable in calculating partnership debt. This is because booking the debt to the balance sheet on Schedule L will cause capital plus debt to exceed assets unless there is a balancing amount added to assets.

For the same reasons, contingent liabilities do not affect basis until they create an asset or are the source of a deduction.[18] Under the principles of balancing inside and outside basis, a nonrecourse obligation is treated as a "liability" for Code Sec. 752 purposes to the same extent that it is treated as a liability for purposes of determining the basis of property or claiming a deduction. If the nonrecourse liability is not recognized as a liability for basis or deduction purposes, it should not be recognized as a liability for Code Sec. 752 purposes.[19]

> **Observation:** Technically, under a strict reading of Code Sec. 752(a) and (b), while debt of a "top tier" partnership increases basis under Code Sec. 752(a) to any partnership holding an interest in the top-tier partnership, there is nothing in the language of Code Sec. 752(a) that would treat that basis as a "liability" to the bottom-tier partnership, so that Code Sec. 752(a) could be reapplied to increase the basis of the partners of the bottom-tier partnership. However, the IRS has applied the "aggregate" theory of partnerships and held that the top-tier-partnership liabilities would be considered liabilities of lower tiers for purpose of reapplication of the debt basis to partners of such lower tiers.[20] This approach, consistent with the "balance inside and outside basis" approach to partnerships, has been adopted in the regulations.[21]

¶ 904 Classification of Partnership Liabilities as Recourse vs. Nonrecourse

The regulations under Code Sec. 752 distinguish between *recourse* and *nonrecourse* liabilities. In general, a partnership liability is deemed a recourse liability to the extent that any partner bears the economic risk of loss for that liability.[22] A nonrecourse loan, in contrast, is one where the lender has no right to demand payment from the borrower in the event of default—the nonrecourse lender's only option is to take possession of the property securing the loan. If the value of the property is not sufficient to satisfy the outstanding debt, the lender has no recourse against the borrower or any other party.

Recourse liabilities are shared among the partners in accordance with the manner in which they share the economic risk of loss associated with partnership

---

[17] *See* former Temp. Reg. § 1.752-1T(k), Ex. 2; *see also* Rev. Rul. 88-77, 1988-2 CB.

[18] *See M. Long v. Commr.*, 71 TC 1, Dec. 35,449 (1978), motion for reconsideration denied, 71 TC 724, Dec. 35,868 (1979), rem'd, aff'd in part, rev'd in part on other issues, CA-10, 81-2 USTC ¶ 9668, 660 F2d 416 (for an accrual-basis taxpayer contingent or contested liabilities are not "liabilities" for Code Sec. 752 purposes until they have become fixed or liquidated). *But see* Reg. § 1.752-7

for rules under which partners must reduce their bases in their partnership interests to reflect contingent liabilities transferred to the partnership.

[19] *See Est. of C.T. Franklin v. Commr.*, 64 TC 752, Dec. 33,359 (1975), aff'd, CA-9, 76-2 USTC ¶ 9773, 544 F2d 1045.

[20] Rev. Rul. 77-309, 1977-2 CB 216.

[21] Reg. § 1.752-4(a).

[22] Reg. § 1.752-1(a)(1).

operations.[23] Nonrecourse liabilities, in contrast, are generally shared in accordance with the way the partners will share in the gain from sale of the property securing the nonrecourse liabilities.

¶ 905 Partner's Share of Partnership Recourse Debt

Under the recourse debt rules, a partner bears the economic risk of loss for a partnership liability only to the extent that the partner (or a person related to the partner) can be required to make a capital contribution to the partnership, restore a deficit in his or her capital account, pay a creditor directly, or reimburse another partner for a payment made by such partner to a creditor of the partnership. As a result, partnership *recourse* liabilities are usually allocable *only* to *general* partners, since limited partners cannot typically be required to contribute additional funds to the partnership. Of course, to the extent a limited partner can be obligated to make additional contributions to the partnership (e.g., a limited partner with a limited deficit restoration obligation), he or she may be allocated a share of the partnership's recourse liabilities (not to exceed his or her obligation to make additional contributions to the partnership).[24]

> **LLC Observation:** Liabilities of an LLC will normally be classified as nonrecourse debts for tax purposes, even if structured as recourse liabilities under state law, unless one or more members of the LLC have guaranteed the debt or are otherwise personally responsible for ensuring that it is repaid.[25]

Generally speaking, in determining whether a partner or related party is obligated to make payments to the partnership (or to a creditor or other partner), all statutory or contractual obligations must be taken into account. This determination is a "facts and circumstances" test under the Regulations.[26] Statutory and contractual obligations that must be considered include:

1. Contractual obligations outside the partnership agreement, such as guarantees, indemnifications, reimbursement agreements, and other obligations owed directly to creditors or to other persons, or to the partnership.[27]

2. Obligations to the partnership that are imposed by the partnership agreement, including the obligation to make a capital contribution and to restore a deficit balance in the partner's capital account upon liquidation of the partner's interest in the partnership (or liquidation of the partnership itself); and

3. Payment obligations imposed by state law, including the governing state partnership statute.

---

[23] Reg. § 1.752-2(a).

[24] The guarantee of a partnership liability that is structured as a *nonrecourse* liability will be sufficient to cause that liability to be classified as a recourse debt, allocable wholly to the guarantor(s). In contrast, the guarantee of a recourse liability will be disregarded, as the guarantor will retain recourse against the other general partners in the event that he/she is required to make good on the guarantee. Reg. § 1.752-2(b)(6).

[25] *See* Field Service Advice 200025018 in which Service concludes that LLC members are "at-risk" for liabilities where they have issued personal guarantees to the lender, unless the guarantor would have recourse against another member of the LLC in the event that she or he were required to make good on the guarantee.

[26] Reg. § 1.752-2(b)(3).

[27] *Id.*

Under the recourse debt rules a limited or general partner bears the economic risk of loss for a partnership liability only if that partner (or person related to that partner) can be required to make a capital contribution to the partnership, restore a capital account deficit, pay a creditor directly, or reimburse another partner for a contribution or payment made by the other partner. In general, the partner's or related party's obligation to make these payments takes into account all statutory and contractual obligations. A partner who has a greater than 10 percent interest in the partnership is also deemed to bear the economic risk of loss for any loan that the partner or person related to that partner makes to the partnership, assuming the loan is nonrecourse to the partnership and the other partners.[28]

.01 Constructive Liquidation of the Partnership

In order to determine a partner's potential economic obligation to make payments to the partnership, the regulations require the partnership to analyze the consequences that would result from a hypothetical "constructive liquidation." Under the regulations, a constructive liquidation is a hypothetical situation in which all the partnership's assets, including cash, become completely worthless and the partnership is left with no funds available to pay its creditors. The partnership's assets are deemed to have been exchanged for no consideration, and the resulting hypothetical losses are allocated among the partners in accordance with their loss-sharing ratios in the partnership agreement. When these hypothetical losses are posted to the partners' capital accounts, the resulting balances reflect the partners' potential risk of loss at that moment in time from partnership operations. Partners with deficit balances in their capital accounts following the hypothetical liquidation would be required to make payments to the partnership. Those hypothetical payments serve as the measure of the partners' individual risks of loss with respect to partnership liabilities.

> **Example 9-6:** A, B and C form a general partnership. Under the terms of the partnership agreement, the partners share profits equally, but losses are allocated 25% to A, 25% to B and 50% to C. Assume the partnership has the following balance sheet:

	Tax Basis	Book Value
Cash	$15,000	$15,000
Accounts Receivable	0	45,000
Land & Buildings	135,000	180,000
Other Assets	60,000	90,000
Total Assets	210,000	330,000
Recourse Liabilities	150,000	150,000
Capital, A	20,000	60,000

---

[28] Reg. § 1.752-2(c)(1) and (d).

Capital, B	20,000	60,000
Capital, C	20,000	60,000
Totals....................	210,000	330,000

In order to determine the partners' individual shares of partnership debt, we must first analyze the consequences of a hypothetical transaction in which all partnership assets became worthless and the resulting losses are passed through the partners' capital accounts. For this purpose, we use the book capital accounts since these are the accounts that govern the partners' legal responsibilities under the partnership agreement and state law. A hypothetical or constructive liquidation would have the following consequences for the partners:

	A	*B*	*C*
Beginning capital balances	$60,000	$60,000	$60,000
Hypothetical loss (book value of partnership assets, shared 25% to A, 25% to B and 50% to C)	(82,500)	(82,500)	(165,000)
Hypothetical capital balances	(22,500)	(22,500)	(105,000)

Thus, in the event the partnership's assets became completely worthless, A would be required to pay $22,500 to the partnership to restore the deficit balance in her capital account, as would B. C would be required to make a payment of $105,000 to the partnership. These payments would be used to repay the partnership's $150,000 outstanding liabilities. Accordingly, A's and B's shares of the partnership's debt are each equal to $22,500, while C's share is equal to $105,000.

As illustrated in the above example, the constructive liquidation test for allocation of partnership recourse liabilities requires an analysis of the partners' capital balances and resulting obligations under the terms of the partnership agreement in connection with the following hypothetical events:

1. All of the partnership's liabilities become payable in full;

2. With the exception of property contributed solely to secure a partnership liability, all of the partnership's assets, including cash, have a zero value;

3. The partnership in fact disposes of all of its assets for no consideration other than the relief of nonrecourse liabilities;

4. All items of partnership gain (e.g., from relief of nonrecourse liabilities) and loss (from sale of all remaining assets for no consideration) are allocated among the partners in accordance with the terms of the partnership agreement; and

5. The partnership liquidates.

Observation: One effect of the constructive liquidation process is the allocation of recourse liabilities based upon the hypothetical ending balances in the partners' capital accounts after allocating the hypothetical loss among the partners. The smaller a partner's capital account balance is before analyzing the effects of the hypothetical loss, the larger the deficit balance in that account following the hypothetical loss. Thus, distributions and special loss allocations have the effect of shifting debt, and therefore basis, to those partners receiving the distributions or special loss allocations (assuming such partners' shares of subsequent partnership loss are not affected by the distribution or special allocation). Accordingly, special allocations of partnership loss or deduction essentially create the tax basis necessary to sustain themselves under the regulations.

LLC Observation: In *Hubert Enterprises,*[29] the Tax Court ruled that a deficit restoration obligation incorporated into the operating agreement of an LLC did not create personal liability for the LLC's recourse liabilities. Although the deficit restoration obligation allowed the entity to allocate recourse liabilities to the affected taxpayer under Reg. § 1.752-2, such allocations did *not* increase the taxpayer's amount at risk with respect to the LLC. The court held that the DRO did not create an "unconditional obligation" on the part of the taxpayer to contribute additional capital to the LLC. Because a recourse creditor lacks the power to force the taxpayer to liquidate its interest in the LLC, the creditor could not force the taxpayer to make good on the recourse debt in the event of an LLC default. Thus, the obligation caused by the DRO was contingent on the taxpayer voluntarily liquidating its interest in the LLC. This decision is consistent with the IRS's position in the regulations that the owner of a single member LLC does *not* bear personal responsibility for otherwise recourse liabilities of the LLC unless the owner personally guarantees those liabilities.[30] The owner's risk of loss is limited to the net value of the assets of the LLC to which creditors will ultimately have recourse in the event of default.

.02 Some "Nonrecourse" Loans Recharacterized as Recourse Loans

Nonrecourse Loans from Partners. Generally speaking, a nonrecourse loan from a partner to the partnership will be recharacterized as a recourse loan allocable entirely to the partner who made the loan.[31] Similarly, if a partnership nonrecourse loan is made by a lender or other person who is related to a partner, it will be recharacterized as recourse and allocated entirely to the related partner. These rules do not apply if the partner from whom the loan is received (or who is related to the lender) owns an interest in *each* item of partnership income, gain, deduction, loss or credit of 10% or less. Nonrecourse loans made by 10% or less partners will retain their characterization as nonrecourse for purposes of the regulations under Code Sec. 752 and will be allocated in accordance with the provisions of Reg. § 1.752-3, discussed later in this chapter.

Where a nonrecourse loan from a partner or related person to the partnership "wraps around" an existing nonrecourse loan from an unrelated lender, only the

---

[29] *Hubert Enterprises, Inc.*, 95 TCM 1194, TC Memo 2008-46, on remand from CA-6, 2007-1 USTC 50,494, *aff'g* in part, *vac'g* and *rem'g* in part TC in an unpublished opinion (125 TC 72).

[30] Reg. § 1.752-2(k)

[31] Reg. § 1.752-2(c)(1) and (d).

excess portion of the wrap around loan is subject to these provisions. For example, assume a partner makes a $1,000,000 nonrecourse loan to the partnership which wraps around an existing $600,000 nonrecourse loan from an unrelated lender. Only the excess $400,000 of the "new" note above the principal amount of the underlying note will be recharacterized as recourse debt allocable to the lending partner.[32]

Reimbursement rights. A partner's obligation to pay a partnership liability is reduced to the extent that the partner is entitled to reimbursement from another partner or a person who is related to another partner. Generally speaking, all general partners are personally liable for all recourse liabilities of a partnership. However, a general partner has a right of recovery against the other general partners to the extent he or she is required to pay more than his or her share of any liability.

Assumed liability to pay. The regulations presume that the partner who has an obligation in fact discharges the obligation on the constructive liquidation of the partnership, notwithstanding that the partner may not in fact possess sufficient assets to do so.[33]

Plan to avoid. An obligation will be disregarded if the facts and circumstances indicate a plan to circumvent or avoid such obligation.[34]

Tantamount to a guarantee. An arrangement need not actually be a "guarantee" under non-tax rules to be considered one for purposes of treating it as a guarantee. If one or more partners or related persons undertake contractual obligations that substantially eliminate a creditor's risk on an otherwise nonrecourse loan, the arrangement may be considered tantamount to a guarantee and treated for all purposes under the regulations as a guarantee.[35]

> ***Example 9-7:*** Assume that partnership ABC has purchased property from *X*, where *X* has provided 100% financing on a nonrecourse basis. Assume that partner *A* has also agreed to lease the property from partnership ABC for an amount that will pay the interest. *A*'s lease may be "tantamount to a guarantee." If so, the loan will be at least partially recharacterized as a recourse loan and allocated to partner A. (See discussion below).

Time of satisfaction. The extent to which a partner or related person bears the economic risk of loss for a partnership obligation is determined by taking into account any delay in the time when an obligation is to be satisfied. If a payment obligation to a third party is taken into account at its face amount, it must be payable within a *reasonable time* after the liability becomes due. An obligation to make a contribution to the partnership must be payable before the later of the end of the year in which the partner's interest is liquidated or 90 days after the liquidation. Otherwise, the obligation is recognized only to the extent of its *value*.[36] The obligation's value equals its face value if the interest rate is equal to the applicable federal rate under Code Sec. 1274(d). Otherwise, it is discounted to

---

[32] Reg. § 1.752-2(c)(2).
[33] Reg. § 1.752-2(b)(6).
[34] Reg. § 1.752-2(j).

[35] Reg. § 1.752-2(j)(2).
[36] Reg. § 1.752-2(g)(1).

present value as calculated under Code Sec. 1274(b).[37] An obligation under local law is deemed to meet the payment time requirements of the regulations.

Assumption. A partner who assumes responsibility for a partnership debt (*e.g.*, upon receipt of a distribution of encumbered property) is considered liable, provided that:

1. The assuming partner is subject to personal liability with respect to such liability; and

2. In case of assumption by the partner, the creditor is aware of the assumption and can directly enforce the partner's obligation.[38]

Guarantees. The partners who bear the economic risk of loss are deemed to bear the risk of loss constituting the obligation. If a partner is only secondarily liable, the person with the primary liability will be considered the party with the risk of loss. The guarantor of a partnership *recourse* liability generally has a "reimbursement right" from the partnership's general partners and is therefore not the person with the ultimate risk of loss.[39] In contrast, the guarantor of a nonrecourse liability does not have the right to reimbursement from the other partners and will be treated as bearing 100% of the risk for the guaranteed nonrecourse liability. This rule does *not* apply unless the guarantor's interest in all items of partnership income, gain, loss, deduction, or credit exceeds 10 percent.[40]

Interest guarantees. If a liability would otherwise be a nonrecourse liability except that one or more partners (or persons related to a partner) are obligated to pay more than 25 percent of the total interest that will accrue on the liability if the partnership fails to pay such interest, and it is "*reasonable to expect*" that the guarantor will be required to pay "*substantially all*" of the future interest if the partnership fails to do so, then the guarantor partners (or partners related to the guarantors) will be treated as having an economic risk of loss with respect to the liability to the extent of the present value of the guaranteed interest payments, with the balance of the liability being treated as nonrecourse.[41]

Generally, it is "reasonable to expect" that the guarantor will be required to pay substantially all of the guaranteed interest if, upon default by the partnership, the lender can enforce the interest guaranty without foreclosing on the property and extinguishing the underlying debt. The assumption is that the lender would assert the foreclosure remedy before a significant portion of the interest guaranty accrued.[42]

The partner's risk of loss is deemed to be equal to the present value of the unpaid guaranteed interest, valued as of the date of determination. The present value determination is made by using the interest rate stated in the liability or, if none is stated, the applicable federal rate compounded semi-annually.[43]

---

[37] Reg. § 1.752-2(g)(2).
[38] Reg. § 1.752-1(d).
[39] Reg. § 1.752-2(b)(5).
[40] Reg. § 1.752-2(d)(2).

[41] Reg. § 1.752-2(e)(1).
[42] *Id.*
[43] Reg. § 1.752-2(e)(2).

The interest guarantee rules do not apply if the guaranty is for a period not greater than the lesser of five years or one-third of the period of the loan.[44] Interest that has already accrued but is unpaid is treated as a separate liability.

Example 9-8: K is the general partner in a limited partnership. The partnership borrowed $2,000,000 on a nonrecourse loan, the proceeds of which are used to finance acquisition of a shopping center. The nonrecourse loan bears interest at eight percent and has a term of 15 years. It calls for payments of interest only for the first five years, after which time, regular payments of principal and interest will be required. To entice the lender to make the nonrecourse loan, K guaranteed the interest payments for the first five years. Because the guarantee is for a period not in excess of five years or one-third of the term of the loan (also five years), it will be disregarded, and the entire $2,000,000 principal balance of the loan will be classified as nonrecourse (sharable by the limited partners).

Had the terms of the loan called for payments of interest only for the first 10 years (rather than 5), and had K guaranteed the payment of interest during this 10-year period, a portion of the loan would be recharacterized as recourse, rather than nonrecourse. In this case, the interest payments are $160,000 per year (eight percent of $2,000,000). The present value of a 10-year annuity of $160,000, using a discount rate of eight percent (the interest rate charged on the loan) is equal to $1,073,616 ($160,000 times a present value factor of 6.7101). Thus, in the first year of the loan, only $926,384 ($2,000,000 less $1,073,616) will be characterized as a nonrecourse loan. The remaining $1,073,616 will be characterized as recourse and will be allocable entirely to K.

Note that in the second year, the present value of the guaranteed interest stream will decline to $999,504 (the present value factor declines to 6.2469), and $74,112 of the loan will be recharacterized from recourse to nonrecourse.

¶ 906 Partner's Share of Partnership Nonrecourse Debt

Nonrecourse liabilities are those liabilities for which *no partner (or related person)* bears personal risk of loss.[45] In the event that the partnership defaults on the loan, the lender can foreclose upon any property serving as collateral for the loan, but has no further recourse against any partner in the partnership, or against the partnership itself.

If the loan is obtained from a partner, or from a related party to a partner, then the lender, who is a partner in the partnership, bears personal risk of loss and the liability will be treated as a recourse loan for purposes of Code Sec. 752, even if it is structured as a nonrecourse loan.[46] Similar consequences apply if the loan is guaranteed by one or more partners. Because the guaranty will require the guarantor(s) to make payment in the event of partnership default, one or more partners (the guarantors) bear personal risk of loss for the loan and it is not classified as a nonrecourse loan.[47]

---

[44] Reg. § 1.752-2(e)(3).
[45] Reg. § 1.752-1(a)(2).

[46] Reg. § 1.752-2(c)(1).
[47] Reg. § 1.752-2(c)(2).

Nonrecourse liabilities create unique problems from a tax policy standpoint. Although none of the partners have any personal obligation for repayment, no lender would make a loan if it did not expect to be repaid, so the debt is real. It therefore is included in basis. The question then becomes how to allocate the debt (and the related tax basis) among the partners. An evaluation of the partners' economic risks is irrelevant to the question—none of them have any economic risk. Thus, the question becomes how the partners will share in the repayment of the loan. Historically, Code Sec. 752 has looked to the partners' interests in partnership profits to answer this question.

.01 Nonrecourse Liabilities Allocated by Reference to Partners' Profits Interests

Prior to January 30, 1990, nonrecourse liabilities were allocated in accordance with the partners' interests in partnership profits. Because no partner bears personal liability with respect to such debts, the only way these liabilities will be repaid is from partnership profits. Thus, every partner's share of profits will be reduced by payments on the nonrecourse debt, and the partners can be viewed as sharing such debt in the same ratios in which they share partnership profits. Unfortunately, these allocation rules created problems in partnerships where deductions, such as depreciation associated with the property encumbered by the nonrecourse liabilities, were allocated in a manner different than the allocation of partnership profits. In such cases, many partners receiving special allocations of depreciation found themselves with insufficient tax basis in their partnership interests to deduct the specially allocated depreciation. New rules proposed in 1990 (and finalized on December 28, 1991) alleviate this problem.

The current regulations address this problem by creating a hierarchy of profits interests to which the partnership must look in allocating nonrecourse debts among the partners. Specifically, they divide the partners' interests in partnership profits into three categories: (1) "book" (or Code Sec. 704(b)) minimum gain; (2) Code Sec. 704(c) minimum gain; and (3) other profits. Under the general rule of the regulations, a partner's share of partnership nonrecourse liabilities equals the sum of:

1. The partner's share of "book" minimum gain determined in accordance with the rules of Code Sec. 704(b) (henceforth referred to as "Code Sec. 704(b) gain");

2. The amount of taxable gain that would be allocated to the partner under Code Sec. 704(c) (or in the same manner as Code Sec. 704(c) in connection with a revaluation of partnership property) if the partnership disposed of (in a taxable transaction) all partnership property subject to one or more nonrecourse liabilities of the partnership in full satisfaction of its liabilities and for no other consideration (this amount will henceforth be referred to as "Code Sec. 704(c) minimum gain"); and

3. The partner's share of the excess nonrecourse liabilities (those not allocated under 1 and 2 above) of the partnership as determined in accordance with the partner's share of partnership profits.

¶906.01

To provide the maximum amount of flexibility, the regulations provide two alternatives to the allocation in step 3. First, they expressly give the partnership the option to allocate nonrecourse liabilities in excess of the two categories of minimum gain (*i.e.*, excess nonrecourse liabilities) "in accordance with the manner in which it is reasonably expected that the deductions attributable to those nonrecourse liabilities will be allocated."[48] Thus, for example, if the partnership agreement allocates depreciation attributable to properties encumbered by nonrecourse liabilities differently than it allocates profits, excess nonrecourse liabilities may be allocated in accordance with the partners' shares of such depreciation.

Additionally, the partnership may first allocate an excess nonrecourse liability to a partner "up to the amount of built-in gain that is allocable to the partner on section 704(c) property (as defined under § 1.704-3(a)(3)(ii)) or property for which reverse section 704(c) allocations are applicable (as described in § 1.704-3(a)(6)(i)) where such property is subject to the nonrecourse liability to the extent that such built-in gain exceeds the gain described" in step 2 above.[49] Thus, the regulations give the partnership sufficient flexibility to ensure that partners with special allocations of depreciation can be allocated sufficient liabilities to sustain those allocations (i.e., to give the partners sufficient tax basis to deduct the specially allocated depreciation). The rules also allow the partnership to allocate sufficient liabilities to a partner contributing built-in gain property to allow him or her to avoid having to recognize income under Code Sec. 731(a) where the liabilities encumbering the contributed property exceed his/her tax basis in the contributed property.

.02 Minimum Gain

Partnership "minimum gain" is the amount of gain which would be recognized by the partnership if it surrendered the property to the nonrecourse lender in satisfaction of the outstanding balance of the debt (*e.g.*, as in a foreclosure). Because such a transaction is treated as a sale or exchange, the partnership will realize gain in an amount equal to the excess of the outstanding balance of the loan over the book value (adjusted for depreciation deductions) of the property. The partnership could realize more gain on disposition of the property (if its fair value exceeds its book value, adjusted for depreciation), but never less.

> **Example 9-9:** Partnership Alpha owns real estate with a book value (net of accumulated depreciation) of $250,000. The property is encumbered by a $375,000 nonrecourse mortgage incurred to finance acquisition of the property. No partner or related person has any personal risk of loss with respect to the loan. Thus, default by the partnership will effectively result in the transfer of the property to the lender in full satisfaction of the $375,000 remaining principal balance of the note. A sale at this price would generate a gain of $125,000.[50] Since default and foreclosure is the worst-case scenario for the partnership with respect to this property, this is the "minimum gain" that will be realized by the partnership with respect to this property.

---

[48] Reg. § 1.752-3(a)(3).
[49] *Id.*

[50] *See* Reg. § 1.1001-2(c), Examples (7) and (8).

¶906.02

Under the section 704(b) regulations, the existence of partnership minimum gain allows partners' capital accounts to fall below zero even in the absence of any requirement on their parts to make additional capital contributions to "restore" these deficit balances. As long as the deficits do not exceed the partners' shares of partnership minimum gain, any deficit in their capital accounts can be made up— restored—with an allocation of minimum gain. This allocation has tax consequences in that it increases the partners' taxable income. These consequences give the underlying loss allocations economic effect under the section 704(b) regulations. Following the same rationale, the regulations under section 752 look to the allocation of minimum gain to support the allocation of the underlying nonrecourse debt associated with that minimum gain.

Example 9-10: *L* and *M* form a limited partnership to acquire a hotel. *L*, the general partner, contributes $80,000 cash, and *M*, the limited partner, contributes $320,000 cash to the partnership. The partnership borrows $3,600,000 on a nonrecourse note from an unrelated lender and purchases the hotel for $4,000,000. The partners agree to share losses 20% to *L* and 80% to *M*. Partnership income is to be shared equally. These allocations are recognized by the IRS under Code Sec. 704(b). Minimum gain is to be shared 20/80 in order to substantiate the loss-sharing arrangement. In each of its first three years, the partnership's revenues just offset its operating expenses giving it net income of $0 before depreciation. Assume an annual depreciation deduction of $100,000, resulting in a ($100,000) annual tax loss, which will impact the partners' capital accounts as follows:

	L	*M*
Beginning Capital	$80,000	$320,000
Loss in years 1-4	(80,000)	(320,000)
Capital, end of year 4	0	0
Year 5 loss	(20,000)	(80,000)
Capital, end of year 5	(20,000)	(80,000)

At the end of year 4, there is no partnership minimum gain so the nonrecourse liability is allocated equally between the partners in accordance with their general profit-sharing ratios. At the end of year 5, however, partnership minimum gain is $100,000 (basis = 4,000,000 – 500,000 depreciation = 3,500,000 vs. principal amount of loan = $3,600,000). Thus, the first $100,000 of the nonrecourse loan is allocated 20% to *L* and 80% to *M* in accordance with their interests in partnership minimum gain. The remaining nonrecourse liability of $3,500,000 is allocated equally. Thus, at the end of year 5, *L*'s share of partnership nonrecourse debt is $1,770,000 ($20,000 share of partnership minimum gain plus $1,750,000 share of the excess) and *M*'s share is $1,830,000 ($80,000 + $1,750,000). Of course, as noted previously, if the partnership chooses, it may elect to allocate the entire nonrecourse debt 20:80, consistent with the allocation of the associated depreciation deductions.

.03 Code Sec. 704(c) Minimum Gain

Code Sec. 704(c) minimum gain arises when a partnership owns property encumbered by nonrecourse debt which has a book value in excess of its tax basis. In such cases, the total amount of "minimum gain" which would be recognized by the partnership in the event of default and foreclosure by the nonrecourse lender is equal to the excess of the principal amount of the note over the *tax basis* of the property. This total minimum gain is divided into two parts. Code Sec. 704(b) minimum gain is equal to the excess of the nonrecourse debt balance over the book value of the property; the remainder of the "minimum gain" will be allocated under Code Sec. 704(c). It is possible to have Code Sec. 704(c) minimum gain, but no "book" minimum gain. Indeed, this is common—since the book value of contributed property is equal to its fair value at the date of contribution (subsequently adjusted for book depreciation), any minimum gain with respect to such property in the years immediately following contribution will generally consist solely of Code Sec. 704(c) minimum gain. Similarly, it is possible to have "Code Sec. 704(b)" minimum gain, but no Code Sec. 704(c) minimum gain. Again, this is common—for example, for property acquired by the partnership via purchase or self-construction, as opposed to contribution from a partner, book value will generally equal tax basis unless the partnership has revalued its properties under Reg. § 1.704-1(b)(2)(iv)(f).

Where minimum gain would be allocated under Code Sec. 704(c) to one or more partners, the allocation of the nonrecourse liability follows the allocations of the minimum gain, to the extent of the minimum gain.

> **Example 9-11:** *G* and *H* form a general partnership to acquire and manage residential properties. *G* contributes $250,000 to the partnership that it uses to acquire an apartment complex. *H* contributes a second apartment building valued at $425,000. The basis of the property contributed by H is $150,000 and it is subject to a nonrecourse debt of $175,000. The two partners share all profits and losses equally. The $175,000 nonrecourse loan, however, is not shared equally by the partners. The first $25,000 of such loan is allocated to *H* because *H* would be allocated $25,000 of partnership gain under Code Sec. 704(c) if the partnership disposed of the apartment building in full satisfaction of the nonrecourse liability. The remainder of the nonrecourse liability is allocated between the partners in proportion to their equal interests in partnership profits. Thus, *G*'s share of the $175,000 nonrecourse liability is $75,000 (½ of $150,000) and *H*'s share is $100,000 ($25,000 + ½ of $150,000). Since the book value ($425,000) is greater than the $175,000 nonrecourse loan, there would be no Code Sec. 704(b) minimum gain.

> **Example 9-12:** CDE Partnership owns depreciable realty with a book value of $250,000 and a tax basis of $140,000. The property is encumbered by a nonrecourse liability of $300,000. (Assume the market value of the property exceeds this amount, and the reason book value is less than the nonrecourse debt is because of book depreciation over the years.) Thus, the total "minimum gain" with respect to this property is $160,000 (the $300,000 balance of the nonrecourse note over its tax basis of $140,000). Of this amount, $50,000 is "book" minimum gain (the $300,000 balance of the nonrecourse mortgage over

¶906.03

its $250,000 book value), and the remainder is Code Sec. 704(c) minimum gain. The book minimum gain will be allocated among the partners in accordance with the manner in which they have shared the book depreciation deductions. The Code Sec. 704(c) minimum gain will be allocated to the partner who contributed the property to the partnership. The allocation of the first $160,000 of the nonrecourse mortgage will follow these allocations of minimum gain. The remainder will be allocated in accordance with the partners' shares of partnership profits. Alternatively, the partnership may choose to allocate the remainder of the nonrecourse note in accordance with the manner in which it expects to allocate future depreciation deductions.

.04 "Excess" Nonrecourse Liabilities

Under the general rule, partnership nonrecourse liabilities in excess of the partnership's book and Code Sec. 704(c) minimum gain (*i.e.*, "excess" liabilities) are allocated in accordance with the partners' interests in general partnership profits. However, rather than base this allocation on the partners' general profits interests, the regulations provide that a partnership *may choose* to allocate *excess* nonrecourse liabilities first to the contributing partner to the extent of built-in gain allocable to that partner under Code Sec. 704(c) which exceeds the amount of Code Sec. 704(c) minimum gain as determined under step 2. Alternatively, it *may choose* to allocate *excess* nonrecourse liabilities among the partners in accordance with the manner in which it expects to allocate depreciation deductions attributable to the properties encumbered by the nonrecourse liabilities.

> **Observation:** The regulations state explicitly that a partnership is not required to use the same method to allocate its excess nonrecourse deductions every year.[51] Thus a partnership that apportions excess nonrecourse liabilities by reference to its partners' general profits interests may choose to change to an allocation based on the partners' interests in depreciation in a year in which a reduction in the principal balance of the nonrecourse debt is reduced.

Nonrecourse liabilities are generally allocated on a liability-by-liability basis, so that accurate measures of book and tax minimum gain, and the partners' interests therein, can be determined.[52] The separately computed amounts are then added together to determine each partner's aggregate share of partnership nonrecourse liabilities.

> **Example 9-13:** Mockingbird Partners was formed several years ago by three partners, *H*, *L* and *G*. *H* contributed depreciable property with a tax basis of $450,000 and a fair market value of $750,000. The property was encumbered by a $600,000 nonrecourse debt. *L* contributed $150,000 cash and *G* contributed $200,000 cash. The partnership agreement allocates partnership profits 30% to *H*, 30% to *L* and 40% to *G*. Depreciation is allocated equally among the partners. For simplicity, assume that each property is depreciated using the straight line method over 15 years.

---

[51] Reg. § 1.752-3(a)(3), last sentence.   [52] Reg. § 1.704-2(d)(1).

Shortly after formation, the partnership borrowed $550,000 on a nonrecourse mortgage and began development of a large real estate project at a total cost of $900,000. At the end of its first year, the book and tax bases of the partnership's assets were as follows:

	Book Value	Tax Basis
Property contributed by H	$750,000	$450,000
Accumulated depreciation	(50,000)	(30,000)
	700,000	420,000
Property acquired by Partnership ..	900,000	900,000
Accumulated depreciation	(60,000)	(60,000)
	840,000	840,000
Total Assets................	$1,540,000	$1,260,000

Assume the partnership has made no payments against the principal balances of the nonrecourse mortgages. The nonrecourse liabilities would be allocated as follows:

	H	L	G
Mortgage on property contributed by H:			
Book minimum gain	0	0	0
Tax minimum gain..............	180,000	0	0
General profits................	126,000	126,000	168,000
Mortgage on acquired property:			
Book minimum gain	0	0	0
Tax minimum gain..............	0	0	0
General profits................	165,000	165,000	220,000
Totals	471,000	291,000	388,000

As an alternative to the third step above, the partnership could allocate its "excess" nonrecourse liabilities equally, in accordance with its allocations of depreciation. (If and when the partnership has book minimum gain, that portion of the nonrecourse liabilities will be allocated equally since book minimum gain will be created as a result of depreciation allocations.)

.05 Multiple Properties Secured by Single Nonrecourse Liability

In cases where a single nonrecourse loan is secured by multiple properties, measurement of minimum gain is problematic. The regulations give partnerships almost complete flexibility in making this determination. Partnerships may use any "reasonable" method to apportion the liability among the different properties securing it, so long as the apportionment does *not* result in the allocation of debt to

¶906.05

any property in excess of its fair market value.[53] However, once the liability has been allocated among the various properties securing the loan, it may *not* be reallocated among those properties using a different method.

The only exception to this prohibition against reallocating the liability among the properties securing that liability arises when the lender releases a property from the debt. If a property to which a portion of the nonrecourse liability has been allocated subsequently becomes no longer subject to the liability, the portion of the nonrecourse debt allocated to that property must be reallocated to the other properties still subject to that debt. The reallocation is still subject to the limitation against allocating debt to a property in excess of its fair value.

Finally, the regulations provide that where the outstanding principal balance of the liability is reduced, the reduction must be allocated among multiple properties in the same proportion as the liability was allocated to those properties.[54] This requirement is consistent with the prohibition described above against changing the method of allocation of the nonrecourse liability among multiple properties securing it.

¶ 907 Reg. § 1.752-7 Liabilities (Contingent Liabilities)

.01 General

Regulations issued in the summer of 2003 prescribe new rules for so-called "§ 1.752-7 liabilities."[55] Although the regulations do not really define these liabilities, it appears that a § 1.752-7 liability is essentially a contingent liability which, due to the uncertainty of either the amount of the debt or the likelihood of repayment, is not treated as a liability for purposes of Code Secs. 752(a) or (b).

The regulations were issued to address a particularly abusive tax-shelter strategy known as "son-of-BOSS" that was becoming widespread in the late 1990s and the early part of this century.[56] In a typical "son-of-BOSS" transaction, a partner would engage in a short sale of relatively riskless securities (e.g., Treasury Notes). He would transfer the proceeds from the short sale to the partnership, along with the obligation to close the short transaction.[57] However, he would treat the obligation to close the transaction as a contingent liability on grounds that the partnership would not actually know the amount required to close the sale until expiration of the contract. Treating the obligation as a contingent (and thus disregarded) liability allowed the partner to claim a large positive adjustment to the basis of the partnership interest (in the amount of the contributed proceeds from the short sale). He could then sell (or otherwise dispose of) his interest in the partnership,

---

[53] Reg. § 1.752-3(b)(1).

[54] Reg. § 1.752-3(b)(2).

[55] Reg. § 1.752-7, effective June 24, 2003. These regulations effectively replace Temporary Reg. § 1.752-6 which applied to assumptions of partnership liabilities after October 18, 1999 and before June 24, 2003.

[56] The IRS also attacked this tax shelter strategy in the courts. *See* for example, *Salman Ranch Ltd.*, 2007-2 USTC ¶ 50,803, in which the scheme was used to pump up basis in partnership interests prior to distributing appreciated ranchland for resale by the partners. *See also Jade Trad-*

ing LLC, 2008-1 USTC ¶ 50,112 (court imposed substantial understatement penalty on taxpayer), *Klamath Strategic Investment Fund, LLC*, 2006-2 USTC ¶ 50,408 (court upheld retroactive application of Regs.), and *Stobie Creek Investments, LLC*, 2008-2 USTC ¶ 50,471 (court upheld accuracy-related penalties imposed by IRS), among many others. Indeed, the success of the IRS in fighting this tax shelter strategy in the courts raises doubts whether the regulations were even necessary.

[57] "Boss" stands for "bond and option sales strategy." This strategy was refuted by the IRS in Notice 99-59, 1999-52 IRB 761.

recognizing little or no gain (or perhaps even a loss), allowing a virtually tax-free exit from the partnership. Moreover, any gain inherent in partnership assets would be left for the remaining partners (if any) to share for tax purposes.

The purpose of the regulations is to prevent a partner from transferring the tax deductions associated with these contingent liabilities to the other partners in the partnership, or to accelerate his or her own loss by selling the partnership interest prior to the partnership's disposal of the property subject to the contingent liability. Accordingly, the regulations apply the principles of Code Sec. 704(c) (relating to built-in gains or losses inherent in contributed property) to transfers of property encumbered by "contingent" debts by a partner to a partnership. Such contingent debts are referred to as § 1.752-7 liabilities.

.02 Mechanics

Under the regulations, when a partner transfers property to a partnership subject to a § 1.752-7 liability, the liability is not treated as a liability for purposes of Code Sec. 752, but instead is treated as built-in loss under Code Sec. 704(c). At a later date, when the partnership satisfies all or part of a contingent liability, any resulting tax deduction or loss must be allocated to the contributing partner to the extent of the built-in loss at the date of contribution.[58] Note that although the regulations were implemented to address abusive tax shelter schemes, they apply to the transfer of *any* contingent liability to the partnership. For example, the transfer to a partnership of property encumbered by potential environmental liabilities would trigger these provisions.

> **Example 9-14:** *J*, *F* and *K* form DumpStation, Ltd. to develop and operate a landfill. *J* contributes vacant land with a fair market value and tax basis of $600,000. The land is subject to potential environmental liabilities in the amount of $150,000. In exchange, *J* receives a 20% interest in the partnership. *F* contributes $675,000 cash in exchange for a 30% interest in the partnership, and *K* contributes $1,125,000 cash in exchange for a 50% interest. The partnership subsequently pays $250,000 to satisfy the environmental liability on the property contributed by *J*. Assume that the $250,000 payment is deductible by the partnership. The first $150,000 of this deduction must be allocated to *J*. The remainder will be allocated in accordance with the partners' loss-sharing ratios (presumably 20:30:50, although a different sharing ratio will be acceptable so long as the requirements of Code Sec. 704(b) are satisfied).

> **Observation:** The regulations imply that § 1.752-7 liabilities are treated as liabilities for "book" (*i.e.*, Code Sec. 704(b)) purposes, but not for tax purposes. Thus, a partner/member's Code Sec. 704(b) capital account must be reduced by the "value" of the contingent liability, while his or her capital account on the entity's tax balance sheet will not be affected.

> **Caution:** The regulations do not explain how to value a § 1.752-7 liability. The regulations provide that the value of such a liability is equal to "the amount of cash that a willing assignor would pay to a willing assignee to

---

[58] Reg. § 1.752-7(c)(1).

assume the § 1.752-7 liability in an arm's length transaction."[59] Thus, at this point, practitioners are on their own for purposes of attempting to measure such liabilities.

.03 Sale or Transfer of an Interest in a Partnership with § 1.752-7 Liabilities

When a partner sells his or her interest in the partnership before the § 1.752-7 liability has been satisfied, the regulations require that the basis of the partnership interest be reduced by the remaining § 1.752-7 liability amount.[60] The basis reduction is triggered immediately before the sale, exchange or other disposition of the interest, thus increasing the selling partner's gain (or reducing his or her loss) on the disposition. Note that in such cases, the partnership retains the § 1.752-7 liability. Under the regulations, if it subsequently makes a payment in partial or full satisfaction of that liability, it is allowed a deduction or capital expense *only* to the extent that the payment exceeds the remaining built-in loss associated with liability immediately prior to the payment. Moreover, the capital accounts of the remaining partners are adjusted only to the extent such payment is deductible (or capitalizable). If the partnership notifies the original contributing partner that the § 1.752-7 liability has been satisfied, the partner will be allowed a loss or deduction to the extent of the lesser of the built-in loss (the reduction in basis) or the amount paid to satisfy the liability.

> **Example 9-15:** Assume the same facts as in Example 9-14. *J* contributes raw land with a tax basis and fair market value of $600,000 to DumpStation, Ltd. in exchange for a 20% interest therein. *J*'s tax basis in her partnership interest will be $600,000. However, due to a contingent environmental liability of $150,000, her interest is worth only $450,000. Assume that *J* later sells her partnership interest for $450,000 cash. Under Reg. § 1.752-7(e)(1), *J* must reduce her tax basis in the partnership interest by the $150,000 potential environment liability. Thus, she will recognize no gain or loss on the sale. If the partnership subsequently satisfies the obligation for $250,000, it will be entitled to a $100,000 deduction (the amount paid to satisfy the obligation over the estimated amount of the liability at the date of *J*'s contribution to the partnership). If the partnership contacts *J*, she will be entitled to a $150,000 deduction for the built-in loss inherent in the property attributable to the environmental liability.

> **Caution:** Nothing in the regulations obligates the partnership or LLC to notify the former partner that the § 1.752-7 liability has been satisfied. Departing partners should be counseled to obtain a commitment from the partnership that it will provide notification in the event that the § 1.752-7 liability is subsequently paid in a future year. The § 1.752-7 partner must attach a copy of the notification received from the partnership to his or her tax return in the year a deduction is claimed. The notification must include the following information:[61]

---

[59] Reg. § 1.752-7(b)(2)(ii).
[60] Reg. § 1.752-7(e)(1).

[61] Reg. § 1.752-7(h).

- The amount paid in satisfaction of the liability;
- Whether the amount(s) paid was in partial or complete satisfaction of such liability;
- The name and address of the person satisfying the liability;
- The date of payment of such liability; and
- The character of the loss triggered by payment of the liability.

.04 Liquidating Distribution to § 1.752-7 Partner or Distribution of Property Secured by § 1.752-7 Liability to Another Partner

Two other types of transactions also trigger the application of the basis adjustment rules described above:

1. Receipt of a liquidating distribution by a § 1.752-7 partner from the partnership;[62] or

2. Assumption of the § 1.752-7 liability by *another partner* of the partnership[63] (*e.g.*, as when the property encumbered by the § 1.752-7 liability is distributed to another partner).

In either of the above circumstances, the partner who contributed the property subject to the contingent liability (the § 1.752-7 partner) is required to reduce his or her basis in the partnership interest by the remaining built-in loss associated with the § 1.752-7 liability. If and when the § 1.752-7 liability is later satisfied, the payor is entitled to a deduction *only to the extent that the amount paid in satisfaction of the liability exceeds the value of the liability (the built-in loss) at the date of the distribution or assumption.*[64] If the partnership notifies the § 1.752-7 partner that the liability has been discharged (fully or partially), the partner will be entitled to a deduction in an amount equal to the lesser of the built-in loss associated with the liability or the amount paid in satisfaction thereof.

Special rules apply where another partner assumes the contributor's responsibility for the § 1.752-7 liability. First, immediately following the assumption of the § 1.752-7 liability from the partnership by a partner other than the § 1.752-7 liability partner, the partnership must reduce its basis in its assets by the remaining built-in loss associated with the liability. The basis adjustment is allocated among the partnership's assets following the rules of Code Sec. 734(b).

The assuming partner, on the other hand, is not allowed to account for the § 1.752-7 liability until such time as the liability is satisfied. At that time, the assuming partner adjusts his or her basis in the partnership interest, any assets distributed by the partnership to such partner, or gain or loss on disposition of the partnership interest as if a recognized liability had been assumed. The amount of the adjustment is equal to the lesser of the amount paid in satisfaction of the debt or the remaining built-in loss associated with the debt. Any amounts paid in excess of

---

[62] Reg. § 1.752-7(f)(1).

[63] Reg. § 1.752-7(g)(1).

[64] As indicated in Example 9-15, a deduction is allowed in the event that the liability is satisfied in exchange for a

payment that exceeds the built-in loss inherent in the liability at the date of the distribution or assumption of such liability by another partner/member. *See* Reg. §§ 1.752-7(f)(2) and 1.752-7(g)(4).

such amount are deductible or treated as a capital expenditure by the assuming partner.[65]

Example 9-16: *Q*, *L* and *R* form the QLR Partnership. *Q* contributes property 1 with a tax basis and fair market value of $3,000,000. The property is subject to a contingent liability valued at $1,200,000. In return, she receives a 25% interest in the partnership. *L* contributes $1,800,000 in cash in exchange for a 25% interest, and *R* contributes $3,600,000 cash in exchange for a 50% interest. The partnership uses the cash provided by *L* and *R* to purchase additional property.

Two years later, the partnership distributes Property 1 to *R* in partial liquidation of *R*'s interest in the partnership. *R* took the property subject to the $1,200,000 § 1.752-7 liability. Upon the distribution of Property 1 to *R*, *Q* is required to reduce her basis in her partnership interest by $1,200,000 (to $1,800,000). Similarly, the QLR Partnership is required to reduce its tax basis in its other properties by $1,200,000. *R* takes a $3,000,000 carryover basis in Property 1, equal to its tax basis in the hands of the partnership. Assuming that *R*'s tax basis in the partnership interest remained $3,600,000 prior to receipt of the distribution, her remaining tax basis in the interest will be reduced to $600,000.

Assume that *R* subsequently pays $900,000 to satisfy the § 1.752-7 liability. *R* will not be entitled to a tax deduction for the payment. Instead, *R* will increase the tax basis of the encumbered property (Property 1) by the $900,000 payment. If *R* notifies *Q* that the debt has been satisfied, *Q* will be allowed a $900,000 ordinary loss for the amount paid by *R* in satisfaction of the debt, and a $300,000 capital loss deduction for the excess of the built-in loss over the amount paid in satisfaction of the § 1.752-7 liability.

.05 Exceptions

The provisions of Reg. § 1.752-7 do not apply to contingent liabilities transferred in the following situations:

- The partnership assumes the liability in connection with a contribution by the partner of the trade or business with which such liability is associated and the entity continues to carry on that trade or business after the contribution; or

- Just prior to the contribution, the remaining built-in loss associated with the § 1.752-7 liability is less than the lesser of 10 percent of the gross value of all partnership assets or $1,000,000; or

- The § 1.752-7 partner transfers his or her interest in the partnership (in whole or in part) in a nonrecognition transaction (*e.g.*, under Code Sec. 351 or 721).

---

[65] Similar rules apply when the encumbered property is contributed by the partnership to another partnership or corporation. *See* Reg. § 1.752-7 (i).

PART III

LIMITATIONS ON PARTNERSHIP DEDUCTIONS

Chapter 10

Limitations on the Deductibility of Partnership Losses

¶ 1001 Introduction

The deductibility of partnership losses passed through to a partner is subject to three separate limitations. First, under Code Sec. 704(d), the loss may not exceed the partner's *tax basis* in the partnership interest. Second, any losses that survive the Code Sec. 704(d) limitation are subject to the *at-risk limitation* of Code Sec. 465. Finally, losses may be disallowed under the *passive loss limitations* of Code Sec. 469 even if they do not exceed the partner's tax basis or amount at-risk in the partnership interest. Note that these limitations are applied *sequentially*—the Code Sec. 704(d) limitation is applied first, followed by the Code Sec. 465 limitation, and finally the Code Sec. 469 limitation. Amounts disallowed under each section are subject to different carryforward provisions.

Example 10-1: *J* is a one-third partner in JDR Partnership. Her tax basis in her partnership interest is $35,000, consisting of her $15,000 investment in partnership capital and her $20,000 share of partnership nonrecourse liabilities. None of these liabilities are qualified nonrecourse liabilities (i.e., they do not increase her amount at risk, as discussed at ¶ 1005). *J*'s interest in the partnership is a passive activity, and she has no passive income from any other source. For the current year, *J*'s distributive share of the partnership's loss, reported on Schedule K-1, is $45,000.

Under Code Sec. 704(d), $10,000 of *J*'s pass-through loss will be disallowed because it exceeds the tax basis of her partnership interest ($45,000 total loss – $35,000 tax basis). Of the $35,000 loss allowed under Code Sec. 704(d), an additional $20,000 will be disallowed under Code Sec. 465 because the non-qualified nonrecourse liabilities are included in her tax basis but not in her amount at risk. Finally, the remaining $15,000 of the pass-through loss will be disallowed under Code Sec. 469, since passive losses can generally only be deducted against passive income from other sources. Thus, none of the $45,000 loss allocated to *J* will be deductible this year. $10,000 will be disallowed (and carried forward) under Code Sec. 704(d), $20,000 will be disallowed (and carried forward) under the at-risk rules of Code Sec. 465, and the remaining $15,000 will be disallowed (and carried forward) under the Code Sec. 469 passive activity loss rules.

Note in the above example that although Carrie's entire pass-through loss was denied under various statutory limitations of the Internal Revenue Code, her tax basis in her partnership interest is still reduced to zero, as is her amount at risk. Because losses were allowed under Code Secs. 704(d) and 465, those losses reduce her basis and at-risk amounts, respectively, even though the losses were subsequently disallowed under different statutes.

¶ 1002 Disallowed Losses Are Carried Forward

.01 Carryforwards Under Code Sec. 704(d)

Any loss passed through to a partner in excess of his basis in the partnership interest is carried forward indefinitely until such time as the partner obtains additional basis sufficient to allow the deduction. Carryforward losses unused as of the date of sale or disposition of the partnership interest are lost—they do *not* carry over to the transferee (if any) of such interest, and they do not reduce the gain (if any) or increase the loss (if any) recognized in connection with sale of the partnership interest.

Example 10-2: *E* is a 25% partner in Lockwood Partners. His original tax basis in his partnership interest was $35,000, but pass-through losses of ($40,000) reduced that basis to zero. The $5,000 excess of his distributive share of partnership losses over his tax basis in the partnership interest is carried forward under Code Sec. 704(d), and will be deductible when (and if) he obtains additional tax basis (e.g., as the result of an additional contribution to partnership capital).

This year, he sold his interest in the partnership for $10,000, recognizing a $10,000 capital gain (recall that his tax basis was zero). The gain does not increase his tax basis in the partnership interest—indeed, he no longer has an interest in the partnership. Thus, the $5,000 carryforward under Code Sec. 704(d) is lost.

Note that the loss carryforward is not deductible against *E*'s capital gain from sale of the partnership interest because it did not reduce the tax basis of that interest. Put another way, had the loss been deductible, *E*'s basis in the interest would presumably have been negative $5,000 ($35,000 tax basis less $40,000 pass-through loss). Sale of the interest for $10,000 would then have triggered a $15,000 capital gain, rather than $10,000 as above. Thus, *E*'s gain from sale of the interest is *already lower than it would have been had the loss been allowed*. Accordingly, the loss carryforward cannot be utilized to offset the gain recognized on sale of the partnership interest.

.02 Carryforwards Under Code Sec. 465

Losses disallowed under the at-risk rules of Code Sec. 465 are carried forward indefinitely just as are those denied under Code Sec. 704(d). Carryforwards under the two statutes have different effects on the partner, however. As noted above, to the extent deductible under Code Sec. 704(d), a partner's allocable share of the partnership's loss reduces her tax basis in the partnership interest *whether or not it is ultimately deductible under Code Secs. 465 and 469*. Thus, a partner's tax basis in her partnership interest is reduced by losses even if they are disallowed under the at-risk rules (Code Sec. 465). As a result, the partner's gain upon a subsequent sale of that interest is increased by losses that have previously been disallowed under the at-risk rules (because these losses reduced tax basis with no corresponding tax benefit). Thus, when a partner sells her interest in the partnership, losses carried forward under Code Sec. 465, unlike those carried forward under Code Sec. 704, are deductible in full, regardless of the amount of gain or loss recognized by the partner/member on the transaction.

> **Example 10-3:** *Q* is a 10% limited partner in Quantum Limited Partnership. She has a zero tax basis in her partnership interest and her amount at risk is also zero. She has an $8,000 loss carryforward under Code Sec. 704(d) and a $3,500 loss carryforward under Code Sec. 465. She sold her interest in the partnership this year for $25,000, recognizing a $25,000 capital gain.
>
> Note that the loss carryforward under Code Sec. 704(d) is disregarded in determining the tax consequences of the sale of *Q*'s partnership interest. The carryforward cannot be deducted against her gain on the sale, and since she is no longer a partner in Quantum, she will never have additional basis in the interest. The Code Sec. 704(d) carryforward is essentially forfeited upon sale of her interest in the partnership.
>
> In contrast, *Q*'s loss carryforward under Code Sec. 465 consists of losses previously allowed under Code Sec. 704(d) before being disallowed by Code Sec. 465. Accordingly, these losses have reduced her tax basis in the partnership interest, even though they have not actually been deducted. As a result, *Q*'s recognized gain of $25,000 exceeds the economic gain actually realized on the investment by the amount of the loss disallowed under Code Sec. 465. This imbalance is corrected by allowing *Q* to deduct her Code Sec. 465 loss carryforward *in full* on sale or disposition of her interest. She will therefore report a $25,000 capital gain and a ($3,500) ordinary loss in the year of sale.

¶1002.02

Example 10-4: T is a 10% partner in Slingshot Partners, a limited partnership. His tax basis in his partnership interest is $50,000, consisting of his $20,000 investment in partnership capital and his $30,000 share of the partnership's non-qualified nonrecourse debt. For the current year, T's distributive share of the partnership's taxable loss was ($65,000). Under Code Sec. 704(d), only ($50,000) of this loss will be deductible; the remaining ($15,000) will be carried forward indefinitely. Because non-qualified nonrecourse debt is not included in T's at-risk amount, however, only ($20,000) of the loss allowed under Code Sec. 704(d) will be deductible under Code Sec. 465. T's tax basis in his partnership interest will be zero at the end of the year, and he will have loss carryforwards of ($15,000) under Code Sec. 704(d) and ($30,000) under Code Sec. 465.

Example 10-5: Assume in the example above that the partnership has positive income in its second year of operations, and that T's share of this income is $28,000. This income gives T additional tax basis and increases his at-risk amount in the partnership interest. Since the additional basis exceeds the ($15,000) loss carryforward under Code Sec. 704(d), that entire carryforward is deductible in year 2. After deducting the Code Sec. 704(d) loss carryforward, T's net income from the partnership in year 2 is $13,000. This income in turn increases T's amount at-risk in the partnership interest, allowing him to use $13,000 of his Code Sec. 465 carryforward. Thus, for year 2, T will report no income from the partnership, and will have a remaining Code Sec. 465 carryforward of ($17,000). His basis in the partnership interest will be $13,000 ($28,000 income minus ($15,000) loss carryforward), and his amount at-risk will be zero ($13,000 net income minus ($13,000) at-risk carryforward utilized).

Example 10-6: Assume the same facts as in the previous two examples. Going into year 3, T has a $13,000 tax basis in his partnership interest, and a ($17,000) carryforward under Code Sec. 465. Assume that in year 3, T sells his interest in the partnership for $18,000 cash, plus assumption of his $30,000 share of the partnership's non-qualified nonrecourse debt. Subtracting his $13,000 tax basis from the $48,000 net selling price yields a $35,000 taxable gain. This gain presumably will be capital in nature. Sale of the partnership interest triggers T's ($17,000) carryforward under Code Sec. 465. This carryforward loss will be deductible in full, and will retain its character as ordinary loss (assuming it was ordinary in nature in years 1 and 2 when originally passed through to T). Thus, in year 3, T will recognize a capital gain of $35,000 and an ordinary loss of ($17,000).

.03 Carryforwards Under Code Sec. 469 (Passive Loss Carryforwards)

For individuals, losses from passive activities are only deductible to the extent of income from other passive activities. Any excess passive losses are not allowed in the current year. Losses disallowed under the passive loss limitations are carried forward indefinitely until such time as the partnership/LLC has sufficient passive income from other sources to absorb the carryforward. If the partner or LLC member completely disposes of his/her interest in the entity, any passive loss

¶1002.03

carryforward attributable to that investment (i.e., the specific investment in the partnership or LLC) is deductible in full in the year of disposition.

> *Example 10-7: C* is a limited partner in Breakout LLP. Her partnership interest in Breakout is a passive activity for *C* and is subject to the passive loss limitations. She has no interest in any other passive activities. Assume that in Year 1, *C*'s distributive share of the partnership's loss is ($18,000). Further assume that her tax basis and at-risk amount are both $20,000. Since Breakout is a passive activity for *C*, she is not allowed a deduction for the pass-through loss. Note that although the loss is disallowed under the passive loss rules, it still reduces her basis and at-risk amounts to $2,000. In year 2, assume *C* sells her entire interest in the LLP, recognizing a $15,000 capital gain. Disposition of her entire interest in the activity will trigger the deduction of her passive loss carryforward. As in the above example, this loss retains the character of the original pass-through loss in year 1, even though her gain on sale of the partnership interest is capital in nature.

¶ 1003 The Basis Limitations of Code Sec. 704(d)

.01 Losses Cannot Exceed Tax Basis

A general rule of taxation is that taxpayers may not claim a deduction for losses or expenses in excess of the amount they stand to lose in connection with the investment. Similarly, losses and/or depreciation deductions cannot be claimed in excess of the taxpayer's actual investment in depreciable property.

> *Example 10-8: R* purchased an office building in the city several years ago for a total cost of $500,000. He claimed depreciation deductions totaling $225,000 prior to this year, when the building was destroyed by a tornado. When the building was destroyed, its fair market value had increased to approximately $650,000. Nonetheless, *R*'s tax loss is limited to $275,000, the remaining unrecovered cost of his investment in the building. He paid $500,000 for the building, and his total deductions with respect to it cannot exceed that figure. Since he has already deducted $225,000 in depreciation expense, his tax basis—the amount he stands to lose with respect to the property—was only $275,000 at the date of the loss. He cannot deduct a loss in excess of his remaining basis even though the building was worth far more at the date of its destruction.

In the partnership context, this means that a partner cannot deduct partnership losses that exceed the tax basis of the partnership interest. For example, assume in the example above that *R* contributed the building to a partnership rather than selling it. For tax purposes, his investment in the partnership would be only $275,000, the remaining unrecovered cost of the building, even though the value of the building was much higher.[1]

---

[1] Note however, that the *book* value of the property on the partnership's Code Sec. 704(b) books would be equal to its fair market value at the date of contribution. This would also be the initial balance in *R*'s Code Sec. 704(b) capital account (assuming no liabilities encumbered the property at the date of contribution).

.02 Accounting for Debt

The fact that a taxpayer has directly paid only a portion of the total cost of an asset as of the date of loss does not affect the computation of his/her tax basis in that asset. Liabilities incurred to finance acquisition of the property are included in tax basis even though they represent amounts not yet paid by the taxpayer. The taxpayer's tax basis in an asset represents the amount which he/she stands to lose should the asset decline in value. The taxpayer's risk of loss encompasses not only amounts which he/she has directly paid in connection with acquisition and improvement of the asset, but also any amounts he/she is obligated to pay in the future.

> **Example 10-9:** *H* purchased real estate for $350,000. She paid $75,000 cash and financed the remainder with a $280,000 mortgage from an unrelated lender. Although *H*'s direct out-of-pocket expenditure for the property was only $75,000, her tax basis in the property is equal to its purchase price of $350,000. This figure includes both the $75,000 she has already paid and the $280,000 she is obligated to pay in the future. Note that if the property declines in value subsequent to Hope's purchase, she will still be obligated to repay the entire $280,000 debt. Thus, her total investment in the property—the amount she stands to lose if it becomes totally worthless—is $350,000.

As noted in an earlier chapter, contingent liabilities are generally disregarded in calculating basis.

.03 Nonrecourse Debt

Inclusion of liabilities in the tax basis of property is conceptually well-founded because debt generally increases a taxpayer's economic risk of loss. The issue becomes less clear, however, when debt is structured as "nonrecourse" to the borrower. A nonrecourse debt is one for which the borrower has no individual responsibility to repay the lender. That is, the lender has no personal recourse against the borrower in the event the debt is not repaid.

Instead, with a nonrecourse debt the lender agrees to look solely to the property serving as collateral for the debt in the event of default. The lender can foreclose on the property, but should the property turn out to be worth less than the remaining debt balance, the lender has no further recourse against the borrower.[2]

> **Example 10-10:** *D* purchased an office building for $750,000. She paid $175,000 down, and borrowed the remaining $575,000 from an unrelated lender. The mortgage was structured as nonrecourse debt. The building subsequently declined in value to $400,000, and *D* stopped making payments on the mortgage. Assume that the outstanding (i.e., unpaid) balance of the mortgage at the date of default was $500,000. *D* cannot be legally compelled to continue making payments on the loan. The lender's only recourse is to foreclose on the office building, taking it in complete satisfaction of the

---

[2] Generally, with a nonrecourse debt, the borrower must make a larger down payment, and pay a higher rate of interest, relative to recourse loans.

¶1003.02

remaining debt. If it can sell the property for no more than $400,000, it will lose the remaining $100,000 of the loan. *D* will not recognize cancellation of indebtedness income, but will instead be treated as having sold the office building to the lender for $500,000, the remaining unpaid balance of the loan.

Although the borrower is not personally liable for repayment of a nonrecourse loan, if the loan is a legitimate economic liability, it will generally be included in the borrower's tax basis for the property. As will be more fully discussed below, nonrecourse debts are generally considered legitimate if they are borrowed from an unrelated lender, or if the borrower can demonstrate that the fair market value of the property exceeded the principal balance of the loan at the time the loan was made (thus indicating that the borrower intends to repay the loan).

¶ 1004 Code Sec. 465—Losses Cannot Exceed Taxpayer's "At-risk" Amount

Obviously, in the above example, *D*'s tax basis in the office building, which includes the entire $500,000 in nonrecourse indebtedness, exceeds her actual risk of loss with respect to the property. The at-risk rules were originally designed to address this issue, excluding nonrecourse debts from the calculation of the taxpayer's "at-risk" amount. Over time, however, the real estate lobby has won a significant exception to these limitations for so-called "qualified" nonrecourse debts.

Code Sec. 465, which applies to individuals and closely held corporations only, provides that a taxpayer may not claim deductions for losses in excess of the amount that the taxpayer actually has "at risk" with respect to the activity generating the losses.[3] For this purpose, a taxpayer's amount at risk is computed in the same manner as is his/her tax basis except that it does not include *nonqualified* nonrecourse debt.

Under Code Sec. 465(b)(6), a qualified nonrecourse debt (i.e., one that is included in the taxpayer's amount at risk) is one which:

1. Is borrowed by the taxpayer with respect to the activity of holding real property, and which is secured by that real property;

2. Is borrowed from a lender who is in the business of lending money and who has no interest in the activity for which the money is borrowed, other than as a creditor; and

3. Is not convertible into stock or other securities of the taxpayer.

In essence, Code Sec. 465 prohibits inclusion of nonrecourse debts in the taxpayer's amount at risk only if the proceeds of the loan are not invested in real estate, or if the lender is related to the borrower, or has an interest in the activity in which the loan proceeds are to be invested.

One of the primary concerns of Congress in enacting Code Sec. 465 was the case in which a seller sells real estate to a buyer, and finances the purchase him/herself by issuing a nonrecourse loan to the buyer. In this case, because the lender

---

[3] Code Sec. 465(b).

is so integrally tied to the transaction, there is no way for the IRS to know whether the sales price is reasonable. The borrower can easily inflate the apparent purchase price and thereby secure larger depreciation deductions, with no risk that the inflated price will ever be paid.

> **Example 10-11:** Jones and Day, both doctors, approach Doris, owner of a motel, with a purchase offer. Although the value of the motel is about $125,000, Jones and Day offer to purchase the property from Doris for $1,250,000. They offer to pay $50,000 down. Doris will finance the remaining $1,200,000 with an "interest-only" nonrecourse note, the terms of which require the doctors to pay $60,000 per year in interest expense for the next 15 years, with a balloon payment of $1,200,000 due at the end of that period. They then propose to lease the motel back to Doris for $60,000 per year. The lease payments owed by Doris will offset the interest owed by Jones and Day, and thus no cash payments will actually be made by either party. At the end of 15 years, if the motel has appreciated sufficiently in value, Jones and Day will make the balloon payment to pay off the loan. If not, then Doris will foreclose, taking back ownership of the motel. In the interim, Jones and Day hope to deduct depreciation expense of $32,000 per year (the motel is depreciable over 39 years). Since they are both in the 35% tax bracket, these deductions would save them $11,200 per year in income taxes. Over 15 years, they would save a total of $168,000 in income taxes, over three times the amount they actually paid to Doris. Doris, unlike an unrelated lender, has not advanced any real funds to Jones and Day, and therefore will be less concerned if they decide not to make the final balloon payment. In the end, she will retain ownership of the motel, and will have $50,000 cash as an incentive for joining in the transaction. Although this transaction is a sham, and would not be recognized for tax purposes if the true value of the motel was known by the IRS, it is often difficult for the IRS to accurately assess value in such cases. Section 465 eliminates this problem. Because Doris is both the seller of the motel and the lender in this case, the nonrecourse debt is not a qualified nonrecourse debt, and is not included in Jones' and Day's amount at risk. Accordingly, their deductions for depreciation and other expenses related to the motel cannot exceed $50,000.

¶ 1005 Passive Loss Limitations—In General

.01 General

Code Sec. 469, implemented in 1986, denies deductions for net losses from so-called "passive" activities.[4] These "passive" loss limitations focus primarily on losses realized from rental activities and with losses "allocated" to nonparticipatory partners (i.e., limited partners) in partnership activities. For example, landlords often recognize tax losses on residential rental property even though out-of-pocket costs (e.g., mortgage payments) are covered by rental proceeds and the underlying property appreciates in value.

---

[4] The statute also applies to tax credits generated by passive activities. Code Sec. 469(a)(1).

Example 10-12: L purchased a rental house at a total cost of $78,000. He rented the house to tenants for $750 per month. This year, he paid mortgage interest of $6,280, insurance of $600 and $1,200 in property taxes. In addition, he is allowed a depreciation deduction of $2,476, giving him total deductions of $10,556. Offsetting these deductions was rental income of $9,000 ($750 × 12 months), yielding a tax loss of ($1,556). Note that although he realizes a tax loss of over $1,500, he actually had a positive cash flow from the rental activity. L's total cash outlays were $8,080, while he received cash rent payments of $9,000. Assuming that principal payments on the mortgage were less than $920, L's cash inflows exceeded his cash outflows. Yet, for tax purposes, he claimed a ($1,500) loss.

The rationale behind the statute is pretty basic. Where a taxpayer is not personally involved in the daily operations associated with an activity (as in the case of a limited partner) or where an activity does not require a substantial amount of personal attention from the taxpayer (as in the case of rental property), the activity is more akin to an investment than to a business activity. Thus, the "true" loss realized by the taxpayer as a result of investment in the activity can be accurately measured only when the investment is liquidated. At that point, the taxpayer can measure his/her total cash outflows against total cash inflows and determine whether the investment resulted in a net gain or a net loss. Accordingly, under Code Sec. 469, *net* losses (passive losses in excess of passive income) from passive activities are disallowed in the current year. Disallowed losses are carried forward and can be deducted only against net passive income generated in future years or when the taxpayer fully disposes of his/her interest in the passive activity.

Consider the facts in Example 10-12. L purchased rental property for $78,000. His total cash outflows were $8,080 and his total cash inflows were $9,000. Assume that at the beginning of next year, he sells the house. If he sells the house for $80,000, he will have realized a total net profit of $2,920: he paid a total of $86,080 ($78,000 original cost plus $8,080 in interest expense, insurance and property taxes), and received a total of $89,000 ($80,000 sales price plus $9,000 rent income), leaving him $2,920 better off. If the passive loss limitations do not apply to this rental activity, he will deduct a ($1,556) loss in year 1, and recognize a $4,476 gain from sale of the house in year 2 ($80,000 selling price less $75,524 adjusted tax basis, measured as the original $78,000 selling price less $2,476 depreciation expense). The net result is a $2,920 profit ($4,476 year 2 gain, less $1,556 year 1 loss). In contrast, if the passive loss rules do apply to L's investment, he will recognize no loss in year 1, and will recognize a $2,920 net gain in year 2, consisting of the $4,476 gain from sale of the house, and the ($1,556) carryforward loss from year 1. Either way, the net results to L and the government are the same. The only difference is in timing.

.02 Passive Activity Losses Can Be Deducted Only Against Passive Activity Income

Under Code Sec. 469, passive activity losses are deductible only from passive activity income. As noted above, excess losses are carried forward indefinitely until the taxpayer has passive income, or until the taxpayer disposes of his/her entire interest in the activity in a fully taxable transaction.

Note that the passive loss limitation is applied *after* application of the at-risk rules. Thus, any loss disallowed under Code Sec. 465 is not considered in applying the passive loss rules. This may result in losses from other activities, including other investments in partnerships or LLCs, being allowed.

> *Example 10-13: Q* owns interests as a limited partner in three partnerships: Limited Partnership X, Limited Partnership Y, and Limited Partnership Z. Assume that all three activities are passive activities for *Q*. Assume that her basis, at-risk amounts, and pass-through income or loss from each activity are as follows:

Partnership	Tax Basis	At-risk Amount	Pass-through Income or Loss
X	$28,000	$22,000	($21,000)
Y	$25,000	$25,000	$15,000
Z	$12,000	0	($7,500)

Because *Q*'s "at-risk amount" in Limited Partnership Z is zero, none of the ($7,500) loss from that partnership is deductible under Code Sec. 465. In contrast, the loss passed through from Limited Partnership X is less than *Q*'s basis and amount at-risk, and therefore the entire loss survives the limitations of Code Secs. 704(d) and 465. Under Code Sec. 469, however, this loss will be allowed only to the extent of the passive income from Limited Partnership Y (assuming that she has no passive income from any other source other than her limited partnership investments). Thus, $15,000 of the Partnership X loss will be deductible under Code Sec. 469. *Q* will have a ($6,000) loss carryforward under that statute. None of the Partnership Z loss carryforward is a passive loss carryforward. Rather, it is a Code Sec. 465 carryforward, although even if it is allowed under the at-risk limitations in a subsequent year, it will still be subject to the passive loss limitations that year (and therefore may not be deductible if *Q* does not have sufficient passive income in that year).

.03 Passive Activity Credits

Similar rules apply to tax credits from passive activities. Credits passed through from passive activities can be applied only against the tax from net passive income. Passive activity credits include the general business credit and other special business credits, such as the credit for fuel produced from a non-conventional source. Like passive losses, credits from passive activities that exceed the tax on net income from passive activities are carried forward indefinitely and may be used to offset income taxes on net passive income in future years. Unlike passive loss carryforwards, however, passive activity credit carryovers are *not* triggered upon the disposition of a partner or LLC member's entire interest in the partnership or LLC. Rather, they continue to be carried forward, indefinitely, to be applied against taxes on passive income in future years.

¶1005.03

¶ 1006 Classification of Income Under Code Sec. 469

.01 General

Net income or loss from a passive activity is computed as the excess of *passive activity income* over *passive activity deductions*. Passive activity income includes all income from passive activities *including gain from disposition* of an interest in a passive activity or from disposition of property used in a passive activity.

Income from the following sources is *not* passive activity income:

- Income from any activity that is not a passive activity (e.g., income from activities in which the taxpayer "materially participates," as defined below).

- Portfolio income—interest, dividends, annuities, and royalties not derived in the ordinary course of a trade or business, including gain or loss from the disposition of property that produces these types of income or that is held for investment.[5]

- "Personal services income"—salaries, wages, commissions, self-employment income from non-passive trade or business activities, deferred compensation, guaranteed payments from partnerships or LLCs, taxable social security and other retirement benefits, and similar payments.

- Income from working interests in oil or gas properties.

- Income from intangible property, such as a patent, copyright, or literary, musical or artistic composition, if the taxpayer's personal efforts significantly contributed to the creation of the property.

- A partner's distributive share of net income from a publicly traded partnership.[6]

.02 Gain from Sale or Disposition of Property

Gain on the sale or disposition of property is generally classified as passive activity income if, at the time of the disposition, the property was used in a passive activity. For property used in more than one activity during the preceding 12 months, the gain must be allocated between the two activities based on the property's use during that period. Any portion of the gain allocated to a passive activity is passive income.

In some cases, it is acceptable to allocate the gain solely to the activity in which the property was primarily used. Such an allocation is allowable if the fair market value of the taxpayer's interest in the property is not more than the lesser of:

- $10,000, or

- 10 percent of the total of the fair market value of all property used in that activity immediately before the disposition (including the property that has been disposed of).[7]

---

[5] The exclusion for portfolio income does not apply to self-charged interest treated as passive activity income. *See* Section 1.469–7 of the regulations.

[6] The passive loss rules are applied separately to each interest owned by a partner in a publicly traded partnership. *See* Code Sec. 469(k).

[7] Reg. § 1.469-2T(c)(2).

.03 Gain from Sale of an Interest in a Partnership

Similar rules apply to the classification of gain recognized on the sale of an interest in a partnership. If the partnership was engaged in a passive activity, any gain or loss recognized on the sale or disposition of the partner's interest in the entity will be classified as passive gain or loss. If the partnership is engaged in more than one activity (e.g., a passive activity and a portfolio activity), the gain or loss must be allocated between the entity's different activities and classified accordingly. The allocation is generally based on the relative amounts of gain or loss which would have been recognized by the partner if the entity had sold its entire interests in each of its activities just prior to the partner's sale of his/her partnership interest.[8]

> **Example 10-14:** C owns a 10% limited partnership interest in a real estate development partnership. Because C is a limited partner, her share of the partnership's income or loss from its rental real estate activities is passive. This year, she sold her interest in the partnership to an unrelated buyer, recognizing a $25,000 gain. A review of the partnership's balance sheet indicates that 20% of this gain is attributable to portfolio assets held by the partnership and 80% is attributable to the partnership's rental real estate activity. C's gain will be allocated between passive and portfolio income in the same ratio—$20,000 passive income and $5,000 portfolio income.

Note that the same rules apply to classification of gain from the sale of an interest in any passive activity.

.04 Special Rule for Substantially Appreciated Property

Gain recognized on the sale of "substantially appreciated" property cannot be classified as passive income unless one of the following conditions applies:[9]

* The property was used in a passive activity for 20% of the time the taxpayer owned the property (or owned an interest therein); or

* The property was used in a passive activity for the entire 24-month period preceding the disposition.

Thus the transfer of appreciated property to a passive activity followed shortly thereafter by sale of such property will not generate passive income. Similar rules apply to the transfer of substantially appreciated property to a partnership, LLC, or other pass-through entity within two years before the contributor sells his/her interest in the entity.[10]

> **Example 10-15:** V is a 50% partner in a partnership formed several years ago to invest in rental residential real estate. The partnership is a passive activity. Last year, V transferred investment property to the partnership that she had held for several years. The investment property was worth $120,000 at the date of the transfer; her tax basis in the property was $50,000. The

---

[8] Reg. § 1.469-2T(e)(3)(ii). Note that a default rule provides that allocation of a partner/member's gain among the entity's activities may be made on the basis of the relative fair market values of each activity if it is not possible to determine how much gain or loss would be allocated to such partner/member from the sale of the entity's entire interest in each of its activities.

[9] Reg. § 1.469-2(c)(2)(iii).

[10] Reg. § 1.469-2T(e)(3)(iv)(B).

partnership planned to construct an additional rent house on the property. This year, *V* sold her partnership interest to an unrelated buyer for $250,000. Her tax basis in the partnership interest was $160,000. Assume that the value of the investment property she had previously contributed to the partnership was unchanged from the date of contribution. *V* will recognize a total gain on sale of her partnership interest of $90,000. Of this, $70,000 is attributable to the appreciated property contributed to the partnership within two years of sale of her interest. Since she did not use the property in a passive activity prior to its contribution to the partnership, this portion of her gain is not classified as passive income. The remainder of her gain, $20,000, is attributable to the sale of her interest in a passive activity and will be classified as passive income.

¶ 1007 Classification of Expenses and Deductions Under Code Sec. 469

Passive activity deductions include both deductions associated with passive activities incurred during the *current* tax year and *prior year* deductions from passive activities that are carried forward to the current tax year. They also include losses from dispositions of property used in a passive activity and losses from the disposition of the taxpayer's interest, or a portion thereof, in a passive activity.

Passive activity deductions do *not* include the following items:

- Deductions for expenses that are clearly and directly allocable to portfolio income.
- Qualified home mortgage interest, capitalized interest expenses, and other interest expenses other than self-charged interest treated as a passive activity deduction.[11]
- Losses from dispositions of property that produce portfolio income or property held for investment.
- State, local, and foreign income taxes.
- Miscellaneous itemized deductions that may be disallowed because of the two percent of adjusted gross income limit.
- Charitable contributions.
- Net operating loss deductions.
- Percentage depletion carryovers for oil and gas wells.
- Capital loss carry-backs and carryovers.
- The deduction for one-half of self-employment tax.

¶ 1008 Taxpayers to Whom Code Sec. 469 Applies

The passive loss rules apply only to individuals, certain trusts and estates, personal service corporations and closely-held corporations.[12] Although the rules do not technically apply to LLCs, partnerships, and S-corporations directly, they do apply to the owners of these entities, assuming the owners would be subject to the

---

[11] Reg. § 1.469-7.

[12] Code Sec. 469(a)(2). Corporations that are not closely held are not subject to these provisions.

limitations if they held their interests in the activity directly rather than through the LLC, partnership, or S corporation.

Unlike individuals, closely held corporations are allowed to deduct net passive losses against active income.[13] Similarly, they can offset the tax attributable to net active income with passive activity credits. However, closely held corporations cannot offset portfolio income with net passive losses. Thus, certain closely held partnerships and LLCs involved in passive activities may consider electing to be taxed as corporations rather than partnerships in order to avoid some of the passive loss limitations.

¶ 1009 Passive Activities Defined

Although targeted primarily at rental real estate activities and activities conducted through limited partnerships, "passive" activities under Code Sec. 469 are rather broadly defined. In fact, the primary standard for determining whether an activity is passive is the level of participation required of the taxpayer with regard to the activity. A passive activity is defined as one in which the taxpayer does not "materially participate" during the taxable year. In addition, most rental activities are deemed to be passive regardless of the taxpayer's level of participation, though there is a rather significant exception for taxpayers who are engaged primarily in the real estate business.[14]

.01 Material Participation—the "500 Hour" Rule

The first step in determining whether the passive loss rules apply to a particular taxpayer is to determine which of his/her activities are passive in nature. As indicated above, Code Sec. 469 is really targeted at real estate activities and limited partnership activities. However, the statute is so broadly written that other activities can easily fall under its umbrella. In general, the statute defines an activity as passive unless the taxpayer "materially participates" in the activity. Material participation is defined as involvement, by the taxpayer or his/her spouse, which is "regular, continuous and substantial."[15] The statute further provides that a limited partner cannot satisfy this requirement. Accordingly, interests held as a limited partner are generally classified as passive.[16]

The "regular, continuous and substantial" standard above is rather ambiguous, but additional guidance is provided in the regulations. The regulations provide that the determination of whether a taxpayer's participation is material is made by reference to the number of hours the taxpayer actually spent participating in the activity. The general standard is 500 hours—that is, taxpayers spending at least 500 hours in an activity during the taxable year are deemed to have materially participated in the activity. In order to make it easier for family-run small businesses to

---

[13] Net active income is the corporation's taxable income computed without regard to any income or loss from a passive activity or any portfolio income or loss.

[14] The Code also provides that working interests in oil and gas properties are not passive activities whether or not the taxpayer materially participates. Code Sec. 469(c)(3).

[15] Code Sec. 469(h)(1).

[16] The regulations provide exceptions in some cases in which the limited partnership interest generates profits rather than losses or in which a formerly nonpassive interest in an activity is converted into a limited partnership interest.

qualify as active, participation by the spouse is treated as participation by the taxpayer.

The 500-hour standard would create problems for taxpayers who are starting a business outside of their regular employment which takes a while to get off the ground. In recognition of this issue, alternative tests impose a 100 hour standard under which, in conjunction with other conditions, a taxpayer's participation in an activity can be deemed material.

Finally, the regulations provide a number of other exceptions under which taxpayers who do not participate in an activity for at least 500 hours during the taxable year will nonetheless be deemed to have materially participated. These rules are designed primarily to prevent taxpayers from classifying profitable activities as passive activities, thereby allowing them to use losses from other passive activities.[17] Taxpayers trying to avoid classification of an activity as passive will not be affected by these provisions. These provisions are discussed more fully below.

.02 Alternative Standards for Material Participation

The regulations establish a number of tests under which taxpayers may be deemed to have "materially participated in an activity." Satisfaction of any one of the following tests constitutes material participation:

1. The taxpayer's participation in the activity exceeded 500 hours (during the tax year);

2. The taxpayer's participation constituted substantially all the participation in the activity, including the participation of individuals who did not own any interest in the activity (e.g., a part-time business with no or very few employees);

3. The taxpayer's participation exceeded 100 hours during the tax year, and was at least as much as any other person's participation in the activity (again, including people who did not own an interest in the activity) (e.g., a part-time business with a minimum level of employees);

4. The activity is a "significant participation activity" as defined below;

5. The taxpayer materially participated in the activity for any 5 of the preceding 10 taxable years (e.g., a retiree or variable-participation activity);

6. The activity is a personal service activity (involving personal services in the fields of health, veterinary services, law, engineering, architecture, accounting, actuarial science, performing arts, consulting, or any other trade or business in which capital is not a material income-producing factor), and the taxpayer has materially participated in it for any three preceding taxable years (e.g., a recent retiree); or

7. The facts and circumstances support that the taxpayer participated in the activity on a "regular, continuous, and substantial basis" during the taxable year.

---

[17] *See* Reg. § 1.469-5T(f).

Example 10-16: R has a full-time job as an accountant. In addition, he and a friend have started a lawn care business which they operate after regular working hours and on weekends. The business is organized as a partnership, owned 50% each by R and his friend. During the current year, R and his partner each worked about 160 hours providing lawn care services. Their income was not sufficient to offset their costs (primarily equipment and fuel), and they incurred a loss for the year. Since R and his friend each worked more than 100 hours, and both worked the same amount of time, their home improvement business is not a passive activity, and they may deduct their loss without limitation.

A partner cannot be deemed to have materially participated in an activity under test 7 above unless he/she participated in the activity for more than 100 hours during the year. Participation in managing the activity does not count in determining material participation under this test if:

- Any other person received compensation for managing the activity, or

- Any other individual spent more hours during the tax year managing the activity (regardless of whether the individual was compensated for such management services).

.03 Defining Participation

In general, any work performed by the taxpayer in connection with an activity is treated as participation in the activity.[18] Work performed by a taxpayer's spouse counts as work performed by the taxpayer, even if the spouse has no direct interest in the activity and even if the taxpayer and spouse do not file a joint return.

There are two exceptions to the general rule that any work performed by the taxpayer or spouse counts as participation. First, work that is *not* of a type customarily done by an owner in that type of activity is not counted as participation unless the taxpayer can demonstrate that avoiding disallowance of related passive losses is *not* a primary reason for doing the work. For example, if a taxpayer's spouse works as a secretary in a real estate developer's office, the taxpayer is *not* deemed to be an active participant in the development activity by reason of his or her spouse's work for the developer.

Second, work performed in the taxpayer's capacity as an investor in an activity does *not* count as participation unless the taxpayer is directly involved in the day-to-day management or operations of the activity. Work performed as an investor includes:

- Studying and reviewing financial statements or reports on operations of the activity;

- Preparing or compiling summaries or analyses of the finances or operations of the activity for the taxpayer's own use; and

---

[18] Taxpayers can use any reasonable method to support their participation in an activity. A daily log, time report, etc. is not necessary, although written records, such as an appointment book or similar document, are recommended.

¶1009.03

- Monitoring the finances or operations of the activity in a non-managerial capacity.

.04 Limited Partners

Limited partners generally are not treated as material participants in the activity conducted by the partnership. This rule does not apply, however, if the limited partner (or LLC member treated as a limited partner) satisfies the requirements of tests (1), (5), or (6) above. These exceptions are meant to prohibit profitable activities from being classified as passive, thereby allowing the taxpayer to deduct passive losses from other sources.

For a number of years, the Service struggled with the issue of how a member in an LLC should be classified for purposes of applying the passive activity loss limitations. Because LLC members are statutorily protected from liability for entity debts and other obligations, the IRS viewed them as limited partners for purposes of the passive activity rules. After a number of taxpayers successfully challenged this position in the courts,[19] the Treasury Department issued proposed regulations amending the definition of limited partner under Code Sec. 469. Under the proposed regulations, an interest in an entity shall be treated as an interest in a limited partnership as a limited partner if—

1. The entity in which such interest is held is classified as a partnership for Federal income tax purposes under § 301.7701-3; and

2. The holder of such interest does not have rights to manage the entity at all times during the entity's taxable year under the law of the jurisdiction in which the entity is organized and under the governing agreement.[20]

If the taxpayer owns interests as both a limited and general partner in the same activity, he or she will not be treated as a limited partner with respect to either interest.[21]

.05 Rental Activities

Code Sec. 469 automatically classifies as passive most rental activities, regardless of the taxpayer's level of participation. For this purpose, a rental activity is one involving the long-term rental of property to tenants and for which the taxpayer does not provide substantial additional services.[22] Thus, rental activities under the

---

[19] For example, see *Gregg v. U.S.*, 186 F.Supp.2d 1123 (DC Or. 2000) (because the regulations under Code Sec. 469 were silent with respect to the status of LLC members, the limited partner exception in section 469(h)(2) does not apply to LLC members); *Garnett v. Comm'r*, 132 T.C. 368 (2009), (the taxpayers' ownership interests in limited liability partnerships and LLCs fit within the general partner exception of § 1.469-5T(e)(3)(ii)); *Thompson v. U.S.*, 87 Fed. Cl. 728 (2009), acq. in decision only, AOD 2010-02, 2010-14 I.R.B. 515 (the regulations under section 469(h)(2) require the taxpayer's ownership interest to be in a partnership under State law rather than Federal tax law); and *Newell v. Comm'r*, T.C. Memo. 2010-23 (Code Sec. 469(h)(2) does not apply to the managing member of an LLC. On April 5, 2010, the IRS issued an Action on Decision acquiescing in the result only in *Thompson v. U.S.*, AOD 2010-02, 2010-14 I.R.B. 515.

[20] Prop. Regs. 1.469-5(e)(3)(i) (issued Nov. 28, 2011). The proposed regulations provide that a taxpayer will be treated as a limited partner under these provisions "for purposes of section 469(h)(2)." In the preamble to the Proposed Regulations, the Service emphasizes that "the rules concerning an interest in a limited partnership in the proposed regulations are provided solely for purposes of section 469 and no inference is intended that the same rules would apply for any other provisions of the Code requiring a distinction between a general partner and a limited partner." Thus, the Service explicitly provides that this provision does not extend, for example, to the classification of an LLC member as a limited or general partner for purposes of the self-employment tax.

[21] Prop. Reg. 1.469-5(e)(3)(ii).

[22] *See* Reg. § 1.469-1T(e)(3).

passive loss rules are primarily those involving the rental of residential and commercial real estate (apartment complexes, rental houses, office buildings, etc.). In contrast, the operation of hotels, motels, golf courses, and the like does not constitute a passive activity, because the rental periods are usually short and the taxpayer is required to provide a substantial amount of personal services in connection with the rental (e.g., cleaning rooms, making beds, maintaining greens, etc.).[23]

An activity is a rental activity if tangible property (real or personal) is used by customers or held for use by customers, and the gross income (or expected gross income) from the activity represents amounts paid (or to be paid) mainly for the use of the property. It does not matter whether the use is under a lease, a service contract, or some other arrangement.

Exceptions. The Regulations provide a number of exceptions under which certain activities are not treated as rental activities. These exceptions primarily apply to situations where the rental activity requires a large degree of necessary participation by the partners, or by their employees. Under the regulations, the following activities are not rental activities:

- The average period of customer use of the property is seven days or less (e.g., hotels, motels, short-term equipment or vehicle rentals, etc.).

- The average period of customer use of the property is 30 days or less and significant personal services are provided with the rentals. The Regulations do not define the term *significant personal services*, indicating only that all relevant facts and circumstances must be taken into consideration, including the frequency of the services, the type and amount of labor required to perform the services, and the value of the services relative to the amount charged for use of the property.[24] The regulations do provide that significant personal services do *not* include:

  — Services necessary to permit the lawful use of the property;

  — Services to repair or improve property that would extend its useful life for a period substantially longer than the average rental; and

  — Services that are similar to those commonly provided with long-term rentals of real estate, such as cleaning and maintenance of common areas or routine repairs.

- Extraordinary personal services are provided by or on behalf of the owner(s) of the property in making such property available for customer use. Services are extraordinary personal services if they are performed by individuals and the customers' use of the property is incidental to their receipt of the services (e.g., medical care provided at a hospital).

- The rental is incidental to a non-rental activity. Rental is incidental if the main purpose of holding the property is either to realize a gain from its

---

[23] One exception to these rules applies where the taxpayer leases property to a partnership, S Corporation or joint venture in which he/she has an interest. In this case, the rental activity does not constitute a passive activity regardless of the length of the rental period.

[24] Reg. § 1.469-1T(e)(3)(iv).

appreciation or for use in a trade or business activity, and the rental income from the property is a minimal percentage of its cost or value. This standard is satisfied if the gross rental income from the property is less than 2% of its *unadjusted* basis (i.e., cost without adjustment for depreciation or other cost recovery) or fair market value, whichever is smaller. For example, leasing grazing rights on raw land held for investment is an incidental rental activity if the lease payments are less than 2% of the cost or value of the property (whichever is less).

- The rental property is customarily made available during defined business hours for nonexclusive use by various customers (e.g., health clubs).

- The property is provided for use in a non-rental activity in the owner's capacity as an owner of an interest in a partnership, S corporation, or joint venture conducting that activity. Thus, an LLC member may not lease property to his/her LLC in the hopes of generating passive income.

.06 Real Estate Professionals

When first enacted, the passive loss limitations created much discomfort among full-time real estate professionals. These taxpayers argued that the acquisition, improvement, and rental of commercial and residential real estate constituted their full-time occupations, and should not be subject to the passive loss limitations. In 1993, Congress agreed, amending Code Sec. 469 so that taxpayers in the "real property business" are no longer subject to the passive loss restrictions.[25] For this purpose, a taxpayer is in the real property business if he/she:

- Spends more than half of his/her time in real property businesses in which he/she materially participates; and

- Performs more than 750 hours of services during the taxable year in real property trades or businesses in which he or she materially participates.

For this purpose, the term **real property trade or business** includes the development or redevelopment, construction or reconstruction, acquisition and sale, conversion, rental, rental management, or brokerage of real property.

For all other taxpayers, rental activities will be treated as passive activities.

.07 Exemption for Rental Activities in which Taxpayer "Actively" Participates

Code Sec. 469 also provides relief for middle-income taxpayers with rental property. For taxpayers who "actively participate" in the management of rental property, the first $25,000 of net losses generated by such property are exempted from Code Sec. 469. Two points must be emphasized here. First, the losses are still passive losses; however, they are not subject to the passive loss limitations. Second, the exemption applies only if the taxpayer "actively" participates in management of the property.

Note that "active" participation is a lesser standard than material participation. Active participation requires the following:

---

[25] Code Sec. 469(c)(7).

1. The taxpayer must have at least a 10% interest in the rental activity;

2. The taxpayer must not own the interest as a limited partner; and

3. The taxpayer must participate in the activity in a significant and bona fide manner.

The latter requirement is usually interpreted as requiring that the taxpayer participate fully in all management decisions made with regard to the property (e.g., establishing rents, approving new tenants, approving repairs, etc.). Limited partners are not treated as actively participating in a partnership's rental real estate activities.[26]

The exemption is targeted at lower and middle-income taxpayers. To insure that higher income individuals do not benefit, the $25,000 exemption amount is phased out as the taxpayer's adjusted gross income (computed before taking into account the rental loss) exceeds $100,000. Specifically, the exemption amount is reduced by 50 cents for each dollar that the taxpayer's "modified AGI" exceeds $100,000. Thus, once "modified AGI" exceeds $150,000, no exemption is allowed.[27]

> *Example 10-17:* P is a limited partner in a real estate partnership. She has a 20% interest in the partnership's profits and losses. This year, her share of the partnership's losses was ($18,000). She also owns a duplex which she holds out for rent. She is the sole owner of the duplex, and makes all management decisions. This year, she realized a ($14,000) loss from renting the duplex. Her adjusted gross income, before considering the above losses, is $130,000. She has no passive income from any other source. She is not a real estate professional. On her current year tax return, P's loss from the limited partnership will be disallowed under the passive loss rules. Her loss on the duplex is also passive, but a portion of that loss will be exempted from the passive loss rules because P actively participates in the rental activity. Ordinarily, her allowable exemption would be $25,000, an amount which would allow the entire ($14,000) loss on the duplex. In this case, however, P's AGI is in the phase-out range, and her allowable exemption amount will be reduced by $15,000 (.5 × $30,000, the excess of her AGI over $100,000). Thus, she will be able to deduct only ($10,000) of her loss from rental of the duplex. Accordingly, her current AGI, after considering her rental losses, will total $120,000, and she will have a ($22,000) passive loss carryover, of which $18,000 is attributable to the limited partnership interest, and $4,000 to the rental duplex.

Calculating Modified Adjusted Gross Income. Modified AGI for the purpose of computing the phase-out is regular AGI, computed without regard to the following:

---

[26] The proposed regulations provide that "if a taxpayer elects under paragraph (g) of this section to treat all interests in rental real estate as a single rental real estate activity, and at least one interest in rental real estate is held by the taxpayer as an interest in a limited partnership as a limited partner (within the meaning of § 1.469-5(e)(3)), the combined rental real estate activity of the taxpayer will be treated as an interest in a limited partnership as a limited partner for purposes of determining material participation." Prop. Reg. 1.469-9(f)(1).

[27] The AGI level at which the phase-out begins is $200,000 for taxpayers claiming the rehabilitation credit, and there is no phase-out for taxpayers claiming the low-income housing credit or the commercial revitalization deduction. Code Sec. 469(i)(3).

- Taxable social security and tier 1 railroad retirement benefits;
- Deductible contributions to individual retirement accounts (IRAs) and Code Sec. 501(c)(18) pension plans;
- The exclusion from income of interest from qualified U.S. savings bonds used to pay qualified higher education expenses;
- The exclusion from income of amounts received from an employer's adoption assistance program;
- Passive activity income or loss included on Form 8582;
- Rental real estate losses allowed because taxpayer is a "real estate professional;"
- Net losses from publicly traded partnerships;
- The deduction for one-half of self-employment tax;
- The deduction for interest on student loans;
- The deduction for qualified tuition and related expenses.

Example 10-18: K is a 20% general partner in a real estate partnership. He is not a real estate professional, but he does actively participate in the partnership's rental real estate activities. For the current year, his share of the partnership's net loss was ($35,000). In addition, he had tax-exempt interest income of $4,800, and net self-employment income of $120,000. He paid self-employment taxes of $16,128, properly claiming a deduction (for AGI) of $8,064 for half of this amount. K's modified AGI is $120,000, computed as follows:

Adjusted gross income:

Self-employment income	$120,000
Tax-exempt income	0
Total income	$120,000
Less ½ SE Tax	(8,064)
Adjusted gross income	$111,936
Add back adjustment for ½ SE Tax	8,064
Modified AGI	$120,000

Thus, the amount of K's loss that is exempt from Code Sec. 469 is reduced by $10,000 (50% of the excess of his modified AGI over $100,000), and he will be allowed to deduct ($15,000) of the pass-through loss from the partnership. The remaining $20,000 loss will be carried forward.

¶ 1010 Activities That Are Not Passive Activities

Because passive losses are deductible only against passive income, it is important to properly classify activities that are not passive. Essentially, there are five categories of *trade or business* activities that will not be treated as passive activities. The following *are not* passive activities:

1. Trade or business activities in which the taxpayer materially participated for the tax year (as defined above).

2. A working interest in an oil or gas well held by the taxpayer directly or through an entity that does not limit liability (such as a general partner interest in a partnership). The taxpayer's level of participation in the activity is irrelevant for this purpose. Thus, losses from working interests in oil and gas properties are always deductible unless the interest is held by a limited partner, or LLC member treated as a limited partner.[28]

3. Rental of a "vacation home"—i.e., a home or other "dwelling unit" both held for rental and used for personal purposes for more than the *greater of* 14 days or 10% of the number of days during the year that the home was rented at a fair rental.

4. Trading activities involving personal property traded for the account of those who own interests in the activity.[29]

5. Rental real estate activities of real estate professionals.

In addition, investment activities are classified as "portfolio" activities and income from these activities may not be offset with losses from passive activities.

¶ 1011 Recharacterization of Certain Passive Activities as Nonpassive

Finally, the regulations provide for reclassification of *profitable* passive activities as non-passive activities. The rationale for these provisions is to prevent passive losses from being deducted against profits from these profitable activities. If a taxpayer has net income from any of the following passive activities, all or part of that income (depending on the type of passive activity below) will be reclassified as non-passive trade or business income:[30]

- Significant participation passive activities (i.e., activities in which the taxpayer's participation exceeds 100 hours during the taxable year);

- Rental of substantially non-depreciable property (i.e., property for which less than 30% of the *unadjusted* basis is depreciable);

- Equity-financed lending activities;

- Rental of property that is incidental to real estate development activities;

- Rental of property to non-passive activities; and

- Licensing of intangible property by pass-through entities.

¶ 1012 Operating Rules

.01 Calculation and Use of Carryforwards

Conceptually, the passive loss limitations are relatively straightforward. Taxpayers first total all their income from passive activities. They then total their losses from passive activities. If the losses exceed the income, they have a net passive

---

[28] *See* Temp. Reg. § 1.469-1T(e)(4)(ii).
[29] *See* Temp. Reg. § 1.469-1T(e)(6).

[30] Reg. § 1.469-2(f)(5).

loss, which is disallowed unless subject to the exemption for rental activities in which the taxpayer actively participates. The taxpayer must then allocate the disallowed passive loss back to the passive activities which generated the loss. These losses carry forward indefinitely, and can be deducted if the taxpayer either earns net passive income in a subsequent year, or sells or otherwise disposes of his/her entire interest in the passive activity to which the loss has been allocated.

Example 10-19: *J* is a member in four different limited liability companies. She is classified as a limited partner in all four companies, and all four are engaged in rental activities. This year, LLC #1 reported a net profit, while the other 3 companies each reported net losses. *J*'s share of these profits and losses were as follows:

LLC #1	$ 24,000
LLC #2	(10,000)
LLC #3	(20,000)
LLC #4	(30,000)
Net loss	($36,000)

As indicated above, *J* has a net passive loss of ($36,000), none of which will be deductible on her current year tax return. Note, however, that $24,000 of the losses attributable to LLCs #2, 3, and 4 were deducted against the $24,000 income attributable to LLC #1. The ($36,000) passive loss carryover generated this year is allocable ($6,000) to LLC #2 (10,000/60,000), ($12,000) to LLC # 3 (20,000/60,000), and ($18,000) to LLC #4 (30,000/60,000). If one of the LLC interests is sold this allocation will affect the amount of the carryover that can be deducted due to the sale.

Code Sec. 469 is relatively taxpayer friendly with respect to the use of passive loss carryovers upon the disposition of a taxpayer's entire interest in a passive activity. Code Sec. 469(g) provides that the loss carryforward from the terminated activity is applied against passive income from other passive activities and that only the excess of such loss over income from other such activities is characterized as loss from non-passive activities. However, Code Sec. 469(g)(1)(A)(ii) provides that passive loss carryovers from other passive activities are applied against passive income from such activities *before* application of the carryover from the terminated activity. In other words, carryover losses from an activity disposed of by a taxpayer do *not* crowd out passive loss carryovers from those activities in which the taxpayer still maintains an interest.

Example 10-20: Assume the same facts as in Example 10-19. *J* has a ($36,000) passive loss carryforward from year 1, of which ($6,000) is attributable to LLC 2, ($12,000) to LLC 3 and ($18,000) to LLC 4. Assume that in year 2, *J* sold her interest in LLC 3, realizing no gain or loss on the sale. In year 2, *J* is allocated a loss of $10,000 from LLC 3 for the period preceding the sale. Her profit and loss allocations from the other three companies are as follows:

LLC #1	$ 55,000
LLC #2	(15,000)
LLC #4	(15,000)
Net profit	$25,000

Although she realized no taxable gain or loss on the sale of her interest in LLC #3, *J*'s passive loss carryover attributable to that interest is fully deductible in year 2. The entire ($12,000) carryover from LLC #3 is allowable in this year, along with the current $10,000 loss from LLC #3. The $22,000 total losses from LLC #3 would first be applied against any gain from the sale of LLC #3. There being no gain from the sale, the entire $22,000 loss is applied against *J*'s net passive income from other activities in year 2, after reducing that net income by any of the loss carryovers from her interests in LLCs #2 and 4. Her net passive income for other activities for year 2 is $25,000 – $6,000 (LLC #2 carryover) – $18,000 (LLC #4 carryover) = $1,000. The $22,000 loss from LLC #3 is used to offset this income, leaving $21,000 of LLC #3 loss that is no longer characterized as passive (and is therefore deductible in full).

Example 10-21: Assume that in year 3 *J* has no income or loss from LLC #1, but has passive losses of $4,000 from LLC #2 and $12,000 from LLC #4. She has no other passive income in year 3, so in year 4 *J* has passive loss carryovers from LLCs #2 and 4 of ($4,000) and ($12,000) respectively. In year 4, she is allocated profit and loss from her remaining LLC investments as follows:

LLC #1	$ 50,000
LLC #2	(25,000)
LLC #4	(15,000)
Net income	$ 10,000

In year 4, *J* has net passive income of $10,000 as noted above. Under Code Sec. 469, she is allowed to deduct ($10,000) of her passive loss carryovers. Of the ($10,000), ($2,500) will come out of the LLC #2 carryover (4,000/(4,000 + 12,000)), and ($7,500) will come out of the LLC #3 carryover (12,000/(4,000 + 12,000)). On her tax return for year 4, then, *J* will report net passive profit/loss of zero. She will have passive loss carryovers from LLC #2 of ($1,500) = (4,000 – 2,500) and ($4,500) from LLC #4 (12,000 – 7,500).

Note that capital losses realized on disposition of an interest in a passive activity are subject to the capital loss limitations. The provisions allowing deduction of passive loss carryovers upon the disposition of a taxpayer's complete interest in a passive activity do not override the capital loss limitations.

Example 10-22: *C* sold her entire interest in a limited partnership activity in the current year to an unrelated person for $30,000. Her adjusted basis in the partnership interest was $42,000, and she had $10,000 of passive loss carryforwards from the activity. *C* also had salary income from her job of

¶1012.01

$75,000. C will be entitled to a ($13,000) deduction on her current year return, computed as follows:

Selling price of the limited partnership interest	$30,000
Basis of the limited partnership interest	(42,000)
Capital loss on sale	(12,000)
Capital loss limitation	(3,000)
Passive loss carryforwards deductible upon disposition of entire interest	(10,000)
Total deductible loss in year of sale	(13,000)

The remaining $9,000 of C's capital loss on sale of the partnership interest will be carried over under the capital loss carryover rules. It will *not* be subject to the passive activity loss limitations in any subsequent year.

.02 Installment Sales

Disposition of a taxpayer's interest in a passive activity in an installment sale transaction is treated as a disposition of the taxpayer's interest in the activity. However, in such cases, the passive loss carryovers or passive activity credit carryovers attributable to that activity will also be subject to the installment method. That is, a ratable portion of any carryforwards will be allowed in each year equivalent to the portion of the taxpayer's gain from sale of the activity that is taken into income in that year.

Example 10-23: This year, E sold her entire interest in a real estate limited partnership for a total gain of $50,000. She will receive payments from the buyer over five years—under the installment method, she will recognize 20% of her gain each year. Her passive loss carryforwards associated with the limited partnership interest will be deductible as a result of the sale; however, following her treatment of the gain recognized on the sale, she will only be allowed to deduct 20% of her passive loss carryforwards in the year of the sale, with an additional 20% being allowed in each of the remaining years in the installment agreement.

.03 Gifts

Passive loss carryforwards are *not* triggered when a taxpayer gives away his/her interest in a passive activity. Instead, the basis of the transferred interest is increased by the amount of the carryforward losses.

Example 10-24: E owns an interest in a limited partnership. His tax basis in the partnership interest is $8,000. He has a $10,000 passive loss carryforward with respect to the interest. The market value of the partnership interest is $30,000. For estate planning purposes, he gave his interest in the partnership to his daughter, M.

M will take a carryover basis in the interest under Code Sec. 1015. Ordinarily, this would be $8,000. However, the passive loss carryover represents losses previously allocated to E that were never actually deducted by him. Previous reductions in his basis in the interest attributable to these losses were therefore artificial, and they must be added back to his basis in the partnership interest for purposes of determining the basis of that interest in *M*'s hands. Thus, her "carryover" basis in the partnership interest will be $18,000.

.04 Dispositions by Death

Death does trigger the deduction of any unused carryforward losses or credits under Code Sec. 469. However, the carryforwards are first reduced by the amount of the step-up in basis of the passive activity interest in the hands of the beneficiaries of the estate.

> **Example 10-25:** *F* died earlier this year, leaving her limited partnership interest in a real estate investment partnership to her son, *S*. *F*'s tax basis in the limited partnership interest prior to her death was $22,000. It was valued at $50,000 in her estate. Thus, *S* will take a $50,000 basis in the interest under Code Sec. 1014. If *F* had passive loss carryforwards of $30,000 from the activity, only $2,000 of those carryforwards will be deductible as a result of her death. This $2,000 will be deducted on her final income tax return. The remainder of the loss carryforward is not assumed by *S*; instead, these carryforwards will simply expire.

¶ 1013 Grouping Activities

.01 General

Taxpayers can aggregate one or more trade or business activities, or rental activities, as a single activity if those activities constitute an appropriate economic unit for measuring gain or loss under the passive activity rules.

Grouping of activities can yield benefits for taxpayers, but may also have unforeseen costs. For example, by grouping two activities into one larger activity, a taxpayer need only show material participation in the activity as a whole, whereas if the two activities are separate, he/she must demonstrate material participation in each one. Similarly, grouping an activity in which a taxpayer owns less than 10% with one in which he/she owns more than 10% may allow the taxpayer to claim 10% ownership in the combined activity. The disposition of the taxpayer's complete interest in one activity but not the other, however, will prevent the taxpayer from claiming a deduction for the carryforward losses associated with that activity (because his/her entire interest in the two activities as a group has not been eliminated).

.02 Appropriate Economic Units

There are no firm rules to determine whether activities form an appropriate economic unit. The regulations provide that any reasonable method can be used to apply the relevant facts and circumstances in grouping activities. The regulations further provide a list of factors which should be accorded the greatest weight in determining whether two or more activities form an appropriate economic unit.[31] All

---

[31] Reg. § 1.469-4(c)(2).

of the following factors do *not* have to be present to group two or more activities, but all should be considered:

- Similarities and differences in types of trades or businesses;
- The extent of common control;
- The extent of common ownership;
- Geographical location; and
- The interdependencies between or among activities—for example, the extent to which the activities buy or sell goods between or among themselves, involve products or services that are generally provided together, have the same customers or employees, or commingle their accounting systems.

Example 10-26: Park Ridge, LLC, is a limited liability company that has elected to be treated as a partnership for federal income tax purposes. The company operates a bookstore and coffee shop in a shopping mall in Texas and a bookstore and coffee shop in California. Considering the factors listed above, Park Ridge may group all of these into a single activity (both the bookstore and coffee shop have the same customers, and likely use the same accounting system). Alternatively, the company may group the activities into a bookstore activity and a coffee shop activity, a Texas activity and a California activity, or four separate activities.

When a partnership groups two or more activities together into a single activity, the partners are bound by this decision. They may not treat the activities as separate activities on their own returns.

.03 Limitations on Grouping Certain Activities

Rental vs. Trade or Business Activities. The regulations generally prohibit grouping rental activities (inherently passive) with trade or business activities (inherently nonpassive for most taxpayers). An exception applies if the two activities constitute an appropriate economic unit and either the rental activity or the trade or business activity is insubstantial in relation to the other. Alternatively, if both activities form an appropriate economic unit and have common ownership, a portion of the rental activity which involves the rental of property to the trade or business activity may be grouped with the trade or business activity.[32]

Example 10-27: Radiology Associates is an S corporation that provides radiology services to the public at large. It is co-owned by *J* and *K*, both of whom are licensed radiology specialists. *J* and *K* are also equal owners of a partnership which owns radiology equipment that it leases to the S corporation. All of the equipment owned by the partnership is installed in the office of the S corporation and the partnership does not lease any equipment to any other customer. The radiology equipment owned by the partnership is heavily leveraged. After deductions for depreciation and interest expense, the partnership reports large losses for tax purposes. Because the two activities are owned by the same taxpayers, and the partnership's activities are complementary to

---

[32] Reg. § 1.469-4(d)(1).

those of the S corporation, the two activities will be considered part of a common economic unit. They can be grouped together if the taxpayers can demonstrate that the partnership's rental activity is insubstantial in relation to the S corporation's radiology services activity. Likely the most effective approach to demonstrating the insubstantiality of the partnership's activities is to compare the partnership's gross income from rental of the equipment to the revenues from the radiology services provided by the S corporation.[33]

Real vs. Personal Property Rentals. Rental real estate activities generally may not be grouped with activities involving the rental of personal property. The only exception applies when the personal property is provided to customers in connection with the rental of real property or when the real property is provided to customers in connection with the rental of personal property. For example, a partnership engaged in the rental of furnished apartments can treat the rental of furniture and the rental of apartments as a single activity.

Limited Partners. Limited partners are not allowed to group activities from an activity in any of the following trades or businesses with any activity in a *different* type of business:

- Holding, producing, or distributing motion picture films or video tapes;
- Farming;
- Leasing Section 1245 property; or
- Exploring for, or exploiting, oil and gas or geothermal resources.

It is acceptable to group more than one limited partnership activity from the same type of trade or business. For example, a limited partner with interests in two separate oil and gas limited partnerships may treat the two limited partnership interests as a single activity, but may not group that activity with an investment in a real estate limited partnership.[34]

Publicly Traded Partnerships. The passive loss rules of Code Sec. 469 are applied separately to each interest in a publicly traded partnership (PTP) owned by a partner. Thus, an activity conducted through a PTP may not be grouped with any other activity in which the partner participates outside the PTP.

.04 Consistency Is Required

Although the IRS has the authority to regroup activities, taxpayers are generally bound by their own grouping decisions. Once a decision has been made to group activities into appropriate economic units, those activities may not be regrouped in a later tax year.

One exception applies when the original grouping was clearly inappropriate or where there is a material change in the facts and circumstances that makes the original grouping clearly inappropriate. In such cases, the taxpayer is required to regroup the activities and to disclose the regrouping and the reason for that regrouping to the IRS.

---

[33] For example, *see Candelaria*, 2007-2 USTC ¶ 50,758 (U.S. District Court, West. Dist. Texas, El Paso Div.), 518 FSupp2d 852 (10/05/2007).

[34] These rules also apply to "limited entrepreneurs," defined as any taxpayer other than a limited partner who does not actively participate in the management of the enterprise. Thus, LLC members, whether or not classified as limited partners, will have to demonstrate that they actively participate in management in order to group certain activities into a single group.

PART IV

SALES AND DISTRIBUTIONS

Chapter 11

Sale of a Partnership Interest

¶ 1101 Introduction

Gain or loss realized on the sale of a partnership interest is equal to the amount realized by the transferor partner for the transfer of the partner's partnership interest less the adjusted basis in his or her partnership interest ("outside basis"). In keeping with the entity approach to the taxation of transfers of partnership interests, this gain or loss is generally considered to be a capital gain or loss.[1] Code Sec. 751(a) provides an important statutory exception to this general rule which, as a practical matter, applies to many sales of partnership interests. Under this exception, the amount of the seller's gain or loss allocable to the seller's share of the net appreciation or depreciation in the partnership's ordinary income assets is taxed as ordinary income or loss on the sale of the partnership interest. Only the remaining gain or loss is capital.

> **S Corporation Observation:** Unless the collapsible corporation rules of Code Sec. 341 apply, all gain from the sale of S corporation stock is capital gain.

Long term gain from the sale of a partnership interest attributable to the appreciation of collectibles is not ordinary income, but it is taxed at a maximum 28 percent rate, not the usual 15 percent maximum rate that generally applies to long term capital gains.[2] In addition, a 25 percent maximum rate

---

[1] Code Sec. 741.

[2] Code Sec. 1(h)(6)(B); Prop. Reg. § 1.1(h)-1.

applies to the long-term gain attributable to the partner's share of the partnership's unrecaptured Code Sec. 1250 depreciation.[3]

When a partnership interest is sold, the selling partner is required to submit with his or her income tax return for the taxable year a statement setting forth:

- The date of sale;
- The amount of any gain attributable to collectibles and partnership unrecaptured Code Sec. 1250 gain; and
- The gain or loss on the sale of the partnership interest.[4]

S Corporation Observation: Gain from the sale of S corporation stock is subject to the same rule for the shareholder's share of collectibles but not for unrecaptured depreciation.[5]

LLC Observation: The rules discussed in this chapter apply equally to state law partnerships and LLCs taxed as partnerships.

¶ 1102 Amount Realized

As is the situation with most sales of property, the amount realized by the transferor partner equals the amount of cash and the fair market value of any property received by the transferor partner, plus the amount of any liability relief realized by the seller in connection with the transaction.[6] In the case of sales of partnership interests, debt relief usually takes the form of a decreased share of partnership liabilities.[7]

> ***Example 11-1:*** Helen is a 10 percent partner in Troy Partners. Her tax basis in her partnership interest is $75,000, consisting of her $35,000 contribution to partnership capital (including re-invested earnings) and her $40,000 share of the partnership's outstanding liabilities. She sells her entire interest to Elroy for $50,000 cash. Elroy assumes responsibility for Helen's share of partnership debts.
>
> The amount realized by Helen in connection with the sale is $90,000, consisting of the $50,000 cash received plus $40,000 in liability relief (her share of partnership debt fell from $40,000 to zero). As noted above, her tax basis in the partnership interest was $75,000. Thus, she will recognize a $15,000 gain on sale of the partnership interest.

¶ 1103 Adjusted Basis in Partnership Interest

The transferor partner's adjusted basis in his or her partnership interest at the time of transfer is the sum of his or her original tax basis on the day he or she acquired an interest, plus adjustments reflecting operations during the transferor

---

[3] Code Sec. 1(h)(7)(A); Prop. Reg. §1.1(h)-1.

[4] Prop. Reg. §1.1(h)-1(e); Reg. §1.751-1(a)(3). The proposed regulations refer to unrecaptured Code Sec. 1250 gain as "Section 1250 gain."

[5] Code Sec. 1(h)(5)(B).

[6] Reg. §1.1001-2(a)(1); Code Sec. 752(d).

[7] Code Secs. 1001(b) and 752(b). Debt relief is determined in accordance with the provisions of Reg. §1.752-1(e) if the debt was incurred before February 1, 1989, or Reg. §§1.752-1 through -4 if incurred on or after December 28, 1992. *See* Reg. §1.752-5 for effective dates and transitional rules.

partner's holding period. The calculation of a partner's initial basis varies according to whether the partner acquired his or her interest through a contribution to the partnership or from another partner and whether the partner is using the statutory general rule for calculating basis or the statutory alternative method.[8]

.01 General Rule

The initial basis in a partnership interest obtained in exchange for the contribution of cash or property is generally equal to the amount of cash plus the tax basis of any property contributed.[9] The initial adjusted basis of the *transferee* partner in his or her partnership interest is determined under the rules generally applicable to acquisition of other types of property.[10] Thus, if a partner purchases a partnership interest, the partner takes a cost basis in that interest.[11] Similarly, a partner who acquires his or her partnership interest by inheritance gets a stepped-up (or stepped-down) basis in the partnership interest equal to its fair market value at the date of the testator's death or at the alternative valuation date, increased by his or her share of the partnership's debt.[12]

The beginning adjusted basis is then increased by the partner's share of partnership taxable income and tax exempt income. Adjustments are made for income reported for the taxable year of transfer as well as for prior years.[13] Additional contributions by the partner made either in the year of the transfer or any prior taxable year are added to that amount. The beginning adjusted basis is decreased by the transferor partner's distributive share of partnership losses and expenses incurred in producing tax-exempt income, and other nondeductible/noncapitalized expenditures for the taxable year of transfer and for prior years,[14] and by any partnership distributions.[15]

For purposes of calculating gain or loss on sale, the regulations require the seller's basis to reflect these adjustments as of the date of sale whether the seller is selling all of his or her partnership interest or just a part of that interest.[16] These increases and decreases to basis include deemed money contributions and distributions reflecting increases and decreases in the partner's share of partnership debt.[17] The effect of the statutory general rule is that the partner must keep a running tally of the cumulative adjustments to the basis of his or her partnership interest after its acquisition. As a practical matter, the partner may not have retained the records needed to make these calculations. Code Sec. 705(b) provides an alternative approach which may be used in the absence of the partner having information necessary to comply with the approach of Code Sec. 705(a).

---

[8] Code Secs. 722 or 742 govern, depending on whether the partner acquired his or her interest by contribution to the partnership or by the transfer to the partner of an existing partnership interest.

[9] *See* Chapter 2.

[10] Code Sec. 742.

[11] Code Sec. 1012. The transferee partner's cost includes his or her share of the partnership's liabilities. Code Sec. 752(d). This is determined under Reg. § 1.752-1(e) if the debt was incurred before February 1, 1989, or Reg. §§ 1.752-1 through -4 if incurred on or after

December 28, 1992. *See* Reg. § 1.752-5 for effective dates and transitional rules.

[12] Code Sec. 1014. The basis of the partnership interest may not include the value of the partnership interest attributable to "income in respect of a decedent" (IRD) assets under Code Sec. 691. Code Sec. 1014(c).

[13] Code Secs. 705(a)(1) and 722. *See* Chapter 9.

[14] Code Sec. 705(a)(2) and (3).

[15] Code Sec. 733.

[16] Reg. § 1.705-1(a)(1).

[17] Code Sec. 752(a) and (b).

.02 Alternate Rule

In addition to the Code Sec. 705(a) "historical approach" to maintaining a partner's basis in that partner's partnership interest, a partner is allowed to treat his or her share of the partnership's basis in its assets as his or her basis in the interest. This alternative appears inviting at first blush when compared to accounting for yearly adjustments to basis as described above. However, as a practical matter, the necessary calculations and adjustments may make it an unappealing— but perhaps necessary—choice for a typical partnership when there have been property contributions and distributions and/or transfers of partnership interests.

The regulations provide that a partner may use the alternative rule of Code Sec. 705(b) to determine the tax basis of his or her partnership interest by reference to the total adjusted basis of partnership property in two circumstances:

1. Where the partner "cannot practicably apply the general rule set forth in Code Sec. 705(a)"; or

2. If, in the opinion of the IRS Commissioner, the result would be the same under the general rule.[18]

Example 11-2: Individuals Charlie, Dawn, and Ed formed the equal CDE Partnership in 1946. Charlie is selling his partnership interest in the current year, but does not have the necessary information to establish his tax basis. The adjusted basis of all partnership property is $300,000. The partnership has liabilities totaling $100,000. What is the tax basis of Charlie's partnership interest?

The partnership has been in existence for over 60 years. It is not practical for Charlie to reconstruct his tax basis in the partnership interest. Charlie would be entitled to one-third of the partnership property on liquidation and therefore has a basis for his interest equal to one-third of the partnership's basis in its assets, $100,000.

The examples in the regulations involve two approaches to finding a partner's share of the basis of partnership property. The first approach, which is the least appealing of the two, is to determine the partner's share of the value of the partnership's assets; this is his or her tentative share of the partnership's basis in its assets. The resulting amount is the partner's tentative basis in his or her interest.

This tentative basis is, as discussed further below, adjusted to take into account (1) inside/outside basis inequalities generated, for example, because the partner purchased his or her interest, and (2) disproportionate sharing of the basis of the partnership's assets. This can happen, for example, when a partner contributes appreciated or depreciated assets and when a partner joins the partnership at a time when the partnership holds appreciated assets.

Adjustments arise from contributions of property, as well as from transfers of a partnership interest or distributions of property to the partners. The regulation requires that adjustments be made to take this discrepancy into account.[19] In general, adjustments are necessary because:

---

[18] Reg. § 1.705-1(b).   [19] *Id.*

¶1103.02

1. The general application of the alternate rule assumes that aggregate inside and outside basis are equal. They may not be equal.

2. Even though aggregate inside and outside basis may be equal, each partner's share of that basis may not equal his or her share of the value of the partnership's assets because of the operation of Code Sec. 704(c) or the lack of a Code Sec. 754 election.

3. The Code Sec. 752 regulations may allocate debt differently than the partner's share of the assets.

Example 11-3: Individuals C, D, and E formed the equal CDE Partnership in 1946. C is selling his partnership interest in the current year, but does not have the necessary information to establish his tax basis. The adjusted basis of all partnership property is $300,000. The partnership has liabilities totaling $100,000. Land and a building still owned by the partnership were contributed by C with a value on contribution of $30,000 and an adjusted basis of $10,000. D and E each contributed $30,000 as their initial and only capital contributions to the partnership.

Here, C contributed property with a basis of $10,000 in exchange for a one-third interest, while D and E contributed property with a basis of $30,000 for a one-third interest. Thus, the aggregate of the initial bases of partnership assets was $70,000. The partnership assets now have an aggregated basis of $300,000. C's initial one-third share of $70,000 is $23,333, or $13,333 more than the $10,000 basis of property contributed by C. Thus, a *permanent* reduction of $13,333 is necessary to compute C's basis under the alternative rule. On the other hand, a permanent increase of $6,667 (*i.e.*, $30,000 – $23,333) is necessary to compute D or E's basis under the alternative rule.

C's FMV share of bases of partnership assets	$100,000
(1/3 × $300,000)	
C's basis adjustment	(13,333)
C's adjusted basis in his partnership interest	*$86,667*
(Code Sec. 705(b))	
D's and E's FMV share of basis of partnership assets	$100,000
(1/3 × $300,000)	
D's or E's basis adjustment	6,667
D's or E's adjusted basis of his partnership interest	*$106,667*
(Code Sec. 705(b))	

When working under Code Sec. 705(b) with the concept of the equality of the total adjusted basis of partnership property and the total adjusted bases of partnership interests, the presence of liabilities generally is neutral because the debt has been taken into account in the basis of each, having been included in the adjusted bases of assets created or purchased with cash from the debt and also included in the bases of the partners' interests in the partnership. Alternatively, if cash had been dispersed for expenses, the increase in adjusted basis by reason of the debt would have been offset by an equal deduction for the expenditures. The presence or absence of liabilities is, in essence, irrelevant under this alternative approach to figuring the basis of a partnership interest. However, even though, in the aggregate, the increase and the decrease are theoretically equal, in reality the debt may be allocable in a different manner than the expenses paid with the debt or the partners' shares of the adjusted basis of partnership assets (their prorated claim on the assets divided by total assets times total adjusted bases of the property to the partnership).

The first alternate method of computing a partner's basis in his or her partnership interest described above focuses on finding the partner's share of the basis of the partnership's assets. This requires that the partner have access to the partnership's books and records or that the partnership does the calculations necessary to find the partner's basis in his or her interest. However, if the partner had inherited or purchased the interest, the partnership may not be able to figure the partner's basis for his or her partnership interest either. This is because the partnership would need to be aware of the partner's original basis to use the alternative rule described immediately above. The partner may not have access to the partnership's books and records, the partnership may be unwilling to do the necessary work, and a partner who was not one of the original partners may be unwilling or unable to reveal the beginning basis for his or her interest.

Fortunately, the regulations include a second approach under Code Sec. 705(b). This method helps to obviate most of the adjustments necessary to avoid a significant discrepancy which may result from simply dividing inside basis by a partner's share of the partnership. The second approach to the alternative method focuses on the liability and equity section of the partnership's balance sheet. This approach is based upon the accounting principle that the assets on the partnership's balance sheet equal the liabilities plus equity. This variation in the alternative method provides that a partner's share of equity plus liabilities equals his or her share of the assets' bases. This information is often readily available to the partners if the partnership uses tax accounting principles for preparing the Form 1065. It is found on the Schedule K-1 issued each year by the partnership. The partner's capital account is found in Item L, and the partner's share of debt is contained in Item K.

Example 11-4: The ABC equal general partnership has the following tax basis balance sheet:

ABC Partnership

Assets	Tax Basis
Land	$100
Building	200
	$300

¶1103.02

Liabilities

(recourse) $900

Capital

   A . . . . $(200)

   B . . . .   (200)

   C . . . .   (200)

                                                                                                                $(600)

Partner *A* receives the partnership Schedule K-1, which shows his ending capital account of $(200) (item J column (e)) and his debt share of $300 (Item F). His basis under Code Sec. 705(b) is $100. Note, however, that this approach only works when using tax basis capital accounts.

The regulations attempt to be more accurate under this modified alternative approach to funding a partner's share of the basis of partnership assets than simply taking into account the asset section of the partnership's balance sheet. In reality, a partner's basis in his or her interest includes the partner's share of the debt. The first approach of the alternative method ignores debt. This second approach to the alternative method takes into account the possibility that debt is shared differently under Code Sec. 752 than the partner's share of partnership assets by first removing all debt and then reallocating it pursuant to the normal sharing rules.

The regulations then treat each partner's tax basis capital account plus each partner's debt share as equaling his or her share of the assets' basis. This figure must still be modified by any relevant inside/outside basis inequalities. For example, a partner who purchased or inherited an interest would add to this figure any difference between the original basis in the partner's partnership interest and his or her original capital account plus debt share. This method of finding a partner's share of the partnership's assets basis naturally presumes that the partner has access to his or her correct tax basis capital account.

If a partner only sells a portion of his or her partnership interest, only that portion of the partner's basis in his or her partnership interest is taken into account in calculating gain or loss on the sale. Care must be taken to properly account for changes in the partner's share of debt, as this change must be included in the amount realized on the partial sale.

    Example 11-5: Joy is a 20 percent partner in Skyland Partnership. Her tax basis in her partnership interest is $80,000, consisting of her $20,000 tax basis capital account and her $60,000 share of partnership debt. She sold one-half of her interest to an unrelated partner for $100,000 cash. Her amount realized on the sale was $130,000 ($100,000 cash plus *half* of her share of partnership debt). Her tax basis in the one-half of her interest sold was $40,000. Thus, she must recognize a $90,000 taxable gain.

¶1103.02

The holding period of the partnership interest may also need to be divided if the partner acquired the partnership interest at different times.[20]

.03 Adjustments to Basis for Changes in Partner's Share of Liabilities

A partner must be able to determine his or her share of the partnership's debt to determine his or her basis in the interest, whether the partner is using the Code Sec. 705(a) "historical approach" to keep track of the basis or the partner is using the alternative method. The preparer of the partnership's Schedule K-1 must separately disclose in Item F each partner's share of:

1. Nonrecourse debt other than that considered qualified nonrecourse debt under Code Sec. 465(b)(6);[21]

2. Qualified nonrecourse financing; and

3. Other—this last category consists of each partner's share of the partnership's recourse debt. Recourse debt is a liability for which any partner or party related to a partner bears the economic risk of loss.[22]

When a partner is using the historical method of keeping track of the basis of his or her partnership interest, any increase or decrease in his or her total share of partnership debt is a deemed money contribution or distribution. The partner can simply compare the prior year's total of the three types of debt on Schedule K-1, Item F, to the current year-end's total. If the total has increased, the partner has a deemed money contribution. If the total has decreased, there is a deemed money distribution.

When the partner is using the first alternative approach under Code Sec. 705(b) to determine his or her basis in the partnership interest, the partner's share of debt is disregarded.

When the partner is using the modified alternative approach, basis in the partnership interest is equal to his or her tax basis capital account plus the total debt shown in Schedule K-1, Item F, and then modified as described above.

Modifications are generally necessary when the partner was not one of the original partners.

¶ 1104 Ordinary Income from the Sale of an Interest in the Partnership

Code Sec. 751(a) provides the major exception to the statutory general rule that gain or loss from the sale of a partnership interest is treated as capital gain or loss. This exception in treatment was originally meant to keep the partners of a cash-method partnership with significant zero basis accounts receivable from selling their partnership interest and essentially converting the ordinary income inher-

---

[20] Code Sec. 1223(1).

[21] The partnership should include in this category debt secured by real estate even though the property was placed in service before the December 31, 1986, effective date of applying the at-risk rules to real estate. The at-risk rules will apply to partners who acquire their interests after December 31, 1986, regardless of when the partner-

ship placed the realty in service. *See* Act § 503(c)(2) of the Tax Reform Act of 1986, P.L. 99-514, 99th Cong., 2d Sess. The partner's Schedule K-1 should include an attachment explaining the nature of the debt, the date it was borrowed, and when the recurring property was placed in service.

[22] Reg. § 1.752-1(a)(1).

ent in those accounts receivable into long-term capital gain. Basically, Code Section 751(a) provides that any amount realized on the sale of a partnership interest which is attributable to unrealized receivables or inventory is treated as an amount realized from the sale of a noncapital asset. Unrealized receivables and inventory are commonly referred to as "Code Sec. 751" or "hot" assets. They are the partnership's assets with built-in ordinary income or loss, and they are generally property other than Code Sec. 1231 and capital assets. A partnership which holds these assets is sometimes referred to as a "collapsible" partnership.

> **LLC Observation:** The rules discussed in this chapter apply equally to state law partnerships and LLCs taxed as partnerships.

> **Observation:** Under the current Code Sec. 751(a) rules, absent a Code Sec. 754 election, the seller's share of the ordinary income is taxed twice: first, on the sale of the partnership interest under Code Sec. 751(a); second, when the partnership itself recognizes the built-in ordinary income.

Code Sec. 751(a) applies only to the sale or exchange of a partnership interest. Code Sec. 751(a), furthermore, is not applicable to amounts received as partnership distributions, since these are taxed under Code Sec. 751(b). Code Sec. 751(a) applies whether the transfer is of all, or part, of an interest or is to another partner or to an outsider. Under Code Sec. 751(a), the amount of money or the fair market value of any property a selling partner receives in exchange for all or part of his or her interest in the partnership attributable to "unrealized receivables" or to "inventory" items is treated as an amount realized from the sale or exchange of property that is not a capital asset.[23]

> **Example 11-6:** A, B, C, and D are equal partners in the ABCD Partnership. The partnership's current balance sheets are as follows:

Assets	**Book Value**	**FMV**
Cash	$2,000	$2,000
Accounts Receivable	0	2,500
Inventory	2,000	2,500
Stock held as an investment	16,000	16,000
Land held as an investment	2,000	5,000
	$22,000	$28,000
Liabilities and Capital		
Recourse liabilities	$18,000	$18,000
Capital, A	1,000	2,500
Capital, B	1,000	2,500
Capital, C	1,000	2,500
Capital, D	1,000	2,500
	$22,000	$28,000

---

[23] Code Sec. 751(a); Reg. § 1.751-1(a)(1). For sales or exchanges of partnership interests prior to August 5, 1997, the provision applies only to "substantially appreci- ated inventory." The Taxpayer Relief Act of 1997, P.L. 105-34, Act § 1062(a).

Partner *A* agrees to sell her interest in the partnership to new partner E for $2,500 cash, plus assumption of her $4,500 share of partnership debt. *A*'s tax basis in her partnership interest is $5,500 (1,000 tax capital account + $4,500 share of partnership debt). The selling price of her interest is $7,000 ($2,500 cash + $4,500 debt relief). Thus, she recognizes a $1,500 gain on the sale. Under Code Sec. 751(a), her gain will be characterized as ordinary income to the extent she would have been allocated ordinary income if the partnership had sold all of its assets. Here, the partnership would recognize $2,500 ordinary income from selling its accounts receivable and $500 from selling its inventory. *A*'s 25% share of the partnership's ordinary income on these assets would be $750. Thus $750 of *A*'s $1,500 gain on sale of her partnership interest will be taxed as ordinary income. The remainder will be treated as capital gain under Code Sec. 741.

The ordinary income or loss realized by a partner upon the sale or exchange of a partnership interest is the amount of ordinary income or loss that would have been allocated to that partner if the partnership sold all its assets, including its Code Sec. 751 property (ordinary income assets).[24] The regulations are silent as to the effect of an arm's length agreement allocating the purchase price among the partnership's underlying assets. The preamble to Reg. § 1.751-1, however, indicates that this would be "inconsistent with the hypothetical sale approach of the regulations."[25] Since capital gains are taxed at a preferred rate, the seller clearly wants to allocate as little as possible to Code Sec. 751 assets in order to minimize his or her ordinary income. The buyer, however, will have tax consequences under Code Sec. 751 only if a Code Sec. 743(b) adjustment of the basis of the partnership property is to be made, or if the buyer receives a Code Sec. 732(d) distribution.[26] In other situations the IRS should not be bound by the "agreement" that affects only one party. However, most circuit courts have taken the position that a party to the agreement (as opposed to the IRS) must have strong proof to upset it.

> *Observation:* If the partnership has a Code Sec. 754 election in effect and there is an adverse bargaining position due to the buyer's Code Sec. 743(b) adjustments and the character of the seller's gain, an agreement would have some evidentiary weight as to the relative values of the partnership assets.

.01 Definition of Unrealized Receivables

As originally enacted, Code Sec. 751(c) included only a single sentence dealing with rights to receive payments (to the extent not previously includible in income under the method of accounting used by the partnership) for goods and services provided or to be provided. Note that Code Sec. 751(a) would not apply to *realized* receivables (generally, accounts receivable of an accrual-basis taxpayer). However, even realized receivables are included in the definition of inventory, as explained

---

[24] Reg. § 1.751-1(a)(2). Note: these regulations were amended by T.D. 8847, 1999-52 IRB 701, effective for transfers of partnership interests occurring after December 15, 1999. This citation refers to the amended regulations.

[25] Preamble, T.D. 8847, 1999-52 IRB 701.

[26] This is a distribution that occurs within two years of the purchase when a Code Sec. 754 election has not been made.

below. Currently the last two sentences of Code Section 751(c) are a history of Congressional exceptions to capital gain treatment enacted over the years. The term "unrealized receivables" under Code Sec. 751(a) now includes the following items:

1. Depreciation recapture under Code Sec. 1245.

2. Excess depreciation under Code Sec. 1250.

3. Mining exploration expenses recapture under Code Sec. 617(d).

4. Stock in a D.I.S.C.[27] or certain foreign corporations.[28]

5. Franchises, trademarks, etc.[29]

6. Oil, gas or geothermal property.[30]

7. Excess farm loss recapture under Code Sec. 1252.

8. Market discount bonds[31] and short-term obligations.[32]

Code Sec. 751(c) does not purport to be an exhaustive list of "unrealized receivables" but merely indicates that the term "includes" the items listed. To date, the IRS has not argued for any other inclusion, but the language to support such an argument is in the section.

As indicated, the term "unrealized receivables" includes the rights to payments for services rendered or to be rendered to the extent not already reported. The term "rights . . . to payment for" is construed liberally, including a noncontractual or equitable right (*quantum meruit*) to payment, whether it is partially or fully earned, and when there is a noncancellable future contract to perform services or deliver goods. However, if the agreement is cancellable at will by the buyer-customer, it is not an unrealized receivable to the seller. Thus, general expectations of profit are likened to goodwill, which is not a Code Sec. 751 asset. Even though goodwill represents future profits to which the purchaser has assigned economic value, the seller will have capital gain on its disposition.

Unrealized receivables include the right to receive payments for goods delivered or to be delivered. The right to be paid for "goods" is defined as the right to receive payment for property other than a capital asset.[33]

The recapture items referred to in the last two sentences of Code Sec. 751(c) are different from the right to receive payments for goods or services in that they do not involve any type of contractual right to receive payments. They are, in effect, the current unrealized potential ordinary income inherent in the property if it were sold at its current fair market value. This unrealized receivable is an amount of ordinary income determined by referring to the fair market value of the asset, its adjusted basis, and the type of gain, ordinary or capital, which would be reported if it were sold.

---

[27] Code Sec. 992(a).

[28] Code Sec. 1248.

[29] Code Sec. 1253.

[30] Code Sec. 1254.

[31] As defined in Code Sec. 1278.

[32] As defined in Code Sec. 1283.

[33] Reg. § 1.751-1(c)(1)(i).

Since Code Sec. 751 assets include only assets that represent potential ordinary income; assets with short-term capital gain potential are not Code Sec. 751 assets, and gain from the sale of the partnership interest attributable to such items will receive long-term capital gain treatment if the partnership interest has been held long term.

Generally, Code Sec. 751(c) defines unrealized receivables for all purposes of partnership taxation (Subchapter K of the Internal Revenue Code). References to "unrealized receivables" may be found in the following sections in Subchapter K:

1. Code Sec. 731(a)(2), which provides for the recognition of loss upon certain distributions in liquidation of a partner's partnership interest;

2. Code Sec. 732(c), which provides for an allocation of adjusted basis to distributed property to be made first to Code Sec. 751 assets;

3. Code Sec. 735(a), which provides that the character of gain or loss realized on a subsequent sale of unrealized receivables received in a distribution is ordinary income; and

4. Code Sec. 724, which provides that the character of partnership gain or loss realized on a subsequent sale of unrealized receivables contributed by a partner is ordinary income.

.02 "Inventory Items" Defined

The second category of Code Sec. 751 assets consists of inventory items. Code Sec. 751(d) sets out three categories of inventory items.[34] The first of the three categories of inventory items is true inventory in terms of Code Sec. 1221(1), and dealer property held primarily for sale to customers in the ordinary course of the partnership's business.[35]

The second category comprises other property which, when sold or exchanged by the partnership, would be considered property other than a capital asset in terms of Code Sec. 1221 and other than a Code Sec. 1231(b) asset.[36] This category is so broad as to apparently encompass all the other categories and specifically includes the accounts receivable of a cash-basis taxpayer,[37] realized accounts receivable of an accrual-basis taxpayer, depreciation recapture, and all unrealized receivables. The inclusion of unrealized receivables in "inventory" has the effect of increasing the aggregate value of partnership inventory without increasing its aggregate basis. Thus, the apparent rationale behind the expanded definition of inventory is to increase the likelihood that the partnership's inventory will be substantially appreciated, and therefore to reduce the likelihood that the selling partner will be able to convert ordinary income into capital gain (by selling his or her partnership interest before the partnership sells its inventory). Nonetheless, this overlapping definition of inventory and unrealized receivables creates

---

[34] Prior to August 5, 1997, the effective date of Act § 1062(a) of the Taxpayer Relief Act of 1997 (P.L. 105-34), the second category of Code Sec. 751 assets was "substantially appreciated" inventory. If the inventory items were, in the aggregate sense, "substantially appreciated" within the guidelines of Code Sec. 751(d)(1), then "substantially appreciated" inventory existed.

[35] Code Sec. 751(d)(1).

[36] Code Sec. 751(d)(2).

[37] Although this would seem unwarranted, the regulations specifically provide for this result. Reg. § 1.751-1(d)(2)(ii).

confusion in applying other provisions of Subchapter K which provide special separate treatment for inventory and unrealized receivables.[38]

The fact that the Code Sec. 751(d)(2) definition of inventory refers to noncapital assets and not to noncapital gains potentially means that Code Sec. 306 stock, Code Sec. 341 gains, gains from original issue discount, and other gains which are from capital assets but are taxed as ordinary income are excluded from the definition of inventory under Code Sec. 751(d)(2). If this were the case, most recapture items would not be inventory items. Code Sec. 64, however, appears to classify these assets as other than Code Sec. 1231(b) or capital assets, and therefore these assets are unlikely to be excluded from the definition of inventory.

The third category is any other partnership property that would be either Code Sec. 1221(1) property, other noncapital assets, or non-Code Sec. 1231(b) property if it were held by the selling partner.[39] Therefore, if the property falls into one of the first two categories "if held by the selling . . . partner," it is considered to be inventory for the purposes of Code Sec. 751(a). The legislative history does not indicate the purpose for this provision which, in effect, requires the property to be tested at two levels.

Whether or not property is "held primarily for sale" under Code Sec. 1221(l) is a factual test focusing on the taxpayer's intent with regard to the property in question. In the context of Code Sec. 751(d)(3), this test is difficult to apply since the partner does not actually own the property. It could be argued that a selling partner, who is otherwise a dealer in the type of assets the partnership owns, can have investment accounts, and that this particular property would be such an investment. A trader or dealer in certain types of property may invest in that property if he or she shows an intent. One method of showing this intent is to set the property aside from other similar property that he or she deals in. Ownership through a partnership that is not controlled by the partner would help show investment motive. However, with respect to a similar provision, Code Sec. 341(e) provides that, if the taxpayer has similar inventory, this is enough to create a presumption that it would be held for sale.[40]

> *Observation:* This rule treating partnership property as inventory if it would be inventory in the hands of the selling partner could have some surprising and unwelcome results. For example, a dealer in unimproved land who is a partner in a partnership which invests in the same type of land will report as capital gain his or her share of the partnership's capital gain when the property is sold. However, under the Code Sec. 751(d)(3) definition of inventory, the IRS can take the position that ordinary income is generated on the

---

[38] Code Secs. 724 and 735.

[39] Code Sec. 751(d)(4).

[40] Code Sec. 341(b)(1) refers to the purchase of property described in Code Sec. 341(b)(3), which defines "Section 341 assets." *See* Rep. No. 781, 82d Cong., 1st Sess. (1951), reprinted in 1951-2 CB 458, 481. *See also Jacobs v. Commr.*, CA-9, 55-2 USTC ¶ 9555, 224 F2d 412.

Reg. § 1.341-6(b)(4). This issue potentially causes additional problems when Code Sec. 751(b) is applicable as it may give ordinary income to the other nondealer partners upon a deemed property distribution to the dealer. The regulations cure this by limiting Code Sec. 751(d)(4) to property retained by the partnership. Reg. § 1.751-1(d)(2)(iii). *See* further discussion of Code Sec. 751(b) under distributions in Chapter 12.

sale of his or her partnership interest if the partner sells the interest rather than waiting for the partnership to sell the investment land.

Often Code Sec. 751(a) has the simple effect of turning part of the gain on the sale of a partnership interest into ordinary income. In some cases, however, the selling partner may be required to recognize ordinary income in an amount that exceeds his or her total gain on the sale. In such cases, the partner will recognize a capital loss in the amount of the excess.

Example 11-7: Alice and Barbara are equal partners in personal service AB Partnership. Barbara transfers her interest in the AB Partnership to Ted for $15,000 when the AB Partnership's balance sheet (reflecting a cash receipts and disbursements method of accounting) is as follows:

AB Partnership

Assets	Adjusted Basis	FMV
Cash	$3,000	$3,000
Loans Receivable	10,000	10,000
Capital Assets	7,000	5,000
Unrealized Receivables	0	14,000
Total	$20,000	$32,000
Liabilities and Capital		
Liabilities	$2,000	$2,000
Capital		
Alice	9,000	15,000
Barbara	9,000	15,000
Total	$20,000	$32,000

None of the assets owned by the AB Partnership is Code Sec. 704(c) property, and the capital assets are nondepreciable. The total amount realized by Barbara is $16,000, consisting of:

Amount Realized

Cash	$15,000
Debt Relief	1,000
	$16,000

Barbara's Adjusted Basis in Her Partnership Interest

Tax Basis Capital Account	$9,000
Debt Share	1,000
	$10,000

If Code Sec. 751(a) did not apply to the sale, Barbara would recognize $6,000 of capital gain from the sale of the interest in the AB Partnership. However, Code Sec. 751(a) does apply to the sale because Barbara's undivided half-interest in the partnership property includes a half-interest in the partnership's unrealized receivables. Barbara's basis in her partnership interest is $10,000.

If the AB Partnership sold all of its Code Sec. 751 property in a fully taxable transaction immediately prior to the transfer of Barbara's partnership interest to Ted, Barbara would have been allocated $7,000 of ordinary income from the sale of the ABC Partnership's unrealized receivables. Therefore, Barbara will recognize $7,000 of ordinary income with respect to the unrealized receivables. The difference between the amount of capital gain or loss that the partner would realize in the absence of Code Sec. 751 ($6,000) and the amount of ordinary income or loss ($7,000) is the transferor's capital gain or loss on the sale of its partnership interest. In this case, Barbara will recognize a $1,000 capital loss.

Character of Barbara's Gain

Amount Realized	$16,000
Partnership Interest Adjusted Basis	(10,000)
Total Gain	*$6,000*
Less Ordinary Income Share	(7,000)
Capital Gain (Loss)	*$(1,000)*

.03 Tiered Partnerships

Code Sec. 751(f) provides that, in determining whether partnership property is an unrealized receivable or an inventory item, a partnership will be treated as owning its proportionate share of the property held by any other partnership in which it is a partner. The purpose of this provision is to assure that the collapsible partnership rules will be applied evenly without regard to whether property is held directly by a partnership or indirectly through another partnership.

The application of Code Sec. 751(f) to the simple situation in which a parent partnership's only significant asset is its interest in a subsidiary is straight forward. For example, the subsidiary partnership's activities, trade or business, intent, and so forth, are attributed directly to the parent partnership along with the ownership of the parent's share of the subsidiary partnership's assets.

However, if the parent partnership is engaged in a separate trade or business, should the character of the subsidiary partnership's assets be determined in its hands and then attributed to the parent partnership along with the ownership of its share of the subsidiary's assets? Should the assets be tested by treating the parent partnership as owning them directly? In keeping with the apparent legislative purpose to neutralize the significance of tiered partnership agreements, most—if not all—of these and similar questions should be resolved by completely ignoring the separate existence of subsidiary partnerships. Accordingly, Code Sec. 751(d) should be applied on a "consolidated" basis, and the parent partnership should be viewed as owning a share of the subsidiary's assets and engaging directly in the subsidiary's business and its own business for purposes of determining the character of its share of the subsidiary's assets. Neither the statute nor the legislative history resolve questions of this type.

.04 Enforcement

Code Sec. 6050K(a) generally requires partnerships to file information returns with the Form 1065, U.S. Partnership Return of Income, for any transfers described in Code Sec. 751(a) for the tax year in which the calendar year of the exchange takes place.[41] These returns must identify the transferor and transferee involved in the exchange and provide such other information as the regulations require. Code Sec. 6050K(b) also requires that the information in the return be disclosed to the transferor and transferee "before January 31 following the calendar year for which the return . . . was made."[42]

Code Sec. 6050K(c)(1) requires that any transferor of a partnership interest give prompt notice of the transfer to the partnership,[43] and Code Sec. 6050K(c)(2) delays the partnership's required filing date until after it is "notified of such exchange." Thus, the burden of triggering the entire reporting process falls on the transferor.

Even though the clear intent of Code Sec. 6050K is to force compliance with Code Sec. 751(a), neither the section itself nor the Form 8308, Report of a Sale or Exchange of Certain Partnership Interests, or its instructions, or Reg. § 1.6050K-1, require the partnership to notify the partner of the information necessary to calculate the seller's ordinary income under Code Sec. 751(a). The partner is merely informed of the requirement to treat a portion of gain or loss from the sale of his or her partnership interest as ordinary in character.[44]

The collapsible partnership rules in Code Sec. 751 are very complex and are frequently overlooked (or ignored) by both practitioners and revenue agents. However, the Code Sec. 751(a) rules are extremely broad and are potentially applicable to a wide variety of common situations. In part, the wide applicability of these rules is a direct consequence of the definition of "unrealized receivables." Thus, any partner who transfers his or her partnership interest is likely to be subject to Code Sec. 751(a) if the partnership owns depreciable personal property or uses the cash method of accounting.

---

[41] Form 8308, Report of a Sale or Exchange of Certain Partnership Interests.

[42] Pub. 541, Tax Information on Partnerships, indicates that "The partnership must also provide a copy of the Form 8308 (or a written statement with the same information) to each transferee and transferor, by the later of

January 31, following the end of the calendar year or 30 days after it receives notice of the exchange."

[43] Within 30 days of the transfer or by January 15 of the year following the year of transfer if earlier.

[44] Reg. § 1.6050K-1(c).

.05 Comparison with Code Sec. 341

The above provisions are comparable to those applicable to collapsible corporations and Code Sec. 751 is similar, in effect, to Code Sec. 341 since both have the same purpose—namely, to preclude the conversion of ordinary income into capital gains. Code Sec. 341, however, has many important differences from Code Sec. 751; for example, it adopts an "all-or-nothing" approach because the shareholder's gain is all ordinary income or all long-term capital gain. Furthermore, unlike Code Sec. 751, which is completely mechanical, Code Sec. 341 is triggered only if a shareholder has the requisite subjective intent described in Code Sec. 341(a). Finally, Code Sec. 751(a) prevents shifting of ordinary income between partners, whereas Code Sec. 341 is aimed mainly at the complete avoidance of ordinary income. If the partnership does not have a Code Sec. 754 election in effect, the selling partner's share of ordinary income is reported twice—first by him, and then by the purchaser.

> **S Corporation Observation:** Code Sec. 341 applies to S corporations as well as C corporations, but Code Sec. 751(a) does not apply to S or C corporations.

¶ 1105 Collectibles and Unrecaptured Code Sec. 1250 Gain

Collectibles and unrecaptured section 1250 gain held by the partnership have similar consequences for partners upon sale of their partnership interests. Although these assets do not cause a portion of the partner's gain on sale of the interest to be taxed as ordinary income, they do cause a portion of that gain to be recharacterized. Consistent with the provisions of Code Sec. 751(a), the differential tax rates applicable to gain from the sale of these assets cannot be avoided by selling them through a partnership rather than selling them directly.

.01 Collectibles Gain

If the partner has held his or her interest in a partnership for more than one year, gain recognized on its sale will ordinarily be characterized as long-term capital gain subject to a maximum tax rate of 15 percent. As discussed previously, to the extent this gain is attributable to the partner's share of partnership ordinary income assets, it will be recharacterized as ordinary income under Code Sec. 751(a). To the extent the gain is attributable to the partner's share of partnership "collectibles," Code Sec. 751(a) is not triggered because such assets are not ordinary income assets. However, Code Sec. 1(h)(5)(B) requires that the gain must be partially or wholly recharacterized as collectibles gain, rather than long-term capital gain. Any portion of the gain classified as collectibles gain will be subject to a maximum tax rate of 28 percent rather than the more favorable 15 percent rate generally applied to long-term capital gains.[45]

The selling partner will recognize "collectibles gain" in an amount equal to the net gain (but not net loss) that would be allocated to that partner if the partnership sold all of its collectibles for cash at their fair market value immediately before the

---

[45] Code Sec. 1(h)(4).

transfer of the interest in the partnership. The term "collectibles" includes assets of the following types that are held for more than one year:[46]

- Works of art,
- Rugs or antiques,
- Precious metals or gems,
- Stamps or coins,[47]
- Alcoholic beverages, and
- Other tangible personal property which may be classified by the IRS as a collectible.

Net collectibles gains are subject to the same tax rates as ordinary income, except that the tax rate on these gains cannot exceed 28 percent.[48] Note that determination of the holding period, and thus determination of whether a portion of the partner's gain will be characterized as collectibles gain, is based on the partner's holding period in the partnership interest, and not the partnership's holding period in the collectibles.[49]

If only a part of the partner's interest has been held for more than one year, then only a ratable portion of the partner's gain will be treated as collectibles gain by the partner. The collectibles gain will reduce the long term capital gain recognized by the partner on the sale of the interest, and might in fact create or increase a residual long term capital loss on the sale.

> **Example 11-8:** Antiques Etc. is a general partnership that invests in artwork. The partnership owns paintings worth $500,000, with a tax basis of $340,000. Carlyn, a 25 percent partner in the partnership, sold her partnership interest for $600,000. Her tax basis in the partnership interest was $400,000, triggering a gain on the sale of $200,000. Had the partnership sold its artwork, it would have recognized a $160,000 gain on the sale ($500,000 value less $340,000 tax basis). Assume that Carlyn would have been allocated a 25 percent share of this gain, equal to her interest in the partnership, and that she has held her interest in the partnership for more than one year. Carlyn will treat $40,000 of her gain on sale of the partnership interest as collectibles gain (25% of $160,000). The remaining $160,000 of gain she recognizes would be long term capital gain.

> Had Carlyn's holding period for the partnership interest been only 50 percent long term, she would have recognized a long-term capital gain of $80,000, a collectibles gain of $20,000 (50% of $40,000), and a short-term capital gain of $100,000 (half of her total gain on the sale). Note that the collectibles gain comes entirely out of the portion of her total gain treated as long-term capital gain.

---

[46] Code Secs. 1(h)(5) and 408(m)(2).

[47] Code Sec. 408(m)(3) provides an exception under which certain coins or bullion defined in Code Sec. 5112 that are held by banks and other qualified trustees. However, under Reg. § 1.1(h)(1)(b)(2)(i), this exception does not apply for purposes of determining the portion of a partner's gain on sale of a partnership interest which is classified as collectibles gain.

[48] Code Sec. 1(h)(4).

[49] Reg. § 1.1(h)-1(b)(2)(ii).

Finally, assume that Carlyn's holding period of the entire partnership interest had been long term, but that her tax basis in the partnership interest had been $590,000. In this case, her total gain would be only $10,000. However, since she would have been allocated a $40,000 share of the partnership's gain from sale of the artwork, her collectibles gain would still be $40,000. She would offset this gain with a long term capital loss ($30,000).

.02 Unrecaptured Section 1250 Gain

Generally speaking, unrecaptured section 1250 gain is the depreciation that has been taken on real property, less the depreciation that is recaptured as ordinary income. Code Sec. 1250 recaptures as ordinary income only the excess of depreciation actually deducted on depreciable real estate over the amount of depreciation that would have been allowed using the straight-line method. Under current law, all depreciable real estate must be depreciated using the straight-line method. Thus, any gain recognized on the sale of depreciable real property will generally be classified as unrecaptured section 1250 gain to the extent of accumulated depreciation deductions on the property. Of course, unrecaptured section 1250 gain cannot exceed the gain recognized on the sale of the asset. Unrecaptured section 1250 gains are subject to a maximum tax rate of 25 percent.[50]

As with collectibles gains, Code Sec. 1(h) requires that any gain recognized on the sale of a partnership interest that is attributable to the partner's share of partnership unrecaptured section 1250 gains will not be eligible for the preferential 15 percent long-term capital gains tax rate. Here, the portion of the partner's gain that is attributable to unrecaptured Code Sec. 1250 gains will be subject to a maximum tax rate of 25 percent (vs. 28 percent for collectibles and 15 percent for long-term capital gains).

Again, these rules only come into play when a partner sells a partnership interest for which her holding period was long term. When an interest in a partnership held for more than one year is sold or exchanged, the transferor is required to recognize the unrecaptured section 1250 gain that would be allocated to that partner if the partnership sold all of its section 1250 property at their fair market value immediately before the transfer of the interest in the partnership. If a portion of the holding period of the partnership interest is not long term, or if the exchange of the interest was not fully taxable, only a *pro rata* portion of the partner's share of the unrecaptured 1250 gain will have to be recognized. As with collectibles gains, unrecaptured section 1250 gains will reduce the long term capital gain recognized by the partner on the sale of the interest, and this reduction can create or increase a residual long term capital loss on the sale.

¶ 1106 Installment Sale of a Partnership Interest

A partner who sells a partnership interest at a gain for consideration that includes the buyer's note must report the sale on the installment method unless he or she elects to report the gain in the year of sale. The gross profit, total contract price, gross profit reporting ratio, and yearly payments are computed based upon

---

[50] Code Sec. 1(h)(1)(D).

the same principles as installment sales of other property. The selling partner's share of partnership liabilities are taken into account as part of the total contract price and as year-of-sale payments only to the extent they exceed the selling partner's basis in his or her interest.[51]

If the sale triggers recognition of both ordinary income and capital gain under Code Sec. 751(a), application of the installment sale rules will depend upon the specific nature of the ordinary income triggered by the sale. If the ordinary income represents the selling partner's share of partnership depreciation recapture, it cannot be reported under the installment method but must be reported in its entirety in the year of sale.[52]

The partner's share of Code Secs. 1245 and 1250 depreciation recapture income may not, as mentioned, be reported under the installment method.[53] Also, the general rule is that the installment method is not available for the sale of inventory.[54] The IRS's position is that the portion of any gain from the sale of a partnership interest attributable to the partner's share of the partnership inventory is not reportable under the installment method.[55] In addition, CCA 200722027 holds that a taxpayer is not permitted to report income from the sale of the taxpayer's interest in the partnership under the installment method to the extent it represents income attributable to Code Sec. 751(c)(2) unrealized receivables for payment for services rendered. The Treasury Department is authorized to prescribe regulations which treat the role of a partnership interest as a "proportionate share of the assets of the partnership" for purposes of Code Sec. 453A.[56] Code Sec. 453A contains restrictions on pledges of installment notes and provides for interest on deferred tax liability under some circumstances. Code Sec. 453(k)(2) authorizes the Treasury Department to prescribe regulations which deny the installment sale method to the sale of a partnership interest when it is an indirect sale of publicly traded stocks and securities. Such regulations have not been issued.

While there is no general authority with respect to the treatment of partnership-level unrecaptured Code Sec. 1250 gain when a partnership interest is sold on the installment method, the treatment of unrecaptured Code Sec. 1250 gain in these circumstances would presumably conform to the usual treatment of such gain in the case of an installment sale. Regulation § 1.453-12(d), Example 1, holds that when an asset with unrecaptured Code Sec. 1250 gain is sold under the installment method, the unrecaptured Code Sec. 1250 gain is recognized before any capital gain on the sale. In fact, the IRS has held, in PLR 200937007, that if an interest in a partnership having assets with unrecaptured Code Sec. 1250 gain is sold, the unrecaptured Code Sec. 1250 gain is recognized before any net capital gain. With respect to the treatment of collectibles gain inherent in partnership property when a partnership interest is sold under the installment method, there is no direct or

---

[51] Rev. Rul. 76-483, 1976-2 CB 131.

[52] Code Sec. 453(i)(2).

[53] Code Sec. 453(i)(2).

[54] Code Sec. 453(b)(2).

[55] Rev. Rul. 89-108, 1989-2 CB 100.

[56] Code Sec. 453(e).

indirect authority. Presumably collectibles gain in this situation should be recognized in the same manner that unrecaptured Code Sec. 1250 gain is recognized.

Example 11-9: The equal ABC general partnership has the following balance sheets:

ABC Partnership

Assets	Tax Basis	FMV
Land	$300	$1,200
Liabilities	$0	$0
Capital		
A	$100	$400
B	100	400
C	100	400
	$300	$1,200

Partner *A*, who has a $100 basis in his partnership interest, sells his interest to *D* for a $100 cash payment and a note for $300. His gross profit reporting ratio of 75% is calculated as follows:

Selling Price (SP)	$400	($100 cash + $300 note)
Basis	(100)	
Gross Profit (GP)	*$300*	

The gross profit reporting ratio is equal to the gross profit (GP) divided by the total contract price (TCP). The TCP in the absence of debt relief exceeding basis is merely the face value of the note plus cash received in the year of sale.

$$\text{Gross Profit Reporting Ratio} = \frac{GP}{TCP} = \frac{\$300}{\$400} = 75\%$$

Partner *A* must report gain of $75 in the year of sale and 75% of each principal payment when received.

Gross Profit Reporting Ratio (75%) × Payment ($100) = $75

Example 11-10: The ABC equal general partnership has the following balance sheet:

ABC Partnership

Assets	*Tax Basis*	*FMV*
Land	$300	$900
Building	0	900
	$300	*$1,800*
Liabilities	$600	$600

Capital Accounts

	Tax Basis	*FMV*
A	$(100)	$400
B	(100)	400
C	(100)	400
	$300	*$1,200*

Partner *A*, who has a $100 basis in his partnership interest, sells his interest to *D* for a $100 cash payment and a note for $300. His gross profit reporting ratio is 100% and he has a deemed $100 payment in the year of sale.

Selling Price (SP) . . .	$600	($100 cash + $200 debt relief + $300 note)
Basis	(100)	

Gross Profit (GP) . . .   *$500*

Note: *The SP includes Partner A's former $200 share of the partnership debt.*

The gross profit reporting ratio is defined as:

$$\frac{\text{Gross Profit (GP)}}{\text{Total Contract Price (TCP)}}$$

Total contract price (TCP) is equal to the cash purchase price received in the year of sale plus the principal amount of the note received, plus debt relief in excess of the basis of the partnership interest, and is equal to:

Down Payment	$100
Note's face value	300
Debt in excess of basis	100
Total Contract Price	*$500*

The gross profit reporting ratio (GPRR) is equal to:

$$\text{GPRR} \quad = \quad \frac{\text{GP}}{\text{TCP}} \quad = \quad \frac{\$500}{\$500} \quad = \quad 100\%$$

Partner A's gain reportable in the year of sale is equal to the product of the gross profit reporting ratio times the year of sale payments. For this purpose, the $100 debt relief in excess of basis is a deemed cash payment in the year of sale.

$$\text{GPRR (100\%)} \quad \times \quad \text{Payments (\$100 + \$100)} \quad = \quad \$200$$

Two hundred dollars is reported as gain in the year partner A sells his interest.

Example 11-11: The ABC equal general partnership has the following balance sheets. The partnership's equipment had originally been purchased for $1,000 and any gain on its sale would be ordinary income under Code Sec. 1245:

ABC Partnership

Assets	**Tax Basis**	**FMV**
Land	$300	$900
Equipment	0	900
	$300	$1,800
Liabilities	$600	$600
Capital Accounts		
A	$(100)	$400
B	(100)	400
C	(100)	400
	$300	$1,200

Partner A, who has a $100 basis in his partnership interest, sells his interest to D for a $100 cash payment and a note for $300. His gross profit reporting ratio is 100%, he has a deemed $100 payment in the year of sale, and he reports $300 of ordinary income for his share of the gain attributable to his share of the partnership's depreciation recapture income which cannot be deferred under the installment method of accounting.

Selling Price (SP)	$600	($100 cash + $200 debt relief + $300 note)
Basis	(100)	
Gross Profit (GP)	$500	

Note: *The SP includes Partner A's former $200 share of the partnership debt.*

The portion of the gain attributable to Partner A's $300 share of the Code Sec. 1245 depreciation recapture related to the equipment is not deferred under the installment method; therefore, the gross profit reportable under the installment method is $200.

The gross profit reporting ratio (GPRR) is the gross profit (GP) divided by the total contract price (TCP). The TCP is equal to any purchase price received in the year of sale, plus the note's principal amount, plus debt relief in excess of basis. Partner A's total contract price is equal to:

Cash down payment	$100
Note's face value	300
Debt in excess of basis	100
Total Contract Price	*$500*

Partner A's gross profit reporting ratio is:

$$\text{GPRR} \quad = \quad \frac{\text{GP}}{\text{TCP}} \quad = \quad \frac{\$200}{\$500} \quad = \quad 40\%$$

Partner A's gain reportable in the year of sale is equal to this gross profit reporting ratio (GPRR) times payments received in the year of sale. For this purpose, Partner A's debt relief in excess of basis of $100 is a deemed principal payment for the sale year. Partner A's capital gain reported under the installment method is as follows:

Year of Sale	=	$80 = 40% × $200*
Future Years	=	120 = 40% × $300**

$200 Total Capital Gain

300 Ordinary income in the year of sale

$500 Total gain from Partner A's sale of his partnership interest

GPRR: 40%; Principal Payments: $100 cash + $100 debt over basis.

**GPRR: 40%; Principal Payments: $300 note paid after sale year.*

¶ 1107 Abandonments and Gifts of a Partnership Interest

The abandonment, forfeiture, or similar disposition of a partnership interest is treated in a manner similar to the taxation of an abandonment, foreclosure, or deed-in-lieu of other property. The same is true of the worthlessness of a partnership interest. If there is no debt relief connected with those types of dispositions, there is no sale or exchange under Code Sec. 1222 and any loss is ordinary in character.[57] The partner establishes worthlessness by showing the partnership interest has no value.[58] Establishing the abandonment or worthlessness of a partnership interest is a question of fact. The partner can establish abandonment by proving that he or she intends to discontinue all investment and other involvement with the partnership.[59]

Example 11-12: Partner A is an equal member of the ABC general partnership. At a meeting of the partners he announces that he will no longer make contributions to the partnership as required by the partnership agreement. He also offers to transfer his interest to anyone interested in acquiring it in exchange for assuming his obligations under the agreement. The Tax Court

---

[57] *G.G. Gannon v. Commr.*, 16 TC 1134, Dec. 18,304 (1951), Acq.; *P. Hutcheson v. Commr.*, 17 TC 14, Dec. 18,430 (1951), Acq.; *J.C. Echols v. Commr.*, CA-5, 91-2 USTC ¶ 50,360, 935 F2d 703; Rev. Rul. 93-80, 1993-2 CB 230.

[58] *E.g., Tejon Ranch Co. v. Commr.*, 49 TCM 1357, Dec. 42,058(M), TC Memo. 1995-207.

[59] *E.g., S. Pallan v. Commr.*, 51 TCM 497, Dec. 42,891(M), TC Memo. 1986-76.

held that this did not establish abandonment of his interest.[60] The Fifth Circuit Court of Appeals held that it did.[61]

When a partner abandons or otherwise disposes of a partnership interest and is relieved of a share of partnership debt, the transaction is treated as a sale for the amount of the debt relief.[62]

In the case of a gift of a partnership interest when the partner does not receive a deemed cash payment for a decrease in his or her share of liabilities, there is no amount realized upon a disposition of property and therefore there can be no gain[63] or loss.[64] In contrast, gain, but not loss, can be incurred when the gift of a partnership interest results in a reduction in the donor's share of the partnership debt. As in the case of an abandonment of a partnership interest, this deemed money distribution under Code Sec. 752(b) is treated as an amount realized in a bargain sale transaction. The transaction will be recharacterized as a partial sale and gain will be recognized to the extent the debt relief exceeds the partner's tax basis of the interest deemed sold.[65] Any loss is disallowed.[66] If the gift is to a charity, the IRS has taken the position that the amount of the charitable contribution deduction is based upon the type of property held by the partnership.[67] For example, the amount of the charitable contribution is reduced to the extent that the partner would recognize ordinary income had he or she sold the partnership interest (*i.e.*, under Code Sec. 751(a)).[68]

¶ 1108 Like-Kind Exchanges of Partnership Interests

.01 Code Sec. 1031(a)(2)(D)

Code Sec. 1031(a)(2)(D) explicitly provides that a partnership interest exchanged for a partnership interest in the same or another partnership does *not* qualify for nonrecognition under that section. This is true even though the underlying properties may be identical.

The regulations specifically provide that Code Sec. 1031 does not apply to any exchange of partnership interests in a partnership regardless of whether the interests exchanged are general or limited partnership interests in the same partnership or in different partnerships.[69] As a result, exchanges of interests in different partnerships are taxable. Exchanges of interests in the same partnerships are taxable, but changes in status (such as from the status of a general partner to the status of a limited partner) are not taxable unless collateral rules apply to cause a taxable event. For example, a change in status could trigger income by creating a negative at-risk amount[70] or cause a deemed money distribution in excess of basis on account of a decrease in a partner's share of liabilities.[71]

---

[60] *J.C. Echols v. Commr.*, 93 TC 533, Dec. 46,141 (1989).

[61] *J.C. Echols v. Commr.*, CA-5, 91-2 USTC ¶ 50,360, 935 F2d 703.

[62] *E.g., N.J. O'Brien v. Commr.*, 77 TC 113, Dec. 38,076 (1981); Rev. Rul. 93-80, 1993-2 CB 239.

[63] Code Sec. 1001(a).

[64] Code Sec. 262.

[65] Code Sec. 1011(b).

[66] Reg. § 1.1001-1(e).

[67] Rev. Rul. 60-352, 1960-2 CB 208.

[68] Code Sec. 170(e)(1).

[69] Reg. § 1.1031(a)-1(a)(1).

[70] Code Sec. 465(e).

[71] Code Sec. 752(b).

LLC Observation: When a partnership is converted to an LLC or an LLP, the same concepts apply. For federal income tax purposes, the new LLC partnership is a continuation of the old partnership. The new liability limitations may, however, affect the continuing partner's shares of the partnership debt.

.02 Planning for Exchanges of Some Partnership Property and Sale of Other Partnership Property

Co-ownership. Although a direct exchange of partnership interests is no longer directly possible, a similar result might be obtained by using the concept of co-ownership. Often the partners will agree that the partnership should dispose of its property but will disagree as to the form of the disposition. Some will prefer a cash sale, others an installment sale, and some will want a tax-free exchange into like-kind property under Code Sec. 1031. One commonly encountered solution to this dilemma is for the partnership to distribute a tenancy-in-common interest in its property to partners who want to custom tailor the tax results of their disposition. Under the current regulations and the case law applicable to Code Sec. 1031, it is possible to exchange a co-ownership interest in property for a co-ownership interest in other property. In Rev. Proc. 2002-22,[72] the IRS has outlined the conditions that generally must be met in order for it to agree to rule on whether an undivided fractional interest in a particular rental real estate co-ownership arrangement will be treated as an interest in a business entity (such as a partnership) or not. Many practitioners have advised that a partnership may make a distribution to a partner of a co-ownership interest in the partnership's property. This co-ownership interest may, in turn, be used for a like-kind exchange, perhaps for a similarly distributed undivided interest in another partnership's property.[73]

This maneuver, while apparently skirting the 1984 amendments in an efficient manner, may nonetheless fall afoul of the regulations that provide that:

> [M]ere co-ownership of property which is maintained, kept in repair, and rented or leased does not constitute a partnership (what might be called "passive co-ownership"). Tenants in common, however, may be partners if they actively carry on a trade, business, financial operation, or venture and divide the profits thereof. For example, a partnership exists if co-owners of an apartment building lease space and in addition provide services to the occupants either directly or through an agent[.][74]

Relevant cases such as *McManus v. Commissioner*[75] and *Allison v. Commissioner*[76] indicate that it is the degree of business activity that determines whether what the parties thought was a co-tenancy is taxed as a partnership. It is thus possible, despite the distribution of a co-ownership interest in the partnership property, that the distributee and the partnership will be taxed as partners and not

---

[72] 2002-1 CB 733.

[73] At a minimum, the transaction's legal form must track its intended tax treatment. *D.G. Chase v. Commr.*, 92 TC 874, Dec. 45,634 (1989) (Code Sec. 1031 treatment denied when the taxpayer did not record the deed from the partnership until shortly before the sale, did not

directly pay his or her share of the property's operating expenses, nor receive the property's rental income).

[74] Reg. § 1.761-1(a).

[75] *T.K. McManus v. Commr.*, 65 TC 197, Dec. 33,483 (1975), aff'd, CA-9, 78-2 USTC ¶ 9748, 583 F2d 443.

[76] *I.T. Allison v. Commr.*, 35 TCM 1069, Dec. 33,968(M), TC Memo. 1976-248.

as co-tenants should they continue to generate sufficient business activity together with regard to the property after the Code Sec. 1031 exchange.[77] Naturally, if the property distributed is being used in the active conduct of a trade or business, as discussed above, co-ownership of the property with the partnership is by definition a partnership. An equal ten-person partnership operating a hardware business could not effectively distribute to one of its partners a one-tenth tenancy-in-common interest in the business. The purported distribution would not cause nine-tenths of the operations to be reported on the partnership's Form 1065 and one-tenth on the partner's Form 1040 Schedule C. Creating a co-tenancy with the partnership through a distribution of an undivided interest in partnership property will require that the property distributed not be used in the active conduct of the partnership's trade or business.[78]

In the event that the distribution and the exchange occur simultaneously, or as one uninterrupted chain of events, it is possible that the "step-transaction doctrine" or "form over substance doctrine" will apply, and the transactions will be telescoped into one transaction comprising an attempt at a like-kind exchange of interests in different partnerships or a partnership interest for a direct interest in property.[79] Under these circumstances, Code Sec. 1031 treatment would be disallowed.

> **Comment:** If a partnership has a buyer for its property and some of the partners wish to cash out and others wish to exchange into replacement property under Code Sec. 1031, the partnership should distribute the portion of property to be sold, not the portion of the property to be exchanged. Then the partnership makes the Code Sec. 1031 exchange. Structuring the transaction in this way avoids the above Code Sec. 1031 issues which arise when it is the distributed property which will be exchanged.

Partnership level combined exchange and installment sale. If a partnership wishes to dispose of partnership property and some of the partners want to cash out while others prefer to roll over their investments in a Code Sec. 1031 exchange, a Code Sec. 1031 exchange combined with a receipt of an installment note should be considered. The note is boot for Code Sec. 1031 purposes, but gain is not recognized until it is paid. The partnership then distributes the note in liquidation of the interest of a partner who wishes to cash out. The distribution of the note is not taxable[80] and the note receives a basis equal to the partner's basis in his or her partnership interest. If it is a current distribution, the note's basis will be the lesser of the partnership basis in the note (likely zero) or the basis of the distributee's partnership interest.[81] When the note is paid, the partner will have capital gain to the extent the partnership would have had capital gain. In effect, the

---

[77] *See also* Rev. Rul. 75-374, 1975-2 CB 261.

[78] *See* ¶ 106 for a discussion of the creation of a co-tenancy interest in partnership property not integrally related to the active conduct of a partnership's trade or business.

[79] *D.G. Chase v. Commr.*, 92 TC 874, Dec. 45,634 (1989) (the Tax Court's denial of Code Sec. 1031 treatment, partially due to the application of the substance over form doctrine).

[80] Reg. § 1.453-9(c)(2).

[81] Code Sec. 732. The note is likely to have a zero basis because the gross profit to be reported is equal to the cash boot which would be reportable if cash in the amount of the face value of the note had been received by the partnership. Cash boot is not taxable only to the extent it exceeds the gain realized from the exchange. This basis of the note is equal to 100% minus the gross profit reporting ratio multiplied by the ratio's principal amount. A zero basis in such a note distributed in a current distribution would normally be unappealing to the partner.

partner will be reporting his or her share of the property's appreciation and, in addition, all or a portion of the other partners' shares of the partnership built-in gain. In the case of a liquidating distribution, the note's basis in the hands of the partnership (normally zero) is replaced by the basis the partner has in his or her partnership interest.

Sale followed by exchange. The partnership may also consider selling a portion of the assets for cash and distributing the cash to the partner who wishes to be cashed out in a liquidating distribution. The partnership year closes with respect to the retiring partner and his or her share of the partnership's income for the portion of the year for which he or she was a partner would include a special allocation of gain from the asset sold. The partnership would then later exchange the remaining assets.

Debt financed liquidation. If the partnership has the ability to borrow enough cash to liquidate interests of the partners who want to cash out, a liquidating cash distribution is a simple solution to the problem.

¶1109 Change in Status

The IRS's position is that a conversion of a limited partnership interest into a general partnership interest or the reverse is not a disposition.[82] The change in status may result in an increase or decrease in the partner's debt share, which will be treated as a deemed distribution or a contribution of property. A deemed distribution of money in excess of basis is taxed under Code Sec. 731. If the conversion results in a negative amount at risk in the activity, it is taxable under Code Sec. 465(e).

¶1110 Miscellaneous Partnership Interest Transfers

The following is a brief list and description of some additional less commonly encountered exchanges:

- *Contribution of Partnership Interest to a Corporation or Partnership.* In the unlikely event that the partner has no share of the partnership debt, or if the partner's share of debt does not exceed his or her partnership interest adjusted basis, Code Sec. 351 (contribution to a corporation) or Code Sec. 721 (contribution to a partnership) will apply and the contribution will not be taxable. When there is a contribution of a partnership interest with liabilities in excess of the basis of the interest to a corporation, application of Code Sec. 357(c) will result in gain.[83] If the partnership interest (Partnership 1) is contributed to another partnership (Partnership 2), the partner's share of Partnership 1's debt is considered a deemed money distribution from Partnership 2. This deemed money distribution is in turn netted with any deemed money contribution to Partnership 2 under Code Sec. 752(a) for the partner's share of Partnership 2's debt.[84] There is gain if and only if the net debt relief is in excess of the basis the partner had in Partnership 1.

---

[82] Rev. Rul. 84-52, 1984-1 CB 157.
[83] *See* Rev. Rul. 81-38, 1981-1 CB 386.

[84] Rev. Rul. 79-205, 1979-2 CB 255; Rev. Rul. 77-309, 1977-2 CB 216.

- *Distribution of a Partnership Interest by a Corporation.* If an appreciated partnership interest is distributed by a corporation it is treated as if it were sold.[85] If this deemed sale results in a loss, the loss is not allowed.

- *Distribution of a Partnership Interest by a Partnership.* Given the absence of any direct authority governing the results of a partnership (Partnership 1) distributing an interest it owns in another partnership (Partnership 2), the general rules of property distributions should apply. If the distributed partnership interest (Partnership 2) has no share of Partnership 2's debt, it is merely treated as a distribution of unencumbered property. If the distributed partnership interest (Partnership 2) shares in that Partnership 2's debt, it is treated as a distribution of encumbered property. The distributee partner has a deemed money contribution to Partnership 1 for his or her share of Partnership 2's debt. The distributee partner has a deemed money distribution for his or her reduced share of Partnership 1's debt, which no longer includes its share of Partnership 2's debt. Any excess of the deemed money contribution over the money distribution is a deemed money contribution to Partnership 1. The partner's share in Partnership 1 is increased by this amount and then reduced by Partnership 1's basis in Partnership 2. In a current distribution, the partner's basis in Partnership 2 is the lesser of what was Partnership 1's basis or the partner's basis in Partnership 1 after the deemed money contribution. In a liquidating distribution, the distributee partner's basis in his or her interest in Partnership 1 becomes his or her basis in the interest in Partnership 2.

---

[85] Code Sec. 311(b).

Chapter 12

Partnership Distributions

¶ 1201 Introduction

Distributions from a partnership to a partner are classified as either current distributions or liquidating distributions. A *current*, or operating, distribution is one that does not liquidate the partner's interest in the partnership. Thus, if the partner retains some or all of his or her interest in partnership capital or profits following receipt of a distribution from the partnership, the distribution is a current distribution.

A liquidating distribution, in contrast, is one that completely terminates the partner's interest in partnership capital and profits. The liquidation may be the result of the partner leaving the partnership or of the partnership itself terminating its operations and distributing its assets to creditors and/or partners. Either way, the recipient partner treats the transaction as a liquidating distribution.

Both types of distributions are generally nontaxable to both the recipient partner and the partnership. If the distribution does not liquidate the partner's interest in the partnership (i.e., it is a current distribution), the partner generally recognizes no gain or loss and takes a carryover basis in the distributed property equal to the partnership's basis immediately before the distribution. These rules are subject to the important limitation that the partner's tax basis in the property cannot exceed his or her tax basis in the partnership interest (their outside basis) before receipt of the distribution. In effect, the partner divides his or her pre-distribution tax basis in the partnership interest between the property received and the remaining interest in the partnership.

Different rules apply when the distribution liquidates the partner's interest in the partnership. In such cases, since there is no remaining interest in the partnership, there can be no remaining basis in the partnership interest. Accordingly, the partner generally takes a "substitute" basis in the distributed property equal to his or her basis in the partnership interest immediately before the distribution.

Where a partner receives a cash distribution in an amount that exceeds his or her basis in the partnership interest, gain must be recognized to the extent of such excess. Gain may also be triggered when the partner receives a deemed cash distribution in the form of liability relief that exceeds his or her basis in the partnership interest.

Partners may even be allowed to recognize losses on the receipt of certain distributions. A distribution in complete liquidation of a partner's interest in the partnership, consisting solely of cash and/or partnership ordinary income assets, will trigger recognition of loss if the amount of cash and the tax basis of any ordinary income property received are lower than the partner's tax basis in the partnership interest.

Of course, many transactions structured as partnership distributions are recharacterized under Subchapter K. For example, distributions that alter the recipient partner's interest in partnership ordinary income property (so-called disproportionate distributions), distributions that compensate the recipient partner for prior or concurrent property transfers or services provided to the partnership, and certain distributions involving contributed property under Code Secs. 704(c) or 737 will be partially recharacterized as sales between the partner and partnership. Similarly, certain payments to retired or retiring partners will be treated outside the general distribution framework. This chapter discusses the general framework applicable to partnership distributions, and also the exceptions and special rules applicable to disproportionate distributions. Disguised sales (Chapter 14), distributions of contributed property (Chapter 14), and payments to retiring partners (Chapter 15) are discussed elsewhere in this book.

> **LLC Observation:** The distribution rules discussed in this chapter apply equally to state law partnerships and LLCs taxed as partnerships.

¶ 1202 Operating or "Current" Distributions

As noted above, a current distribution is one that does not completely terminate the partner's interest in the partnership. Thus, a current distribution encompasses transactions ranging from the *pro rata* distribution of partnership profits among the partners to the redemption of a portion of a partner's interest in the partnership. So long as the recipient partner retains some interest in partnership capital or profits, the distribution will not liquidate his or her entire interest in the partnership and will be characterized as a current distribution.[1]

Generally speaking, a current distribution of either cash or property is a nontaxable transaction for the partnership. The partnership accounts for the distribution by writing off the cash or property distributed against the recipient partner's capital account.[2] Unlike in the corporate and S corporation framework, partnership distributions are generally not treated as taxable exchanges and the partnership recognizes neither gain nor loss.

Receipt of a current distribution is generally a nontaxable event for the partner as well. The partner merely reduces his or her tax basis in the partnership interest by the amount of cash or the basis of property received. Only if the partner receives *cash* in excess of the tax basis of the partnership interest will he or she be required to recognize taxable gain. In such cases, the basis of the partnership interest is not sufficient to absorb the entire cash distribution and the basis of cash received cannot be adjusted to account for the shortfall. Thus, gain must be recognized. In all other transactions constituting a current distribution from the partnership to a partner, neither gain nor loss will be recognized.

.01 Cash Distributions—Effect on Basis and Recognition of Gain

A cash distribution is generally treated as a return of the partner's capital investment in the partnership. The partner must reduce his or her tax basis in the partnership interest by the amount of the money received.[3] If the amount of money received exceeds the partner's tax basis in the partnership interest, basis is reduced to zero and the partner must recognize taxable gain to the extent of the excess.[4] This gain is generally treated as gain from sale of the partnership interest, which is a capital asset; therefore, the partner's gain will usually be treated as a capital gain.[5]

> ***Example 12-1:*** Angie is a one-third partner in the ABC Partnership. Her tax basis in her partnership interest at year-end is $5,000. At that date, the partnership distributed $30,000 cash to Angie. The distribution was not part of a disguised sale and it did not terminate her interest in the partnership. Under Code Sec. 731(a), Angie must recognize a $25,000 gain. Under Code Sec. 741, this gain has the same character as if Angie had sold her interest in the partnership. Thus, assuming Angie has held her partnership interest for more than 12 months, the gain will be a long-term capital gain. Her remaining basis in the partnership interest will be zero.

---

[1] Where the complete liquidation of a partner's interest is accomplished through a series of payments, scheduled by the partner and partnership and intended to terminate the partner's interest in the partnership, each payment will be treated as part of a liquidating distribution. *See* ¶ 1203.

[2] In many situations, writing the distributed cash or property off against the partner's capital account results in a deficit in that capital account. Alternatively, in cases involving liquidating distributions, writing the property or cash off against the partner's capital account may be insufficient to completely eliminate that partner's capital account. In such cases, the partnership may be required to adjust its basis in its assets in order to balance its tax balance sheet. Basis adjustments are discussed in Chapter 13.

[3] Code Sec. 733(1).

[4] Code Sec. 731(a).

[5] Code Sec. 741. An important exception applies if the partnership owns unrealized receivables or appreciated inventory. In such cases, a portion of the partner's gain will be characterized as ordinary income. *See* Chapter 11.

.02 Mid-year Advances and Partner "Draws"

Distributions of money or property during the partnership taxable year may be treated as "advances or drawings of money or property against a partner's distributive share of income."[6] For tax purposes, such "draws" are treated as distributions made on the last day of the *partnership's* taxable year.[7] Of course, to the extent a mid-year distribution exceeds the recipient partner's distributive share of the partner's income, the excess may be taxable if the total distributions exceed the partner's tax basis in the partnership interest, adjusted for his or her distributive share of partnership income.[8]

> **Example 12-2:** As of January 1, Austin's tax basis in his 25% interest in ABC Partnership was $50. Austin receives a monthly draw of $10 from the partnership. ABC is a calendar year partnership. Its profit for the year is $400.
>
> If each draw were treated as a distribution made on the date received, Austin's tax basis would be reduced to zero on receipt of the May distribution. All subsequent draws would trigger taxable gain. However, as discussed above, the draws are treated as made on the last day of the partnership's taxable year. On that day, Austin's basis in his partnership interest is $150, consisting of his beginning tax basis of $50, plus his $100 share of the partnership's taxable income. Accordingly, the $120 in draws reduce his tax basis to $30 and he recognizes no gain under Code Sec. 731(a). Of course, his $100 share of ABC's taxable income must be included on his individual tax return.

Deemed money distributions caused by a reduction in a partner's share of partnership liabilities also receive draw treatment, assuming they meet the other requirements.[9]

Distribution of a note payable from the partnership to the partner is not treated as a cash distribution. Indeed, partners need to be careful in structuring such transactions—if the distribution is recognized as a legitimate transaction, the partner will take a zero basis in the note (the partnership's tax basis would be zero) and may be required to recognize income when the note is subsequently paid.

> **Example 12-3:** Hank's basis in his interest in Gilmore Partners is $75. When the partnership planned to distribute $100 to each partner, Hank asked that he be distributed a note rather than cash, in order to avoid recognition of

---

[6] Reg. § 1.731-1(a)(1)(ii).

[7] *Id.*

[8] *See* Rev. Rul. 81-241, 1981-2 CB 146, in which a construction partnership used the completed contract method of accounting. The partnership received progress payments during the year, but did not include these in its income under the completed contract method. Accordingly, the progress payments did not increase the partners' bases in their partnership interests. Draws taken by the partners from their shares of such progress payments exceeded their tax bases in their partnership interests in the years preceding completion of the contract and were taxable to the extent of such excess.

[9] Rev. Rul. 99-4, 1994-1 CB 195. *See also* Rev. Rul. 81-242, 1981-2 CB 147. When a building owned by a partnership was condemned by the city, the partnership elected to defer recognition of gain under the involuntary conversion provisions of Code Sec. 1033. The partnership used condemnation payments received from the city to pay off the mortgage encumbering the condemned building. The resulting reduction in the partners' shares of partnership liabilities were deemed distributions triggering recognition of income under Code Sec. 731(a) to the extent of the partners' bases in their partnership interests. Gain was required to be recognized even though the partnership's gain on the transaction was deferred under Code Sec. 1033.

$25 gain. In the next year, Hank's distributive share of the partnership's income is $50, and the partnership pays off the note.

Hank's tax basis in the note is zero. Accordingly, when the partnership pays it off, he will recognize a $100 gain. He would have recognized less gain had the partnership simply distributed the $100 to him in the prior year, when it made distributions to the other partners.

Alternatively, Hank could simply have refused the distribution last year without taking the note. Assuming the agreement between the partners requires proper maintenance of partner capital accounts as required by Code Sec. 704(b), the distributions received by the other partners will reduce their capital account balances by $100 relative to Hank's. Thus, deferring the distribution will not give the other partners an economic advantage relative to Hank; even if he does not receive a "catch-up" distribution in the next year, he will be entitled to an additional $100 relative to the other partners upon liquidation of the partnership.

The substance of this type of transaction will in most cases depend on how the partnership accounts for the initial distribution. In the above example, if the partnership reduces Hank's Code Sec. 704(b) capital account at the date the note is distributed (by the face value of the note), then the consequences will be as described above. In contrast, if the transaction is informal, with no contractual obligation between the partnership and the recipient partner (Hank in the above example), then the partnership's promise to make a subsequent distribution will be disregarded for tax purposes. The subsequent payment will be treated as a cash distribution subject to the provisions of Code Sec. 731. Of course, treating the partnership's obligation to make a subsequent distribution informally will preclude the payment of interest on the "debt."

¶ 1203 Property Distributions—Consequences to the Partnership

A significant difference between the taxation of partnerships and that of S corporations (and regular corporations) is the treatment of property distributions. In the partnership context, property distributions are generally nontaxable to both the partnership and the distributee-partner.[10] The partnership merely takes the property off its books and reduces the partner's capital account by a like amount. It recognizes neither taxable gain nor deductible loss on the transaction (although any book gain or loss should be recognized for book purposes, and will affect the partners' capital accounts). Moreover, there are no restrictions on the amount by which the partner's capital balance can be reduced. The partner's capital account, unlike his or her tax basis in the partnership interest, can be negative.[11] Thus, the partnership can reduce partner capital for the distribution regardless of the pre-distribution balance in the partner's capital account.

---

[10] In contrast, under Code Sec. 361(c) the distribution of appreciated property by either a regular corporation or an S corporation is treated as a sale of such property followed by a distribution of the proceeds. As such, it is fully taxable to the corporation or S corporation.

[11] Note that a partner is required to "restore" any deficit balance in his or her Code Sec. 704(b) "book" capital account at liquidation of either his/her interest or the partnership itself. *See* Chapter 6.

Example 12-4: JDR Partners has three partners, *J*, *D* and *R*. Assume that the partnership's book and tax balance sheets look as follows:

	Basis	Value
Total Assets	$900	$1,500
Liabilities	0	0
Capital, *J*	300	500
Capital, *D*	300	500
Capital, *R*	300	500
Total Liabilities & Capital	$900	$1,500

The partnership distributes property with a tax basis of $100 and fair market value of $175 to Partner *R*. Assuming the distribution does not trigger the provisions of Code Secs. 751(b), 704(c)(1)(B), 707, or 737, it will recognize no gain. Its post-distribution balance sheets will be as follows:

	Basis	Value
Total Assets	$800	$1,325
Liabilities	0	0
Capital, *J*	300	500
Capital, *D*	300	500
Capital, *R*	200	325
Total Liabilities & Capital	$800	$1,325

Had *R*'s tax capital account been less than $100, it would have a deficit balance on the partnership's post-distribution balance sheet.

Where the distribution to a partner triggers the recognition of gain or loss by that partner, the partnership may elect to adjust its tax basis in its remaining assets under Code Sec. 734(b). Similarly, where the distributee-partner takes a different basis in the distributed property than such property had in the partnership's hands prior to the distribution, an adjustment to the basis of remaining assets may be required. (See Chapter 13 for a discussion of basis adjustments under Code Sec. 734(b).)

¶ 1204 Partner's Basis in Distributed Property

.01 General Rule—Carryover Basis

As noted above, receipt of a non-liquidating (i.e., current) property distribution is generally a nontaxable transaction to the partner as well as the partnership. Under the general rule of Code Sec. 732(a)(1), the partner takes a *carryover* basis in the property received equal to the basis the partnership had in the property just prior to the distribution. The partner must reduce his or her tax basis in the partnership interest by the same amount.[12]

Example 12-5: Arthur is a 20 percent partner in Warlock Partnership. His tax basis in his partnership interest at December 31 was $25,000. He received a distribution of property from the partnership with a fair market value of $50,000 and a tax basis of $18,000. The distribution did not liquidate Arthur's interest in the partnership. Arthur will recognize no gain on receipt of the distribution. He will take an $18,000 tax basis in the property and reduce his basis in his partnership interest to $7,000.

The basis taken by the distributee-partner in distributed property cannot exceed his or her basis in the partnership interest prior to the distribution. If the partnership's basis in the distributed property exceeds the partner's basis in the partnership interest, then the basis of the partnership interest becomes the substituted basis of the property. The result is a zero basis in the partnership interest and step down in the property's basis.[13]

Example 12-6: Mooney has a basis in his partnership interest of $15,000. In a nonliquidating distribution, he receives a tract of raw land worth $60,000. Its basis in the partnership's hands prior to the distribution was $32,000. Mooney will recognize no gain on receipt of the distribution and will take a $15,000 tax basis in the land received. His basis in his partnership interest will be reduced to zero.

.02 Effect of Prior Partnership-level Basis Adjustments

The partnership's basis in the distributed property includes basis adjustments made in prior years under Code Sec. 734(b) (arising from prior distributions) but does *not* include basis adjustments under Code Sec. 743(b) (arising from prior transfers of interests in the partnership).[14] An exception applies to Code Sec. 743(b) adjustments applicable to the distributee partner—any basis adjustments attributable to the distributed property will be included in the partnership's tax basis of such property if the adjustments relate to the previous acquisition of an interest in the partnership by the distributee partner.[15] Code Sec. 743(b) adjustments to the property's basis which are personal to other partners are reallocated to the partnership's remaining like-kind property.[16]

Special rules apply to property distributions occurring within two years of the distributee-partner's acquisition of his or her partnership interest. In such cases, the distributee-partner may elect to compute the partnership's basis in the distributed property as if a Code Sec. 754 election had been in effect at the date he or she acquired the interest in the partnership, whether or not the partnership actually made such an election (or had one in effect).[17] This election allows the distributee-partner to treat the partnership's basis in the distributed property as if it included any basis adjustment that would have been made under Code Sec. 743(b) had the partnership had a Code Sec. 754 election in effect.

---

[12] Code Sec. 733.
[13] Code Secs. 732(a)(2) and 733(2).
[14] Reg. § 1.732-2(b).

[15] Reg. §§ 1.743-1(g)(1) and 1.732-2(b).
[16] Reg. § 1.743-1(g)(2)(ii).
[17] Code Sec. 732(d).

Example 12-7: Abel purchased a 25 percent interest in Cruz Partners for $125,000. The partnership did not have a Code Sec. 754 election in effect and chose not to make one. Thus, it was not allowed to increase its basis in its assets even though Abel paid fair market value for his interest in those assets. One year later, Abel received a non-liquidating distribution consisting of a tract of undeveloped real estate with a tax basis to the partnership of $14,000 and a fair market value of $50,000. Had the partnership had a Code Sec. 754 election in effect when Abel acquired his partnership interest, it would have increased its basis in this asset by $9,000 [0.25($50,000 − $14,000)]. Under Code Sec. 732(d), Abel will take a $23,000 tax basis in the real property received and his basis in the partnership interest will be reduced to $102,000 ($125,000 original basis − $23,000 basis in distributed property).

.03 Character and Holding Period of Distributed Property

As a result of these modified carryover basis rules, any unrealized appreciation or depreciation inherent in the property distributed by the partnership will be taxed to the partner when he or she subsequently disposes of the property. The partner's holding period for the property includes the partnership's holding period (i.e., the partnership's holding period for the property is "tacked" onto the partner's holding period), ensuring that gains that would have been long-term if realized by the partnership will continue to receive long-term treatment when sold by the partner.[18] If the partnership acquired the distributed property by contribution from another partner, the distributee partner's holding period for the distributed property also includes the period for which the property was held by the contributing partner.[19]

Example 12-8: The ABC Partnership distributes land to partner *C* with a tax basis of $180 and a fair market value of $200. *C* has been a partner in ABC Partnership for several years. Her tax basis in her partnership interest is $150 at the date of the distribution. Assume that the partnership purchased the land on September 30 of Year 2 and distributed it to *C* on January 1 of Year 3. *C's* tax basis in the land will be limited to her $150 tax basis in her partnership interest. Although she substitutes her basis in the partnership interest for her basis in the land, she cannot substitute her holding period for the partnership interest as her holding period for the land. Her holding period for the land will begin on September 30 of Year 2, the date the partnership acquired the land. Thus, if she sells the land before September 30 of Year 3, any gain she recognizes will be characterized as short-term capital gain. Note that this characterization will apply to any portion of her gain that is attributable to the step-down in her tax basis in the land as well as to any appreciation inherent in the value of the land at the date of distribution.

Assume that the partnership had acquired the land via contribution from Partner *A* on September 30, Year 2, rather than via purchase on that date. Further assume that Partner *A* had purchased the land in February of Year 1. Now *C's* holding period for the land will date back to February, Year 1 and any

---

[18] Code Sec. 735(b).

[19] Code Sec. 1223(2); Reg. § 1.735-1(b).

gain she recognizes on sale of the land will be characterized as long-term capital gain, regardless of when she sells it.

The character of income, gain or loss subsequently recognized by the partner on disposition of the distributed property depends on the nature of the property distributed. Unrealized receivables received by a partner from the partnership retain their character as ordinary income property regardless of the purpose for which they are held by the distributee-partner.[20] Of course, any income realized on the collection of uncollected accounts receivable by a partner will always be characterized as ordinary, so this provision has significance primarily with respect to depreciation recapture, and other similar assets such as farmland, oil & gas property, etc. Determination of the amount of ordinary income to be recognized on subsequent disposition of assets subject to recapture can be complicated when the partner is required to step down their basis as a result of the distribution rules.

> *Example 12-9: J* is a partner in JDR Partners. Her tax basis in her partnership interest is $25,000. She received a non-liquidating distribution of Code Sec. 1245 property with a tax basis of $30,000, and a fair market value of $50,000 from the partnership. The property originally cost the partnership $45,000, so that $15,000 of depreciation recapture under Code Sec. 1245 is inherent in the property (original cost of $45,000 less partnership's tax basis of $30,000). Following the distribution, the property will take an adjusted basis of only $25,000 in *J*'s hands. Assume that she uses the property for personal purposes only and claims no additional depreciation deductions. If she subsequently sells the property for $43,000, she will recognize taxable gain of $18,000: $15,000 of this amount will be taxable as ordinary recapture income, and the remainder will be characterized as capital gain.[21]

Unlike unrealized receivables, inventory items distributed by the partnership retain their character as ordinary income items only for five years following the distribution.[22] After five years, the character of such property depends on how it is held or used by the distributee partner. For example, real estate held for resale by the partnership may be converted by the partner into business- or personal-use property, or may be held for investment. If the real estate is not held by the partner as inventory, it will be converted to capital gain property if held by the partner for more than five years. At first blush, these provisions appear to be rather straightforward, but partners need to carefully consider the implications of Code Sec. 735(a) before disposing of distributed property.

> *Example 12-10:* ABC Partnership was formed in October of Year 1. Prior to formation, Partner *A* was in the business of building and selling single family homes as a developer; he contributed to the partnership a number of single family homes held for sale to customers. The partnership held the homes for rental purposes. On December 31 of Year 4, the partnership distributed one of the homes to Partner *C*, who continued to use it as rental

---

[20] Code Sec. 735(a)(1).

[21] *See* Example 12-14 (¶ 1204) for an illustration of how to account for the step down in tax basis of distributed property subject to Code Sec. 1245 recapture.

[22] Code Sec. 735(a)(2). For purposes of measuring the five-year holding period, the partnership's holding period for the distributed inventory does *not* tack. Code Sec. 735(b).

property.[23] C subsequently sold the home on July 30 of Year 9 for a substantial profit.

Because the single family homes were inventory items to A, any gain or loss on their disposition by the partnership within five years after receipt is treated as ordinary income or loss under Code Sec. 724(b). Code Sec. 724(b) does not carry over to the partnership the character of the property but only the character of the gain or loss. Thus, these homes are not inventory to the partnership under Sec. 724(b), nor are they held by the partnership as inventory. However, they remain classified as inventory items under Code Sec. 751(d)(2): Code Sec. 64 provides that if gain from the sale of property is treated as ordinary income, then the property is neither a capital asset nor Code Sec. 1231 property, and Code Sec. 751(d)(2) provides that inventory is all property other than capital assets or Code Sec. 1231 property.

Thus, the single family homes contributed to the partnership by Partner A constitute inventory items to the partnership even though the partnership does not hold the homes for resale. When the partnership distributes one of these homes to Partner C, the home continues to be treated as an inventory item for five years following the distribution. Because Partner C sold the home within five years of the distribution, his or her recognized gain is characterized as ordinary income under Code Sec. 735(a)(2). The characterization of C's gain as ordinary is not limited to the potential ordinary income inherent in the home in partnership's hands just prior to the distribution. Rather, C's entire gain will be characterized as ordinary, even that portion (if any) that arises from continued appreciation in the value of the home after the distribution.

It is worth noting that unrealized receivables and inventory cannot be transformed into capital gain property through a nonrecognition transaction such as a like-kind exchange. Except in the case of C corporation stock received in a Code Sec. 351 transaction, the Code Sec. 735 "taint" carries over to the exchanged basis property received in the nonrecognition transaction.[24]

> **Example 12-11:** Assume the same facts as in Example 12-10. Partnership ABC distributes rental real estate to Partner C that was previously contributed to the partnership by a partner in the home construction business. The property was inventory to the contributing partner, and retains that taint in the partnership's hands for 5 years. The property was distributed to Partner C on December 31 of Year 4. Assume that C exchanged the property for property of a like kind on June 30 of Year 8, and sold the like-kind property on September 30 of Year 9 for a substantial profit. C's gain on sale of the like-kind property is characterized as ordinary income because the property received in the like-kind exchange is treated as inventory under Code Sec. 735(c)(2)(A).

---

[23] Note that the distribution to partner C will trigger recognition *by partner A* of any built-in gain inherent in the property at the date of its contribution. Under Code Sec. 704(c)(1)(B), the distribution of contributed built-in gain property within 7 years of the date of its contribution to the partnership triggers recognition of any remaining built-in gain inherent in the property at the date of distribution.

[24] Code Sec. 735(c)(2).

Example 12-12: Assume the same facts as in Example 12-11 except that rather than exchange the rental property received from the partnership for like-kind property, *C* transferred the property to a corporation in exchange for stock in a Code Sec. 351 transaction. *C* subsequently sold the corporate stock for a substantial gain on September 30 of Year 9. *C*'s gain would now be capital. Code Sec. 735(c)(2)(A) provides an explicit exception to the "tainted character" rules for stock received in a nontaxable 351 exchange. Of course, since the property retains its carryover basis in the hands of the corporation, the cost of converting *C*'s ordinary income into capital gain is to subject the gain inherent in the rental property to double taxation.

If the distributed property did not constitute inventory or unrealized receivables in the hands of the partnership prior to the distribution, its character in the partner's hands will depend on the partner's use of such property or purpose for holding it. For example, real property held by the partnership for investment purposes may constitute inventory in the hands of a distributee partner who is a professional real estate developer.

.04 Receipt of Multiple Properties

If more than one property is distributed in a single distribution and the partnership's aggregate basis in the properties exceeds the partner's tax basis in the partnership interest, the partner's aggregate basis in the properties received will be limited to his or her tax basis in the partnership interest. The allocation of basis to the distributed properties is governed by Code Sec. 732(c).

Code Sec. 732(c) is designed to protect the partner from the possibility that capital gain will be inadvertently converted into ordinary income. Accordingly, it allocates tax basis first to any ordinary income property received by the partner and then to capital gain property, ensuring that any step-down in tax basis is borne most heavily by capital gain property. Under these provisions, the partner's tax basis in the partnership interest is first reduced by the amount of any cash received as part of the distribution (including liability relief). Remaining basis is next allocated to unrealized receivables and inventory received in the distribution, to the extent of the partnership's pre-distribution tax basis in these assets.[25] Any remaining basis is then allocated to capital gain property received.

Example 12-13: Susan's tax basis in her partnership interest is $20,000. In a non-liquidating distribution, she receives the following assets:

	Tax Basis	*FMV*
Cash	$10,000	$10,000
Accounts Receivable	0	15,000
Inventory	7,500	17,500
Capital Asset	12,000	20,000
	$29,500	*$62,500*

[25] Code Sec. 732(c).

Susan will recognize no gain on the distribution. Her aggregate tax basis in the distributed assets will be $10,000 (tax basis in partnership interest of $20,000 less $10,000 cash received in the distribution), and her basis in her partnership interest will be reduced to zero. This basis will first be allocated to ordinary income assets received (accounts receivable and inventory) to the extent of the partnership's basis in such assets. In this case, she will take a carryover basis of zero in the receivables and $7,500 in the inventory. The remaining $2,500 will be allocated to the capital asset. The net result in this case is that the entire $9,500 "step-down" in basis from the partnership to Susan will be allocated to the capital asset.

Application of these provisions can be especially important when the partnership distributes depreciable property the basis of which must be stepped down by the partner. In such cases, these rules should work to ensure that the basis decrease is allocated to the Code Sec. 1231 portion of the distributed asset rather than to the depreciation recapture portion, thus preventing the partner from subsequently being required to recognize more recapture income on disposition of the asset than the partnership would have recognized had it sold the asset rather than distributing it.

> **Example 12-14:** Ethel is a partner in Mertz Aviation. Her tax basis in her partnership interest is $60,000. Earlier this year, the partnership distributed an airplane to Ethel in a non-liquidating distribution. The plane had a tax basis to the partnership of $67,000 and fair market value of $75,000. Its original acquisition price was $85,000. Had the partnership sold the plane, it would have recognized an $8,000 gain, all of which would have been taxable as ordinary depreciation recapture income under Code Sec. 1245.
>
> The distribution to Ethel is nontaxable to both Ethel and the partnership. (Assume the distribution is not disproportionate and does not trigger the provisions of Code Sec. 751(b)). Her basis in the plane is limited to her $60,000 tax basis in the partnership interest prior to the distribution. Under Code Sec. 732(c), the distribution is deemed to consist of two assets: an unrealized receivable (depreciation recapture) with a tax basis of zero and a fair market value of $8,000, and a Code Sec. 1231 asset with a tax basis and fair market value of $67,000. Ethel will take a carryover basis of zero in the unrealized receivable (depreciation recapture). Her basis in the partnership interest is insufficient to allow full carryover basis in the Code Sec. 1231 portion of the plane; accordingly, her tax basis in this portion of the plane will be $60,000. Thus, the entire step-down in tax basis is allocated to the Code Sec. 1231 portion of the plane.
>
> Assume that Ethel uses the plane for personal purposes and does not depreciate it. Further assume that she later sells the plane for $75,000, recognizing a taxable gain of $15,000. Even though prior depreciation deductions with respect to the plane totaled $18,000 ($85,000 purchase price less $67,000 partnership basis in the asset), only $8,000 of Ethel's taxable gain will be classified as ordinary recapture income, because she was not allowed to step down the basis of the unrealized receivable received from the partnership, and

she did not further depreciate the plane following receipt of the distribution. The entire step-down in the plane's tax basis was attributable to the Code Sec. 1231 portion of the plane and thus her remaining taxable gain will be characterized as capital gain.

Of course, in many cases, the partner will have insufficient basis in the partnership interest to allow a full carryover basis in ordinary income property received. In such cases, the partner's basis in these assets will be lower than the basis the partnership had in such assets just prior to the distribution. This "step-down" in basis is allocated first to properties with unrealized depreciation, in proportion to the amount of the unrealized depreciation.[26] Any remaining step-down is allocated in proportion to the respective bases of the unrealized receivables and inventory (after adjustment for unrealized depreciation per above).[27] This formula is designed to reduce the partner's basis in depreciated property, and will reduce loss when the property is subsequently sold or otherwise disposed of.

> **Example 12-15:** Julian is a one-third partner in Weldonshire Partnership. His tax basis in his partnership interest is $25,000. He receives a nonliquidating distribution consisting of the following properties:
>
> | | Tax Basis | FMV |
> |---|---|---|
> | Cash | $10,000 | $10,000 |
> | Inventory 1 | 16,000 | 10,000 |
> | Inventory 2 | 10,000 | 18,000 |
> | | $36,000 | $38,000 |

Julian's tax basis in the partnership interest is first reduced by the $10,000 cash received. His remaining $15,000 tax basis in the partnership interest is not sufficient to allow a carryover basis in the two inventory items received. The resulting ($11,000) step-down in the basis of these two assets is allocated first to Inventory 1 to the extent of the excess of its basis to the partnership over its fair value at the date of the distribution, ($6,000). This reduces the tax basis of this asset to $10,000. The remaining ($5,000) reduction in basis is then allocated equally between Inventory items 1 and 2 since the basis of each asset is now $10,000. Thus, $8,500 of the basis reduction is allocated to Inventory 1 ($6,000 in step 1 plus $2,500 in step 2) and $2,500 is allocated to Inventory 2 ($0 in step 1 plus $2,500 in step 2). Following the distribution, Julian will have a tax basis of $7,500 in each asset, and his tax basis in the partnership interest will be reduced to zero.

Basis remaining after allocations to inventory and receivables is allocated to other properties (Code 1221/1231 property) to the extent of the partnership's basis in those properties. Any decrease in the basis of these properties is allocated under the same framework as described above: basis is first decreased in proportion to

---

[26] Code Sec. 732(c)(3)(A).   [27] Code Sec. 732(c)(1)(A) and (3)(B).

the inherent depreciation in distributed assets, with any remaining step-down being allocated in proportion to the remaining adjusted bases of the properties received.[28]

Example 12-16: Blum Partnership distributes the assets below to Lowe, a 20-percent partner. The distribution does not liquidate Lowe's interest in the partnership. Both Asset 1 and Asset 2 are Code Sec. 1231 assets. Lowe's basis in her partnership interest is $25,000. The distributed assets have bases and FMVs as follows:

	Tax Basis	*FMV*
Cash	$10,000	$10,000
Inventory Item A	8,000	10,000
Inventory Item B	16,000	15,000
Asset 1	40,000	30,000
Asset 2	60,000	70,000
Totals	*$134,000*	*$135,000*

Lowe has insufficient basis in her partnership interest to allow full carryover basis in the distributed assets. The distribution of the cash decreases her remaining basis to $15,000. The inventory will be allocated basis next, but since the basis of the inventory to the partnership totals $24,000, a reduction of $9,000 must be made to the basis of the inventory. This decrease will first be allocated to Inventory Item B in the amount of $1,000, its unrealized depreciation. The remaining $8,000 of the $9,000 adjustment will be allocated to the Inventory Items based on their relative remaining bases, or $2,783 to Item A [($8,000/$23,000) × $8,000] and $5,217 to Item B [($15,000/$23,000) × $8,000]. The basis of the assets to Lowe after the distribution will be:

	Tax Basis
Cash	$10,000
Inventory Item A ($8,000 − $2,783)	5,217
Inventory Item B ($16,000 − $1,000 − $5,217)	9,783
Asset 1	0
Asset 2	0
Total	*$25,000*

What if Lowe's basis in her partnership interest is $120,000, rather than $25,000? She will be required to decrease the basis of Assets 1 and 2 by $14,000 ($134,000 total basis − $120,000 partnership interest basis) in the aggregate. The first $10,000 of this decrease will be allocated to Asset 1, reflecting the excess of its basis in the partnership's hands over its fair market value at the date of distribution. The remaining $4,000 of the step-down in basis will be allocated one-third ($30,000/$90,000) to Asset 1 (which now has a

---

[28] Code Sec. 732(c)(3)(A) and (B).

¶1204.04

tax basis of $30,000) and two-thirds ($60,000/$90,000) to Asset 2 (carryover basis of $60,000). The basis of the assets to Lowe after the distribution will be:

	Tax Basis
Cash	$10,000
Inventory Item A	8,000
Inventory Item B	16,000
Asset 1 ($40,000 – $10,000 – $1,333)	28,667
Asset 2 ($60,000 – $2,667)	57,333
Total	*$120,000*

Her tax basis in the partnership interest will be reduced to zero.

¶ 1205 Liquidating Distributions

A liquidating distribution is one that completely terminates the partner's interest in partnership capital and profits. The liquidation may be the result of the partner leaving the partnership or of the partnership itself terminating its operations and distributing its assets to creditors and/or partners. Either way, the consequences are the same.

Generally, the distribution of property in liquidation of a partner's interest in the partnership is a nontaxable transaction both to the partner and to the partnership. The partner takes a tax basis in the distributed property equal to his or her tax basis in the partnership interest just prior to the distribution; recognition of gain or loss is thus deferred until the partner sells or otherwise disposes of the property.

There are a number of exceptions to the general framework outlined above. Receipt of cash (including liability relief) in excess of the partner's tax basis in the partnership interest will trigger recognition of gain by the partner just as it does with a current distribution. Loss may also be recognized by a partner upon receipt of an all-cash liquidating distribution where the amount of cash received (including liability relief) is less than the tax basis of the partnership interest. Loss may also be recognized where the partner receives nothing but cash and/or partnership ordinary income assets where the amount of cash received plus the tax basis of the ordinary income assets received is less than the partner's tax basis in the partnership interest. In such cases, the partner is prohibited from increasing the tax basis of either the cash or the ordinary income assets received – recognition of loss is thus the only way that he or she can fully recover the tax basis of the partnership interest.

Finally, there are a number of circumstances under which gain will be triggered to the partner even though he or she does not receive a distribution of cash in excess of the basis of the partnership interest. Gain may be recognized if the liquidating distribution alters the partner's interest in partnership "hot" assets, as defined in Code Sec. 751. In such cases, both the partner and the partnership may be required to recognize income or gain. The tax consequences of such "disproportionate" distributions are discussed later in this chapter. Similarly, gain may be recognized under Code Sec. 704(c)(1)(B) or 737 if contributed property is distributed in liquidation of the partner's interest in the partnership. (See Chapter 14.) Finally, as discussed in Chapter 15, certain distributions to a retiring or retired partner may be recharacterized as guaranteed payments, taxable to the partner as ordinary income and deductible by the partnership (see Code Sec. 736(b)).

> **LLC Observation:** The liquidating distribution rules discussed in this chapter apply equally to state law partnerships and LLCs taxed as partnerships.

.01 Recognition of Gain or Loss by Distributee Partner

As with operating distributions, also known as current or non-liquidating distributions, a partner receiving a liquidating distribution recognizes gain only to the extent that the cash received (including liability relief) exceeds the partner's outside basis in the partnership interest.[29] If both cash (in an amount not in excess of basis) and other property are distributed, Code Secs. 731 and 732 work in tandem to minimize gain recognized by the partner on the distribution. First, the partner reduces basis in the partnership interest by the cash received and then, in effect, exchanges his or her remaining partnership interest for the other assets received in the distribution. Code Sec. 731 affords nonrecognition treatment to the partner and the partnership on the distribution, and Code Sec. 732(b) provides the partner with an aggregate basis in the distributed property equal to his or her predistribution outside basis in the partnership interest less any cash received in the liquidation. This exchanged basis mechanism preserves any gain or loss inherent in the partner's interest for recognition when the partner subsequently disposes of the distributed assets. If more than one asset is received, Code Sec. 732(c) once again prescribes the method for allocating aggregate exchanged basis.[30]

Liquidating distributions usually involve a complete termination of liability for any share of partnership debt because either the partnership ceases to exist or the partner is no longer responsible for the partnership's debts. This reduced share of partnership debt is netted with any liabilities the partner takes over from the partnership. Net debt relief is treated as additional money received.[31] If the partner takes over more than his or her share of partnership liabilities, the partner's basis in the partnership will be increased by the net increase and will be allocated among the distributed assets as described previously. If the partner takes over his or her *pro rata* share of the partnership debt, there will be no deemed cash receipt or payment.

But consider the partner who receives solely cash, unrealized receivables and inventory items in a liquidating distribution. In that event, unlike the case with operating distributions, Code Sec. 731(a)(2) provides that the partner recognizes a loss to the extent that his or her outside basis exceeds the sum of the cash distributed plus the partner's Code Sec. 732 transferred basis in the receivables and inventory items. The loss is deemed to result from the sale or exchange of a

---

[29] This discussion assumes that neither Code Secs. 736(a) nor 751(b) apply.

[30] If the retired partner received cash in excess of his or her outside basis in the partnership interest, the part-ner would recognize capital gain to the extent of the excess and any distributed assets would take a zero basis in the partner's hands.

[31] Code Sec. 752(a) and (b).

partnership interest and thus is a capital loss under Code Sec. 741. Where a partner receives only cash, any realized loss must be recognized because the partner may not defer recognition by way of an exchanged basis for cash. If the partner also receives ordinary income assets, the basis of these assets cannot be increased above the partnership's basis for those assets prior to the distribution.[32] The excess of the partner's former basis in his or her partnership interest in excess of the basis allocated among the ordinary income assets is recovered as loss. The immediate recognition of loss is required to prevent the partner from converting a capital loss into an ordinary loss on the sale of the distributed assets.

The converse, however, is not true. If the partner's basis in his or her partnership interest is less than the partnership's basis in the ordinary income assets, the distributee partner's basis in those assets will be less than the partnership's basis. In that case, the ordinary income reported from any subsequent sale of these assets by the partner will exceed the amount of ordinary income that would have been reported by the partnership.

To illustrate, assume that a retiring partner with an outside basis of $60 receives $20 cash and ordinary income assets with an inside basis to the partnership of $25 in a liquidating distribution to which Code Sec. 751(b) does not apply.[33] The partner first reduces his or her outside basis by the $20 cash received and, without more, the partner would be left with a $40 exchanged basis to spread among the ordinary income assets, which would result in less ordinary income or more ordinary loss when the partner sells those assets. But recall that Code Sec. 732(c)(1) limits the partner's basis in ordinary income assets to the partnership's pre-distribution inside basis—$25 in this example. As a corollary to this rule, Code Sec. 731(a)(2) provides that the partner recognizes a ($15) capital loss—the excess of his or her $60 outside basis over the sum of the $20 cash received and the $25 transferred basis in the ordinary income assets.

Example 12-17: Richard is a partner in the equal RHK partnership. His tax basis in his partnership interest is $90,000. Richard received a liquidating distribution from the partnership consisting of the following assets:

	Tax Basis
Cash	$10,000
Inventory	60,000

The cash distribution reduces Richard's basis to $80,000, of which only $60,000 can be allocated to the inventory items. The remaining $20,000 of basis, not allocable to the distributed property, is deductible as a capital loss to Richard under Code Sec. 731(a)(2).[34]

Observation: When a liquidating distribution will cause a capital loss to the partner, the parties should consider distributing low value Code Sec. 1231 property in addition to cash and ordinary income assets. The capital loss can

---

[32] Code Sec. 732(c)(1)(A)(i).

[33] Code Secs. 751(b) and 736(a) are both inapplicable if the retiring partner receives a *pro rata* distribution of partnership properties.

[34] In addition, if the partnership has a Code 754 election in effect, or chooses to make one, it will be required to adjust its tax basis in its remaining assets under Code Sec. 734(b). *See* Chapter 13.

thereby be converted to tax basis in the Code Sec. 1231 property. Assuming the property remains Code Sec. 1231 property to the partner, any subsequent sale at a loss will be converted to ordinary loss.

.02 Property Distributions and Determination of Basis

On receipt of a liquidating distribution, the distributee partner generally takes a "substitute" basis in property(ies) received equal to his or her tax basis in the partnership interest, reduced by any cash received as part of the distribution.[35] Note that the partner's tax basis in the partnership interest immediately prior to the liquidating distribution must first be adjusted for the partner's allocable share of partnership income or loss for the period preceding the liquidation. This adjusted basis in the partnership interest is then reduced by the amount of cash (if any) received as part of the liquidating distribution (including deemed cash distributions resulting from the decrease in the partner's share of partnership liabilities). The remainder becomes the partner's tax basis in property received in the distribution.

> **Example 12-18:** Calvin was a 20 percent partner in Hobbes Properties until June 3 of the current year. On that date, he received a liquidating distribution consisting of $15,000 cash and two properties with an aggregate fair market value of $250,000.
>
> At the beginning of the year, Calvin's tax basis in his partnership interest was $200,000, consisting of his capital contributions (and share of reinvested earnings) of $90,000 and his $110,000 share of partnership debt. Assume that his share of partnership income for the year of the distribution was $22,500. Assuming that the properties received by Calvin were *not* encumbered by liabilities, Calvin's tax basis in the distributed properties will be calculated as follows:

Initial basis in partnership interest	$200,000
Share of partnership income for period preceding the liquidating distribution	22,500
Reduction in share of partnership debt	(110,000)
Cash received as part of liquidating distribution	(15,000)
Remaining basis in partnership interest	*$97,500*

This becomes Calvin's tax basis in the distributed properties.

The tax basis calculated in the above example must be allocated between the properties received by the partner. The allocation of basis is governed by Code Sec. 732(c). Where only one property is received, of course, no allocation is necessary. Where the distribution consists of multiple properties, however, the allocation will depend upon the types of property received and upon whether the partner takes a decreased basis in such properties (relative to the partnership's basis) or an increased basis. If the partner takes a decreased basis in the assets distributed (in other words, the basis of the partner's partnership interest exceeds the partnership's bases in the assets distributed) in a liquidating distribution, the allocation of

---

[35] Code Sec. 732(b).

¶1205.02

basis to the distributed properties is done in the same manner as if the distribution is nonliquidating. Refer back to Example 12-16. None of the results in that example would be any different if the distribution was a liquidating distribution, rather than a nonliquidating distribution.

Allocation of basis to assets in a liquidating distribution does differ from a nonliquidating distribution, however, when the partner's basis in their partnership interest exceeds the total basis the partnership had in the property distributed. First, if only cash, inventory, and unrealized receivables are distributed, the excess of the partner's interest basis over the partnership's basis in the assets distributed would be recognized as a loss in the case of a liquidating distribution, but not in the case of a nonliquidating distribution. Second, if the partner's interest basis exceeds the basis of the assets distributed and any of the distributed assets are capital or Code Sec. 1231 assets, the basis of the capital/Code Sec. 1231 assets will be increased. The increase in the basis of the capital/Code Sec. 1231 assets will equal the excess of the partner's interest basis over the total basis (to the partnership) of the assets distributed. The increase will first be allocated to assets that have appreciated, in proportion to the relative amount of appreciation inherent in each. Any remaining increase will be allocated in proportion to their relative fair market values.

Example 12-19: Recall that in Example 12-16 Blum Partnership distributed the assets below to Lowe, a 20-percent partner. Rather than assuming the distribution is nonliquidating, as in Example 12-16, assume that the distribution liquidates Lowe's interest in the partnership. Both Asset 1 and Asset 2 are Code Sec. 1231 assets. The distributed assets have bases and FMVs as follows:

	Tax Basis	*FMV*
Cash	$10,000	$10,000
Inventory Item A	8,000	10,000
Inventory Item B	16,000	15,000
Asset 1	40,000	30,000
Asset 2	60,000	70,000
Totals	*$134,000*	*$135,000*

If Lowe's basis in her partnership interest is $120,000, the allocation of basis to the assets in this liquidating distribution will be the same as when the distribution was nonliquidating (as in Example 12-16). She will be required to decrease the basis of Assets 1 and 2 by $14,000 ($134,000 total basis – $120,000 partnership interest basis) in the aggregate. The first $10,000 of this decrease will be allocated to Asset 1, reflecting the excess of its basis in the partnership's hands over its fair market value at the date of distribution. The remaining $4,000 of the step-down in basis will be allocated one-third ($30,000/$90,000) to Asset 1 (which now has a tax basis of $30,000) and two-thirds ($60,000/$90,000) to Asset 2 (carryover basis of $60,000). The basis of the assets to Lowe after the liquidating distribution will be:

	Tax Basis
Cash	$10,000
Inventory Item A	8,000
Inventory Item B	16,000
Asset 1 ($40,000 – $10,000 – $1,333)	28,667
Asset 2 ($60,000 – $2,667)	57,333
Total	*$120,000*

Her tax basis in the partnership interest will be reduced to zero, which is appropriate since she is no longer a partner.

If Lowe's basis in her partnership interest is $150,000, the excess (of Lowe's partnership basis over the basis of the distributed property) of $16,000 ($150,000 – $134,000) will be allocated first to Asset 2 in the amount of $10,000. The remaining $6,000 will be allocated between Assets 1 and 2 in proportion to their relative fair market values, so $1,800 will be allocated to Asset 1 [($30,000/$100,000) × $6,000]. Asset 2 will be allocated $4,200 [($70,000/$100,000) × $6,000].

The basis of the assets to Lowe after the liquidating distribution under these circumstances will be:

	Tax Basis
Cash	$10,000
Inventory Item A	8,000
Inventory Item B	16,000
Asset 1 ($40,000 + $1,800)	41,800
Asset 2 ($60,000 + $10,000 + $4,200)	74,200
Total	*$120,000*

The above rules for distributions are summarized in the following table:

Treatment of Partnership Distributions
Nonliquidating distributions

Basis in distributed property > basis in partnership interest

1. Cash distributed	Gain recognized if cash distribution is greater than basis in partnership interest
2. Cash, inventory, and unrealized receivables distributed	a. Basis allocated first to cash, then inventory and unrealized receivables.
	b. Deficiency allocated to inventory and unrealized receivables in proportion to (1) inherent depreciation, then (2) relative bases.

¶1205.02

| 3. Cash, inventory, unrealized receivables and capital/Sec. 1231 assets distributed | a. Basis allocated first to cash, then inventory and unrealized receivables, then capital/Sec. 1231 assets. |
| | b. Deficiency allocated to (i) inventory and unrealized receivables or (ii) capital/Sec. 1231 assets (as the case may be) in proportion to (1) inherent depreciation, then (2) relative bases. |

Basis in partnership interest > basis in distributed property

| 4. Cash, inventory, unrealized receivables and capital/Sec. 1231 assets distributed | Carryover basis for all assets. No increase in basis for assets, partnership interest retains some basis |

Liquidating distributions

Basis in distributed property > basis in partnership interest

Same as for nonliquidating distributions, see 1-3, above.

Basis in partnership interest > basis in distributed property

| 5. Only cash and/or inventory and/or unrealized receivables distributed. | Loss recognized. No change in basis of distributed assets. |
| 6. At least some capital/Sec. 1231 assets distributed (could be combined with cash, inventory, and unrealized receivables) | No gain or loss recognized. Excess of partnership interest basis over basis of property distributed is allocated to capital/Sec. 1231 assets based first (1) in proportion to their relative appreciation, then (2) in proportion to their relative fair market values. |

¶ 1206 Disproportionate Distributions—Results to Partner and Partnership When the Partner's Share of Ordinary Income Assets Is Affected

Code Sec. 751(b) is intended to preclude a partner from obtaining the potential tax benefits of distribution treatment when, in reality, the economic effect of the transaction is an exchange of the partner's share of the ordinary income assets to the other partners in exchange for a distribution of cash or capital gain property. It also applies when the distributee is, in effect, trading to the other partners his or her share of the capital gain property in exchange for a distribution of ordinary income property.

Rules similar to those in Code Sec. 751(a) are triggered when a distribution changes the partner's proportionate share of "unrealized receivables" and "substantially appreciated inventory," as defined in Code Secs. 751(b)(3), (c) and (d). These ordinary income assets are sometimes referred to as Code Sec. 751 assets or "hot" assets. When a partner receives more or less than his or her share in value of these ordinary income assets in a distribution in exchange for an increased or decreased interest in capital assets, Code Sec. 1231 assets, or cash, the distribution is partially recast as a taxable exchange. Thus, for example, a partner is required to report his or her share of the potential ordinary income from this portion of the substantially appreciated inventory and unrealized receivables when the partner receives a liquidating cash distribution. The partnership obtains a fair market value basis in the partner's preliquidation share of these assets.

When a partner receives more than his or her share of the ordinary income assets, the partner is treated as receiving the excess through a sale to the partnership of his or her share of the non-ordinary income assets for the excess ordinary income assets the partner received. The partner will report capital gains for his or her share of the appreciation in capital gain assets relinquished to the other partners. The portion of the ordinary income assets received in the deemed exchange will have a cost basis to the distributee equal to their fair market value.

Code Sec. 751(b) is triggered when a distribution results in an exchange of some portion of the partner's interest in partnership ordinary income property for an increased interest in partnership capital gain and other property, or vice-versa. The exchange is measured in terms of the partner's interest in the *values* of the assets in each class before and after the distribution.

Example 12-20: QLR Partners has the following balance sheets at September 30:

	Tax Basis	FMV
Cash	$15,000	$15,000
Accounts Receivable	0	15,000
Inventory	30,000	60,000
Capital Assets	27,000	45,000
	$72,000	$135,000
Capital, *Q*	$24,000	$45,000
Capital, *L*	24,000	45,000
Capital, *R*	24,000	45,000
	$72,000	$135,000

On that date, the partnership distributed the capital assets to partner *L* in complete liquidation of her interest in the partnership. Prior to the distribution, *L* was an equal one-third partner. An analysis of her interest in the partnership's assets is as follows:

	Pre-distribution	Post-distribution	Change
Ordinary Income Assets:			
Accounts Receivable	$5,000	-0-	
Inventory	20,000	-0-	
	25,000	-0-	(25,000)

Other Assets:

Cash.....................	$5,000	-0-
Capital Assets	$15,000	45,000
	20,000	45,000 25,000

Thus, the distribution has the effect of exchanging L's $25,000 share of the *value* of the partnership's ordinary income assets for an additional $25,000 worth of the partnership's capital assets. Code Sec. 751(b) will recharacterize this portion of the distribution as a taxable exchange. The remainder of the transaction will be treated as a liquidating distribution of $20,000 worth of capital assets.

Note that Code Sec. 751(b) applies only to the extent that a distribution results in the intentional or unintentional shift of the distributee partner's relative interests in partnership ordinary income vs. other assets. It does *not* apply when the distribution has the effect of shifting gain (or loss) among partners with respect to two or more assets in the same class. It remains possible, therefore, to shift gain (and thus tax liability) among partners through distributions of disproportionately appreciated assets of the same class. It also remains possible to shift gain among partners through distributions of disproportionately appreciated assets of a different class if they have equal values.

Example 12-21: Lactose Ltd. is a three-person equal partnership with the following balance sheets:

	Tax Basis	*FMV*
Cash	$75,000	$75,000
Accounts Receivable	0	25,000
Inventory	40,000	50,000
Capital Asset 1	30,000	50,000
Capital Asset 2	5,000	25,000
	$150,000	$225,000
Capital, B	$50,000	$75,000
Capital, L...........................	50,000	75,000
Capital, T	50,000	75,000
	$150,000	$225,000

The partnership distributed half its inventory and Capital Asset 1 to T in complete liquidation of her interest. The distribution affected T's interest in the partnership's ordinary vs. other assets as follows:

	Pre-distribution	Post-distribution	Change
Ordinary Income Assets:			
Accounts Receivable	$8,333	-0-	(8,333)
Inventory	16,667	25,000	8,333
			-0-
Other Assets:			
Cash.	$25,000	-0-	(25,000)
Capital Asset 1	16,667	50,000	33,333
Capital Asset 2	8,333	-0-	8,333
			-0-

Since the distribution did not alter *T*'s interest in the aggregate value of each class of partnership assets, it is not a disproportionate distribution, and Code Sec. 751(b) will not apply. This is true even though *T* will recognize only $5,000 of ordinary income on any subsequent sale of the distributed inventory for its $25,000 value, while the remaining partners will recognize $30,000 ordinary income upon sale of the partnership's remaining inventory (FMV $25,000; basis $20,000) and collection of the accounts receivable (FMV $25,000; basis -0-).[36]

Comment: From the distributee partner's point of view, if he or she receives a liquidating distribution, Code Sec. 751(b) produces a result which is similar to the Code Sec. 751(a) result to a selling partner. Each partner will have ordinary income in an amount equal to their share of the partnership's ordinary income appreciation. However, from the standpoint of the partnership, the result is very different. Under Code Sec. 751(b), the partnership (consisting of the remaining partners who have purchased the liquidated partner's share of the ordinary income assets) will have a fair market value basis in these assets. Under Code Sec. 751(a), the partnership receives a fair market value basis for the purchaser's share of the assets only if there is a Code Sec. 754 election in effect.

LLC Observation: The disproportionate distribution rules discussed in this chapter apply equally to state law partnerships and LLCs taxed as partnerships.

¶ 1207 Definition of Unrealized Receivables

As noted above, Code Sec. 751(b) applies when a distribution alters the distributee partner's share of the aggregate value of the partnership's "unrealized receivables" and "substantially appreciated inventory." The first step, then, is to define these terms so that partnership assets can be properly classified.

---

[36] Note that a Code Sec. 754 election will not help the remaining partners in this case as *T* is not taking a stepped-up or down basis in either asset received from the partnership.

Generally, Code Sec. 751(c) defines unrealized receivables for all purposes of partnership taxation (Subchapter K of the Internal Revenue Code). References to "unrealized receivables" may be found in the following sections in Subchapter K:

1. Code Sec. 731(a)(2), which provides for the recognition of loss upon certain distributions in liquidation of a partner's partnership interest;

2. Code Sec. 732(c), which provides for an allocation of adjusted basis to distributed property to be made first to Code Sec. 751 assets; and

3. Code Sec. 735(a), which provides that the character of gain or loss realized on a subsequent sale of unrealized receivables received in a distribution is ordinary income.

As originally enacted, Code Sec. 751(c) included only a single sentence dealing with rights to receive payments for goods and services provided or to be provided. Currently, however, the last two sentences of the section are representative of Congressional exceptions to capital gain treatment enacted over the years. Other than for purposes of Code Sec. 736(a), the term "unrealized receivables" now includes the following items:

1. Depreciation recapture under Code Sec. 1245.

2. Excess depreciation under Code Sec. 1250.

3. Mining exploration expenses recapture under Code Sec. 617(d).

4. Stock in a D.I.S.C.[37] or certain foreign corporations.[38]

5. Franchises, trademarks, etc.[39]

6. Oil, gas or geothermal property.[40]

7. Excess farm loss recapture under Code Sec. 1252.

8. Market discount bonds[41] and short-term obligations.[42]

Code Sec. 751(c) does not purport to be an exhaustive list of "unrealized receivables" but merely indicates that the term "includes" the items listed. To date, the IRS has not argued for any other inclusion, but the language to support such an argument is in the section.

As indicated, the term "unrealized receivables" includes the rights to payments for services rendered or to be rendered to the extent not already reported. The term "rights ... to payment for" is construed liberally, including a non-contractual or equitable right (*quantum meruit*) to payment, whether it is partially or fully earned, and when there is a noncancellable future contract to perform services or deliver goods. However, if the agreement is cancellable at will by the buyer/customer, it is not an unrealized receivable to the seller. Thus, general expectations of profit are likened to goodwill, which is not a Code Sec. 751 asset. Even though goodwill represents future profits on which the purchaser has put economic value, the seller will have capital gain on its disposition.

---

[37] Code Sec. 992(a).
[38] Code Sec. 1248.
[39] Code Sec. 1253.

[40] Code Sec. 1254.
[41] As defined in Code Sec. 1278.
[42] As defined in Code Sec. 1283.

Unrealized receivables include the right to receive payments for goods delivered or to be delivered. However, to the extent these constitute accounts receivable for financial accounting purposes, they most likely will have been recognized by the partnership because taxpayers selling inventoried goods generally must use the accrual method of accounting for sale of goods. Accrual method partnerships will often have a right to be paid for goods that have been ordered but not yet delivered.

The recapture items referred to in the last two sentences of Code Sec. 751(c) are different from the right to receive payments for goods or services in that they do not involve any type of contractual right to receive payments. They are, in effect, the current, unrealized, potential ordinary income inherent in the property if it were sold at its current fair market value. This unrealized receivable is an amount determined by referring to the fair market value of the asset, its adjusted basis, and the type of gain, ordinary or capital, which would be reported if it were sold. The unrealized receivable is the ordinary income the partnership would realize if it sold the asset. An arm's-length agreement between the partnership and the distributee may be used in certain circumstances to establish what is exchanged.[43]

> *Observation:* It must be remembered that it is the ordinary income asset's value and basis that controls the results to the distributee partner and distributing partnership. For example, a cash basis partnership's accounts receivable are an unrealized receivable to the extent of the value the buyer and seller of the partnership's business would agree upon. This amount could very likely be less than the receivables' face value. In the case of an accrual basis partnership, that value is likely to be less than the basis of the receivables.

Note that depreciable property subject to recapture potential is classified as an unrealized receivable only to the extent of the recapture income inherent in the asset. For most such assets, this will result in dual classification: to the extent of its tax basis, the asset will be classified as Code Sec. 1231 property (i.e., "other" property), while the excess of the value of the asset over its tax basis will be classified as Code Sec. 1245 (or other recapture) property. For example, assume a partnership owns depreciable personal property with an original cost of $75,000, a tax basis of $50,000 (indicating $25,000 of accumulated depreciation), and a fair value of $60,000. Only $10,000 of this property will be classified as an unrealized receivable. The remaining $50,000 will be treated as Code Sec. 1231 (other) property.

Since Code Sec. 751 assets include only assets that represent potential ordinary income, assets with short-term capital gain potential are not Code Sec. 751 assets, and gain from the sale of the partnership interest attributable to such items may receive long-term capital gain treatment.

¶ 1208 Definition of Substantially Appreciated Inventory Items

The second category of Code Sec. 751 assets consists of substantially appreciated inventory items. This requires a two part analysis: first, the asset must

---

[43] Reg. § 1.751-1(g), Exs. (3)(c), (3)(d)(1) and (5)(c).

constitute inventory—Code Sec. 751(d) sets out four categories of inventory items. Second, the inventory must be substantially appreciated.

The first of the four categories of inventory items is true inventory in terms of Code Sec. 1221(1) and dealer property held primarily for sale to customers in the ordinary course of the partnership's business.[44]

The second category comprises other property which, when sold or exchanged by the partnership, would be considered property other than a capital asset in terms of Code Sec. 1221 and other than a Code Sec. 1231(b) asset.[45] This category is so broad as to apparently encompass all the other categories and specifically includes the accounts receivable of a cash-basis taxpayer,[46] realized accounts receivable of an accrual-basis taxpayer, depreciation recapture, and all other unrealized receivables. When there is a disproportionate distribution involving unrealized receivables, the fact that an asset is an unrealized receivable will alone result in characterizing a part of the distribution as a sale of these unrealized receivables. In addition, however, classifying this same asset as an inventory item may result in the partnership's other inventory being deemed substantially appreciated when they otherwise might not have been, or not substantially appreciated when it otherwise would have been.

> *Observation:* The inclusion of unrealized receivables as inventory (in this second category) has an effect on only the "substantial appreciation test." The result is that, in the case of a cash-basis partnership, it is more likely that the traditional category of inventory will be appreciated, while the opposite is often true of an accrual-basis partnership.

The fact that Code Sec. 751(d)(2) refers to noncapital assets and not to noncapital gains could potentially mean that Code Sec. 306 stock, Code Sec. 341 gains, gains from original issue discount, and other gains which are from capital assets but are taxed as ordinary income, are excluded from the definition of inventory under Code Sec. 751(d)(2). Recapture items would not be inventory items. Code Sec. 64, however, appears to classify recapture items as other than Code Sec. 1231(b) or capital assets, and therefore these assets are unlikely to be excluded from status as inventory.

The third category of inventory items comprises the potential gain from the sale of Code Sec. 1246 stock.[47]

The fourth category is any other partnership property that would be either Code Sec. 1221(1) property, other noncapital assets or non-Code Sec. 1231(b) property, or property giving rise to potential gain from the sale of Code Sec. 1246 stock if it were held by the distributee partner.[48] Therefore, if the property would fall into one of the first three categories "if held by the selling or distributee partner," it will be considered to be inventory for the purposes of Code Sec. 751.

---

[44] Code Sec. 751(d)(1).

[45] Code Sec. 751(d)(2).

[46] Although this would seem unwarranted, the regulations specifically provide for this result. Reg. § 1.751-1(d)(2)(ii).

[47] Foreign investment company stock. Code Sec. 751(d)(3).

[48] Code Sec. 751(d)(4).

The legislative history does not indicate the purpose for this provision which, in effect, requires the property to be tested at two levels.

> *Observation:* This fourth category of inventory has the potential to produce unexpected tax consequences. For example, it is clear that a dealer in real estate who is a limited partner in a partnership which invests in real estate incurs capital gains for his share of the profits if the partnership produces capital gains from the sale of its real estate investments. However, under Code Secs. 751(b) and 751(d)(4), if the limited partner receives a liquidating cash distribution from the partnership, the IRS could recharacterize some or all of the distribution as ordinary income.

Whether or not property is "held primarily for sale" in terms of Code Sec. 1221(1) is a factual test focusing on the taxpayer's intent with regard to the property in question. In the context of Code Sec. 751(d)(4), this test is difficult to apply since the partner does not actually own the property. It could be argued that a selling partner, who is otherwise a dealer in the type of assets the partnership owns, can have investment accounts, and that this particular property would be such an investment. A trader or dealer in certain types of property may invest in that type of property if he or she shows such an intent. One method of showing investment intent is to set the property aside from other similar property that he or she does deal in. Ownership through a partnership that is not controlled by the partner would help show investment motive. However, with respect to a similar provision, the Code Sec. 341(e) rules provide that, if the taxpayer has similar inventory, this is enough to create a presumption that it would be held for sale.[49]

For distributions, partnership inventory items are not Code Sec. 751 assets unless they are "substantially appreciated" in the aggregate. Code Sec. 751(b)(3) lays down a mechanical test for determining whether inventory is substantially appreciated. The total fair market value of the inventory must exceed 120 percent of the total adjusted basis of all the inventory items to the partnership.[50]

Before the August 5, 1997, effective date of Act § 1062(a) of the Taxpayer Relief Act of 1997,[51] only substantially appreciated inventory could generate ordinary income on both sales of partnership interests under Code Sec. 751(a) and disproportionate distributions under Code Sec. 752(b). Since that date, the substantial appreciation requirement affects only disproportionate distributions. Inventory is considered substantially appreciated for this purpose only if the aggregate fair market value of these assets exceeds their aggregate basis by 120 percent.[52] For this purpose, inventory is disregarded if a principle purpose for acquiring it was to

---

[49] Code Sec. 341(b) refers to the purchase of property described in Code Sec. 341(b)(3) which defines "Section 341 assets." See also S. Rep. No. 781, 82d Cong., 1st Sess. (1951), reprinted in 1951-2 CB 458, 481. This issue potentially causes additional problems when Code Sec. 751(b) is applicable, as it may give ordinary income to the other nondealer partners upon a deemed property distribution to the dealer. The regulations cure this by limiting Code Sec. 751(d)(2)(D) to property retained by the partner-

ship. Reg. § 1.751(d)(2)(iii). See further discussion of Code Sec. 751(b) under distributions.

[50] Special basis adjustments under Code Secs. 743(b) and 732(d) are ignored in calculating the basis of partnership property. Reg. § 1.751-1(d)(1). The Taxpayer Relief Act of 1997, P.L. 105-34, Act § 1062(a).

[51] P.L. 105-34.

[52] Code Sec. 751(b)(3); Reg. § 1.751-1(d)(1).

prevent the partnership's inventory items from being substantially appreciated (*e.g.*, if it was depreciated at the date of acquisition or contribution by a partner).[53]

Example 12-22: A, B, C, and D formed the calendar year ABCD partnership, each with a one-fourth interest in partnership capital, profits, and losses. The original contributions to ABCD were $100 in cash from each partner. A, B, C, and D derive their income exclusively from the partnership. The current balance sheet is as follows:

Assets	*Book Value and Adjusted Basis*	*FMV*
Cash	$240	$240
Inventory	60	100
Capital Asset *X*	100	260
	$400	*$600*
Capital		
A	$100	$150
B	100	150
C	100	150
D	100	150
	$400	*$600*

The adjusted basis of each partner's partnership interest is $100. The partnership distributes $150 in liquidation of Partner *A*'s interest.

The distribution of the cash to *A* results in a Code Sec. 751(b) distribution because *A* is exchanging part of his interest in Code Sec. 751 property (the inventory) for cash, a non-Code Sec. 751 asset. In order to determine the amount of the exchange and the amount of the distribution, it is helpful to proceed as follows.

Initially, one must classify the assets. The cash and Capital Asset *X* are not Code Sec. 751 property because neither is within the definition of Code Sec. 751(c) or (d). The inventory is Code Sec. 751 property because it is inventory within the definition of Code Sec. 751(d), and meets the substantial appreciation test of Code Sec. 751(b)(3)(A).

Next, one must determine *A*'s interest in the respective assets before and after the distribution in order to determine which assets are being exchanged:

---

[53] Code Sec. 751(b)(3)(B).

1. *A's pre-distribution* interest in:

Cash	=	1/4	×	$240	=	$60
Inventory	=	1/4	×	$100	=	$25
Asset X	=	1/4	×	$260	=	$65

2. *A*'s *post-distribution* interest in each asset retained by the partnership is $0 because *A* is no longer a partner.

3. Property distributed to *A* is cash of $150.

As *A* receives only cash, he has relinquished his interest in Capital Asset *X* worth $65 and his interest in inventory worth $25 for cash of $90. Only the relinquishment of the inventory for cash is a Code Sec. 751(b) exchange. *A* has relinquished an interest in inventory worth $25 for cash of $25. The exchange of an interest in a capital asset for cash is irrelevant as the statutory focus is on a relinquishment of his share of Code Sec. 751 property.[54]

The basis of the *hot assets* (the inventory) deemed exchanged for the cash is determined under Code Sec. 732(a) as if *A* had received the assets in a current distribution immediately before the exchange. *A* exchanged an interest in inventory worth $25 for cash in the same amount. The basis of the inventory to *A* is $25/$100 × $60 or $15. Thus, *A* must recognize $10 ordinary income: the difference between the cash he received in the exchange and his basis in the relinquished *hot assets*.

The partnership does not recognize gain because it is deemed to have purchased the inventory assets with cash. The character of *A*'s gain is ordinary since he is deemed to have sold to the partnership the inventory deemed distributed to him. Sale of the inventory immediately after a distribution results in ordinary income.[55]

The remaining cash distributed to *A* is treated as a distribution to which Code Secs. 731 through 735 apply. *A* has gain under Code Sec. 731(a)(1) because he received cash in excess of his basis in his partnership interest. The amount of the distribution is $125 (the total of $150 minus the amount allocated ($25) to the sale of inventory). *A*'s basis in his partnership interest at the time of the cash distribution ($100) must be reduced by *A*'s share of the basis for the inventory ($15) which was deemed to have been distributed to him immediately before the Code Sec. 751(b) exchange. This reduction occurs under Code Sec. 733 and reduces *A*'s basis in his partnership interest to $85. Thus, *A* has a capital gain on the distribution of $125 minus $85, or $40. In summary:

1. *A*'s taxable gain on the distribution is $50. Ten dollars of the gain is ordinary from the deemed sale of the inventory and $40 of it is capital gain from the cash distribution in excess of basis.

---

[54] The exchange of *A*'s $65 share of Capital Asset *X* for cash is accounted for under Code Sec. 734(b)(1)(A) if the partnership has a Code Sec. 754 election in effect. See Chapter 13.

[55] Code Sec. 735(a)(2).

2. The partnership has no gain on the distribution. It did not *sell* Code Sec. 751(b) property, but only *bought* the inventory from *A* with cash.

3. The partnership's adjusted basis in the inventory is $60 (its beginning basis) minus the adjusted basis of the portion of the inventory that was deemed to be distributed to *A* ($15), plus the purchase price of that same portion of the inventory that it bought from *A* for $25. The total thus is $70 ($60 – $15 + $25).

4. Assuming the partnership does not have a Code Sec. 754 election in effect, its post-distribution balance sheet is as follows:

Assets	*Basis*	*FMV*
Cash	$90	$90
Inventory	70	100
Capital Asset *X*	100	260
	$260	*$450*
Capital		
B	100	150
C	100	150
D	100	150
	$300	*$450*

The preceding example is the clearest application of Code Sec. 751(b). The partner leaves the partnership with a liquidating distribution of cash and gives up his interest in all other assets. The liquidated partner has received his share of the cash and the other partners have also given a portion of their shares of the partnership's cash for the liquidated partner's share of the noncash assets. This is a clear case of the other partners purchasing the liquidated partner's share of the noncash assets. In other cases, the partnership, rather than the partner, will recognize ordinary income under Code Sec. 751(b).

Example 12-23: *A, B, C,* and *D* are equal partners of the ABCD Partnership. At the present time, ABCD's balance sheet is as follows:

Assets	*Basis*	*FMV*
Inventory	$40	$150
Capital Asset *X*	360	650
	$400	*$800*
Capital		
A	$100	$200
B	100	200

Capital

C	100	200
D	100	200
	$400	*$800*

The adjusted basis of each partner's partnership interest is $100.

It is agreed that the partnership will distribute the inventory to *A*. Following the distribution, *A*'s overall interest in profits and capital will be reduced from one-fourth to one-thirteenth. The interests of *B*, *C*, and *D* each will be increased from one-fourth to four-thirteenths.

The distribution of the inventory to *A* is a Code Sec. 751(b) distribution because *A* is exchanging part of his interest in the non-Code Sec. 751 property (Capital Asset *X*) for Code Sec. 751 property (inventory). To determine the amount of the exchange and the amount of the distribution, one should proceed as follows.

Initially, one must classify the assets. The inventory is Code Sec. 751 property because it is inventory within the definition of Code Sec. 751(d) and meets the substantial appreciation test of Code Sec. 751(b)(3). Capital Asset *X* is not Code Sec. 751 property because it is a capital asset.

Next, one must determine *A*'s interests in the respective assets before and after the transaction in order to determine which assets are being exchanged.

1. *A*'s pre-distribution interest in:

Inventory	=	1/4	×	$150	=	$37.50
Asset *X*	=	1/4	×	$650	=	$162.50

2. *A*'s post-distribution interest in each asset retained by ABCD:

Asset *X*	=	1/13	×	$650	=	$50

3. Property distributed to *A* is inventory of $150

Since *A* received only inventory, he has relinquished an interest in Capital Asset *X* worth $112.50 for an interest in the inventory worth $112.50. The remaining $37.50 of inventory *A* received was a distribution of his share of that inventory and is not subject to the provisions of Code Sec. 751(b).

The basis of the asset exchanged is determined under Code Sec. 732(a) as if *A* had received the asset in a current distribution immediately before the exchange. *A* exchanged an interest in Asset *X* worth $112.50. The basis of the asset is $112.50/$650 × $360 or $62.30 (fair market value of the exchanged asset deemed distributed over the total value of the asset times the basis of the asset).

A recognizes taxable gain in an amount equal to the difference between the value of the property received by him in the exchange, the inventory, and his basis in the relinquished asset, Capital Asset *X*.

Amount realized	$112.50	Value of inventory received in the exchange
Basis	62.30	Basis of the portion of Asset X deemed exchanged by A
Gain (capital gain)	*$50.20*	*A*'s gain on the Code Sec. 751(b) exchange is characterized as capital since *A* is treated has having disposed of a portion of a capital asset for the inventory. Whether the gain should be long-term or short-term depends upon the asset's holding period.

The partnership has gain equal to the difference between the value of the property received (Capital Asset X) and the basis of the property exchanged (the inventory).

Amount realized	$112.50	Value of Asset X "purchased" in the exchange
Basis	30.00	Basis of the portion of inventory exchanged*
Gain (ordinary income) .	*$82.50*	ABCD's ordinary income on the Code Sec. 751(b) exchange

*The adjusted basis is the remaining share (3/4) of the basis ($40) of the inventory after reduction by A's share of the inventory distributed to him.

The character of ABCD's gain is ordinary since it is deemed to have "exchanged" inventory. ABCD's gain on this transaction will be allocated to *B*, *C*, and *D* on the basis of each partner's postdistribution interest in profits and loss.[56]

The remaining portion of the inventory is treated as a distribution to which Code Secs. 731 through 735 apply. *A* has no gain on the distribution of inventory worth $37.50 (1/4 of the inventory which was his portion before the distribution) under Code Sec. 731(a). His basis in this portion of the inventory is $10.

Comment: Code Sec. 751(b) applies only if the distributee partner is both (1) receiving a distribution of one class of assets, and (2) relinquishing a share in the value of the other class of assets. In Example 12-22, Partner *A*'s share of capital and profits was reduced by the distribution. In some cases, receipt of a nonliquidating distribution may reduce the distributee partner's capital account, but have no impact on his or her interest in profits and losses. In such cases, the distribution may not affect the distributee partner's future share of income. The regulations are silent on how a distributee partner determines his or her pre-and post-distribution share of partnership assets when that partner's profit/loss sharing ratios are not the same as his or her share of capital.

Example 12-24: Partner *A* of the equal AB Partnership has a $95 basis in his partnership interest. The partnership has $300 of ordinary income property

---

[56] Reg. § 1.751-1(b)(2)(ii) and (3)(ii).

and $100 of capital gain property, with bases of $150 and $40, respectively. *A* receives a distribution of the capital gain property in a nonliquidating distribution, reducing his interest in partnership profits, losses and capital to one-third. Before the distribution, *A* had an indirect $150 interest in the ordinary income property and a $50 interest in the capital gain property for a total interest valued at $200. After the distribution, the value of *A*'s interest is $100 and is comprised entirely of a reduced interest in the ordinary income property. The distribution results not only in *A*'s obtaining an undivided direct interest in *his* share of the capital gain property, but also in his receiving a direct undivided ownership in the *other* partner's share of the capital gain property in exchange for giving the other partner $50 in value of his indirect interest in the ordinary income property.

If the rate of tax imposed upon capital gains is lower than that imposed upon ordinary income, *A*'s motivation for the distribution in the previous example is obvious. Before the distribution, his share of the partnership's potential taxable income consists of $30 of capital gains and $75 of ordinary income. In the absence of Code Sec. 751(b), he will, after distribution, have a $60 interest in the unrealized capital gain and a $50 share of the partnership's ordinary income. Thus, *A* exchanged an ordinary income potential of $25 for an additional $30 of potential capital gains. In addition, if the ordinary income assets are sold, and *A* receives $100 as a liquidating distribution, he will be entitled to a $5 loss after adjusting his basis for his share of the gain and distributions.[57] With a long-term capital gain rate of 15%, and ordinary tax rates up to 35%, this is a good trade.

In this example, Code Sec. 751(b) treats the disproportionate distribution as the distributee partner's sale of his reduced share of the ordinary income assets to the other partners. Technically, he is treated as if he received the other partners' shares of capital gains property by purchasing it with the share of inventory he relinquished to them. The regulations specify the mechanics of this exchange.[58] He is treated as if he receives, in a current distribution, the share of ordinary income assets given up and immediately sells them to the partnership. He has ordinary income for the appreciation of his relinquished share of ordinary income assets and a fair market value basis for the disproportionate segment of the capital asset received in the exchange. The remaining portion of the distribution, the distribution of his prorated share of capital assets, is taken into account under the normal distribution rules. *A*'s deemed distribution of ordinary income property is as follows:

$50 Value ($150.00 share before distribution less $100.00 share after)

$25 Basis (Basis to the partnership of 1/6 of the inventory)

His basis in his interest is reduced by $25 to $70.

---

[57] First, the nonliquidating property distribution reduces *A*'s initial basis in his partnership interest ($95) by the partnership's basis in the distributed property ($40) to $55. Second, his share of the income resulting from a liquidation of the partnership's assets (ordinary income of $50) increases his basis to $105. Last, upon a liquidation of the partnership *A* is entitled to a $100 cash distribution (1/3 of the partnership assets). A $100 liquidating cash distribution to a partner with a $105 basis in his interest results in a $5 loss. Code Sec. 731(a)(2).

[58] Reg. § 1.751-1(b)(2).

A's deemed exchange of this inventory with the partnership for $50 of capital gain property results in $25 of ordinary income and a basis of $50 in that portion of the asset. The partnership's basis in this portion of the inventory is increased by $25 to $50. The $25 increase is for *B*'s benefit only.

The $50 remaining portion of the capital asset distribution is governed by the normal distribution rules. *A*'s basis in this portion is $20. His ending basis in the $100 capital asset is $70. His ending basis in his partnership interest is $50. *A*'s pre-distribution ordinary income share was $75. He has recognized $25. If the partnership sells the ordinary income asset, his share of the gain is $50 (1/3 of $150) and *B*'s share is $75 (2/3 of $150 less $25).

The partnership is, in turn, treated as if it used a share of the capital gain property to purchase the ordinary income property. AB incurs capital gains to the extent of the appreciated portion of the capital asset considered to be disproportionately distributed. The partnership receives a fair market value basis in the ordinary income assets deemed acquired in the exchange. The basis increase to the ordinary income asset is normally equal to the amount of ordinary gain the distributee reports. The basis increase to the distributed capital assets is normally equal to the capital gain the partnership recognizes.

¶ 1209 Distribution of Marketable Securities

For purposes of Code Secs. 731(a)(1) and 737, the term "money" generally includes "marketable securities."[59] As a result, a partner generally recognizes gain to the extent the value of the distributed securities exceeds the partner's basis in his or her partnership interest.

However, the provision permits a partner to receive marketable securities attributable to *his or her share* of the net appreciation of the partnership's marketable securities without recognizing gain. This is done by reducing the amount of marketable securities treated as money by:

1. The excess of the partner's share of net gain that would be recognized if all securities of the type distributed held by the partnership immediately *before* the transaction were sold for fair market value, over

2. The partner's share of gain that would be taken into account if the securities held by the partnership immediately *after* the transaction had been sold.

As a result, Code Sec. 731(c) generally applies only when a partner receives a distribution of marketable securities in exchange for the partner's share of appreciated assets other than marketable securities—*i.e.*, a distribution consisting of more than his or her share of marketable securities from the partnership.

In conformance with legislative intent, all marketable securities retained by the partnership are considered to be of the same type as the distributed securities.[60] A

---

[59] Code Sec. 731(c). Code Sec. 731(c) was enacted as part of the Uruguay Round Agreements Act, P.L. 103-465. This provision does not apply to securities distributed before January 1, 1995, if held by the partnership on July 27, 1994. P.L. 103-465, Act § 741(c)(2).

[60] Reg. § 1.731-2(b)(1); Code Sec. 731(c)(3)(B).

simple example adapted from the legislative history of Code Sec. 731(c) illustrates the general concept.

Example 12-25: ABC Partnership holds 300 shares of publicly traded stock; it also owns other assets. Each share has a basis of $10 and a value of $100. *A*'s adjusted basis in his partnership interest is $5,000. *A*'s 1/3 interest in the partnership is liquidated in exchange for the 300 shares of stock worth $30,000.

The $30,000 of stock treated as money is reduced by $9,000. This is the excess of (1) *A*'s $9,000 share of the net gain in the partnership's securities before the distribution, over (2) *A*'s $0 share of the net gain in partnership securities after the distribution. It is the amount of gain that would have been allocated to *A* if the partnership sold the shares. Consequently, *A* recognizes a gain of $16,000 which is the amount of stock treated as money ($21,000) reduced by *A*'s $5,000 basis in the partnership. This reduction of gain equals the reduced share of partnership gain which is built into the basis of the distributed securities.

If ABC's share of *X* stock had a fair market value and tax basis of $100 per share, all of the $30,000 value of *X* stock distributed to *A* would be treated as cash. Because the stock would have no built-in gain, *A* would not derive any benefit from this gain limitation despite the fact that *A* may have owned his interest in ABC, and ABC may have owned its *X* stock for several years.

Code Sec. 731(c) provides no relief with respect to a distribution to a partner of his or her pro rata share of that partnership's marketable securities if such securities are not appreciated. Code Sec. 731(c) was amended, in part, to address the deficiencies in Code Sec. 751(b) since the latter provision does not apply to intra-character exchanges of assets in partnership solution.[61] If Code Sec. 731(c) was meant only to tax an exchange by a partner of his or her interest in other appreciated partnership assets for an increased interest in marketable securities, however, it would seem logical for the statute to exclude from the provision a partner's pro rata share of the distributed securities (regardless of whether appreciated) to which he or she would have been entitled absent any shifting of ownership in other partnership assets. However, the approach taken in this limitation on recognized gain seems to indicate that Congress felt that Code Secs. 704(c)(1)(B), 707(a)(2)(B), 737, and 751(b) did not adequately prevent a distributee partner from shifting the economic appreciation in his or her partnership interest into a highly liquid, easily valued security that provided such partners with much potential for realizing value on a tax deferred (or tax eliminated) basis. Only to the extent that the existing appreciation in a distributee partner's partnership interest reflected such partner's share of appreciation in marketable securities already owned by the partnership did Congress apparently believe the distributee partner deserved relief from gain recognition under Code Sec. 731(c). Only in this case can it be assured that no appreciation attributable to other assets (other than appreciation already

---

[61] S. Rep. No. 103d Cong., 2d Sess., 155 (1994).

inherent in marketable securities) is shifted from those assets to highly liquid marketable securities.

As long as a partner's inside basis in the assets of a partnership are in parity with the partner's outside basis in his or her partnership interest, a partner should be able to withdraw his or her full distributive share of marketable securities without recognizing any gain under Code Sec. 731. If such partner is foregoing a non-appreciated interest in other partnership assets in return for the distribution of marketable securities, the partner should still not recognize gain under Code Sec. 731(a) to the extent the partner has outside basis in the partnership interest that matches his or her share of inside basis in such other assets. The built-in gain limitation is designed to result in gain recognition under Code Sec. 731(a) only when the distributee partner is distributed marketable securities in return for his or her share of unrealized appreciation in such other assets (*i.e.*, shifting built-in gain attributable to those other assets into the marketable securities).

Problems arise, however, under this approach when an inside-outside basis disparity exists with respect to a distributee partner's interest. For example, a partner may have purchased an interest in a partnership at a time when the value of marketable securities held by the partnership was well below their original cost (*i.e.*, reflecting a built-in loss). Later, at a time when the securities had substantially appreciated in value to their original cost, the partnership distributes to such partner his or her pro rata share of such securities. Assuming the partnership had not made a Code Sec. 754 election, the Code Sec. 731(c)(3)(B) limitation would provide the distributee partner with no protection from gain recognition. This would be true even if there were no appreciation in other assets being shifted to the marketable securities (or even if there were no other assets owned by the partnership). These same inequities can arise in any other situation in which an inside-outside basis disparity exists.

Under the statute, the reduction in marketable securities treated as money provided by Code Sec. 731(c)(3)(B) turned on a partner's share of appreciation in marketable securities of the same *class* and *issuer* as the distributed securities. This would severely restrict the application of this limitation on gain somewhat unfairly because part of the reason for the enactment of Code Sec. 731(c) was the view that all marketable securities were cash equivalents. The regulations provide that for purposes of Code Sec. 731(c)(3)(B), all marketable securities held by a partnership are treated as marketable securities of the same class and issuer as the distributed securities.[62] The IRS and Treasury proposed this rule because "treating all marketable securities as a single asset for this purpose is consistent with the basic rationale of Code Sec. 731(c) that marketable securities are the economic equivalent of money. As a result, the amount of the distribution that is not treated as money will depend on the partner's share of the net appreciation in all partnership securities, not on the partner's share of the appreciation in the type of securities distributed."[63]

The effect of the final regulations' expansive definition of the "same class and issuer" rule in the statute is illustrated in the following example.

---

[62] Reg. § 1.731-2(b)(1).

[63] Preamble to Prop. Reg. § 1.732-2.

Example 12-26: One class rule. Assume that Partnership ABC owns securities issued by two different companies. One block of securities issued by *X* Co. has a fair market value of $400 and a tax basis of $400. The other block of securities issued by *Y* Co. has a fair market value of $400 and a tax basis of $100. ABC has liabilities of $500 that had originally been used to purchase the securities (in other words, the securities were 100% debt financed).

ABC distributes to *A*, in liquidation of her one-third interest, $100 of the securities issued by *Y* Co. *A*'s one-third share of ABC's $300 built-in gain in the *Y* Co. securities before the distribution is $100. Since this distribution will completely retire *A*'s interest in ABC, *A*'s share of ABC's built-in gain in the *Y* Co. securities after the distribution is zero. Thus, *A*'s reduction in her share of built-in gain in the *Y* Co. securities is $100. As a result, no portion of the value of the *Y* Co. securities distributed to *A* is characterized as cash under Code Sec. 731(c)(3)(B).

If, instead, ABC distributes $100 of *X* Co. securities (*i.e.*, the non-appreciated securities) in liquidation of *A*'s interest in ABC, the same result should follow. Even though the *X* Co. securities are of a different class and issuer from the *Y* Co. securities that reflect all of ABC's built-in gain, the regulations require that the *X* Co. securities and *Y* Co. securities be treated as securities of the same class and issuer as the distributed securities.[64] Thus, no portion of the distributed *X* Co. securities (up to $100 in value) should be characterized as cash under Code Sec. 731(c).

The single-class-of-stock rule is almost always favorable to taxpayers. However, it does have an adverse result when built-in-loss securities are aggregated with built-in-gain securities to reduce or eliminate the net built-in gain for purposes of the reduction in cash distribution rule.

¶ 1210 Definition of Marketable Securities

The term "marketable securities" is very broad; it generally means financial instruments and foreign currencies which are actively traded within the meaning of the straddle provisions of Code Sec. 1092(d)(1). The term "financial instrument" means stocks, other equity interests, debt, options, forward or futures contracts, notional principal contracts, and derivatives. Marketable securities also include interests in actively traded precious metals and other financial instruments specified in the Internal Revenue Code and Treasury regulations.[65] [66] There are four exceptions to the general rule that distributions of marketable securities are treated as money distributions:

1. The provision does not apply if the security was contributed to the partnership by the distributee-partner.

2. To the extent provided in regulations, the provision does not apply if the property distributed was not a marketable security when acquired by the partnership.[67]

---

[64] Reg. § 1.731-2(b)(1).
[65] Code Sec. 731(c)(2).

[66] Code Sec. 731(c)(3)(A) and (C).
[67] Reg. § 1.731-2(d)(1)(iii).

3. This provision does not apply to distributions of marketable securities received in a nonrecognition provision such as a Code Sec. 351 contribution or a qualified reorganization under Code Sec. 368 if additional requirements are met.[68]

4. Finally, the provision is inapplicable if the partnership is an investment partnership and the partner is an eligible partner. Look-through rules are provided for tiered partnerships.[69]

An investment partnership is a partnership that has never been engaged in a trade or business and substantially all of the assets of which have always consisted of investment assets specified in the Internal Revenue Code and Treasury regulations.[70] A partnership is not treated as engaged in a trade or business by reason of activity as an investor, trader, or dealer in an investment asset.

The term eligible partner is defined in the negative. An eligible partner is any partner who did not contribute any property other than the specified investment asset before the date of distribution.[71] However, a transferee in a nonrecognition transfer is not an eligible partner if the transferor was not an eligible partner.

¶ 1211 Basis in Securities Distributed, Partnership Interest, and Assets Remaining in the Partnership

The basis to the partner of the distributed securities is increased by the amount of gain recognized under this provision. The basis increase is allocated to individual securities received in proportion to the amounts of unrealized appreciation inherent in each. Neither the deemed money distribution nor the gain recognized under this provision affect the distributee's basis in his or her partnership interest. In addition, Code Sec. 734(b) is applied as if no gain were recognized.

> **Example 12-27:** ABC Partnership holds 300 shares of publicly traded stock; it also owns other assets which are not marketable securities. Each share has a basis of $10 and a value of $100. A's adjusted basis in his partnership interest is $5,000. A's one-third interest in the partnership is liquidated in exchange for the 300 shares of stock worth $30,000.
>
> The $30,000 of stock treated as money is reduced by $9,000, the amount of gain that would have been allocated to A if the partnership sold the shares. Consequently, A recognizes a gain of $16,000 which is the amount of stock treated as money ($21,000) reduced by A's $5,000 basis in the partnership.
>
> A's basis in the stock is $21,000. This is the $5,000 basis he would have in the stock without Code Sec. 731(c) plus the $16,000 gain he recognized because of Code Sec. 731(c). His basis in his partnership interest is his beginning basis of $5,000 and is not adjusted for the deemed money distribution of $21,000, but is adjusted for a distribution of property with a basis of $3,000. This is a liquidating distribution and therefore his basis in his partnership becomes the basis in the securities which is then increased by the $16,000

---

[68] *See* Reg. § 1.731-2(d)(1)(ii) and (3).
[69] Code Sec. 731(c)(3)(C)(iv).

[70] Code Sec. 731(c)(3)(C)(i).
[71] Code Sec. 731(c)(3)(C)(iii).

gain recognized under Code Sec. 731(c).[72] Had this been a current distribution, his partnership interest basis would have been reduced from $5,000 by the partnership's $3,000 basis for the securities to $2,000, and the securities would have a basis equal to the partnership basis of $3,000 plus the Code Sec. 731(c) gain of $16,000, or $19,000.

If *A* sold the shares for their value his gain would be:

Shares Received in a Liquidating Distribution		Shares Received in a Current Distribution
$30,000	. . . . Sales price	$30,000
(21,000)	. . . . Basis	(19,000)
$9,000	. . . . Gain from sale of shares	*$11,000*
16,000	. . . . Gain on stock distribution	16,000
$25,000	. . . . Total	*$27,000*

$25,000 is equal to the gain *A* would have had if the partnership distributed $30,000 cash to him in a liquidating distribution with or without selling the stock.

¶ 1212 Coordination with Other Provisions

Code Sec. 731(c) is not the only provision that applies when a partnership distributes marketable securities to a partner. In addition to Code Sec. 731, the partnership must consider the following provisions:

- Code Sec. 704(c)(1)(B) may simultaneously apply if another partner contributed the marketable securities. If so, any basis increase generated by Code Sec. 704(c)(1)(B) is taken into account before Code Sec. 731(c) is applied.[73]

- The Internal Revenue Code and the legislative history are silent on the application of the provision to a termination under Code Sec. 708(b)(1)(B). However, the regulations treat the newly reconstituted partnership as if it were the terminated partnership for purposes of Code Sec. 731(c).[74]

- The disguised sale rules of Code Sec. 707(a)(2)(B) take precedence over the new provision.

- To the extent that marketable securities are treated as money, that amount also is treated as money for purposes of Code Sec. 737. This reduces the amount of gain recognized under Code Sec. 737. In addition, the portion of the marketable securities not treated as money is treated as property for purposes of Code Sec. 737.[75]

- Code Sec. 751(b) takes precedence over the provisions of Code Sec. 731(c).

---

[72] If the partnership has a Code Sec. 754 election in effect, it will be required to reduce its basis in remaining assets by the $2,000 step-up in the basis of the securities received by *A*.

[73] Reg. § 1.731-2(g)(1).
[74] Reg. § 1.731-2(g)(2).
[75] Code Sec. 731(c)(1); Reg. §§ 1.731-2(g)(1)(ii) and 1.704-4(e)(1).

The regulations contain several examples of the application of the rules, some of which are analyzed below.[76] In these examples, it is assumed that the deemed sale rules of Code Secs. 707(a)(2)(B), 704(c)(1)(B), 737, and 751(b) do not apply unless otherwise provided. It is further assumed that none of the exceptions to Code Sec. 731(c) apply to the distributed securities, unless otherwise provided.

Example 12-28: *Recognition of gain.* A and B form partnership AB as equal partners. A contributes property with a fair market value of $1,000 and an adjusted tax basis of $250. B contributes $1,000 cash. AB subsequently purchases Security X for $500 and immediately distributes the security to A in a current distribution. A's basis in her partnership interest at the time of distribution is $250.

The distribution of Security X is treated as a distribution of money in an amount equal to the fair market value of Security X on the date of distribution ($500). As a result, A recognizes $250 of gain under Code Sec. 731(a)(1) on the distribution ($500 distribution of money less $250 adjusted tax basis in A's partnership interest).

Because there was no built-in gain or loss inherent in Security X at the date of distribution, the amount of the distribution that is treated as money is not reduced under Code Sec. 731(c)(3)(B). The transaction is treated as a cash distribution in its entirety.

Example 12-29: *Reduction in amount treated as money.* A and B form partnership AB as equal partners. AB subsequently distributes Security X to A in a current distribution. Immediately before the distribution, AB held securities with the following fair market values, adjusted tax bases, and unrecognized gain or loss:

	FMV	Tax Basis	Gain (Loss)
Security X (distributed)	$100	$70	$30
Security Y	$100	$80	$20
Security Z	$100	$110	$(10)

If AB had sold the securities for fair market value immediately before the distribution to A, the partnership would have recognized $40 of net gain ($30 gain on Security X plus $20 gain on Security Y, minus $10 loss on Security Z). A's distributive share of this gain would have been $20 (one-half of $40 net gain). If AB had sold the remaining securities immediately after the distribution of Security X to A, the partnership would have $10 of net gain ($20 of gain on Security Y minus $10 loss on Security Z). A's distributive share of this gain would have been $5 (one-half of $10 net gain). As a result, the distribution resulted in a decrease of $15 in A's distributive share of the net gain in AB's securities ($20 net gain before distribution minus $5 net gain after distribution).

---

[76] Reg. § 1.731-2(j).

The amount of the distribution of Security X that is treated as a distribution of money is reduced by $15. The distribution of Security X is therefore treated as a distribution of $85 of money to A ($100 fair market value of Security X minus $15 reduction).

Example 12-30: *Reduction in amount treated as money—Change in partnership allocations.* A is admitted to partnership ABC as a partner with a 1% interest in partnership profits. At the time of A's admission, ABC held no securities. ABC subsequently acquires Security X. A's interest in partnership profits is subsequently increased to 2% for securities acquired after the increase in A's profits interest. A retains a 1% interest in all securities acquired before the increase. ABC then acquires Securities Y and Z and later distributes Security X to A in a current distribution. Immediately before the distribution, the securities held by ABC had the following fair market values, adjusted tax bases, and unrecognized gain or loss:

	FMV	Tax Basis	Gain (Loss)
Security X	$1,000	$500	$500
Security Y	$1,000	$800	$200
Security Z	$1,000	$1,100	$(100)

If ABC had sold the securities for fair market value immediately before the distribution to A, the partnership would have recognized $600 of net gain ($500 gain on Security X plus $200 gain on Security Y, minus $100 loss on Security Z). A's distributive share of this gain would have been $7 (1% of $500 gain on Security X plus 2% of $200 gain on Security Y, minus 2% of $100 loss on Security Z).

If ABC had sold the remaining securities immediately after the distribution of Security X to A, the partnership would have $100 of net gain ($200 gain on Security Y minus $200 loss on Security Z). A's distributive share of this gain would have been $2 (2% of $200 gain on Security Y minus 2% of $200 loss on Security Z). As a result, the distribution resulted in a decrease of $5 in A's distributive share of the net gain in ABC's securities ($7 net gain before distribution minus $2 net gain after distribution).

The amount of the distribution of Security X that is treated as a distribution of money is reduced by $5. The distribution of Security X is therefore treated as a distribution of $995 of money to A ($1,000 fair market value of Security X minus $5 reduction).

Example 12-31: *Basis consequences—Distribution of marketable security.* A and B form partnership AB as equal partners. A contributes nondepreciable real property with a fair market value and adjusted tax basis of $100.

AB subsequently distributes Security X with a fair market value of $120 and an adjusted tax basis of $90 to A in a current distribution. At the time of distribution, A's basis in her partnership interest is $100. The amount of the distribution that is treated as money is reduced under Code Sec. 731(c)(3)(B) by $15 (one-half of $30 net gain in Security *X*). As a result, *A* recognizes $5 of gain under Code Sec. 731(a) on the distribution (excess of $105 distribution of money over $100 adjusted tax basis in *A*'s partnership interest).

A's adjusted tax basis in Security *X* is $95 ($90 adjusted basis of Security *X* determined under Code Sec. 732(a)(1) plus $5 of gain recognized by *A* by reason of Code Sec. 731(c)). The basis in *A*'s interest in the partnership is $10 as determined under Code Sec. 733 ($100 pre-distribution basis minus $90 basis allocated to Security *X* under Code Sec. 732(a)(1)).

Example 12-32: *Basis consequences—Distribution of marketable security and other property.* *A* and *B* form partnership AB as equal partners. *A* contributes nondepreciable real property, with a fair market value of $100 and an adjusted tax basis of $10.

AB subsequently distributes Security *X* with a fair market value and adjusted tax basis of $40 to *A* in a current distribution *not subject to Code Sec. 737* and, as part of the same distribution, AB distributes Property *Z* to *A* with an adjusted tax basis and fair market value of $40. At the time of distribution, *A*'s basis in her partnership interest is $10. *A* recognizes $30 of gain under Code Sec. 731(a) on the distribution (excess of $40 distribution of money over $10 adjusted tax basis in *A*'s partnership interest).

A's adjusted tax basis in Security *X* is $35 ($5 adjusted basis determined under Code Sec. 732(a)(2) and (c)(2), plus $30 of gain recognized by *A* by reason of Code Sec. 731(c)). *A*'s basis in Property *Z* is $5, as determined under Code Sec. 732(a)(2) and (c)(2).

The basis in *A*'s interest in the partnership is $0 as determined under Code Sec. 733 ($10 pre-distribution basis minus $10 basis allocated between Security *X* and Property *Z* under Code Sec. 732). Code Sec. 731(c)(5) provides that Code Sec. 733 is applied in determining a distributee partner's basis in its partnership interest following a distribution of marketable securities as if no gain was recognized under Code Sec. 731(c) and as if the basis of the distributed securities had not been adjusted for any such gain recognition.

AB's adjusted tax basis in the remaining partnership assets is unchanged unless the partnership has a Code Sec. 754 election in effect. If AB made such an election, the aggregate basis of AB's assets would be increased by $70 (the difference between the $80 combined basis of Security *X* and Property *Z* in the hands of the partnership before the distribution and the $10 combined basis of the distributed property in the hands of *A* under Code Sec. 732 after the distribution, but before the basis increase under Code Sec. 731(c)(4)). Under Code Sec. 731(c)(5), Code Sec. 734 (like Code Sec. 733) shall be applied as if no gain had been recognized by *A* by reason of Code Sec. 731(c), and as if no step-up in basis in the distributed marketable securities in the hands of *A* had occurred by reason of Code Sec. 731(c).

Determination of basis when both marketable securities and other property are distributed is not as simple as this example indicates. Example 12-32, set forth

¶1212

below, illustrates the interaction of Code Secs. 731(c) and 737 in a situation in which the other property distributed has no basis to the partnership.

If the other property has a positive basis, it is not possible to allocate the basis of both properties under Code Sec. 732(a)(2) and (c)(2) because Code Sec. 737(c)(1) (second sentence) states that the basis of the distributed Code Sec. 737 property reflects the increase in the basis of the partnership interest because of gain recognized under Code Sec. 737(a). As a result of this basis increase, neither Code Sec. 732(a)(2) nor (b) will apply to the distributed Code Sec. 737 property. As a result, it is necessary to first apply Code Sec. 732 to the distributed marketable security and then apply Code Secs. 737(c)(1) (second sentence) and 732 to the distributed Code Sec. 737 property. This computation may be illustrated as follows:

Security X FMV	=	$40		Property Z FMV	=	$40
Tax Basis	=	$40		Tax Basis	=	$40

Partnership interest basis	=	$10
Security X basis	=	$10 (Code Sec. 732(a)(2))
		+ 30 (Code Sec. 731(c)(4))
		_____
		$40
Property Y basis	=	$40 (Code Sec. 737(c)(1) increases the adjusted tax basis of A's partnership interest by $40 of Code Sec. 737(a) gain)

Example 12-33: *Coordination with Code Sec. 737. A* and *B* form partnership AB. *A* contributes Property *A*, nondepreciable real property with a fair market value of $200 and an adjusted basis of $100, in exchange for a 25% interest in partnership capital and profits. AB owns marketable Security *X*.

Within seven years of the contribution of Property *A*, AB subsequently distributes Security *X*, with a fair market value of $120 and an adjusted tax basis of $100 to *A* in a current distribution that is subject to Code Sec. 737. As part of the same distribution, AB distributes Property *Y* to *A* with a fair market value of $20 and an adjusted tax basis of $0. At the time of distribution, there has been no change in the fair market value of Property *A* or the adjusted tax basis in *A*'s interest in the partnership.

If AB had sold Security *X* for fair market value immediately before the distribution to *A*, the partnership would have recognized $20 of gain. *A*'s distributive share of this gain would have been $5 (25% of $20 gain). Because AB has no other marketable securities, *A*'s distributive share of gain in partnership securities after the distribution would have been $0. As a result, the distribution resulted in a decrease of $5 in *A*'s share of the net gain in AB's securities ($5 net gain before distribution minus $0 net gain after distribution). The amount of the distribution of Security *X* that is treated as a distribution of money is reduced by $5. The distribution of Security *X* is therefore treated as a distribution of $115 of money to *A* ($120 fair market value of Security *X* minus $5 reduction). The portion of the distribution of the marketable security that is

¶1212

not treated as a distribution of money ($5) is treated as other property for purposes of Code Sec. 737.

A recognizes total gain of $40 on the distribution. *A* recognizes $15 of gain under Code Sec. 731(a)(1) on the distribution of the portion of Security *X* treated as money ($115 distribution of money less $100 adjusted tax basis in *A*'s partnership interest). *A* recognizes $25 of gain under Code Sec. 737 on the distribution of Property *Y* (FMV $20) and the portion of Security *X* that is not treated as money ($5). *A*'s Code Sec. 737 gain is equal to the lesser of (1) *A*'s precontribution gain ($100), or (2) the excess of the fair market value of property received ($20 fair market value of Property *Y* plus $5 portion of Security *X* not treated as money) over the adjusted basis in *A*'s interest in the partnership immediately before the distribution ($100) reduced (but not below zero) by the amount of money received in the distribution ($115).

A's adjusted tax basis in Security *X* is $115 ($100 basis of Security *X* determined under Code Sec. 732(a)(2) plus $15 of gain recognized by reason of Code Sec. 731(c)). *A*'s adjusted tax basis in Property *Y* is $0 under Code Sec. 732(a)(2). The basis in *A*'s interest in the partnership is $25 ($100 basis before distribution minus $100 basis allocated to Security *X* under Code Sec. 732(a) (and Code Sec. 733), plus $25 gain recognized under Code Sec. 737(a) and (c)(1)).

This example, taken from the regulations, illustrates the interaction between Code Secs. 731(c) and 737, but only in the context where the basis of the other property in the hands of the partnership was zero. In Example 12-32, if Property *Y* had a basis greater than zero (*e.g.* $20) and $25 of gain was recognized under Code Sec. 737(a), does the $5 of securities treated as property for purposes of Code Sec. 737 obtain a basis step-up to $120 pursuant to the operation of Code Secs. 737(c)(1) and 732? Presumably yes, although this situation should be made clear.

Example 12-34: *Comprehensive.* Equal ABC Partnership has 600 shares of *X* stock (per-share FMV = $100, Adjusted Basis = $10). *A*'s basis for his partnership interest is $5,000. The partnership distributes 300 shares to *A* with a fair market value equal to $30,000. *A* remains an equal profits and loss member of the partnership.

General rule of Code Sec. 731(c)(1).

$30,000	Stock's value	
(5,000)	Basis of *A*'s partnership interest	
$25,000	Gain	

Gain is reduced under Code Sec. 731(c)(3)(B).

$18,000	*A*'s share of appreciation before	($600 × $90/3)
(9,000)	*A*'s share of appreciation after	($300 × $90/3)
$9,000	Gain reduction	

$25,000   Gain under Code Sec. 731(c)(1)

(9,000)   Reduced under Code Sec. 731(c)(3)(B)

_____

$*16,000*   Gain

Basis of distributed stock. Add gain to what the basis would have been under Code Sec. 732:

$3,000 Carryover basis for current distribution*

16,000 Plus gain under Code Sec. 731(c)

_____

$*19,000* Stock's basis

*Code Sec. 733.

Note: Allocate basis increase according to relative appreciation if shares are not identical.[77]

Partnership interest adjusted basis. Apply Code Sec. 733 only—*i.e.*, partnership interest adjusted basis is decreased by basis of stock, but not deemed money distribution under Code Sec. 731(c) (FMV Securities). *A*'s partnership interest adjusted basis is:

$5,000   Adjusted basis before distribution

(3,000)   Basis reduction for current distribution disregarding *Code Sec. 731(c)*

_____

$*2,000*   Ending basis

Basis in remaining property. The gain does not generate a Code Sec. 754/734(b) adjustment.

Coordination with Code Sec. 737. To the extent securities are considered money under Code Sec. 731(c), they are not property under Code Sec. 737 and any basis step-up under Code Sec. 737(c) is not allocated to the securities.

The term "marketable securities" is very broad; it generally means financial instruments and foreign currencies which are actively traded within the meaning of the straddle provisions of Code Sec. 1092(d)(1). The term "financial instrument" means stocks, other equity interests, debt, options, forward or futures contracts, notional principal contracts, and derivatives. Marketable securities also include interests in actively traded precious metals and other financial instruments specified in the Internal Revenue Code and Treasury regulations.[78] [79] There are four exceptions to the general rule that distributions of marketable securities are treated as money distributions:

1. The provision does not apply if the security was contributed to the partnership by the distributee-partner.

---

[77] Code Sec. 731(c)(4); *see* Reg. § 1.731-2(f)(1).

[78] Code Sec. 731(c)(2).

[79] Code Sec. 731(c)(3)(A) and (C).

2. To the extent provided in regulations, the provision does not apply if the property distributed was not a marketable security when acquired by the partnership.[80]

3. This provision does not apply to distributions of marketable securities received in a nonrecognition provision such as a Code Sec. 351 contribution or a Code Sec. 368 reorganization if additional requirements are met.[81]

4. Finally, the provision is inapplicable if the partnership is an investment partnership and the partner is an eligible partner. Look-through rules are provided for tiered partnerships.[82]

An investment partnership is a partnership that has never been engaged in a trade or business and substantially all of the assets of which have always consisted of investment assets specified in the Internal Revenue Code and Treasury regulations.[83] A partnership is not treated as engaged in a trade or business by reason of activity as an investor, trader, or dealer in an investment asset.

The term eligible partner is defined in the negative. An eligible partner is any partner who did not contribute any property other than the specified investment asset before the date of distribution.[84] However, a transferee in a nonrecognition transfer is not an eligible partner if the transferor was not an eligible partner.

---

[80] Reg. § 1.731-2(d)(1)(iii).
[81] *See* Reg. § 1.731-2(d)(1)(ii) and (3).
[82] Code Sec. 731(c)(3)(C)(iv).

[83] Code Sec. 731(c)(3)(C)(i).
[84] Code Sec. 731(c)(3)(C)(iii).

Chapter 13

Basis Adjustments to Partnership Property—Code Secs. 734(b), 743(b)

¶ 1301 Basis Adjustment to Partnership Property—Code Sec. 743(b) Basis Adjustments

Under an aggregate approach to partnership taxation, a partner who acquires his or her partnership interest by purchase would receive a cost basis in his or her share of the partnership assets. The partner's position would be similar to that of a tenant-in-common.

Under an entity approach to partnership taxation, however, the price paid by the purchasing partner affects only the partner's adjusted basis in his or her partnership interest, not the basis of his or her share of the partnership assets. A shareholder's acquisition of corporate stock is an example of the operation of the entity approach.

Prior to 1954, neither the aggregate nor the entity approach had been completely accepted by the courts, but the weight of authority came down on the side of the entity approach. The rationale for not allowing a change in the adjusted basis of the partnership assets on the transfer of a partnership interest was that the purchasing partner had not acquired an interest in the partnership property itself, but only in the partnership as an entity. Code Sec. 743(a) codified this approach.

Code Sec. 743(b), however, provides that if an election under Code Sec. 754 is in effect for the year of sale or if the partnership has a substantial built-in loss (as defined in Code Sec. 743(d)) immediately after the transfer, the entity rules of Code Sec. 743(a) give way to the modified aggregate rules of Code Sec. 743(b). In such cases, the transfer of a partnership interest will trigger a required adjustment to the basis of partnership assets. This adjustment affects the transferee partner only, effectively giving the transferee a FMV basis in his or her share of each of the partnership's assets.

.01 Code Sec. 743(b) Transfers

Code Sec. 743(b) is applicable only to certain transfers of partnership interests. It applies to sales, exchanges, and transfers of partnership interests upon death. It applies to any transfer considered a sale or exchange. For example, Code Sec. 743(b) applies to distributions of a partnership interest by a corporation or a partnership.[1] It does *not* apply to the gift of a partnership interest, nor to the contribution of cash or property to a partnership in exchange for an interest in that partnership.

Partner dies with community property partnership interest. When property is held as community property and either the husband or wife dies, the decedent's share of the partnership interest is includable in his or her gross estate at its value on the applicable valuation date.[2] The devisee will take a tax basis for the partnership interest equal to its value plus his or her share of the partnership's debt.[3] The surviving spouse's community property portion of the partnership interest is not included in the decedent's gross estate and is not transferred to the surviving spouse by reason of the decedent's death. The surviving spouse's share of the partnership interest, however, also receives a basis equal to its value at the appropriate valuation date.[4] The IRS has ruled that in spite of the absence of a partnership interest being transferred, the surviving spouse's share of the assets is adjusted if the partnership has a Code Sec. 754 election in effect for the partnership year in which the decedent's death occurred.[5]

Purchase of economic rights only. With respect to a transfer of the economic rights to a partnership interest when the new owner of the economic rights is not formally admitted to the partnership, the IRS has ruled that the economic owner is the partner for tax purposes.[6] Although there is no authority directly on this point, such a transfer should qualify as a sale of a partnership interest for Code Sec. 743(b) purposes.

.02 Code Sec. 743(b) Adjustments—Overview

Code Sec. 743(b) serves to protect the purchasing partner from being allocated gain or loss for tax purposes when no gain or loss has been economically realized by that partner. In effect, it prevents the purchasing partner from being allocated taxable gain or loss on the subsequent disposition of partnership assets that was previously recognized by the *selling* partner on the initial transfer of the partnership interest. Under Code Sec. 743(b), the partnership computes a basis adjustment amount which is allocated among its assets, increasing or decreasing their individual bases to reflect the amount paid by the purchaser for his or her interest therein. The amount of gain, loss, depreciation, etc. reported by the partnership with

---

[1] Code Sec. 761(e). H.R. Rep. No. 801, 98th Cong., 2d Sess., 863-865 (1984).

[2] Code Sec. 2031 or 2032.

[3] Code Secs. 1014(a), 642, and 752.

[4] Code Sec. 1014(b)(6).

[5] Rev. Rul. 79-124, 1979-1 CB 224.

[6] Rev. Rul. 77-137, 1977-1 CB 178.

respect to future use or disposition is computed taking these basis adjustments into account.

The total amount of the adjustment to all the partnership property is the difference between the incoming partner's basis for his or her partnership interest and that partner's share of the adjusted basis of the partnership property at the time of purchase. If the purchasing partner's initial adjusted basis in the partnership interest is greater than his or her share of the adjusted basis of partnership assets, the total basis adjustment to the partnership assets is upward in an amount equal to the excess. Conversely, the adjustment is downward where the reverse is true. The adjustment thus results in the partner's adjusted basis in his or her partnership interest being equal to the adjusted basis of his or her share of the partnership assets. The total adjustment is then allocated among the partnership properties in accordance with rules contained in Code Sec. 755.

Code Sec. 743(b) adjustments may affect the timing, and occasionally the character, of income or loss to be recognized by the incoming partner, but they generally will not affect the total amount of income or loss ultimately reported by the partner. For example, a partner purchasing an interest in a partnership that has not made (and does not make) an election under Code Sec. 754 will not be allocated a step-up (or step-down) in the basis of partnership assets. As a result, such partner will be allocated lesser depreciation deduction (assuming appreciation in partnership property) over the operating life of the partnership's depreciable property. One result of these reduced depreciation allocations, however, is that the partner's outside basis in his or her partnership interest will be higher than it would be had the partner received larger depreciation allocations. The partner will therefore recognize a lower gain when (s)he later disposes of the interest in the partnership.

> **Example 13-1:** J purchases a 20 percent interest in Buffalo Partners, a general partnership. At the date of purchase, the partnership had the following assets:

	Tax Basis	*FMV*
Cash	$100	$100
Depreciable property	300	500
Other assets	400	400
	$800	$1,000

J paid $200 for her 20 percent interest in the partnership. Her share of the tax basis of the partnership's assets is $160 (20% of $800). Thus, if the partnership has a Code Sec. 754 election in effect (or chooses to make one), it will increase its tax basis in its assets by $40 ($200 purchase price less $160 share of "inside" basis). As will be discussed later in this chapter, this increase will be allocated entirely to the partnership's depreciable property (its only appreciated asset) and will be made solely for J's benefit.

Assume the partnership breaks even before depreciation every year. If the partnership does *not* increase its tax basis in its depreciable property, J will be allocated $60 of depreciation expense over the operating life of the partnership's depreciable property (20% of $300). Her basis in her partnership interest at the end of this period will be $140 ($200 initial tax basis less $60 depreciation allocations). If she subsequently sells the interest for $250, she will recognize a taxable gain of $110. Her net gain from the investment is $50 and her total recognized income is also $50 ($110 gain on sale less $60 depreciation deductions).

Compare these results to those that would arise if the partnership had a Code Sec. 754 election in effect (or chose to make one). If the partnership increases its basis in the depreciable property by $40 under §743(b), this increase will be made solely for J's benefit. Over the operating life of the depreciable property, she will be allocated depreciation deductions of $100 ($60 attributable to the partnership's existing basis in the depreciable property, plus the $40 basis adjustment). These deductions will reduce her tax basis in the partnership interest to $100 (original purchase price of $200 less $100 in depreciation allocations). If she sells that interest for $250, she will recognize a taxable gain of $150. Her net gain will still be $50—the $150 gain on sale of the interest, less the $100 in depreciation deductions claimed over the operating life of the depreciable assets. The basis adjustment under Code Sec. 743(b) changes the timing and character of J's income or gain from Buffalo Partners, but not the total amount ultimately reported.

The amount of income the partner ultimately receives is usually affected only if the partner dies before selling his or her partnership interest. In such an event, the partner's heirs may receive a "stepped-up" basis in the partnership interest under Code Sec. 1014 that is equal to the fair market value of the partnership interest at the date of the partner's death, or at the alternative valuation date plus his or her share of the partnership's debt. Nobody is required to include in income the additional amount by which the adjusted basis in the partnership interest would have been reduced, owing to the Code Sec. 743(b) adjustment.

.03 Partnerships with "Substantial Built-in Loss" Immediately Following Transfer of an Interest

Basis adjustments under Code Sec. 743(b) are triggered by the sale or transfer of an interest in a partnership in two circumstances:

1. The partnership makes an election under Code Sec. 754 (or has such an election in effect at the date of the transfer); or

2. The partnership has a "substantial built-in loss" immediately following the transfer.

A partnership has a substantial built-in loss if, immediately following the transfer of an interest in the partnership, the adjusted basis of partnership property exceeds by more than $250,000 the fair market value of such property.[7] In such cases, the partnership is required to adjust its basis in its assets under Code Sec. 743(b) even if no Code Sec. 754 election has been made.

---

[7] Code Sec. 743(d).

Exception for "securitization" partnerships. Code Sec. 743(f) provides that the built-in loss rules do not apply to "securitization partnerships." Thus, unless these partnerships have a Code Sec. 754 election in effect (or make one), no adjustment to the basis of partnership assets is required under Code Sec. 743(b) following the sale or transfer of a partnership interest.

A "securitization partnership" is defined as any partnership whose sole business activity "is to issue securities which provide for a fixed principal (or similar) amount and which are primarily serviced by the cash flows of a discrete pool (either fixed or revolving) of receivables or other financial assets that by their terms convert into cash in a finite period, but only if the sponsor of the pool reasonably believes that the receivables and other financial assets comprising the pool are not acquired so as to be disposed of."[8]

Special rules for electing investment partnerships. Eligible investment partnerships can elect to be treated as if they do not have substantial built-in losses following the sale or transfer of a partnership interest. If an eligible partnership so elects, it will not be required to adjust its basis in partnership property following the sale of an interest.[9] However, when the partnership subsequently disposes of depreciated securities, the transferee partner (the purchaser) will only be allowed to deduct his or her share of such losses to the extent that they exceed the loss recognized by the transferor, including any prior transferor, on the sale or transfer of the partnership interest.[10] Disallowed losses under this provision do not reduce the transferee partner's basis in his or her partnership interest.[11] These provisions apply without regard to whether or not the sale or transfer of the partnership interest results in a technical termination of the partnership under Code Sec. 708(b)(1)(B).

In computing the amount of the loss recognized by the transferor partner, and thus the amount of the transferee partner's share of subsequent partnership losses which is disallowed, Code Sec. 743(e)(5) allows adjustment for "step-downs" in basis under Code Sec. 732(a)(2) on property distributed to the transferee partner following his or her acquisition of the partnership interest. To the extent that the transferee partner's basis in property distributed to him or her by the partnership is lower than the basis of such property in the partnership's hands, the "built-in" loss associated with the earlier acquisition of the partnership interest is reduced.

> ***Example 13-2:*** GDF Partners is an investment partnership with a depreciated portfolio. *G*, a one-fifth partner, has a tax basis in his partnership interest of $250,000. He sells it to *K* for $175,000, recognizing a ($75,000) capital loss. This loss represents 20% of the partnership's $350,000 unrealized loss inherent in its investment portfolio. The partnership does not have a Code Sec. 754 election in effect, and elects under Code Sec. 743(e)(5) not to adjust its basis in its assets to reflect the loss recognized by *G*. *K* will take a $175,000 tax basis in the newly acquired partnership interest. Assume that the partnership subsequently sells securities with a tax basis of $500,000 for $300,000, recognizing a

---

[8] Code Sec. 743(f)(2).
[9] Code Sec. 743(e)(1).

[10] Code Sec. 743(e)(2).
[11] Code Sec. 743(e)(3).

($200,000) loss on the transaction. *K*'s 20% share of this loss is ($40,000). This loss is not deductible by *K*, and does not reduce her basis in the partnership interest.

Comment: The limitation of Code Sec. 743(e) is applied to the transferee partner's share of the gross amount of loss recognized by the partnership on any subsequent sale of depreciated assets (to the extent of the loss previously recognized by the transferor partner on sale of the partnership interest). If the partnership sells some assets for a loss, and other assets for a gain, the transferee partner must report his or her share of the gain, but cannot deduct his or her share of the loss.[12]

Only eligible investment partnerships may make the election under Code Sec. 743(e). To be eligible, a partnership must satisfy the following criteria:

- The partnership would be an investment company under section 3(a)(1)(A) of the Investment Company Act of 1940 but for an exemption under paragraph (1) or (7) of section 3(c) of such Act;

- The partnership has never been engaged in a trade or business;

- The partnership holds substantially all of its assets for investment;

- At least 95 percent of the assets contributed to such partnership consist of money;

- No assets contributed to such partnership had an adjusted basis in excess of fair market value at the time of contribution;

- All partnership interests of such partnership are issued by such partnership pursuant to a private offering before the date which is 24 months after the date of the first capital contribution to such partnership;

- The partnership agreement of such partnership has substantive restrictions on each partner's ability to cause a redemption of the partner's interest; and

- The partnership agreement of such partnership provides for a term that is not in excess of 15 years.

Once made, an election under Code Sec. 743(e) is irrevocable except with the consent of the Secretary.

.04 Partnerships Without Substantial Built-in Losses

If the partnership does not have a substantial built-in loss immediately after the sale or transfer of a partnership interest, no basis adjustment is required or allowed unless the partnership has a Code Sec. 754 election in effect or chooses to make one effective for the year of the transfer.

It is important to note that the basis adjustments required by both Code Sec. 743(b) and Code Sec. 734(b) are activated by a single Code Sec. 754 election, and that the taxpayer cannot limit his or her election to one section or the other.[13]

---

[12] Code Sec. 743(e)(2).

[13] Code Sec. 734(b) adjustments are discussed later in this chapter.

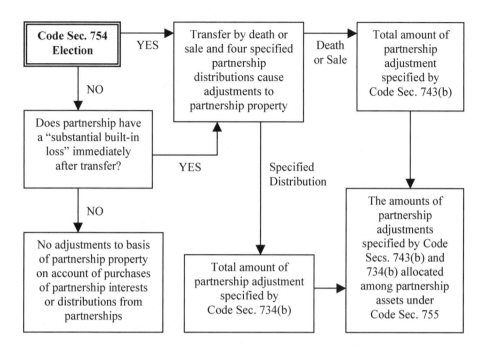

Comment: The election can only be made in a year in which a Code Sec. 743(b) transfer or a Code Sec. 734(b) distribution is made. The election cannot be made in contemplation of such a transfer or distribution in a future year.[14]

Making the election. The election is made by attaching a statement to the partnership's Form 1065, U.S. Partnership Return of Income, declaring a Code Sec. 754 election which includes the partnership's name, address and taxpayer identification number and is signed by any partner.[15] The election applies to all sales, exchanges, transfers upon death, and the four distributions listed in Code Sec. 734(b) until it is terminated. Since it is the partnership that makes the election, any purchasing partner, in order to ensure the benefits of the Code Sec. 743(b) adjustment, should have the partnership amend its partnership agreement to include an obligation to make such an election. It may be prudent to require the partnership to allow the affected partner to mail the partnership's Form 1065 after inspecting the election and getting a power of attorney to make the election on behalf of the partnership if it is not properly executed. However, the other partners should obtain an agreement on the part of the new partner to bear any additional accounting expenses.

Observation: This could provide for some lively negotiation as the new partner may then be obligated to pay the extra expenses to account for all future Code Sec. 743(b) and 734(b) adjustments. This is because future adjustments are required for most transfers of partnership interests and some distributions. When a Code Sec. 754 election is the result of the demands of an

---

[14] Reg. § 1.754-1(b)(1).   [15] Reg. § 1.754-1(b).

incoming partner, that partner is the cause of all future adjustments the partnership is required to make. A new incoming partner may not be willing to accept responsibility for paying for the partnership's accounting for the new adjustments required by his or her purchase. This would be especially true if the adjustment is negative or immaterial in amount. Of course, the continuing partners receive no tax benefit or detriment derived from a Code Sec. 743(b) adjustment. It may be a reasonable compromise to require that the incoming partner who initiates the Code Sec. 754 election pay for the accounting for his adjustment, negative adjustments and *de minimis* adjustments.

Deadline for election. As to the timing of the Code Sec. 754 election, the regulations require that it be made with a "timely return for the taxable year during which the distribution or transfer occurs."[16] This is interpreted to include extensions. An application for revocation of an election must be filed no later than 30 days after the close of the partnership's taxable year with respect to which the election is intended to take effect.

The IRS has the general power to grant an extension beyond the deadline for filing elections when:[17]

- The filing deadline is not expressly provided by statute;[18]
- The request for extension is filed before the time fixed by regulations or within such time after the time fixed by regulations that the IRS considers reasonable under the circumstances;[19] and
- It is shown to the IRS's satisfaction that granting the extension would not jeopardize the interests of the government.[20]

Taxpayers are granted an automatic 12-month extension of time in which to file the election under Code Sec. 754 provided they take corrective action within that 12-month extension period.[21] No request for a private letter ruling is required to obtain the extension.[22] The partnership need merely file an amended or original return for the year the election should have been made, attaching the appropriate statement making the election.[23]

An extension of time to make the election should be available even after the partnership terminates under Code Sec. 708. For example, where an equal partner of a two-man partnership died on January 1, and no election was filed on the partnership's return for the year ending on December 31 of the same year, the election could be filed for the January 1 transfer, even though the estate of the deceased partner sold its interest to the other partner, thereby terminating the partnership[24]

Revoking the election. An application for revocation of a Code Sec. 754 election must, as previously stated, be filed no later than 30 days after the close of

---

[16] Reg. § 1.754-1(b)(1).
[17] Reg. § 301.9100-1(a).
[18] Reg. § 301.9100-1(a)(1).
[19] Reg. § 301.9100-1(a)(2).
[20] Reg. § 301.9100-1(a)(3).
[21] Reg. § 301.9100-2T(a)(2).

[22] Accordingly, the partnership does not have to pay a user fee or any other type of fee to take advantage of the extension of time. Rev. Proc. 92-85, § 4.03, 1992-2 CB 490, obsoleted by Treasury Decision 8680 (implementing Regs. § 301.9100-1T through 3T).
[23] Reg. § 301.9100-2T(c).
[24] Rev. Rul. 86-139, 1986-2 CB 95.

the partnership's taxable year with respect to which the election is intended to take effect. The approval of a District Director of the IRS is needed for a revocation of the Code Sec. 754 election.[25] The regulations suggest the following acceptable reasons for revocation:

1. A change in the nature of partnership trade or business.

2. A substantial increase in assets.

3. A change in the nature of assets.

4. An increasing administrative burden.

A potential decrease in the basis of partnership assets, owing to the effect of the Code Sec. 754 election, is *not* a sufficient reason for permission for a revocation to be granted.

Termination of the partnership under Code Sec. 708 terminates the "old" partnership's Code Sec. 754 election because the "new" partnership is treated as a separate and distinct entity for tax purposes from the partnership that made the election.

In light of the nature of the Code Sec. 743 and 734 adjustments, it is important, before the election is made, to consider the cost of accounting for the adjustment and the possibility that the continued existence of a Code Sec. 754 election may require a future downward adjustment in basis. Furthermore, record keeping problems can be significant.

.05 Making the Code Sec. 743(b) Adjustment

Total amount of Code Sec. 743(b) adjustment. The total basis adjustment which must be made by the partnership is equal to the difference between the initial adjusted basis[26] of the incoming partner's interest in the partnership and that partner's proportionate share of the adjusted basis to the partnership of the partnership's property.[27] In general, this difference (and the amount of the adjustment) will be the same as the income the selling partner would have earned if the partnership had sold all of its assets for their fair market value at the date of the sale of the partnership interest.

Alternatively, one can compute the incoming partner's share of the adjusted basis of partnership property as the sum of that partner's interest in the partnership's previously taxed capital, plus his or her share of partnership liabilities. Then the total basis adjustment will be the difference between the incoming partner's basis in the partnership interest and his or her share of the adjusted basis of partnership property.

Generally, an incoming partner's interest in the partnership's previously taxed capital[28] is equal to:

1. The amount of cash that the incoming partner would receive if the partnership sold all of its assets for cash and liquidated;[29] increased by

---

[25] Reg. § 1.754-1(c).

[26] Determined by applying the rules of Code Sec. 742.

[27] Reg. § 1.743-1(b).

[28] To the extent attributable to the acquired partnership interest.

[29] Reg. § 1.743-1(d)(2).

2. The amount of tax loss[30] that would be allocated to the transferee from the hypothetical transaction; or decreased by

3. The amount of tax gain[31] that would be allocated to the transferee from the hypothetical transaction.

Example 13-3: *A* is a member of the ABC Partnership in which the partners have equal interests in capital and profits. The partnership has made an election under Code Sec. 754. *A* sells her interest to *T* for $22,000. The balance sheet of the partnership at the date of sale shows the following:

Assets	*Adjusted Basis*	*FMV*
Cash	$5,000	$5,000
Accounts receivable	10,000	10,000
Inventory................................	20,000	21,000
Depreciable assets	20,000	40,000
Total	*$55,000*	*$76,000*

Liabilities and Capital		
Liabilities..............................	$10,000	$10,000
Capital		
A.......................................	15,000	22,000
B.......................................	15,000	22,000
C.......................................	15,000	22,000
Total	*$55,000*	*$76,000*

The amount of the basis adjustment under Code Sec. 743(b) is the difference between the basis of *T*'s interest in the partnership and *T*'s share of the adjusted basis to the partnership of the partnership's property. The income *A* would have recognized on the sale of all of the assets of the partnership would have been $76,000 − $55,000 = $21,000 ÷ 3 partners = $7,000. As you will see below, this is the same as the adjustment arrived at under the calculation suggested by the regulations.

Under Code Sec. 742 *T*'s tax basis in the newly acquired partnership interest is $25,333.[32] *T*'s interest in the partnership's previously taxed capital is equal to his $15,000 capital balance on the partnership's tax balance sheet[33] plus his $3,333 share of partnership liabilities, or $18,333.

---

[30] Including any remedial allocations under Reg. § 1.704-3(d).

[31] *Id.*

[32] $22,000 (cash paid by income Partner *T* to outgoing Partner *A*) plus $3,333 (Partner *T*'s share of partnership liabilities).

[33] In the absence of a basis adjustment under Code Sec. 743(b), the partnership is unaffected by T's acquisition of A's interest; T merely assumes A's capital balances on both the book and tax balance sheets.

¶1301.05

The amount of the basis adjustment under Code Sec. 743(b) to partnership property, therefore, is $7,000. Note that this is also equal to the gain that would have been recognized by partner *A* if there had been a sale of all of the partnership assets immediately before the sale of the partnership interest.

T's basis in his partnership interest	$25,333
T's share of the adjusted basis of the partnership property	(18,333)
T's total Code Sec. 743(b) adjustment	*$7,000*

Where the selling partner previously contributed built-in gain property to the partnership, the purchasing partner will be treated as the contributing partner for purposes of Code Sec 704(c). These provisions must be taken into account in measuring the purchasing partner's share of the basis of partnership assets.

Example 13-4: *S*, *B*, and *C* form the SBC Partnership, to which *S* contributes land with a fair market value of $1,000 and an adjusted basis to *S* of $400, and *B* and *C* each contribute $1,000 cash. Each partner has $1,000 credited to him on the books of the partnership as his capital contribution. The partners share in profits equally.

The SBC Partnership has the following initial balance sheets:

Assets	*Basis*	*FMV*
Cash	$2,000	$2,000
Land	400	1,000
	$2,400	$3,000
Liabilities.................................	$ 0	$ 0
Capital		
S......................................	$400	$1,000
B......................................	1,000	1,000
C......................................	1,000	1,000
Total	$2,400	$3,000

During the partnership's first taxable year, the land appreciates in value to $1,300. *S* sells her one-third interest in the partnership to *P* for $1,100 when an election under Code Sec. 754 is in effect. The amount of tax gain that would be allocated to *S* from a cash sale of the partnership's assets is $700 ($600 Code Sec. 704(c) built-in gain plus one-third of the additional gain). Thus, *P*'s share of the inside basis of partnership property is only $400 ($1,100, the amount of cash *P* would receive if ABC liquidated immediately after the cash sale of its assets, decreased by $700, *P*'s share of gain from a cash sale of the partnership's assets). The amount of *P*'s basis adjustment under Code Sec. 743(b) to partnership property is $700 (the excess of $1,100, *P*'s cost basis for the interest, over $400, *P*'s share of the adjusted basis to the partnership of partnership property). Note that this is the same as the income *S* would have recognized had the assets of the partnership been sold immediately before the sale of the partnership interest.

In cases where there has been more than one transfer of a partnership interest, a transferee's basis adjustment is determined without regard to any prior transferee's basis adjustment. In the case of a gift of an interest in a partnership, the donor is treated as transferring, and the donee as receiving, that portion of the basis adjustment attributable to the gifted partnership interest.

> **Example 13-5:** *A*, *B*, and *C* form the ABC Partnership. *A* and *B* each contribute $1,000 cash, and *C* contributes land with a basis and fair market value of $1,000.

The ABC Partnership has the following initial balance sheet:

Assets	Basis	FMV
Cash	$2,000	$2,000
Land	1,000	1,000
	$3,000	$3,000
Liabilities	$0	$0
Capital		
A	1,000	1,000
B	1,000	1,000
C	1,000	1,000
Total	$3,000	$3,000

> When the land has appreciated in value to $1,300, *C* sells her interest to *D* for $1,100 (one-third of $3,300, the fair market value of the partnership property). An election under Code Sec. 754 is in effect; therefore, *D* has a basis adjustment under Code Sec. 743(b) of $100.

> After the land has further appreciated in value to $1,600, *D* sells his interest to *E* for $1,200 (one-third of $3,600, the fair market value of the partnership property). *E* has a basis adjustment under Code Sec. 743(b) of $200. This amount is determined without regard to any basis adjustment under Code Sec. 743(b) that *D* may have had in the partnership assets.

Allocating the Code Sec. 743(b) adjustment between Code Sec. 1221/1231 assets and ordinary income assets. The total basis adjustment determined under Code Sec. 743(b) is allocated among the partnership's assets under Code Sec. 755. The regulations, effective for transfers of partnership interests on or after December 15, 1999, first allocate the total Code Sec. 743(b)

¶1301.05

adjustment between the two classes of property described in Code Sec. 755(b). These classes of partnership property are:[34]

1. Capital gain property;[35] and

2. Ordinary income property.[36]

The basis adjustment allocated to each class is then allocated among the items within each class.

The portion of the basis adjustment allocated to ordinary income property would be equal to the total income, gain and loss (including remedial allocations) that would be allocated to the transferee upon the sale of the partnership's ordinary income property if the partnership sold all its assets in a fully taxable transaction.[37] The basis adjustment to capital gain property is equal to the total adjustment less the amount allocated to ordinary income property. If the basis adjustment to capital gain property is negative, it cannot exceed the partnership's basis[38] in capital gain property.[39] Any excess is applied to reduce the basis of ordinary income property. This allocation method has the effect of treating the capital asset class as the spillover category that absorbs basis adjustments in excess of those that must be allocated to the ordinary income class of assets.

> **Example 13-6:** A and B form equal AB Partnership. A and B each contribute $1,000 cash which the partnership uses to purchase land and a building which are Code Sec. 1231 assets and wine and cheese which are inventory assets. After one year, A sells her partnership interest to T for $1,200. The net amount of T's basis adjustment is $200. However, it is possible that the partnership would be required to make a positive adjustment to the basis of one class of assets in an amount greater than $200, offset by a negative basis adjustment to the other class.
>
> For example, assume that immediately after the transfer of the partnership interest to T, the adjusted basis and fair market value of AB Partnership's assets are as follows:

Assets	Adjusted Basis	FMV	Built-in Gain/ (Loss)	T's Share of Gain/ (Loss)
Capital Gain Property:				
Building	$500	$1,000	$500	$250
Land	500	500	0	0
	$1,000	*$1,500*	*$500*	*$250*

---

[34] Reg. § 1.755-1(a).

[35] Capital assets and Code Sec. 1231(b) property.

[36] All property which is not capital gain property or Code Sec. 1231(b) property. Unrealized receivables as defined by Code Sec. 751(c) are considered separate ordinary income property. For this purpose, depreciation recapture under Code Secs. 1245 and 1250 is considered to be a zero basis unrealized receivable with a value equal to the built-in gain.

[37] Reg. § 1.755-1(b)(2). The regulations refer to this deemed sale of all partnership assets as the "hypothetical transaction." Reg. § 1.755-1(b)(1)(ii).

[38] Or in the case of property subject to the remedial allocation method, the transferee's share of any remedial loss from the hypothetical transaction under Reg. § 1.704-3(d).

[39] Reg. § 1.755-1(b)(2)(i).

Assets	Adjusted Basis	FMV	Built-in Gain/ (Loss)	T's Share of Gain/ (Loss)
Ordinary Income Property:				
Wine	$500	$600	$100	$50
Cheese..............	500	300	(200)	(100)
	$1,000	$900	$(100)	$(50)
Total..................	$2,000	$2,400	$ 400	$ 200

If, immediately after the transfer of the partnership interest to *T*, the ABC Partnership sold all of its assets in a fully taxable transaction at fair market value, *T* would be allocated a loss of $50 from the sale of the ordinary income property. Thus, the amount of the basis adjustment to ordinary income property is $(50). The amount of the basis adjustment to capital gain property is $250 ($200, the amount of the total basis adjustment under Code Sec. 743(b), increased by the $50 negative adjustment to the basis of the ordinary income property).

Allocating the adjustment among ordinary income assets. Among ordinary income assets, the amount of the basis adjustment allocated to each item of property within the class of ordinary income property is equal to the amount of income, gain or loss (including any remedial allocations)[40] that would be allocated to the transferee from the hypothetical sale of the item. Within the class of ordinary income property, then, the purchaser's share of the basis of each item of ordinary income property is generally equal to the purchaser's share of the fair market value of each such property.[41]

Allocating the adjustment among Code Sec. 1221/1231 assets. Allocation of the basis adjustment among the different assets in the capital gain category follows a similar process: the basis adjustment to each item of property is generally equal to the amount of gain or loss that would be allocated to the purchasing partner if such property were immediately sold by the partnership for its fair market value. Recall, however, that the total basis adjustment allocated to capital gain property is the residual of the total basis adjustment remaining after allocation to the ordinary income property. Thus, in cases where the purchase price of the partnership interest was less than the purchasing partner's share of the aggregate net value of partnership assets, the residual basis adjustment allocated to the partnership's capital gain property will be less than the amount of gain that would be allocated to the purchasing partner upon a hypothetical sale of the partnership's

---

[40] Reg. § 1.704-3(d).

[41] Where the positive allocation to the ordinary class of assets exceeds the total basis adjustment, a negative adjustment to the basis of capital gain property will be necessary. The regulations specifically allow for this situation. However, the adjusted basis of capital gain assets may not be reduced below zero. In rare and unusual circumstances, a negative adjustment to capital gain prop-

erty may exceed the basis of such property. In such cases, the regulations provide that the excess negative adjustment to the capital asset class (i.e., the portion in excess of the tax basis of those assets) must be subtracted from the positive adjustment to the ordinary class of assets. This subtraction is allocated among the assets in the ordinary income class of assets in proportion to their relative fair market values. Reg. § 1.755-1(b)(3)(i).

assets. In such cases, the shortfall is allocated among the partnership's capital gain properties in proportion to the fair market values of those assets.[42]

Example 13-7: *A* and *B* form equal AB Partnership. *A* contributes $50,000 cash and Blackacre, a capital asset with a fair market value of $50,000 and an adjusted tax basis of $25,000. *B* contributes $100,000. The AB Partnership uses the cash to purchase Whiteacre, which is a capital asset, and wine and cheese, which are inventory assets. After a year, *A* sells her interest in the AB Partnership to *T* for $120,000. At the time of the transfer, *A*'s share of the partnership's basis in partnership assets is $75,000. Therefore, *T* receives a $45,000 basis adjustment.

Immediately after the transfer of the partnership interest to *T*, the adjusted basis and fair market value of the AB Partnership's assets are as follows:

Assets	Adjusted Basis	FMV	Built-in Gain/ (Loss)	T's Share of Gain/ (Loss)
Capital Gain Property:				
Blackacre	$25,000	$75,000	$50,000	$37,500 *
Whiteacre	100,000	117,500	17,500	8,750
	$125,000	$192,500	$67,500	$46,250
Ordinary Income Property:				
Wine	$40,000	$45,000	$5,000	$2,500
Cheese	10,000	2,500	(7,500)	(3,750)
	$50,000	$47,500	$2,500	($1,250)
Total	$175,000	$240,000	$65,000	$45,000

*$25,000 Code Sec. 704(c) gain + $12,500 share of post-contribution gain.

Allocating the $45,000 Code Sec. 743(b) Adjustment Between Classes of Partnership Property*

Ordinary Income Assets:

Wine

Amount Realized	$45,000
Adjusted basis	(40,000)
Gain	*$5,000*

Cheese

Amount Realized	$2,500
Adjusted Basis	(10,000)
Loss	*$(7,500)*

---

[42] Reg. § 1.755-1(b)(3)(ii).

Net loss from sale of the ordinary income property		*$(2,500)*
T's share of ordinary loss (50%)		$(1,250)
Capital Gain Property:		
Blackacre		
Amount Realized	$75,000	
Adjusted basis	(25,000)	
Gain		*$50,000*
Whiteacre		
Amount Realized	$117,500	
Adjusted Basis	(100,000)	
Gain		*$17,500*
Net gain from sale of the capital gain property		*$67,500*
T's share of Code Sec. 704(c) built-in gain		$25,000
Fifty percent of the remainder		
"50% × ($67,500 – $25,000)"		21,250
T's share of capital gain		*$46,250*

*Deemed fair market value sale of all partnership assets.

The amount of the basis adjustment that is allocated to ordinary income property is equal to $(1,250) (the amount of the loss allocated to *T* from the hypothetical sale of the ordinary income property).

The amount of the basis adjustment that is allocated to capital gain property is equal to $46,250 (the amount of the total basis adjustment increased by the ($1,250) negative adjustment to the basis of the ordinary income property).

Example 13-8: Assume the same facts as Example 13-7 above. Of the $45,000 basis adjustment, $46,250 was allocated to capital gain property. The amount allocated to ordinary income property was $(1,250).

Blackacre is a capital gain asset, and *T* would be allocated $37,500 from the sale of Blackacre in the hypothetical transaction. Therefore, the amount of the adjustment to Blackacre is $37,500.

Whiteacre is a capital gain asset, and *T* would be allocated $8,750 from the sale of Whiteacre in the hypothetical transaction. Therefore, the amount of the adjustment to Whiteacre is $8,750.

The wine is ordinary income property, and *T* would be allocated $2,500 from the sale of the wine in the hypothetical transaction. Therefore, the amount of the adjustment to the wine is $2,500.

The cheese is ordinary income property, and T would be allocated $(3,750) from the sale of the cheese in the hypothetical transaction. Therefore, the amount of the adjustment to the cheese is $(3,750).

The allocation is more complex when the basis adjustment to a class of assets differs from the amount of gain or loss the acquiring partner would be allocated from the hypothetical sale of the assets in that class.

Example 13-9: Assume the same facts as Example 13-8 above, except that A sold her interest in the AB Partnership to T for $110,000 rather than $120,000. T, therefore, receives a basis adjustment under Code Sec. 743(b) of $35,000, rather than $45,000. Of the $35,000 basis adjustment, $(1,250) is allocated to ordinary income property, and $36,250 is allocated to capital gain property.

The AB Partnership allocates the $36,250 basis adjustment to capital gain property among assets in this class as follows:

To Blackacre

$37,500	Partner T's share of Blackacre's built-in gain before the adjustment
(3,896)	[$10,000 × $75,000 ÷ $192,500]*
$33,602	Adjustment to Blackacre

To Whiteacre

$8,750	Partner T's share of Whiteacre's gain before the adjustment
(6,104)	$10,000 × $117,500 ÷ $192,500**
$2,646	Adjustment to Whiteacre

*The total gain built into all capital gain property after the adjustment ($10,000), multiplied by the value of Blackacre ($75,000) divided by the value of all capital gain property ($192,500).

**The total gain built into all capital gain property after the adjustment ($10,000), multiplied by the value of Whiteacre ($117,500) divided by the value of all capital gain property ($192,500).

Income in respect of a decedent. Where a partnership interest is transferred as a result of the death of a partner, under Code Sec. 1014(c) the transferee's basis in its partnership interest is not adjusted for that portion of the interest, if any, which is attributable to items representing income in respect of a decedent under Code Sec. 691.[43] If a partnership interest is transferred as a result of the death of a partner, and the partnership holds assets representing income in respect of a decedent, no adjustment under Code Sec. 743(b) can be made to the basis of these assets.[44]

Example 13-10: A and B are equal partners in personal service AB Partnership. As a result of B's death, B's partnership interest is transferred to

---

[43] Reg. § 1.742-1.   [44] *See* Reg. § 1.743-1(b).

T. At the date of B's death, the AB Partnership's tax basis and fair market value balance sheets (reflecting a cash receipts and disbursements method of accounting) are as follows:

Assets	**Basis**	**FMV**
Capital Asset	$2,000	$5,000
Unrealized Receivables	0	15,000
	$2,000	*$20,000*

Capital		
A	$1,000	$10,000
B	1,000	10,000
	$2,000	*$20,000*

None of the assets owned by the AB Partnership is Code Sec. 704(c) property, and the capital asset is nondepreciable. The fair market value of *T*'s partnership interest on the applicable date of valuation set forth in Code Sec. 1014 is $10,000. Of this amount, $2,500 is attributable to *T*'s 50% share of the partnership's capital asset, and $7,500 is attributable to *T*'s 50% share of the partnership's unrealized receivables. The partnership's unrealized receivables represent income in respect of a decedent. Accordingly, under Code Sec. 1014(c), *T*'s basis in its partnership interest is not adjusted for that portion of the interest which is attributable to the unrealized receivables. Therefore, *T*'s basis in her partnership interest is $2,500.

At the time of the transfer, *B*'s share of the partnership's basis in partnership assets is $1,000. Accordingly, *T* receives a $1,500 basis adjustment under Code Sec. 743(b). The entire basis adjustment is allocated to the partnership's capital asset.

Special rules for miscellaneous transfers. Special rules apply to the allocation of Code Sec. 743(b) adjustments resulting from transferred basis exchanges, such as partnership interests contributed to corporations and other partnerships.[45] These special rules generally are modeled on the rules for allocating basis adjustments under Code Sec. 734(b). The regulations do not contain a specific anti-abuse rule regarding the special basis allocation rules which are applicable to such transfers. However, there may be situations where taxpayers will attempt to undertake abusive transactions using these special rules. For instance, a partner could acquire a partnership interest during a year in which no Code Sec. 754 election is in effect, and then (in a related transaction) contribute the property to a wholly-owned corporation in order to take advantage of the basis allocation rules applicable to transferred basis exchanges. In appropriate situations, the IRS may attack such

---

[45] Reg. § 1.755-1(b)(5).

abusive transactions under a variety of judicial doctrines, including substance over form or step transactions, or under Reg. § 1.701-2.

Code Sec. 743(b) adjustment made for benefit of transferee partner only. The basis adjustment constitutes an adjustment to the basis of partnership property with respect to the transferee only. No adjustment is made to the common basis of partnership property. Thus, for purposes of calculating income, deduction, gain, and loss, the transferee will have a special basis for those partnership properties, the bases of which are adjusted under Code Sec. 743(b). The adjustment to the basis of partnership property under Code Sec. 743(b) has no effect on the partnership's computation of any partnership item under Code Sec. 703.

The partnership first computes its partnership items of income, deduction, gain or loss at the partnership level under Code Sec. 703. It then allocates these items among the partners, including the transferee, in accordance with Code Sec. 704, and adjusts the partners' capital accounts accordingly. The partnership then adjusts the transferee's distributive share of the items of partnership income, deduction, gain, or loss to reflect the effects of the transferee's basis adjustment under Code Sec. 743(b). These adjustments to the transferee's distributive shares must be reflected on Schedules K and K-1 of the partnership tax return (Form 1065, U.S. Partnership Return of Income). These adjustments to the transferee's distributive shares do not affect the transferee's book capital account.[46]

Sale of property with Code Sec. 743(b) basis adjustment. The amount of a transferee's income, gain, or loss from the sale or exchange of a partnership asset in which the transferee has a basis adjustment is equal to:

- The transferee's share of the partnership's common gain or loss from the sale of the asset;[47]

- Minus the amount of the transferee's positive basis adjustment for the partnership asset (adjusted for previously claimed deductions for depreciation or other cost recovery); or

- Plus the amount of the transferee's negative basis adjustment for the partnership asset.[48]

> **Example 13-11:** *Negative Code Sec. 743(b) adjustments—Code Sec. 704(c) property sold for a tax loss.* A and B form the equal AB Partnership. A contributes nondepreciable property with a fair market value of $50 and an adjusted tax basis of $100. The AB Partnership will use the traditional allocation method under Reg. § 1.704-3(b). B contributes $50 cash.

---

[46] Reg. § 1.743-1(j)(2).). For this purpose, book capital accounts are those maintained under Reg. § 1.704-1(b)(2)(iv). *See also* Reg. § 1.704-1(b)(2)(iv)(m)(2).

[47] Including any remedial allocations under Reg. § 1.704-3(d).

[48] Determined by taking into the account the recovery of the basis adjustment under Reg. § 1.743-1(j)(4)(ii)(B).

Assets	Basis	FMV
Cash	$50	$50
Property	100	50
	$150	$100
Liabilities................................	$0	$0
Capital		
A.....................................	100	50
B.....................................	50	50
	$150	$100

A sells his interest to T for $50. The AB Partnership has an election in effect to adjust the basis of partnership property under Code Sec. 754. T receives a negative $50 basis adjustment under Code Sec. 743(b) that, under Code Sec. 755, is allocated to the nondepreciable property. The AB Partnership then sells the property for $60. The AB Partnership recognizes a book gain of $10 (allocated equally between T and B) and a tax loss of $40. Because Partner T steps into the shoes of Partner A who contributed the built-in loss property, Partner T will receive an allocation of $40 of tax loss under the principles of Code Sec. 704(c). However, because T has a negative $50 basis adjustment in the nondepreciable property, T recognizes a $10 gain from the sale of the partnership's property. The calculations are as follows:

Partnership's Gain on Sale of Property

	Tax	Book
Amount realized...........................	$60	$60
Adjusted basis	(100)	(50)
The AB Partnership's Gain/(Loss)	$(40)	$10

Partner T's share of tax loss:

Before Code Sec. 743(b) adjustment	$40
Code Sec. 743(b) adjustment................	(50)
Partner T's recognized Gain/(Loss)	$10

Comment: Note that partner T is recognizing the entire gain in the above example. This is a consequence of the partnership's use of the traditional method under the Code Sec. 704(c) regulations. If the partnership used the remedial allocations method, partners B and T would each recognize $5 gain on the transaction—fifty percent (each) of the appreciation in value of the partnership's property occurring after original partner A sold her interest to T.

¶1301.05

Example 13-12: Positive Code Sec. 743(b) adjustments—Code Sec. 704(c) property sold for a tax gain. A and B form the equal AB Partnership. A contributes nondepreciable property with a fair market value of $100 and an adjusted tax basis of $50. B contributes $100 cash. The AB Partnership will use the traditional allocation method under Reg. § 1.704-3(b).

Assets	*Basis*	*FMV*
Cash	$100	$100
Property	50	100
	$150	$200
Liabilities..............................	$ 0	$ 0
Capital		
A.....................................	100	100
B.....................................	50	100
	$150	$200

A sells his interest to T for $100. The AB Partnership has an election in effect to adjust the basis of partnership property under Code Sec. 754. Therefore, T receives a $50 basis adjustment under Code Sec. 743(b) that, under Code Sec. 755, is allocated to the nondepreciable property. The AB Partnership then sells the nondepreciable property for $90. The AB Partnership recognizes a book loss of $10 (allocated equally between T and B) and a tax gain of $40. Because Partner T steps into the shoes of Partner A who contributed the built-in gain property, Partner T will receive an allocation of the entire $40 of tax gain under the principles of Code Sec. 704(c). However, because T has a $50 basis adjustment in the property, T recognizes a $10 loss from the partnership's sale of the property.

Gain on Sale of Property

	Tax	*Book*
Amount realized...........................	$90	$90
Adjusted basis	(50)	(100)
The AB Partnership's Gain/(Loss)	$*(40)*	$*10*
Partner T's share of tax loss:		
Before Code Sec. 743(b) adjustment	$40	
Code Sec. 743(b) adjustment................	(50)	
Partner T's Gain/(Loss)......................	$*(10)*	

Example 13-12 is the inverse of Example 13-11. Here, partner T recognizes all of the post-acquisition depreciation in value of the partnership's nondepreciable property. As in the previous example, if the partnership used the remedial allocations method to allocate its built-in gain or loss under Code Sec. 704(c), the loss would be allocated equally between partners *B* and *T*.

> **Example 13-13:** *Negative Code Sec. 743(b) adjustment and Code Sec. 704(c) property sold for a tax loss.* *A* and *B* form the equal AB Partnership. The AB Partnership will make allocations under Code Sec. 704(c) using the remedial allocation method.[49] *A* contributes nondepreciable property with a fair market value of $100 and an adjusted tax basis of $150. *B* contributes $100 cash.

Assets	Basis	FMV
Cash	$100	$100
Property	150	100
	$250	$200
Liabilities	$ 0	$ 0
Capital		
A	150	100
B	100	100
	$250	$200

A sells his partnership interest to *T* for $100. The AB Partnership has an election in effect to adjust the basis of partnership property under Code Sec. 754. *T* receives a negative $50 basis adjustment under Code Sec. 743(b) that, under Code Sec. 755, is allocated to the property. The partnership then sells the property for $120. The partnership recognizes a $20 book gain and a $30 tax loss. The book gain will be allocated equally between the partners. The entire $30 tax loss will be allocated to *T* under the principles of Code Sec. 704(c) because Partner *T* steps into the shoes of Partner *A* who contributed the built-in loss property. To match his $10 share of book gain, *B* will be allocated $10 of remedial gain, and *T* will be allocated an offsetting $10 of remedial loss. *T* was allocated a total of $40 of tax loss with respect to the property. However, because *T* has a negative $50 basis adjustment to the property, *T* recognizes a $10 gain from the partnership's sale of the property.

Gain on Sale of Property

	Tax	Book
Amount realized...........................	$120	$120
Adjusted basis	(150)	(100)
The AB Partnership's Gain/(Loss)	$(30)	$20

---

[49] Described in Reg. § 1.704-3(d).

	Tax	*Book*
Partner T's *share of tax loss:*	$(30)	
Remedial Allocation	(10)	
Code Sec. 743(b) adjustment	50	
Partner *T*'s Gain/(Loss)	*$10*	

Thus, partners *B* and *T* are each allocated $10 gain for tax purposes.

The amount of any positive basis adjustment to depreciable (or amortizable) property is depreciable (or amortizable) in the transferee's hands. Depreciation or amortization of this portion of the basis adjustment in any year is added to the transferee's distributive share of the partnership's depreciation or amortization deductions for that year. The basis adjustment is adjusted under Code Sec. 1016(a)(2) to reflect depreciation or other cost recovery.

Depreciation of Code Sec. 743(b) adjustments. Generally, if the basis of a partnership's recovery property is increased as a result of the transfer of a partnership interest, then the increased portion of the basis is taken into account as if it were newly-purchased recovery property placed in service when the transfer occurs. Consequently, any applicable recovery period and method may be used to determine the recovery allowance with respect to the increased portion of the basis. However, no change is made for purposes of determining the recovery allowance under Code Sec. 168 for the portion of the basis for which there is no increase.[50]

The one exception to the described rule above applies when a partnership elects to use the remedial allocation method[51] with respect to an item of the partnership's recovery property; in such cases, the portion of any increase in the basis of the item of the partnership's recovery property under Code Sec. 743(b) that is attributable to Code Sec. 704(c) built-in gain is recovered over the remaining recovery period for the partnership's excess book basis in the property.[52] Any remaining portion of the basis increase is recovered as described above.

> **Example 13-14:** *A, B* and *C* are equal partners in the ABC Partnership, which owns depreciable equipment with a useful life of five years. The equipment was purchased two years ago for $45,000 and is being depreciated using the straight-line method. Assume that *C* sold her interest in the partnership to *T* on January 1 of Year 3. The partnership had a Code Sec. 754 election in effect and adjusted the basis of the equipment by $4,000 with respect to *T*.
>
> For Year 3, *T* will be allocated a one-third share of depreciation with respect to the equipment. Depreciation expense for the unadjusted basis of the equipment will be $9,000 (one-fifth of the $45,000 cost of the equipment). *T*'s share of this amount will be $3,000. In addition, *T* will depreciate the $4,000 basis adjustment as if it were a newly-acquired asset with a 5-year life. This will yield additional depreciation expense of $800. *T*'s total depreciation deduction for Year 3, the year of purchase, will therefore be $3,800.[53]

[50] Reg. § 1.743-1(j)(4)(i).

[51] Reg. § 1.704-3(d).

[52] Determined in the final sentence of Reg. § 1.704-3(d)(2).

[53] Had the depreciable property been 704(c) property, and the partnership used the remedial allocations method, the Code Sec. 743(b) adjustment would be depreciated over the remaining 3-year life of the partnership's depreciable property rather than as a newly acquired asset with a 5-year useful life.

For purposes of Code Sec. 168, if the basis of an item of partnership depreciable property is decreased as the result of the transfer of an interest in the partnership, then the transferee must reduce his or her allocable share of depreciation with respect to such property to reflect the negative basis adjustment to the transferee's share of the property. That is, the "cost recovery" (depreciation or amortization) deduction with respect to the property must be reduced to reflect the basis reduction under Code Sec. 743(b). The reduction in depreciation or amortization for any year during the recovery period is equal to the product of:

1. The amount of the decrease to the item's adjusted basis (determined as of the date of the transfer); multiplied by

2. A fraction, the numerator of which is the portion of the adjusted basis of the item recovered by the partnership in that year, and the denominator of which is the adjusted basis of the item on the date of the transfer (determined prior to any basis adjustments).[54]

The amount of any negative basis adjustment allocated to an item of depreciable or amortizable property that is recovered in any year first decreases the transferee's distributive share of the partnership's depreciation or amortization deductions from that item of property for the year. If the amount of the basis adjustment recovered in any year exceeds the transferee's distributive share of the partnership's depreciation or amortization deductions from the item of property, then the transferee's distributive share of the partnership's depreciation or amortization deductions from other items of partnership property is decreased. The transferee then recognizes ordinary income to the extent of the excess, if any, of the amount of the basis adjustment recovered in any year over the transferee's distributive share of the partnership's depreciation or amortization deductions from all items of property.[55]

> ***Example 13-15:*** *J*, *D* and *R* are equal partners in the JDR Partnership. The partnership owns depreciable real estate with an original cost of $315,000 and a 31.5-year useful life. It uses the straight-line method of depreciation.
>
> In the partnership's 10th year of operations, *D* sold her one-third interest in the partnership to *Q*. The partnership had a Code Sec. 754 election in effect and was required to make a negative basis adjustment to the real estate in the amount of ($30,000). This adjustment is made solely with respect to *Q*.
>
> In the year of the purchase, the partnership's tax basis in the depreciable realty was $225,000 (original cost of $315,000 less 9 years' depreciation expense of $10,000 per year). Annual depreciation expense is $10,000. The amortization of the negative basis adjustment will therefore be $1,333.33 [(10,000/225,000) X 30,000]. This adjustment will be attributable entirely to new partner *Q*. Thus, her share of depreciation expense will be $2,000 (one-third of the partnership's 10,000 depreciation allocation less $1,333.33 amortization of the negative Code Sec. 743(b) adjustment.)

(Footnote Continued)

ship's depreciable property rather than as a newly acquired asset with a 5-year useful life.

[54] Reg. § 1.743-1(j)(4)(ii)(B).
[55] Reg. § 1.743-1(j)(4)(ii).

.06 Distribution of Property with Code Sec. 743(b) Adjustments

The consequences of distributing partnership property that is subject to a Code Sec. 743(b) basis adjustment depend partly upon to which partner the property is distributed. If the property is distributed to the partner for whom the special basis adjustment was made, that partner's basis under Code Sec. 732 will take into account the special basis adjustment.[56] If, however, the property subject to a special basis adjustment is distributed to a partner(s) other than the one for whom the adjustment was made, the special basis adjustment is shifted to property of like kind still remaining in the partnership. The Code Sec. 743(b) adjustment will continue to affect only the same partner.[57] When the interest of a partner with respect to whom a special basis adjustment is in effect is completely liquidated, the partner's entire remaining adjustments in all partnership property must be allocated to the distributed property.[58] However, the partner will have a total adjusted basis in the distributed property equal to the adjusted basis of his or her partnership interest. The total basis of the distributed property is not affected by the Code Sec. 743(b) adjustment. Property distributed in complete liquidation of a partnership interest has a total basis equal to the partner's pre-distribution basis in his or her partnership interest. This total amount is allocated among the distributed properties in a manner which takes into account their bases to the partnership, including special basis adjustments due to the Code Sec. 754 election.

> **Example 13-16:** A, B, and C are equal partners in the ABC Partnership. Each partner originally contributed $10,000 in cash, and the ABC Partnership used the contributions to purchase five nondepreciable capital assets. The ABC Partnership has no liabilities. After five years, the ABC Partnership's balance sheet appears as follows:

Assets	Basis	FMV
Property 1	$10,000	$10,000
Property 2	4,000	6,000
Property 3	6,000	6,000
Property 4	7,000	4,000
Property 5	3,000	13,000
Total	$30,000	$39,000
Capital	**Basis**	**FMV**
A	10,000	13,000
B	10,000	13,000
C	10,000	13,000
Total	$30,000	$39,000

---

[56] Reg. § 1.743-1(g)(1)(i).
[57] Reg. § 1.743-1(g)(2).
[58] Reg. § 1.743-1(g)(3).

Partner *A* sells his interest to *T* for $13,000 when the ABC Partnership has an election in effect under Code Sec. 754. *T* receives a basis adjustment under Code Sec. 743(b) in the partnership property that is equal to $3,000 (the excess of *T*'s basis in the partnership interest, $13,000, over *T*'s share of the adjusted basis to the partnership of partnership property, $10,000). The basis adjustment is allocated under Code Sec. 755, and the partnership's balance sheet appears as follows:

Assets	Adjusted Basis	FMV	Basis Adjustment
Property 1	$10,000	$10,000	$ 0.00
Property 2	4,000	6,000	666.67
Property 3	6,000	6,000	0.00
Property 4	7,000	4,000	(1,000.00)
Property 5	3,000	13,000	3,333.33
Total	*$30,000*	*$39,000*	*$3,000.00*

Capital	Adjusted Per Books	FMV	Special Basis Adjustment
T	$10,000	$13,000	$3,000
B	10,000	13,000	0
C	10,000	13,000	0
Total	*$30,000*	*$39,000*	*$3,000*

Current distribution to T. Assume that the ABC Partnership distributes Property 2 to *T* in partial liquidation of *T*'s interest in the partnership. *T* has a basis adjustment under Code Sec. 743(b) of $666.67 in the property. *T* takes the basis adjustment into account under Code Sec. 732. Therefore, *T* will have a basis in Property 2 of $4,666.67 following the distribution.

Distribution not to T. Assume instead that the ABC Partnership distributes Property 5 to **Partner** *C* in complete liquidation of *C*'s interest in the ABC Partnership. *T* has a basis adjustment under Code Sec. 743(b) of $3,333.33 in Property 5. *C* does not take *T*'s basis adjustment into account under Code Sec. 732. Therefore, the partnership's basis for purposes of Code Secs. 732 and 734 is $3,000. *T*'s $3,333.33 basis adjustment is reallocated among the remaining partnership assets under Reg. § 1.755-1(c).

Liquidating distributions to T. Assume instead that the ABC Partnership distributes Property 5 to *T* in complete liquidation of her interest in the ABC Partnership. Immediately prior to the distribution of Property 5 to *T*, the ABC Partnership must adjust the basis of the property. Therefore, immediately prior to the distribution, ABC Partnership's basis in Property 5 is equal to $6,000, which is the sum of:

¶1301.06

1. $3,000, the ABC Partnership's common basis in Property 5, plus

2. $3,333.33, *T*'s basis adjustment to Property 5, plus

3. $(333.33), the sum of *T*'s basis adjustments in Properties 2 and 4.

For purposes of Code Secs. 732 and 734, therefore, the ABC Partnership will be treated as having a basis in Property 5 equal to $6,000.

When the partner who has a special basis adjustment in partnership property receives a liquidating distribution entirely in cash, the partnership succeeds to the special basis adjustment as part of its common basis.[59] Also, where a distribution gives rise to a Code Sec. 734(b) adjustment, the Code Sec. 743(b) adjustment is used in calculating the amount of the adjustment.

.07 Transfer of Partnership Interests with Existing Code Sec. 743(b) Adjustments

Transfers by sale. A new partner who acquires his or her partnership interest from an outgoing partner, in respect of whom a Code Sec. 743(b) adjustment was in effect, does not succeed to the selling partner's basis adjustment because it does not carry over to him or her on the transfer of the partnership interest. However, unless the Code Sec. 754 election has been terminated, a new basis adjustment is calculated with reference to the new partner's purchase price for the partnership interest and the new partner's share of the partnership's common basis for its assets. A partner who sells a part of his or her partnership interest will be required to eliminate the special basis adjustment proportionately.

Contribution of property with existing Code Sec. 743(b) adjustment to another partnership. If a partnership contributes to another partnership property with respect to which a basis adjustment has been made, the basis adjustment is treated as contributed to the lower-tier partnership, regardless of whether the lower-tier partnership makes a Code Sec. 754 election. The lower tier partnership's basis in the contributed assets and the upper tier partnership's basis in the partnership interest received in the transaction are determined with reference to the basis adjustment. However, that portion of the basis of the upper tier partnership's interest in the lower tier partnership attributable to the basis adjustment must be segregated and allocated solely to the transferee partner for whom the basis adjustment was made. Similarly, that portion of the lower tier partnership's basis in its assets attributable to the basis adjustment must be segregated and allocated solely to the upper tier partnership and the transferee. A partner with a basis adjustment in property held by a partnership that terminates under Code Sec. 708(b)(1)(B) will continue to have the same basis adjustment with respect to property deemed contributed by the terminated partnership to the new partnership, regardless of whether the new partnership makes a Code Sec. 754 election.[60]

Contribution of property with existing Code Sec. 743(b) adjustment to a corporation. A corporation's adjusted tax basis in property transferred to it by a partnership

---

[59] Reg. § 1.734-2(b)(1).

[60] Reg. §§ 1.743-1(h)(1) and 1.708-1(b)(1)(iv).

in a transaction described in Code Sec. 351 is determined with reference to any basis adjustments to the property under Code Sec. 743(b).[61]

The amount of gain, if any, recognized by the partnership on a transfer of property by the partnership to a corporation in a transfer described in Code Sec. 351 is determined without reference to any basis adjustment to the transferred property under Code Sec. 743(b). The amount of gain, if any, recognized by the partnership on the transfer that is allocated to a partner with a basis adjustment in the transferred property is adjusted to reflect the partner's basis adjustment in the transferred property.[62]

The partnership's adjusted tax basis in stock received from a corporation in a transfer described in Code Sec. 351 is determined without reference to the basis adjustment in property transferred to the corporation in the Code Sec. 351 exchange. A partner with a basis adjustment in property transferred to the corporation, however, has a basis adjustment in the stock received by the partnership in the Code Sec. 351 exchange in an amount equal to the partner's basis adjustment in the transferred property, reduced by any basis adjustment that reduced the partner's gain.[63]

> **Example 13-17:** *A*, *B*, and *C* are equal partners in the ABC Partnership. The partnership's only asset, investment land, has an adjusted tax basis of $60 and a fair market value of $120. The land is a nondepreciable capital asset and is not Code Sec. 704(c) property. *A* has a basis in his partnership interest of $40, and a positive Code Sec. 743(b) adjustment of $20 in the land. In a transaction to which Code Sec. 351 applies, the ABC Partnership contributes the land to *X*, a corporation, in exchange for $15 in cash and *X* stock with a fair market value of $105.
>
> The ABC Partnership realizes $60 of gain on the transfer of the land to *X*. It recognizes only $15 of that gain under Code Sec. 351(b)(1). Of this amount, $5 is allocated to each partner. *A* must use $5 of the basis adjustment in the land to offset his share of the ABC Partnership's gain.
>
> The ABC Partnership's basis in the stock received from *X* is $60. However, *A* has a basis adjustment in the stock received by the ABC Partnership equal to $15 (his basis adjustment in the land, $20, reduced by the portion of the adjustment which reduced *A*'s gain, $5).
>
> *X*'s basis in the land equals $90.
>
> | $60 | Partnership ABC's common basis in the land |
> |---|---|
> | 15 | Gain recognized by ABC under Code Sec. 351(b)(1) |
> | 20 | *A*'s Code Sec. 743(b) adjustment |
> | (5) | Portion of *A*'s adjustment which reduced *A*'s share of the Code Sec. 351(b)(1) gain |
> | —— | |
> | *$90* | |

---

[61] Other than any basis adjustment that reduces a partner's gain under Reg. § 1.743-1(h)(2)(ii).

[62] Reg. § 1.743-1(h)(2)(ii).
[63] Reg. § 1.743-1(h)(2)(iii).

.08 Compliance Requirements Under Code Sec. 754

A partnership that adjusts the bases of partnership properties under Code Sec. 743(b) must attach a statement to the partnership return for the year of the transfer setting forth the name and taxpayer identification number of the transferee, as well as the computation of the adjustment and the partnership properties to which the adjustment has been allocated.

A transferee that acquires, by sale or exchange, an interest in a partnership with an election under Code Sec. 754 in effect for the taxable year of the transfer must notify the partnership, in writing, within 30 days of the sale or exchange. The written notice to the partnership must be signed under penalties of perjury and must include:

- The names and addresses of the transferee and (if ascertainable) of the transferor;
- The taxpayer identification numbers of the transferee and (if ascertainable) of the transferor;
- The relationship (if any) between the transferee and the transferor;
- The date of the transfer;
- The amount of any liabilities assumed or taken subject to by the transferee;
- The amount of any money, the fair market value of any other property delivered or to be delivered for the transferred interest in the partnership; and
- Any other information necessary for the partnership to compute the transferee's basis.

A transferee that acquires, on the death of a partner, an interest in a partnership with an election under Code Sec. 754 in effect for the taxable year of the transfer must notify the partnership, in writing, within one year of the death of the deceased partner. The written notice to the partnership must be signed under penalties of perjury and must include:

- The names and addresses of the deceased partner and the transferee;
- The taxpayer identification numbers of the deceased partner and the transferee;
- The relationship (if any) between the transferee and the transferor, the deceased partner's date of death;
- The date on which the transferee became the owner of the partnership interest;
- The fair market value of the partnership interest on the applicable date of valuation set forth in Code Sec. 1014; and
- The manner in which the fair market value of the partnership interest was determined.

In making the adjustments under Code Sec. 743(b) and filing any statement or return relating to such adjustments under this section, a partnership may rely on the written notice provided by a transferee to determine the transferee's basis in a partnership interest, unless any partner who has responsibility for federal income tax reporting by the partnership has knowledge of facts indicating that the statement is clearly erroneous.

A partnership is not required to make the adjustments under Code Sec. 743(b) (or any statement or return relating to those adjustments) with respect to any transfer until it has been notified of the transfer. For purposes of this section, a partnership is notified of a transfer when either:

1. The partnership receives the required written notice from the transferee; or

2. Any partner who has responsibility for federal income tax reporting by the partnership has knowledge that there has been a transfer of a partnership interest.

Comment: The current regulations make it clear that it is the partnership and not the partners who takes the Code Sec. 743 (b) adjustments into account.[64] The prior regulations were ambiguous in this respect and it was common practice for the partnership to prepare Form 1065 and Schedules K-1 without the Code Sec. 743(b) adjustment and the various partners would make the adjustments for purposes of reporting their shares of the partnership income.

If the transferee fails to provide the partnership with written notice of the transfer, the partnership must attach a statement to its return in the year that the partnership is otherwise notified of the transfer. This statement must set forth the name and taxpayer identification number (if ascertainable) of the transferee. In addition, the following statement must be prominently displayed in capital letters on the first page of the partnership's return for such year, and on the first page of any schedule or information statement relating to such transferee's share of income, credits, deductions, etc.: "RETURN FILED PURSUANT TO SECTION 1.743-1(k)(5)." The partnership is then entitled to report the transferee's share of partnership items without adjustment to reflect the transferee's basis adjustment in partnership property. If, following the filing of a return, the transferee provides the applicable written notice to the partnership, the partnership must make the adjustments necessary to adjust the basis of partnership property (as of the date of the transfer) in any amended return otherwise to be filed by the partnership or in the next annual partnership return of income to be regularly filed by the partnership. At such time, the partnership must also provide the transferee with such information as is necessary for the transferee to amend its prior returns to properly reflect the adjustment under Code Sec. 743(b).

.09 Partner-Level Code Sec. 743(b) Adjustments—Code Sec. 732(d)

Although it is the partnership that must invoke Code Secs. 743 and 734 by making a Code Sec. 754 election, Code Sec. 732(d) provides that a transferee partner, to whom a distribution of partnership property (other than money) is made within two years of the date the transferee partner acquired his or her partnership

---

[64] Reg. § 1.743-1(j)(2).

interest, can make an election to treat the adjusted basis of the distributed partnership property as if a Code Sec. 743(b) adjustment were in effect with respect to the partnership property. This adjustment is allocated among the distributed properties under the provisions of Code Sec. 755. Code Sec. 732(d), however, unlike Code Secs. 754 and 743(b), does not require the partnership to make further basis adjustments for subsequent transfers and distributions. If at the time of the purchase there would have been a positive adjustment to the partnership's property basis on behalf of the purchasing partner, the Code Sec. 732(d) election has the effect of providing the purchasing partner with a higher basis in the distributed property and a lower basis in his or her partnership interest.

> **Example 13-18:** *D* has a basis in his one-third interest in the profits, losses, and capital account of the ABD Partnership of $40,000. He bought his interest in the prior year from retiring Partner *C*. The partnership decided not to make an election under Code Sec. 754. ABD makes a current distribution to *D* of an asset with a basis of $10,000. *D*'s capital account is appropriately reduced, but his interest in all items of partnership profit and loss is unchanged. At the time *D* bought his interest, the asset was worth $45,000 (his share was $15,000) and *D* would have been entitled to a $5,000 basis adjustment if Code Sec. 754 were in effect. What are the tax consequences to *D* on a current distribution of the asset?

> The Code Sec. 732(d) election is applicable to current and liquidating distributions.[65] Thus, *D* can elect to have Code Sec. 732(d) apply and receive a special basis adjustment for the distributed asset which is equal to the adjusted basis the asset would have had if the Code Sec. 754 election were in effect with respect to the partnership property when *D* bought his interest. *D* received the distribution within two years after the transfer as required. Therefore, *D*'s basis for the asset is $15,000 ($10,000 basis to the partnership plus the $5,000 special basis adjustment under Code Sec. 732(d)). *D*'s basis for his partnership interest is reduced by $15,000 after the distribution to $25,000.

¶ 1302 Technical Terminations

The continuing partners, those partners who remain members of the partnership after the transferor partner has transferred his or her interest in the partnership to the transferee partner, are generally not affected by the transfer even when there is a substantial built-in loss or a Code Sec. 754 election in effect. However, the transfer of a partnership interest can have a significant tax impact on the continuing partners if the transfer causes the "termination" of the partnership under Code Sec. 708(b). Assuming that the business and financial operations of the partnership continue to be carried on by the partnership, a termination occurs only when 50 percent or more of the total interest in the partnership's capital and profits is sold or exchanged within a 12-month period. Thus, the partnership will not be terminated provided the partnership interest sold or exchanged, together with any other partnership interests sold or exchanged within a 12-month period, constitutes less than a 50 percent interest in partnership capital and profits. There is no guidance in

---

[65] Reg. § 1.732-1(d)(4), Ex. 2.

the Internal Revenue Code or Treasury regulations as to the definitions of capital account and profits interest. Percent of capital is probably the percent of the value of the assets the partner would be entitled to receive upon a liquidating distribution. It is not clear how different profits interests in various aspects of the partnership's operations should be taken into account. However, if capital accounts are taken into account at their fair market values, a profits interest in existing built-in gain would be part of the capital account test of Code Sec. 708(b).[66]

The term "sale or exchange" includes:

1. Sales violating an anti-assignment agreement;[67]

2. Taxable and tax-free exchanges;[68]

3. The distribution of a partnership interest from a partnership or a corporation;[69]

4. The contribution of a partnership interest to a corporation;[70]

5. The contribution of a partnership interest to another partnership;[71]

6. Abandonment of a partnership interest when the partner is relieved of a share of partnership debt under Code Sec. 752(b) in excess of his or her basis in his or her interest; and

7. The sale of a partnership interest to new or existing partners.[72]

The term "sale or exchange" does *not* include:

1. Bequests and inheritances;[73]

2. Gifts when the donor has no debt relief under Code Sec. 752(b).[74] Debt relief suggests a part gift/part sale analysis; and

3. Entry of a new partner.[75]

.01 Consequences of Partnership Termination

If a partnership is terminated by a sale or exchange of an interest, the following is deemed to occur:

1. The partnership contributes all of its assets and liabilities to a new partnership in exchange for an interest in the new partnership; and,

2. Immediately thereafter, the terminated partnership liquidates, distributing interests in the new partnership to the purchasing partner and the other

---

[66] The Service has yet to issue guidance regarding the proper treatment of an interest in future appreciation of partnership assets or future profits for purposes of §708(b). Presumably such "contingent" interests can safely be disregarded.

[67] *D.L. Evans v. Commr.*, 54 TC 40, Dec. 29,915 (1970), aff'd, CA-7, 71-2 USTC ¶ 9597, 447 F2d 547.

[68] *A.E. Long v. Commr.*, 77 TC 1045, Dec. 38,402 (1981) (taxable exchange of partnership interests); *D.L. Evans v. Commr.*, 54 TC 40, Dec. 29,915 (1970) (contribution under Code Sec. 351 to a corporation).

[69] Code Sec. 761(e). However, a partnership interest deemed distributed by a partnership terminated under

Code Sec. 708(b) is not treated as a sale or exchange for purposes of terminating the subsidiary partnership. Reg. §1.761-1(e).

[70] Rev. Rul. 81-38, 1981-1 CB 386; *D.L. Evans v. Commr.*, 54 TC 40, Dec. 29,915 (1970), aff'd CA-7, 447 F2d 547.

[71] IRS Letter Rulings 8929003, 8229034.

[72] Reg. §1.708-1(b)(1)(ii).

[73] *Id.*

[74] *Id.*

[75] *Id.*

remaining partners in proportion to their respective interests in the terminated partnership.

Example 13-19: *A* and *B* each contribute $10,000 cash to form AB, a general partnership, as equal partners. AB purchases depreciable Property *X* for $20,000. Property *X* increases in value to $30,000, at which time *A* sells her entire 50% interest to *C* for $15,000 in a transfer that terminates the partnership under Code Sec. 708(b)(1)(B). At the time of the sale, Property *X* had an adjusted tax basis of $16,000 and a book value of $16,000 (original $20,000 tax basis and book value reduced by $4,000 of depreciation). In addition, *A* and *B* each had capital account balances of $8,000 (original $10,000 capital account reduced by $2,000 of depreciation allocations with respect to Property *X*).

Following the deemed contribution of assets and liabilities by the terminated AB partnership to a new partnership (new BC) and the liquidation of the terminated AB partnership, the adjusted tax basis of Property *X* in the hands of new BC is $16,000.[76] The book value of Property *X* in the hands of new partnership AB is also $16,000 (the book value of Property *X* immediately before the termination), and *B* and *C* each have a capital account of $8,000 in new AB (the balance of their capital accounts in AB prior to the termination).[77]

Property *X* was not Code Sec. 704(c) property in the hands of terminated AB and is therefore not treated as Code Sec. 704(c) property in the hands of new AB, even though Property *X* is deemed contributed to new AB at a time when the fair market value of Property *X* ($30,000) was different from its adjusted tax basis ($16,000).[78] However, if a Code Sec. 754 election is in effect, new partnership BC will be required to increase its basis in Property X by $7,000 (gain recognized by A on sale of the partnership interest). This basis adjustment will be made solely for the benefit of new partner C. (See ¶ 1301.)

If a partnership is terminated by the sale or exchange of an interest therein, a Code Sec. 754 election by the new partnership on its initial return, or a Code Sec. 754 election previously made by the terminated partnership that is in effect for the taxable year in which the sale occurs, applies with respect to the incoming partner. Therefore, the bases of partnership assets are adjusted pursuant to Code Secs. 743 and 755 prior to their deemed contribution to the new partnership.[79] If the terminated partnership has previously made Code Sec. 743(b) adjustments to its property, these carry over to the new partnership as well.[80]

---

[76] Code Sec. 723.

[77] *See* Reg. § 1.704-1(b)(2)(iv)(*l*) (providing that the deemed contribution and liquidation with regard to the terminated partnership are disregarded in determining the capital accounts of the partners and the books of the new partnership). Additionally, under Reg. § 301.6109-1(d)(2)(iii), new BC partnership retains the taxpayer identification number of the terminated AB partnership.

[78] *See* Reg. § 1.704-3(a)(3)(i) (providing that property contributed to a new partnership under Reg.

§ 1.708-1(b)(1)(iv) is treated as Code Sec. 704(c) property only to the extent that the property was Code Sec. 704(c) property in the hands of the terminated partnership immediately prior to the termination).

[79] Different rules applied to technical terminations occurring before May 9, 1997. Practitioners dealing with terminations occurring before this date should be careful to consult the regulations in effect at that time.

[80] Reg. § 1.743-1(h)(1).

.02 Other Consequences

Although a technical termination can have adverse consequences for the unwary, in many ways it does not affect the partnership's continuing operations or status. The consequences of a technical termination can be summarized as follows:

1. The termination does not require that the new partnership get a new taxpayer identification number.[81]

2. The termination requires the terminated partnership to file a "Final Return" for the short year ending with the date of sale.

3. The termination requires the new partnership to file an initial short year partnership tax return.

4. The termination continues any remaining Code Sec. 704(c) gain for the continuing partners.[82]

5. The old partnership's taxable year, accounting method, and other elections do *not* carry over to the new partnership.

6. The termination is disregarded in determining the capital accounts of the partners.[83]

7. The holding period of the new partnership in its assets is the same as the terminated partnership.[84]

8. Code Sec. 724 taint. It is unclear whether the new partnership retains the Code Sec. 724 taint. This code provision simply provides that the character of gain from the sale of contributed assets, which are ordinary income assets to the contributing partner, will be ordinary income to the old partnership. Code Sec. 724 does not treat these assets as inventory or unrealized receivables to the old partnership. These contributions to the new partnership by the old partnership are not literally subject to Code Sec. 724. Absent this, Code Sec. 724 does not cause the new partnership's disposition to be affected by its provisions. However, application of Code Sec. 64 may result in all the old partnership's hot assets being treated as subject to Code Sec. 724.

9. Any Code Sec. 465, at-risk loss carryover, and Code Sec. 469, passive activity loss carryover, continue if the activity continues.

10. Code Sec. 704(d) carryover losses are probably lost because the partner no longer has an interest in the partnership which generated the loss.[85]

11. The terminated partnership is entitled to make a Code Sec. 754 election in its final return which applies with respect to the incoming partner.[86]

12. The new partnership is entitled to make a Code Sec. 754 election in its initial return which applies to the incoming partner.[87]

---

[81] Reg. § 1.708-1(b)(1)(iv), Ex.

[82] Reg. § 1.704-3(a)(3)(i).

[83] Reg. §§ 1.704-1(b)(2)(iv)(*l*), and 1.708-1(b)(1)(iv), Ex. (ii).

[84] Code Secs. 722 and 1223.

[85] Cf. *W. Sennett v. Commr.*, 80 TC 825, Dec. 40,077 (1983), aff'd, CA-9, 85-1 USTC ¶ 9153, 752 F2d 428.

[86] Reg. § 1.708-1(b)(1)(v). The basis of the assets are adjusted prior to their deemed contribution to the new partnership.

[87] Reg. § 1.761-1(e).

13. It is the Treasury Department's opinion that the "property deemed contributed to the new partnership will continue to be subject to the anti-churning provisions of Code Sec. 168(f)(5), which will generally require the new partnership to depreciate the property as if it were newly acquired property under the same depreciation system used by the terminated partnership."[88] However, the new partnership steps into the shoes of the terminated partnership's amortization of Code Sec. 197 assets.[89]

14. The tax basis of the assets in the hands of the new partnership is the same as the basis to the terminated partnership.[90]

15. There is no guidance on the treatment of unamortized Code Sec. 709 costs. The organization costs of the terminated partnership may be considered an interest of the new partnership.

16. Depreciation recapture under Code Secs. 1245 and 1250 is not triggered by a termination.

¶ 1303 Partnership Basis Adjustments Following Distributions of Property

The impact, or lack thereof, that a distribution has on the partnership is largely determined by whether a Code Sec. 754 election is in effect for the year of the distribution. If there is not a disproportionate distribution, a partnership incurs neither gain nor loss because of a cash distribution.[91] In addition, without a Code Sec. 754 election, and assuming no disproportionate distribution or other deemed sale event, there is no effect on the basis of the partnership's remaining property.[92] Therefore, as long as Code Secs. 704(c)(2), 707(a)(2)(B), 737, 751(b) and 754 do not apply, a cash distribution is treated by the partnership in much the same manner as a Subchapter C or S corporation treats a cash distribution. There is no partnership gain or loss and there is no basis adjustment to the partnership's remaining property.

An exception to the general rule that no basis adjustments are allowed or required absent a Code Sec. 754 election by the partnership applies when a distribution results in a "substantial basis reduction" as defined in Code Sec. 734(d). Under this statute, added by the American Jobs Creation Act of 2004, a "substantial basis reduction" exists when the sum of:

i. The amount of loss recognized by the distributee partner under Code Sec. 731(a) on receipt of the distribution; and

ii. The step-up in basis of distributed property in the distributee partner's hands under Code Sec. 732

---

[88] Preamble to Prop. Reg. § 1.708-1(b), adopted by T.D. 8717, 1996-1 CB 877, 878.

[89] Code Sec. 197(f)(2)(B).

[90] Reg. § 1.708-1(b)(1)(iv), Ex. (ii).

[91] Code Sec. 731(b).

[92] Code Sec. 734(a).

exceeds $250,000. In such cases, the partnership is required to adjust its basis in remaining partnership properties under Code Sec. 734(b) whether or not the partnership has a Code Sec. 754 election in effect.[93]

For example, if there is no Code Sec. 754 election in effect for the year of the distribution, the partnership is not allowed to increase its basis in its remaining property for any gain a distributee partner reports as a result of the distribution.[94] In the case of a partner who receives a liquidating cash distribution resulting in a gain, it is readily apparent that the gain (the excess of the cash distributed over the partner's outside basis) represents the distributee partner's share of the appreciation in value of the assets which the partnership retains. The partner has "cashed out" all or a portion of his or her share of the value of the partnership assets.

Because the basis in his or her partnership interest is generally equal to the partner's share of the costs of the partnership's assets, the gain on liquidation is equal to the gain on the indirect sale of his or her share of the assets. However, the partnership's adjusted basis in the assets remains the same (because there is no Code Sec. 754 election in effect). This is true even though the remaining partners have in effect used their share of the partnership's cash to purchase the liquidated partner's share of the assets. If the partnership sells its remaining assets, the gain will be taxed again when the property is sold. This double reporting of gain will ultimately be rectified upon liquidation of the partnership or of the remaining partners' interests therein (because the increase in the adjusted bases of the partners in their partnership interests will cause a reduction in the gain on the ultimate sale or liquidation of their partnership interests). However, a timing difference will exist in the absence of a Code Sec. 734 adjustment. Thus, although the overall taxable income will ultimately be the same, tax by the remaining partners may be paid considerably sooner should the partnership sell the appreciated assets a long time before the remaining partners sell their partnership interests. The Code Sec. 734(b) adjustment in effect gives the partnership a cost basis in the liquidated partner's share of partnership assets purchased by the remaining partners.

> ***C and S Corporation Observation:*** When a corporation distributes appreciated property to a shareholder, the corporation recognizes gain (but not loss) as if the corporation sold the property to the shareholder and distributed the cash.[95]

> ***LLC Observation:*** The distribution rules discussed in this chapter apply equally to state law partnerships and LLCs taxed as partnerships.

¶ 1304 No Code Sec. 754 Election in Effect

Generally speaking, unless the partnership has a Code Sec. 754 election in effect, or chooses to make one, the distribution of property or cash to a partner has no tax consequences for the partnership. There are numerous exceptions of course—the partnership may be required to recognize gain or adjust the basis of its

---

[93] Code Sec. 734(d). Note, however that this exception does not apply to "securitization partnerships" as defined in Code Sec. 743(f). See Code Sec. 743(e) and ¶ 1301.03.

[94] Code Secs. 311(b) and 1239.
[95] Code Sec. 734(b)(1).

assets if the distribution triggers the disproportionate distribution rules of Code Sec. 751(b) or the deemed sale provisions of Code Secs. 704(c)(2), 707(a)(2)(B), or 737 (each discussed elsewhere in this book). But as a general rule, distributions are nontaxable events for the partnership.[96]

¶ 1305 Code Sec. 754 Election in Effect or Substantial Basis Reduction

The mechanics of making the Code Sec. 754 election are not affected by whether adjustments result because of a transfer of a partnership interest or a distribution. The mechanics of making the Code Sec. 754 election are discussed in ¶ 1301.04.

Similar to the provisions of Code Sec. 743 which provide that there is no change in the basis of partnership assets on a sale of a partnership interest, Code Sec. 734(a) provides the general rule that the basis of retained partnership property will not be adjusted following a distribution to a partner unless the partnership makes a Code Sec. 754 election or unless there is a substantial basis reduction; in that event, a Code Sec. 734(b) basis adjustment will be made to the retained partnership property. The adjustment process has two steps:

- Computing the total adjustment, and
- Allocating the total adjustment to the partnership assets.

.01 Amount of the Adjustment

The amount of the required Code Sec. 734(b) basis adjustment to partnership property is determined as follows:

1. In the case of a distribution to a partner of money that is greater than the adjusted basis the partner has in his or her partnership interest, the partnership will increase the adjusted basis of its assets ("partnership property") by the amount of gain recognized by the distributee partner under Code Sec. 731(a).[97]

2. In the case of a distribution to a partner consisting solely of money, unrealized receivables, and/or inventory in complete liquidation of his or her partnership interest when the distributee partner recognizes a loss under Code Sec. 731(a)(2), the partnership will reduce the adjusted basis of its undistributed assets by the amount of the loss.[98]

3. In the case of a distribution of property in which the partner takes a *lower* basis in the property than the partnership had, the partnership will *increase* its basis in remaining properties by a like amount.[99]

4. The converse situation to that outlined in (3) above occurs when, upon the complete liquidation of a partner's interest, the total adjusted basis of the

---

[96] Code Sec. 731(b).

[97] Code Sec. 734(b)(1)(A).

[98] Code Sec. 734(b)(2)(A).

[99] A partner's basis in property received in a current distribution cannot exceed his or her basis in the partner-

ship interest. Code Sec. 732(a)(2). Similarly, a partner's tax basis in property received in a liquidating distribution is equal to his or her basis in the partnership interest reduced by the amount of cash and the basis of ordinary income property received as part of the distribution. Code Sec. 732(b).

assets in the distributee partner's hands is greater than it was in the hands of the partnership immediately before the distribution. The partnership must decrease the adjusted basis of its retained partnership property by the amount of this difference.[100]

If a Code Sec. 754 election is in effect, the partnership adjusts its basis in its assets to allow its remaining members to avoid any distortion in reporting their future shares of partnership taxable income. In the case of a purchase or inheritance of a partnership interest, the Code Sec. 743(b) adjustment attempts to ensure that inside and outside basis run in tandem and that a purchaser or successor in interest of a partnership interest does not recognize gain or loss built into the partnership assets before his or her tenure (see ¶ 1301). Its companion adjustment, that of Code Sec. 734(b), attempts to effectuate the same policy in the context of partnership distributions.

In contrast to the Code Sec. 743(b) adjustment which is personal to the new partner who acquires his or her interest by purchase, bequest, or devise, the Code Sec. 734(b) adjustment is made for the benefit of all remaining partners. This includes the distributee if he or she remains a partner. A distribution of partnership assets, unless pro rata among the members, often reflects an exchange or purchase of some portion of the non-distributed assets by the remaining partners for the relinquishment of their share of the distributed assets.[101] The Code Sec. 734(b) adjustment attempts to treat such a transaction accordingly. For example, when a partner receives a cash distribution resulting in a gain, the gain (the excess of the cash distributed over the partner's outside basis) represents the distributee partner's share of the appreciation in value of the assets that the partnership retains.

Example 13-20: The JDR Partnership has the following balance sheets:

	Basis	*FMV*
Cash	$30,000	$30,000
Property 1	20,000	20,000
Property 2	10,000	40,000
	$60,000	$90,000

The partnership has three equal partners. If it sold Property 2 for its $40,000 fair market value, each would be allocated a $10,000 share of the gain.

Assume that the partnership distributes $30,000 cash to *J* in complete liquidation of her interest. *J*'s tax basis in her partnership interest was $20,000. Thus, she will recognize a $10,000 gain on receipt of the distribution just as she would have had the partnership sold Property 2.

While Code Sec. 731(b) ensures that *J* cannot avoid recognizing her share of the inherent gain in the partnership's assets upon receipt of the liquidating distribution, it does *not* protect the other partners. Absent an adjustment to the basis of the partnership's assets, the partnership will *still* recognize a $30,000

---

[100] Code Sec. 734(b)(2)(B).

[101] This is similar to the treatment of Code Sec. 751(b) distributions.

gain upon the eventual sale of Property 2. Since there are only two remaining partners, however, *D* and *R* will now be required to recognize $15,000 gain each, vs. the $10,000 each would have been allocated prior to *J*'s departure. This is the problem that Code Sec. 734(b) is designed to remedy.

When a partnership makes a liquidating cash distribution under circumstances resulting in a loss to the distributee, that loss represents the difference between the distributee partner's share of the fair market value of the partnership property and the distributee partner's share of its basis, which in turn is equal to the adjusted basis of his or her partnership interest. If the distributee partner can deduct the loss, and if the partnership is also able to recognize a loss on the sale of the partnership assets (since the fair market value of the assets will have depreciated below the partnership's adjusted basis in the assets), the same issue arises in reverse: the remaining partners' shares of built-in partnership losses are increased following the cash liquidation of the distributee partner. This is later rectified through adjustments to the partners' outside bases, but it may cause a significant timing difference in the absence of a Code Sec. 734(b) adjustment.

Example 13-21: The RHC Communities Partnership has the following balance sheet:

Assets	Adjusted Basis	FMV
Greenacre	$50,000	$10,000
Blackacre	40,000	25,000
Whiteacre	60,000	30,000
Redacre	50,000	35,000
	$200,000	$100,000
Liabilities	0	0
Capital Accounts		
Richard	$50,000	25,000
Helen	50,000	25,000
Cassandra	100,000	50,000
	$200,000	$100,000

Richard's tax basis in his partnership interest is $50,000. It is worth only $25,000. Assume that the partnership borrows $25,000, giving the bank a lien against Redacre, and distributes the money to Richard in liquidation of his partnership interest. (His share of the debt will increase his basis, but this increase will be only temporary as he is leaving the partnership immediately.)

Richard will recognize a $25,000 loss on the distribution under Code Sec. 731(a). Assume the partnership does not have a Code Sec. 754 election in effect, and that it chooses not to make one for the year of the liquidating distribution. Thus, the basis of the partnership's assets remains $200,000 (and their value remains $100,000). The partnership's built-in loss remains un-

¶1305.01

changed, though it will now be allocated between only two partners. Again, Code Sec. 734(b) is designed to remedy this problem, but only if the partnership has a Code Sec. 754 election in effect.[102]

In other cases, the distributee partner will recognize no income on receipt of the distribution, but will take a stepped-down basis in property received from the partnership. The ultimate result of such distributions is that the distributee will ultimately recognize more gain (or less loss) on disposition of the distributed property than the partnership would have recognized had it sold the property rather than distributing it.

Example 13-22: Assume that Partnership JDR has the following balance sheets:

	Basis	*FMV*
Cash	$10,000	$10,000
Property 1	30,000	40,000
Property 2	20,000	70,000
	$60,000	$120,000
Capital, *J*	$20,000	$40,000
Capital, *D*	20,000	40,000
Capital, *R*	20,000	40,000
	$60,000	$120,000

The three partners each have tax bases of $20,000 in their partnership interests and each would be allocated a $20,000 share of gain if the partnership sold Properties 1 and 2 for their fair market values (total gain of $60,000; each partner would be allocated one-third).

Assume that the partnership distributes Property 1 to *R* in complete liquidation of his interest. Although the partnership's basis in Property 1 is $30,000, *R*'s basis in the property will be limited to his $20,000 basis in his partnership interest. He recognizes no gain on receipt of the distribution but will recognize a $20,000 gain if he later sells Property 1 for its $40,000 fair market value. Thus, the basis rules of Code Sec. 732 have worked with respect to *R*: he will recognize the same amount of gain from sale of Property 1 as he would have recognized had the partnership sold all its property and liquidated.

The same is not true for *J* and *D*, however. The partnership's basis in its remaining assets is $30,000 and their aggregate fair market value is $80,000. Thus, their shares of the partnership's built-in gains have increased from $20,000 each prior to *R*'s departure (one-third of $60,000) to $25,000 each following his departure (one-half of $50,000). This increase can be eliminated if

---

[102] In this case, Code Sec. 734(b) would require that the partnership *reduce* its basis in remaining assets, so it is unlikely to make a Code Sec. 754 election in the current year. If the election had been made in a previous year, however, and was still in effect, the basis reduction under Code Sec. 734(b) would be mandatory.

the partnership makes a Code Sec. 754 election. If such an election is made (or is already in effect). Code Sec. 734(b) will allow the partnership to increase its tax basis in its remaining asset (Property 2) by the $10,000 difference between its pre-distribution basis in Property 1 and the basis *R* took in that asset following the distribution.

Finally, Code Sec. 734(b) may require the partnership to decrease its basis in remaining assets following certain liquidating distributions, even where the distributee partner does not recognize a loss. Under the substitute basis rules of Code Sec. 732(b), a partner's tax basis in property received in a liquidating distribution is generally equal to his or her pre-distribution basis in the partnership interest, regardless of the bases such property had in the partnership's hands.[103] In many cases, these rules may result in the distributee partner taking a stepped-up basis in property received in the liquidating distribution. What that happens, the partnership will be required to reduce its tax basis in its remaining assets by a like amount *if* it has a Code Sec. 754 election in effect from a prior year, or if it chooses to make one for the year of the distribution.

Example 13-23: CLT Partnership has the following balance sheets at Dec. 31:

	Basis	FMV
Cash	$10,000	$10,000
Property 1	10,000	60,000
Property 2	70,000	110,000
	$90,000	$180,000
Capital, *C*	$30,000	$60,000
Capital, *L*	30,000	60,000
Capital, *T*	30,000	60,000
	$90,000	$180,000

The three partners each have tax bases of $30,000 in their partnership interests, and would be allocated a $30,000 share of gain if the partnership sold Properties 1 and 2 for their fair market values (one-third of $90,000 gain inherent in partnership's assets).

Assume that the partnership distributes Property 1 to *T* in complete liquidation of her interest. Although the partnership's basis in Property 1 is $10,000, *T* will take a substitute basis in this property equal to her $30,000 tax basis in the partnership interest. This basis will preserve *T*'s $30,000 share of the built-in-gain inherent in partnership assets prior to the distribution (sale of the property for its $60,000 fair value will trigger a $30,000 gain to *T*).

---

[103] Basis in the partnership interest is first reduced by the amount of any cash received before assigning basis to property received. Code Sec. 732(b).

However, the remaining built-in gain inherent in partnership assets following the distribution to T will be only $40,000 ($110,000 fair market value of Property 2 over its $70,000 tax basis). Thus, C and L have each seen their shares of partnership built-in gain decline by $10,000, their shares of the amount by which the tax basis of Property 1 was increased in the hands of Partner T. If the partnership has a Code Sec. 754 election in effect, it will be required under Code Sec. 734(b) to reduce its basis in its remaining property by $20,000, the amount of the step-up to T. Note that if the partnership does not already have a Code Sec. 754 election in effect, it would be unwise to make one for the current year.[104]

.02 Allocation of Code Sec. 734(b) Adjustment Among Partnership Property

Allocation of the Code Sec. 734(b) adjustment among the partnership's assets is governed by Code Sec. 755. Although the rules for allocating Code Sec. 734(b) adjustments differ slightly from those governing the allocation of adjustments under Code Sec. 743(b) (arising from the sale or transfer of a partnership interest), the underlying rationale of both sets of rules is the same. Basis adjustments are allocated among partnership assets in a way that eliminates or reduces the difference between the fair market value and tax basis of partnership properties.[105] As noted previously, Code Sec. 734(b) adjustments are not made with respect to any particular partner, but apply to the common basis of partnership assets.

Allocation of total adjustment between the Code Sec. 1221/1231 and ordinary income classes of partnership property. The allocation rules first apportion the total Code Sec. 734(b) adjustment between two classes of partnership property: ordinary income property and Code Sec. 1221/1231 "capital gain" property. After this bifurcation of the total adjustment, the amount of the adjustment allocated to each class is further allocated among the assets within each class.

The allocations are made according to the following rules:[106]

1. If a positive Code Sec. 734(b)(1)(A) adjustment arises when the distributee partner recognizes gain under Code Sec. 731(a)(1), or a negative adjustment arises under Code Sec. 734(b)(2)(A) if he or she recognizes a loss under Code Sec. 731(a)(2), then the upward or downward adjustment is to be allocated *only* to "capital gain assets."[107] The adjustment is allocated in such a way as to reduce the difference between the fair market values and the adjusted bases of the assets of that class that have appreciated in value, in the case of an upward basis adjustment, or have depreciated in value, for a downward basis adjustment.[108] In applying these rules, the basis of an asset may not be reduced below zero,[109] and, if the partnership either has no retained capital gain property, or has insufficient basis in the property in the class to fully absorb a negative adjustment allocated to that class, the

---

[104] It should also be noted that avoiding a negative basis adjustment does not constitute valid grounds for terminating an existing Code Sec. 754 election from a prior year. Reg. § 1.754-1(c).

[105] Reg. § 1.755-1(b)(1).

[106] Reg. § 1.755-1(c).

[107] Code Secs. 1221 and 1231 property; Reg. § 1.755-1(c)(1)(ii).

[108] Code Sec. 755(a).

[109] Reg. § 1.704-1(c)(3).

balance of the adjustment is to be applied to subsequently acquired capital gain property.[110]

2. If the Code Sec. 734(b) adjustment is caused by the distributee partner's adjusted basis in the distributed property being less than or greater than the partnership's adjusted basis in that property immediately before the distribution, then the increase or decrease is allocated to the remaining partnership assets that are of a character similar to that of the distributed property. For example, when the partnership's adjusted basis in distributed "capital assets" immediately before the distribution exceeds that of the distributee partner after the distribution, the upward adjustment in undistributed partnership assets will be allocated entirely to the undistributed "capital assets" of the partnership. If the distributed assets that produced the upward Code Sec. 734(b) adjustment were "inventory," the adjustment would be allocated solely to the partnership's remaining inventory.[111] In applying these rules, the basis of an asset may not be reduced below zero,[112] and, if an adjustment is allocated to a class in which the partnership either has no retained property or has insufficient basis in the property in the class to fully absorb a negative adjustment allocated to that class, the balance of the adjustment is to be applied to subsequently acquired property of that class.[113]

Allocation of adjustment among partnership property within a class. If there is an increase in basis to be allocated to a group of properties within a class, the increase must be allocated first to properties with unrealized appreciation in proportion to their respective amounts of unrealized appreciation before such increase (but only to the extent of each property's unrealized appreciation). Any remaining increase must be allocated among the properties within the class in proportion to their fair market values.[114]

If there is a decrease in basis to be allocated to a group of properties within a class, the decrease must be allocated first to properties with unrealized depreciation in proportion to their respective amounts of unrealized depreciation before such decrease (but only to the extent of each property's unrealized depreciation).

Any remaining decrease must be allocated among the properties within the class in proportion to their adjusted bases (as adjusted under the preceding sentence).[115] Where a decrease in the basis of partnership assets is required under Code Sec. 734(b)(2) and the amount of the decrease exceeds the adjusted basis to the partnership of property of the required character, the basis of such property is reduced to zero (but not below zero).[116]

Where, in the case of a distribution, an increase or a decrease in the basis of undistributed property cannot be made because the partnership owns no property

---

[110] Reg. § 1.755-1(c)(4).

[111] Reg. § 1.755-1(c)(1)(i).

[112] Reg. § 1.704-1(c)(3).

[113] Reg. § 1.755-1(c)(4).

[114] Reg. § 1.755-1(c)(2)(i). The regulations governing distributions prior to December 15, 1999, had no provision for handling positive adjustments which created basis in excess of value.

[115] Reg. § 1.755-1(c)(2)(ii).

[116] Reg. § 1.755-1(c)(3).

of the character required to be adjusted, or because the basis of all the property of a like character has been reduced to zero, the adjustment is made when the partnership subsequently acquires property of a like character to which an adjustment can be made.

Example 13-24: A, B, and C form equal ABC Partnership. Partner A contributes $50,000 and Asset 1—capital gain property with a fair market value of $50,000 and an adjusted tax basis of $25,000. Partners B and C each contribute $100,000. The ABC Partnership uses the cash to purchase Assets 2, 3, 4, 5, and 6. Assets 4, 5, and 6 are the only ordinary income assets held by the partnership which are subject to Code Sec. 751. The partnership has an election in effect under Code Sec. 754. After seven years, the adjusted basis and fair market value of ABC Partnership's assets are as follows:

Assets	Adjusted Basis	FMV
Capital Gain Property:		
Asset 1	$25,000	$75,000
Asset 2	100,000	117,500
Asset 3	50,000	60,000
Ordinary Income Property:		
Asset 4	40,000	45,000
Asset 5	50,000	60,000
Asset 6	10,000	2,500
Total	*$275,000*	*$360,000*

Assume that the ABC Partnership distributes Assets 3 and 5 to A in complete liquidation of Partner A's interest in the partnership. Partner A's basis in the partnership interest was $75,000. The partnership's basis in Assets 3 and 5 was $50,000 each. Partner A's $75,000 basis in his partnership interest is allocated between Assets 3 and 5 under Code Secs. 732(b) and (c). Partner A will, therefore, have a basis of $25,000 in Asset 3 (capital gain property), and a basis of $50,000 in Asset 5 (ordinary income property). The distribution results in a $25,000 decrease in the basis of capital gain property. There is no change in the basis of ordinary income property. Therefore, the partnership is required to increase the basis of its remaining property by $25,000. This increase is allocated to the partnership's remaining Code Sec. 1221/1231 property and must be allocated among partnership property within that class.

The amount of the basis increase to capital gain property is $25,000 and must be allocated among the remaining capital gain assets in proportion to the difference between the fair market value and basis of each. The fair market value of Asset 1 exceeds its basis by $50,000. The fair market value of Asset 2 exceeds its basis by $17,500. Therefore, the basis of Asset 1 will be increased by $18,519 ($25,000 × $50,000 ÷ $67,500), and the basis of Asset 2 will be increased by $6,481 ($25,000 × $17,500 ÷ $67,500).

¶1305.02

Example 13-25: The ABC partnership is a cash-method, calendar-year partnership that has made the Code Sec. 754 election. The profit and loss ratios of the partners are not equal. It has the following balance sheet:

Assets	Book Value and Adjusted Basis	FMV	Appreciation (Depreciation)
Cash...........................	$18,000	$18,000	$ 0
Parcel X	23,000	22,000	(1,000)
Parcel Y	19,000	29,000	10,000
	$60,000	$69,000	$9,000

Capital Accounts			
A	$20,000	$18,000	$(2,000)
B	20,000	22,000	2,000
C	20,000	29,000	(9,000)
	$60,000	$69,000	$9,000

What are the tax consequences to the partners and the partnership if Partner *A* receives the cash in complete liquidation of his partnership interest which has an adjusted basis of $20,000?

A partner recognizes loss if the partnership distributes only money in liquidation of the partner's interest in the partnership to the extent that the partner's adjusted basis in his partnership interest exceeds the sum of money distributed.[117] *A* received $18,000 and had an adjusted basis of $20,000. He therefore recognizes a $2,000 loss. Partner *A*'s $2,000 loss creates a negative $2,000 partnership adjustment.

Code Sec. 734(b)(2)(A) is applicable when the Code Sec. 754 election is in effect and provides that the amount of loss recognized to a distributee partner with respect to distributions under Code Sec. 731(a)(2) must be reflected by a decrease in the adjusted basis of partnership property in accordance with the rules provided in Code Sec. 755.[118] A decrease in basis must first be allocated to the assets whose bases exceed their value and in proportion to the difference between the basis and value of each.[119]

Parcel *X*'s basis is first reduced from $23,000 to $22,000. The $1,000 of remaining basis reduction is then allocated between Parcel *X* and Parcel *Y* based on their relative adjusted bases.

---

[117] Code Sec. 731(a)(2)(A).

[118] Code Sec. 734(c).

[119] The former regulation apparently did not intend that decreases be made if the fair market value of any asset will equal or exceed the resulting adjusted basis. Reg. §1.755-1(a)(1)(i). Thus, the basis of Parcel *X* was reduced by only $1,000 to $22,000. See Code Sec. 755(b) for the special rule when decreases in adjusted basis are prevented. Former Reg. §1.755-1(a)(1)(iii).

Adjustment Allocation	Parcel X	Parcel Y
Per relative depreciation	$1,000	$ 0
Per relative basis	537	436
Total negative adjustment	$1,537	$436

Non-liquidating distributions of property can often result in the distributed property taking a basis to the distributee partner which is less than the partnership's former basis. This occurs whenever the distributed property's basis to the partnership exceeds the partner's basis in his or her partnership interest. If there is no Code Sec. 754 election in effect for the year of the distribution, this basis is lost. If there is an effective Code Sec. 754 election, the basis step-down becomes an upward adjustment to the partnership's remaining property.[120] The basis step-down to distributed property which includes capital and Code Sec. 1231 assets is added to the basis of capital and Code Sec. 1231 assets remaining with the partnership.[121] It is allocated first in accordance with the relative appreciation inherent in each asset.[122] Any remaining increase is allocated among the Code Sec. 1221/1231 assets in proportion to their respective values.[123] The basis step-down in distributed ordinary income assets is added to the basis of ordinary income assets still held by the partnership and is allocated in the same manner.[124]

Usually, a partner who receives a liquidating distribution of property takes a basis in that property either above or below that of the partnership since Code Sec. 732(b) provides that the partner's basis in the distributed property is determined with reference to the adjusted basis of the partner's interest in the partnership (reduced by any money distributed in the same transaction). Even where the partner's outside basis is equal to his or her pro rata share of the partnership's basis for its assets, it is unlikely the partner will receive a distribution of a *pro rata* cross section of the assets. The partnership will merely choose assets that have a value equal to the partner's partnership interest. This step-up or step-down in basis represents unrealized appreciation or depreciation that will never be recognized if a Code Sec. 754 election is not in effect, since the gain or loss inherent in the distributed property escapes taxation, owing to the tax-free basis step-up or step-down. Also note that without this adjustment, inside and outside bases will be out of alignment.

> **Example 13-26:** The ABC partnership is a cash-method, calendar-year partnership that has made the Code Sec. 754 election. The profit and loss ratios of the partners are not equal. It has the following balance sheet:

---

[120] Code Sec. 734(b)(1)(B).
[121] Reg. § 1.755-1(c)(1)(i).
[122] Reg. § 1.755-1(c)(2)(i).
[123] *Id.*
[124] Reg. § 1.755-1(c)(2)(ii).

Assets	Book Value and Adjusted Basis	FMV	Appreciation (Depreciation)
Cash............................	$18,000	$18,000	$ 0
Parcel X	23,000	22,000	(1,000)
Parcel Y	19,000	29,000	10,000
	$60,000	$69,000	$9,000

Capital Accounts			
A	$20,000	$18,000	$(2,000)
B	20,000	22,000	2,000
C	20,000	29,000	9,000
	$60,000	$69,000	$9,000

Partner B receives Parcel X in complete liquidation of his partnership interest.

Code Sec. 732(b) provides that the basis of property distributed by a partnership to a partner in liquidation of the partner's interest shall be an amount equal to the adjusted basis of such partner's interest in the partnership reduced by any money distributed in the same transaction. Since B received no cash in the transaction, his adjusted basis in Parcel X is equal to his adjusted basis in his partnership interest of $20,000.

The consequences to the partnership are governed by Code Sec. 734(b)(1)(B), which provides that when Code Sec. 732(b) applies to a distribution of property, there will be an increase in the adjusted basis of the partnership property to the extent of the excess of the adjusted basis of the partnership property to the partnership immediately before the distribution over the partner's basis in such property immediately after the distribution. In this case, the excess is $3,000. Therefore, the partnership will increase its basis in Parcel Y (the only like-kind asset) by $3,000 in accordance with the rule set forth in Code Sec. 755.[125] If there were appreciated like-kind assets other than Parcel Y, in that class, the adjustments would be allocated first in proportion to their relative appreciation and then any excess positive adjustment is allocated based on their relative values.[126]

Example 13-27: Assume the same facts as above, except that Partner C receives Parcel Y, rather than Parcel X, in complete liquidation of his partnership interest. Partner C's basis in Parcel Y is $20,000. The $1,000 increase in the basis of Parcel Y over the partnership's pre-distribution basis in that asset precipitates the application of Code Sec. 734(b). The partnership will reduce its basis in Parcel X by $1,000 to $22,000.[127]

---

[125] Code Sec. 734(c).
[126] Reg. § 1.755-1(c).

[127] Code Sec. 734(b)(2)(B); Reg. § 1.755-1(a)(1)(iii).

Example 13-28: Assume the pre-distribution balance sheet of the EFG Partnership is as follows:

Assets	Book Value and Adjusted Basis	FMV	Appreciation (Depreciation)
Accounts Receivable	$50,000	$50,000	$ 0
Cash	$50,000	$50,000	$ 0
Inventory	20,000	30,000	10,000
Investment Stock	20,000	60,000	40,000
Business Automobiles	60,000	30,000	(30,000)
Land	30,000	40,000	10,000
Building*	70,000	160,000	90,000
	$300,000	$420,000	$120,000

Capital Accounts			
Ed	$100,000	$140,000	$40,000
Frank	100,000	140,000	40,000
George	100,000	140,000	40,000
	$300,000	$420,000	$120,000

*No Code Sec. 1250 recapture.

Assume that each of the partners has an adjusted basis in his partnership interest of $100,000. In complete liquidation of his partnership interest, Ed receives the inventory, the investment stock, the business automobiles and $20,000. Assume that a Code Sec. 754 election is in effect.

Ed's basis in his partnership interest prior to distribution is $100,000.[128] Code Sec. 732(b) provides that the basis of property distributed by a partnership to a partner in liquidation of a partner's interest shall be an amount equal to the adjusted basis of such partner's interest in the partnership reduced by any money distributed in the same transaction. Ed received $20,000 in the transaction. Therefore, the $80,000 remaining basis will be allocated pursuant to Code Sec. 732(c)—$20,000 will be allocated first to the inventory items in an amount equal to the adjusted basis of those assets to the partnership.[129] Under Code Sec. 732(c)(2), the balance of Ed's basis in his partnership interest, $60,000, will be allocated to the investment stock and the business automobiles.

---

[128] Code Sec. 751 does not apply because the inventory (accounts receivable and inventory) is not substantially appreciated.

[129] Code Sec. 732(c)(1).

The $60,000 total basis to be allocated to the assets is $20,000 less than the pre-distribution basis of the assets to the partnership. This is a basis decrease. The $20,000 decrease is allocated to the only depreciated asset, the business automobile.

Ed's basis in each asset is:

Assets	Basis	FMV
Stock..............................	$20,000	$60,000
Automobiles	40,000	30,000
	$60,000	*$90,000*

The Code Sec. 734 adjustment is computed by comparing any increase or decrease in the respective Code Sec. 755 classes. Here the distributed property class consists of capital assets and Code Sec. 1231 property. The partnership has a Code Sec. 734(b)(1)(B) upward adjustment of $20,000, since this is the excess of the adjusted basis of distributed property to the partnership immediately before the distribution ($100,000) over the basis of the distributed property to the distributee partner ($80,000). The entire Code Sec. 734(b) increase is allocated only to the retained capital and Code Sec. 1231(b) assets.[130]

This increase is allocated between the land and building as follows:[131]

Assets	Adjusted Basis	FMV	Excess of Value over Basis
Land...................	$30,000	$40,000	$10,000
Building	70,000	160,000	90,000
	$100,000	*$200,000*	*$100,000*

To Land = 10% × $20,000 = $2,000 Adjustment

To Building = 90% × $20,000 = $18,000 Adjustment

.03 Substantial Basis Reduction

Whether or not the partnership has a Code Sec. 754 election in effect, Code Sec. 734(a) requires the partnership to adjust its basis in remaining assets following a distribution that results in a "substantial basis reduction." A substantial basis reduction is deemed to result from a distribution if the sum of the loss recognized by the partner (if any) on receipt of the distribution plus the step-up in basis of the distributed property in the distributee partner's hands exceeds $250,000. In such cases, the partnership is required to decrease its tax basis in its remaining properties in order to ensure that remaining partners are not allowed to artificially inflate their shares of subsequent partnership losses.[132]

---

[130] Code Sec. 755(b); Reg. § 1.755-1(c)(1)(ii).
[131] Code Sec. 755(a)(2); Reg. § 1.755-1(c)(2)(i).

[132] This requirement does not apply to securitization partnerships as defined in Code Sec. 734(f). See ¶ 1301.03 for a definition of securitization partnerships.

Example 13-29: Caprock Partners has the following balance sheets at year-end:

	Basis	*FMV*
Cash	$100,000	$100,000
Property 1	1,500,000	1,000,000
Property 2	3,800,000	1,900,000
	$5,400,000	$3,000,000
Capital, *F*	$1,800,000	$1,000,000
Capital, *H*	1,800,000	1,000,000
Capital, *K*	1,800,000	1,000,000
	$5,400,000	$3,000,000

K has decided to leave the partnership. To that end, the partnership distributes Property 1 to *K* in liquidation of her interest. *K* will take a substitute basis in Property 1 equal to her $1,800,000 basis in the partnership interest. Because this results in a step-up in the basis of Property 1 of more than $250,000, the partnership will be required to reduce its basis in Property 2 by $300,000 (the step-up in basis of Property 1 in *K*'s hands) whether or not a Code Sec. 754 election is in effect. The entire adjustment in this case is allocated to Property 2 because that is the only property the partnership has left.

Note that had the partnership distributed $50,000 cash plus *half* of Property 2 in liquidation of *K*'s interest (rather than Property 1), no adjustment would be triggered under Code Sec. 734, unless the partnership had a Code Sec. 754 election in effect (or chose to make one). In this case, *K* would recognize no gain or loss on the distribution and would take a stepped-*down* basis in the portion of Property 2 received in the distribution. Thus, there would not be a substantial basis reduction as defined in Code Sec. 734(d). The partnership would almost certainly want to make the Code Sec. 754 election in this case in order to preserve the other partners' shares of the pre-distribution built-in loss, but absent the election, no adjustment would be required (or allowed).

It is not clear whether these provisions are triggered when two or more distributions are made, neither of which constitutes a "substantial basis reduction" by itself, but when combined would result in a loss or stepped-up basis of more than $250,000. Code Sec. 734(d) reads as follows:

> For purposes of this section, there is a substantial basis reduction with respect to *"a" distribution* if . . .
> (emphasis added)

A literal reading of the statute suggests that each distribution must be analyzed individually, so that no adjustment is required (absent a Code Sec. 754 election)

¶1305.03

unless at least one distribution triggers a "substantial basis reduction" by itself. It is worth noting, however, that the statute defines the phrase "substantial basis reduction" as the *sum* of the loss recognized by the partner on receipt of the distribution and the basis step-up taken by the distributee partner in any property received. It is not possible for a partner to both step up the basis of property received in a partnership distribution and recognize a loss in the same transaction. Thus, this apparent anomaly may suggest that any future regulations issued under this statute aggregate multiple distributions made by a partnership within a specified time period. If they do not, partners or their advisors will surely recognize that dividing a planned distribution into two or more transactions will allow the partnership to avoid a mandatory reduction in the basis of its assets.

PART V

ADVANCED TOPICS

Chapter 14

Disguised Sales

¶ 1401 Introduction

In keeping with the entity/aggregate tension of the partnership taxation rules, transfers between the partnership and the partner are subject to rules which recognize the partnership as an entity separate from the partner, but take into account the fact that the partner is to some extent dealing with him- or herself. This chapter discusses the tax treatment of actual and deemed sales between the partnership and partner.

¶ 1402 Tax Treatment of Sale of Property to the Partnership by a Partner

.01 Sale at a Gain

If any person considered to be related to the partnership, whether a partner or not, sells property to the partnership that does not qualify as a capital asset in the *partnership's* hands, the gain will be treated as ordinary income.[1] The same result occurs when the sale is by the partnership to the related party. Examples of property commonly affected by this provision are depreciable realty and subdivided real estate which will be developed and sold to the public. The purpose of this provision is to make sure partners/partnerships can't avoid ordinary income by having a separate partnership/partner develop the property that is contributed/distributed.

Persons are considered to be related to the partnership if they own, directly or indirectly, more than 50 percent of the partnership's profit *or* capital interests. A person is considered to indirectly own partnership interests if those interests are owned by the following other persons:

---

[1] Code Sec. 707(b)(2).

1. Brothers,

2. Sisters,

3. Spouse,

4. Ancestors, or

5. Lineal descendants.[2]

A partnership interest held by a corporation, partnership, estate, or trust is considered to be owned proportionately by, or for, its shareholders, partners, or beneficiaries.[3]

.02 Sale at a Loss

No loss may be recognized on the sale of property between a partnership and a person owning, directly or indirectly, more than 50 percent of the interest in capital or profits of the partnership.[4] Indirect ownership is defined under Code Sec. 267(c) as described above.[5] Following the structure of Code Sec. 267, the buyer of property in this situation takes a cost basis equal to the price he, she or it paid to acquire the property even though the loss realized by the seller is not recognized.

However, when the buyer subsequently disposes of the property, any gain realized in that transaction may be offset by the disallowed loss previously realized by the seller. The gain offset should be treated as tax exempt income for purposes of adjusting the basis of the partnership interest of the partners to whom the gain is allocated. If the disallowed loss exceeds the subsequently realized gain (or if there is no gain subsequently realized on disposition), the excess loss is permanently erased.

> **Example 14-1:** Hilary Martin owns 60% of the capital and profits interests in Marlow Partners. This year, her son, Steve, sold property to the partnership for its appraised value of $275,000. Steve's tax basis in the property was $315,000. Because he is deemed to own the 60% interest in the partnership owned by Hilary, his $(40,000) loss is disallowed under Code Sec. 707(b)(1). However, the partnership's tax basis in the property will be equal to the $275,000 price it paid. If it subsequently sells the property for, say, $325,000, it will report gain of only $10,000 (its $50,000 realized gain offset by Steve's $40,000 disallowed loss). Note that if it later sells the property for only $300,000, it will report no gain or loss. Its $25,000 realized gain will be offset by the previously disallowed loss, but no deduction will be allowed for the remaining, "unused" loss.

> **Observation:** A question remaining unanswered is whether the partner who had the burden of the disallowed loss can be specially allocated the benefit of the offset to the partnership's taxable income. Although the situation

---

[2] Code Secs. 707(b)(3) and 267(c).

[3] Code Secs. 707(b)(3) and 267(c)(1).

[4] Code Sec. 707(b)(1). Losses are also disallowed on the sale of property between two partnerships if the same

persons own (directly or indirectly) more than 50 percent of the profits or capital interests in the two partnerships.

[5] For this purpose, Code Sec. 707(b)(3) provides for the application of Code Sec. 267(c), "other than paragraph (3) of such section."

is very much like a built-in Code Sec. 704(c) loss, neither the Code Sec. 704(b) or (c) regulations address the issue.

It should be noted that a sale of property at a loss between a partnership and a person other than a partner shall be considered as occurring between the other person and the members of the partnership separately.[6] This means that even if the other person is not related to the partnership, part of the loss, as opposed to the whole loss, will be disallowed if the other person is related to one of the partners.

> **Example 14-2:** *A*, an equal partner in the ABC partnership, personally owns all the stock of M Corporation. Partners *B* and *C* are not related to partner *A* or M Corporation. During the year the partnership sold property to M Corporation, sustaining a loss on the sale. The sale is considered as occurring between M Corporation and the partners separately. The sale considered as occurring between *A* and the M Corporation falls within the scope of Code Sec. 267(a) and (b), but the sales considered as occurring between partners *B* and *C* and the M Corporation do not. The latter two partners may, therefore, deduct their distributive shares of the partnership loss. However, no deduction shall be allowed to *A* for his 1/3 distributive share of the partnership loss. Furthermore, *A*'s adjusted basis for his partnership interest must be decreased by the amount of his distributive share of the loss.[7]
>
> Likewise, if M Corporation sold property to ABC for a loss, then only 2/3 of the loss (the part that was not "sold" to *A*) would be deductible by M Corporation.[8]

¶ 1403 Property Contributions Treated as Disguised Sales

.01 In General

The traditional method of tax accounting for property transfers between the partnership and a partner allowed the parties to treat the transfers as separate transactions: a contribution of property to the partnership and a subsequent distribution of property from the partnership. The partner and the partnership could take the position that a bona fide contribution and an unrelated distribution had occurred minimizing the tax consequences associated with what is, in substance, a disguised sale between the partner and the partnership.

The IRS was left the difficult task of detecting the "plan" and proving that the transactions taken as a whole amounted to a sale. These disguised sales could take the form of money sales when funds were "distributed" soon after a property "contribution." The sale could also be made in exchange for other property. For example, a taxpayer could contribute property *A* to a partnership and receive property *B* as a distribution in liquidation of his interest. Or, property *A* could be distributed to another partner in liquidation of his interest, leaving the partnership with only property *B* as its principal asset and the taxpayer as its principal partner.

Under the traditional contribution and distribution rules of partnership taxation, the swap would be tax-free. Three provisions have been enacted to treat these

---

[6] Reg. § 1.267(b)-1(b)(1).
[7] Reg. § 1.267(b)-1(b)(2), Example (1).

[8] Reg. § 1.267(b)-1(b)(2), Example (2).

types of transactions as disguised sales: Code Secs.707(a)(2)(B), 704(c)(1)(B) and 737.

    S Corporation Observation: There is no counterpart to the partnership disguised sale rules in the S corporation arena. However, the potential for abuse is much lower due to the very different rules applicable to distributions from an S Corp to its shareholders. If a shareholder receives any property other than stock in exchange for a contribution of property to a regular or S corporation, such property is treated as "boot" and generates immediate tax consequences. Distributions to a shareholder subsequent to the contribution of property to the S corporation must generally be *pro rata* unless they are structured as a stock redemption. Stock redemptions are treated by the shareholder as a sale of his or her stock, which trigger immediate tax consequences. In addition, distributions of appreciated property are a taxable event to an S or C corporation.[9]

.02 Contributions Related to Distributions—The Facts and Circumstances Test of Code Sec. 707(a)(2)(B)

Code Sec. 707(a)(2)(B) deals with disguised sales carried out by means of a contribution to the partnership entity followed by a subsequent distribution to the partner by recharacterizing the transaction as a sale.[10] The "disguised sale between partners" technique demonstrated in the example below was used by taxpayers in a number of reported cases.[11]

    Example 14-3: A owns land with a $100,000 fair market value and basis of $60,000. B is interested in developing the land but A does not want to recognize taxable gain from sale of the land. They form an equal partnership in which A contributes the land and B contributes $50,000 and a financing commitment. After the money is obtained to finance the development, the partnership distributes $50,000 of cash to A. Since A's basis is $60,000, A recognizes no gain on the transaction. This is true even though in the IRS's view A had, in essence, sold a half interest in this property to B, which should have resulted in a gain of $20,000. A would be effectively using his entire basis in the land to offset a gain on sale of one-half the land.

    Example 14-4: A owns land with a $100,000 fair market value and a basis of $60,000. The BC partnership is interested in developing the land and A is willing to sell it for BC's installment note. Under the installment method of reporting this sale, A's reporting ratio would be 60% and A would report 60% of each payment as capital gain. ABC instead arranged the sale as a contribution to the ABC partnership and an installment liquidation of A's interest. Under the

---

[9] Code Sec. 311(b).

[10] Under proposed regulations a transfer of money, property or other consideration (including the assumption of a liability) by a partner (purchasing partner) to a partnership and a transfer of consideration by the partnership to another partner (selling partner) would in many cases be treated as a sale, in whole or in part, of the selling partner's interest in the partnership to the purchasing partner. However, these proposed regulations

have been controversial, and as a result there is some doubt that they will be finalized in their current form. Prop. Regs. §§ 1.707-7, 1.07-9.

[11] See, for example, *J.H. Otey, Jr. v. Commr.*, 70 TC 312, Dec. 35,167 (1978), aff'd per curiam, CA-6, 80-2 USTC ¶ 9817, 634 F2d 1046; *Barenholtz v. Commr.*, 77 TC 85, Dec. 38,070 (1981) (holding that there was a taxable sale).

partnership distribution rules, cash distributions are first treated as recoveries of A's $60,000 basis in his interest before he reports any capital gain.[12] A would in effect be receiving cost recovery reporting for the installment sale.

Prior to implementation of Code Sec. 707(a)(2)(B), the IRS was explicitly authorized in the regulations under Code Sec. 731 to recharacterize as sales contributions which were followed by related distributions.[13] The IRS argued that the substance of such transactions was a sale and that the tax treatment should correspond to the substance. The courts, however, often held that taxpayers had simply structured a transaction to achieve favorable tax results. The cases hinged on the importance of the particular property to the business of the partnership and the necessity of financial success before the partner contributing property could recover his or her entire investment. As an example, in *Otey v. Commissioner*,[14] ithe Tax Court pointed out that, without the contributed property, the partnership would have no property at all, and Otey had no guarantee of recovering his property's value from a buyer. Code Sec. 707(a)(2)(B) now states, as did the prior regulations, that when such a transaction, viewed as a whole, is properly characterized as a sale, then the transaction is treated as a sale and governed by Code Sec. 707(a)(1).

General rules. The general rules provide that a transfer of property to a partnership, coupled with a concurrent or subsequent transfer of money or other consideration to the contributing partner (including the assumption of the partner's liability or taking the property subject to the liability), will be treated, not as two separate transactions, but as a *sale*, in whole or in part, of the property to the partnership if:

1. The transfer of money or other consideration would *not* have been made but for the transfer of property; and

2. In cases in which the transfers are not made simultaneously, the subsequent transfer is not dependent on the entrepreneurial risks of partnership operations.[15]

The regulation adopts a test of ten facts and circumstances to determine whether either of the foregoing two rules apply.[16]

The facts and circumstances taken into account in determining whether a disguised sale has occurred are:

1. The reciprocal transfer's timing and amount are determinable with reasonable certainty;

2. The partner has a legally enforceable right to the reciprocal transfer;

3. The right to the reciprocal transfer is secured;

4. Another party is legally obligated to make contributions to the partnership to permit the partnership to make the reciprocal transfer;

---

[12] Code Sec. 731(a).

[13] Reg. § 1.731-1(c)(3).

[14] *J.H. Otey, Jr. v. Commr.*, 70 TC 312, Dec. 35,167 (1978), aff'd per curiam, CA-6, 80-2 USTC ¶ 9817, 634 F2d 1046.

[15] Reg. § 1.707-3(b)(1).

[16] Reg. § 1.707-3(b)(2).

5. Another party is legally obligated to loan money to the partnership to permit the partnership to make the reciprocal transfer;

6. The partnership is obligated to borrow amounts necessary to permit the reciprocal transfer;

7. The partnership holds money or other liquid assets, beyond the reasonable needs of the business, that are expected to be available to make the reciprocal transfer;

8. The partnership distributions, allocations, or control of partnership operations is designed to effect an exchange of the burdens and benefits of ownership of property;

9. Transfers of money or other consideration by the partnership to the partner which are disproportionately large in relationship to the partner's general and continuing interest in partnership profits indicates a reciprocal transfer; and

10. A distribution that is in no event returnable indicates a reciprocal transfer.[17]

Presumptions. If within two years of a property contribution to a partnership the partnership transfers money or other property to the partner, the transfers are presumed to be a sale of the property to the partnership unless the facts and circumstances clearly establish that the transfers do not constitute a sale.[18] With certain exceptions, the regulations require tax return disclosure of any distributions to a property contributor made within two years of the property contribution.[19]

See sample Form 8275, Disclosure Statement, in the Appendix.

If the transfers of property and money are *more* than two years apart, the regulations create a rebuttable presumption that a "sale" did *not* take place. However, if two years or *less* separate the transactions, the contribution and subsequent distribution are presumed to be related and they will be treated as a disguised sale. The presumption places the burden of proof on the taxpayer to substantiate that the two transfers were not related, or that the subsequent distribution was subject to the risk of entrepreneurial operations by the partnership. Where the two transactions occur more than two years apart, the burden of proof shifts to the IRS.

> *Example 14-5:* [20] *A* transfers property to a partnership with a value of $4,000, and receives an interest in the partnership plus $3,000 in cash. His basis in the property is $1,200. Under Code Sec. 707(a)(2)(B):
>
> - Three-fourths of the transaction is treated as a "sale" ($3,000/$4,000), and one-fourth as a "contribution."

---

[17] *Id.*

[18] Reg. § 1.707-3(c).

[19] Either the distributee partner files Form 8275, Disclosure Statement, or an attachment to his or her Form 1040, U.S. Individual Income Tax Return, described in the regulations in lieu of Form 8275. Reg. §§ 1.707-3(c)(2) and 1.707-8.

[20] Reg. § 1.707-3(f), Ex. 1.

- A must recognize gain as follows:

Sale proceeds	$3,000
Basis (3/4 × $1,200)	(900)
Gain	*$2,100*

- *A* has made a contribution of property with a value of $1,000 and a basis of $300 (one-fourth each of $4,000 and $1,200, respectively). Note that *A*'s percentage interest in the partnership is ignored, and indeed not even mentioned, in the above results.

- The partnership has purchased a three-fourths interest in the property and has a basis of $3,300 ($3,000 cost basis plus a $300 transferred basis) in the property.

If multiple properties are transferred to the partnership, the computation of the "sale" and "contribution" amounts are allocated to the various properties in proportion to their respective fair market values.

.03 Special Rules for Guaranteed Payments, Preferred Returns, Cash Flow Distributions, and Pre-formation Expenditures

The legislative history of Code Sec. 707(a)(2)(B) indicates that the disguised sale rules are not intended to prevent partners from receiving guaranteed priority or preferential distributions in return for their capital contributions.[21] In the context of disguised sale determinations, the critical issue relating to preferred returns and guaranteed payments is whether they represent merely a return *on* the recipient's contributed capital or, instead, are designed to serve as a return *of* all or a portion of the recipient's contributed capital. In the case of a return *on* capital, such an interest does not provide a means of withdrawing the transferor's equity in the contributed property and can be disregarded in the disguised sale analysis. In the case of a return *of* capital, the payment does reduce the transferor-partner's equity interest in the partnership and must be taken into account in the disguised sale analysis.

Guaranteed payments and preferred returns—definition. The term "guaranteed payment for capital," as used in the regulations, means any payment to a partner by the partnership that is determined without regard to partnership income and is for the use of that partner's capital.[22] The term "preferred return," as used in the regulations, refers to a partner's right to preferential distributions of partnership cash flow matched, to the extent available, by an allocation of partnership income.[23]

Guaranteed payments presumed not to be sales proceeds. A guaranteed payment for capital made to a partner will not be treated as part of a sale of property under the regulations.[24] This exclusion applies whether or not the guaranteed payment is made within two years of the transferor's contribution of property to the partnership.[25]

For purposes of Code Sec. 707(a)(2) and the regulations thereunder, a payment is presumed to be a guaranteed payment for capital[26] if it is:

---

[21] *See* H.R. Rep. No. 432, Pt. 2, 98th Cong., 2d Sess., 1216, 1218, 1221 (1984); S. Rep. at 231.
[22] Reg. § 1.707-4(a)(1).
[23] Reg. § 1.707-4(a)(2).

[24] Reg. § 1.707-4(a)(1)(i).
[25] Reg. § 1.707-4(a)(1)(ii).
[26] *Id.*

- Characterized by the parties as a guaranteed payment for capital;
- Determined without regard to income of the partnership; and
- Reasonable.

This presumption can be rebutted only by facts and circumstances clearly establishing that the payment is not a guaranteed payment for capital and is part of a sale.[27] Note that if the deduction for the guaranteed payment is specially allocated to the recipient partner, the transaction is not properly characterized as a guaranteed payment.[28] The deduction exactly offsets the recipient partner's income from receipt of the guaranteed payment, essentially making the payment nontaxable. Moreover, the deduction reduces the partner's capital account. Thus, the payment is properly classified as a distribution rather than as a guaranteed payment. If it occurs within two years of a contribution of property by the partner to the partnership, the disguised sale rules will be triggered.

A payment to a partner that is characterized by the parties as a guaranteed payment for capital but that is not reasonable will be presumed not to be a guaranteed payment for capital.[29] This presumption will apply whether or not the guaranteed payments are made within two years of the transferor's contribution of property to the partnership.[30] This presumption can be rebutted only by facts and circumstances clearly establishing that the payment is a guaranteed payment for capital.[31]

Reasonable preferred payments presumed not sales proceeds. A transfer of money to a partner that is characterized by the parties as a preferred return and that is reasonable is presumed not to be part of a sale of property to the partnership.[32] This presumption can be rebutted only by facts and circumstances (including the likelihood and expected timing of the matching allocation of income or gain to support the preferred return) clearly establishing that the transfer is part of a sale.[33]

Reasonable in amount. A transfer of money that is made to a partner that is characterized as a guaranteed payment for capital or a preferred return is reasonable only to the extent that:

- The transfer is made to the partner pursuant to a written provision of a partnership agreement that provides for payment for the use of capital in a reasonable amount; and
- The payment is made for the use of capital only after the date on which that provision is added to the partnership agreement.[34]

A transfer of money that is made to the partner during any partnership taxable year and is characterized as a preferred return or guaranteed payment for capital is reasonable in amount if the sum of any preferred return and any guaranteed payment for capital that is payable for that year does not exceed the amount determined by multiplying either (1) the partner's unreturned capital at the *begin-*

---

[27] *Id.*

[28] Reg. § 1.707-4(a)(1)(i).

[29] Reg. § 1.707-4(a)(1)(iii).

[30] *Id.*

[31] *Id.*

[32] Reg. § 1.707-4(a)(2).

[33] *Id.*

[34] Reg. § 1.707-4(a)(3)(i).

ning of the year or, at the partner's option, (2) the partner's weighted average capital balance for the year (with either amount appropriately adjusted, taking into account the relevant compounding periods, to reflect any unpaid preferred return or guaranteed payment for capital that is payable to the partner) by the safe harbor interest rate for that year.[35] Regardless of the partnership's risk profile, the safe harbor interest rate for a partnership's taxable year equals 150 percent of the highest applicable federal rate in effect at any time from the time that the right to the preferred return or guaranteed payment for capital is first established pursuant to a binding, written agreement among the partners through the end of the taxable year.[36] A partner's unreturned capital equals the excess of the aggregate amount of money and the fair market value of other consideration (net of liabilities) contributed by the partner to the partnership over the aggregate amount of money and the fair market value of other consideration (net of liabilities) distributed by the partnership to the partner other than transfers of money that are presumed to be guaranteed payments for capital, reasonable preferred returns, or operating cash flow distributions (described below).[37]

A partner is likely to elect to use the weighted average capital balance where a partner contributes additional capital to the partnership after the beginning of the year, exceeding any distributions received during the year, inasmuch as this method will increase the amount of reasonable guaranteed payments and/or preferred returns. Conversely, a partner who makes no additional contributions and receives distributions reducing capital during the year would prefer to use the unreturned capital at the beginning of the year.

Presumption rebutted. As stated, the presumption that a reasonable preferred return is not part of a disguised sale and the presumption that a reasonable guaranteed payment is a guaranteed payment for capital are both subject to rebuttal based upon a showing of facts and circumstances that clearly establish to the contrary. In rebutting these presumptions, the regulations appear to be most focused on whether the preferred return or guaranteed payment is merely an income preference or has the potential to return to the recipient some portion of his or her investment. The regulations, in the case of preferred returns and guaranteed payments, do not seem concerned with the degree of entrepreneurial risk associated with any such income preference. Since, absent special circumstances, neither a preferred return nor a guaranteed payment has the capacity to reduce the recipient's capital investment, they are distinguishable from other cash flow distributions that do have such capacity. There is nothing inherently offensive about a preferred return or a guaranteed payment, assuming reasonableness, whether received with respect to cash or property. As with preferred stock, they merely represent an income preference generally found in a situation where one partner has traded off a participation in the upside in return for a more secure cash flow.[38]

---

[35] Reg. § 1.707-4(a)(3)(ii).

[36] *Id.*

[37] *Id.*

[38] Thus, a preferred return that is matched with gross income (a low risk source) should be as acceptable as a preferred return matched with net income (a potentially high risk source, depending upon its components). A preferred return matched with gross income is similar to many guaranteed payments (though still less secure than others).

If, however, the deduction for a reasonable guaranteed payment is dispropor-tionately allocated to the recipient thereof, the payment effectively reduces the partner's equity interest and is therefore converted from a return *on* capital to a return *of* capital. The same is true when the parties agree to a reasonable preferred return that is not expected to be matched with income, or such matching is not expected to occur until the distant future. Once the character of these income preferences has been changed in this manner, as in the case of any other distribu-tion of capital, entrepreneurial risk considerations must be applied. In such cases, if the IRS can also establish that the funding of such income preferences has been secured or supported by arrangements with a partner or third parties that insulate such payments from the risks of the partnership's business, the favorable presump-tions would likely be overridden and the provisions of Reg. § 1.707-3 applied.

For example, a partnership agreement may provide for a guaranteed payment paid with respect to a transferor partners' capital which is (1) limited in duration, (2) charged entirely against the cash flow otherwise distributable to the transferee partner, and (3) expressly subject to credit support provided by the transferee partner. Moreover, if the partnership or the partner had purchased the property from the contributing partner in an installment sale, applying a market interest rate would have resulted in payments approximating the guaranteed payments. Such arrangement insures a reduction in the transferor partner's capital and a concomi-tant build-up in the transferee partner's capital of a predetermined amount (much like the shift of equity accompanying a sale). Therefore, the combination of these circumstances are sufficient to override the favorable presumption otherwise ex-tended to a guaranteed payment that is reasonable in amount. The payments actually result in a return of, rather than a return on, capital due to the economic effect of disproportionately burdening the transferee partner's cash flow.[39]

In addition, though the regulations do not address this circumstance, when a nonsimultaneous distribution is found to be a related transfer and a portion of the partner's contributed property is deemed sold, it would appear that any preferred returns or guaranteed payments previously made with respect to that portion of the recipient partner's capital that is deemed sold would also be characterized, in whole or in part, as payments with respect to such sale. The partner would be treated as receiving installment sale payments and the partnership would get basis for its obligation to make the payments.[40]

Operating cash flow distributions. An operating cash flow distribution received in connection with a contribution of property to a partnership is presumed not to be part of a sale of such property to the partnership.[41] This presumption will apply whether or not the operating cash flow distributions are made within two years of the transferor's contribution of property to the partnership.[42] Such presumption can be rebutted only by facts and circumstances clearly establishing that the distribu-tion is part of a sale transaction.[43]

---

[39] Reg. § 1.707-4(a)(4), Ex. 2.

[40] *Id.* The only undesirable aspect of the example is that it did not provide insight into the relative weight given to each of the above circumstances.

[41] Reg. § 1.707-4(b)(1).

[42] *Id.*

[43] *Id.*

¶1403.03

Operating cash flow distribution defined. Transfers of money by a partnership to a partner during the taxable year will be presumed to be operating cash flow distributions for purposes of the regulations to the extent that:

- Such distributions are not presumed to be guaranteed payments for capital;
- Such distributions are not reasonable preferred returns;
- Such distributions are not characterized by the parties as distributions to the recipient partner acting in a capacity other than as a partner; and
- Such distributions do not exceed the product of (1) the net cash flow of the partnership from operations from the year, multiplied by (2) the lesser of the partner's percentage interest in overall partnership profits for that year or the partner's percentage interest in overall partnership profits for the life of the partnership.[44]

The net cash flow of the partnership from operations for a taxable year is an amount equal to the taxable income or loss of the partnership arising in the ordinary course of the partnership's business and investment activities, *increased* by:

- Tax exempt interest;
- Depreciation;
- Amortization;
- Cost recovery allowances; and
- Other non-cash charges deducted in determining such taxable income;

and *decreased* by:

- Principal payments made on any partnership indebtedness;
- Property replacement or contingency reserves actually established by the partnership;
- Capital expenditures when made from other than these reserves or from borrowings, the proceeds of which are not included in operating cash flow; and
- Any other cash expenditures (including preferred returns) not deducted in determining such taxable income or loss.[45]

In determining a partner's operating cash flow distributions for any taxable year, the partner may use the partner's smallest percentage interest under the terms of the partnership agreement in any material item of partnership income or gain that the partnership may realize in the three-year period beginning with such taxable year.[46] This provision is intended to serve merely as a safe harbor for taxpayers and is not intended to preclude a taxpayer from using a different percentage in determining its operating cash flow distributions.[47]

The preamble to the final regulations states that, if a transfer of operating cash flow exceeds the amount allowed under the operating cash flow distribution

---

[44] Reg. § 1.707-4(b)(2)(i).
[45] *Id.*

[46] Reg. § 1.707-4(b)(2)(ii).
[47] *Id.*

presumption described above,[48] the transfer will qualify for the presumption up to the amount allowed under the presumption.[49] The excess or portion of the transfer that does not qualify as an operating cash flow distribution is tested under the facts and circumstances test, subject to any presumptions that may apply.[50]

Example 14-6: Joe Baxter contributed property with a tax basis of $100,000 and a fair market value of $200,000 to newly formed Baxter Brothers Partnership. In exchange, Joe received a 20% general partnership interest. For the partnership's first year of operations, it reported $200,000 of taxable income, of which $40,000 (20%) was allocated to Joe. At year-end, he received a distribution of $60,000 from partnership cash flows. Because this distribution exceeded Joe's share of cash flows, the excess will likely be treated by the IRS as a disguised payment under Code Sec. 707. Joe will likely be treated as having sold 10% (20,000/200,000) of the contributed asset, and will be required to recognize a $10,000 gain (10% of the built-in gain interest in the property at the date of contribution).

Post-year-end distribution requirement. The proposed regulations provided that excludible guaranteed payments for capital, preferred returns, and operating cash flow distributions would lose their character unless distributed no later than 75 days after the end of a taxable year.[51] The final regulations eliminate this distribution deadline. Therefore, a payment that initially qualifies for an exclusion will not lose the benefit of qualification even if it is retained for distribution in a later year.

Special rule for reimbursements of pre-formation expenditures. A transfer of money or other consideration by a partnership to a partner will not be treated as part of a sale of property by the partner to the partnership under the regulations to the extent that the transfer to the partner is made to reimburse the partner for certain capital expenditures incurred before property is contributed to the partnership.[52]

Pre-formation capital expenditures defined. To qualify for this special rule, the capital expenditures must meet the following conditions:

- The capital expenditures are incurred during the two-year period preceding the transfer by the partner to the partnership; and
- The capital expenditures are incurred by the partner with respect to:
  - Partnership organization and syndication costs described in Section 709 of the Internal Revenue Code; or
  - Property contributed to the partnership by the partner, but only to the extent the reimbursed capital expenditures do not exceed 20 percent of the fair market value of such property at the time of the contribution. However, the 20 percent of value limitation does not apply if the fair market value of the contributed property does not exceed 120 percent of the partner's adjusted basis in the contributed property at the time of

---

[48] Reg. § 1.707-4(b)(2)(i).

[49] *See* the Preamble to Final Regulations, T.D. 8439, 1992-2 CB 126.

[50] *Id.*

[51] Prop. Reg. § 1.707-4(c).

[52] Reg. § 1.707-4(d).

¶1403.03

contribution. If these rules are satisfied, 100 percent of the reimbursement of capital expenditures that otherwise satisfy the requirements of the regulations are excepted from disguised sale treatment.[53]

The proposed regulations left some question as to whether the exception would apply at all if the reimbursement exceeded 20 percent of the fair market value. The language was modified in the final regulations to provide that in the case of a reimbursement that exceeds 20 percent of the fair market value of the contributed property, the reimbursement qualifies for the exception to the extent of 20 percent of value.

Planning. The pre-formation expenditure rule provides substantial flexibility to taxpayers holding appreciated property in need of capital improvements. In tandem with the disguised sale rules governing the sale/contribution of encumbered property with qualified liabilities incurred in the acquisition or improvement of a contributed property,[54] these rules allow a taxpayer to withdraw potentially all of his or her equity in a property acquired and/or improved within the preceding 24 months (assuming the taxpayer could finance up to 80 percent of its acquisition costs and improvement with a qualified liability). However, this rule is in need of clarification on several points.

The pre-formation expenditure rule is clearly related to the disguised sale qualified liability rule,[55] and yet there is no expressed interface between the two rules. As a result, a literal application of the two rules can result in a doubling-up of the benefits realized by a taxpayer. For example, it would appear that the 20-percent limitation in the pre-formation expenditure rule can be literally read to relate to the full fair market value of the contributed property, not reduced by qualified liabilities incurred in funding the same capital expenditures being reduced under such rule. If the transferor financed more than 80 percent of the acquisition and improvement of the contributed property within 24 months of its transfer to a partnership, it would appear that the transferor can actually use this rule as a means of withdrawing equity from the improved property itself or other property contributed along with the improved property.

Example 14-7: *A* owns a property that has appreciated from $2 million to $5 million in value. *A* spends $5 million on improvements to such property financed 100% with a qualified (recourse) liability. The property has a value of $10 million, as improved. *B* contributes $7 million of cash to partnership AB for a 70% interest therein. *A* contributes the improved property to AB for a 30% interest therein. AB assumes the $5 million liability and distributes $2 million cash to *A*. AB immediately repays the $5 million assumed liability. Technically, the pre-formation expenditure rule should safe harbor the $2 million distribution from disguised sale treatment even though all of the capital expenditures were funded with a qualified liability.[56] The $2 million distribution is actually a withdrawal of a portion of *A*'s "historic" equity in the property and should be taxable as disguised sales proceeds.

---

[53] *See* the Preamble to Final Regulations, T.D. 8439, 1992-2 CB 126.

[54] Reg. § 1.707-5(a)(6)(i)(C).

[55] *Id.*

[56] Otherwise exempted from disguised sale treatment under Reg. § 1.707-5.

Example 14-8: *A* owns unencumbered property *X* with a fair market value of $5 million and a tax basis of $2 million. *A* acquires property *Y* with a fair market value of $5 million—financing 100% of such purchase on a recourse basis. *A* contributes *X* and *Y* (subject to the debt) to partnership AB and receives from AB a distribution of $2 million and a Code Sec. 704(b) book capital account of $3 million. *B* contributes $5 million to AB and AB immediately repays the qualified liability transferred by *A*. Though it would appear that *A* has effectively sold 40% of property *X* to AB for a $1.2 million gain, this transaction does not appear to be subject to recharacterization under the final regulations.

Though it seems that the 20-percent fair market value limitations should apply to the value of only the property upon which the capital expenditures were incurred, it is not clear whether improvements to real property should be treated as separate property for this purpose.

The reference to capital expenditures should be clarified as to whether a capital expenditure (*i.e.*, a cost giving rise to a benefit extending over a 12-month or greater period) that is currently deductible for federal income tax purposes due to a special allowance still qualifies as a capital expenditure under this rule (*e.g.*, intangible drilling cost deductions). Since the character of these expenditures is not affected by the allowance of the deduction such items should qualify.

Clarification should also be provided in the case where the property to be contributed to a partnership is an interest in another existing partnership. More specifically, in this context, do capital contributions made within the prior 12 months constitute capital expenditures with respect to the contributed partnership interest? Does it matter when the expenditure at the level of the existing partnership being funded through such capital contributions is itself a capital expenditure? In this context, are capital expenditures limited to organizational costs, syndication costs, and other "outside" costs associated with the acquisition of such interest?

It is difficult to understand the limitations imposed on the pre-formation expenditure rule (*i.e.*, the 24-month and 20-percent value limitations) in light of the fact that no such limitations are applied to the related qualified liability rule under the disguised sale rules.[57] Assuming that it is clarified under the pre-formation expenditure rule that historical equity cannot be withdrawn from an encumbered property using the double-dipping method outlined above, there does not appear to be justification for such bias. It merely encourages taxpayers to fund their capital expenditures with as much debt financing as possible.

Other exceptions. The regulations provide that other types of transfers or payments to a partner may be excepted from treatment as part of a sale, by revenue ruling or other guidance published in the Internal Revenue Bulletin. The Preamble to the final regulations suggests that disguised sale payments do not include loans, repayments, and guaranteed payments for services.[58]

---

[57] Code Sec. 1.707-5(a)(6)(i)(C).   [58] Reg. § 1.707-4(e); T.D. 8439, 1992-2 CB 126.

¶1403.03

.04 Effect of Liabilities

General. Regulation § 1.707-5 addresses the treatment of liability transfers to the partnership in connection with the transfer of property. Recall that Section 752(b) treats the partnership's assumption of a partner's liabilities as a cash payment to the partner. In some cases, these deemed payments trigger the disguised sale rules, depending on whether or not the liability is a "qualified liability."

Unless the liability is a "qualified liability" (see below), the "deemed distribution" arising from allocation of a portion of such liability among the other partners will be treated as a payment subject to the disguised sale rules. For purposes of Reg. § 1.707-3, the "disguised sale" amount is not the total deemed distribution, but only the portion thereof which is attributable to the liability shares of the other partners.[59] That is, the deemed distribution associated with the partnership's assumption of the partner's liability is offset by the deemed contribution associated with the contributing partner's share of such debt. Note that this offset applies only to the contributing partner's share of his or her own debt. To the extent the partner is allocated a share of other partnership liabilities, there is no offset against the debt relief associated with the disguised sale portion of the exchange. The key to understanding the application of the disguised sale rules is recognizing that the transfer to the partnership is broken into two separate transactions: a disguised sale of a portion of the "contributed" property (governed by § 707) and a contribution to the partnership of the remainder of the property (governed by § 721).

Example 14-9: Kali transfers property to a partnership in which she is a one-third partner with a value of $4,000. Her tax basis in the property is $2,500. Assume that just prior to the transfer, Kali borrowed $3,000 against the property, which she used to pay an unrelated debt. She transfers the property to the partnership subject to this new debt. Because the debt was not incurred to acquire the property and the proceeds were not invested in the property, the debt is not a qualified liability (as discussed below). The assumption of the debt by the partnership is treated as a distribution of money to Kali under Section 752(b). Moreover, because this deemed cash payment occurs within two years of Kali's contribution of property to the partnership, the transfer to the partnership will be partially re-characterized as a disguised sale.

Assume that Kali is allocated one-third of the debt (reflecting her one-third interest in the partnership). Thus, only 2/3rds of the deemed cash payment under Section 752(b), or $2,000, will be treated as a payment received by Kali in connection with her transfer of the property to the partnership. Kali will be treated as selling half the property to the partnership ($2,000 deemed cash payment received ÷ $4,000 FMV of property). Her basis in half the property is $1,250 and she will recognize a gain on the disguised sale of $750, as follows:

---

[59] Reg. § 1.707-5(b). Note that the rules of Temp. Reg. § 1.163-8T apply to "trace" the financing proceeds into the hands of the partner.

Sales price	$2,000
Cost (50% × $2,500)	(1,250)
Gain	*$750*

The remainder of the transfer, consisting of half the property (basis $1,250 and FMV $2,000) and subject to the remainder of the liability ($1,000), will be treated as a contribution to the partnership under Section 721. Kali will take a $1,250 tax basis in her partnership interest, computed as follows:

Basis in property contributed	$1,250
Liability relief	(1,000)
Share of partnership liabilities (1/3 of $3,000)	1,000
Basis in partnership interest	$1,250

Qualified liability relief not deemed sales proceeds. A "qualified liability" is one which is not greater than the fair market value of the property and was incurred by a partner:

- More than two years prior to the transfer of the property and which has encumbered the property during this period; or
- Within two years of the property transfer, which has encumbered the property during the period, and was *not* incurred in anticipation of the transfer and based on the facts and circumstances was incurred:[60]
  1. For the purpose of providing funds, the expenditure of which was capitalized to the property; or
  2. In the ordinary course of the business in which the property was used, and substantially all of the assets used in such business are transferred to the partnership.[61]

    Example 14-10: A contributed property with a tax basis of $500,000 and a FMV of $750,000 to limited liability company AB in exchange for a 50% partnership interest. The property is encumbered by a $350,000 recourse mortgage incurred several years ago to finance its acquisition. The LLC's assumption of the mortgage is treated under §752 as a distribution of cash to A. However, for purposes of §707, the mortgage is a qualified liability (incurred more than two years before the contribution and used to finance acquisition of the encumbered property). Accordingly, the deemed distribution under §752(b) is not treated as a partial payment for the property contributed by A to the LLC.

.05 Treatment of Qualified Liabilities when Transfer Is Treated as Part of a Sale

    General. If a transfer is treated as a sale without regard to the shifting of liabilities from the partner/member to the partnership or LLC, then the amount of

---

[60] There are requirements of notification to the IRS under Reg. §1.707-5 that are similar to those under Reg. §1.707-3. See fn 19.

[61] Reg. §1.707-5(a)(6).

qualified liabilities shifted will increase the amount realized by the partner or LLC member on the sale. For this purpose, the amount of qualified liabilities deemed shifted by virtue of the contribution to the entity is limited to the lesser of:[62]

1. The amount determined under §752(b) (with adjustment for the different allocation rules for nonrecourse liabilities under §707); or

2. The product of the partner/member's *net equity percentage* in the contributed property and the outstanding balance of the debt.

The partner/member's *net equity percentage* in the contributed property is equal to the FMV of other consideration received from the entity divided by the net FMV of the contributed property.

> ***Example 14-11:*** *D* contributes Property 1 to a partnership. Property 1 has a FMV of $165,000 and a tax basis of $96,000. It is encumbered by a $75,000 liability incurred more than two years ago to finance acquisition of the property. In exchange, *D* receives a 1/3 partnership interest, and $30,000 in cash.
>
> Because the $30,000 cash distribution occurs within two years of *D*'s contribution of the property to the partnership, the two transfers are treated as related. In addition, the partnership's assumption of the mortgage is treated as a distribution related to *D*'s contribution. Since the mortgage is a qualified liability, however, only a portion of the deemed distribution under §752(b) is treated as part of the sale of the property to the partnership.
>
> The amount of the transfer under §707 with regard to the liability is limited to the lesser of the amount shifted under §752 ($50,000 = $75,000 liability × 2/3), or the product of *D*'s "net equity percentage" in the transferred property times the outstanding balance of the debt. *D*'s net equity percentage is the ratio of the FMV of the other property transferred to *D* ($30,000 cash) over the *net* FMV of the property contributed to the partnership by *D* ($165,000 FMV – $75,000 debt = $90,000). Thus, *D*'s net equity percentage is 1/3, and the amount of the qualified liability included in *D*'s amount realized from the disguised sale is $25,000 ($75,000 liability × 1/3). *D* must recognize a $23,000 gain under §707:

Cash received	$30,000
Liability relief included in deemed sale portion of transaction	25,000
Total deemed sales price	$55,000
Basis in property included in deemed sale (1/3 x $96,000) . .	32,000
Gain recognized	$23,000

.06 Disguised Payment for Services

Another area of contention is "disguised payments for services." Here, the concern is that ordinary-income compensation for services is converted to capital

---

[62] Reg. §1.707-5(a)(5).

gain, or that the partnership is avoiding capitalizing service compensation. However, proposed regulations on the subject have not yet been issued.[63]

> ***Example 14-12:*** The ABC partnership engages *C*, an architect, to design and supervise construction of improvements to its properties. If the partnership paid *C* with cash, the payments would be capitalized into the basis of the improvements. Instead, they admit him as a partner for rendering the future services of designing and construction supervision. His income allocation would have the effect of allowing the other partners a deduction for his services and if he sells his interest, he will have capital gain.

The "disguised sale" rationale is also manifested in Code Sec. 704(c)(1)(B) (Distribution of Contributed Property to Partners other than the Contributing Partner) and in Code Sec. 737 (Distribution of Property to a Partner with Built-In Gain). These provisions are discussed below.

¶ 1404 Partner Contributes Property and Partnership Distributes It to Another Partner—Code Sec. 704(c)(1)(B)

Prior to the implementation of Code Sec. 704(c)(1)(B),[64] it was relatively simple for a seller of property to avoid gain by contributing it to a partnership that distributed it to another partner (the buyer) leaving the partnership with the property the buyer had contributed (the purchase price).

> ***Example 14-13:*** *A* owns Blackacre, which has a fair market value of $1,000,000 and basis of $100,000. The BCDE Partnership wishes to buy and develop Blackacre, but *A* neither wants to recognize gain on the property's sale nor to participate in a Code Sec. 1031 like-kind exchange. A new ABCDE Limited Partnership is formed with *A* contributing Blackacre, *B* contributing $1,000,000, and *C, D* and *E* each contributing $100,000. Blackacre is then distributed to *B* in liquidation of his interest. *B* recognizes no gain and takes a basis of $1,000,000 in Blackacre. The ACDE partnership continues as an investment partnership with *A* as the general partner holding a 99% interest. Its sole asset is cash in the amount of $1,300,000. *B* has effectively purchased Blackacre for $1,000,000, with *A* attempting to defer her gain until liquidation of the partnership.

The stated purpose of Code Sec. 704(c)(1)(B) is to prevent partners from escaping the anti-gain shifting rule of Code Sec. 704(c)(1)(A) by simply distributing the contributed property to another partner who may receive a full basis step-up in the property in a liquidating distribution.[65] The effect of the statute is to trigger recognition of the gain inherent in the distributed property to the partner from whom such property was originally received by the partnership. The consequences

---

[63] Reg. §1.707-2 has been reserved for purposes of later rule-making on this topic.

[64] The Omnibus Budget Reconciliation Act of 1989, P.L. 101-239, 101st Cong., 1st Sess. Code Sec. 704(c)(1)(B) applies to any property contributed to a partnership after October 3, 1989. The regulations apply to distributions on or after January 9, 1995.

[65] H.R. Rep. No. 101-247, 101st Cong., 1st Sess., 406 (1989). In this case, the continuing partners could avoid a Code Sec. 734(b) step-down in the basis of the retained noncontributed property by not making a Code Sec. 754 election in such year.

are very similar to (but not exactly the same as) those under the disguised sale rules of Code Sec. 707(a)(2)(B).

.01 Recognition of Gain or Loss

If property contributed by one partner is distributed to another partner within seven years of its contribution, the contributing partner (or his or her successor)[66] recognizes gain or loss in an amount (and character) equal to the gain or loss that would have been allocated to the contributing partner under Code Sec. 704(c)(1)(A) (remaining precontribution gain) if the partnership had sold the property to the distributee at its fair market value at the time of the distribution.[67]

The amount of gain or loss recognized by the contributing partner may vary depending on the particular method the partnership uses in making allocations of built-in gain or loss[68] because the amount of remaining built-in gain or loss may vary depending on the particular method of allocation adopted.[69]

The regulations provide that property a partnership receives in exchange for contributed property in a nonrecognition transaction is treated as the contributed property. This result is consistent with the built-in gain or loss rules in general.[70] The regulations also provide that the successor in interest of a contributing partner is treated as the contributing partner.[71] For example, if the contributing partner subsequently sells his or her interest to another partner, the new partner will be treated as the contributor of any property previously contributed by the selling partner.

> **Tax Planning Point:** This outcome can be alleviated if the partnership or LLC had a § 754 election in effect when the original contributor sold his or her interest to the successor or agrees to make one in the year of transfer. Thus, it is very important that the purchaser of an interest in an existing partnership or LLC consider whether or not the entity has a § 754 election in effect when deciding to make the purchase. If no election has previously been made, the purchaser should attempt to convince the other partners/members to make one.[72]

.02 Character of Gain or Loss

The regulations provide that the character of the contributing partner's gain or loss is determined as if the property had been sold by the partnership to the distributee partner. Thus, if the distributee partner holds more than a 50-percent capital or profits interest in the partnership, any gain recognized by the contributing partner is ordinary income if the property is not a capital asset when held by the distributee partner.[73]

---

[66] Code Sec. 704(c)(1).

[67] Code Sec. 704(c)(1)(B)(i) and (ii). For property contributed to the partnership prior to June 9, 1997, the time period was five years rather than seven years. The Taxpayer Relief Act of 1997, P.L. 105-34, Act § 1063(a) increased the trigger window to 7 years.

[68] Code Sec. 704(c)(1)(B); Reg. § 1.704-3.

[69] See Reg. § 1.704-4(a)(5), Exs. 1-3.

[70] Reg. §§ 1.704-4(d)(1) and 1.704-3(a)(8).

[71] Reg. § 1.704-4(d)(2).

[72] Reg. §§ 1.704-4(e)(3) and 1.704-3(a)(7).

[73] Reg. § 1.704-4(b)(2); Code Sec. 707(b)(2).

In addition, because the property is treated as having been sold by the partnership to the distributee partner, the regulations provide that any loss that would have been disallowed under the related party rules[74] had the distributed property actually been sold to the distributee partner will be disallowed under Code Sec. 704(c)(1)(B) as well.[75]

.03 Basis Rules

Contributing partner's basis in his or her partnership interest. The contributing partner recognizing gain or loss under Code Sec. 704(c)(1)(B) is entitled to increase the basis, or required to decrease the basis, of his or her partnership interest by the amount of gain or loss recognized under Code Sec. 704(c)(1)(B).

Partnership's basis in Code Sec. 704(c) built-in gain or loss property. The partnership is entitled to increase the basis, or required to decrease the basis, of the contributed property by the gain or loss required to be recognized by the contributing partner under Code Sec. 704(c)(1)(B). The basis adjustment to the property is deemed made prior to the distribution, after which the usual distribution rules are applied to the distributee.[76]

> *Example 14-14:* Christine Williams contributed nondepreciable realty with a tax basis of $45,000 and a fair market value of $75,000 to the Williams Sisters Partnership in exchange for a 25% interest therein. Three years later, when the property's value had increased to $90,000, it was distributed to another partner in partial liquidation of her interest in the partnership. Upon distribution of this property to the other partner, Christine will be required to recognize the still remaining built-in gain of $30,000 inherent in the property at the date she initially contributed it to the partnership. This gain will increase both Christine's basis in her partnership interest and the partnership's basis in the property she contributed. Thus, subject to the limitations of Code Sec. 732(a)(2),[77] the distributee partner will take a $75,000 basis in the property received.

These adjustments are taken into account in determining (1) the noncontributing partner's basis in the property distributed to that partner, (2) the contributing partner's basis in any property distributed to that partner in the same transaction (except to the extent that the distributed property is like-kind property subject to a special rule discussed below), (3) the basis adjustments, if any, to partnership property by a partnership with a Code Sec. 754 election in effect, and (4) the amount of the contributing partner's gain under Code Sec. 731 or Code Sec. 737 on a related distribution of money or property, respectively, to the contributing partner.

---

[74] Code Sec. 707(b)(1).

[75] Reg. § 1.704-4(b)(2), Ex.

[76] Reg. § 1.704-4(e)(2); S. Rep. No. 101, 101st Cong., 1st Sess., 197 (1989). This portion of the legislative history and Code Sec. 737 regulations will have less importance because the current Code Sec. 708 regulations do not create a deemed property distribution as part of a technical termination occurring after May 9, 1997.

[77] Under Code Sec. 732(a)(2), the distributee partner's basis in the distributed property cannot exceed her basis in her partnership interest immediately prior to receipt of the distribution.

.04 Special Rules for Constructive Termination of Partnerships

By statute, a constructive termination of the partnership or LLC under Section 708(b)(1), and the deemed distribution of the partnership/LLC's property that accompanies it, does not trigger gain or loss to the contributors of property under Section 704(c)(1)(B). As a corollary to this rule, the statute requires that investors' sharing ratios in any Section 704(c) gain or loss inherent in partnership or LLC property before the constructive liquidation remain unchanged by Section 708. In other words, termination of the entity under Section 708 cannot serve to shift pre-contribution built-in gain or loss away from the contributed property or the contributing partner/member(s). Moreover, termination under Section 708 cannot serve to create additional built-in gain.[78]

On May 8, 1997, the regulations were modified and now provide that in the case of a technical termination, after May 9, 1997, under Code Sec. 708(b)(1)(B), "A subsequent distribution of Section 704(c) property by the new partnership to a partner of the new partnership is subject to Section 704(c)(1)(B) to the same extent that the distribution by the terminated partnership would have been subject to Section 704(c)(1)(B)."[79]

.05 Exceptions

Code Sec. 704(c)(1)(B) will not apply in the following cases:

- A distribution of the contributed property back to the contributing partner (or his or her successor in interest);[80]
- A distribution of contributed property to a noncontributing partner, if coupled with the distribution of a noncontributed property of a like kind (under Code Sec. 1031) to the contributing partner not later than the earlier of 180 days after the date of distribution of the contributed property or the due date for the contributing partner's tax return for the year in which the distribution was made;[81]
- An election under Code Sec. 761(a) to be excluded from Subchapter K;
- The distribution of a contributed property more than seven years after its contribution;
- The distribution of a noncontributed property to a contributing partner;[82]
- Distributions to a partner other than in his or her capacity as a partner (e.g., transactions or distributions subject to Code Sec. 707(a) or Code Sec. 751(b));[83]
- Transfers by the transferee partnership of all of its assets to a second partnership coupled with the transferee partnership's distribution of the second partnership's interests to its partners. However, the second partnership is subject to Code Sec. 704(c)(2);[84] and
- Incorporation of the partnership.[85]

---

[78] Regs. §§ 1.708-1(b)(4) and 1.704-3(a)(3)(i).
[79] Reg. § 1.704-4(b)(3); *see also* Reg. § 1.704-4(a)(4)(i).
[80] Code Sec. 704(c)(1)(B).
[81] Code Sec. 704(c)(2).

[82] *But see* Code Sec. 737.
[83] Reg. § 1.704-4(a)(2).
[84] Reg. § 1.704-4(c)(4).
[85] Reg. § 1.704-4(c)(5).

The regulations also provide that Code Sec. 704(c)(1)(B) does not apply to the distribution of a portion of contributed property to a noncontributing partner in a complete liquidation of the partnership if a portion of the contributed property is distributed to the contributing partner and that portion has unrecognized gain or loss in the hands of the contributing partner, determined immediately after the distribution, at least equal to the built-in gain or loss that would have been allocated to the contributing partner under Code Sec. 704(c)(1)(A) on a sale of the contributed property by the partnership at the time of the distribution. This exception is consistent with the purpose of Code Sec. 704(c)(1)(B) to prevent the shifting of built-in gain or loss among partners because no shift has occurred in this limited situation.[86]

.06 Contributor Receives Like-kind Property in Same Distribution

The statute provides a special rule where the distribution of property originally contributed by one partner or LLC member (the contributor) to another partner/ member (the distributee) is accompanied by a distribution of property of a like-kind to the contributor.[87] A similar exchange would not be taxable if made outside the partnership or LLC, and the 1989 amendment to § 704(c) will not make it taxable merely because it occurs through the entity.

> **Tax Planning Point:** This special rule essentially allows a like-kind exchange to take place through a partnership or LLC without triggering recognition of gain under § 704(c)(1)(B). The rationale is that a similar exchange outside the entity (under § 1031) would not trigger recognition of income. Instead, any gain inherent in property given up (the contributed property in this case) is built into the basis of the like-kind property received and can be deferred until the like-kind property is sold.

The "like-kind" exception applies in cases in which the contributing partner receives like-kind property no later than the earlier of (1) 180 days following the date of the distribution of contributed property to another partner, or (2) the due date (determined with regard to extensions) of the contributing partner's income tax return for the taxable year of the distribution to the other partner.

Accordingly, under the regulations, the built-in gain that would ordinarily be recognized under § 704(c)(1)(B) is deferred to the extent that it can be built into the basis of the like-kind property received. That is, the built-in gain to be recognized by the original contributor on the distribution is "reduced by the amount of built-in gain or loss [inherent] in the distributed like-kind property in the hands of the contributing partner [or LLC member] immediately after the distribution."[88] Gain is recognized under § 704(c) only to the extent the built-in gain inherent in the original contributed property (now distributed to another partner or LLC member)

---

[86] Reg. § 1.704-4(c)(2).

[87] Code § 704(c)(2). This special rule does not apply where the property received by the contributing partner/ member is of a type described in §§ 1031(a)(2) or (e)

(property not eligible for like-kind treatment under § 1031).

[88] Reg. § 1.704-4(d)(3).

exceeds the difference between the FMV of the like-kind property received by the contributor and the basis such property takes in his/her hands.[89]

> *Example 14-15:* J, D, and R form limited liability company JDR. J contributes land with a tax basis of $20,000 and a fair market value of $35,000. D and R each contribute $35,000 cash. The LLC uses some of the cash contributed by members D and R to purchase another tract of land (tract 2) for $25,000. Two years later, the LLC distributes tract 1, originally contributed by J, to member D in partial liquidation of her interest in the entity. Six days later, the LLC distributes tract 2, originally purchased for $25,000, to J. At the date of the distribution to J, tract 2 is valued at $28,000. Assume that LLC income just equaled expenses during years 1 and 2, and that no additional contributions or distributions have been made by or to the members.
>
> Under Section 732(a)(1), J would ordinarily take a carryover basis in tract 2. Section 732(a)(2), however, limits J's basis in tract 2 to her basis in her interest in the LLC at the date of the distribution (substitute basis). Thus, J will take a tax basis of $20,000 in tract 2 received from the LLC. There will therefore be an $8,000 built-in gain inherent in tract 2 in J's hands ($28,000 fair market value less $20,000 tax basis). This built-in gain will reduce the gain required to be recognized by J upon the distribution of tract 1 to D. Ignoring the distribution received by J, the distribution to D would trigger recognition of J's $15,000 built-in gain under Section 704(c)(1)(B). Under Section 704(c)(2), and the proposed regulations thereunder, J's recognized gain is reduced by the $8,000 built-in gain inherent in tract 2 in J's hands. Consequently, J must recognize only $7,000 of the original built-in gain inherent in tract 1 on the distribution to D.

¶ 1405 Partner Contributes Property and Partnership Distributes Other Property to the Partner—Code Sec. 737

Code Sec. 737[90] addresses partnership distributions of property to a partner within seven years of a contribution of other property to the partnership by the same partner.[91] The 1992 legislative history (the "legislative history") accompanying the enactment of Code Sec. 737 noted that "the committee is concerned that a partner who contributes appreciated property to a partnership may be able to avoid or defer the recognition of gain with respect to that property through the mechanism of having the partnership distribute other partnership property to him in partial or complete redemption of his interest while the partnership continues to own the contributed property."[92] Code Sec. 737 thus appears to have been intended to serve as a backstop to the gain recognition provisions under Code Sec.

---

[89] This rule applies only if the like-kind property distributed to the contributor is received by him within 180 days of the distribution of the contributed property to the distributee, or by the due date of the contributor's individual tax return, if sooner. Extensions of time are considered in determining the due date of the contributor's tax return.

[90] Enacted by the Energy Policy Act of 1992, P.L. 102-486. Code Sec. 737 applies to partnership distribu-

tions of appreciated property on or after June 25, 1992. The regulations apply to distributions on or after January 9, 1995.

[91] For property contributed to the partnership prior to June 9, 1997, the time period is five years rather than seven years. The Taxpayer Relief Act of 1997, P.L. 105-34, Act § 1063(a) increased the trigger window to 7 years.

[92] *See* H.R. Rep. No. 11, 102d Cong., 2nd Sess. Code Sec. 3004.

704(c)(1)(B) which are primarily concerned with taxpayers avoiding the recognition of Code Sec. 704(c) built-in gain by distributing a contributed (appreciated) property to a noncontributing partner. Both Code Sec. 737 and Code Sec. 704(c)(1)(B), in turn, serve as back-ups to the disguised sale rules in Code Sec. 707(a)(2)(B). The effective date of Code Sec. 737 was retroactive in that it piggybacks off of the effective date rule of Code Sec. 704(c)(1)(B). Code Sec. 737 therefore applies to any property contributed to the partnership after October 3, 1989.

Section 704(c)(1)(B) prevents partners from avoiding Section 704(c) by having the partnership distribute contributed property to another partner rather than selling it. Section 704(c)(1)(B) is triggered, however, only if the contributing partner remains a partner at the date of the distribution to another partner. If the contributing partner is no longer a partner at the date of the distribution, the partnership distribution would not affect her. If she terminates her interest in the partnership by selling or otherwise transferring ownership of that interest to another, the provisions of Section 704(c)(1)(B) are preserved and applied to her successor in interest. But Section 704(c) is silent with regard to the consequences of a transfer by a contributing partner of her interest in the partnership back to the partnership. That is, Section 704(c) does not provide for the preservation of the contributing partner's built-in gain or loss if the partnership distributes other property to her in liquidation of her interest in the partnership.

Section 737 fulfills this role. It acts as a corollary to Section 704(c)(1)(B), triggering recognition of the contributing partner's built-in gain upon her receipt of other partnership property with a value in excess of her basis in her partnership interest. The statute prevents the contributing partner from avoiding the requirements of §704(c) by liquidating her interest in the partnership prior to the partnership's distribution or other disposition of the contributed property. Section 737 closes this loophole.

Both Code Sec. 737 and Code Sec. 704(c)(1)(B), in turn, serve as back-ups to the disguised sale rules in Code Sec. 707(a)(2)(B). The effective date of Code Sec. 737 was retroactive in that it piggybacks off of the effective date rule of Code Sec. 704(c)(1)(B). Code Sec. 737 therefore applies to any property contributed to the partnership after October 3, 1989.

The Tax Reform Act of 1984[93] made mandatory the application of Code Sec. 704(c) allocations as a means of prohibiting the shifting of a contributed property's built-in gain or loss from a contributing partner to a noncontributing partner. In 1989, Code Sec. 704(c)(1)(B) was enacted to prohibit the avoidance of Code Sec. 704(c) by requiring that built-in gain or loss be recognized upon the distribution of a contributed property having Code Sec. 704(c) built-in gain or loss to a noncontributing partner. (This recognition avoidance potential was generally present only if the partnership had failed to make a Code Sec. 754 election such that no Code Sec. 734(b) adjustment was available to adjust the inside basis of the noncontributed property). The policy of Code Sec. 737, enacted in 1992, if related at all to the Code

---

[93] P.L. 98-369.

Sec. 704(c) rules, seems to be to prohibit the shifting of Code Sec. 704(c) built-in gain or loss from a contributed property kept by the partnership to a noncontributed property distributed to the former owner of the contributed property. It is akin to the Code Sec. 707(a)(2)(B) disguised sale rules.

.01 Mechanics

If a partner contributes appreciated property to a partnership and receives a distribution of other property from the partnership within seven years of such contribution, the contributing partner shall recognize gain equal to the lesser of:[94]

1. An amount equal to the excess, if any, of the fair market value of the distributed property (other than money) over the part ner's adjusted tax basis in his or her partnership interest, immediately prior to the distribution, reduced (but not below zero) by any money received in the distribution; and

2. The net remaining precontribution gain of the contributing partner.[95]

.02 Net Pre-contribution Gain

The net precontribution gain of the contributing partner is equal to the net gain (if any) that the contributing partner would have recognized, pursuant to Code Sec. 704(c)(1)(B), if all property that the contributing partner had contributed to the partnership within seven years of the distribution, and which the partnership still held immediately prior to the distribution, was distributed by the partnership to another partner.[96] For this purpose, built-in losses inherent in any property contributed within the preceding seven-year period will be netted against built-in gains in any other such property in determining net precontribution gain.[97]

.03 Basis Rules Following Application of Code Sec. 737

Contributing partner's basis in partnership interest. The adjusted basis of a partner's interest in a partnership is increased by any gain which that partner is required to recognize under Code Sec. 737. For purposes of determining the basis of distributed property, the increase in the contributing partner's basis in his or her partnership interest is deemed to occur immediately prior to the distribution of property.[98]

Partnership's basis in contributed property following application of Code Sec. 737. The partnership is entitled to increase the basis of the contributed built-in gain property by any gain the contributing partner is required to recognize pursuant to Code Sec. 737.[99]

> **Example 14-16:** Alfred Johnson contributed non-depreciable real estate with a fair market value of $150,000 (tax basis $80,000) to the Sun Country Partnership in exchange for a 20% partnership interest. Three years later, he received a distribution of other real estate from Sun Country with a tax basis of $70,000 and a fair market value of $115,000. This distribution reduced his

---

[94] Code Sec. 737(b).

[95] Reg. § 1.737-1(a)(1); Code Sec. 737(a)(1) and (2).

[96] Code Sec. 737(b)(1).

[97] *See* legislative history, H.R. Rep. No. 11, 102nd Cong., 2nd Sess., § 3004 (1992).

[98] Code Sec. 737(c)(1); Reg. § 1.737-3(b).

[99] Code Sec. 737(c)(2); Reg. § 1.737-3(c).

interest in the partnership from 20% to 10%. At the date of the distribution, Sun Country still owned the property contributed by Alfred. Under Code Sec. 737, Alfred must recognize $25,000 gain on receipt of the property distribution from Sun Country. This gain, which reflects the excess of the value of the property received by Alfred ($115,000) over his basis in his partnership interest ($90,000) will increase the partnership's tax basis in the property Alfred originally contributed. The tax basis of this property is now $105,000 ($80,000 + $25,000), leaving a remaining Code Sec. 704(c) built-in gain for Alfred of only $45,000 ($150,000 date of contribution value minus $105,000 adjusted tax basis).

.04 Character of Gain

Any gain recognized under Code Sec. 737 is in addition to gain recognized under Code Sec. 731 and the character of gain is determined by the "proportionate character of the net precontribution gain."[100] The character is determined at the partnership level as if the distributed property had been sold to an unrelated party.[101]

.05 Code Sec. 737 not Triggered if Contributed Property Distributed Back to the Contributor

The purpose of Code Sec. 737 is to tax disguised sales; its provisions should not apply to distributions of the same property contributed to the partnership. Code Sec. 737(a), however, has application to all distributions. Code Sec. 737(d) provides an exception to any gain recognition if the property distributed was previously contributed by the same partner.

If a contributed asset is distributed back to the contributing partner, that asset will neither be:

- Taken into account in determining the fair market value of the distributed property for purposes of calculating Code Sec. 737 gain, nor
- Taken into account in determining net precontribution gain.[102]

If the contributed asset that is distributed back to a contributing partner consists of an interest in an entity (*e.g.*, a corporation) the exception noted above shall not apply to the extent the value of the entity is attributable to property contributed to it after such property was contributed to the partnership.[103]

.06 Constructive Terminations of the Partnership

The legislative history of Code Sec. 737 and the regulations make clear that a constructive distribution of partnership property to a contributing partner pursuant to a Code Sec. 708(b)(1)(B) termination under the pre-May 8, 1997, Code Sec. 708 regulations will not result in a recognition of Code Sec. 704(c) gain to the contributing partner under Code Sec. 737.[104] In fact, the Conference Report states that a

---

[100] Code Sec. 737(a); Reg. § 1.737-1(d).

[101] Compare Code Sec. 704(c)(1)(B).

[102] Code Sec. 737(d)(1); Reg. § 1.737-2(d)(1).

[103] Code Sec. 737(d)(1); Reg. § 1.737-2(d)(1) and (2). Presumably, this exception to the exception applies only

if the property contributed by the partnership to the entity is not itself property that was originally contributed by the contributing partner to which the interest in the entity is distributed.

[104] Reg. § 1.737-2(a).

constructive termination under Code Sec. 708(b)(1)(B) does not change the application of the sharing requirements of Code Sec. 704(c) to precontribution gain with respect to property contributed to the partnership before the termination.

The legislative history further states that "parties will recognize gain in connection with the distribution of partnership property within 5 years following the constructive termination, *to the extent of their respective shares of the pretermination appreciation in the value of the partnership property that is not already required to be allocated to the original contributor (if any) of the property.*"[105] Thus, the legislative history appears to indicate that a Code Sec. 708(b)(1)(B) termination will start a new seven-year period running with respect to built-in gain (*i.e.*, appreciation), even gain accruing in property between the date it was acquired by the terminated partnership and the date it was deemed contributed to the reconstituted partnership pursuant to the Code Sec. 708(b)(1)(B) termination.[106] This concept of a new seven-year period with respect to this post-acquisition appreciation leads to several problems.

The legislative history appears to require that there be maintained with respect to a contributed property two or more seven-year periods whenever a Code Sec. 708(b)(1)(B) termination occurs prior to the lapse of the original seven-year period maintained under Code Sec. 737.

> **Example 14-17:** Assume that Partner *A* contributes Blackacre, with a fair market value of $1,000,000 and a basis of $100,000, to partnership AB on January 1 of Year 1. If AB is terminated on January 1 of Year 2, when Blackacre has a fair market value of $1,500,000, it would appear that AB must maintain under Code Sec. 737 two separate seven-year periods with respect to Blackacre (with a fair market value of $1,500,000 and a basis of $100,000):
>
> 1. A seven-year period that expires on January 1 of Year 7, with respect to the precontribution appreciation of $900,000; and
>
> 2. A seven-year period that expires on January 1 of Year 8, with respect to the postcontribution appreciation of $500,000.

In fact, AB could technically have as many as seven separate seven-year periods maintained with respect to Blackacre under Code Sec. 737 (assuming a termination occurs every 12 months).

On May 8, 1997, however, the Code Sec. 737 regulations were modified and now provide that in the case of a technical termination, after the date under Code Sec. 737, "[a] subsequent distribution of Section 704(c) property by the new partnership to a partner of the new partnership is subject to Section 737 to the same extent that the distribution by the terminated partnership would have been subject to Section 737."[107]

---

[105] Emphasis added. *See* legislative history, H.R. Rep. No. 11, 102nd Cong., 2nd Sess., §3004 (1992). For property contributed to the partnership after June 9, 1997, the time period is seven years. The Taxpayer Relief Act of 1997, P.L. 105-34, Act §1063(a). This portion of the legislative history and Code Sec. 737 regulations will have less importance because the current Code Sec. 708 regulations do not create a deemed property distribution as part of a technical termination occurring after May 9, 1997.

[106] The regulations seem to adopt this approach indirectly through a cross reference to the Code Sec. 704(c)(1)(B) rules. *See* Reg. §1.737-2(a) cross reference to "similar" rules of Reg. §1.704-4(c)(3).

[107] Reg. §1.737-2(a).

.07 Hierarchy of Statutes

Overlap of Code Sec. 704(c)(1)(B) and Code Sec. 707(a)(2)(B). Under the disguised sale rules of Code Sec. 707(a)(2)(B), the determination of whether a sale, rather than a contribution, of an asset has occurred depends largely upon the entrepreneurial risk to which such asset is subject in the hands of the partnership and the degree of certainty as to timing and amount with which the contributing partner can forecast the ultimate distribution of cash or some other asset to such partner in the future (taking into account the entrepreneurial risks that exist during the period preceding such distribution).[108]

If, based on relevant facts and circumstances, a sale is found to have occurred under Code Sec. 707(a)(2)(B), the regulations are clear that such sale is deemed for all tax purposes to have occurred at the outset on the initial conveyance of the property to the partnership.[109] The regulations deem the contributing partner to have received a payment right, rather than a partnership interest, at the time and any subsequent related distribution of cash or property to the contributing partner will be characterized as a payment in satisfaction of the partnership's obligation arising out of the sale and not as a distribution.[110] Thus, the related distribution of cash or property that constitutes part of a disguised sale transaction is not a distribution to a partner acting in his or her capacity as a partner. Any such distribution is not subject to Code Sec. 731.

There appears to be no overlap between the disguised sale regulations and Code Sec. 704(c)(1)(B). Once the IRS is successful in recharacterizing a transaction as a disguised sale of the appreciated property, all Code Sec. 704(c)(1)(B) built-in gain with respect to that property is eliminated. The contributing partner would already be characterized as having sold the property to the partnership (or the other partner) at the outset and having triggered a recognition of the built-in gain. Because the timing and magnitude of the gain recognition under the two rules usually will differ, and because the IRS's opportunity to successfully apply the disguised sale recharacterization will vary greatly depending upon the facts of each case, the IRS can be expected to assert both theories of recharacterization as alternatives on audit or in litigation. They should not, however, overlap.

Overlap of Code Sec. 704(c)(1)(B) and Code Sec. 737. Code Sec. 737 applies when a partner receives a distribution from the partnership of property other than property he or she originally contributed. Under Code Sec. 737, upon receipt of the distributed property, any built-in Code Sec. 704(c) gain inherent in the property originally contributed by such partner is triggered to the extent that the value of the property received in the distribution exceeds the partner's tax basis in his or her partnership interest. Like Code Sec. 704(c)(1)(B), Code Sec. 737 applies only to distributions received in the seven-year period following the initial contribution of appreciated property to the partnership.

Code Sec. 704(c)(1)(B) and Code Sec. 737 will often overlap. Certainly, if the property distributed to the contributing partner itself contains built-in (precontribu-

---

[108] Reg. § 1.707-3(b)(2).
[109] Reg. § 1.707-3(a)(2).
[110] *Id.*

tion) appreciation and such property was originally contributed to the partnership by another partner, the distribution of any portion of such property to the contributing partner during the seven years following the contribution of such distributed property will result in the partner who contributed such distributed property also recognizing Code Sec. 704(c) gain under Code Sec. 704(c)(1)(B).

Overlap of Code Sec. 737 and Code Sec. 707(a)(2)(B). The determination for Code Sec. 707(a)(2)(B) purposes of whether a sale, rather than a contribution, of an asset to a partnership has occurred depends largely upon the entrepreneurial risk to which the contributing partner is subject while a participant in the partnership. The more entrepreneurial risk such partner is subject to, and the lesser the degree of certainty with which the contributing partner can predict the amount and timing of any ultimate distribution of cash or some other asset in the future, the higher the probability that such partner's initial conveyance to the partnership will be characterized as a contribution and not a sale.[111]

If, based on relevant facts and circumstances, a sale is found to have occurred, the Code Sec. 707 regulations are clear that such sale is deemed for all tax purposes to have occurred at the time of the initial conveyance of the property to the partnership.[112] Those same regulations deem the contributing partner to have received a payment right, rather than a partnership interest, at that time and any subsequent related transfer of cash or property to the contributing partner will be characterized as a payment in satisfaction of the partnership's purchase obligation arising out of the disguised sale.[113]

Thus, the related distribution of cash or property that constitutes part of a disguised sale transaction is not a distribution to a partner acting in a partner capacity. No such distribution is subject to characterization as a partnership distribution under Code Sec. 731.

An interface between the disguised sale regulations and Code Sec. 737 is not required. Once the IRS is successful in recharacterizing a suspect contribution to a partnership as a disguised sale or exchange of the contributed property to the partnership, Code Sec. 737 should have no application to the partnership's related transfer to the partner taxable under Code Sec. 707(a)(2)(B). The contributing partner would already be characterized as having engaged in a taxable exchange of the appreciated property with the partnership (or the other partner) at the outset and having triggered a recognition of the built-in gain. In other words, there would be no net precontribution gain to recognize under Code Sec. 737; nor would there be a distribution to the contributing partner (in a partner capacity) to trigger application of Code Sec. 737.

Because the timing and magnitude of the gain recognition under the two rules likely will differ, and because the IRS's opportunity to successfully apply the disguised sale recharacterization will vary greatly depending upon the particular facts of each case, the IRS can be expected frequently to assert both theories of

---

[111] Reg. § 1.707-3(b)(2).
[112] Reg. § 1.707-3(a)(2).
[113] *Id.*

recognition independently (assuming the suspect distribution is within the prescribed seven-year period). The two provisions should not, however, overlap.

Planning. Code Sec. 737 requires only that the contributing partner recognize gain if the fair market value of the property distributed exceeds the adjusted basis of the distributee partner's interest in the partnership. Thus, for example, a contribution of property to increase that partner's basis in its partnership interest in order to avoid recognition of gain under Code Sec. 737 will be respected. A partner may be able to contribute built-in loss property, immediately prior to a partnership distribution, in order to reduce the net precontribution gain inherent in that partner's contributed properties. Such self-help strategies, however, would still need to avoid the disguised sale rules in Code Sec. 707(a)(2)(B). The partnership could consider also obtaining loans which increase the partners' bases in their interests.

A distributee partner is not taxed under Code Sec. 737 to the extent that the partner receives a distribution of property he or she previously contributed.[114] Further guidance may be warranted in this area. To the extent that the partnership makes modifications to the contributed property (*i.e.*, land developed and held for resale), it is not clear whether such property retains its character as previously contributed property or is somehow fragmented into contributed and noncontributed components. In addition, though not clear, Code Sec. 737 should not apply to the extent a partner receives a distribution of property fungible with the property that he or she contributed.

Code Sec. 737 does not except certain distributions of partnership property other than distributions of previously contributed property.[115] Assuming the partnership were incorporated within seven years after the contribution of appreciated property, the substituted basis property is the functional equivalent (at least to the extent of the value associated with the exchanged property) of the property contributed by the partner. The exception for distributed property under Code Sec. 737(d)(1) takes into account substituted basis property where the partnership received this substituted basis property in exchange for property contributed by the partner and the partnership later distributes the substituted basis property to the contributing partner.[116] Therefore, Code Sec. 737 does not apply to a distribution of the stock of a corporation which owns as its only asset, property previously contributed by the distributee.

Code Sec. 737 applies to an incorporation of the partnership involving an actual distribution of property by the partnership to the partners followed by a contribution to a corporation.[117] Code Sec. 737 does not apply, however, to the extent that the property actually distributed to a partner was previously contributed to the partnership by that partner.[118] Code Sec. 737 does not apply to an incorporation of a partnership by methods not involving an actual distribution of partnership property to the partners, provided that the incorporation is followed by a complete liquida-

---

[114] Code Sec. 737(d)(1).
[115] *Id.*
[116] Reg. §§ 1.737-2(d)(3) and 1.757-2(e), Ex. 2.

[117] Reg. § 1.737-2(c).
[118] Reg. § 1.737-2(d).

tion of the partnership as part of the same plan or arrangement as the incorporation.[119] The explanation of provisions to the proposed regulations states that Code Sec. 737 does not apply to these situations because the partners are converting their partnership interests into a stock interest in the corporation in a nonrecognition transaction and, under the rules of either Code Sec. 732 or Code Sec. 358, the built-in gain in a partner's partnership interest is preserved in the stock received by the contributing partner. While incorporation by means of a distribution of partnership property to the partners results in the same conversion of a partnership interest into stock of a corporation, that method of incorporation involves an actual distribution of property to the partners.[120] In this case, the form of incorporation the partners choose governs the tax consequences of incorporation, including the application of Code Sec. 737.

The regulations provide that a related distribution of property the distributee partner previously contributed to the partnership is not taken into account in determining the amount of the excess distribution or the partner's net precontribution gain.[121]

> **Example 14-18:** [122] On January 1 of Year 1, *A, B,* and *C* form partnership ABC as equal partners. *A* contributes the following nondepreciable real property to the partnership:
>
> | | *FMV* | *Adjusted Tax Basis* |
> |---|---|---|
> | Property A1 .... | $20,000 | $10,000 |
> | Property A2 .... | 10,000 | 6,000 |
>
> *A*'s total net precontribution gain on the contributed property is $14,000 ($10,000 on Property A1 plus $4,000 on Property A2). *B* contributes $10,000 cash and Property B, nondepreciable real property with a fair market value and adjusted tax basis of $20,000. *C* contributes $30,000 cash. On December 31 of Year 3, Property A2 and Property B are distributed to *A* in complete liquidation of *A*'s interest in the partnership. Property A2 was previously contributed by *A* and is therefore not taken into account in determining the amount of the excess distribution or *A*'s net precontribution gain. The adjusted tax basis of Property A2 in the hands of *A* is also determined under Code Sec. 732 as if that property were the only property distributed to *A*. As a result of excluding Property A2 from these determinations, the amount of the excess distribution is $10,000 ($20,000 fair market value of distributed Property B less $10,000 adjusted tax basis in *A*'s partnership interest). *A*'s net precontribution gain is also $10,000 ($14,000 total net precontribution gain less $4,000 gain with respect to previously contributed Property A2). *A* therefore recognizes $10,000

---

[119] Reg. § 1.737-2(c).

[120] *See* Explanation of Provisions, NPRM PS-76-92 and PS-51-93, 60 FR 2352, 2355 (1/9/95).

[121] Reg. § 1.737-2(d)(1).

[122] Reg. § 1.737-2(e), Ex. 1. Assume, for purposes of the example, unless otherwise indicated, that partnership

income equals partnership expenses (other than depreciation deductions for contributed property) for each year of the partnership, the fair market value of the partnership property does not change, all distributions by the partnership are subject to Code Sec. 737, and all partners are unrelated.

of gain on the distribution, the lesser of the excess distribution or the net precontribution gain.

Consistent with Code Sec. 737(d)(1), the regulations also provide for a limitation in the case of a distribution of a previously contributed interest in an entity. It is intended to prevent a partner from avoiding Code Sec. 737 by contributing an interest in an entity to the partnership and having the partnership contribute property to that entity, followed by a distribution of an interest in the entity to the contributing partner under the previously contributed property exception.[123] This rule does not apply to the extent that the property contributed by the partnership to the entity was contributed by the same partner that contributed the interest in the entity because, in that case, the distributee partner is receiving only a distribution of property that it previously contributed to the partnership.

Code Sec. 737 does not apply to the extent that Code Sec. 751(b) applies to a distribution.[124] Thus, Code Sec. 751 will supersede Code Sec. 737 to the extent a portion of the distribution is recharacterized as a sale or exchange under Code Sec. 751(b). Code Sec. 737 would still appear to apply to the portion of any distribution actually treated as a Code Sec. 731 distribution under Code Sec. 751(b).

Where the partner receives a distribution of other property encumbered by a liability, the partner's assumption of responsibility for that liability is treated under Code Sec. 752(a) as a contribution of cash to the partnership. This deemed contribution increases the partner's basis in his or her partnership interest. This basis increase technically occurs upon the distribution (and not immediately before such distribution). Since Code Sec. 737 refers to the contributing partner's basis in the partnership interest "immediately prior" to the distribution, it may be unclear whether the deemed contribution alleviates the partner's recognition of gain under Code Sec. 737. However, in two previous (unrelated) revenue rulings, the IRS has indicated that the basis adjustment associated with a deemed contribution under Code Sec. 752(a) occurs immediately prior to the distribution of encumbered property which triggers that adjustment.[125] Thus, the assumption of debt by a partner in connection with a Code Sec. 737 distribution should alleviate the gain recognized under that section as well.

There are certain instances where Code Sec. 737 will require recognition of built-in gain which is still embedded in the contributed property (i.e., no shift of such gain to the distributed property has occurred). This generally occurs when the noncontributed property being distributed to the contributing partner has appreciated since its acquisition by the partnership. In this case, gain recognition by Code Sec. 737 cannot be justified on any tax policy ground but, by its terms, it applies nonetheless.

---

[123] Reg. § 1.737-2(d)(2). *See* Explanation of Provisions, NPRM PS-76-92 and PS-51-93, 60 FR 2352, 2355 (1/9/95).

[124] Code Sec. 737(d)(2).

[125] *See* Rev. Rul. 79-205, 1979-2 CB 255, and Rev. Rul. 87-120, 1987-2 CB 161.

Chapter 15

Death or Retirement of a Partner

¶ 1501 Introduction

When a partner voluntarily or involuntarily discontinues his or her participation in a partnership, there are several available alternatives that put the partner in substantially the same economic position but have different tax consequences:

1. The partner can sell his or her interest to one or more remaining partners and/or to an unrelated party;

2. The partnership can liquidate the partner's interest in the partnership; or

3. The partnership itself can liquidate.

Tax planning most often involves a choice between the first and second alternatives if the business is to be continued without interruption. The tax consequences of selling a partnership interest are discussed in Chapter 11. The consequences of liquidating the partnership are discussed in Chapter 12. This chapter covers the tax consequences when a partnership continues but a partner's interest is terminated not by sale but by receipt of a liquidating distribution or series of distributions from the partnership. The tax rules governing these circumstances are found in Code Sec. 736. The following table contains a brief comparison of the tax consequences of a partner's retirement by a continuing partnership through a liquidation versus a cross-purchase.

Liquidation by Partnership	*Sale to Other Partner(s)*
1. Partnership makes payments to retiring partner (or deceased partner's successor in interest.	1. Partner(s) make payments to retiring partner.

Liquidation by Partnership	Sale to Other Partner(s)
2. Difference between tax basis and FMV of distributed property (other than cash) not taxed until sold by distributee partner.	2. Cash and FMV of property received treated as sales proceeds. Difference between proceeds and partnership interest tax basis is realized gain.
3. Installment payments for share of partnership property not taxed until proceeds exceed outside basis (however, may elect to prorate basis).	3. All installment payments taxed. Outside basis is prorated and applied against each payment.
4. Can produce both capital gain and ordinary income for retiring partner.	4. Usually produces capital gain for retiring partner—unless collapsible partnership rules apply (Code Sec. 751(a)).
5. Can often be structured so some of the payments are deductible by the partnership.	5. Payments increase purchasing partner's basis in his or her interest and may result in a Code Sec. 754 step-up, but payments are usually not immediately deductible by the purchasing partner.
6. Not considered to be a sale or exchange that can terminate the partnership under Code Sec. 708.	6. The sale of 50% or more of the partnership's capital and profits interests within a 12-month period terminates the partnership under Code Sec. 708.
7. Installment payments are not subject to the OID rules (i.e., the payments can include no interest or below-market interest).	7. Any deferred payments must provide for "adequate" interest or interest will be imputed under the OID rules.

LLC Observation: The statute, legislative history and regulations are silent with respect to which members, if any, of an LLC are considered general partners for Code Sec. 736 purposes.[1]

In general, payments made in liquidation of the interest of a retiring partner or a deceased partner will be treated according to the normal rules for partnership distributions, to the extent these payments are made for the partner's interest in partnership property.[2] The valuation placed by the partners upon a partner's interest in partnership property in an arm's length agreement will generally be

---

[1] In 1997, the IRS issued proposed regulations addressing the classification of LLC members as limited vs. general partners for purposes of the self-employment tax (Prop. Reg. § 1.1402(a)-2). Congress reacted by prohibit-ing the IRS from issuing further regulations on this subject before July 1, 1998. No further regulations have yet been issued.

[2] Code Sec. 736(b)(1).

regarded as correct.[3] These payments made for the retiring partner's interest in partnership property are commonly referred to as "Code Sec. 736(b) payments." Any distributions in excess of the partner's interest in partnership property will be treated as either a distributive share of partnership income or as a guaranteed payment, and are referred to as "Code Sec. 736(a) payments."

If the amounts of Code Sec. 736(a) payments are based on the income of the partnership, they are treated as a distributive share of partnership income, and will reduce the amount of the other partners' distributive shares.[4] As distributive shares, the character of the resulting income to the retiring partner will depend on its character to the partnership. If the amounts of Code Sec. 736(a) payments are *not* based on the income of the partnership (if they are fixed, for example), they are treated as guaranteed payments.[5] As such, they are ordinary income to the retiring partner, and create an ordinary deduction for the partnership.

> ***Example 15-1:*** Partner *A* of the equal ABC Partnership retires from the partnership on December 31 of last year, when his basis in his partnership interest is $150,000. The partnership will pay him a total of $300,000 to retire his partnership interest this year. The total fair market value of partnership property is $600,000, and the partnership and *A* agree that his share is $200,000, 1/3 of that. $200,000 of the $300,000 payment is a Code Sec. 736(b) payment (in exchange for *A*'s share of partnership property), and will be treated as a distribution. It will therefore result in $150,000 tax free return of capital (the amount of his basis) and capital gain of $50,000. If the partnership owns inventory or unrealized receivables, part or all of the $50,000 might be characterized as ordinary income under Code Sec. 751. The other $100,000 will be treated as a guaranteed payment (since it is fixed), and will result in ordinary income to *A* and an ordinary deduction to the partnership.

If the retiring partner (or deceased partner's successor in interest) receives payments that are not fixed in amount, these variable payments will first be treated as payments in exchange for her interest in partnership property under Code Sec. 736(b) to the extent of the value of her interest in partnership property. Any payments in excess of the partner's share in partnership property are treated as payments under Code Sec. 736(a).[6]

> ***Example 15-2:*** Partner *D* of the equal DEF Partnership retires from the partnership on December 31 of last year, when her basis in her partnership interest was $200,000. The partnership will pay her a fixed amount of $300,000 to retire her partnership interest this year. In addition, she will also receive a payment equal to 1/6 of partnership income for the current year and the next two years. Partnership income for the current year and the next two years turns out to be $120,000 each year. The total fair market value of partnership property is $720,000, and the partnership and *D* agree that her share is $240,000, 1/3 of that. $240,000 of the $300,000 payment is a Code Sec. 736(b) payment (in exchange for *D*'s share of partnership property), and will be

---

[3] Reg. § 1.736-1(b)(1).
[4] Code Sec. 736(a)(1).
[5] Code Sec. 736(a)(2).
[6] Reg. § 1.736-1(b)(5)(ii).

treated as a distribution. It will therefore result in $200,000 tax free return of capital (the amount of her basis) and capital gain of $40,000. If the partnership owns inventory or unrealized receivables part or all of the $40,000 might actually be characterized as ordinary income under Code Sec. 751, depending on the amount of D's share of ordinary income. The other $60,000 of the $300,000 fixed payment is a Code Sec. 736(a) payment, will be treated as a guaranteed payment (since it is fixed), and will result in ordinary income to D and an ordinary deduction to the partnership. The $20,000 payment D receives (1/6 × $120,000) each year will also be a Code Sec. 736(a) payment, will be treated as a distributive share of partnership income (since the amount is based on partnership income), and the character of each payment will depend on the character of the income earned by the partnership.

Instead of the above rules, the allocation of each annual payment between Code Sec. 736(a) and (b) can be made in any manner agreed to by all the remaining partners and the withdrawing partner or his successor in interest, provided that the total amount allocated to property under Code Sec. 736(b) does not exceed the fair market value of the retiring partners share of property at the date of death or retirement.[7]

If a fixed amount (whether or not supplemented by any additional amounts) is to be received over a fixed number of years, the fraction of each fixed payment that is treated as a distribution under Code Sec. 736(b) for the taxable year will be the total fixed payments under Code Sec. 736(b) divided by the total fixed payments under both Code Sec. 736(a) and (b). The balance, if any, of the fixed amount received in the same taxable year will be treated as a distributive share or a guaranteed payment under Code Sec. 736(a)(1) or (2). However, if the total amount received in any one year is less than the amount considered as a distribution under Code Sec. 736(b) for that year, then any unapplied portion will be added to the portion of the payments for the following year or years which are to be treated as a distribution under Code Sec. 736(b).

>   **Example 15-3:** Retiring partner W, who is entitled to an annual payment of $6,000 for 10 years for his interest in partnership property, receives only $3,500 in 2009. In 2010, he receives $10,000. Of this $10,000 amount, $8,500 ($6,000 plus $2,500 from 2009) is treated as a distribution under section 736(b) for 2010; $1,500 will be treated as a payment under Code Sec. 736(a).[8]

>   **Example 15-4:** Partner D of the equal DEF Partnership retires from the partnership on December 31 of last year, when her basis in her partnership interest was $200,000. The partnership will pay her a fixed amount of $100,000 each year for three years (beginning in the current year) to retire her partnership interest. In addition, she will also receive a payment equal to 1/6 of partnership income for the current year and the next two years. Partnership income for the current year and the next two years turns out to be $120,000 each year. The total fair market value of partnership property is $720,000, and the partnership and D agree that her share is $240,000, 1/3 of that. $240,000 of

---

[7] Reg. § 1.736-1(b)(5)(iii).　　　　　　[8] Reg. Sec. 1.736-1(b)(5)(i).

the $300,000 in fixed payments are Code Sec. 736(b) payments. Of each fixed $100,000 payment received, 80% ($240,000 Code Sec. 736(b) payments/total fixed payments) will be treated as a Code Sec. 736(b) payment. The first two fixed payments will therefore result in an $80,000 ($100,000 × 80%) return of capital each year. The third $100,000 payment will result in a $40,000 return of capital ($200,000 basis – $80,000 – $80,000) and a $40,000 capital gain ($80,000 Code Sec. 736(b) payment – $40,000 return of capital). If the partnership owns inventory or unrealized receivables part or all of the $40,000 might actually be characterized as ordinary income under Code Sec. 751. The other 20% ($20,000 of each payment) will be treated as a Code Sec. 736(a) payment, and will, since the amount is fixed, be treated as a guaranteed payment. The $20,000 payment D receives (1/6 × $120,000) each year will also be Code Sec. 736(a) payments, will be treated as distributive shares of partnership income (since the amount is based on partnership income), and the character of these payments will depend on the character of the income earned that year by the partnership.

The amount of any payments under Code Sec. 736(a) will be included in the income of the retiring partner for his taxable year with or within which ends the partnership taxable year for which the payment is a distributive share, or in which the partnership is entitled to deduct the payment as a guaranteed payment. This is consistent with the payments' treatment as distributive shares or guaranteed payments. On the other hand, payments under Code Sec. 736(b) will be taken into account by the retiring partner in his taxable year in which the payments are made. This treatment is consistent with the treatment of these payments as distributions.[9]

Code Sec. 736 does not apply when the continuing partners purchase the interest of the retiring or deceased partners. It also does not apply to distributions when the partnership itself liquidates (even though the economic consequences may be similar), whether the withdrawing partner is bought out by the partnership or by all the remaining partners.[10]

The Code Sec. 736 rules do apply when there is a complete liquidation of one general partner's interest in a two-partner service partnership.[11] With respect to the withdrawal of one member of a two-person partnership, the parties should be particularly careful in the manner in which payments to the withdrawing partner are made. If Code Sec. 736 (retirement) treatment is desired, the partnership agreement should clearly provide that the payments will be made from funds of the business rather than from the separate funds of the remaining partner. In addition, the Code Sec. 736 payments to the withdrawing partner should be reflected in the books of the continuing business. These precautions are suggested because, upon the withdrawal of one of two partners, the "partnership" continues as a federal income tax entity as long as Code Sec. 736 payments are made to the withdrawing partner by the partnership. If the payments are considered to come from the remaining partner, the IRS could claim that, rather than a liquidation of the withdrawing partner's interest by the partnership, the remaining partner actually purchased the withdrawing partner's interest. If such a recharacterization were

---

[9] Reg. § 1.736-1(a)(5).
[10] Reg. § 1.736-1(a)(1)(i).
[11] Reg. § 1.736-1(a)(6).

successful, Code Sec. 736 would not apply to the payments and the partnership would terminate for federal income tax purposes at the time of the "purchase" (*i.e.*, when the partner withdraws).

The characterization of payments from a partnership to a withdrawing partner is significant because it determines:

1. Whether the withdrawing partner recognizes capital gain or loss or ordinary income with respect to the payments;

2. The timing of the gain, loss, or income recognition by the withdrawing partner;

3. Whether the partnership is entitled to a deduction with respect to the payments; and

4. Whether the remaining partners are entitled to exclude from their own share of partnership income amounts paid to the retiring partner.

Classification under Code Sec. 736 also determines whether the amounts paid to the successors of a deceased partner constitute income in respect of a decedent.[12]

---

[12] Code Secs. 691 and 753.

Overview of Code Sec. 736's Designation of Liquidating Distributions

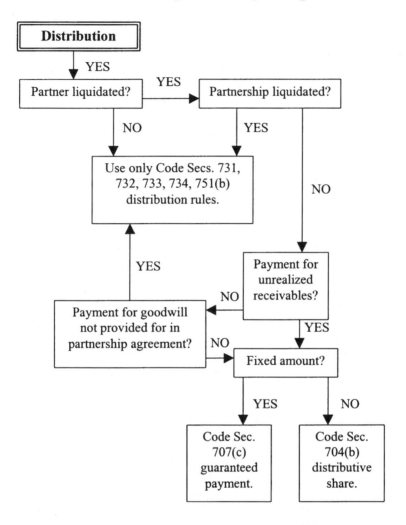

¶ 1502 Payment for Retiring General Partner's Interest in a Partnership When Capital Is Not a Material Income-Producing Factor

Additional complications arise when capital is not a material income producing factor for the partnership, and the retiring partner is a general partner—in other words, when retirement payments are made from a service partnership to a general partner. In cases such as this, unrealized receivables and goodwill are not treated as payments for property (except in the case of goodwill, where the partnership agreement specifically directs that payment for goodwill should be treated as payments for property), and are therefore treated as Code Sec. 736(a) payments.[13]

Example 15-5: General partner *G* of the equal GHI Partnership retires from the partnership on December 31 of last year, when her basis in her partnership interest is $11,000. The partnership will pay her a fixed amount of $60,000 to retire her partnership interest this year. The partnership agreement is silent with respect to the treatment of goodwill. The partnership balance sheet shows the following:

	Basis	*FMV*
Cash	$21,000	$21,000
Unrealized Receivables	$0	$90,000
Inventory	$3,000	$6,000
Equipment (Accum. Depr. = $6,000)	$9,000	$21,000
Goodwill	$0	$12,000
Total	$33,000	$150,000

If capital is a material income-producing factor for the partnership (or if *G* had been a limited partner), the part of the $60,000 in retirement payments to *G* that would have constituted Code Sec. 736(b) payments would have been $50,000, *G*'s share of partnership property. Of this $50,000, $11,000 would be return of capital. The other $39,000 (using the distribution rules when "hot" assets are owned by the partnership) would be ordinary income to the extent of $33,000 [1/3 × ($90,000 + $3,000 + $6,000)]. The remaining $6,000 of the Code Sec. 736(b) payments would be capital gain. The Code Sec. 736(a) payment of $10,000 would be treated as a guaranteed payment, since it is fixed.

If capital is *not* a material income-producing factor for the partnership, the part of the $60,000 in retirement payments to *G* that would have constituted Code Sec. 736(b) payments would have been $16,000, *G*'s share of the cash, inventory and equipment.[14] Of this $16,000, $11,000 would be return of capital. The other $5,000 (using the distribution rules when "hot" assets are owned by the partnership) would be ordinary income to the extent of $3,000 [1/3 × ($3,000 inventory appreciation + $6,000 depreciation recapture potential)]. The remaining $2,000 of the 736(b) payment would be capital gain. The Code Sec. 736(a) payment of $44,000 ($60,000 – $16,000) would be treated as a guaranteed payment, since it is fixed. If the partnership agreement had stipulated that payments for goodwill would be treated as payments for property, the Code Section 736(b) payments, and the capital gain, would have been $4,000 (1/3 × $12,000) higher. Accordingly, the Code Sec. 736(a) payment, and the resulting guaranteed payment, would have been $4,000 lower.

---

[13] Code Sec. 736(b)(2) and (3).

[14] It should be noted that the term "unrealized receivables" under Code Sec. 736 does not include inventory or depreciation recapture.

LLC Comment: In the case of a service-oriented LLC there is no guidance that identifies which members are considered general or limited partners for purposes of Code Sec. 736. Until the IRS or the Treasury issues guidance, it would be reasonable to treat members who act as general partners as such for Code Sec. 736 purposes. For example, member managers who have the authority to operate the LLC's business and are actively involved in its business should be treated as general partners for Code Sec. 736 purposes.

.01 When Is Capital a Material Income-Producing Factor?

The legislative history of the Revenue Reconciliation Act of 1993 provides that capital is not a "material income-producing factor" when substantially all of the gross income of the partnership business consists of fees, commissions or other compensation for personal services performed by an individual. The practice of a doctor, dentist, lawyer, architect, or accountant will not, as such, be treated as a trade or business in which capital is a material income-producing factor although a partnership may have made substantial capital investments incidental to the professional practice. The legislative history of the Revenue Reconciliation Act of 1993 states that the determination of whether capital is a material income-producing factor will be made under principles of present and prior law (under Code Secs. 401(c)(2), 911(d), and former Code Sec. 1348(b)(1)(A)).[15]

Code Sec. 401(c)(2) defines "earned income" for purposes of determining whether a self-employed person may make a contribution to a qualified plan. Code Sec. 401(c)(2) provides that the term "earned income" means net earnings from self-employment, but that such net earnings will be determined only with respect to a trade or business in which personal services of the taxpayer are a material income-producing factor.[16]

Code Sec. 911(d) defines "earned income" for purposes of deciding what income of a U.S. citizen or resident living abroad can be excluded from gross income. Code Sec. 911(d)(2)(A) provides that earned income includes amounts received as compensation for personal services actually rendered. Code Sec. 911(d)(2)(B) provides special treatment for income earned in connection with a trade or business in which both personal services and capital are material income-producing factors.

Former Code Sec. 1348 (repealed by the Economic Recovery Tax Act of 1981[17]) imposed a maximum tax of 50 percent on "personal service income." Code Sec. 1348(b)(1) provided that the term "personal service income" meant any income that was earned income within the meaning of Code Sec. 401(c)(2)(C) or Code Sec. 911(b). As with Code Sec. 911, Code Sec. 1348 afforded special treatment if an individual was engaged in a trade or business in which both personal services and capital were "material income-producing factors."[18]

Under former Code Sec. 1348, capital was a material income-producing factor if a "substantial portion" of the gross income of the business was attributable to the

---

[15] H. Rept. No. 103-111 (P.L. 103-66), p. 782.

[16] Code Sec. 401(c)(2)(A)(i).

[17] P.L. 97-34.

[18] Reg. § 1.1348-3(a)(3)(i).

¶1502.01

employment of capital in the business, as reflected, for example, by a substantial investment in inventories, plant, machinery or other equipment.[19] In general, capital was not deemed a material income-producing factor where the gross income of the business consisted principally of fees, commissions, or other compensation for personal services performed by an individual.[20]

The key issue in determining whether Code Sec. 736 will apply is whether a capital investment is merely incidental to a business or whether a substantial portion of the gross income of a business is produced from capital. Such determination must be decided by reference to all the facts of each case. The cases under Code Sec. 1348 typically looked at such facts as: (1) the amount of capital investment in the business; (2) its relation to the amount of personal services performed; (3) how the capital was used; (4) how critical it was to the business; and (5) for what (*i.e.*, providing services or capital) the business received gross income.[21]

The outcome of cases tended to be fairly predictable. In the majority of cases involving businesses that used capital of any sort (such as inventories, equipment, or buildings) in a nontrivial and nonincidental way (rather than providing little beyond services), capital was held to be a material income-producing factor. Perhaps the key point was that, under the standard, the use of capital did not have to be more significant than the use of labor but merely of some significance.

Examples of situations where capital has been found to be a material income-producing factor include the funeral services business, contracting business, wholesale distribution of jewelry business, development business, wholesale and retail bowling supply business, grocery store business, and auto repair facility business.[22]

Examples of situations where capital has been found to be incidental include construction and design of wrought-iron rails, manufacture and sale of taxidermy supplies, investment brokerage business, bail bondsmen, and a real estate brokerage firm.[23]

---

[19] Reg. § 1.1348-3(a)(3)(ii).

[20] *Id.*

[21] *See, e.g., Curry v. U.S.*, CA-FC, 86-2 USTC ¶ 9744, 804 F2d 647.

[22] Among the businesses that were held, under the facts of the particular cases, to use capital as a material income-producing factor, were *Parker v. Commr.*, CA-9, 87-2 USTC ¶ 9441, 822 F2d 905 (designing, producing and using slot machines); *Hicks v. U.S.*, CA-5, 86-1 USTC ¶ 9355, 787 F2d 1018 (general contracting); *Holland v. Commr.*, CA-4, 80-2 USTC ¶ 9469, 622 F2d 95 (maintenance contracting); *Gullion v. Commr.*, TC Memo. 1982-106 (concrete flatwork); *McGowan v. Commr.*, TC Memo. 1982-65 (making landfill); *Hardy v. U.S.*, 589 FSupp 330 (E.D. Wis. 1984) (estate development); *Nelson v. Commr.*, CA-10, 85-2 USTC ¶ 9504, 767 F2d 667 (painting business); *Treatman v. Commr.*, TC Memo. 1981-74 (mail order business); *Friedlander v. U.S.*, CA-9, 83-2 USTC ¶ 9632, 718 F2d 294 (jewelry store); *Whaley v. U.S.*, 84-1 USTC ¶ 9395 (W.D. Miss. 1984) (pharmacy); *Moore v. Commr.*, 71 TC 533, Dec. 35,823 (1979) (retail grocery store); *Block v. U.S.*, 569 FSupp 981 (W.D. Tenn. 1983)

(cotton merchant); *Weiss v. U.S.*, 78-2 USTC ¶ 9734 (N.D. Ohio 1978) (metal treating); *Thomas v. Commr.*, 92 TC 206, Dec. 45,460 (1989) (book publishing); *Harris v. Commr.*, TC Memo. 1984-189 (publishing cookbooks); *Wilson v. Commr.*, TC Memo. 1982-289 (eggs); *Gaudern v. Commr.*, 77 TC 1305, Dec. 38,504 (1981) (selling bowling supplies); *Crowell v. Commr.*, TC Memo. 1988-305 (securities brokerage); *Herman v. Commr.*, TC Memo. 1985-396 (operating motels); *Curry v. U.S.*, CA-FC, 86-2 USTC ¶ 9744, 804 F2d 647 (funeral home); *Pilkington v. Commr.*, TC Memo. 1983-111 (bars and lounges); *Novikoff v. Commr.*, TC Memo. 1980-330 (movie theaters); and *Bender v. Commr.*, TC Memo. 1985-375.

[23] Capital was not held a material income-producing factor for particular businesses involved in *Van Dyke v. U.S.*, CA-FC, 696 F2d 9057 (taxidermy supply); *Bruno v. Commr.*, 71 TC 191, Dec. 35,529 (1978) (bail bonding); *Fried v. Commr.*, TC Memo. 1989-430 (promoting tax shelters); *Barnes v. Commr.*, TC Memo. 1987-544 (securities brokerage); *Roselle v. Commr.*, TC Memo. 1981-394 (providing management services); and *Van Kalker v. Commr.*, CA-7, 84-2 USTC ¶ 9727, 804 F2d 967 (fabricating and installing ornamental iron railings).

¶1502.01

Capital does not have to be directly invested in a business to be a material income-producing factor (*e.g.*, capital lent to a business).[24]

Assuming that the legal standard of whether capital is a material income-producing factor in a business is exactly the same under Code Sec. 736 as under former Code Sec. 1348, these cases are not firm precedent regarding the same types of businesses today, since each was decided under its particular facts. Nonetheless, the cases as a whole support two conclusions. First, relatively few activities, outside those specifically listed in the material participation regulations (*i.e.*, health, law, engineering, architecture, accounting, actuarial science, performing arts, and consulting) are likely to be treated as personal service activities. A business's deployment of significant capital (such as buildings, inventory, or equipment) tends to establish that capital is a material income-producing factor and, thus, that it is not a personal service activity for purposes of the regulations. Second, while a wide range of taxpayers are entitled to be fairly certain that they are not engaged in personal services activities, complete certainty about this (or even sufficient certainty for a cautious practitioner to issue an opinion letter) is hard to come by. The standard remains too amorphous and case-specific to support certainty in cases that are close to the line.

.02 Retired Partner Defined

The term "retiring" partner refers to any partner who is departing from a partnership, voluntarily or involuntarily, regardless of the circumstances. A partner is treated as a "retired" partner when such partner ceases to be a partner under local law.[25] Section 736 applies to distributions made in liquidation of a partner's interest in the partnership regardless of why the partner is departing. For example, the rules apply to payments made to a partner who is leaving a partnership due to advancing age, but they also apply to payments to a partner who is being forced out of the partnership for violation of terms of the partnership agreement (e.g., a law partner taking on clients outside the partnership in violation of the terms of the partnership agreement). Neither the age of the "retiring" partner or the reasons for his or her departure are relevant in determining whether Section 736 will apply.

It is not clear from the wording of Code Sec. 736 or the corresponding regulations whether the partner must have actually ceased to be a partner for local law purposes at the time of a payment in order for Code Sec. 736 to apply, or, alternatively, whether the payment must only be in contemplation that the withdrawing partner will cease to be a partner for local law purposes. The statute refers to a "retiring" rather than a "retired" partner. However, the regulations state that Code Sec. 736 does not apply to the successor of a deceased partner that "continues to be a partner in its own right under local law."[26] The implication may be that a "retiring" partner similarly may not continue to be a partner for local law purposes, since there is no justification for distinguishing the successors of a deceased partner from another retiring partner in this context. The wording of the statute (and the regulations in the case of a "retiring" partner) could be interpreted as not

---

[24] Rev. Rul. 78-306, 1978-2 CB 218.

[25] Reg. § 1.736-1(a)(1)(ii).

[26] Reg. § 1.736-1(a)(1)(i).

requiring that the withdrawing partner cease his or her status as a partner for local law purposes in order for Code Sec. 736 to apply (if, for example, the partner were under a binding contract to withdraw under local law in the future). However, if Code Sec. 736 treatment is desired, it would be advisable for the partner to withdraw from the partnership under local law at or before the time the partner receives his or her first liquidation payment.

If a general partner ceases to be a partner under local law and receives payments from the service partnership in liquidation of his or her partnership interest, Code Sec. 736 applies regardless of the reason for the partner's ceasing to be a partner.[27] The regulations under Code Sec. 736 are not concerned with the reasons or the circumstances surrounding a partner's ceasing to be a member of the partnership and the courts have concluded that Code Sec. 736 applies whether the withdrawal is voluntary or involuntary.[28] Code Sec. 736 does not apply to any distributions made to a continuing partner (*e.g.*, distributions that only partially liquidate a partner's interest).[29]

.03 Payments for Retiring Partner's Share of Unrealized Receivables—Code Sec. 736(a)

The tax treatment of payments received by a retired partner (or his or her successor in interest) for that retired partner's share of partnership unrealized receivables depends upon whether the payments to be received are fixed in amount or whether they are instead contingent upon future partnership income. Where the payments are fixed in amount, the portion of each payment attributable to the retired partner's share of partnership unrealized receivables (*e.g.*, accounts receivable and unbilled work in process) is treated as a Code Sec. 707(c) guaranteed payment, deductible by the partnership and taxed as ordinary income to the recipient.[30] Note that total payments received by the retired partner (or his or her successor in interest) include deemed payments from a reduction in the partner's share of partnership debt.[31] Because this deemed payment is fixed in amount it is a guaranteed payment if it is for the retired partner's share of unrealized receivables. Amounts treated as guaranteed payments under these rules are taxable to the recipient in his or her taxable year "within or with which ends the partnership year in which the partnership deducted such payment."[32]

If the amount of the payments to be received by the withdrawing partner is contingent on future partnership income, the parties treat the portion of the payments attributable to unrealized receivables as a continuing profit share.[33] Partnership income, up to the amount of such payments, is allocated to the retired

---

[27] Reg. § 1.736-1(a)(1)(ii).

[28] For example, in *V.Z. Smith*, 37 TC 1033, Dec. 25,383 (1962), *aff'd*, CA-10, 63-1 USTC ¶ 9211, 313 F2d 16, taxpayer was expelled from an aerial photography company and reported payments received in excess of his investment in the partnership as capital gain. Both the Tenth Circuit Court of Appeals and the Tax Court analyzed the payments under the provisions of Section 736.

[29] Reg. § 1.736-1(a)(1)(i).

[30] If a partnership terminates before all guaranteed payments have been made, successors to the partnership who continue to make such payments are entitled to a deduction for such payments. *See* Rev. Rul. 75-154, 1975-1 CB 186; Rev. Rul. 83-155, 1983-2 CB 38; IRS Letter Ruling 7939099 (6-28-79) (undivided shareholders entitled to the deduction for their payments after partnership incorporated).

[31] Code Sec. 752(b).

[32] Reg. §§ 1.736-1(a)(5) and 1.707-1(c).

[33] Code Sec. 736(a)(1).

partner, and the continuing partners exclude the payments from their share of the partnership's income. The retired partner is, for tax purposes, treated as a continuing member of the partnership while such payments continue. Therefore, the character (*e.g.*, ordinary income versus capital gain) of the payments representing a continuing profit share are treated the same as under the normal distributive share rules of Code Sec. 702. It may be more beneficial for a withdrawing partner to receive a distributive share of partnership items that may include capital gain rather than to receive a guaranteed payment that will represent ordinary income.

The regulations create some confusion about when the withdrawing partner includes a distributive share of income under Code Sec. 736(a)(1). The withdrawing partner is required to include a "payment" as a distributive share.[34] It therefore could be argued that the implication of the regulation is that a Code Sec. 736(a)(1) payment must be included only when paid by the partnership. The regulations further provide that the withdrawing partner is to claim the payments as income "for his taxable year with or within which ends the partnership taxable year for which the *payment* is a distributive share."[35] This regulation could be read to mean that it is the partnership's taxable year in which the payment is actually made that determines the year of inclusion for the withdrawing partner. However, the accepted practice is to treat the timing of Code Sec. 736(a)(1) payments the same as the payment of any other share of partnership income and require inclusion in the partner's year with or within which the partnership year ends.[36]

For purposes of Code Sec. 736 the term "unrealized receivables" is limited to rights to be paid for services rendered or to be rendered and goods delivered or to be delivered not previously includible in the partnership's income.[37] As a practical matter, this will include mainly cash basis accounts receivable and unbilled work in process.[38] Partnership payments for the retiring partner's share of depreciation recapture will be treated under Code Sec. 736(b) as a distribution for the retiring partner's interest in partnership property. In a liquidating cash distribution, payments for the retired partner's share of recapture will generally cause a disproportionate distribution within the meaning of Code Sec. 751(b). Therefore, that portion of the Code Sec. 736(b) payments representing depreciation recapture will trigger ordinary income for the retired partner and a basis step-up for the partnership under the rules of Code Sec. 751(b).

.04 Payments for Retiring Service Partner's Share of Goodwill—Code Sec. 736(a) or (b)

Under Code Sec. 736, a partnership in which capital is *not* a material income-producing factor has the discretion to treat a payment to a general partner for goodwill as either:

1. A Code Sec. 736(a) payment (*i.e.*, a distributive income share or guaranteed payment depending upon whether the amount is fixed or contingent), or

2. A Code Sec. 736(b) payment (*i.e.*, a distribution).[39]

---

[34] Reg. § 1.736-1(a)(4).

[35] Reg. § 1.736-1(a)(5) (emphasis added).

[36] Code Sec. 706(a).

[37] Code Sec. 751(c), second sentence.

[38] P.L. 103-66, Act § 13262(b); Code Sec. 751(c).

[39] Code Sec. 736(b)(2)(B).

The partnership and the retiring partner may "elect" to treat the payment as a distribution by simply providing in the partnership agreement that a retiring partner is to be paid for goodwill.[40] If such a provision is absent and the partnership pays a fixed sum, the portion attributable to goodwill is considered a guaranteed payment under Code Sec. 707(c). If the amount paid for goodwill is contingent on partnership income, the absence of such a provision in the partnership agreement results in the payment being considered a distributive share of the partnership's income.

Code Sec. 707(a) specifically provides that the deduction by a partnership of a guaranteed payment under Code Sec. 162(a) is subject to Code Sec. 263 (which disallows a current deduction with respect to capital expenditures). The purchase of goodwill is a capital expenditure; however, the limitation on deductions set forth in Code Sec. 263 does not apply to Code Sec. 707(c) payments that are treated as such by Code Sec. 736(a)(2).[41] Therefore, Code Sec. 736(a)(2) payments are always deductible by a partnership under Code Sec. 162(a).[42] Guaranteed payments made to a withdrawing partner under Code Sec. 736(a)(2) are deductible by the paying party when the partnership terminates for a reason other than the withdrawal of the partner, and the former partners, or a successor to the partnership, continue payment to the withdrawing partner.[43]

Classifying a portion of the payments as expressly for goodwill need not affect the amount that the retiring partner receives. The parties are free to negotiate the amount of the retirement payments by considering or disregarding goodwill. Whether payments for goodwill to a retiring partner in a "service partnership" will be treated as a Code Sec. 736(a) payment or a Code Sec. 736(b) payment depends entirely on whether the "partnership agreement" specifically allocates liquidation payments to goodwill. If it does, the payments will be treated as Code Sec. 736(b) payments. The courts have shown a tendency to strictly apply Code Sec. 736 (*i.e.*, the partners can decide the classification of distributions, apart from the "true" nature of the distribution payments).[44] However, if a written allocation is ambiguous, the courts will look beyond the partnership agreement to find out the intent of the partners.[45] Frequently, partnership agreements do not address the issue of the character of payments to be made to a retiring partner in liquidation of the partner's interest in the partnership (*i.e.*, Code Sec. 736(a) verses Code Sec. 736(b)). Instead,

---

[40] *Id.*

[41] Reg. § 1.707-1(c).

[42] The Tax Reform Act of 1976, P.L. 94-455, Act § 213(b)(3), amended Code Sec. 707(c) and clarified that deductibility of Code Sec. 707(c) payments under Code Sec. 162(a) is subject to the capitalization mandate of Code Sec. 263. Prior to that amendment, taxpayers argued that a Code Sec. 707(c) guaranteed payment was deductible even if the expenditure was capital in nature. *See, e.g., J.E. Cagle, Jr. v. Commr.,* 63 TC 86, Dec. 32,828 (1974), aff'd, CA-5, 76-2 USTC ¶ 9672, 539 F2d 409. The legislative history of the 1976 amendment to Code Sec. 707(c) states that the amendment "is not intended to affect adversely the deductibility to the partnership of a payment described in Code Sec. 736(a)(2) to a retiring partner." S. Rep. No. 938, 94th Cong., 1st Sess., 94, n. 7 (1976). This concept of continuing to allow a partnership deduction for a Code Sec. 736(a)(2) payment, notwithstanding the 1976 amendment to Code Sec. 707(c), is reflected in Reg. § 1.707-1(c).

[43] Rev. Rul. 75-154, 1975-1 CB 186; IRS Letter Ruling 7939099 (6-28-79).

[44] *V.Z. Smith v. Commr.,* 37 TC 1033, Dec. 25,383 (1962), aff'd, CA-10, 63-1 USTC ¶ 9211, 313 F2d 16; *Miller v. U.S.,* CtCls, 67-2 USTC ¶ 9685, 181 CtCls 331.

[45] *Jackson Investment Co. v. Commr.,* 41 TC 675, Dec. 26,664 (1964), rev'd on other grounds, CA-9, 65-2 USTC ¶ 9451, 346 F2d 187; *Julian E. Jacobs v. Commr.,* 33 TCM 848, Dec. 32,702(M), TC Memo. 1974-196.

¶ 1502.04

the parties will often negotiate a liquidation agreement that specifies amounts and timing. It is important that such agreements expressly provide how much, if any, of the agreed upon amount is paid for goodwill.[46] If the agreement clearly includes or omits payments for goodwill, the underlying intentions of the partners are not controlling.[47] Goodwill payments for which the partners desire Code Sec. 736(a) treatment should not mention the words "goodwill" and such payments will be classified as "Code Sec. 736(a) payments."

The "partnership agreement" must specify a payment for goodwill if it is to qualify as a Code Sec. 736(b) payment. The term "partnership agreement" includes "any modifications of the partnership agreement made prior to, or at, the time prescribed by law for the filing of the partnership return for the taxable year (not including extension . . .)."[48] Therefore, an amendment to the partnership agreement providing for goodwill payments to a withdrawing partner should be effective as long as the amendment is entered into on or before the earlier of the due date (without extensions) of the partnership tax return for the year in which the partner withdraws for purposes of local law or in which the partner receives the first potential Code Sec. 736(b) payment.[49] If, for example, a partner withdraws from a calendar year partnership (or receives the first Code Sec. 736(b) payment) in Year 1, an amendment providing for goodwill payments must be entered into no later than April 15, Year 2, in order to be effective.[50]

Certainly the original partnership agreement as amended will qualify as the agreement which must specify for a payment for goodwill. It has also been held that a collateral agreement between the withdrawing partner and the remaining partner specifying a payment for goodwill is effective to qualify the payment as a Code Sec. 736(a) payment.[51] For purposes of Subchapter K of the Internal Revenue Code, the term "partnership agreement" includes modifications to the agreement "which are agreed to by all of the partners, or which are adopted in such other manner as may be provided by the partnership agreement."[52] However, in view of the controversy as to what is considered as part of the partnership amendment for Code Sec. 736 purposes, any collateral agreement between the partners regarding goodwill payments to a withdrawing partner should be signed by all partners or otherwise comply strictly with the terms of the partnership agreement relating to amendments, even if the collateral agreement does not strictly constitute an amendment to the partnership agreement for state law purposes.

The regulations indicate that a modification to the partnership agreement may be written or oral.[53] Therefore, if applicable law allows for oral modifications to a written agreement, if the partnership agreement is itself oral, or if the partnership

---

[46] Id.

[47] Is a partnership agreement amendment on this point effective which is entered into after the death of a withdrawing partner? There is little guidance on this issue. However, Code Sec. 761(c) does provide that the partnership agreement includes any amendments adopted on or before the filing date of the partnership tax return.

[48] Code Sec. 761(c).

[49] It is unclear whether an amendment to the agreement for a tax year subsequent to the retirement year is effective.

[50] Code Sec. 6072.

[51] *Jackson Investment Company v. Commr.*, CA-9, 65-2 USTC ¶ 9451, 346 F2d 187, rev'g, 41 TC 675, Dec. 26,664 (1964).

[52] Code Sec. 761(c).

[53] Reg. § 1.761-1(c).

agreement provides for oral modifications, an oral agreement providing for good-will payments should be respected.[54]

If a partnership has a tax basis in capitalized goodwill (*e.g.*, because of a business purchased by the partnership or a prior basis adjustment pursuant to Code Sec. 743(b)) payments to the extent of such basis are Code Sec. 736(b) payments, regardless of the language in the partnership agreement.[55]

Goodwill payments treated as Code Sec. 736(b) payments will be treated under the normal partnership distribution rules. The partnership is not entitled to a deduction for any Code Sec. 736(b) payment made to a withdrawing partner. Such a distribution will trigger an adjustment to the partnership's basis in goodwill under Code Sec. 734(b) only if there is a Code Sec. 754 election in effect. In the absence of an election under Code Sec. 754 by the partnership, a Code Sec. 736(b) payment to a withdrawing partner has no tax effect on the remaining partners if the partnership does not have substantially appreciated inventory. However, if a Code Sec. 754 election applies to the Code Sec. 736(b) payment and gain is recognized by the withdrawing partner, the partnership is entitled to increase the basis of its remaining property to the extent of the withdrawing partner's gain.[56]

.05 Payments for Property Other Than Unrealized Receivables and Goodwill—Code Sec. 736(b)

Payments up to the fair market value of a partner's share of partnership property other than unrealized receivables and goodwill are always classified by Code Sec. 736 as distributions. As a rule, if cash distributions are made to a partner for an interest in partnership property, the partner is normally allowed to recover his or her basis in the partnership free of tax, and any payments over such basis result in capital gain.[57] There are exceptions to this general rule. One exception applies when a partnership has substantially appreciated inventory or items of recapture (*e.g.*, depreciation recapture); in such cases, the retiring or deceased partner will be required to recognize ordinary income from the constructive sale of his or her interest in such substantially appreciated inventory or recapture items.[58] Under these circumstances the continuing partnership will receive a fair market value basis for the departing partner's share of these assets. A second exception allows the partner to elect to apportion payments made over several years between the recovery of partnership interest basis and gain recognition.[59] A partner is allowed a capital loss if the partner's basis in the partnership interest is not recovered by such payments.[60]

The partnership is not entitled to a deduction for any Code Sec. 736(b) payment made to a withdrawing partner. In the absence of an election under Code Sec. 754 by the partnership, a Code Sec. 736(b) payment to a withdrawing partner

---

[54] Consistent treatment of the payment for goodwill by both the partnership and the retiring partner in filing their tax returns should be sufficient to indicate the presence of an oral agreement.

[55] Reg. § 1.736-1(b)(3).

[56] Code Sec. 734(b).

[57] The provisions of Code Sec. 751(b) will apply if a portion of the cash distribution is payment for the retiring partner's share of the partnership's substantially appreciated inventory.

[58] Reg. § 1.736-1(b)(6); Code Sec. 751(b).

[59] Reg. § 1.736-1(b)(6).

[60] *Id.*

has no tax effect on the remaining partners if the partnership does not have substantially appreciated inventory or assets subject to recapture. However, if the partnership has a Code Sec. 754 election in effect and gain is recognized by the withdrawing partner, the partnership is entitled to increase the basis of its remaining property to the extent of the withdrawing partner's gain.[61]

Property distributions are governed by the normal rules applicable to liquidating property distributions. The partnership can be adversely affected by Code Sec. 736(b) liquidation payments if a retiring partner originally acquired the partnership interest by purchase or inheritance and a Code Sec. 754 election was not made in connection with the original acquisition of such interest. If a Code Sec. 754 election is made in connection with Code Sec. 736(b) liquidating property distributions, the partnership could be required to reduce the basis of its assets pursuant to Code Sec. 734(b)(2) to the extent the retiring partner takes a stepped-up basis in distributed property.

.06 Allocating the Payment Among Code Sec. 736 Categories

Typically, liquidating distributions include payments for all three categories of property (unrealized receivables, goodwill, and other property). If there is one lump-sum payment, it is allocated to the different categories of payments based upon their relative values.

While the IRS should ordinarily respect the partners' determination of the value of the withdrawing partner's share of partnership property because of the competing interests of the withdrawing partner and the continuing partners, it will not necessarily respect the valuation in every case. Generally, the valuation the partners place upon a partner's interest in partnership property in an arm's-length agreement will be regarded as correct.[62] If the partners are not dealing at arm's length (for example, if the withdrawing partner and the continuing partners are members of the same family), the IRS may question the value of the withdrawing partner's interest in partnership property agreed to by the parties. If the partners do not attempt to value the withdrawing partner's interest in the partnership property, however, the courts may do so.[63] It is therefore advisable to agree to a value and to formalize the agreement in a written document.

A partner increases his or her basis in the partnership interest by increases in his or her share of partnership indebtedness[64] and is required to decrease his or her basis to the extent that the partner's share of partnership indebtedness is reduced.[65] The valuation of a partner's interest in partnership property should be on a gross, rather than a net, basis (*i.e.*, total value without reduction for liabilities),

---

[61] Code Sec. 734(b).

[62] Reg. § 1.736-1(b)(1).

[63] The Tax Court valued a withdrawing partner's interest in partnership property where the partners failed to allocate liquidation payments between Code Sec. 736(a) and (b) payments in *A.O. Champlin v. Commr.*, 36 TCM 802, Dec. 34,476(M), TC Memo. 1977-196. The determination by the court was based on a "careful examination of the record and all the factors affecting the negotiations between the parties." *See also Est. of T.P. Quirk v.*

Commr., 55 TCM 1188, Dec. 44,870(M), TC Memo. 1988-286, aff'd, CA-6, 91-1 USTC ¶ 50,148, 928 F2d 751. Value and character of retiring partner's interest determined even though such issues were the subject of litigation in state court; values on partnership's financial statements adopted because taxpayer failed to produce contrary evidence.

[64] Code Sec. 752(a).

[65] Code Sec. 752(b).

because the reduction in the partner's share of liabilities will itself be treated as part of the liquidating payment(s) received by the partner.

.07 Accounting for a Series of Payments

When there is an installment liquidation, the partner treats part of each payment as a distributive share of partnership income, and/or a guaranteed payment (depending upon whether the amount was fixed or contingent),[66] and any remainder as a liquidating distribution.[67] The retiring partner and the partnership may agree upon an allocation of each payment between Code Sec. 736(a) and Code Sec. 736(b) amounts.[68] Lacking such an agreement, the ordering depends upon whether the amount of the total payments is fixed or contingent upon future partnership income. If the amount is contingent, the payments treated as distributions are accounted for first.[69] The remainder of the fixed payments are accounted for as a share of partnership income. If the amount is fixed, the portion of each payment treated as a distribution is the amount that the total of the Code Sec. 736(b) payments bears to the total of all payments. The remainder of each payment is treated as a Code Sec. 707(c) guaranteed payment.[70] If the withdrawing partner receives less than the amount the parties had agreed would be the fixed amount to be paid as a Code Sec. 736(b) payment in any year, the deficit amount is carried over to the next year and added to the fixed amounts paid in the succeeding year in determining the Code Sec. 736(b) amount in the later year.[71]

> **Example 15-6:** *A* is a general partner in the equal ABCDE Partnership. He is retiring on June 15, Year 1. In liquidation of his interest he is to receive $4,000 per year for the next eight years. The partnership agreement does not provide for a payment to a retiring partner for goodwill. The partnership does not have a Code Sec. 754 election in effect and uses the cash method of accounting. *A*'s basis for his interest is $9,400.[72]

ABCDE Balance Sheet 6/15/Year 1

Assets	Tax Basis	FMV
Cash	$17,000	$17,000
Accounts Receivable	0	80,000
Building (No Recapture)	16,000	25,000
Land	14,000	24,000
Goodwill	0	55,000
	$47,000	$201,000

---

[66] Code Sec. 736(a).
[67] Code Sec. 736(b).
[68] Reg. § 1.736-1(b)(5)(iii).
[69] Reg. § 1.736-1(b)(5)(ii).
[70] Reg. § 1.736-1(b)(5)(i).
[71] *Id.*
[72] $1,200 tax basis capital account plus *A*'s $8,200 debt share.

Liabilities and Capital

Mortgage (Recourse)	$41,000	$41,000
Capital—*A*	1,200	32,000
Capital—Other Partners	4,800	128,000
Total Liabilities and Capital.............	*$47,000*	*$201,000*

The total payments to be received by *A* must be increased by the deemed payment for liability relief. Thus, in determining the consequences under Code Sec. 736, *A* is treated as liquidating his partnership interest for a total of $40,200 ($32,000 cash payments over eight years, plus $8,200 debt relief). The debt relief occurs at the time of *A*'s withdrawal from the partnership. Thus, his Year 1 payments total $12,200 ($4,000 cash payment, plus $8,200 debt relief). Each subsequent year's payment will be $4,000.

Of the total payments to be received, $13,200 will be treated as Code Sec. 736(b) payments (*A*'s 20% share of the value of the cash, building and land). The remainder will be governed by Code Sec. 736(a). Thus, $4,006 of the first year's total payments will be classified under 736(b) (13,200/40,200 × 12,200), and $8,194 under Code Sec. 736(a) (27,000/40,200 × 12,200). Of the $4,000 payment received in each subsequent year, $1,313 will be classified as a Code Sec. 736(b) payment and $2,687 as a Code Sec. 736(a) payment.

Assume that in Years 3, 4, and 5 the partnership is unable to make the agreed upon $4,000 payments, but it catches up with additional payments of $4,000 in Years 6, 7, and 8. Classification of the payments received by *A* would be as follows:[73]

Year	*Code Sec. 736(b)*	*Code Sec. 736(a)*	*Total*
1	$4,006	$8,194	$12,200
2	1,313	2,687	4,000
3	0	0	0
4	0	0	0
5	0	0	0
6	5,252	2,748	8,000
7	1,313	6,687	8,000
8	1,313	6,687	8,000
	$13,200 *	*$27,000* *	*$40,200*

*Note: slight difference due to rounding.

A's Code Sec. 736(b) payments are first recovery of his $9,400 basis in his partnership interest. Starting in Year 6, *A* will recognize capital gain. With the sixth payment he will have recovered his $9,400 basis and have received $1,171

---

[73] Reg. § 1.736-1 (b) (5) (i).

in excess of that basis. During Years 7 and 8, *A* will have $1,313 capital gain each year.

Had *A* been a partner in a partnership in which capital was a material income-producing factor, all retirement payments would have been treated as Code Sec. 736(b) payments for partnership property (which would include the unrealized receivables and goodwill). To the extent the payments are deemed to be for unrealized receivables, *A* would recognize ordinary income under the Code Sec. 751(b) hot asset rules. To the extent the Code Sec. 754 election results in an increase in the partnership's goodwill, an amortizable asset would be created.

Because *A* continues to be treated as a partner until his liquidation payments cease, he will continue to receive Schedules K-1 through Year 8. For each year, the Code Sec. 736(b) payment should be shown on *A*'s Schedule K-1 as a cash distribution in the capital account reconciliation. The Code Sec. 736(a) payments should be treated as guaranteed payments—*i.e.*, deducted on Form 1065, U.S. Partnership Return of Income, Page 1, line 10, and reported as income on box 4 of *A*'s Schedule K-1.

Example 15-7: *A* is a general partner in the equal ABCDE Partnership. He is retiring on June 15, Year 1. In liquidation of his interest he is to receive 20% of the partnership's net income per year for the next eight years. The partnership agreement does not provide for a payment to a retiring partner for goodwill. The partnership does not have a Code Sec. 754 election in effect and uses the cash method of accounting. *A*'s basis for his interest is $9,400.[74]

ABCDE Balance Sheet 6/15/Year 1

Assets	*Tax Basis*	*FMV*
Cash	$17,000	$17,000
Accounts Receivable	0	80,000
Building (No Recapture)	16,000	25,000
Land	14,000	24,000
Goodwill	0	55,000
	$47,000	$201,000

Liabilities and Capital		
Mortgage (Recourse)	$41,000	$41,000
Capital—*A*	1,200	32,000
Capital—Other Partners	4,800	128,000
Total Liabilities and Capital	$47,000	$201,000

As before, $13,200 of *A*'s retirement payments will be classified as Code Sec. 736(b) payments. *A* must treat all of the payments as Code Sec. 736(b)

---

[74] $1,200 tax basis capital account plus *A*'s $8,200 debt share.

payments until he has received $13,200. Assuming partnership net income of $20,000 per year, *A* accounts for the payments as follows:

Year	*Code Sec. 736(b)*	*Code Sec. 736(a)*	*Total*
1	$12,200	$ 0	$12,200
2	1,000	3,000	4,000
3	0	4,000	4,000
4	0	4,000	4,000
5	0	4,000	4,000
6	0	4,000	4,000
7	0	4,000	4,000
8	0	4,000	4,000
	$13,200	*$27,000*	*$40,200*

If a withdrawing partner receives both fixed and contingent payments over time in liquidation of his or her interest in the partnership and the fixed amounts to be received over the entire payout period (whether or not supplemented by any additional amounts) equal or exceed the value of the withdrawing partner's interest in partnership properties, a proportionate share of each fixed payment is considered to be a Code Sec. 736(b) amount in the manner described above. The balance of each fixed payment and the entire amount of each contingent payment will constitute Code Sec. 736(a) amounts.[75] If the total amount of the fixed payments a withdrawing partner is to receive over the payout period is less than the value of the partner's interest in partnership property, the entire amount of each fixed payment is considered to be a Code Sec. 736(b) amount. In addition, each contingent payment is considered to be a Code Sec. 736(b) amount until the full amount of fixed payments to be received plus the contingent amounts allocated to Code Sec. 736(b) equal the value of the withdrawing partner's interest in partnership property.[76]

When a withdrawing partner receives a series of Code Sec. 736(b) cash distributions in the absence of a contrary election, he or she recognizes gain or loss and reports it in accordance with a cash basis, cost recovery method of accounting.[77] The partner recovers his or her entire basis in his or her partnership interest before recognizing any gain, and a loss is not recognized until the final Code Sec. 736(b) distribution is made to the withdrawing partner.[78] As an alternative, the regulations allow a withdrawing partner to elect to include the total gain or loss to be recognized ratably over all Code Sec. 736(b) distributions if the total amount of Code Sec. 736(b) distributions to be received is fixed.[79]

A withdrawing partner who elects to apportion the gain or loss attributable to Code Sec. 736(b) must attach a statement to his or her tax return for the first

---

[75] *Id.*
[76] *Id.*
[77] Reg. §§ 1.736-1(b)(6), 1.731-1(a)(1) and (2).
[78] Reg. § 1.731-1(a)(2).
[79] Reg. § 1.736-1(b)(6).

taxable year he or she receives a Code Sec. 736(b) distribution, indicating his or her election and showing the computation of the gain or loss included in or deducted from gross income.[80]

.08 Allocating Property Distributions Between Code Sec. 736(a) Payments and Code Sec. 736(b) Payments

Since Code Sec. 736 applies to "payments," the implication of the provision as well as the implication of the regulations[81] is that Code Sec. 736 applies to cash payments. It is not clear whether Code Sec. 736 also applies to a partnership distribution of property. While Code Sec. 736 uses the term "payment," the provision is not specifically limited to a distribution of cash. Neither the legislative history of Code Sec. 736 nor the regulations provides any guidance as to whether Code Sec. 736 applies to in-kind distributions. On the other hand, the Code Sec. 736 regulations as originally proposed specifically provided that Code Sec. 736 applied only to cash payments and not to property distributions.[82] While there is no explanation set forth in the Treasury Decision that adopted the final regulations[83] for the deletion of the language in the proposed regulations limiting the application of Code Sec. 736 to cash payments, the deletion provides at least an inference that Code Sec. 736 applies to both property and cash distributions.[84]

Unfortunately, neither the Internal Revenue Code nor the Treasury regulations provide any guidance on how to account for distributions consisting, in whole or part, of property. The method of allocation between Code Sec. 736(a) and (b) payments (*e.g., pro rata*, property distribution first treated as Code Sec. 736(b) distributions, etc.) is important because treating a distribution of appreciated property as a Code Sec. 736(a) payment will seemingly require the partnership to recognize the appreciation as gain. Arguably, the partners can, and should, allocate each distribution, whether in cash or property, between Code Sec. 736(a) and Code Sec. 736(b).[85]

.09 Passive Gain or Loss

The portion of the Code Sec. 736(a) payments that are allocable to unrealized receivables (as defined in Code Sec. 751(c)) and goodwill that is treated as passive activity gross income may not exceed the percentage of the passive activity gross income that would be included in the gross income that the retiring partner or deceased partner would have recognized if the unrealized receivables and goodwill had been sold when the liquidation of the interest commenced.[86] Gain or loss triggered by receipt of a Code Sec. 736(b) payment is treated as passive activity

---

[80] *Id.*

[81] Only cash payments are used as examples in the Code Sec. 736 regulations, which arguably could be read to mean that Code Sec. 736 applies only to cash payments and not to distributions of other property.

[82] Prop. Reg. § 1.736-1(a)(2), NPRM (1954), 20 FR 5854 (August 12, 1955).

[83] T.D. 6175, 1956-1 CB 211.

[84] An additional indication that the IRS believes that Code Sec. 736 applies to property distributions is provided by IRS Letter Ruling 8538094 (6-27-85), which dis-

cusses the tax consequences of the incorporation of a general partnership. Some of the partners withdrew from the partnership as part of the same transaction which culminated in incorporation. Property was distributed to the withdrawing partner in kind. The ruling recognizes that Code Sec. 736 may apply to the property distributions but sidesteps the issue by excepting from the ruling the tax consequences to the extent that the property distributions to the withdrawing partners constituted payments under Code Sec. 736.

[85] Reg. § 1.736-1(b)(5)(iii).

[86] Reg. § 1.469-2(e)(2)(iii)(B).

gross income or a passive activity deduction to the extent that the gain or loss would have been passive activity gross income or a passive activity deduction of the retiring or deceased partner if it had been recognized when the liquidation of the interest commenced.[87]

.10 Effect of Code Sec. 754 Election

A Code Sec. 754 election generally has no effect when the partnership itself is liquidating.[88] But when partnership operations continue and a particular partner's interest is liquidated, a Code Sec. 754 election may benefit remaining partners. The portion of the payments to the retiring partner treated as distributions under Code Sec. 736(b) can be the source of a Code Sec. 734(b) adjustment to remaining partnership property.

1. The retired partner's gain from a cash distribution in excess of his or her basis in the partnership interest generates an increase in the partnership's basis for its capital and Code Sec. 1231 assets in a like amount.[89]

2. Any loss recognized by the retiring partner causes the partnership to reduce its basis in its remaining capital and Code Sec. 1231 assets.[90]

3. If a retired partner's basis in distributed property after the distribution exceeds the partnership's former basis, the partnership decreases its basis in remaining similar property by the same amount.[91]

4. If a retired partner's basis in distributed property after the distribution is less than the partnership's former basis, the partnership increases its basis in remaining similar property by the same amount.[92]

See Chapter 15 for a discussion of how Code Sec. 734(b) adjustments are determined and how they are allocated among remaining partnership assets.

.11 Classification of Retirement Payments as Self-Employment Income

Code Sec. 1402(a), which defines net earnings from self-employment, specifically excludes retirement payments to a partner if the following requirements are satisfied:

1. The payments must be made on a periodic basis by the partnership pursuant to a written plan that provides for payments on account of retirement to partners generally or to a class or classes of partners to continue at least until the partner's death;[93]

2. The retired partner to whom the payments are made must not render services with respect to any trade or business carried on by the partnership (or its successors) during the taxable year of the partnership (or its successors), which ends within or with the taxable year of the partner and in which the payment was received;

---

[87] Reg. § 1.469-2(e)(2)(iii)(A).

[88] In the case of a technical termination under Code Sec. 708 caused by a sale of 50% or more of the partnership interests in a 12-month time period, the adjustments under Code Sec. 743(b) may affect the way basis is allocated to the distributed property in the deemed liquidating distribution.

[89] Code Sec. 734(b)(1)(A).

[90] Code Sec. 734(b)(2)(A).

[91] Code Sec. 734(b)(2)(B).

[92] Code Sec. 734(b)(2)(A).

[93] Code Sec. 1402(a)(10) and Reg. § 1.1402(a)-17.

3. No obligation exists (as of the close of the partnership year referred to in item 2 above) from the other partners to the retired partner except with respect to retirement payments under the plan or rights such as benefits payable on account of sickness, accident, hospitalization, medical expenses, or death; and

4. The retired partner's share of the capital of the partnership has been paid to him in full before the close of the partnership's taxable year referred to in item 2 above.

Under the regulations, if the above requirements are satisfied, all payments received by the partner on account of retirement are excluded from the partner's self-employment income. If any of the above requirements are not satisfied, none of the payments will be excluded. The regulations further provide that the effect of the conditions set forth in items 3 and 4 above is that the exclusion may apply with respect to such payments received by the retired partner during the taxable year only if at the close of the partnership taxable year the retired partner has no financial interest in the partnership except for the right to retirement payments.

¶ 1503 Payment for Retiring Partner's Interest When Capital Is a Material Income-Producing Factor or Partner Is a Limited Partner

Code Sec. 736(a) is inapplicable for post-1992 liquidating payments made to limited partners and general partners of partnerships having capital as a material income-producing factor.[94] All payments are governed by the distribution rules described immediately above in connection with Code Sec. 736(b) payments for other than unrealized receivables and goodwill.

The Revenue Reconciliation Act of 1993 amendments to Code Sec. 736 generally apply to partners retiring or dying on or after January 5, 1993.[95] However, if a written contract to purchase a partner's interest was binding on January 4, 1993, and at all times after that, the 1993 Act amendments are not applicable.[96] The legislative history adds that a written contract is to be considered binding only if the contract specifies the amount to be paid for the partnership interest and the timing of any such payments.[97] Many partnership agreements provide for the partnership to purchase a deceased partner's interest based on a formula price. It is unclear if a formula price will be deemed to represent a "specified amount." It seems that such a formula price buy-out should qualify the parties to use Code Sec. 736 as it existed before the 1993 Act. This is because informed partnerships have based their formulas, in part, upon the tax laws in existence when the agreement was reached. A change in the tax laws doesn't automatically grant any partner a right to change the agreement.

The House Committee Report to the Revenue Reconciliation Act of 1993 states that the changes to Code Sec. 736 are not intended to affect the deductibility of

---

[94] Specifically, Code Sec. 736(a) is inapplicable to payments made to these types of partners retiring after January 15, 1993, the effective date of the Revenue Reconciliation Act of 1993, P.L. 103-66, Act § 13262(b).

[95] P.L. 103-66, Act § 13262(b).

[96] The Revenue Reconciliation Act of 1993, P.L. 103-66, Act § 13262(c)(2).

[97] H.R. Rep. N. 102-11, 103rd Cong., 1st Sess. (1993).

compensation to a retiring partner for past services. Therefore, legitimate and reasonable compensation for past services paid to a retiring partner whose interest is being liquidated in a partnership in which capital is a material income-producing factor will be governed by the principles of Code Sec. 707 (*e.g.*, as a deductible guaranteed payment under Code Sec. 707(c) or (a)). Therefore, though Code Sec. 736 will no longer permit capital-intensive partnerships the right to classify retirement payments as deductible guaranteed payments; the partnership may still obtain a deduction for payments to the extent they represent reasonable compensation for past services.

¶ 1504 Partnership Interest Sale Compared to Liquidation

	Liquidation Approach	*Sale Approach*
Depreciation recapture		
All partners..............................	736(b), 751(b)	751(a)
Unrealized receivables (other than depreciation recapture)		
Service partner	736(a)	751(a)
Other partner	736(b), 751(b)	751(a)
Substantially appreciated inventory (other than unrealized receivables)		
All partners..............................	736(b), 751(b)	751(a)

Chapter 16

S Corporations

¶ 1601 Eligibility, Election, and Formation

S corporations, like partnerships, are flow-through entities and are generally not subject to any federal income tax. Instead, in a manner very much like that of a partnership, the income of the S corporation flows through to the individual shareholders and is recognized by them. In fact, S corporations were created in order to give closely held corporations the ability to avoid income tax on corporate income at the entity level. Like a partnership, the S corporation must file a tax return, and in fact the tax return contains Schedule K and also K-1s that must be distributed to the S corporation shareholders. While the treatment of income items by a partnership and S corporation are strikingly similar, there are several differences in other areas of tax treatment. For example, while the distributions of appreciated property from a partnership are generally nontaxable, a distribution of appreciated property from an S corporation will generally result in income to the S corporation to the extent of the amount of the appreciation.

Although most S corporations are legal corporations under state law, it is not necessary that an S corporation (a tax entity for which there is no state law equivalent) be a statutory corporation. In fact, a statutory partnership or LLC that has elected to be taxed as an association can subsequently elect to be taxed as an S corporation rather than a regular C corporation.

.01 Eligibility

An S corporation is defined as a "small business corporation" for which an election under Code Sec. 1362(a) is in effect for the taxable year. A C corporation, on the other hand, is defined as a corporation which is not an S corporation for a taxable year.[1] A "small business corporation" is a domestic corporation which is not an "ineligible corporation" and which does not—

---

[1] Code Sec. 1361(a).

 A. have more than 100 shareholders,

 B. have as a shareholder a person (other than an estate, a trust described in Code Sec. 1361(c)(2), or an organization described in Code Sec. 1361(c)(6)) who is not an individual,

 C. have a nonresident alien as a shareholder, and

 D. have more than one class of stock.[2]

The term "ineligible corporation" (which may not be treated as an S orporation) means any corporation which is—

 A. a financial institution which uses the reserve method of accounting for bad debts described in Code Sec. 585,

 B. an insurance company subject to tax under subchapter L,

 C. a corporation to which an election under Code Sec. 936 applies, or

 D. a DISC or former DISC.

One hundred shareholder limitation. For purposes of computing the number of shareholders, a husband and wife (and their estates) will be treated as one shareholder, and all members of a family (and their estates) will also be treated as one shareholder. For this purpose the term "members of a family" means a common ancestor, any lineal descendant of such common ancestor, and any spouse or former spouse of such common ancestor or any such lineal descendant. Any legally adopted child of an individual, any child who is lawfully placed with an individual for legal adoption by the individual, and any eligible foster child of an individual (within the meaning of Code Sec. 152(f)(1)(C)), will be treated as a child of the individual.[3]

It should be noted that the 100 shareholder limitation in many cases is not an effective limitation on the number of owners of an enterprise, even where the owners of the enterprise will all be better served by being S corporation shareholders. This is because the Service has taken the position that multiple S corporations can be partners in the same partnership.[4] The Service in Revenue Ruling 94-43 concluded that three S corporations formed for the principal purpose of avoiding the S corporation shareholder limitation should not be considered a single corporation.

Types of shareholders allowed. Certain trusts can be shareholders in an S corporation, but rules have been created to ensure that these trusts don't provide a vehicle for investment for foreign shareholders. The following trusts may be shareholders:

 a. A trust all of which is owned by an individual who is a citizen or resident of the United States.

 b. A trust which was "owned" by a citizen or resident immediately before the death of the deemed owner and which continues in existence after such

---

[2] Code Sec. 1361(b)(1).   [4] Rev. Rul. 94-43, 1994-2 CB 199.
[3] Code Sec. 1361(c).

¶1601.01

death, but only for the 2-year period beginning on the day of the deemed owner's death.

c. A trust with respect to stock transferred to it pursuant to the terms of a will, but only for the 2-year period beginning on the day on which such stock is transferred to it.

d. A trust created primarily to exercise the voting power of stock transferred to it.

e. the estate of an individual in bankruptcy.[5]

In general, qualified retirement plan trusts (described in Code Sec. 401(a)) and charitable organizations (described in Code Sec. 501(c)(3)) may be shareholders in an S corporation.[6]

More than one class of stock. Although S corporations are not allowed to have more than one class of stock, an exception to this rule is allowed with respect to voting rights. An S corporation will not be treated as having more than one class of stock solely because there are differences in voting rights among the shares of common stock.[7] In addition, a safe harbor provision allows that straight debt is not treated as a second class of stock if certain requirements are met.[8]

Shareholder recognition of income. In general, each shareholder's pro rata share of any item for any taxable year will be determined based on the number of days the shareholder held the shares and the percentage ownership the shareholder had on the days they held the shares.[9]

> ***Example 16-1:*** The Able Corporation elected S status for the year, and their taxable income was $730,000 for the year. Each day of the year would be allocated $730,000/365 = $2,000, and each shareholder on those days would share the income allocated to that day ($2,000) based on their ownership percentage on that day. If shareholder Mark had a 25% interest for the first 100 days of the year, Mark would be allocated $2,000 X 25% X 100 days = $50,000 of the income from the S corporation, and that would be reflected on his Schedule K-1. If the $730,000 in income was 20% long term capital gain, then Mark's K-1 would reflect $40,000 of ordinary income from the S corporation and $10,000 of long term capital gain.

If any shareholder terminates their interest in the corporation during the taxable year and all "affected shareholders" (the shareholder whose interest is terminated and all shareholders to whom such shareholder has transferred shares during the taxable year) and the corporation agree, income will be allocated to the shareholders as if the taxable year consisted of two taxable years, the first of which ends on the date of the termination.[10]

Fringe benefits. With respect to employee fringe benefits, an S corporation is treated as a partnership, and any 2-percent shareholder of the S corporation will be treated as a partner of the partnership. A "2-percent shareholder" is any person who

---

[5] Code Sec. 1361(c)(2) and (3).
[6] Code Sec. 1361(c)(6).
[7] Code Sec. 1361(c)(4).
[8] Code Sec. 1361(c)(5).
[9] Code Sec. 1377(a)(1).
[10] Code Sec. 1377(a)(2).

owns (or is considered as owning) on any day during the taxable year more than 2 percent of the outstanding stock of the corporation or stock possessing more than 2 percent of the total combined voting power of all stock of the corporation.[11]

.02 Election

An S corporation election is valid only if all shareholders as of the day on which the election is made consent to the election.[12] An S corporation election may be made for the current taxable year:

A. at any time during the preceding taxable year, or

B. at any time on or before the 15th day of the third month of the current taxable year.[13]

On the other hand, if the election is made after the 15th day of the third month of the current taxable year and on or before the 15th day of the third month of the following taxable year, then the election will be treated as made for the following taxable year.[14]

Example 16-2: A calendar year small business corporation begins its first taxable year on January 7, 2013. To be an S corporation beginning with its first taxable year, the corporation must make the election during the period that begins January 7, 2013, and ends before March 22, 2013. Because the corporation had no taxable year immediately preceding the taxable year for which the election is to be effective, an election made earlier than January 7, 2013, would not be valid.[15]

If the election is made on or before the 15th day of the third month of the year, but for at least one day on or prior to the election day the corporation did not qualify as an S corporation, then the election will be treated as made for the following taxable year. Similarly, if there was at least one day on or prior to the election day when one or more of the shareholders for any day during the taxable year before the election was made did not consent to the election, then the election is treated as made for the following taxable year.[16]

If the taxable year of the S corporation election has less than two and one half months, the election will be considered timely if it is made during the first two and one half months following the beginning of the short taxable year.[17]

Example 16-3: A calendar year small business corporation begins its first taxable year on November 8, 2013. To be an S corporation beginning with its first taxable year, the corporation must make the election during the period that begins November 8, 2013, and ends before January 23, 2014.

If an untimely election is made, the IRS can allow the election to be considered timely if it determines that there was reasonable cause for the failure to make a timely election.[18] Once made, an S corporation election is effective for the taxable

---

[11] Code Sec. 1372.

[12] Code Sec. 1362(a).

[13] Code Sec. 1362(b)(1).

[14] Code Sec. 1362(b)(3).

[15] Reg. § 1362-6(a)(2)(iii), Example (1).

[16] Code Sec. 1362(b)(2)(B).

[17] Code Sec. 1362(b)(4).

[18] Code Sec. 1362(b)(5).

year of the corporation for which it is made and for all succeeding taxable years of the corporation, until the election is terminated.[19]

A corporation must make the S corporation election by filing a completed Form 2553, Election by a Small Business Corporation. The election form must be filed with the service center designated in the instructions applicable to Form 2553. The election is not valid unless all shareholders of the corporation at the time of the election consent to the election. However, once a valid election is made, new shareholders need not consent to the election.[20] An eligible entity that timely elects to be an S corporation is treated as having made an election to be classified as an association, provided that the entity meets all other requirements to qualify as a small business corporation.[21]

> **Example 16-4:** On January 1, 2013, two individuals and a partnership own all of the stock of a calendar year subchapter C corporation. On January 31, 2013, the partnership dissolved and distributed its shares in the corporation to its five partners, all individuals. On February 28, 2013, the seven shareholders of the corporation consented to the corporation's election of subchapter S status. The corporation files a properly completed Form 2553 on March 2, 2013. The corporation is not eligible to be a subchapter S corporation for the 2013 taxable year because during the period of the taxable year prior to the election it had an ineligible shareholder, the partnership. However, the election is treated as made for the corporation's 2014 taxable year.

.03 Corporate Contributions

Except for the treatment related to the passthrough of income, S corporations are generally treated the same as C corporations for tax purposes. They are therefore subject to the rules of Code Sec. 351 when it comes to the taxability of contributions to the corporation in exchange for stock of the corporation. Under Code Sec. 351, no gain or loss is recognized by the shareholder if (1) property is transferred to the corporation (2) solely in exchange for stock in the corporation and (3) immediately after the exchange the participants to the exchange are in control of the corporation.[22] For this purpose the term "control" means the ownership of stock possessing at least 80 percent of the total combined voting power of all classes of stock entitled to vote and at least 80 percent of the total number of shares of all other classes of stock of the corporation.[23]

If "boot" (money or property that is not stock of the S corporation) is received by the contributing shareholder in the exchange, the shareholder will recognize any realized gain (but not loss) on the exchange, up to the amount of boot (fair market value of property or the amount of money) received.[24]

> **Example 16-5:** Judy contributes land (value = $300,000, basis = $250,000) to the Spa Corporation (an S corporation for tax purposes) in exchange for 1000 shares of its stock, $5,000 cash, and a painting worth $10,000 and a basis to the corporation of $9,000. After the exchange she owns 85% of the stock of

---

[19] Code Sec. 1362(c).
[20] Reg. § 1362-6(a)(2)(i).
[21] Reg. § 301.7701-3(c)(1)(v)(C).

[22] Code Sec. 351(a).
[23] Code Sec. 368(c).
[24] Code Sec. 351(b).

Spa. Her realized gain is $300,000 - $250,000 = $50,000 (assuming the value of the stock she receives is $285,000). The exchange meets the requirements of Code Sec. 351, so her recognized gain will be the lesser of the boot received, $15,000 ($5,000 cash plus $10,000 value of the painting), or the gain realized $50,000. Her recognized gain will therefore be $15,000. Her basis in the painting will be its fair market value, $10,000, and her basis in the stock received will be $250,000 [$250,000 (basis in the property contributed) + $15,000 gain recognized - $15,000 boot received].

The value of services contributed by the shareholder in exchange for stock will always be recognized as income by the shareholder, and is not considered "property" for purposes of Code Sec. 351.[25] If services is all that is contributed by a shareholder, their ownership is not considered when determining whether the 80% control test is met. However, if a significant portion of their contribution is also property, the ownership of a service-providing shareholder will still be considered in the determination of whether or not the control requirement is met.

> *Example 16-6:* E, an individual, owns property with a basis of $10,000 and a fair market value of $18,000. E also had rendered services valued at $2,000 to Corporation F, an S corporation. Corporation F has outstanding 100 shares of common stock, all of which are held by G. Corporation F issues 400 shares of its common stock (having a fair market value of $20,000) to E in exchange for his property worth $18,000 and in compensation for the services he has rendered worth $2,000. Immediately after the transaction, E owns 80 percent of the outstanding stock of Corporation F, so no gain is recognized upon the exchange of the property for the stock. However, E will recognize $2,000 of ordinary income as compensation for services rendered to Corporation F.[26]

In general, the assumption of a shareholder's liability by the corporation in an exchange of property for stock will not be considered to be boot to the shareholder,[27] unless tax avoidance is a motive for the transfer of the liability.[28] However, if the sum of the amount of the liabilities assumed by the corporation in the exchange exceeds the total of the adjusted basis of the property transferred in the exchange, then the excess will be treated as gain from a sale or exchange. Whether it is a capital gain or not will depend on the nature of the associated assets transferred.[29]

> *Example 16-7:* Barry transfers to an S corporation, under section 351, properties having a total basis in his hands of $20,000. One of the properties has a basis of $10,000, but is subject to a mortgage of $30,000. If Barry controls the corporation he will be subject to tax with respect to $10,000, the excess of the amount of the liability over the total adjusted basis of all the properties in his hands.[30]

---

[25] Code Sec. 351(d).
[26] Reg. § 1.351-1(a)(2), Example (3).
[27] Code Sec. 357(a)(1).

[28] Code Sec. 357(b).
[29] Code Sec. 357(c)(1).
[30] Reg. § 1.357-2(a).

If the liability is transferred to the corporation for tax-avoidance purposes, the entire amount of the liabilities is treated as money received, or boot.[31]

.04 S Corporation Method of Accounting and Taxable Year

S corporations, unlike most regular corporations, are allowed to use the cash method of accounting. The accounting method is elected by the entity itself[32] and does not have to match the accounting method used by the shareholders. In contrast, regular, or "C" corporations are required to use the accrual method of accounting if their gross receipts exceed $5 million.[33]

The taxable year of an S corporation must be one of the following:

1. the "required" taxable year (i.e., a taxable year ending on December 31),

2. a taxable year elected under section 444,

3. a 52-53-week taxable year ending with reference to the required taxable year, or a taxable year elected under section 444, or

4. a natural business year.[34]

An S corporation that elects a fiscal tax year under section 444 must make a "required payment", in the same manner a partnership would. The required payments are intended to represent the value of the tax deferral obtained by the S corporation shareholders through the use of a tax year different from the required year. These payments are not deductible by the S corporation or its shareholders. Instead, they are similar to refundable deposits. These payments are not passed through to S corporation shareholders and are not allowed as a credit against the federal income tax liabilities of S corporation shareholders.[35]

A "natural business year" is a year for which an S corporation satisfies the "25-percent gross receipts test." The 25-percent gross receipts test is satisfied if, for the current year and the prior two years, total gross receipts from sales and services for the last two months of the 12-month period exceed 25% of total gross receipts for that year.[36]

¶ 1602 Taxation of S Corporations

.01 Built-in Gains Tax

In the absence of any statutory provisions to prevent it, regular C corporations would find it easy to avoid entity-level tax on appreciated property by electing S corporation status, then selling the appreciated property. To prevent this, Congress provided for the taxation of the net built-in gains of S corporations.[37] The amount of the built-in gains tax is computed by applying the highest corporate tax rate (currently 35%) to the "net recognized built-in gain" of the S corporation for the taxable year. Understandably, the built-in gains tax does not apply to a corporation that was originally and always has remained an S corporation.[38]

---

[31] Code Sec. 357(b)(1).

[32] Code Sec. 1363(c)(1). If the S corporation is a tax shelter, it is prohibited from using the cash method of accounting. Code Sec. 448(a)(3).

[33] Code Sec. 448(b)(3).

[34] Reg. § 1.378-1(a), Rev. Proc. 2006-46, 2006-2 CB 859.

[35] Reg. § 1.7519-2T.

[36] Rev. Proc. 2006-46, 2006-2 CB 859, Section 5.07(1).

[37] Code Sec. 1374(a).

[38] Code Sec. 1374(c)(1).

Example 16-8: The Able Corporation elected S status for the year, and its taxable income was $100,000 for the year. During the year Able sold land (sale price = $130,000, basis = $100,000) for a gain of $30,000. Able had owned the land at the beginning of the year, and at that time it had a fair market value of $130,000. The built-in gains tax on the sale would be $30,000 X 35% = $10,500. This tax would be paid by Able, while the $30,000 gain itself would pass through to the Able shareholders.

The tax is assessed only on the amount of "net recognized built-in gain" that an S corporation has for the year. The term "net recognized built-in gain" means, with respect to any taxable year, the lesser of

a. the amount which would be the taxable income of the S corporation for the taxable year if only recognized built-in gains and recognized built-in losses were taken into account, or

b. the corporation's taxable income for the taxable year.[39]

However, any excess of the amount in (a) above over the amount in (b) will be carried over until the next year, so the built-in gains tax can't be avoided by recognizing the built-in gains in years in which there is no taxable income.[40]

Example 16-9: The Best Corporation elected S status three years ago, and its taxable income was $70,000 for the current year. During the current year Best sold one parcel of land (sale price = $230,000, basis = $100,000) for a gain of $130,000, and another parcel (sale price = $120,000, basis = $140,000) for a loss of $20,000. These parcels of land have been owned by Best since before the S election, and their fair market values have not changed over the last four years. The "net recognized built-in gain" for the year is $70,000, the lesser of (a) $130,000 - $20,000 = $110,000 or (b) $70,000 current year taxable income. The built-in gains tax for the year would be $70,000 X 35% = $24,400. This tax would be paid by Best, while the $110,000 net gain itself would pass through to the Able shareholders in the current year. The $110,000 - $70,000 = $40,000 of recognized built in gain not used in the calculation of built-in gains tax this year will be carried forward indefinitely to future years until it is either subject to the built in gains tax or offset by future built-in losses.

The built-in gains tax is not assessed against appreciation in an asset that occurred after the beginning of the first S corporation year. Accordingly, a "recognized built-in gain" is any gain recognized on the disposition of any asset which was held at the beginning of the first S corporation taxable year, except to the extent that the gain exceeds the appreciation (fair market value minus basis) in the asset at the beginning of the first S corporation year.[41] Similarly, a "recognized built-in loss" is any loss recognized on the disposition of any asset which was held at the beginning of the first S corporation taxable year, except to the extent that the loss exceeds the depreciation (basis minus fair market) value at that time.[42]

---

[39] Code Sec. 1374(d)(2).
[40] Code Sec. 1374(d)(2)(B).

[41] Code Sec. 1374(d)(3).
[42] Code Sec. 1374(d)(4).

Example 16-10: The Groover Corporation elected S status two years ago, and during the current year sold one parcel of land (sale price = $210,000, basis = $100,000) for a gain of $110,000, and another parcel (sale price = $70,000, basis = $80,000) for a loss of $10,000. These parcels of land have been owned by Groover since before the S election, and their fair market values at the beginning of the first S corporation year were $190,000 and $74,000, respectively. The built-in gain and loss, respectively, for these two parcels is $190,000 - $100,000 = $90,000 and $74,000 - $80,000 = <$6,000>, for a total "net recognized built-in gain" (before considering current taxable income) for the year of $90,000 - $6,000 = $84,000.

Once the cumulative amount of built-in gains recognized equals the *original net unrealized* built-in gains, no more built-in gains will be subject to the tax. This prevents an S corporation that recognizes all of their built-in gains first (and their losses last) from recognizing more income from built-in gains than they would have if they had sold all of their properties before making the S election. Specifically, the amount of the net recognized built-in gain taken into account in computing the built-in gains tax for any taxable year can't exceed the excess (if any) of—

A. the original net *unrealized* built-in gain (from all C corporation years), over

B. the *cumulative* net *recognized* built-in gains for prior taxable years.[43]

The term "net unrealized built-in gain" means the amount (if any) by which—

A. the fair market value of the assets of the S corporation as of the beginning of its first taxable year for which an S election is in effect, exceeds

B. the aggregate adjusted bases of all of the assets at such time.[44]

Example 16-11: The Hobart Corporation elected S status four years ago, when its only assets were land parcels A, B, and C, with fair market values and bases as follows:

Parcel	FMV	Basis
A	$300,000	$200,000
B	$550,000	$350,000
C	$600,000	$850,000

The net unrealized built-in gain for Hobart is $100,000 + $200,000 - $250,000 = $50,000. That is the maximum cumulative built-in gain it will recognize. Should it sell Parcel B alone, the built-in gains tax will be $50,000 (the net unrealized built-in gain) X .35 = $17,500 (assuming Hobart's taxable income is at least $50,000 for the year, and the actual gain from the sale is at least $50,000). After that, it can sell Parcel A at any time and not have any built-in gains tax, since the total cumulative built-in gain has already been recognized.

---

[43] Code Sec. 1374(c)(2). [44] Code Sec. 1374(d)(1).

Since the corporation, in one of its prior C corporation years, could have used a net operating loss carryforward to offset some or all of the gain from the sale of appreciated property, any net operating loss carryforward arising in a taxable year for which the corporation was a C corporation is allowed as a deduction (for built-in gains tax purposes) against the net recognized built-in gain of the S corporation for the taxable year. Similar rules apply in the case of a capital loss carryforward arising in a taxable year for which the corporation was a C corporation.[45]

Under certain circumstances a business credit carryforward under section 39 or a minimum tax credit under section 53 arising in a taxable year for which the corporation was a C corporation is allowed as a credit against the built-in gains tax.[46]

Any item of income which is recognized during an S corporation year but which is attributable to periods before the first S corporation year is treated as a recognized built-in gain for the year in which it is recognized. Similarly, any deduction which is allowable during an S corporation year but which is attributable to periods before the first S corporation year is treated as a recognized built-in loss for the year in which it is allowable as a deduction. Before realization these amounts will be treated as adjustments to net unrealized built in gain.[47]

Recall that the purpose of the built-in gains tax is to keep corporations from avoiding double taxation of gains by electing S status before a sale of appreciated property. Lawmakers apparently decided that if the property was held for ten years after the beginning of the first S election year, this motive was somewhat unlikely because of the length of time between the election and the sale. Therefore, if any property is sold later than ten years after the beginning of the first S corporation year, its gain or loss will not be considered a built-in gain or loss. This means that the built-in gains tax will not be assessed on property held for at least ten years after the first S corporation year. In order to encourage the sale of appreciated property and the resultant recognition of the gain by S corporation shareholders, for 2009 and 2010 this period was shortened to seven years, and for 2011 it was shortened to five years. Neither the 5-year, 7-year, or 10-year periods apply to gains recognized because of distributions to shareholders.[48]

> ***Example 16-12:*** The Jonas Corporation, a calendar year corporation, elected S status effective on 1/1/2002. If it sells any property on which there is a built-in gain before 1/1/2012, it could be subject to the built-in gains tax. After that date it will not be subject to the built-in gains tax.

.02 Tax on Excess Net Passive Investment Income

Without a tax on passive investment income, a regular C corporation with significant passive assets could avoid the personal holding company and accumulated earnings taxes by electing to be an S corporation. A tax is therefore imposed on any S corporation that for any taxable year has (1) accumulated earnings and profits at the close of the taxable year, and (2) passive investment income that

---

[45] Code Sec. 1374(b)(2).
[46] Code Sec. 1374(b)(3).

[47] Code Sec. 1374(d)(5).
[48] Code Sec. 1374(d)(7).

makes up more than 25% of gross receipts.[49] If these two conditions are met, the tax imposed on the S corporation is the product of (1) the S corporation's *excess net passive income* and (2) the highest corporate tax rate (currently 35%).

Excess net passive income (ENPI) can be calculated as follows:

ENPI = Net Passive Income X (Passive Investment Income - 25% of Gross Receipts)/Passive Investment Income

Essentially ENPI is a percent of net passive income (NPI), and that percent is the percent of passive investment income (PII) that exceeds 25% of gross receipts. Excess net passive income for any taxable year is limited to the amount of the corporation's taxable income for the taxable year.[50]

Passive investment income is defined to be gross receipts derived from royalties, rents, dividends, interest (including tax-exempt interest), and annuities. For this purpose PII does not include any income identified by the Commissioner as income derived in the ordinary course of a trade or business.[51] PII also does not include any recognized built-in gain or loss of the S corporation for any taxable year.[52]

Net passive income is passive investment income reduced by the deductions which are directly connected with passive investment income, other than certain deductions such as for NOL, dividends received, and organization expenses.[53]

The sales of capital assets (other than stock and securities) will increase gross receipts only to the extent of the resulting capital gain net income therefrom. In the case of sales or exchanges of stock or securities, gross receipts will be increased only to the extent of the resulting gains.[54]

> **Example 16-13:** Assume Corporation M, an S corporation, has for its taxable year total gross receipts of $200,000, passive investment income of $100,000, $60,000 of which is interest income, and expenses directly connected with the production of this interest income in the amount of $10,000. Assume also that at the end of the taxable year Corporation M has Subchapter C earnings and profits. Since more than 25 percent of the Corporation M's total gross receipts ($200,000 X .25 = $50,0000) are passive investment income ($100,000), and since Corporation M has Subchapter C earnings and profits at the end of the taxable year, Corporation M will be subject to the tax on excess net passive investment income. The amount of excess net passive investment income is $45,000 ($90,000 NPI × [($100,000 PII - 50,000)/100,000]).[55]

> **Example 16-14:** Assume an S corporation with subchapter C earnings and profits has tax-exempt income of $400,000, its only passive income, gross receipts of $1,000,000 and taxable income of $250,000, and there are no expenses associated with the tax-exempt income. The corporation's excess net income for the taxable year would total $150,000 (400,000 × ((400,000 -

---

49 Code Sec. 1375(a).
50 Code Sec. 1375(b)(1).
51 Reg § 1.1362-2(c)(5)(ii)(G).
52 Code Sec. 1375(b)(4).

53 Code Sec. 1375(b)(2).
54 Code Sec. 1362(d)(3)(B).
55 Reg § 1.1375-1(f), Example (1).

250,000/400,000)). This amount is subject to the tax on excess net passive investment income, notwithstanding that this amount is otherwise tax-exempt income.[56]

The IRS may waive the tax on ENPI if the S corporation establishes to the satisfaction of the IRS that—

1. it determined in good faith that it had no accumulated earnings and profits at the close of a taxable year, and

2. during a reasonable period of time after it was determined that it did have accumulated earnings and profits at the close of the taxable year the earnings and profits were distributed.[57]

.03 LIFO Recapture

If a C corporation that had been using the LIFO method of valuing inventory makes an S election, the *LIFO recapture amount* will have to be included in the gross income of the corporation. In addition, appropriate adjustments to the basis of inventory will also be made to take into account the amount included in gross income. Any increase in the tax caused by this inclusion of income will be payable in four equal installments. The first installment will be due on or before the due date (determined without regard to extensions) of the income tax return for the last C corporation taxable year. The three succeeding installments must be paid on or before the due date for the corporation's return for the 3 succeeding taxable years.

The "LIFO recapture amount" is the amount (if any) by which—

A. the inventory amount of the inventory asset under the FIFO method exceeds

B. the inventory amount of the assets under the LIFO method.

For this purpose the inventory amounts must be determined as of the close of the last C corporation taxable year.[58]

.04 Penalties for Failure to File

If any S corporation required to file a return for any taxable year—

1. fails to file the return at the required time, or

2. files a return which fails to show the information required, the S corporation will have to pay a penalty for each month (or fraction thereof - but not to exceed 12 months in total) it doesn't file or provide the required information, unless it is can show that the failure is due to reasonable cause.[59]

In one case, the Tax Court ruled that an S corporation met this reasonable cause exception where the S corporation exercised "ordinary business care and prudence" in its efforts to timely file its Form 1120S. The Tax Court found that the S corporation's president apparently forgot to file the return, but thought he did. He usually signed and mailed the returns on time, and the S corporation's accountant

---

[56] Reg § 1.1375-1(f), Example (2).
[57] Code Sec. 1375(d).
[58] Code Sec. 1363(d).
[59] Code Sec. 6699(a).

had sent him the return in time for him to file it by the deadline. The president retained a copy of the Form 1120S in his files, erroneously thinking he had mailed the original, and he mailed the Schedules K-1 to the shareholders. Under these circumstances, the Court found that the S corporation was not liable for the failure to file penalty.[60] The amount of the penalty per month is $195 for each person who was a shareholder in the S corporation during any part of the taxable year.[61]

.05 General Business Credit Recapture

Election of S corporation status will not trigger recapture of the general business credit. However, the S corporation will continue to be liable for any general business credit recapture attributable to credits allowed for taxable years before the S corporation election, should the S corporation dispose of the related property. Any recapture of the credit by the S corporation will reduce the earnings and profits of the S corporation, since the credit originally effectively increased those earnings and profits by decreasing the tax liability of the predecessor C corporation.[62]

The adjusted basis of stock in an S corporation will be appropriately adjusted to take into account adjustments to the basis of property held by an S corporation due to the recapture of the general business credit.[63]

¶ 1603 Treatment of Income by the Shareholder

.01 Allocation Among Shareholders

In general the treatment of items of income, deductions, and credits of the S corporation by its shareholders closely follows the treatment of those items by partners in a partnership.[64] One primary difference is the allocation of items of income, deduction, and credit to the S corporation shareholders. Where a partnership can use special allocations to allocate income, and the allocation of some items depends on when during the year the item occurred, the allocation of income by S corporations is much more mechanical. For an S corporation, each shareholder's share of any item for any taxable year is determined on a per share, per day basis. This is done by first assigning an equal portion of each S corporation item of income, deduction, or credit to each day of the taxable year, and then by allocating those items for the day pro rata to the shares outstanding on that day.[65] The sum of the items of income, deduction and credit for the days the shareholder owned shares are then summed for each shareholder.

> **Example 16-15:** AB Corporation is a calendar-year S corporation with 1000 shares outstanding, 100 of which are owned by A and 900 of which are owned by B. During the year AB has ordinary business income of $730,000 and a long term capital gain of $365,000 from a transaction that occurred on 1/1. The ordinary income allocated to each day would be $730,000/365 = $2,000 and the long term capital gain allocated to each day would be $365,000/365 =

---

[60] *Ensyc Technologies v. Commr.*, TC Summary Opinion 2012-55.

[61] Code Sec. 6699(b).

[62] Code Sec. 1371(d).

[63] Code Sec. 50(c)(5).

[64] Code Sec. 1366(a)(1).

[65] Code Sec. 1377(a)(1).

$1,000. For each day, then, A would be allocated $200 of ordinary income and $100 of long term capital gain, and B would be allocated the rest. A's ordinary income using this calculation would be $200 X 365 = $73,000, and A's long term capital gain would be $36,500. Of course, a simpler calculation in this straightforward example where the outstanding shares and the ownership remains the same during the year would be, for example, to multiply $730,000 by A's 10% ownership to get A's $73,000 share of ordinary income.

Example 16-16: Assume that with 74 days left in the year (October 19), B sells 450 shares to C. C's share of the ordinary income for the year will be determined by multiplying the ordinary income and long term capital gain for each day she owned the shares by 450/1000. This would result in an allocation of ordinary income and long term capital gain to C of $65,700 ($2,000 X 73 days X 450/1000 shares) and $32,850 ($1,000 X 73 X 450/1000 shares), respectively. Note: the day a share is sold is allocated to the seller.[66]

Example 16-17: Assume that instead of B selling shares to C, AB issues 450 shares to C with 74 days left in the year (October 19). C's share of the ordinary income for the year will be determined by multiplying the ordinary income and long term capital gain for each day she owned the shares by 450/1450. This would result in an allocation of ordinary income and long term capital gain to C of $45,931 ($2,000 X 74 days X 450/1450 shares) and $22,966 ($1,000 X 74 X 450/1450 shares), respectively. Note that the days allocated to C are different in this case because it is no longer a sale.[67]

Termination. If any shareholder terminates their entire interest in the corporation during the taxable year and all affected shareholders and the corporation agree, items of income, deduction, and credit will be allocated to the affected shareholders as if the taxable year consisted of 2 taxable years, the first of which ends on the date of the termination. The term "affected shareholders" means the shareholder whose interest is terminated, and also all shareholders to whom the terminated shareholder has transferred shares during the taxable year.[68]

.02 Pass-through of Items to Shareholders

Similar to the treatment of income from a partnership by a partner, the character of any item passed through from an S corporation to one of its shareholder will be determined as if the item were realized directly from the source from which it was realized by the corporation, or incurred in the same manner as incurred by the corporation.[69] For example, if an S corporation has capital gain on the sale or exchange of a capital asset, a shareholder's pro rata share of that gain will also be characterized as a capital gain regardless of whether the shareholder is otherwise a dealer in that type of property. Similarly, if an S corporation engages in an activity that is not for profit, a shareholder's pro rata share of the S corporation's deductions will be characterized as not for profit.[70]

---

[66] Reg. § 1.1377-1(a)(2)(ii).
[67] See, for example, Reg. § 1.1377-1(c), Example (1).
[68] Reg. § 1.1377-1(b).

[69] Code Sec. 1366(b).
[70] Reg. § 1.1366-1(b)(1)(i).

There are, however, a couple of exceptions to the rule above. If an S corporation is formed or availed of for a principal purpose of selling or exchanging contributed property that in the hands of the shareholder or shareholders would not have produced capital gain if sold or exchanged by the shareholder or shareholders, then the gain on the sale or exchange of the property recognized by the corporation is not treated as a capital gain. In addition, If an S corporation is formed or availed of for a principal purpose of selling or exchanging contributed property that in the hands of the shareholder or shareholders would have produced capital loss if sold or exchanged by the shareholder or shareholders, then the loss on the sale or exchange of the property recognized by the corporation is treated as a capital loss to the extent that, immediately before the contribution, the adjusted basis of the property in the hands of the shareholder or shareholders exceeded the fair market value of the property.[71]

An S corporation has to report (and each shareholder has to take into account) each shareholder's pro rata share of an S corporation's items of income, loss, deduction, or credit with respect to each separate activity as defined in the passive activity rules of Code Sec. 469.[72]

Gross income. A shareholder's gross income includes the shareholder's pro rata share of the gross income of the corporation.[73] For example, for purposes of determining the applicability of the 6-year period of limitation on assessment and collection relating to omission of more than 25 percent of gross income, a shareholder's gross income includes the shareholder's pro rata share of S corporation gross income.[74]

> **Example 16-18:** Shareholder A, an individual, owns 30 percent of the stock of Corporation N, an S corporation that has $300,000 gross income and $100,000 taxable income. A reports only $20,000 as A's pro rata share of N's taxable income. A should have reported $30,000 as A's pro rata share of taxable income, derived from A's pro rata share, $90,000, of N's gross income. Because A's return included only $20,000, A is regarded as having reported on the return only $60,000 ($20,000/$30,000 of $90,000) as gross income from N.[75]

Similarly, an individual shareholder's pro-rata share of an S corporation's gross income from farming or fishing is treated as gross income from farming or fishing to the shareholder.[76] On the other hand, the Ninth Circuit Court of Appeals has determined that shareholders couldn't deduct their S corporation's pass-through losses for purposes of calculating their self-employment tax liability. S corporation income is likewise not included in the calculation of a shareholder's self-employment income.[77]

If an individual who is a member of the family of one or more shareholders of an S corporation performs services for the corporation or furnishes capital to the corporation without receiving reasonable compensation, the IRS can make adjust-

---

[71] Reg. § 1.1366-1(b)(2) and (3).
[72] Reg. § 1.1366-1(a)(4).
[73] Code Sec. 1366(c).
[74] Reg. § 1.1366-1(c)(2)(i).

[75] Reg. § 1.1366-1(c)(2)(ii).
[76] Rev. Rul. 87-121, 1987-2 CB 217.
[77] *Ding v. Comm.*, 84 AFTR 2d 99-7517 (200 F3d 587).

ments in the items allocated to the individual and the other S corporation shareholders as may be necessary in order to reflect the value of the services or capital.[78] This is similar to the treatment of family partnerships under Code Sec. 704(e), and is intended to prevent high-income taxpayers from shifting taxable income to relatives in lower tax brackets.

If any tax is imposed on built-in gains of an S corporation, the amount of the tax on built-in gains will be treated as a loss sustained by the S corporation during the taxable year. The character of the loss (from the tax) will be determined by allocating the loss proportionately among the recognized built-in gains giving rise to the tax.[79]

Similarly, if an S corporation is required to pay a tax on excess net passive income, each item of passive investment income for the taxable year will be reduced by an amount which bears the same ratio to the amount of the tax as—

A. the amount of such item, bears to

B. the total passive investment income for the taxable year.[80]

.03 Deduction or Exclusion Limitations at the Shareholder Level

A shareholder must aggregate the shareholder's separate deductions or exclusions with the shareholder's pro rata share of the S corporation's separately stated deductions or exclusions in determining the amount of any deduction or exclusion allowable to the shareholder after any limitation that might apply.[81]

> **Example 16-19:** In 2013, Corporation M, a calendar year S corporation, purchases and places in service section 179 property costing $400,000. Corporation M elects to expense the entire cost of the property. Shareholder A owns 50 percent of the stock of Corporation M. Shareholder A's pro rata share of this item after Corporation M applies the section 179(b) limitations is $200,000. Because the aggregate amount of Shareholder A's pro rata share and separately acquired section 179 expense may not exceed $500,000 (the aggregate maximum cost that may be taken into account under section 179(a) for the applicable taxable year), Shareholder A may elect to expense up to $300,000 of separately acquired section 179 property that is purchased and placed in service in 2013, subject to the taxable income limitations of section 179.[82]

.04 Loss Limitations - Basis

The amount of S corporation losses and deductions taken by an S corporation shareholder for any taxable year can't exceed the sum of the shareholder's adjusted basis in the S corporation stock and the shareholder's adjusted basis of any indebtedness of the S corporation to the shareholder.[83] However, any disallowed loss or deduction retains its character and is treated as incurred by the corporation in the corporation's first succeeding taxable year, and subsequent taxable years, with respect to the shareholder.[84] Note that, unlike with partnerships, an S corpora-

---

[78] Code Sec. 1366(e).
[79] Code Sec. 1366(f)(2).
[80] Code Sec. 1366(f)(3)
[81] Reg. § 1.1366-1(a)(5)(i).

[82] Reg. § 1.1366-1(a)(5)(ii).
[83] Code Sec. 1366(d)(1).
[84] Reg. § 1.1366-2(a)(2).

¶1603.03

tion shareholder's basis in their stock is not increased by their share of S corporation debt.

If a shareholder holds more than one indebtedness at the close of the corporation's taxable year or, if applicable, immediately prior to the termination of the shareholder's interest in the corporation, the reduction in basis is applied to each indebtedness in the same proportion that the basis of each indebtedness bears to the aggregate bases of the indebtedness to the shareholder.[85]

> **Example 16-20:** A has been the sole shareholder in Corporation S since 2002. In 2003, A loans S $1,000 (Debt No. 1), which is evidenced by a ten-year promissory note in the face amount of $1,000. In 2006, A loans S $5,000 (Debt No. 2), which is evidenced by a demand promissory note. On December 31, 2006, the basis of A's stock is $1,000. For S's 2007 taxable year the corporation has a net loss of $4,000. The basis of A's stock is reduced by $1,000, to zero. The basis of Debt No. 1 is reduced in an amount equal to $500 ($3,000 (remaining excess) × $1,000 (basis of Debt No. 2) / $6,000 (total basis of all debt)). The basis of Debt No. 2 is reduced in an amount equal to $2,500 ($3,000 (remaining excess) × $5,000 (basis of Debt No. 2) / $6,000 (total basis of all debt)). Accordingly, on December 31, 2007, A's basis in his stock is zero and his bases in the two debts are as follows:

Debt	1/1/06 basis	12/31/07 reduction	1/1/08 basis
No. 1	$1,000	$ 500	$ 500
No. 2	5,000	2,500	2,500

A shareholder generally determines the adjusted basis of stock for purposes of limiting losses and deductions after taking into account (1) increases in basis from income earned during the period, and from depletion in excess of the depletable property's basis; and (2) decreases in basis relating to distributions, nondeductible expenses, and certain oil and gas depletion deductions for the taxable year.[86]

Restoration of reduction. If S corporation losses or deductions result in a reduction in a shareholder's basis in the indebtedness of the S corporation to the shareholder, any subsequent net increase in basis from net income of the S corporation will first increase the basis of the debt (but only up to its prior amount) before increasing the shareholder's basis in the stock of the S corporation.[87]

More than one debt. If a shareholder holds more than one indebtedness as of the beginning of an S corporation's taxable year, any net increase is applied first to restore the reduction of basis in any indebtedness repaid (in whole or in part) in that taxable year to the extent necessary to offset any gain that would otherwise be realized on the repayment. Any remaining net increase is applied to restore each outstanding indebtedness in proportion to the amount that the basis of each outstanding indebtedness has been reduced and not restored.[88]

---

[85] Reg. § 1.1367-2(b)(3).
[86] Reg. § 1.1366-2(a)(3)(i).

[87] Code Sec. 1367(b)(2)(B).
[88] Reg. § 1.1367-2(c)(2).

Example 16-21: The facts are the same as in the prior example. For S's 2008 taxable year, the net increase in basis (from S corporation net income) with respect to A equals $2,000. The net increase is applied first to restore the bases in the debts held on January 1, 2008, before any of the net increase is applied to increase A's basis in his shares of S stock. Any net increase is applied to restore the bases of the outstanding debts in proportion to the amount that each of these outstanding debts have been reduced previously and have not been restored. As of December 31, 2008, the total reduction in A's debts held on January 1, 2008 equals $3,000. The net increase of $2,000 is applied to restore the bases of Debt No. 1 and Debt No. 2. As of December 31, 2008, the total reduction in these outstanding debts is $3,000. The basis of Debt No. 1 is restored in an amount equal to $333 ($2,000 × $500/$3,000). Similarly, the basis in Debt No. 2 is restored in an amount equal to $1,667 ($2,000 × $2,500/$3,000). On December 31, 2008, A's basis in his S stock is zero and his bases in the two remaining debts are as follows:

	Original basis	Amount reduced	1/1/08 basis	Amount restored	12/31/08 basis
No. 1	$ 1,000	$500	$500	$ 333	$ 833
No. 2	5,000	2,500	2,500	1,667	4,167

If an S corporation shareholder's losses and deductions exceed the sum of the adjusted basis of the shareholder's stock in the S corporation and the adjusted basis of any indebtedness of the corporation to the shareholder, then the limitation on losses and deductions must be allocated among the shareholder's pro rata share of each loss or deduction. The amount of the limitation allocated to any loss or deduction is an amount that bears the same ratio to the amount of the limitation as the loss or deduction bears to the total of the losses and deductions. For this purpose, the total of losses and deductions for the taxable year is the sum of the shareholder's pro rata share of losses and deductions for the taxable year, and the losses and deductions disallowed and carried forward from prior years.[89]

Any loss or deduction disallowed because of lack of basis is personal to the shareholder and can't in any manner be transferred to another person. If a shareholder transfers some but not all of the shareholder's stock in the corporation, the amount of any disallowed loss or deduction under due to lack of basis is not reduced and the transferee does not acquire any portion of the disallowed loss or deduction. If a shareholder transfers all of the shareholder's stock in the corporation, any disallowed loss or deduction is permanently disallowed. If a shareholder transfers S corporation stock to a spouse or former spouse stock in transaction that is incident to a divorce, and is nontaxable under Code Sec. 1041(a), any loss or deduction with respect to the transferred stock that was previously disallowed to the transferring shareholder due to lack of basis will carry over to the transferee spouse or former spouse.[90]

---

[89] Reg. § 1.1366-2(a)(4).   [90] Reg. § 1.1366-2(a)(5).

.05 Loss Limitations - At Risk

The at risk rules currently do not apply to S corporations, although they do apply to S corporation shareholders. However, proposed regulations would require them to be applied at the corporation and shareholder level. Therefore, under the proposed regulations losses from an activity could be deducted by the corporation only to the extent that the corporation is at risk in the activity. In addition, each shareholder would be allowed a loss in the activity only to the extent that the shareholder is at risk in the activity.[91] Under the proposed regulations, an S corporation's amount at risk in an activity would be determined in the same manner as that of any other taxpayer.[92]

Under the proposed regulations amounts borrowed by an S corporation from one or more of its shareholders would increase the corporation's amount at risk, notwithstanding the fact that the shareholders have an interest in the activity other than that of a creditor.[93]

Currently the general at risk rules apply to the S corporation shareholder's at risk amount in the S corporation. Any loans from the shareholder to the corporation increase the shareholder's at risk amount. Under proposed regulations this rule would be formalized, and the amount at risk of a shareholder of an S corporation would specifically be adjusted to reflect any increase or decrease in the adjusted basis of any indebtedness of the corporation to the shareholder.[94]

> **Example 16-22:** A is the single shareholder in X, an electing S corporation engaged in a business activity. A contributed $50,000 to X in exchange for its stock. In addition, A borrowed $40,000, for which A assumed personal liability. A then loaned the entire amount to X for use in the activity. During its taxable year, X had a net operating loss of $75,000. At the close of the taxable year (without reduction for any losses of X) A's amount at risk is $90,000 ($50,000 + $40,000). However, under the proposed regulations, it is also necessary to determine X's amount at risk in the activity. X is also at risk for the $40,000 borrowed from A and expended in the activity. Therefore, X's amount at risk in the activity is $90,000 ($50,000 + $40,000). Because X's amount at risk in the activity ($90,000) exceeds the net operating loss ($75,000), the entire loss is allowed to the corporation and allocated to A. Since A's amount at risk ($90,000) also exceeds the loss ($75,000) A will be allowed the entire loss deduction.[95]

In order for the guarantee of a debt of the S corporation by one of its shareholders to increase the amount the shareholder has at risk with respect to the S corporation, the shareholder must be primarily liable for the debt.[96]

.06 Loss Limitations - Passive Activity

The passive activity rules do not apply to S corporations, but they do apply to S corporation shareholders. Under the passive activity rules, the determination of

---

[91] Prop. Reg. § 1.465-10(a).
[92] Prop. Reg. § 1.465-10(b)(1).
[93] Prop. Reg. § 1.465-10(b)(2).

[94] Prop. Reg. § 1.465-10(c).
[95] Prop. Reg. § 1.465-10(d).
[96] *Goatcher v. U.S.,* 68 AFTR 2d 91-5596 (944 F2d 747), (CA10) 09/10/1991.

whether an activity of the S corporation is material with respect to an S corporation shareholder depends on the participation of the shareholder in the activity. The shareholder's participation is determined for the taxable year of the S corporation (and not the taxable year of the taxpayer).[97] The following example illustrates the application of this paragraph (e)(1):

> **Example 16-23:** A, a calendar year individual, is a partner in a partnership that has a taxable year ending January 31. During its taxable year ending on January 31, 2013, the partnership engages in a single trade or business activity. For the period from February 1, 2012, through January 31, 2013, A does not materially participate in this activity. In A's calendar year 2013 return, A's distributive share of the partnership's gross income and deductions from the activity must be treated as passive activity gross income and passive activity deductions, without regard to A's participation in the activity from February 1, 2013, through December 31, 2013.

¶ 1604 Treatment of S Corp Distributions to Shareholders

.01 Overview

Because the S Corp is a flow-through entity, its income is taxed to shareholders as it is earned, without regard to the amount, if any, distributed to shareholders. Consequently, most distributions to shareholders are of income that has already been taxed to them. Not surprisingly, then, Code Sec. 1368 provides that distributions from an S corporation to its shareholders, made "with respect to" their stock, are generally taxable only to the extent that such distributions exceed the shareholders' tax bases in their stock in the S corporation. In this respect, Code Sec. 1368, governing distributions from an S corporation to its shareholders, is similar to Code Sec. 731 which governs partnership distributions to partnerships.

There are a number of significant differences between the tax treatment of distributions from S corporations and partnerships, however. First, Code Sec. 1368(c)(2) provides that distributions of earnings & profits from prior tax years in which the S corporation was treated as a regular corporation ("C" corporation) are taxable as dividends to the recipient shareholder(s). This provision is relevant when the corporation operated as a regular corporation for some period of time before making the S election.

Other differences arise from the limited scope of subchapter S. Generally speaking, where subchapter S is silent with respect to the proper treatment of a particular transaction, the provisions of subchapter C (or other parts of the Internal Revenue Code) apply. With respect to distributions to shareholders, Code Sec. 1368 applies to distributions of property "with respect to its stock to which (but for this subsection) section 301(c) would apply ... "[98] Thus, Code Sec. 1368 does not apply to distributions to a shareholder in redemption of all or part of his or her stock (distributions "in exchange for," rather than "with respect to" stock). The tax consequences of a distribution in redemption of stock are governed by Code Sec. 302.

---

[97] Reg § 1.469-2T(e)(1).   [98] Code Sec. 1368(a).

Moreover, Code Sec. 1368 addresses the consequences to the shareholder on receipt of a distribution from the S corporation. It does not address the consequences to the corporation itself. The tax consequences to the corporation are governed by Code Sec. 311(b) which provides that the corporation must recognize gain on the distribution of appreciated property as if it had sold such property to the shareholder(s) for fair market value, and then distributed the net proceeds from the hypothetical sale. In the S corporation context, this gain flows through to the shareholders and is reflected in their stock basis before accounting for the deemed distribution of the proceeds. Thus, the shareholder takes a fair market value basis in property received as a distribution from the S corporation. The amount of the distribution is equal to the fair market value of the property received, reduced by any liabilities assumed by the shareholder in connection with the distribution. This is a substantial departure from the rules governing distributions from a partnership to a partner.

In summary, the tax treatment of S corporation distributions depends on both the nature of the distribution and the nature of the S corporation making the distribution. The tax consequences of a cash distribution can differ substantially from those associated with a distribution of appreciated property. Likewise, the tax consequences of a distribution by a corporation that has been classified as an S corporation since its inception may differ from those associated with a distribution by a corporation that operated as a regular corporation for a period of time before making the S election. Taxpayers and their advisers who understand these provisions can avoid potentially costly tax traps, and in many cases may be able to use the special rules governing distributions from an S corporation to their advantage.

.02 Distributions—S Corp has no Prior Year E&P

Under Code Sec. 1368(b), the receipt of a distribution from a corporation with no earnings & profits from prior years as a regular corporation ("C" corporation) does not trigger recognition of income to the shareholder unless it exceeds the basis of the shareholder's stock in the S corporation from which the distribution is received. The shareholder must reduce his or her tax basis in the S corporation stock by the amount of the distribution.[99] Basis in the stock may not be reduced below zero (which is why gain is recognized).

The gain, if any, recognized by a shareholder upon the receipt of a distribution in excess of stock basis is treated as gain from the sale or exchange of property (in this case, the shareholder's stock in the corporation), and thus will generally be taxable as long-term capital gain.[100] Unlike in the partnership context, there is no look-through rule in subchapter S under which gain on the sale or receipt of certain distributions in entities with "hot" assets must be recharacterized as ordinary income.[101]

---

[99] Code Sec. 1368(b)(1).

[100] Code Sec. 1368(b)(2).

[101] Code Sec. 341 used to play a role in corporate taxation similar to that played by Code Sec. 751 for partnerships. Under section 341(b)(1), the proceeds received by a shareholder from certain distributions or sale transactions involving corporations "formed or availed of for the manufacture, construction, production or purchase of certain property *with a view* to (i) the sale or exchange of the stock by its shareholders, or a distribution to them prior to the realization of two-thirds of the taxable income from the property, and (ii) the realization by the shareholders of gain attributable to that property" were taxable to the recipient(s) as ordinary income (em-

Example 16-24: K and D are equal shareholders in KD, Inc., which has been an S corporation since its inception. This year, the S corporation distributed $85,000 to each of the shareholders. The distributions did not alter the shareholders' interests in the corporation. Each owned 1,000 shares of KD stock both before and after the distribution. Assume that K's tax basis in her KD stock just prior to the distribution was $80,000, while D's basis in her KD stock was $125,000. The tax consequences to each shareholder will be as follows:

	K	D
Stock basis just prior to distribution	$80,000	$125,000
Amount received	(85,000)	(85,000)
Gain recognized on receipt of distribution	$5,000	0
Remaining basis in stock	0	$40,000

Under Code Sec. 1368(b)(2), K's gain will be characterized as gain from the sale of her stock in KD. Assuming she has held all of her shares for more than one year, her gain should be classified as long-term capital gain.

A second, often more important, difference between the tax treatment of distributions from S corporations versus partnerships involves the effect of debt on the shareholder's basis in stock. Recall that Code Sec. 752 treats a partner's share of partnership debt as a contribution of money by the partner to the partnership, such that a partner's tax basis in his or her partnership interest includes his or her share of partnership liabilities. In contrast, liabilities of the S corporation are *not* included in the shareholders' basis in their S corporation stock. This is true even when the shareholder is the lender, or when he or she guarantees the S corporation's liabilities to a third party. Debt of the S corporation is never included in the shareholders' bases in their S corporation stock, regardless of the characteristics of the debt.

Example 16-25: J and D are equal shareholders in JD, Incorporated, which has been an S corporation since its inception. Each shareholder has a tax basis of $75,000 in her JD Inc. stock. In addition, J has personally guaranteed the corporation's $300,000 loan from the First National Bank. Assume each shareholder receives an $100,000 distribution from the S corporation.

(Footnote Continued)

phasis added). Code Sec. 341 was repealed by the Jobs & Growth Reconciliation Act of 2003 (JGTRRA), effective for years beginning after 2002. Under a sunset provision of JGTRRA, repeal of these so-called "collapsible corporation" provisions was effective only through 2010 (Act Sec. 303 of P.L. 108-27, as amended by Act Sec. 102 of P.L. 109-222). The repeal of section 341 was subsequently extended through the end of 2012 by the Tax Relief, Unemployment Insurance Reauthorization and Job Creation Act of 2010. Even if repeal of the statute is not extended beyond 2012, however, its application is limited to circumstances in which the corporation (and thus the S corporation) was "formed or availed of" with the intent to convert ordinary income to capital gain through sale or redemption of the stock prior to corporate realization of at least 2/3rds of the ordinary income inherent in its property. Note that other statutes also trigger ordinary income upon the sale of regular or S corporation stock in certain transactions. Sections 304 and 306 trigger recognition of ordinary income to the shareholder in certain parent-subsidiary and brother-sister stock redemptions. Section 1254 recharacterizes a portion of the shareholder's gain as ordinary income upon the disposition of shares in a corporation possessing certain oil, gas, geothermal or other mineral properties. None of these statutes possesses the breadth of Code Sec. 751 in subchapter K.

¶1604.02

Since the distribution received by each shareholder exceeds her tax basis in her JD stock, each will recognize a $25,000 upon receipt of the distribution. The fact that J has guaranteed a sizable liability of the S corporation, and thus may someday have to use some or all of the proceeds of the distribution to satisfy the guarantee is disregarded. J's guarantee is treated as a contingent liability and will be accounted for when and if the contingency occurs.

Note that the consequences in the above example would be the same if J had loaned the $300,000 to JD Inc. directly, rather than guaranteeing the S corporation's loan from a third party. The loan from J to the S corporation is accounted for separately from J's investment in corporate stock. She would have a $75,000 tax basis in her stock (prior to receipt of the distribution) and a $300,000 tax basis in her loan. Under Code Sec. 1368, the distribution proceeds can be offset against her tax basis in her stock only; no offset is allowed against her basis in the debt.[102]

.03 Distributions—S Corp has Prior Year E&P

The tax consequences of S corporation distributions are a little more complex when the S corporation has accumulated earnings & profits (E&P) from prior years as a regular corporation.[103] Under Code Sec. 301, distributions from a regular corporation are taxable as dividends to the extent of the corporation's E&P. Congress was concerned that closely held and highly profitable regular corporations might choose to make an S election before making sizable distributions to their shareholders in hopes that the distributions would receive nontaxable treatment under subchapter S. Code Sec. 1368(c) avoids this possibility, providing that distributions from earnings & profits generated before a corporation made the S election (i.e., while it was a regular, or "C" corporation) retain their character as dividend income, regardless of when the distribution occurs.

Code Sec. 1368(c) does allow shareholders to withdraw profits from S corporation years on which they have already been taxed before withdrawing accumulated E&P from prior years as a regular corporation. The statute provides that distributions from an S corporation with accumulated E&P are deemed to come from the following sources in the following sequence:

1. Distributions come first from the S corporation's accumulated adjustments account (AAA), which is essentially the accumulated taxable income from its years as an S corporation, as described more fully below. Distributions from AAA are nontaxable to the shareholder, but reduce his or her tax basis in S corporation stock.

2. Once AAA is fully distributed, the next dollar of distributions is deemed to come from accumulated E&P. Distributions from E&P are taxable as dividend income and have no effect on the shareholder's stock basis.

---

[102] Note that in the event J is allocated a share of S corporation loss, she can deduct her share of the loss against her basis in the debt (after her stock basis is reduced to zero). This treatment is not extended to distributions.

[103] An S corporation may also obtain accumulated E&P in connection with the acquisition of a regular corporation, if the acquisition is structured as a merger with the S corporation as survivor. Code Sec. 381(c)(2).

3. Distributions in excess of the sum of the AAA and E&P accounts are treated as a return of capital. They are nontaxable to the extent of the shareholder's remaining basis in his or her S corporation stock.

4. To the extent the return of capital portion of the distribution exceeds his or her remaining basis in S corporation stock, the excess is taxable as capital gain from the sale of property (stock in the S corporation).

Note that, because a shareholder's share of S corporation income increases her tax basis in her S corporation stock, stock basis should never be less than the portion of AAA attributable to the shareholder's stock. Thus, distributions from AAA will almost always be nontaxable and will reduce stock basis dollar for dollar.

> *Example 16-26:* AB, Inc. was established twelve years ago, but has only been an S corporation for five years. It has accumulated E&P of $86,000 from years prior to making the S election. The balance in its accumulated adjustments account (AAA), representing its accumulated taxable income since making the election, is $40,000. This year it distributed $200,000 to its two shareholders ($100,000 each). Assume that shareholder A has a tax basis in her AB stock of $45,000 and that B has a tax basis in her AB stock of $80,000. The shareholders will report their respective distributions on their individual tax returns as follows:

	A	B	Totals
Amount received from AAA, treated as nontaxable return of capital	20,000	20,000	40,000
Amount received from E&P, treated as taxable dividend income	43,000	43,000	86,000
Remainder, treated as return of capital, nontaxable to the extent of remaining basis in stock	25,000	37,000	62,000
Capital gain (equal to excess over stock basis)	12,000	0	12,000
Total distribution received	$100,000	$100,000	$200,000

Recall that A's tax basis in her AB stock just prior to the distribution was $45,000. The first $20,000 received by her, representing her share of AB's AAA account, was nontaxable, reducing her tax basis in her AB stock to $25,000. The next $43,000 was taxable as a dividend, and had no effect on her stock basis. The remaining $37,000 was a return of capital, reducing her tax basis in her AB stock to zero and triggering a $12,000 capital gain ($37,000 less remaining $25,000 tax basis). A will recognize a total of $55,000 in income in connection with receipt of the distribution—$43,000 dividend income and $12,000 capital gain.

¶1604.03

Because B's stock basis was higher than A's ($80,000 vs. $45,000), she will not recognize any capital gain. She will report $43,000 in dividend income, representing the portion of her distribution paid from accumulated E&P, and will reduce her stock basis by $57,000. Her tax basis in her stock, after accounting for the distribution, will be $23,000 ($80,000 - $57,000).

Under Code Sec. 1368(e)(3), the corporation may elect to distribute accumulated E&P first. All affected shareholders (i.e., those receiving distributions from E&P) must consent to the election. There are a variety of reasons that an S corporation and its shareholders may wish to make this election. The shareholders may choose to accelerate the recognition of dividend income in a year before the tax rate on dividends is expected to change.[104] Alternatively, a shareholder who is purchasing stock in an existing S corporation may wish to have the selling shareholder take a distribution of the corporation's E&P prior to the sale, ensuring that the dividend income is reported by the shareholder who owned the stock when the E&P was generated. In other cases, S corporations with a relatively small amount of E&P may choose to make the election in order to eliminate the E&P account and reduce administrative costs in future years.[105]

Example 16-27: Q is the sole shareholder of Q, Inc. She established the company several years ago, but only made the S election in recent years. At the beginning of the year, the company had accumulated E&P from prior years as a regular corporation of $40,000. On July 1 of this year, she sold half her stock in Q, Inc. to L. The corporation made distributions as follows during the year:

February 15	$50,000
September 15	100,000

The first distribution was received entirely by Q, since she was the only shareholder at that date. The second distribution was split equally between Q and L, the new shareholder. The shareholders both agree to have the S corporation elect to make distributions first from E&P and then from AAA. Because accumulated E&P is allocated chronologically to distributions made during the tax year,[106] the effect of this election will be to attribute the first $40,000 of the February 15 distribution to accumulated E&P. Since this entire distribution went to Q, the election will result in Q recognizing 100% of the taxable dividend distributed by the S corporation. The remaining $10,000 of the February 15 distribution, and the entire $100,000 distributed in September, will be deemed to come from the corporation's AAA account, and/or from capital contributions by the shareholders.

---

[104] For example, the tax rate on dividends increased from 15% to 23.8% in 2013.

[105] S corporations concerned about the Code Sec. 1375 tax on excess passive income (passive income in excess of 25 percent of gross receipts) may choose to distribute

their E&P in order to avoid the tax. See Code Sec. 1375. Tax Imposed When Passive Investment Income of Corporation having Accumulated Earnings & Profits Exceeds 25 Percent of Gross Receipts.

[106] Reg. § 1.316-2(b).

.04 Accumulated Adjustments Account (AAA)

The accumulated adjustments account (AAA) represents the accumulated post-1982 taxable income of the S corporation.[107] The AAA reflects the amount of income reported by the S corporation, but not yet distributed, on which the shareholders have already paid income tax. Thus, the AAA account is similar in concept to E&P for regular corporations. The only difference is that E&P reflects all undistributed income, net of expenses, of the regular corporation, while AAA reflects only the net taxable income of the S corporation.[108] S corporations with accumulated earnings and profits must maintain the AAA in order to determine the portion, if any, of distributions to shareholders that should be classified as dividends. S corporations with no accumulated earnings and profits are not required to maintain an accumulated adjustments account because no portion of distributions to their shareholders will ever be classified as dividends.

The AAA balance begins at zero on the first day of the corporation's first tax year as an S corporation, and is adjusted every year thereafter. The account is increased and decreased as follows:

The AAA is increased in every tax year by:

1. income other than tax-exempt income; and

2. the excess of the deduction for depletion over the basis of the property subject to the depletion (unless the property is oil and gas property, the basis of which has been allocated to the shareholders).

After increases are made to the AAA, the account is decreased by the following items, in the order listed.

1. deductible losses and expenses and nondeductible expenses other than expenses related to tax-exempt income and federal taxes attributable to a C corporation year;

2. the sum of the shareholders' deductions for depletion for oil or gas property held by the corporation;

3. distributions of cash and property (measured at fair market value as described previously); and

4. any net negative adjustment (resulting from a net taxable loss reported on Form 1120-S).

Adjustments are made at the end of each year. As indicated above, positive adjustments (reflecting positive S corporation taxable income) are taken into account before determining the proper classification of distributions. Net negative adjustments, however, representing net taxable losses reported by the S corporation, are not subtracted from the balance in AAA until after distributions have been accounted for.[109]

---

[107] Accumulated taxable income of the S corporation for pre-1983 years is maintained in the "previously taxed income" (PTI) account.

[108] Code Sec. 1368(e)(1)(A). Note that nontaxable income and non-deductible expenses are maintained in another balance sheet account on Form 1120-S called the

"other adjustments account." This account is not statutorily defined or required, but is merely an accounting device to segregate nontaxable from taxable net profits on the S corporation's balance sheet.

[109] Code Sec. 1368(e)(1)(C).

Example 16-28: At the beginning of the year, Becker Corporation had accumulated E&P of $100,000 and AAA of $25,000. For the current year, it reported the following on Form 1120-S:

Net ordinary income (reported on page 1)	$42,000
Separately stated items:	
Interest on municipal bonds (tax-exempt), net of related expenses	7,000
Charitable contributions	(9,000)
Section 179 deduction	(11,000)

On July 1, the company distributed $50,000 to its shareholders. For purposes of determining the source of the distribution, it is treated as made at the end of the year. At that time, the balance in the corporation's AAA is $47,000, computed as follows:

Beginning balance	$25,000
Income other than taxable income	42,000
Deductible losses and expenses	(20,000)
Balance prior to distribution	$47,000
Distribution to shareholders from AAA	(47,000)
Ending balance in AAA	0

The remaining $3,000 of the distribution comes from accumulated E&P and will be classified as a dividend. The ending balance in accumulated E&P will be $97,000 ($100,000 less the $3,000 dividend).

The balance in the AAA may be negative if the S corporation incurs a taxable loss. However, it may not be reduced below zero as the result of a distribution, because the amount of the distribution in excess of AAA is deemed to come from accumulated E&P, as illustrated in the example above.

Example 16-29: QLR, Inc. was established several years ago, but has been an S corporation for only five years. The company has accumulated E&P from its regular corporation years of $150,000. At the beginning of the current year, it had a balance in AAA of $38,000. This year, it reported a net loss on Form 1120-S of ($28,000). It distributed $21,000 to its 3 shareholders ($7,000 each). Because distributions are taken from AAA before the account is adjusted for net losses, the entire distribution comes from AAA, and will thus be nontaxable to the shareholders. The balance in AAA at the beginning of next year will be ($11,000), computed as follows:

Beginning balance in AAA	$ 38,000
Distribution from AAA	(21,000)
Net taxable loss	(28,000)
Ending balance (beginning balance next year)	($11,000)

¶1604.04

Because the entire distribution came from AAA, the balance in accumulated E&P will remain unchanged at $150,000.

.05 Distributions of Property

As discussed previously, the distribution by an S corporation of appreciated property triggers income to the S corporation as if the property had been sold for its fair market value. Under Code Sec. 311(b), the corporation is treated as if it had sold the property to the shareholder(s) for fair market value, and then immediately distributed the proceeds of sale. The corporation recognizes gain, but not loss, on the deemed sale, which flows through to the shareholders, increasing both their taxable incomes and their tax basis in the S corporation stock. The distribution is then accounted for at fair market value, reducing their stock basis (but not below zero), and potentially triggering recognition of additional capital gain if the distribution exceeds the basis of their stock.

Example 16-30: G is the sole shareholder of Slate Inc., which has made a valid S election. G's tax basis in her Slate stock at the beginning of the year was $25,000. On its Form 1120-S for the current year, Slate reported a net ordinary loss of ($30,000), and a gain of $42,000 in connection with the distribution of appreciated real estate to G. The basis of the real estate to the S corporation was $18,000. Its fair market value was $60,000. Thus, G's tax basis in her Slate stock before accounting for the distribution was $37,000, computed as follows:

Beginning basis	$25,000
Ordinary loss passed through on Schedule K-1	(30,000)
Gain on deemed sale of distributed property, also passed through to G	42,000
Tax basis in Slate stock before accounting for distribution	$37,000
Distribution (equals hypothetical proceeds from deemed sale of real estate	(60,000)
Gain on excess distribution	$23,000

Thus, G will recognize total capital gain of $65,000 ($42,000 + $23,000) in connection with the distribution, along with an ordinary loss of ($30,000) from the S corporation's normal business operations. Her remaining tax basis in her Slate shares will be zero. Compare this outcome with that which would have been associated with a similar transaction between a partnership and a partner. Under Code Sec. 731, neither the partner nor the partnership would recognize gain on the distribution.[110] The partner would take a carryover basis in the distributed property, limited to her tax basis in the partnership interest.[111] In this case, the partner would recognize no capital gain and, assuming the distribution occurred at year-end, would take a tax basis in the distributed real

---

[110] Code Secs. 731(a) (no gain is recognized by the partner) and 731(b) (no gain is recognized by the partnership).

[111] Code Sec. 732.

estate equal to zero (the pass-through loss reduces her tax basis in the partnership interest to zero).[112]

If the distributed property is encumbered by a liability, the consequences to the S corporation are unchanged: the property is deemed to have been sold for its full fair market value, with the assumption of the corporation's liability being included in the deemed sale price. The amount of the distribution received by the shareholder, however, is reduced by the liability. In effect, the net proceeds from the deemed sale are reduced by the amount of the liability assumed by the shareholder.

> **Example 16-31:** K is the sole shareholder of S corporation Karma. K's basis in his Karma stock is $50,000. He receives a distribution from the S corporation of property with a tax basis of $32,000 and a fair market value of $70,000. The property is encumbered by a liability of $40,000 for which K assumes responsibility. Assume that the S corporation has no other income or loss for the year other than that triggered by the distribution. The distribution will affect K as follows for tax purposes:
>
> | | |
> |---|---:|
> | Initial tax basis in Karma shares | $50,000 |
> | Gain recognized by S corporation on distribution ($70,000 minus $32,000, passed through to K) | 38,000 |
> | Tax basis in Karma shares before accounting for the distribution | $88,000 |
> | Distribution ($70,000 FMV less $40,000 liability assumed) | (30,000) |
> | Ending basis in Karma shares | $58,000 |
>
> K will report the $38,000 gain from the deemed sale of the property on his individual tax return for the year. His tax basis in the property will be equal to its fair market value of $70,000, and his remaining tax basis in his S corporation stock will be $58,000 as calculated above.

.06 Distributions in Redemption of Stock

Recall that under Code Sec. 1361, an S corporation may have only one class of stock. An S corporation is treated as having only one class of stock if "all outstanding shares of stock of the corporation confer identical rights to distribution and liquidation proceeds."[113] Thus, the regulations under section 1361 require that the governing provisions of the S corporation (corporate charter, articles of incorporation, bylaws, applicable state law, etc.) confer identical distribution rights to each share of stock in the S corporation. The upshot of this requirement is that an S corporation is generally not allowed to make a distribution to one or more shareholders without making a comparable, simultaneous distribution to all shareholders. In cases where an S corporation with more than one shareholder wants to

---

[112] Note that if the distribution occurred before year-end, the partner would take a $25,000 tax basis in the property, reducing her tax basis in the partnership interest to zero; none of the pass-through loss would be deductible on the partner's current year tax return under Code Sec. 704(d) (pass-through losses deductible only to extent of basis in partnership interest).

[113] Regs. § 1.1361-1(*l*)(1).

make distribution to only a single shareholder, or a subset of all shareholders, the transaction often must be structured as a stock redemption—the shareholder(s) receiving the distribution must forfeit some of their stock to prevent the corporation from violating the single class of stock requirement.

As noted previously, Code Sec. 1368 generally does not apply to distributions in redemption of a shareholder's stock. Instead, if the requirements of Code Sec. 302 are satisfied, the transaction will be treated by the shareholder as a sale of the redeemed shares. He or she will recognize gain in an amount equal to the excess of the payment received over the tax basis of the redeemed shares.

> **Example 16-32:** L and M are equal shareholders in LM, Inc., an S corporation. L's tax basis in her LM shares is $100,000. This year, L encountered a financial emergency and had to withdraw funds from the corporation. Rather than make distributions to both shareholders, the corporation distributed $60,000 to L in redemption of 20 percent of her shares. Her tax basis in the redeemed shares was $20,000 (20% of $100,000). Thus, she will report the transaction on her individual tax return as a sale of LM stock with a tax basis of $20,000 for $60,000, and will recognize a capital gain of $40,000. L's tax basis in her remaining LM shares will be $80,000 ($100,000 initial basis less $20,000 basis in the redeemed shares).
>
> Note that had LM been organized as a partnership, the transaction would have been treated as a current (i.e., non-liquidating) distribution, and L would have recognized no gain. She would reduce her tax basis in her partnership interest to $40,000 ($100,000 less $60,000).

A distribution of appreciated property in redemption of shares will be somewhat more complicated because the corporation must first recognize gain on the distribution as if it had sold the property for fair market value, using the proceeds from the deemed sale to redeem the shareholder's stock. The gain flows through to the shareholders and increases their stock basis before accounting for the subsequent redemption transaction. The net result will be more income for both the redeeming and non-redeeming shareholders.

> **Example 16-33:** Assume the same facts as in Example 16-32, except that LM Inc. distributes property to L with a fair market value of $60,000 and a tax basis of $18,000 in redemption of 20% of her shares. The distribution of appreciated property will trigger a $42,000 gain to LM, half of which will flow through to each shareholder (they are still equal shareholders at the time the gain is triggered). The tax consequences to L are as follows:
>
> | | |
> |---|---:|
> | Initial basis in LM stock | $100,000 |
> | Share of S corporation gain on distribution (50%) | 21,000 |
> | Adjusted basis in stock just prior to redemption | $121,000 |
> | Tax basis of redeemed shares (20% of $121,000) | 24,200 |
> | Amount received in redemption (FMV of property) | 60,000 |
> | Gain on redemption of stock | $ 35,800 |

Total gain reported on L's return (21,000 + 35,800)	$ 56,800
Pre-redemption basis in stock (per above)	$121,000
Basis of redeemed shares	(24,200)
Tax basis in remaining shares after redemption	$ 96,800

Note that M will also recognize a $21,000 capital gain (her 50% share of the S corporation gain on the distribution). Her tax basis in her LM shares will be increased accordingly.

Planning Pointer: There may be situations in which the shareholders in an S corporation would like to shift the tax burden associated with the distribution of accumulated E&P to one shareholder, or one group of shareholders, and away from others. This type of allocation is seldom possible in an S corporation setting because there are no special allocation provisions in subchapter S. Indeed, under subchapter S, every share of S corporation stock must be entitled to identical rights in all items of corporate income, deduction, loss, distribution, etc. This is a substantial difference between partnerships and S corporations. However, in some cases, it may be possible to use a non-qualified stock redemption to shift the tax burden of dividends distributed from accumulated E&P among the shareholders. Under Code Sec. 302, stock redemptions which do not substantially alter the shareholders' relative interests in the corporation are subject to the provisions of Code Sec. 301, rather than 302.[114] In the S corporation context, then, distributions received in a non-qualified redemption of the shareholder's stock will be subject to Code Sec. 1368. Thus, for example, where shares in a family corporation are all attributed to, say, the patriarch of the family, a redemption of some of the patriarch's shares will generally not qualify for treatment as a sale of those shares under Code Sec. 302. The redemption is economically real, so the single class of stock requirement is not violated, but the transaction will be treated as a distribution under Code Sec. 1368. If the corporation elects to treat distributions as coming from E&P first (as discussed previously), the net effect of the transaction will be to distribute E&P disproportionately to the patriarch. In some tax planning scenarios (e.g., estate planning, succession planning, etc.), such an arrangement may provide a net tax benefit to the family in the longer term.

Example 16-34: RQJ, Inc. is a family corporation established several years ago, which made the S election relatively recently. R and Q are J's parents. The S corporation has accumulated E&P of $300,000 and AAA of $300,000. R and Q each own 4,000 shares of stock in the company, and J owns 2,000 shares. R's aggregate tax basis in his shares is $500,000. This year, the corporation agrees to redeem half of R's shares for $400,000. Under the family attribution rules of Code Sec. 318, R is attributed ownership of shares owned by his spouse (Q) and his child (J). Thus, he is a 100% shareholder both before and after the redemption, and the transaction will be treated as a distribution

---

[114] Code Sec. 302(d).

(rather than a sale of his stock) for tax purposes under Code Sec. 302. If the S corporation elects to distribute E&P before AAA, this transaction will allow the entire E&P balance to be distributed to R without violating the single class of stock requirement:

Distribution	$400,000
From E&P	(300,000)
From AAA (remainder)	(100,000)

R will recognize $300,000 of dividend income and will reduce his tax basis in his RQJ stock by $100,000 (the portion of the distribution from AAA). In addition, J's relative interest in the corporation will increase from 20% (2,000 shares out of 10,000) to 23.25% (2,000 shares out of 8,600). Increasing her interest in future appreciation of corporate assets reduces the portion of such future appreciation that will be potentially subject to the estate tax. Likewise, shifting the entire burden of the tax liability on the dividend to R reduces the size of his potential estate. Since the maximum tax rate on dividend income is 23.8%, regardless of the taxpayer's other income, the immediate tax burden on the family is not affected by who pays the tax, but the family may achieve significant long-term estate tax savings.

¶ 1605 Termination of Election

.01 General

The S election can be terminated in a variety of ways, both intentionally and unintentionally. First, the S corporation can simply revoke its S election under Code Sec. 1362(d)(1). Termination under section 1362 is always voluntary. But this is not the only way to terminate the election. The election is automatically terminated if it becomes invalid—that is, if the corporation ceases to satisfy the qualifications for S status. For example, the corporation may issue a second class of stock, or may be determined by the IRS to have a second class of stock (e.g., as the result of disproportionate distributions as discussed above). Alternatively, it may add additional shareholders beyond the 100 shareholder maximum of Code Sec. 1361(b)(1) or it may issue shares (or another shareholder may sell shares) to an ineligible shareholder (e.g., another corporation, a nonresident alien, etc.). A third option is for the corporation to lose its eligibility as a consequence of violating statutory restrictions on passive investment income. Any of these invalidation activities can occur either voluntarily or involuntarily, although the corporation's governing documents often prohibit activities that might inadvertently terminate the S election.

.02 Revocation

Code Section 1362(d)(1) permits a corporation to revoke its S corporation election. An affirmative revocation requires the consent of shareholders holding more than half the stock of the corporation on the day of the revocation. In determining whether consenting shareholders hold more than half of the corporation's stock, both voting and nonvoting shares are counted, but Treasury shares are not.[115] Thus, one way a corporation may reach the 50% threshold is to purchase (redeem) the shares of reluctant shareholders.

> **Example 16-35:** The outstanding shares of Z, Inc., an S corporation, are owned by individuals A, B and C. A and B each own 100 shares of Z voting stock. C owns 100 shares of nonvoting stock. All the shares are common, and all have identical rights to corporate income and assets. Thus, the differences in voting rights do not violate the single class of stock requirement. Although C's shares do not entitle her to vote on management issues, the corporation cannot terminate its S election under Code Sec. 1362 without C's consent, because A and B do not own "more than" fifty percent of the outstanding shares of Z, Inc. stock. Note that both A and B do not have to consent—it will be sufficient if C, along with either A or B, consent to revocation of the S election.

To revoke the S election, the corporation must file a statement affirmatively revoking the election with the service center where the election was originally properly filed. The revocation statement should refer to Code Sec. 1362(a) and must include the total number of shares of stock (including non-voting stock) issued and outstanding at the time the revocation is made along with signed, written consents from each shareholder who consents to the revocation.[116] Each consent should provide the following information:

1. The name, address and taxpayer identification number of each consenting shareholder;

2. The number of shares of stock (including non-voting stock) held by each consenting shareholder as of the date of the revocation;

3. The acquisition date(s) of the stock held by each consenting shareholder;

4. The taxable year of each consenting shareholder; and

5. The name and taxpayer identification number of the S corporation.[117]

The statement must be signed by each consenting shareholder under penalty of perjury.

The regulations also define the shareholders whose consent is required. While this may seem self-evident, there are interesting questions raised with respect to shares jointly held by spouses, shares held by minors, and shares held by estates and trusts. The regulations provide that when shares are jointly held by spouses, both spouses must consent. For shares held by a minor, either the minor or the minor's legal representative may sign the consent form. Where shares are held by an estate, the executor of the estate must sign the consent statement. Finally, where shares are held in trust, the signature of the person (i.e., the beneficiary) who is treated as the shareholder is required.[118]

---

[115] Only issued and outstanding shares are taken into account. Reg. § 1.1362-6(a)(3)(i).

[116] Reg. § 1.1362-6(a)(3)(i).

[117] Reg. § 1.1362-6(b)(1).

[118] Reg. § 1.1362-6(b)(2)(i)-(iv).

.03 Termination via Violation of Eligibility Requirements

If a corporation violates the eligibility requirements for classification as a small business corporation (i.e., an S corporation), its S corporation status on the first date the violation occurred as described above. Termination by disqualification, whether intentional or unintentional, must be reported to the IRS upon discovery. The regulations state that the corporation must attach to its return for the tax year in which the termination occurs a statement both notifying the Service of the termination and setting forth the date of termination.[119] If the violation is unintentional, the corporation may not be aware of the violation when it files its tax return. In such cases, the corporation can petition the Internal Revenue Service to have its termination disregarded, provided that it takes steps within a reasonable period following discovery to remedy the violation.[120]

To be granted relief, the taxpayer must demonstrate that the violation of the eligibility requirements was "inadvertent."[121] The regulations provide that circumstances that suggest the violation was inadvertent include:

- election events not reasonably within the control of the corporation, and
- terminations not part of a plan to terminate the election or that took place without the corporation's knowledge and despite its due diligence to avoid such terminations.[122]

To be eligible for relief, the corporation must, within a "reasonable period" after discovering the circumstances that led to the violation, take steps to rectify the situation, including acquiring necessary shareholder consents and making necessary adjustments to deal with the eligibility issue. The corporation can then request a ruling for relief.

.04 Termination Due to Excess Passive Investment Income

S status is intended by Congress to ease the tax burden on business activities carried out through small business corporations. Congress has long been concerned, however, that regular corporations might choose not to distribute excess profits in order to allow shareholders to avoid dividend taxes. That concern is the basis for the accumulated earnings tax of Code Sec. 531, which imposes a tax on the corporation equal to 20 percent of "excess accumulations," measured as the excess of a corporation's retained profits over its reasonable needs. Code Section 1362 (d) prohibits a corporation from avoiding the accumulated earnings tax by electing to be taxed as an S corporation. Under Code Sec. 1362(d)(3)(A)(i), an S corporation which has accumulated E&P and for which more than 25 percent of its gross receipts are derived from "passive investment income" for three consecutive years is no longer eligible for S status.[123] Under Code Sec. 1362(d)(3)(A)(ii) termination caused by violation of the prohibition against excess passive investment income is effective "on and after the first day of the first taxable year

---

[119] Reg. § 1.1362-2(b)(1).
[120] Code Sec. 1362(f).
[121] Code Sec. 1362(f)(2).
[122] Reg. § 1.1362-4(b).

[123] Code Section 1362(d)(3)(C)(i) defines passive investment income as income from royalties, rents, dividends, interest and annuities. For years beginning after 2006, Section 1362(d)(3)(B) provides that gains from the sale of certain capital assets do not constitute passive investment income.

beginning after" the third tax year of excess passive income. Note that for termination to be triggered as a result of excess passive income, the corporation must have accumulated E&P as well as excess passive income in each of the three years.

Example 16-36: Styrene, Inc. was established many years ago as a regular corporation. Six years ago, it elected to be taxed as an S corporation. Four years ago, passive investment income comprised 32% of the company's gross receipts. The following year, passive income was 30% of gross receipts and last year, passive income made up 28% of gross receipts. Effective as of the first day of the current year, Styrene will be classified as a regular corporation, rather than an S corporation for federal tax purposes.

Note that there are three ways that a company can avoid triggering termination of its S status under the excess passive investment income provisions. It can reduce its passive income, perhaps by distributing its excess cash to shareholders rather than investing those funds itself. Alternatively, it can increase its gross receipts such that its passive income falls below 25 percent. The third option is for the company to distribute all its E&P to its shareholders. It does not matter what portion of an S corporation's gross receipts are comprised of investment income if the company has no E&P. This is a primary reason that S corporations are allowed to elect under Code Section 1368(d)(3) to make distributions from earnings and profits before the accumulated adjustments account. This election is discussed in an earlier section of this chapter.

.05 Effective Date of Termination

The effective date of termination of an S election depends on the nature of the revocation event. If the corporation becomes ineligible for S status (e.g., by exceeding the maximum number of shareholders), its S status is terminated as of the date that it first becomes ineligible.[124] If the violation is unintentional, the corporation may be required to file amended Form 1120 for prior periods when it was ineligible to file Form 1120-S. If the violation is intentional, the corporation will file Form 1120-S for the short period (if any) between the first day of the corporation's tax year and the date of termination. It will Form 1120 for the period beginning on the date of ineligibility. If that date occurs in the midst of its tax year, its first Form 1120 will be filed for the short period beginning on the date of ineligibility and ending on the last day of the corporation's tax year.

If the S corporation files an affirmative revocation statement under Code Sec. 1362, it has two options. It can designate a specific date for the termination to be effective—e.g., July 1 of the current year. The corporation may choose a specific date to follow a planned asset sale so that the gain on the sale will pass through to the shareholders before the election is terminated, or it may simply choose the first day of its tax year. If no date is specified, the termination will be effective as of the first day of the corporation's current tax year if the statement is made "on or before the 15th day of the third month" of the corporation's tax year, and on the first day of the corporation's following tax year if it is filed after that day.[125] For example, if a corporation were on a calendar tax year and it revoked its election on January 31,

---

[124] Reg. § 1.1362-2(b)(2).   [125] Code Sec. 1362(d)(1)(D); Reg. § 1.1362-2(a)(2)(i).

2011, but did not state when the revocation was effective, the election would be effective on January 1, 2011, but if the revocation were made on June 3, 2011, the revocation would be effective on January 1, 2012.

The election to revoke a corporation's S status may be rescinded. The rescission must be made before the revocation becomes effective and must include the consent of all shareholders who consented to the revocation as well as anyone who became a shareholder of the corporation after the day the revocation was made.[126]

.06 Reelection of S Status Following a Termination

A corporation is allowed to reelect S corporation following a termination of its S election, but it must generally wait at least five years after the year in which the termination was effective.[127] This restriction applies to both the corporation whose S election was terminated as well as to a successor corporation. In unusual circumstances, the Service has the authority to allow an earlier election.[128] As noted above, the Service can choose to ignore the termination (essentially consenting to immediate reelection) if the event causing the termination was not reasonably within the control of the corporation or of the shareholders possessing "substantial interests" in the corporation and was not part of a plan of either to terminate the election.[129] In cases where the termination was voluntary and intentional, consent to reelect S status before the expiration of the five year waiting period is more likely to be granted if the corporation can demonstrate circumstances such as a change in ownership of more than 50 percent of the corporation's stock since the date of the termination or other facts and circumstances that suggest that the rationale for the earlier termination is no longer valid.

¶ 1606 Tax Administration

Under Code Sec. 6037, the tax treatment of S corporation income, deduction, gain, loss, or credits is generally determined at the entity level, and all shareholders are required to file their returns in a manner consistent with the treatment on the Form 1120-S. Shareholders choosing to file their individual returns in a manner inconsistent with the corporate return must disclose the inconsistency on their properly filed return.

When the Service disputes an item reported on the S corporation tax return, the procedures for resolving this dispute are dependent on the size of the S corporation. Under the unified audit procedures, an S corporation shareholder's treatment of corporate items on his or her individual return cannot be changed except through the unified audit procedures. So long as the shareholder's treatment of the item on his or her return is consistent with the treatment of the item on the S corporation return, the IRS can only adjust the treatment of the item through an entity-level proceeding. Similarly, the shareholder cannot place in issue in an individual proceeding the proper treatment of an item on the S corporation return.[130] As noted above, a shareholder can treat an item inconsistently with the

---

[126] Reg. § 1.1362-6(a)(4).

[127] Code Sec. 1362(g).

[128] Consent for an earlier election is not necessary if as of the first day of its first tax year, either the corporation revoked its election or failed to qualify as a small business corporation.

[129] Reg. § 1.1362-2(b)(1).

[130] Reg. § 301.6221-1(a)

treatment of the item on the corporation's return, provided that the shareholder notifies the IRS of the inconsistent treatment.[131]

These rules are unnecessarily onerous for relatively small entities, so Congress implemented an exception to the unified audit rules in Code Sec. 6231(a)(1)(B), allowing partners in small partnerships to address disputes with the IRS directly rather than requiring the resolution to take place through an audit of the partnership. The Tax Court has ruled that the small partnership exception contained in section 6231(a)(1)(B), which exempts partnerships with 10 or fewer partners from the TEFRA partnership procedures, also applies to S corporations, and that a notice of final S corporation administrative adjustment (FSAA) issued under the unified audit and litigation provisions of sections 6241-6245 with respect to an S corporation having only one shareholder was invalid.[132] The Court further determined, however, that due to the differences between S corporations and partnerships, the statute does not necessarily define a small S corporation for purposes of the exception as one having 10 or fewer shareholders, but left the task of setting the size of the small S corporation to the Treasury Department.

In a subsequent decision, rendered before the Service had addressed the issue, the Court agreed that the Service properly exercised its discretion in applying the unified audit and litigation provisions of sections 6241-6245 with respect to an S corporation having 3 shareholders for a tax year (1983) for which regulations did not set an exception.[133] The Court stated that in the absence of regulations the small S corporation exception to the unified audit and litigation procedures is limited to one shareholder S corporations. For returns due after January 29, 1987, Temporary Regs. § 301.6241-1T(c)(2)(i) provide that the small S corporation applies to S corporations with 5 or fewer shareholders.

[131] Code Sec. 6222(b).
[132] *Blanco Investments & Land, Ltd. v. Commr.*, 89 T.C. No. 82 (Dec. 10, 1987) [CCH Dec. 44,377].
[133] *111 West 16 Street Owners, Inc. v. Commr.*, 90 T.C. No. 80 (June 23, 1982) [CCH Dec. 44,852].

Appendix

Caution: Before using any of these appendices,
consult the laws in the jurisdiction
where the material will be used.

¶ 2501 Form 1065, U.S. Partnership Return of Income

Form **1065** Department of the Treasury Internal Revenue Service	**U.S. Return of Partnership Income** For calendar year 2012, or tax year beginning _____ , 2012, ending _____ , 20 _____ . ▶ Information about Form 1065 and its separate instructions is at *www.irs.gov/form1065.*	OMB No. 1545-0099 **2012**

A Principal business activity		Name of partnership	D Employer identification number
B Principal product or service	**Print or type.**	Number, street, and room or suite no. If a P.O. box, see the instructions.	E Date business started
C Business code number		City or town, state, and ZIP code	F Total assets (see the instructions) $

G Check applicable boxes: **(1)** ☐ Initial return **(2)** ☐ Final return **(3)** ☐ Name change **(4)** ☐ Address change **(5)** ☐ Amended return
(6) ☐ Technical termination - also check (1) or (2)
H Check accounting method: **(1)** ☐ Cash **(2)** ☐ Accrual **(3)** ☐ Other (specify) ▶ _____
I Number of Schedules K-1. Attach one for each person who was a partner at any time during the tax year ▶ _____
J Check if Schedules C and M-3 are attached . . . . ☐

Caution. *Include only trade or business income and expenses on lines 1a through 22 below. See the instructions for more information.*

Income	1a	Gross receipts or sales	1a	
	b	Returns and allowances	1b	
	c	Balance. Subtract line 1b from line 1a	1c	
	2	Cost of goods sold (attach Form 1125-A)	2	
	3	Gross profit. Subtract line 2 from line 1c	3	
	4	Ordinary income (loss) from other partnerships, estates, and trusts (attach statement) . .	4	
	5	Net farm profit (loss) (attach Schedule F (Form 1040))	5	
	6	Net gain (loss) from Form 4797, Part II, line 17 (attach Form 4797)	6	
	7	Other income (loss) (attach statement)	7	
	8	**Total income (loss).** Combine lines 3 through 7	8	
Deductions (see the instructions for limitations)	9	Salaries and wages (other than to partners) (less employment credits)	9	
	10	Guaranteed payments to partners	10	
	11	Repairs and maintenance	11	
	12	Bad debts	12	
	13	Rent	13	
	14	Taxes and licenses	14	
	15	Interest	15	
	16a	Depreciation (if required, attach Form 4562)	16a	
	b	Less depreciation reported on Form 1125-A and elsewhere on return	16b	16c
	17	Depletion **(Do not deduct oil and gas depletion.)**	17	
	18	Retirement plans, etc.	18	
	19	Employee benefit programs	19	
	20	Other deductions (attach statement)	20	
	21	**Total deductions.** Add the amounts shown in the far right column for lines 9 through 20 .	21	
	22	**Ordinary business income (loss).** Subtract line 21 from line 8	22	

Sign Here

Under penalties of perjury, I declare that I have examined this return, including accompanying schedules and statements, and to the best of my knowledge and belief, it is true, correct, and complete. Declaration of preparer (other than general partner or limited liability company member manager) is based on all information of which preparer has any knowledge.

▶ _____   ▶ _____
Signature of general partner or limited liability company member manager   Date

May the IRS discuss this return with the preparer shown below (see instructions)? ☐ **Yes** ☐ **No**

Paid Preparer Use Only	Print/Type preparer's name	Preparer's signature	Date	Check ☐ if self- employed	PTIN
	Firm's name ▶			Firm's EIN ▶	
	Firm's address ▶			Phone no.	

For Paperwork Reduction Act Notice, see separate instructions.   Cat. No. 11390Z   Form **1065** (2012)

Form 1065 (2012) Page **2**

Schedule B — Other Information

				Yes	No
1	What type of entity is filing this return? Check the applicable box:				

a ☐ Domestic general partnership   **b** ☐ Domestic limited partnership

c ☐ Domestic limited liability company   **d** ☐ Domestic limited liability partnership

e ☐ Foreign partnership   **f** ☐ Other ▶

2 At any time during the tax year, was any partner in the partnership a disregarded entity, a partnership (including an entity treated as a partnership), a trust, an S corporation, an estate (other than an estate of a deceased partner), or a nominee or similar person? . . . .

3 At the end of the tax year:

a Did any foreign or domestic corporation, partnership (including any entity treated as a partnership), trust, or tax-exempt organization, or any foreign government own, directly or indirectly, an interest of 50% or more in the profit, loss, or capital of the partnership? For rules of constructive ownership, see instructions. If "Yes," attach Schedule B-1, Information on Partners Owning 50% or More of the Partnership . . . .

b Did any individual or estate own, directly or indirectly, an interest of 50% or more in the profit, loss, or capital of the partnership? For rules of constructive ownership, see instructions. If "Yes," attach Schedule B-1, Information on Partners Owning 50% or More of the Partnership . . . .

4 At the end of the tax year, did the partnership:

a Own directly 20% or more, or own, directly or indirectly, 50% or more of the total voting power of all classes of stock entitled to vote of any foreign or domestic corporation? For rules of constructive ownership, see instructions. If "Yes," complete (i) through (iv) below . . . .

(i) Name of Corporation	(ii) Employer Identification Number (if any)	(iii) Country of Incorporation	(iv) Percentage Owned in Voting Stock

b Own directly an interest of 20% or more, or own, directly or indirectly, an interest of 50% or more in the profit, loss, or capital in any foreign or domestic partnership (including an entity treated as a partnership) or in the beneficial interest of a trust? For rules of constructive ownership, see instructions. If "Yes," complete (i) through (v) below . .

(i) Name of Entity	(ii) Employer Identification Number (if any)	(iii) Type of Entity	(iv) Country of Organization	(v) Maximum Percentage Owned in Profit, Loss, or Capital

		Yes	No
5	Did the partnership file Form 8893, Election of Partnership Level Tax Treatment, or an election statement under section 6231(a)(1)(B)(ii) for partnership-level tax treatment, that is in effect for this tax year? See Form 8893 for more details		

6 Does the partnership satisfy **all four** of the following conditions?

a The partnership's total receipts for the tax year were less than $250,000.

b The partnership's total assets at the end of the tax year were less than $1 million.

c Schedules K-1 are filed with the return and furnished to the partners on or before the due date (including extensions) for the partnership return.

d The partnership is not filing and is not required to file Schedule M-3 . . . .

If "Yes," the partnership is not required to complete Schedules L, M-1, and M-2; Item F on page 1 of Form 1065; or Item L on Schedule K-1.

7 Is this partnership a publicly traded partnership as defined in section 469(k)(2)? . . . .

8 During the tax year, did the partnership have any debt that was cancelled, was forgiven, or had the terms modified so as to reduce the principal amount of the debt? . . . .

9 Has this partnership filed, or is it required to file, Form 8918, Material Advisor Disclosure Statement, to provide information on any reportable transaction? . . . .

10 At any time during calendar year 2012, did the partnership have an interest in or a signature or other authority over a financial account in a foreign country (such as a bank account, securities account, or other financial account)? See the instructions for exceptions and filing requirements for Form TD F 90-22.1, Report of Foreign Bank and Financial Accounts. If "Yes," enter the name of the foreign country. ▶

Form **1065** (2012)

Form 1065 (2012)   Page **3**

Schedule B	Other Information *(continued)*	Yes	No
11	At any time during the tax year, did the partnership receive a distribution from, or was it the grantor of, or transferor to, a foreign trust? If "Yes," the partnership may have to file Form 3520, Annual Return To Report Transactions With Foreign Trusts and Receipt of Certain Foreign Gifts. See instructions		
12a	Is the partnership making, or had it previously made (and not revoked), a section 754 election? . . . . . . See instructions for details regarding a section 754 election.		
b	Did the partnership make for this tax year an optional basis adjustment under section 743(b) or 734(b)? If "Yes," attach a statement showing the computation and allocation of the basis adjustment. See instructions		
c	Is the partnership required to adjust the basis of partnership assets under section 743(b) or 734(b) because of a substantial built-in loss (as defined under section 743(d)) or substantial basis reduction (as defined under section 734(d))? If "Yes," attach a statement showing the computation and allocation of the basis adjustment. See instructions.		
13	Check this box if, during the current or prior tax year, the partnership distributed any property received in a like-kind exchange or contributed such property to another entity (other than disregarded entities wholly-owned by the partnership throughout the tax year) . . . . ▶ ☐		
14	At any time during the tax year, did the partnership distribute to any partner a tenancy-in-common or other undivided interest in partnership property?		
15	If the partnership is required to file Form 8858, Information Return of U.S. Persons With Respect To Foreign Disregarded Entities, enter the number of Forms 8858 attached. See instructions ▶		
16	Does the partnership have any foreign partners? If "Yes," enter the number of Forms 8805, Foreign Partner's Information Statement of Section 1446 Withholding Tax, filed for this partnership. ▶		
17	Enter the number of Forms 8865, Return of U.S. Persons With Respect to Certain Foreign Partnerships, attached to this return. ▶		
18a	Did you make any payments in 2012 that would require you to file Form(s) 1099? See instructions		
b	If "Yes," did you or will you file required Form(s) 1099?		
19	Enter the number of Form(s) 5471, Information Return of U.S. Persons With Respect To Certain Foreign Corporations, attached to this return. ▶		
20	Enter the number of partners that are foreign governments under section 892. ▶		

Designation of Tax Matters Partner (see instructions)

Enter below the general partner or member-manager designated as the tax matters partner (TMP) for the tax year of this return:

Name of designated TMP ▶		Identifying number of TMP ▶
If the TMP is an entity, name of TMP representative ▶		Phone number of TMP ▶
Address of designated TMP ▶		

Form **1065** (2012)

Form 1065 (2012) Page **4**

Schedule K	Partners' Distributive Share Items		Total amount

Income (Loss)

1	Ordinary business income (loss) (page 1, line 22)	1	
2	Net rental real estate income (loss) (attach Form 8825)	2	
3a	Other gross rental income (loss)	3a		
b	Expenses from other rental activities (attach statement)	3b		
c	Other net rental income (loss). Subtract line 3b from line 3a	3c	
4	Guaranteed payments	4	
5	Interest income	5	
6	Dividends: a Ordinary dividends	6a	
	b Qualified dividends	6b		
7	Royalties	7	
8	Net short-term capital gain (loss) (attach Schedule D (Form 1065))	8	
9a	Net long-term capital gain (loss) (attach Schedule D (Form 1065))	9a	
b	Collectibles (28%) gain (loss)	9b		
c	Unrecaptured section 1250 gain (attach statement) .	9c		
10	Net section 1231 gain (loss) (attach Form 4797)	10	
11	Other income (loss) (see instructions) Type ▶	11	

Deductions

12	Section 179 deduction (attach Form 4562)	12	
13a	Contributions	13a	
b	Investment interest expense	13b	
c	Section 59(e)(2) expenditures: **(1)** Type ▶_____ **(2)** Amount ▶	13c(2)	
d	Other deductions (see instructions) Type ▶	13d	

Self-Employ-ment

14a	Net earnings (loss) from self-employment	14a	
b	Gross farming or fishing income	14b	
c	Gross nonfarm income	14c	

Credits

15a	Low-income housing credit (section 42(j)(5))	15a	
b	Low-income housing credit (other)	15b	
c	Qualified rehabilitation expenditures (rental real estate) (attach Form 3468)	15c	
d	Other rental real estate credits (see instructions) Type ▶_____	15d	
e	Other rental credits (see instructions) Type ▶_____	15e	
f	Other credits (see instructions) Type ▶_____	15f	

Foreign Transactions

16a	Name of country or U.S. possession ▶_____		
b	Gross income from all sources	16b	
c	Gross income sourced at partner level	16c	
	Foreign gross income sourced at partnership level		
d	Passive category ▶_____ e General category ▶_____ f Other ▶	16f	
	Deductions allocated and apportioned at partner level		
g	Interest expense ▶_____ h Other . . . . ▶	16h	
	Deductions allocated and apportioned at partnership level to foreign source income		
i	Passive category ▶_____ j General category ▶_____ k Other ▶	16k	
l	Total foreign taxes (check one): ▶ Paid ☐ Accrued ☐	16l	
m	Reduction in taxes available for credit (attach statement)	16m	
n	Other foreign tax information (attach statement)		

Alternative Minimum Tax (AMT) Items

17a	Post-1986 depreciation adjustment	17a	
b	Adjusted gain or loss	17b	
c	Depletion (other than oil and gas)	17c	
d	Oil, gas, and geothermal properties—gross income	17d	
e	Oil, gas, and geothermal properties—deductions	17e	
f	Other AMT items (attach statement)	17f	

Other Information

18a	Tax-exempt interest income	18a	
b	Other tax-exempt income	18b	
c	Nondeductible expenses	18c	
19a	Distributions of cash and marketable securities	19a	
b	Distributions of other property	19b	
20a	Investment income	20a	
b	Investment expenses	20b	
c	Other items and amounts (attach statement)		

Form **1065** (2012)

Analysis of Net Income (Loss)

1	Net income (loss). Combine Schedule K, lines 1 through 11. From the result, subtract the sum of Schedule K, lines 12 through 13d, and 16l			**1**	

2	Analysis by partner type:	(i) Corporate	(ii) Individual (active)	(iii) Individual (passive)	(iv) Partnership	(v) Exempt organization	(vi) Nominee/Other
a	General partners						
b	Limited partners						

Schedule L   Balance Sheets per Books

	Assets	Beginning of tax year		End of tax year	
		(a)	(b)	(c)	(d)
1	Cash				
2a	Trade notes and accounts receivable . . .				
b	Less allowance for bad debts				
3	Inventories				
4	U.S. government obligations				
5	Tax-exempt securities				
6	Other current assets (attach statement) . .				
7a	Loans to partners (or persons related to partners)				
b	Mortgage and real estate loans				
8	Other investments (attach statement) . . .				
9a	Buildings and other depreciable assets . .				
b	Less accumulated depreciation				
10a	Depletable assets				
b	Less accumulated depletion				
11	Land (net of any amortization)				
12a	Intangible assets (amortizable only) . . .				
b	Less accumulated amortization				
13	Other assets (attach statement)				
14	Total assets				
	Liabilities and Capital				
15	Accounts payable				
16	Mortgages, notes, bonds payable in less than 1 year				
17	Other current liabilities (attach statement) .				
18	All nonrecourse loans				
19a	Loans from partners (or persons related to partners)				
b	Mortgages, notes, bonds payable in 1 year or more				
20	Other liabilities (attach statement)				
21	Partners' capital accounts				
22	Total liabilities and capital				

Schedule M-1   Reconciliation of Income (Loss) per Books With Income (Loss) per Return

Note. Schedule M-3 may be required instead of Schedule M-1 (see instructions).

1	Net income (loss) per books		6	Income recorded on books this year not included on Schedule K, lines 1 through 11 (itemize):	
2	Income included on Schedule K, lines 1, 2, 3c, 5, 6a, 7, 8, 9a, 10, and 11, not recorded on books this year (itemize):		a	Tax-exempt interest $ _____	
3	Guaranteed payments (other than health insurance)		7	Deductions included on Schedule K, lines 1 through 13d, and 16l, not charged against book income this year (itemize):	
4	Expenses recorded on books this year not included on Schedule K, lines 1 through 13d, and 16l (itemize):		a	Depreciation $ _____	
a	Depreciation $ _____		8	Add lines 6 and 7	
b	Travel and entertainment $ _____		9	Income (loss) (Analysis of Net Income (Loss), line 1). Subtract line 8 from line 5 .	
5	Add lines 1 through 4				

Schedule M-2   Analysis of Partners' Capital Accounts

1	Balance at beginning of year . . .		6	Distributions: a Cash	
2	Capital contributed: a Cash . . .			b Property	
	b Property . .		7	Other decreases (itemize): _____	
3	Net income (loss) per books				
4	Other increases (itemize): _____		8	Add lines 6 and 7	
5	Add lines 1 through 4		9	Balance at end of year. Subtract line 8 from line 5	

Form **1065** (2012)

¶ 2502 Schedule K-1 (Form 1065), Partner's Share of Income, Credits, Deductions, etc.

651112

☐ Final K-1	☐ Amended K-1		OMB No. 1545-0099	

Schedule K-1 **(Form 1065)** Department of the Treasury Internal Revenue Service	20**12** For calendar year 2012, or tax year beginning _____ , 2012 ending _____ , 20 ____	**Part III** **Partner's Share of Current Year Income,** **Deductions, Credits, and Other Items**

Part III fields		
1 Ordinary business income (loss)	15 Credits	
2 Net rental real estate income (loss)		
3 Other net rental income (loss)	16 Foreign transactions	
4 Guaranteed payments		
5 Interest income		
6a Ordinary dividends		
6b Qualified dividends		
7 Royalties		
8 Net short-term capital gain (loss)		
9a Net long-term capital gain (loss)	17 Alternative minimum tax (AMT) items	
9b Collectibles (28%) gain (loss)		
9c Unrecaptured section 1250 gain		
10 Net section 1231 gain (loss)	18 Tax-exempt income and nondeductible expenses	
11 Other income (loss)		
12 Section 179 deduction	19 Distributions	
13 Other deductions		
	20 Other information	
14 Self-employment earnings (loss)		

Partner's Share of Income, Deductions, Credits, etc. ▶ See back of form and separate instructions.

Part I **Information About the Partnership**
A Partnership's employer identification number
B Partnership's name, address, city, state, and ZIP code
C IRS Center where partnership filed return
D ☐ Check if this is a publicly traded partnership (PTP)

Part II **Information About the Partner**
E Partner's identifying number
F Partner's name, address, city, state, and ZIP code

G ☐ General partner or LLC member-manager   ☐ Limited partner or other LLC member

H ☐ Domestic partner   ☐ Foreign partner

I1 What type of entity is this partner? (see instructions) _____

I2 If this partner is a retirement plan (IRA/SEP/Keogh/etc.), check here (see instructions) . . . . ☐

J Partner's share of profit, loss, and capital (see instructions):

	Beginning	Ending
Profit	%	%
Loss	%	%
Capital	%	%

K Partner's share of liabilities at year end:

Nonrecourse	$ _____
Qualified nonrecourse financing .	$ _____
Recourse	$ _____

L Partner's capital account analysis:

Beginning capital account . . .	$ _____
Capital contributed during the year	$ _____
Current year increase (decrease) .	$ _____
Withdrawals & distributions . .	$ (_____)
Ending capital account	$ _____

☐ Tax basis   ☐ GAAP   ☐ Section 704(b) book
☐ Other (explain)

M Did the partner contribute property with a built-in gain or loss?
☐ Yes   ☐ No
If "Yes," attach statement (see instructions)

*See attached statement for additional information.

For IRS Use Only

For Paperwork Reduction Act Notice, see Instructions for Form 1065.   IRS.gov/form1065   Cat. No. 11394R   Schedule K-1 (Form 1065) 2012

Schedule K-1 (Form 1065) 2012   Page **2**

This list identifies the codes used on Schedule K-1 for all partners and provides summarized reporting information for partners who file Form 1040. For detailed reporting and filing information, see the separate Partner's Instructions for Schedule K-1 and the instructions for your income tax return.

1. Ordinary business income (loss). Determine whether the income (loss) is passive or nonpassive and enter on your return as follows.

	Report on
Passive loss	See the Partner's Instructions
Passive income	Schedule E, line 28, column (g)
Nonpassive loss	Schedule E, line 28, column (h)
Nonpassive income	Schedule E, line 28, column (j)

2. Net rental real estate income (loss)   See the Partner's Instructions

3. Other net rental income (loss)

Net income	Schedule E, line 28, column (g)
Net loss	See the Partner's Instructions

4. Guaranteed payments   Schedule E, line 28, column (j)
5. Interest income   Form 1040, line 8a
6a. Ordinary dividends   Form 1040, line 9a
6b. Qualified dividends   Form 1040, line 9b
7. Royalties   Schedule E, line 4
8. Net short-term capital gain (loss)   Schedule D, line 5
9a. Net long-term capital gain (loss)   Schedule D, line 12
9b. Collectibles (28%) gain (loss)   28% Rate Gain Worksheet, line 4 (Schedule D instructions)
9c. Unrecaptured section 1250 gain   See the Partner's Instructions
10. Net section 1231 gain (loss)   See the Partner's Instructions

11. Other income (loss)

Code		Report on
A	Other portfolio income (loss)	See the Partner's Instructions
B	Involuntary conversions	See the Partner's Instructions
C	Sec. 1256 contracts & straddles	Form 6781, line 1
D	Mining exploration costs recapture	See Pub. 535
E	Cancellation of debt	Form 1040, line 21 or Form 982
F	Other income (loss)	See the Partner's Instructions

12. Section 179 deduction   See the Partner's Instructions

13. Other deductions

Code		Report on
A	Cash contributions (50%)	
B	Cash contributions (30%)	
C	Noncash contributions (50%)	
D	Noncash contributions (30%)	See the Partner's
E	Capital gain property to a 50% organization (30%)	Instructions
F	Capital gain property (20%)	
G	Contributions (100%)	
H	Investment interest expense	Form 4952, line 1
I	Deductions—royalty income	Schedule E, line 19
J	Section 59(e)(2) expenditures	See the Partner's Instructions
K	Deductions—portfolio (2% floor)	Schedule A, line 23
L	Deductions—portfolio (other)	Schedule A, line 28
M	Amounts paid for medical insurance	Schedule A, line 1 or Form 1040, line 29
N	Educational assistance benefits	See the Partner's Instructions
O	Dependent care benefits	Form 2441, line 12
P	Preproductive period expenses	See the Partner's Instructions
Q	Commercial revitalization deduction from rental real estate activities	See Form 8582 Instructions
R	Pensions and IRAs	See the Partner's Instructions
S	Reforestation expense deduction	See the Partner's Instructions
T	Domestic production activities information	See Form 8903 instructions
U	Qualified production activities income	Form 8903, line 7b
V	Employer's Form W-2 wages	Form 8903, line 17
W	Other deductions	See the Partner's Instructions

14. Self-employment earnings (loss)

Note. *If you have a section 179 deduction or any partner-level deductions, see the Partner's Instructions before completing Schedule SE.*

Code		Report on
A	Net earnings (loss) from self-employment	Schedule SE, Section A or B
B	Gross farming or fishing income	See the Partner's Instructions
C	Gross non-farm income	See the Partner's Instructions

15. Credits

Code		Report on
A	Low-income housing credit (section 42(j)(5)) from pre-2008 buildings	
B	Low-income housing credit (other) from pre-2008 buildings	
C	Low-income housing credit (section 42(j)(5)) from post-2007 buildings	
D	Low-income housing credit (other) from post-2007 buildings	See the Partner's Instructions
E	Qualified rehabilitation expenditures (rental real estate)	
F	Other rental real estate credits	
G	Other rental credits	
H	Undistributed capital gains credit	Form 1040, line 71; check box a
I	Alcohol and cellulosic biofuels credit	See the Partner's Instructions

Code		Report on
J	Work opportunity credit	
K	Disabled access credit	
L	Empowerment zone and renewal community employment credit	
M	Credit for increasing research activities	See the Partner's Instructions
N	Credit for employer social security and Medicare taxes	
O	Backup withholding	
P	Other credits	

16. Foreign transactions

Code		Report on
A	Name of country or U.S. possession	
B	Gross income from all sources	Form 1116, Part I
C	Gross income sourced at partner level	

Foreign gross income sourced at partnership level

Code		Report on
D	Passive category	
E	General category	Form 1116, Part I
F	Other	

Deductions allocated and apportioned at partner level

Code		Report on
G	Interest expense	Form 1116, Part I
H	Other	Form 1116, Part I

Deductions allocated and apportioned at partnership level to foreign source income

Code		Report on
I	Passive category	
J	General category	Form 1116, Part I
K	Other	

Other information

Code		Report on
L	Total foreign taxes paid	Form 1116, Part II
M	Total foreign taxes accrued	Form 1116, Part II
N	Reduction in taxes available for credit	Form 1116, line 12
O	Foreign trading gross receipts	Form 8873
P	Extraterritorial income exclusion	Form 8873
Q	Other foreign transactions	See the Partner's Instructions

17. Alternative minimum tax (AMT) items

Code		Report on
A	Post-1986 depreciation adjustment	
B	Adjusted gain or loss	See the Partner's
C	Depletion (other than oil & gas)	Instructions and
D	Oil, gas, & geothermal—gross income	the Instructions for
E	Oil, gas, & geothermal—deductions	Form 6251
F	Other AMT items	

18. Tax-exempt income and nondeductible expenses

Code		Report on
A	Tax-exempt interest income	Form 1040, line 8b
B	Other tax-exempt income	See the Partner's Instructions
C	Nondeductible expenses	See the Partner's Instructions

19. Distributions

Code		Report on
A	Cash and marketable securities	
B	Distribution subject to section 737	See the Partner's Instructions
C	Other property	

20. Other information

Code		Report on
A	Investment income	Form 4952, line 4a
B	Investment expenses	Form 4952, line 5
C	Fuel tax credit information	Form 4136
D	Qualified rehabilitation expenditures (other than rental real estate)	See the Partner's Instructions
E	Basis of energy property	See the Partner's Instructions
F	Recapture of low-income housing credit (section 42(j)(5))	Form 8611, line 8
G	Recapture of low-income housing credit (other)	Form 8611, line 8
H	Recapture of investment credit	See Form 4255
I	Recapture of other credits	See the Partner's Instructions
J	Look-back interest—completed long-term contracts	See Form 8697
K	Look-back interest—income forecast method	See Form 8866
L	Dispositions of property with section 179 deductions	
M	Recapture of section 179 deduction	
N	Interest expense for corporate partners	
O	Section 453(l)(3) information	
P	Section 453A(c) information	
Q	Section 1260(b) information	See the Partner's
R	Interest allocable to production expenditures	Instructions
S	CCF nonqualified withdrawals	
T	Depletion information—oil and gas	
U	Amortization of reforestation costs	
V	Unrelated business taxable income	
W	Precontribution gain (loss)	
X	Section 108(i) information	
Y	Other information	

¶ 2503 Form 1128, Application To Adopt, Change, or Retain a Tax Year

Form **1128** (Rev. January 2008) Department of the Treasury Internal Revenue Service	**Application To Adopt, Change, or Retain a Tax Year** ▶ See separate instructions.	OMB No. 1545-0134 Attachment Sequence No. **148**

Part I   **General Information**

Important: All filers must complete Part I and sign below. See instructions.

<table>
<tr><td rowspan="6" style="writing-mode:vertical-rl">Type or Print</td><td>Name of filer (if a joint return is filed, also enter spouse's name) (see instructions)</td><td>Filer's identifying number</td></tr>
<tr><td>Number, street, and room or suite no. (if a P.O. box, see instructions)</td><td>Service Center where income tax return will be filed</td></tr>
<tr><td>City or town, state, and ZIP code</td><td>Filer's area code and telephone number/Fax number
(   )   / (   )</td></tr>
<tr><td>Name of applicant, if different than the filer (see instructions)</td><td>**Applicant's identifying number** (see instructions)</td></tr>
<tr><td>Name of person to contact (if not the applicant or filer, attach a power of attorney)</td><td>Contact person's area code and telephone number/Fax number
(   )   / (   )</td></tr>
</table>

1   Check the appropriate box(es) to indicate the type of applicant (see instructions).

- ☐ Individual
- ☐ Partnership
- ☐ Estate
- ☐ Domestic corporation
- ☐ S corporation
- ☐ Personal service corporation (PSC)
- ☐ Cooperative (sec. 1381(a))
- ☐ Controlled foreign corporation (CFC) (sec. 957)
- ☐ Foreign sales corporation (FSC) or Interest-charge domestic international sales corporation (IC-DISC)
- ☐ Specified foreign corporation (SFC) (sec. 898)
- ☐ 10/50 corporation (sec. 904(d)(2)(E))
- ☐ Trust
- ☐ Passive foreign investment company (PFIC) (sec. 1297)
- ☐ Other foreign corporation
- ☐ Tax-exempt organization
- ☐ Homeowners Association (sec. 528)
- ☐ Other _____ (Specify entity and applicable Code section)

2a Approval is requested to (check one) (see instructions):

- ☐ Adopt a tax year ending ▶ .... (Partnerships and PSCs: Go to Part III after completing Part I.)
- ☐ Change to a tax year ending ▶ ....   ☐ Retain a tax year ending ▶ ....

b If changing a tax year, indicate the date the present tax year ends. ▶ ....

c If adopting or changing a tax year, the first return or short period return will be filed for the tax year beginning ▶ _____ , 20____ , and ending ▶ _____ , 20____

3   Is the applicant's present tax year, as stated on line 2b above, also its current financial reporting year? ▶ ☐ **Yes** ☐ **No**

If "No," attach an explanation.

4   Indicate the applicant's present overall method of accounting.
- ☐ Cash receipts and disbursements method   ☐ Accrual method
- ☐ Other method (specify) ▶ ....

5   State the nature of the applicant's business or principal source of income.

Signature—All Filers (See **Who Must Sign** in the instructions.)

Under penalties of perjury, I declare that I have examined this application, including accompanying schedules and statements, and to the best of my knowledge and belief, it is true, correct, and complete. Declaration of preparer (other than filer) is based on all information of which preparer has any knowledge.

Filer*	**Preparer (other than filer)**
_____ Signature and date	_____ Signature of individual preparing the application and date
_____ Name and title (print or type)	_____ Name of individual preparing the application
*If the application is filed on behalf of a controlled foreign corporation or a 10/50 corporation by a controlling domestic shareholder, see instructions.	_____ Name of firm preparing the application

For Privacy Act and Paperwork Reduction Act Notice, see separate instructions.   Cat. No. 21115C   Form **1128** (Rev. 1-2008)

Form 1128 (Rev. 1-2008) Page **2**

Part II | **Automatic Approval Request** (see instructions)

● Identify the revenue procedure under which this automatic approval request is filed ▶ . . . . . .

Section A—Corporations (Other Than S Corporations or Personal Service Corporations) (Rev. Proc. 2006-45, or its successor)

		Yes	No
1	Is the applicant a corporation (including a homeowners association (section 528)) that is requesting a change in tax year **and** is not precluded from using the automatic approval rules under section 4 of Rev. Proc. 2006-45 (or its successor)? (see instructions) . . . . ▶		
2	Does the corporation intend to elect to be an S corporation for the tax year immediately following the short period? If "Yes" and the corporation is electing to change to a permitted tax year, file Form 1128 as an attachment to Form 2553.		
3	Is the applicant a corporation requesting a concurrent change for a CFC, FSC or IC-DISC? (see instructions) ▶		

Section B—Partnerships, S Corporations, Personal Service Corporations (PSCs), and Trusts (Rev. Proc. 2006-46, or its successor)

4	Is the applicant a partnership, S corporation, PSC, or trust that is requesting a tax year **and** is not precluded from using the automatic approval rules under section 4 of Rev. Proc. 2006-46 (or its successor)? (see instructions) . ▶		
5	Is the partnership, S corporation, PSC, or trust requesting to change to its required tax year or a partnership, S corporation, or PSC that wants to change to a 52-53 week tax year ending with reference to such tax year? ▶		
6	Is the partnership, S corporation, or PSC (other than a member of a tiered structure) requesting a tax year that coincides with its natural business year described in section 4.01(2) of Rev. Proc. 2006-46 (or its successor)? Attach a statement showing gross receipts for the most recent 47 months. (See instructions for information required to be submitted) . . . . ▶		
7	Is the S corporation requesting an ownership tax year? (see instructions) . . . . ▶		
8	Is the applicant a partnership requesting a concurrent change pursuant to section 6.09 of Rev. Proc. 2006-45 (or its successor) or section 5.04(8) of Rev. Proc. 2002-39 (or its successor)? (see instructions) . . . . ▶		

Section C—Individuals (Rev. Proc. 2003-62, or its successor) (see instructions)

9	Is the applicant an individual requesting a change from a fiscal year to a calendar year? . . . . ▶		

Section D—Tax-Exempt Organizations (Rev. Proc. 76-10 or 85-58) (see instructions)

10	Is the applicant a tax-exempt organization requesting a change? . . . . ▶		

Part III | **Ruling Request** (All applicants requesting a ruling must complete Section A and any other section that applies to the entity. See instructions.) **(Rev. Proc. 2002-39, or its successor)**

Section A—General Information | | Yes | No

		Yes	No
1	Is the applicant a partnership, S corporation, personal service corporation, or trust that is under examination by the IRS, before an appeals office, or a Federal court?. . . . . ▶ If "Yes," see the instructions for information that must be included on an attached explanation.		
2	Has the applicant changed its annual accounting period at any time within the most recent 48-month period ending with the last month of the requested tax year? . . . . ▶ If "Yes" and a letter ruling was issued granting approval to make the change, attach a copy of the letter ruling, or if not available, an explanation including the date approval was granted. If a letter ruling was not issued, indicate when and explain how the change was implemented.		
3	Within the most recent 48-month period, has any accounting period application been withdrawn, not perfected, denied, or not implemented? . . . . ▶ If "Yes," attach an explanation.		
4a	Is the applicant requesting to establish a business purpose under section 5.02(1) of Rev. Proc. 2002-39 (or its successor)?. . . . . ▶ If "Yes," attach an explanation of the legal basis supporting the requested tax year (see instructions).		
b	If your business purpose is based on one of the natural business year tests under section 5.03, check the applicable box. ☐ Annual business cycle test ☐ Seasonal business test ☐ 25-percent gross receipts test Attach a statement showing gross receipts from sales and services (and inventory cost if applicable) for the test period. (see instructions)		
5	Enter the taxable income or (loss) for the 3 tax years immediately preceding the year of change and for the short period. If necessary, estimate the amount for the short period. Short period $ .... First preceding year $ .... Second preceding year $ .... Third preceding year $ .... **Note:** Individuals, enter adjusted gross income. Partnerships and S corporations, enter ordinary income. Section 501(c) organizations, enter unrelated business taxable income. Estates, enter adjusted total income. All other applicants, enter taxable income before net operating loss deduction and special deductions.		

Form **1128** (Rev. 1-2008)

		Yes	No
6	Corporations only, enter the losses or credits, if any, that were generated or that expired in the short period:		

Generated   Expiring

Net operating loss . . . . $ _____ $ _____
Capital loss . . . . $ _____ $ _____
Unused credits . . . . $ _____ $ _____

7 Enter the amount of deferral, if any, resulting from the change (see section 5.05(1), (2), (3) and 6.01(7) of Rev. Proc. 2002-39, or its successor) . . . . ▶ $ _____

8a Is the applicant a U.S. shareholder in a CFC? . . . . ▶

If "Yes," attach a statement for each CFC providing the name, address, identifying number, tax year, the percentage of total combined voting power of the applicant, and the amount of income included in the gross income of the applicant under section 951 for the 3 tax years immediately before the short period and for the short period.

b Will each CFC concurrently change its tax year? . . . . ▶
If "Yes" to line 8b, go to Part II, line 3.
If "No," attach a statement explaining why the CFC will not be conforming to the tax year requested by the U.S. shareholder.

9a Is the applicant a U.S. shareholder in a PFIC as defined in section 1297? . . . . ▶

If "Yes," attach a statement providing the name, address, identifying number, and tax year of the PFIC, the percentage of interest owned by the applicant, and the amount of distributions or ordinary earnings and net capital gain from the PFIC included in the income of the applicant.

b Did the applicant elect under section 1295 to treat the PFIC as a qualified electing fund? . . . . . . ▶

10a Is the applicant a member of a partnership, a beneficiary of a trust or estate, a shareholder of an S corporation, a shareholder of an IC-DISC, or a shareholder of an FSC? . . . . ▶

If "Yes," attach a statement providing the name, address, identifying number, type of entity (partnership, trust, estate, S corporation, IC-DISC, or FSC), tax year, percentage of interest in capital and profits, or percentage of interest of each IC-DISC or FSC and the amount of income received from each entity for the first preceding year and for the short period. Indicate the percentage of gross income of the applicant represented by each amount.

b Will any partnership concurrently change its tax year to conform with the tax year requested? . . . . ▶
c If "Yes" to line 10b, has any Form 1128 been filed for such partnership? . . . . ▶

11 Does the applicant or any related entity currently have any accounting method, tax year, ruling, or technical advice request pending with the IRS National Office?. . . . . ▶

If "Yes," attach a statement explaining the type of request (method, tax year, etc.) and the specific issues involved in each request.

12 Is **Form 2848,** Power of Attorney and Declaration of Representative, attached to this application? . . ▶

13 Does the applicant request a conference of right (in person or by telephone) with the IRS National Office, if the IRS proposes to disapprove the application? . . . . ▶

14 Enter amount of **user fee** attached to this application (see instructions) . . . . ▶ $

Section B—Corporations (other than S corporations and controlled foreign corporations) (see instructions)

15 Enter the date of incorporation. ▶

		Yes	No
16a	Does the corporation intend to elect to be an S corporation for the tax year immediately following the short period? . . . . ▶		

b If "Yes," will the corporation be going to a permitted S corporation tax year? . . . . ▶
If "No" to line 16b, attach an explanation.

17 Is the corporation a member of an affiliated group filing a consolidated return? . . . . ▶

If "Yes," attach a statement providing **(a)** the name, address, identifiying number used on the consolidated return, tax year, and Service Center where the applicant files the return; **(b)** the name, address, and identifying number of each member of the affiliated group; **(c)** the taxable income (loss) of each member for the 3 years immediately before the short period and for the short period; and **(d)** the name of the parent corporation.

18a Personal service corporations (PSCs): Attach a statement providing each shareholder's name, type of entity (individual, partnership, corporation, etc.), address, identifying number, tax year, percentage of ownership, and amount of income received from the PSC for the first preceding year and the short period.

b If the PSC is using a tax year other than the required tax year, indicate how it obtained its tax year.
☐ Grandfathered (attach copy of letter ruling)   ☐ Section 444 election (date of election _____)
☐ Letter ruling (date of letter ruling _____ (attach copy))

Form **1128** (Rev. 1-2008)

Section C—S Corporations (see instructions)

		Yes	No
19	Enter the date of the S corporation election. ▶		
20	Is any shareholder applying for a corresponding change in tax year? . . . . ▶		
	If "Yes," each shareholder requesting a corresponding change in tax year must file a separate Form 1128 to get advance approval to change its tax year.		

21 If the corporation is using a tax year other than the required tax year, indicate how it obtained its tax year.
   ☐ Grandfathered (attach copy of letter ruling)   ☐ Section 444 election (date of election _____)
   ☐ Letter ruling (date of letter ruling _____(attach copy))

22 Attach a statement providing each shareholder's name, type of shareholder (individual, estate, qualified subchapter S Trust, electing small business trust, other trust, or exempt organization), address, identifying number, tax year, percentage of ownership, and the amount of income each shareholder received from the S corporation for the first preceding year and for the short period.

Section D—Partnerships (see instructions)

		Yes	No
23	Enter the date the partnership's business began. ▶		
24	Is any partner applying for a corresponding change in tax year? . . . . ▶		

25 Attach a statement providing each partner's name, type of partner (individual, partnership, estate, trust, corporation, S corporation, IC-DISC, etc.), address, identifying number, tax year, and the percentage of interest in capital and profits.

26 Is any partner a shareholder of a PSC as defined in Regulations section 1.441-3(c)? . . . . ▶
   If "Yes," attach a statement providing the name, address, identifying number, tax year, percentage of interest in capital and profits, and the amount of income received from each PSC for the first preceding year and for the short period.

27 If the partnership is using a tax year other than the required tax year, indicate how it obtained its tax year.
   ☐ Grandfathered (attach copy of letter ruling)   ☐ Section 444 election (date of election _____)
   ☐ Letter ruling (date of letter ruling _____ (attach copy))

Section E—Controlled Foreign Corporations (CFC)

28 Attach a statement for each U.S. shareholder (as defined in section 951(b)) providing the name, address, identifying number, tax year, percentage of total value and percentage of total voting power, and the amount of income included in gross income under section 951 for the 3 tax years immediately before the short period and for the short period.

Section F—Tax-Exempt Organizations

		Yes	No
29	Type of organization: ☐ Corporation ☐ Trust ☐ Other (specify) ▶		
30	Date of organization. ▶		
31	Code section under which the organization is exempt. ▶		
32	Is the organization required to file an annual return on Form 990, 1120-C, 990-PF, 990-T, 1120-H, or 1120-POL? ▶		
33	Enter the date the tax exemption was granted. ▶ .... Attach a copy of the letter ruling granting exemption. If a copy of the letter ruling is not available, attach an explanation.		
34	If the organization is a private foundation, is the foundation terminating its status under section 507? . . ▶		

Section G—Estates

35 Enter the date the estate was created. ▶

36a Attach a statement providing the name, identifying number, address, and tax year of each beneficiary and each person who is an interested party of any portion of the estate.

   b Based on the adjusted total income of the estate entered in Part III, Section A, line 5, attach a statement showing the distribution deduction and the taxable amounts distributed to each beneficiary for the 2 tax years immediately before the short period and for the short period.

Section H—Passive Foreign Investment Companies

37 If the applicant is a passive foreign investment company, attach a statement providing each U.S. shareholder's name, address, identifying number, and percentage of interest owned.

Form **1128** (Rev. 1-2008)

¶ 2504   **Instructions for Form 1128**

Instructions for Form 1128

 Department of the Treasury
Internal Revenue Service

(Rev. January 2008)

Application To Adopt, Change, or Retain a Tax Year

Section references are to the Internal Revenue Code unless otherwise noted.

What's New

Trusts. A checkbox was added to Part I, line 1 for trusts. Certain types of trusts are now permitted to use the automatic approval request procedures. Refer to Section B of Part II for the details.

General Instructions

Purpose of Form

File Form 1128 to request a change in tax year. Partnerships, S corporations, personal service corporations (PSCs), or trusts may be required to file the form to adopt or retain a certain tax year.

Who Must File

Generally, all taxpayers must file Form 1128 to adopt, change, or retain a tax year. However, see *Exceptions* below.

The common parent of a consolidated group that files a consolidated return files one Form 1128 for the consolidated group. In addition, the common parent corporation must (a) indicate that the Form 1128 is for the common parent corporation and all its subsidiaries and (b) answer all relevant questions on the application for each member of the consolidated group.

If a consolidated group filing a consolidated return wants to change its tax year by using Rev. Proc. 2006-45, every member of the group must meet the revenue procedure requirements.

If a controlled foreign corporation (CFC) or 10/50 corporation (noncontrolled section 902 corporation) does not have a U.S. trade or business, then the CFC's controlling domestic shareholder(s) must file Form 1128 on behalf of such foreign corporation to change its tax year (except as provided above with respect to a controlling domestic shareholder that is a member of a consolidated group). See Temporary

Regulations section 1.964-1T(c)(5) for the definition of controlling domestic shareholders of a CFC or 10/50 corporation.

If Form 1128 is filed on behalf of a CFC or 10/50 corporation, each controlling domestic shareholder must attach to its tax return a copy of the form and all other domestic shareholders must be provided a written notice of the election. See Temporary Regulations section 1.964-1T(c)(3) for details.

Exceptions

Do not file Form 1128 in the following circumstances.

Corporations
- A corporation adopting its first tax year.
- A corporation required to change its tax year to file a consolidated return with its new common parent (see Regulations sections 1.442-1(c) and 1.1502-76(a)).
- A foreign sales corporation (FSC) or an interest charge domestic international sales corporation (IC-DISC) changing to the tax year of the U.S. shareholder with the highest percentage of voting power (see section 441(h)). Also see Temporary Regulations section 1.921-1T(b)(4). However, a FSC or IC-DISC must file Form 1128 to change its tax year concurrently, if a tax year change has been made by the U.S. shareholder.

Partnerships, S Corporations, and Personal Service Corporations
- A newly formed partnership adopting a required tax year or a 52-53 week tax year with reference to such required tax year.
- A partnership, S corporation, or PSC terminating its section 444 election (see Temporary Regulations section 1.444-1T(a)(5)).
- A newly formed partnership, an electing S corporation, or a newly formed PSC that elects under section 444 a tax year other than the required tax year by filing Form 8716, Election To Have a Tax Year Other Than a Required Tax Year.

- A corporation electing to be treated as an S corporation by filing Form 2553, Election by a Small Business Corporation, and requesting to change or retain its tax year.

Individuals
Newly married individuals changing to the tax year of the other spouse in order to file a joint return (Regulations section 1.442-1(d) must be followed).

Exempt Organizations
An organization exempt under section 501(a) does not file Form 1128 unless the organization has changed its tax year at any time within a 10-calendar-year period, and the organization has had an annual filing requirement during that 10-year period (see Rev. Proc. 85-58, 1985-2 C.B. 740). This exception does not apply to organizations exempt from tax under section 521, 526, 527, or 528; organizations described in section 401(a); and organizations involved in a group change in tax year for all its subordinate organizations.

Trusts
- A trust (other than a tax-exempt trust, charitable trust, or a grantor trust under Rev. Rul. 90-55, 1990-2 C.B. 161) that adopts the calendar year as required by section 644.
- Certain revocable trusts electing to be treated as part of an estate.
- An employee plan or trust filing Form 5308, Request for Change in Plan/Trust Year, to change its plan or trust year.

When To File

Tax Year Adoption, Change, or Retention
- To request a ruling to adopt, change, or retain a tax year, file Form 1128 by the due date (not including extensions) of the federal income tax return for the first effective year. Do not file earlier than the day following the end of the first effective year. In the case of a change in tax year, the first effective year is the short period required to effect the change.
- To request automatic approval to change a tax year under Rev. Proc.

Cat. No. 61752V

2006-45 (Part II, Section A) or Rev. Proc. 2006-46 (Part II, Section B), file by the due date of the return (including extensions) for the short period required to effect the change. A Form 1128 filed by a controlling domestic shareholder (or its common parent) on behalf of a CFC or 10/50 corporation is due no later than the due date (including extensions) of that shareholder's (or its common parent's) income tax return for its tax year with or within which ends the first effective year of the CFC or 10/50 corporation.

• For an individual filing to change to a calendar year under Rev. Proc. 2003-62, 2003-32 I.R.B. 299 (Part II, Section C), Form 1128 must be filed on or before the due date (including extensions) for filing the federal income tax return for the short period required to effect the change.

• To change a tax year under Rev. Proc. 85-58 (Part II, Section D), file by the 15th day of the 5th calendar month after the end of the short period.

Late Applications

Generally, an application filed after the appropriate due date stated above is considered late.

However, applications filed within 90 days after the due date may be considered as timely filed under Regulations section 301.9100-1 when the applicant establishes that:

1. The taxpayer acted reasonably and in good faith and
2. Granting relief will not prejudice the interests of the government.

Applications that are filed more than 90 days after the due date are presumed to jeopardize the interests of the Government, and will be approved only in unusual and compelling circumstances.

Under either circumstance, an extension request must be filed under Procedure and Administration Regulations section 301.9100-3 and is a ruling request under Rev. Proc. 2007-7, 2007-1 I.R.B. 1 (updated annually), and is subject to public inspection under section 6110. See section 7 of Rev. Proc. 2007-1 for information on requesting a ruling.

Note. An extension request under Rev. Proc. 2007-1 (or its successor) requires payment of a user fee.

Early Applications

Generally, an application to adopt or change a tax year will not be

considered if it is submitted before the end of the short period.

Where To File

Part II—Automatic Approval Request

If Part II (automatic approval request) applies to the applicant, file Form 1128 with the Internal Revenue Service Center, Attention: Entity Control, where the applicant's income tax return is filed. The applicant also must attach a copy of Form 1128 to the federal income tax return filed for the short period required to effect the change.

CFCs and 10/50 corporations. If the form is filed on behalf of a CFC or 10/50 corporation, the controlling domestic shareholder who retains the jointly executed consent described in Temporary Regulations section 1.964-1T(c)(3)(ii) must file Form 1128 with its tax return for its tax year with or within which ends the first effective year of the CFC or the 10/50 corporation. The other controlling domestic shareholder(s) must attach a copy of the form to its income tax return for its tax year with or within which ends the tax year of the CFC or 10/50 corporation.

Note. If a corporation is required to file Form 1128 with its tax return and is a member of an affiliated group of corporations filing a consolidated return, the common parent must file the Form 1128 with the consolidated return.

Applications prior to an election to become an S corporation. If a corporation is requesting to change its tax year prior to making an election to become an S corporation and the requested tax year is a permitted tax year for S corporations (for example, a calendar tax year), file Form 1128 as an attachment to Form 2553 to ensure that the S corporation is permitted the tax year requested on Form 2553. See line 2 of Part II on Form 1128. Do not file Form 1128 with the above address for automatic approval requests. For information on where to file Form 2553, see the Instructions for Form 2553.

 Do not file a request for automatic approval with either address below. Doing so will result in a significant delay in the processing of your request.

Part III—Ruling Request

If Part III (ruling request) applies to the applicant, file Form 1128 and the

appropriate user fee with the IRS National Office. Mail Form 1128 to:

> Internal Revenue Service
> Associate Chief Counsel (Income Tax and Accounting)
> Attention: CC:PA:LPD:DRU
> P.O. Box 7604
> Ben Franklin Station
> Washington, DC 20044-7604

The IRS will acknowledge receipt of the application within 45 days. You can inquire about the status of the application by writing to:

> Control Clerk, CC:ITA
> Internal Revenue Service
> Room 4516
> 1111 Constitution Ave., NW
> Washington, DC 20224-0002

The applicant will receive notification of its approval or denial. If no communication is received from the IRS regarding the application within 90 days, contact the Control Clerk.

Exempt organizations requesting a ruling should send Form 1128 and the application user fee to:

> Internal Revenue Service
> Attention: EO Letter Rulings
> P.O. Box 27720
> McPherson Station
> Washington, DC 20038

You can inquire about the status of an application for exempt organizations by calling 1-877-829-5500.

Who Must Sign

Except as discussed below (regarding automatic approval requests filed on behalf of a CFC or 10/50 corporation), Form 1128 must be signed by the filer as discussed below. A valid signature by the individual or an officer of the organization is required on Form 1128. If the form does not have a valid signature, it will not be considered.

Individuals

If this application is for a husband and wife, enter both names on the line "Name of filer." Both husband and wife must sign the application on the line "Signature and date."

Partnerships

Show the partnership name, followed by the signature of a general partner on behalf of a state law partnership, or a member-manager on behalf of a limited liability company.

-2-

Estates

Show the name of the estate and the signature and title of the fiduciary or other person legally authorized to sign.

Trusts

Show the name of the trust and the signature and title of the fiduciary or other person legally authorized to sign.

Tax-Exempt Organizations

Show the name of the organization and the signature of a principal officer or other person authorized to sign, followed by his or her title.

CFC or 10/50 Corporation

For a CFC or 10/50 corporation with a U.S. trade or business and filing Form 1128 as the applicant, follow the same rules as other corporations (see *All Other Filers* below). If the form is being filed on behalf of a CFC or 10/50 corporation by its controlling domestic shareholder(s), follow the instructions below for ruling requests and automatic approval requests.

Ruling request. A ruling request application that is filed on behalf of a CFC or 10/50 corporation must be signed by an authorized officer of the designated (controlling domestic) shareholder that retains the jointly executed consent as provided for in Temporary Regulations section 1.964-1T(c)(3)(ii). A schedule listing the name(s) and identifying number(s) of the controlling domestic shareholder(s) must be attached to the application. Also, the controlling domestic shareholder(s) must satisfy the requirements of Temporary Regulations section 1.964-1T(c)(3). If the designated (controlling domestic) shareholder is a member of a consolidated group, then an authorized officer of the common parent must sign. Do not sign the copy of Form 1128 filed with the income tax return.

Automatic approval request. An automatic ruling request application that is filed on behalf of a CFC or 10/50 corporation does not have to be signed. However, the controlling domestic shareholder completing the form must satisfy the requirements of Temporary Regulations section 1.964-1T(c)(3) and retain the jointly executed consent described in Temporary Regulations section 1.964-1T(c)(3)(ii).

All Other Filers

The application must show the name of the company and the signature of the president, vice president, treasurer, assistant treasurer, or chief accounting officer (such as tax officer) authorized to sign, and their official title. Receivers, trustees, or assignees must sign any application they are required to file. For a consolidated group filing a consolidated return with its common parent, the form should be signed by an authorized officer of the common parent corporation.

Preparer (Other Than Filer/Applicant)

If the individual preparing Form 1128 is not the filer or applicant, the preparer also must sign. However, in the case of an automatic approval request, the Form 1128 attached to the income tax return does not need to be signed.

Specific Instructions

Part I—General Information

All applicants must complete Part I. Attachments to Form 1128 must show the applicant's name, identifying number, and address. Also indicate that the statement is an attachment to Form 1128.

Name

If the application is filed for a husband and wife who file a joint income tax return, the names of both should appear in the heading.

In general, the filer of the form is the applicant. However, for members of a consolidated group of corporations and certain foreign corporations, Form 1128 may be filed on behalf of the applicant. For a consolidated group of corporations, enter the name and EIN of the parent corporation on the first line as the filer and enter the name(s) and EIN(s) of the member corporations applying for a change in accounting period on the fourth line. For CFCs and 10/50 corporations, enter the name and EIN of the controlling domestic shareholder(s) (common parent, if applicable) on the first line and the name and EIN, if any, of the foreign corporation on the fourth line. If there is more than one filer or applicant, attach a statement listing each filer's or applicant's name and EIN.

Identifying Number

Individuals enter their social security number (SSN). If the application is for a husband and wife who file a joint return, enter both SSNs. However, if one or both are engaged in a trade or business, enter the employer identification number (EIN) instead of the SSNs. All other applicants enter their EIN.

Except as discussed below (regarding foreign corporations), if the applicant does not have an EIN or SSN, it must apply for one. An EIN may be applied for:
• Online—Click on the EIN link at *www.irs.gov/businesses/small*. The EIN is issued immediately once the application information is validated.
• By telephone at 1-800-829-4933 from 7:00 am to 10:00 pm in the corporation's local time zone.
• By mailing or faxing Form SS-4, Application for Employer Identification Number.

A limited liability company must determine which type of federal tax entity it will be (that is, partnership, corporation, or disregarded entity) before applying for an EIN (see Form 8832, Entity Classification Election, for details).

Note. The online application process is not yet available for the following types of entities: Entities with addresses in foreign countries or Puerto Rico, limited liability company (LLC) without entity type, REMICs, state and local governments, Federal government/military entities, and Indian Tribal Government/Enterprise entities. Please call the toll-free Business and Specialty Tax Line at 1-800-829-4933 for assistance in applying for an EIN.

An SSN must be applied for on Form SS-5, Application for a Social Security Card. Form SS-5 can be obtained at SSA offices or by calling the SSA at 1-800-772-1213. It is also available from the SSA website at *www.socialsecurity.gov*.

If the applicant has not received its EIN or SSN by the time the application is due, write "Applied for" in the space for the identifying number. See Pub. 583, Starting a Business and Keeping Records.

Foreign corporations. If the applicant is a foreign corporation that is not otherwise required to have or obtain an EIN, enter "Not applicable" in the space provided for the identifying number.

-3-

¶2504

Address

Include the suite, room, or other unit number after the street address. If the Post Office does not deliver mail to the street address and the filer has a P.O. box, show the box number instead.

If the filer receives its mail in care of a third party (such as an accountant or attorney), enter on the street address line "C/O" followed by the third party's name and street address or P.O. box.

Person To Contact

The person to contact must be the person authorized to sign the Form 1128, or the applicant's authorized representative. If the person to contact is not the filer or the applicant, attach Form 2848, Power of Attorney and Declaration of Representative.

Line 1. Check all applicable boxes to indicate the type of entity filing this application. For example, an entity that is a domestic corporation may also be a regulated investment company (RIC). That entity would check both the "Domestic corporation" box and the "Other" box, and write, "RIC under sec. 851" on the dotted line.

Lines 2a and 2b. If the requested year is a 52-53-week tax year, describe the year (for example, last Saturday in December or Saturday nearest to December 31). A 52-53-week tax year must end on the date a specified day of the week last occurs in a particular month or on the date that day of the week occurs nearest to the last day of a particular calendar month.

A newly formed partnership or PSC that wants to adopt a tax year other than its required tax year must go to Part III after completing Part I.

Line 2c. The required short period return must begin on the day following the close of the old tax year and end on the day before the first day of the new tax year. An applicant's first tax year generally starts when business operations begin.

A corporation's tax year begins at the earliest date it first:
- Has shareholders,
- Has assets, or
- Begins doing business. The initial year ends on the day before the first day of the new tax year.

Part II—Automatic Approval Request

Part II is completed by applicants requesting automatic approval of a change in tax year under:
- Rev. Proc. 2006-45 (corporations),
- Rev. Proc. 2006-46 (pass-through entities),
- Rev. Proc. 2003-62 (individuals),
- Rev. Proc. 76-10, 1976-1 C.B. 548 and Rev. Proc. 85-58 (exempt organizations), and
- Rev. Proc. 85-15, 1985-1 C.B. 516 (all filers), to correct the adoption of an improper tax year to a calendar or fiscal year by (1) filing an amended return on a calendar year basis and attach Form 1128, or (2) file a Form 1128 under the procedures of either Rev. Proc. 2006-45, 2006-46, 2002-39, or its successor.

Note. Applicants requesting an automatic approval must complete Parts I and II only.

 A user fee is not required if requesting an automatic approval under any of the sections of Part II listed below.

Complete Part II if the applicant can use the automatic approval rules under one of the sections listed below and the application is filed on time.

If the applicant is:	Complete only
A corporation (other than an S corporation or a PSC)	Section A
A partnership, S corporation, PSC, or a trust	Section B
An individual	Section C
A tax-exempt organization	Section D

If the applicant does not qualify for automatic approval, a ruling must be requested. See Part III for more information.

If the Service Center denies approval because Form 1128 was not filed on time, the applicant can request relief under Regulations section 301.9100-3, discussed earlier under *Late Applications* on page 2, by completing Part III, as discussed on page 7, and sending Form 1128 to the IRS National Office for consideration.

Section A—Corporations (Other than S Corporations or Personal Service Corporations)

Rev. Proc. 2006-45 provides exclusive procedures for certain corporations to obtain automatic approval to change their annual accounting period under section 442 and Regulations section 1.442-1(b). A corporation complying with all the applicable provisions of this revenue procedure will be deemed to have established a business purpose and obtained the approval of the IRS to change its accounting period. See Rev. Proc. 2006-45 for more information.

Line 1. A corporation is precluded from using the automatic approval rules under section 4 of Rev. Proc. 2006-45 if it:

1. Has changed its annual accounting period at any time within the most recent 48-month period ending with the last month of the requested tax year. For exceptions, see section 4.02(1) of Rev. Proc. 2006-45.

2. Has an interest in a pass-through entity as of the end of the short period. For exceptions, see section 4.02(2) of Rev. Proc. 2006-45.

3. Is a shareholder of a FSC or IC-DISC, as of the end of the short period. For exceptions, see section 4.02(3) of Rev. Proc. 2006-45.

4. Is a FSC or an IC-DISC.

5. Is an S corporation.

6. Attempts to make an S corporation election for the tax year immediately following the short period, unless the change is to a permitted S corporation tax year.

7. Is a PSC.

8. Is a CFC. For exceptions, see section 4.02(8) of Rev. Proc. 2006-45.

9. Is a tax-exempt organization, other than an organization exempt from tax under section 521, 526, 527, or 528.

10. Is a cooperative association (within the meaning of section 1381(a)) with a loss in the short period required to effect the change of annual accounting period, unless the patrons of the cooperative association are substantially the same in the year before the change of annual accounting period, in the short period required to effect the change, and in the year following the change.

-4-

11. Is a corporation leaving a consolidated group. The corporation is precluded from using the automatic approval request procedures during the consolidated group's tax year in which the corporation ceased to be a member of the consolidated group. See Rev. Proc. 2007-64, 2007-42 I.R.B. 818 for details.

12. Has a required tax year (for example, a real estate investment trust), unless the corporation is changing to its required tax year and is not described in items (1) through (11), above.

Note. If the corporation is precluded from using the automatic approval rules because of items (2) or (3), listed above, it can nevertheless automatically change to a natural business year that meets the 25-percent gross receipts test described in section 5.04 of Rev. Proc. 2006-45.

If the answer to question 1 is "Yes," sign Form 1128 and see *Part II—Automatic Approval Request* earlier under *Where To File*. Do not complete Part III. If the corporation is requesting to change to a natural business year that satisfies the 25-percent gross receipts test, also include its gross receipts for the most recent 47 months (or for any predecessor).

If the answer to question 1 is "Yes" because the applicant is a CFC that wants to make a one-month deferral election under section 898(c)(2), see Rev. Proc. 2007-64 which modifies the terms and conditions for this election provided in Rev. Proc. 2006-45. If a CFC wants to revoke its one-month deferral election under section 898(c)(2) and change its tax year to the majority U.S. shareholder year (as defined in section 898(c)(3)), attach a statement providing the names, addresses, and identifying numbers for each U.S. shareholder of the foreign corporation.

If the answer to question 1 is "No," go to Part III after completing Section A.

Line 3. If a corporation's interest in a pass-through entity, CFC, FSC, or IC-DISC (related entity) is disregarded under section 4.02(2) or 4.02(3) of Rev. Proc. 2006-45 because the related entity is required to change its tax year to the corporation's new tax year (or, in the case of a CFC, to a tax year beginning one month earlier than the corporation's new tax year), the related entity must change its tax

year concurrently with the corporation's change in tax year, either under Rev. Proc. 2006-45, 2006-46, or 2002-39. This related party change is required notwithstanding the testing date provisions in section 706(b)(4)(A)(ii), section 898(c)(3)(B), Temporary Regulations section 1.921-1T(b)(6), and the special provision in section 706(b)(4)(B).

Section B—Partnerships, S Corporations, Personal Service Corporations, and Trusts

Rev. Proc. 2006-46 provides exclusive procedures for a partnership, S corporation, PSC, or trust within its scope to adopt, change, or retain its annual accounting period under section 442 and Regulations section 1.442-1(b).

The automatic approval request procedures apply to trusts, with the exception of trusts exempt from taxation under section 501(a), charitable trusts described in section 4947(a)(1), and grantor trusts described in Rev. Rul. 90-55, changing to a calendar year.

The rev. proc. only applies to trusts that are using an incorrect tax year and want to change to the required calendar tax year.

Line 4. A partnership, S corporation, PSC, or trust is precluded from using the automatic approval rules under section 4 of Rev. Proc. 2006-46 if any of the following apply:

1. The entity is under examination, unless it obtains consent of the appropriate director as provided in section 7.03(1) of Rev. Proc. 2006-46.

2. The entity is before an appeals office with respect to any income tax issue and its annual accounting period is an issue under consideration by the appeals office.

3. The entity is before a Federal court with respect to any income tax issue and its annual accounting period is an issue under consideration by the Federal court.

4. On the date the partnership or S corporation would otherwise file its application, the partnership's or S corporation's annual accounting period is an issue under consideration in the examination of a partner's or shareholders's federal income tax return or an issue under consideration by an area office or by a Federal court with respect to a

partner's or shareholder's federal income tax return.

Note. If any of the above circumstances apply, you may still be eligible under the automatic approval request procedures if you comply with the procedures explained following item 5 below. See section 7.03 of Rev. Proc. 2006-46 for more information.

5. The entity is requesting a change to, or retention of, a natural business year as described in section 4.01(2) of Rev. Proc. 2006-46 if the entity has changed its annual accounting period at any time within the most recent 48-month period ending with the last month of the requested tax year. For this purpose, the following changes are not considered prior changes in annual accounting period: (a) a change to a required tax year or ownership tax year; (b) a change from a 52-53 week tax year to a non-52-53 week tax year that ends with reference to the same calendar month, and vice versa; or (c) a change in accounting period by an S corporation or PSC, in order to comply with the common tax year requirements of Regulations sections 1.1502-75(d)(3)(v) and 1.1502-76(a).

If the answer to question 4 is "Yes," and any of the following situations apply, the applicable additional procedures described below must be followed.

• The applicant is under examination and has obtained the consent of the appropriate director to the change or retention of the applicant's annual accounting period. The applicant must attach to the application a statement from the director consenting to the change or retention. The applicant must also provide a copy of the application to the director at the same time it files the application with the Service Center. The application must contain the name(s) and telephone number(s) of the examination agent(s).

• The applicant is before an appeals (area) office and the applicant's annual accounting period is not an issue under consideration by the appeals (area) office. The applicant must attach to the application a separate statement signed by the applicant certifying that, to the best of the applicant's knowledge, the applicant's annual accounting period is not an issue under consideration by the appeals (area) office. The applicant must also provide a copy of the application to the appeals officer

-5-

at the same time it files the application with the Service Center. The application must contain the name and telephone number of the appeals officer.

• The applicant is before a Federal court and the applicant's annual accounting period is not an issue under consideration by the Federal court. The applicant must attach to the application a separate statement signed by the applicant certifying that, to the best of the applicant's knowledge, the applicant's annual accounting period is not an issue under consideration by the Federal court. The applicant must also provide a copy of the application to the government counsel at the same time it files the application with the Service Center. The application must contain the name and telephone number of the government counsel.

If the answer to question 4 is "No" because the applicant (or a partner or shareholder) is under examination and has not obtained the appropriate director's consent to the change or retention of the applicant's annual accounting period or the applicant is before an appeals office or Federal court and the applicant's annual accounting period is an issue under consideration by the appeals office or Federal court, do not complete Part III.

If the answer to question 4 is "No" solely because of a prior change as described in item (5) above, go to Part III after completing Section B.

If the answer to question 4 is "Yes" (and the answer to question 5, 6, or 7 is also "Yes"), sign Form 1128 and see *Part II—Automatic Approval Request* under *Where To File*, above. Do not complete Part III. If the answer to question 4 is "Yes" (and the answer to question 5, 6, or 7 is "No"), go to Part III after completing Section B.

Line 6. A partnership, S corporation, electing S corporation, or PSC establishes a "natural business year" under Rev. Proc. 2006-46 by satisfying the following "25-percent gross receipts test." The applicant must supply its gross receipts for the most recent 47 months (or for any predecessor) to compute the 25 percent gross receipts test.

1. Prior 3 years gross receipts:

a. Gross receipts from sales and services for the most recent 12-month period that ends with the last month of the requested annual accounting period are totaled and then divided

into the amount of gross receipts from sales and services for the last 2 months of this 12-month period.

b. The same computation as in a, above is made for the two preceding 12-month periods ending with the last month of the requested annual accounting period.

2. Natural business year:

a. Except as provided in b, below, if each of the three results described in 1 above equals or exceeds 25 percent, then the requested annual accounting period is deemed to be the taxpayer's natural business year.

b. The taxpayer must determine whether any annual accounting period other than the requested annual accounting period also meets the 25-percent test described in a, above. If one or more other annual accounting periods produce higher averages of the three percentages (rounded to 1/100 of a percent) described in 1 above than the requested annual accounting period, then the requested annual accounting period will not qualify as the taxpayer's natural business year.

3. Special rules:

a. To apply the 25-percent gross receipts test for any particular year, the taxpayer must compute its gross receipts under the method of accounting used to prepare its federal income tax returns for such tax year.

b. If the taxpayer has a predecessor organization and is continuing the same business as its predecessor, the taxpayer must use the gross receipts of its predecessor for purposes of computing the 25-percent gross receipts test.

c. If the taxpayer (including any predecessor organization) does not have a 47-month period of gross receipts (36-month period for the requested tax year plus an additional 11-month period for comparing the requested tax year with other potential tax years), then it cannot establish a natural business year under this revenue procedure.

d. If the requested tax year is a 52-53-week tax year, the calendar month ending nearest to the last day of the 52-53-week tax year is treated as the last month of the requested tax year for purposes of computing the 25-percent gross receipts test.

Line 7. For an S corporation, an "ownership tax year" is the tax year other than a calendar year (if any) that, as of the first day of the first effective year, constitutes the tax year of one or more shareholders

(including any shareholder that concurrently changes to such tax year) holding more than 50 percent of the corporation's issued and outstanding shares of stock. For this purpose, a shareholder that is tax-exempt under section 501(a) is disregarded if such shareholder is not subject to tax on any income attributable to the S corporation. Tax-exempt shareholders are not disregarded, however, if the S corporation is wholly-owned by such tax-exempt entities. A shareholder in an S corporation that wants to concurrently change its tax year must follow the instructions generally applicable to taxpayers changing their tax years contained in Regulations section 1.442-1(b), Rev. Proc. 2002-39, or any other applicable administrative procedure published by the IRS.

Line 8. Answer "Yes" if the partnership is a related entity that must concurrently change its tax year as a term and condition of the approval of the taxpayer's request to change its tax year.

Section C—Individuals

Line 9. If the answer to question 9 is "Yes," and the restrictions of section 4.02 of Rev. Proc. 2003-62 (or its successor) do not apply, sign Form 1128 and see *Part II—Automatic Approval Request* above under *Where To File*. Do not complete Part III. If the answer to question 9 is "No," go to Section A of Part III.

Section D—Tax-Exempt Organizations

A tax-exempt organization can request a change to its tax year under the simplified method of either Rev. Proc. 85-58 or Rev. Proc. 76-10.

Under Rev. Proc. 85-58, an organization exempt under section 501(a) does not have to file Form 1128 unless the following conditions described in section 3.03 of Rev. Proc. 85-58 apply:

1. The organization was required to file an annual information return or Form 990-T, Exempt Organization Business Income Tax Return, at any time during the last 10 calendar years, and

2. The organization has changed its tax year at any time within the last 10 calendar years ending with the calendar year that includes the beginning of the short period resulting from the change of tax year.

-6-

An organization described in section 501(c) or (d) is exempt from tax under section 501(a) unless the exemption is denied under section 502 or 503.

Rev. Proc. 85-58 does not apply to:
• Farmers' cooperatives exempt from federal income tax under section 521,
• Organizations described in sections 526, 527, and 528,
• Organizations described in section 401(a), and
• Organizations requesting a change in a tax year on a group basis.

A central organization should follow Rev. Proc. 76-10 to apply for a group change in tax year for all its subordinate organizations.

Rev. Proc. 76-10 does not apply to:
• Farmers' cooperatives exempt from federal income tax under section 521,
• Certain organizations that have unrelated business taxable income defined in section 512(a), and
• Organizations that are private foundations defined in section 509(a).

Line 10. If the answer to question 10 is "Yes," and the organization is a section 501(a) organization to which section 3.03 of Rev. Proc. 85-58 applies or a central organization to which Rev. Proc. 76-10 applies, sign Form 1128 and see *Part II— Automatic Approval Request* above under *Where To File.* Do not complete Part III. If the answer to question 10 is "Yes," and Rev. Procs. 85-58 and 76-10 do not apply, go to Part III.

Part III—Ruling Request

Part III is completed only by applicants requesting to adopt, change, or retain a tax year that cannot use the automatic procedures listed in Part II.

Also, the applicant must complete the specific section(s) in Part III that applies to that particular applicant.

If the applicant is:	Complete only
A corporation (other than an S corporation, 10/50 corporation, or CFC)	Sections A and B, plus any other applicable section in Part III
An S corporation	Sections A and C
A partnership	Sections A and D
A CFC or 10/50 corporation	Sections A and E

 Do not file a tax return using the requested tax year until this application is approved.

Rev. Proc. 2002-39 provides the general procedures for obtaining approval to adopt, change, or retain a tax year for taxpayers not qualifying under the automatic approval rules or if the application is late.

Section A—General Information

All applicants must complete this section to request a ruling on an adoption of, change to, or retention of a tax year.

Line 1. If the applicant is a partnership, S corporation, personal service corporation, or trust and any of the following situations apply, the applicable additional procedures described below must be followed.
• The applicant is under examination and has obtained the consent of the appropriate director to the change or retention of the applicant's annual accounting period. The applicant must attach to the application a statement from the director consenting to the change or retention of its annual accounting period. The applicant must also provide a copy of the application to the director at the same time it files the application with the IRS National Office. The application must contain the name(s) and telephone number(s) of the examination agent(s).
• The applicant is before an appeals (area) office and the applicant's annual accounting period is not an issue under consideration by the appeals (area) office. The applicant must attach to the application a separate statement signed by the appropriate person certifying that, to the best of that person's knowledge, the entity's annual accounting period is not an issue under consideration by the appeals (area) office. The applicant must also provide a copy of the application to the appeals officer at the same time it files the application with the IRS National Office. The application must contain the name and telephone number of the appeals officer.
• The applicant is before a Federal court and the applicant's annual accounting period is not an issue under consideration by the Federal court. The applicant must attach to the application a separate statement signed by the appropriate person certifying that, to the best of that person's knowledge, the entity's annual accounting period is not an

issue under consideration by the Federal court. The applicant must also provide a copy of the application to the government counsel at the same time it files the application with the IRS National Office. The application must contain the name and telephone number of the government counsel.

Line 4a. Attach an explanation of the legal basis supporting the requested tax year. Include all authority (statutes, regulations, etc.) supporting the requested year. The applicant is encouraged to include all relevant facts and circumstances that may establish a business purpose.

Line 4b. If the applicant requests to establish a natural business year under the annual business cycle test or seasonal business test of sections 5.03(1) and 5.03(2) of Rev. Proc. 2002-39, it must provide its gross receipts from sales or services and approximate inventory costs (where applicable) for each month in the requested short period and for each month of the three immediately preceding tax years.

If the applicant is requesting to change to a natural business year that satisfies the 25-percent gross receipts test described in section 5.03(3) of Rev. Proc. 2002-39, the applicant must supply its gross receipts for the most recent 47 months (or for any predecessor).

Line 14. Applicants filing to request an automatic approval for a change in tax year under Rev. Procs. 2006-45, 2006-46, 2003-62, 85-58, or 76-10 (Part II) are not required to pay a user fee when Form 1128 is filed on time.

Applicants filing to request a letter ruling on a change in tax year under Rev. Proc. 2007-1 and Rev. Proc. 2002-39 must pay a $1,500 user fee. A request for an exempt organization letter ruling on a change in tax year under Rev. Proc. 2007-8, 2007-1 I.R.B. 230, requires payment of a $350 user fee.

 You can find Rev. Proc. 2007-1 and Rev. Proc. 2007-8 on pages 1 and 230, respectively, of Internal Revenue Bulletin 2007-1 at www.irs.gov/pub/ irs-irbs/irb07-01.pdf.

A separate $1,500 user fee is also required for applicants filing a letter ruling request for an extension of time to file under Regulations section 301.9100-3 (including requests under Rev. Procs. 2006-45, 2006-46, and 2003-62 (Part II, Sections A, B, and C)).

-7-

¶2504

Note. The user fees referred to in the above paragraphs are published in Rev. Proc. 2007-1 (exempt organizations, see Rev. Proc. 2007-8), or an annual update. The annual updates are published as revenue procedures in the Internal Revenue Bulletin. The Internal Revenue Bulletins can be accessed at *www.irs.gov/irb*. The fees for 2008 are in Internal Revenue Bulletin 2008-1.

Payment of the user fee (check or money order made payable to the Internal Revenue Service) must be attached to Form 1128 at the time the form is filed. See Rev. Proc. 2007-1 for more information.

Section B—Corporations (Other Than S Corporations and Controlled Foreign Corporations)

Corporations must complete this section and any other section in Part III that applies to that particular entity.

For example, a Passive Foreign Investment Company (PFIC) completes Section B and attaches the statement required by Section H. Complete Sections B and F for a tax-exempt organization that is a corporation.

Note. In addition to excluding CFC's from Section B, 10/50 corporations are also excluded.

Section C—S Corporations

An S corporation must have a permitted tax year unless it has elected under section 444 to have a tax year other than the required tax year. A "permitted tax year" is:

1. A tax year that ends on December 31 or
2. Any other tax year if the corporation can establish a business purpose to the satisfaction of the IRS.

For purposes of 2, above, any deferral of income to shareholders will not be treated as a business

purpose. For more information, see Rev. Proc. 2006-46.

If any shareholder is applying for a corresponding change in tax year, that shareholder must file a separate Form 1128 to get advance approval to change its tax year.

Section D—Partnerships

A partnership must obtain advance approval from the IRS to adopt, change, or retain a tax year unless it is not required to file Form 1128, or it meets one of the automatic approval rules discussed in Part II, Section B on page 5. See *Exceptions* on page 1.

Partners must also get separate advance approval to change their tax years.

Line 23. Enter the first date a business transaction resulted in a tax consequence, such as receiving income or incurring an expense.

Privacy Act and Paperwork Reduction Act Notice. We ask for the information on this form to carry out the Internal Revenue laws of the United States. Section 442 says that you must obtain IRS approval if you want to adopt, change, or retain a tax year. To obtain approval, you are required to file an application to adopt, change, or retain a tax year. Section 6109 requires that you disclose your taxpayer identification number (SSN or EIN). Failure to provide this information in a timely manner could result in approval of your application being delayed or withheld. Providing false information could subject you to penalties.

Our authority to ask for information is sections 6001, 6011, and 6012(a) and their regulations, which require you to file a return or statement with us for any tax for which you are liable. Your response is mandatory under these sections. Section 6109 requires that you provide your SSN or EIN on what you file. This is so we know who you are, and can process your return and other papers. You must fill in all parts of the form that apply to you.

You are not required to provide the information requested on a form that is subject to the Paperwork Reduction Act unless the form displays a valid OMB control number. Books or records relating to a form or its instructions must be retained as long as their contents may become material in the administration of any Internal Revenue law. Generally, tax returns and return information are confidential, as required by section 6103.

However, section 6103 allows or requires the Internal Revenue Service to disclose or give the information shown on your application to others as described in the Code. For example, we may disclose your tax information to the Department of Justice to enforce the tax laws, both civil and criminal, and to cities, states, the District of Columbia, U.S. commonwealths or possessions, and certain foreign governments to carry out their laws. We may also disclose this information to federal and state agencies to enforce federal nontax criminal laws and to combat terrorism.

Keep this notice with your records. It may help you if we ask you for other information. If you have any questions about the rules for filing and giving information, call or visit any Internal Revenue Service office.

The time needed to complete and file this form will vary depending on individual circumstances. The estimated burden for individual taxpayers filing this form is approved under OMB control number 1545-0074 and is included in the estimates shown in the instructions for their individual income tax return. The estimated burden for all other taxpayers who file this form is shown below.

	Recordkeeping	Learning about the law or the form	Preparing and sending the form to the IRS
Parts I and II	8 hr., 36 min.	5 hr., 51 min.	6 hr., 15 min.
Parts I and III	22 hr., 14 min.	5 hr., 37 min.	7 hr., 26 min.

If you have comments concerning the accuracy of these time estimates or suggestions for making this form simpler, we would be happy to hear from you. You can write to the Internal Revenue Service, Tax Products Coordinating Committee, SE:W:CAR:MP:T:T:SP, 1111 Constitution Ave. NW, IR-6526, Washington, DC 20224. Do not send the tax form to this office. Instead, see *Where To File* on page 2.

-8-

¶ 2505 Form 8275, Disclosure Statement

Form **8275**	**Disclosure Statement**	OMB No. 1545-0889
(Rev. August 2008)	Do not use this form to disclose items or positions that are contrary to Treasury regulations. Instead, use Form 8275-R, Regulation Disclosure Statement. See separate instructions.	
Department of the Treasury Internal Revenue Service	▶ Attach to your tax return.	Attachment Sequence No. **92**
Name(s) shown on return		Identifying number shown on return

Part I General Information (see instructions)

	(a) Rev. Rul., Rev. Proc., etc.	(b) Item or Group of Items	(c) Detailed Description of Items	(d) Form or Schedule	(e) Line No.	(f) Amount
1						
2						
3						
4						
5						
6						

Part II Detailed Explanation (see instructions)

1

2

3

4

5

6

Part III Information About Pass-Through Entity. To be completed by partners, shareholders, beneficiaries, or residual interest holders.

Complete this part only if you are making adequate disclosure for a pass-through item.

Note: *A pass-through entity is a partnership, S corporation, estate, trust, regulated investment company (RIC), real estate investment trust (REIT), or real estate mortgage investment conduit (REMIC).*

1 Name, address, and ZIP code of pass-through entity	2 Identifying number of pass-through entity
	3 Tax year of pass-through entity / / to / /
	4 Internal Revenue Service Center where the pass-through entity filed its return

For Paperwork Reduction Act Notice, see separate instructions.	Cat. No. 61935M	Form **8275** (Rev. 8-2008)

Form 8275 (Rev. 8-2008)   Page **2**

Part IV	**Explanations** *(continued from Parts I and/or II)*

Form **8275** (Rev. 8-2008)

¶ 2506   **Instructions for Form 8275**

Instructions for Form 8275

Department of the Treasury
Internal Revenue Service

(Rev. February 2011)

(Use with the August 2008 revision of Form 8275.)

Disclosure Statement

Section references are to the Internal Revenue Code unless otherwise noted.

What's New

An underpayment attributable to a transaction lacking economic substance, as defined under section 7701(o), or failing to meet the requirements of any similar rule of law is subject to a 20% accuracy-related penalty. The penalty increases to 40% if the transaction is not adequately disclosed. See *Accuracy-Related Penalty* on this page.

General Instructions

Purpose of Form

Form 8275 is used by taxpayers and tax return preparers to disclose items or positions, except those taken contrary to a regulation, that are not otherwise adequately disclosed on a tax return to avoid certain penalties. The form is filed to avoid the portions of the accuracy-related penalty due to disregard of rules or to a substantial understatement of income tax for non-tax shelter items if the return position has a reasonable basis. It can also be used for disclosures relating to preparer penalties for understatements due to unreasonable positions or disregard of rules and the economic substance penalty.

 The portion of the accuracy-related penalty attributable to the following types of misconduct cannot be avoided by disclosure on Form 8275.
• *Negligence.*
• *Disregard of regulations.*
• *Any substantial understatement of income tax.*
• *Any substantial valuation misstatement under chapter 1.*
• *Any substantial overstatement of pension liabilities.*
• *Any substantial estate or gift tax valuation understatements.*
• *Any claim of tax benefits from a transaction lacking economic substance (within the meaning of*

section 7701(o)) or failing to meet the requirements of any similar rule of law.
• *Any otherwise undisclosed foreign financial asset understatement.*

Who Should File

Form 8275 is filed by individuals, corporations, pass-through entities, and tax return preparers. If you are disclosing a position taken contrary to a regulation, use Form 8275-R, Regulation Disclosure Statement, instead of Form 8275.

For items attributable to a pass-through entity, disclosure should be made on the tax return of the entity. If the entity does not make the disclosure, the partner (or shareholder, etc.) can make adequate disclosure of these items.

Exception to filing Form 8275. Guidance is published annually in a revenue procedure in the Internal Revenue Bulletin. This can be found on the Internet at IRS.gov. The revenue procedure identifies circumstances when an item reported on a return is considered adequate disclosure for purposes of the substantial understatement aspect of the accuracy-related penalty and for avoiding the preparer's penalty relating to understatements due to unreasonable positions. See the *Example* below. You do not have to file Form 8275 for items that meet the requirements listed in this revenue procedure.

Example. Generally, you will have met the requirements for adequate disclosure of a charitable contribution deduction if you complete the contributions section of Schedule A (Form 1040) and supply all the required information. If you make a contribution of property other than cash that is over $500, the form required by the Schedule A instructions must be attached to your return.

How To File

File Form 8275 with your original tax return. Keep a copy for your records.

You may be able to file Form 8275 with an amended return. See Regulations sections 1.6662-4(f)(1) and 1.6664-2(c)(3) for more information.

To make adequate disclosure for items reported by a pass-through entity, you must complete and file a separate Form 8275 for items reported by each entity.

Carrybacks, carryovers, and recurring items. Carryover items must be disclosed for the tax year in which they originated. You do not have to file another Form 8275 for those items for the tax years in which the carryover is taken into account.

Carryback items must be disclosed for the tax year in which they originated. You do not have to file another Form 8275 for those items for the tax years in which the carryback is taken into account.

However, if you disclose items of a recurring nature (such as depreciation expense), you must file Form 8275 for each tax year in which the item occurs.

If you are disclosing a position that is contrary to a rule, and the position relates to a reportable transaction as defined in Regulations section 1.6011-4(b), you must also make the disclosure as indicated in Regulations section 1.6011-4(d). See Form 8886, Reportable Transaction Disclosure Statement, its instructions, Notice 2006-6, 2006-5 I.R.B. 385, available at *http://www.irs.gov/irb/2006-05_IRB/ar10.html*, and Notice 2010-62, 2010-40 I.R.B. 411, available at *www.irs.gov/irb/2010-40_IRB/ar09.html*.

Accuracy-Related Penalty

Generally, the accuracy-related penalty is 20% of any portion of a tax underpayment attributable to:

   1. Negligence or disregard of rules or regulations,
   2. Any substantial understatement of income tax,

Cat. No. 62063F

¶2506

3. Any substantial valuation misstatement under chapter 1 of the Internal Revenue Code,

4. Any substantial overstatement of pension liabilities,

5. Any substantial estate or gift tax valuation understatement, or

6. Any claim of tax benefits from a transaction lacking economic substance, as defined by section 7701(o), or failing to meet the requirements of any similar rule of law.

The penalty is 40% of any portion of a tax underpayment attributable to one or more gross valuation misstatements in (3), (4), or (5) above if the applicable dollar limitation under section 6662(h)(2) is met. The penalty also increases to 40% for failing to adequately disclose a transaction that lacks economic substance in (6) above. See *Economic Substance* on this page. The penalty is 40% of any portion of an underpayment that is attributable to any undisclosed foreign financial asset understatement.

Reasonable basis. Generally, you can avoid the disregard of rules and substantial understatement portions of the accuracy-related penalty if the position is adequately disclosed and the position has at least a reasonable basis. Reasonable basis is a relatively high standard of tax reporting that is significantly higher than not frivolous or not patently improper. The reasonable basis standard is not satisfied by a return position that is merely arguable.

The penalty will not be imposed on any part of an underpayment if there was reasonable cause for your position and you acted in good faith in taking that position.

 The reasonable cause and good faith exception does not apply to any portion of an underpayment attributable to a transaction that lacks economic substance under section 7701(o).

If you failed to keep proper books and records or failed to substantiate items properly, you cannot avoid the penalty by disclosure.

Substantial Understatement

An understatement is the excess of:

1. The amount of tax required to be shown on the return for the tax year, over

2. The amount of tax shown on the return for the tax year, reduced by any rebates.

There is a substantial understatement of income tax if the amount of the understatement for any tax year exceeds the greater of:

1. 10% of the tax required to be shown on the return for the tax year, or

2. $5,000.

An understatement of a corporation (other than an S corporation or a personal holding company, as defined in section 542) is substantial if it exceeds in any year the lesser of:

1. 10% of the tax required to be shown on the return for the tax year (or, if greater, $10,000), or

2. $10,000,000.

For purposes of the substantial understatement portion of the accuracy-related penalty, the amount of the understatement will be reduced by the part that is attributable to the following items.

• An item (other than a tax shelter item) for which there was substantial authority for the treatment claimed at the time the return was filed or on the last day of the tax year to which the return relates.

• An item (other than a tax shelter item) that is adequately disclosed on this form if there is a reasonable basis for the tax treatment of the item. (In no event will a corporation be treated as having a reasonable basis for its tax treatment of an item attributable to a multi-party financing transaction entered into after August 5, 1997, if the treatment does not clearly reflect the income of the corporation.)

For corporate tax shelter transactions (and for tax shelter items of other taxpayers for tax years ending after October 22, 2004), the only exception to the substantial understatement portion of the accuracy-related penalty is the reasonable cause exception. For more details, see section 6662(d) and Regulations section 1.6664-4.

Tax shelter items. A tax shelter, for purposes of the substantial understatement portion of the accuracy-related penalty, is a partnership or other entity, plan, or arrangement, with a significant purpose to avoid or evade federal income tax. For transactions on or before August 5, 1997, a tax shelter is a partnership or other entity, plan, or arrangement, whose principal purpose is to avoid or evade federal income tax.

A tax shelter item is any item of income, gain, loss, deduction, or credit that is directly or indirectly attributable to the principal or significant purpose of the tax shelter to avoid or evade federal income tax.

Economic substance. To satisfy the disclosure requirements under section 6662(i), you may adequately disclose with a timely filed original return (determined with regard to extensions) or a qualified amended return (as defined under Regulations section 1.6664-2(c)(3)) the relevant facts affecting the tax treatment of the transaction.

Note. If you filed a Schedule UTP, you may not need to file Form 8275 to satisfy the disclosure requirements of section 6662(i). See the Instructions for Schedule UTP.

Tax Return Preparer Penalties

A preparer who files a return or claim for refund is subject to a penalty in an amount equal to the greater of $1,000 or 50 percent of the income derived (or to be derived) by the tax return preparer, with respect to the return or claim, for taking a position which the preparer knew or reasonably should have known would understate any part of the liability if:

• There is or was no substantial authority for the position.

• The position is a tax shelter (as defined in section 6662(d)(2)(C)(ii)) or a reportable transaction to which section 6662A applies and it was not reasonable to believe that the position would more likely than not be sustained on its merits.

• The position was disclosed as provided in section 6662(d)(2)(B)(ii), is not a tax shelter or a reportable transaction to which section 6662A applies, and there was no reasonable basis for the position.

The penalty will not apply if it can be shown that there was reasonable cause for the understatement and that the preparer acted in good faith.

In cases where any part of the understatement of the liability is due to a willful attempt by the return preparer to understate the liability, or if the understatement is due to reckless or intentional disregard of rules or regulations by the preparer, the preparer is subject to a penalty equal to the greater of $5,000 or 50 percent of the income derived (or to be derived) by the tax return preparer with respect to the return or claim. This penalty shall be reduced by the

-2-

amount of the penalty paid by such person for taking an unreasonable position, or a position with no reasonable basis, as described immediately above.

A preparer is not considered to have recklessly or intentionally disregarded a rule if a position is adequately disclosed and has a reasonable basis.

Note. For more information about the accuracy-related penalty and preparer penalties, and the means of avoiding these penalties, see the regulations under sections 6662, 6664, and 6694.

Specific Instructions

Be sure to supply all the information for Parts I, II, and, if applicable, Part III. Your disclosure will be considered adequate if you file Form 8275 and supply the information requested in detail.

Use Part IV on page 2 if you need more space for Part I or II. Indicate the corresponding part and line number from page 1. You can use a continuation sheet(s) if you need additional space. Be sure to put your name and identifying number on each sheet.

Part I

Column (a). If you are disclosing a position contrary to a rule (such as a statutory provision or IRS revenue ruling), you must identify the rule in column (a).

Column (b). Identify the item by name.

If any item you disclose is from a pass-through entity, you must identify the item as such. If you disclose items from more than one pass-through entity, you must complete a separate Form 8275 for each entity. Also, see *How To File* on page 1.

Column (c). Enter a complete description of the item(s) you are disclosing.

Example. If entertainment expenses were reported in column (b), then list in column (c) "theater tickets, catering expenses, and banquet hall rentals."

If you claim the same tax treatment for a group of similar items in the same tax year, enter a description identifying the group of items you are disclosing rather than a separate description of each item within the group.

Columns (d) through (f). Enter the location of the item(s) by identifying the form number or schedule and the line number in columns (d) and (e) and the amount of the item(s) in column (f).

Part II

Your disclosure statement must include a description of the relevant facts affecting the tax treatment of the item. To satisfy this requirement you must include information that reasonably can be expected to apprise the IRS of the identity of the item, its amount, and the nature of the controversy or potential controversy. Information concerning the nature of the controversy can include a description of the legal issues presented by the facts.

⚠ **CAUTION** *Unless provided otherwise in the General Instructions above, your disclosure will not be considered accurate unless the information described above is provided using Form 8275. For example, your disclosure will not be considered adequate if you attach a copy of an acquisition agreement to your tax return to disclose the issues involved in determining the basis of certain acquired assets. If Form 8275 is not completed and attached to the return, the disclosure will not be considered valid even if the information described above is provided using another method, such as a different form or an attached letter.*

Part III

Line 4. Contact your pass-through entity if you do not know where its return was filed. However, for partners and S corporation shareholders, information for line 4 can be found on the Schedule K-1 that you received from the partnership or S corporation.

If the pass-through entity filed its return electronically using *e-file*, enter "e-file" on line 4.

Paperwork Reduction Act Notice. We ask for the information on this form to carry out the Internal Revenue laws of the United States. You are required to give us the information if you wish to use this form to make adequate disclosure to avoid the portion of the accuracy-related penalty due to a substantial understatement of income tax or disregard of rules, or to avoid certain preparer penalties. We need it to ensure that you are complying with these laws and to allow us to figure and collect the right amount of tax.

You are not required to provide the information requested on a form that is subject to the Paperwork Reduction Act unless the form displays a valid OMB control number. Books or records relating to a form or its instructions must be retained as long as their contents may become material in the administration of any Internal Revenue law. Generally, tax returns and return information are confidential, as required by section 6103.

The time needed to complete and file this form will vary depending on individual circumstances. The estimated burden for individual taxpayers filing this form is approved under OMB control number 1545-0074 and is included in the estimates shown in the instructions for their individual income tax return. The estimated burden for all other taxpayers who file this form is shown below.

Recordkeeping . . . . 3 hr., 35 min.
**Learning about the law
or the form** . . . . 1 hr.

**Preparing and sending
the form to the IRS** . . . 1 hr., 6 min.

If you have comments concerning the accuracy of these time estimates or suggestions for making this form simpler, we would be happy to hear from you. See the instructions for the tax return with which this form is filed.

¶ 2507   Form 8832, Entity Classification Election

Form **8832** (Rev. January 2012) Department of the Treasury Internal Revenue Service	**Entity Classification Election**	OMB No. 1545-1516

Type or Print	Name of eligible entity making election	Employer identification number
	Number, street, and room or suite no. If a P.O. box, see instructions.	
	City or town, state, and ZIP code. If a foreign address, enter city, province or state, postal code and country. Follow the country's practice for entering the postal code.	

▶ Check if: ☐ Address change   ☐ Late classification relief sought under Revenue Procedure 2009-41
          ☐ Relief for a late change of entity classification election sought under Revenue Procedure 2010-32

Part I	**Election Information**

1   Type of election (see instructions):

a ☐ Initial classification by a newly-formed entity. Skip lines 2a and 2b and go to line 3.
b ☐ Change in current classification. Go to line 2a.

2a Has the eligible entity previously filed an entity election that had an effective date within the last 60 months?

  ☐ **Yes.** Go to line 2b.
  ☐ **No.** Skip line 2b and go to line 3.

2b Was the eligible entity's prior election an initial classification election by a newly formed entity that was effective on the date of formation?

  ☐ **Yes.** Go to line 3.
  ☐ **No.** Stop here. You generally are not currently eligible to make the election (see instructions).

3 Does the eligible entity have more than one owner?

  ☐ **Yes.** You can elect to be classified as a partnership or an association taxable as a corporation. Skip line 4 and go to line 5.
  ☐ **No.** You can elect to be classified as an association taxable as a corporation or to be disregarded as a separate entity. Go to line 4.

4 If the eligible entity has only one owner, provide the following information:

a Name of owner ▶ ....
b Identifying number of owner ▶ ....

5 If the eligible entity is owned by one or more affiliated corporations that file a consolidated return, provide the name and employer identification number of the parent corporation:

a Name of parent corporation ▶ ....
b Employer identification number ▶ ....

For Paperwork Reduction Act Notice, see instructions.   Cat. No. 22598R   Form **8832** (Rev. 1-2012)

Form 8832 (Rev. 1-2012)   Page **2**

| **Part I** | **Election Information** (Continued) |

6 **Type of entity** (see instructions):

a ☐ A domestic eligible entity electing to be classified as an association taxable as a corporation.

b ☐ A domestic eligible entity electing to be classified as a partnership.

c ☐ A domestic eligible entity with a single owner electing to be disregarded as a separate entity.

d ☐ A foreign eligible entity electing to be classified as an association taxable as a corporation.

e ☐ A foreign eligible entity electing to be classified as a partnership.

f ☐ A foreign eligible entity with a single owner electing to be disregarded as a separate entity.

7 If the eligible entity is created or organized in a foreign jurisdiction, provide the foreign country of
organization ▶ --

8 Election is to be effective beginning (month, day, year) (see instructions) . . . . ▶ _____

| **9** Name and title of contact person whom the IRS may call for more information | **10** Contact person's telephone number |

Consent Statement and Signature(s) (see instructions)

Under penalties of perjury, I (we) declare that I (we) consent to the election of the above-named entity to be classified as indicated above, and that I (we) have examined this election and consent statement, and to the best of my (our) knowledge and belief, this election and consent statement are true, correct, and complete. If I am an officer, manager, or member signing for the entity, I further declare under penalties of perjury that I am authorized to make the election on its behalf.

Signature(s)	Date	Title

Form **8832** (Rev. 1-2012)

Part II   Late Election Relief

11   Provide the explanation as to why the entity classification election was not filed on time (see instructions).

Under penalties of perjury, I (we) declare that I (we) have examined this election, including accompanying documents, and, to the best of my (our) knowledge and belief, the election contains all the relevant facts relating to the election, and such facts are true, correct, and complete. I (we) further declare that I (we) have personal knowledge of the facts and circumstances related to the election. I (we) further declare that the elements required for relief in Section 4.01 of Revenue Procedure 2009-41 have been satisfied.

Signature(s)	Date	Title

Form **8832** (Rev. 1-2012)

¶ 2508   Instructions for Form 8832

General Instructions

Section references are to the Internal Revenue Code unless otherwise noted.

What Is New:

A checkbox was added for explanatory language of the Rev. Proc. 2010-32, foreign entities that meet the requirements of Rev. Proc. 2010-32, 2010-36 I.R.B. 320.

The IRS has created a page on IRS.gov for information about Form 8832 and its instructions at *www.irs.gov/form8832*. Information about any future developments affecting Form 8832 (such as legislation enacted after we release it) will be posted on that page.

Purpose of Form

An eligible entity uses Form 8832 to elect how it will be classified for federal tax purposes, as a corporation, a partnership, or an entity disregarded as separate from its owner. An eligible entity is classified for federal tax purposes under the default rules described below unless it files Form 8832 or Form 2553, Election by a Small Business Corporation, to elect a classification or change its current classification. See *Who Must File* below.

The IRS will use the information entered on this form to establish the entity's filing and reporting requirements for federal tax purposes.

 A new eligible entity should not file Form 8832 if it will be using its default classification (see Default Rules below).

Eligible entity. An eligible entity is a business entity that is not included in items 1, or 3 through 9, under the definition of **corporation** provided under *Definitions.* Eligible entities include limited liability companies (LLCs) and partnerships.

Generally, corporations are not eligible entities. However, the following types of corporations are treated as eligible entities:

1. An eligible entity that previously elected to be an association taxable as a corporation by filing Form 8832. An entity that elects to be classified as a corporation by filing Form 8832 can make another election to change its classification (see the *60-month limitation rule* discussed below in the instructions for lines 2a and 2b).

2. A foreign eligible entity that became an association taxable as a corporation under the foreign default rule described below.

Default Rules

Existing entity default rule. Certain domestic and foreign entities that were in existence before January 1, 1997, and have an established federal tax classification generally do not need to make an election to continue that classification. If an existing entity decides to change its classification, it may do so subject to the 60-month limitation rule. See the instructions for lines 2a and 2b. See Regulations sections 301.7701-3(b)(3) and 301.7701-3(h)(2) for more details.

Domestic default rule. Unless an election is made on Form 8832, a domestic eligible entity is:

1. A partnership if it has two or more members.

2. Disregarded as an entity separate from its owner if it has a single owner.

A change in the number of members of an eligible entity classified as an **association** (defined below) does not affect the entity's classification. However, an eligible entity classified as a partnership will become a disregarded entity when the entity's membership is reduced to one member and a disregarded entity will be classified as a partnership when the entity has more than one member.

Foreign default rule. Unless an election is made on Form 8832, a foreign eligible entity is:

1. A partnership if it has two or more members and at least one member does not have limited liability.

2. An association taxable as a corporation if all members have limited liability.

3. Disregarded as an entity separate from its owner if it has a single owner that does not have limited liability.

However, if a qualified foreign entity (as defined in section 3.02 of Rev. Proc. 2010-32) files a valid election to be classified as a partnership based on the reasonable assumption that it had two or more owners as of the effective date of the election, and the qualified entity is later determined to have a single owner, the IRS will deem the election to be an election to be classified as a disregarded entity provided:

1. The qualified entity's owner and purported owners file amended returns that are consistent with the treatment of the entity as a disregarded entity;

2. The amended returns are filed before the close of the period of limitations on assessments under section 6501(a) for the relevant tax year; and

3. The corrected Form 8832 is filed and attached to the amended tax return. Corrected Form 8832 must include across the top the statement "FILED PURSUANT TO REVENUE PROCEDURE 2010-32;"

Also, if the qualified foreign entity (as defined in section 3.02 of Rev. Proc. 2010-32) files a valid election to be classified as a disregarded entity based on the reasonable assumption that it had a single owner as of the effective date of the election, and the qualified entity is later determined to have two or more owners, the IRS will deem the election to be an election to be classified as a partnership provided:

1. The qualified entity files information returns and the actual owners file original or amended returns consistent with the treatment of the entity as a partnership;

2. The amended returns are filed before the close of the period of limitations on assessments under section 6501(a) for the relevant tax year; and

3. The corrected Form 8832 is filed and attached to the amended tax returns. Corrected Form 8832 must include across the top the statement "FILED PURSUANT TO REVENUE PROCEDURE 2010-32"; see Rev. Proc. 2010-32, 2010-36 I.R.B. 320 for details.

Definitions

Association. For purposes of this form, an association is an eligible entity taxable as a corporation by election or, for foreign eligible entities, under the default rules (see Regulations section 301.7701-3).

Business entity. A business entity is any entity recognized for federal tax purposes that is not properly classified as a trust under Regulations section 301.7701-4 or otherwise subject to special treatment under the Code regarding the entity's classification. See Regulations section 301.7701-2(a).

Corporation. For federal tax purposes, a corporation is any of the following:

1. A business entity organized under a federal or state statute, or under a statute of a federally recognized Indian tribe, if the statute describes or refers to the entity as incorporated or as a corporation, body corporate, or body politic.

2. An association (as determined under Regulations section 301.7701-3).

3. A business entity organized under a state statute, if the statute describes or refers to the entity as a joint-stock company or joint-stock association.

4. An insurance company.

5. A state-chartered business entity conducting banking activities, if any of its deposits are insured under the Federal Deposit Insurance Act, as amended, 12 U.S. C. 1811 et seq., or a similar federal statute.

6. A business entity wholly owned by a state or any political subdivision thereof, or a business entity wholly owned by a foreign government or any other entity described in Regulations section 1.892-2T.

7. A business entity that is taxable as a corporation under a provision of the Code other than section 7701(a)(3).

8. A foreign business entity listed on page 7. See Regulations section 301.7701-2(b)(8) for any exceptions and inclusions to items on this list and for any revisions made to this list since these instructions were printed.

9. An entity created or organized under the laws of more than one jurisdiction (business entities with multiple charters) if the entity is treated as a corporation with respect to any one of the jurisdictions. See Regulations section 301.7701-2(b)(9) for examples.

Disregarded entity. A disregarded entity is an eligible entity that is treated as an entity not separate from its single owner for income tax purposes. A "disregarded entity" is treated as separate from its owner for:

• Employment tax purposes, effective for wages paid on or after January 1, 2009; and

• Excise taxes reported on Forms 720, 730, 2290, 11-C, or 8849, effective for excise taxes reported and paid after December 31, 2007.

See the employment tax and excise tax return instructions for more information.

Limited liability. A member of a foreign eligible entity has limited liability if the member has no personal liability for any debts of or claims against the entity by reason of being a member. This determination is based solely on the statute or law under which the entity is organized (and, if relevant, the entity's organizational documents). A member has personal liability if the creditors of the entity may seek satisfaction of all or any part of the debts or claims against the entity from the member as such. A member has personal liability even if the member makes an agreement under which another person (whether or not a member of the entity) assumes that liability or agrees to indemnify that member for that liability.

Partnership. A partnership is a business entity that has at least two members and is not a corporation as defined above under *Corporation.*

Who Must File

File this form for an eligible entity that is one of the following:

• A domestic entity electing to be classified as an association taxable as a corporation.

• A domestic entity electing to change its current classification (even if it is currently classified under the default rule).

• A foreign entity that has more than one owner, all owners having limited liability, electing to be classified as a partnership.

• A foreign entity that has at least one owner that does not have limited liability, electing to be classified as an association taxable as a corporation.

• A foreign entity with a single owner having limited liability, electing to be an entity disregarded as an entity separate from its owner.

• A foreign entity electing to change its current classification (even if it is currently classified under the default rule).

Do not file this form for an eligible entity that is:

• Tax-exempt under section 501(a);

• A real estate investment trust (REIT), as defined in section 856; or

• Electing to be classified as an S corporation. An eligible entity that timely files Form 2553 to elect classification as an S corporation and meets all other requirements to qualify as an S corporation is deemed to have made an election under Regulations section 301.7701-3(c)(v) to be classified as an association taxable as a corporation.

All three of these entities are deemed to have made an election to be classified as an association.

Effect of Election

The federal tax treatment of elective changes in classification as described in Regulations section 301.7701-3(g)(1) is summarized as follows:

• If an eligible entity classified as a partnership elects to be classified as an association, it is deemed that the partnership contributes all of its assets and liabilities to the association in exchange for stock in the association, and immediately thereafter, the partnership liquidates by distributing the stock of the association to its partners.

• If an eligible entity classified as an association elects to be classified as a partnership, it is deemed that the association distributes all of its assets and liabilities to its shareholders in liquidation of the association, and immediately thereafter, the shareholders contribute all of the distributed assets and liabilities to a newly formed partnership.

• If an eligible entity classified as an association elects to be disregarded as an entity separate from its owner, it is deemed that the association distributes all of its assets and liabilities to its single owner in liquidation of the association.

• If an eligible entity that is disregarded as an entity separate from its owner elects to be classified as an association, the owner of the eligible entity is deemed to have contributed all of the assets and liabilities of the entity to the association in exchange for the stock of the association.

Note. For information on the federal tax consequences of elective changes in classification, see Regulations section 301.7701-3(g).

When To File

Generally, an election specifying an eligible entity's classification cannot take effect more than 75 days prior to the date the election is filed, nor can it take effect later than 12 months after the date the election is filed. An eligible entity may be eligible for late election relief in certain circumstances. For more information, see *Late Election Relief,* later.

Where To File

File Form 8832 with the Internal Revenue Service Center for your state listed below.

In addition, attach a copy of Form 8832 to the entity's federal tax or information return for the tax year of the election. If the entity is not required to file a return for that year, a copy of its Form 8832 must be attached to the federal tax returns of all direct or indirect owners of the entity for the tax year of the owner that includes the date on which the election took effect. An indirect owner of the electing entity does not have to attach a copy of the Form 8832 to its tax return if an entity in which it has an interest is already filing a copy of the Form 8832 with its return. Failure to attach a copy of Form 8832 will not invalidate an otherwise valid election, but penalties may be assessed against persons who are required to, but do not, attach Form 8832.

Each member of the entity is required to file the member's return consistent with the entity election. Penalties apply to returns filed inconsistent with the entity's election.

If the entity's principal business, office, or agency is located in:	Use the following Internal Revenue Service Center address:
Connecticut, Delaware, District of Columbia, Illinois, Indiana, Kentucky, Maine, Maryland, Massachusetts, Michigan, New Hampshire, New Jersey, New York, North Carolina, Ohio, Pennsylvania, Rhode Island, South Carolina, Vermont, Virginia, West Virginia, Wisconsin	Cincinnati, OH 45999

If the entity's principal business, office, or agency is located in:	Use the following Internal Revenue Service Center address:
Alabama, Alaska, Arizona, Arkansas, California, Colorado, Florida, Georgia, Hawaii, Idaho, Iowa, Kansas, Louisiana, Minnesota, Mississippi, Missouri, Montana, Nebraska, Nevada, New Mexico, North Dakota, Oklahoma, Oregon, South Dakota, Tennessee, Texas, Utah, Washington, Wyoming	Ogden, UT 84201
A foreign country or U.S. possession	Ogden, UT 84201-0023

Note. Also attach a copy to the entity's federal income tax return for the tax year of the election.

Acceptance or Nonacceptance of Election

The service center will notify the eligible entity at the address listed on Form 8832 if its election is accepted or not accepted. The entity should generally receive a determination on its election within 60 days after it has filed Form 8832.

Care should be exercised to ensure that the IRS receives the election. If the entity is not notified of acceptance or nonacceptance of its election within 60 days of the date of filing, take follow-up action by calling 1-800-829-0115, or by sending a letter to the service center to inquire about its status. Send any such letter by certified or registered mail via the U.S. Postal Service, or equivalent type of delivery by a designated private delivery service (see Notice 2004-83, 2004-52 I.R.B. 1030 (or its successor)).

If the IRS questions whether Form 8832 was filed, an acceptable proof of filing is:

• A certified or registered mail receipt (timely postmarked) from the U.S. Postal Service, or its equivalent from a designated private delivery service;

• Form 8832 with an accepted stamp;

• Form 8832 with a stamped IRS received date; or

• An IRS letter stating that Form 8832 has been accepted.

Specific Instructions

Name. Enter the name of the eligible entity electing to be classified.

Employer identification number (EIN). Show the EIN of the eligible entity electing to be classified.

 Do not put "Applied For" on this line.

Note. Any entity that has an EIN will retain that EIN even if its federal tax classification changes under Regulations section 301.7701-3.

If a disregarded entity's classification changes so that it becomes recognized as a partnership or association for federal tax purposes, and that entity had an EIN, then the entity must continue to use that EIN. If the entity did not already have its own EIN, then the entity must apply for an EIN and not use the identifying number of the single owner.

A foreign entity that makes an election under Regulations section 301.7701-3(c) and (d) must also use its own taxpayer identifying number. See sections 6721 through 6724 for penalties that may apply for failure to supply taxpayer identifying numbers.

If the entity electing to be classified using Form 8832 does not have an EIN, it must apply for one on Form SS-4, Application for Employer Identification Number. The entity must have received an EIN by the time Form 8832 is filed in order for the form to be processed. An election will not be accepted if the eligible entity does not provide an EIN.

 Do not apply for a new EIN for an existing entity that is changing its classification if the entity already has an EIN.

Address. Enter the address of the entity electing a classification. All correspondence regarding the acceptance or nonacceptance of the election will be sent to this address. Include the suite, room, or other unit number after the street address. If the Post Office does not deliver mail to the street address and the entity has a P.O. box, show the box number instead of the street address. If the electing entity receives its mail in care of a third party (such as an accountant or an attorney), enter on the street address line "C/O" followed by the third party's name and street address or P.O. box.

Address change. If the eligible entity has changed its address since filing Form SS-4 or the entity's most recently-filed return (including a change to an "in care of" address), check the box for an address change.

Late-classification relief sought under Revenue Procedure 2009-41. Check the box if the entity is seeking relief under Rev. Proc. 2009-41, 2009-39 I.R.B. 439, for a late classification election. For more information, see *Late Election Relief,* later.

Relief for a late change of entity classification election sought under Revenue Procedure 2010-32. Check the box if the entity is seeking relief under Rev. Proc. 2010-32, 2010-36 I.R.B. 320. For more information, see *Foreign default rule,* earlier.

Part I. Election Information

Complete Part I whether or not the entity is seeking relief under Rev. Proc. 2009-41 or Rev. Proc. 2010-32.

Line 1. Check box 1a if the entity is choosing a classification for the first time (i.e., the entity does not want to be classified under the applicable default classification). Do not file this form if the entity wants to be classified under the default rules.

Check box 1b if the entity is changing its current classification.

Lines 2a and 2b. 60-month limitation rule. Once an eligible entity makes an election to *change* its classification, the entity generally cannot change its classification by election again during the 60 months after the effective date of the election. However, the IRS may (by private letter ruling) permit the entity to change its classification by election within the 60-month period if more than 50% of the ownership interests in the entity, as of the effective date of the election, are owned by persons that did not own any interests in the entity on the effective date or the filing date of the entity's prior election.

Note. The 60-month limitation does not apply if the previous election was made by a newly formed eligible entity and was effective on the date of formation.

Line 4. If an eligible entity has only one owner, provide the name of its owner on line 4a and the owner's identifying number (social security number, or individual taxpayer identification number, or EIN) on line 4b. If the electing eligible entity is owned by an entity that is a disregarded entity or by an entity that is a member of a series of tiered disregarded entities, identify the first entity (the entity closest to the electing eligible entity) that is not a disregarded entity. For example, if the electing eligible entity is owned by disregarded entity A, which is owned by another disregarded entity B, and disregarded entity B is owned by partnership C, provide the name and EIN of partnership C as the owner of the electing eligible entity. If the owner is a foreign person or entity and does not have a U.S. identifying number, enter "none" on line 4b.

Line 5. If the eligible entity is owned by one or more members of an affiliated group of corporations that file a consolidated return, provide the name and EIN of the parent corporation.

Line 6. Check the appropriate box if you are changing a current classification (no matter how achieved), or are electing out of a default classification. Do not file this form if you fall within a default classification that is the desired classification for the new entity.

Line 7. If the entity making the election is created or organized in a foreign jurisdiction, enter the name of the foreign country in which it is organized. This information must be provided even if the entity is also organized under domestic law.

Line 8. Generally, the election will take effect on the date you enter on line 8 of this form, or on the date filed if no date is entered on line 8. An election specifying an entity's classification for federal tax purposes can take effect no more than 75 days prior to the date the election is filed, nor can it take effect later than 12 months after the date on which the election is filed. If line 8 shows a date more than 75 days prior to the date on which the election is filed, the election will default to 75 days before the date it is filed. If line 8 shows an effective date more than 12 months from the filing date, the election will take effect 12 months after the date the election is filed.

Consent statement and signature(s). Form 8832 must be signed by:

1. Each member of the electing entity who is an owner at the time the election is filed; or

2. Any officer, manager, or member of the electing entity who is authorized (under local law or the organizational documents) to make the election. The elector represents to having such authorization under penalties of perjury.

If an election is to be effective for any period prior to the time it is filed, each person who was an owner between the date the election is to be effective and the date the election is filed, and who is not an owner at the time the election is filed, must sign.

If you need a continuation sheet or use a separate consent statement, attach it to Form 8832. The separate consent statement must contain the same information as shown on Form 8832.

Note. Do not sign the copy that is attached to your tax return.

Part II. Late Election Relief

Complete Part II only if the entity is requesting late election relief under Rev. Proc. 2009-41.

An eligible entity may be eligible for late election relief under Rev. Proc. 2009-41, 2009-39 I.R.B. 439, if **each** of the following requirements is met.

1. The entity failed to obtain its requested classification as of the date of its formation (or upon the entity's classification becoming relevant) or failed to obtain its requested change in classification solely because Form 8832 was not filed timely.

2. Either:

a. The entity has not filed a federal tax or information return for the first year in which the election was intended because the due date has not passed for that year's federal tax or information return; or

b. The entity has timely filed all required federal tax returns and information returns (or if not timely, within 6 months after its due date, excluding extensions) consistent with its requested classification for all of the years the entity intended the requested election to be effective and no inconsistent tax or information returns have been filed by or with respect to the entity during any of the tax years. If the eligible entity is not required to file a federal tax return or information return, each affected person who is required to file a federal tax return or information return must have timely filed all such returns (or if not

Form 8832 (Rev. 1-2012)

timely, within 6 months after its due date, excluding extensions) consistent with the entity's requested classification for all of the years the entity intended the requested election to be effective and no inconsistent tax or information returns have been filed during any of the tax years.

3. The entity has reasonable cause for its failure to timely make the entity classification election.

4. Three years and 75 days from the requested effective date of the eligible entity's classification election have not passed.

Affected person. An affected person is either:

• with respect to the effective date of the eligible entity's classification election, a person who would have been required to attach a copy of the Form 8832 for the eligible entity to its federal tax or information return for the tax year of the person which includes that date; or

• with respect to any subsequent date after the entity's requested effective date of the classification election, a person who would have been required to attach a copy of the Form 8832 for the eligible entity to its federal tax or information return for the person's tax year that includes that subsequent date had the election first become effective on that subsequent date.

For details on the requirement to attach a copy of Form 8832, see Rev. Proc. 2009-41 and the instructions under *Where To File.*

To obtain relief, file Form 8832 with the applicable IRS service center listed in *Where To File,* earlier, within 3 years and 75 days from the requested effective date of the eligible entity's classification election.

If Rev. Proc. 2009-41 does not apply, an entity may seek relief for a late entity election by requesting a private letter ruling and paying a user fee in accordance with Rev. Proc. 2011-1, 2011-1 I.R.B. 1 (or its successor).

Line 11. Explain the reason for the failure to file a timely entity classification election.

Signatures. Part II of Form 8832 must be signed by an authorized representative of the eligible entity and each affected person. See *Affected Persons,* earlier. The individual or individuals who sign the declaration must have personal knowledge of the facts and circumstances related to the election.

Foreign Entities Classified as Corporations for Federal Tax Purposes:

American Samoa—Corporation
Argentina—Sociedad Anonima
Australia—Public Limited Company
Austria—Aktiengesellschaft
Barbados—Limited Company
Belgium—Societe Anonyme
Belize—Public Limited Company
Bolivia—Sociedad Anonima
Brazil—Sociedade Anonima
Bulgaria—Aktsionerno Druzhestvo
Canada—Corporation and Company
Chile—Sociedad Anonima
People's Republic of China—Gufen Youxian Gongsi

Republic of China (Taiwan) —Ku-fen Yu-hsien Kung-szu
Colombia—Sociedad Anonima
Costa Rica—Sociedad Anonima
Cyprus—Public Limited Company
Czech Republic—Akciova Spolecnost
Denmark—Aktieselskab
Ecuador—Sociedad Anonima or Compania Anonima
Egypt—Sharikat Al-Mossahamah
El Salvador—Sociedad Anonima
Estonia—Aktsiaselts
European Economic Area/European Union —Societas Europaea
Finland—Julkinen Osakeyhtio/Publikt Aktiebolag
France—Societe Anonyme
Germany—Aktiengesellschaft
Greece—Anonymos Etairia
Guam—Corporation
Guatemala—Sociedad Anonima
Guyana—Public Limited Company
Honduras—Sociedad Anonima
Hong Kong—Public Limited Company
Hungary—Reszvenytarsasag
Iceland—Hlutafelag
India—Public Limited Company
Indonesia—Perseroan Terbuka
Ireland—Public Limited Company
Israel—Public Limited Company
Italy—Societa per Azioni
Jamaica—Public Limited Company
Japan—Kabushiki Kaisha
Kazakstan—Ashyk Aktsionerlik Kogham
Republic of Korea—Chusik Hoesa
Latvia—Akciju Sabiedriba
Liberia—Corporation
Liechtenstein—Aktiengesellschaft
Lithuania—Akcine Bendroves
Luxembourg—Societe Anonyme
Malaysia—Berhad
Malta—Public Limited Company
Mexico—Sociedad Anonima
Morocco—Societe Anonyme
Netherlands—Naamloze Vennootschap
New Zealand—Limited Company
Nicaragua—Compania Anonima
Nigeria—Public Limited Company
Northern Mariana Islands—Corporation
Norway—Allment Aksjeselskap
Pakistan—Public Limited Company
Panama—Sociedad Anonima
Paraguay—Sociedad Anonima
Peru—Sociedad Anonima
Philippines—Stock Corporation
Poland—Spolka Akcyjna
Portugal—Sociedade Anonima
Puerto Rico—Corporation

Romania—Societe pe Actiuni
Russia—Otkrytoye Aktsionernoy Obshchestvo
Saudi Arabia—Sharikat Al-Mossahamah
Singapore—Public Limited Company
Slovak Republic—Akciova Spolocnost
Slovenia—Delniska Druzba
South Africa—Public Limited Company
Spain—Sociedad Anonima
Surinam—Naamloze Vennootschap
Sweden—Publika Aktiebolag
Switzerland—Aktiengesellschaft
Thailand—Borisat Chamkad (Mahachon)
Trinidad and Tobago—Limited Company
Tunisia—Societe Anonyme
Turkey—Anonim Sirket
Ukraine—Aktsionerne Tovaristvo Vidkritogo Tipu
United Kingdom—Public Limited Company
United States Virgin Islands—Corporation
Uruguay—Sociedad Anonima
Venezuela—Sociedad Anonima or Compania Anonima

 CAUTION *See Regulations section 301.7701-2(b)(8) for any exceptions and inclusions to items on this list and for any revisions made to this list since these instructions were printed.*

Paperwork Reduction Act Notice

We ask for the information on this form to carry out the Internal Revenue laws of the United States. You are required to give us the information. We need it to ensure that you are complying with these laws and to allow us to figure and collect the right amount of tax.

You are not required to provide the information requested on a form that is subject to the Paperwork Reduction Act unless the form displays a valid OMB control number. Books or records relating to a form or its instructions must be retained as long as their contents may become material in the administration of any Internal Revenue law. Generally, tax returns and return information are confidential, as required by section 6103.

The time needed to complete and file this form will vary depending on individual circumstances. The estimated average time is:

Recordkeeping . . . . 2 hr., 46 min.

Learning about the law or the form . . . . 3 hr., 48 min.

Preparing and sending the form to the IRS . . . . 36 min.

If you have comments concerning the accuracy of these time estimates or suggestions for making this form simpler, we would be happy to hear from you. You can write to the Internal Revenue Service, Tax Products Coordinating Committee, SE:W:CAR:MP:T:M:S, 1111 Constitution Ave. NW, IR-6526, Washington, DC 20224. Do not send the form to this address. Instead, see *Where To File* above.

Case Table

This table lists all cases that are cited as authorities in *Practical Guide to Partnerships and LLCs*. The citations appear at the paragraphs indicated.

References are to paragraph (¶) numbers.

Case Name	Paragraph No.
G.S. Sorrell, Jr. v. Commr.	408
G.T. Helvering v. G.A. Eubank	802.02
G.T. Helvering v. G.B. Clifford, Jr.	802.02; 802.05
G.T. Helvering v. P.R.G. Horst	802.02
Garnett v. Commr.	104; 1009.04
Gaudern v. Commr.	1502.01
Gibson Products Co. v. U.S.	903.01
Goatcher v. U.S.	1603.05
Graham Flying Service v. Commr.	802.03
Gregg v. U.S	104; 1009.04
Gross	802.09
Gullion v. Commr.	1502.01
Gus Grissman Co., Inc. v. Commr.	802.03
H. Feldman v. Commr.	802.02
H.K. Stevens v. Commr.	403
H.S. Reddig	802.05
Hardy v. U.S.	1502.01
Harris v. Commr.	1502.01
Herman v. Commr.	1502.01
Hicks v. U.S.	1502.01
Holland v. Commr.	1502.01
Hubert Enterprises, Inc.	1004.01
I. Garnets v. Commr.	802.03
I.L. Rosenburg v. Commr.	106.04
I.T. Allison v. Commr.	1108.02

Case Name	Paragraph No.
J. Maiatico v. Commr.	802.05
J. Prizant v. Commr.	402.02; 403
J. Smith	802.05
J.C. Echols v. Commr.	1107
J.D. Ballou v. U.S.	802.05
J.E. Cagle, Jr. v. Commr.	1502.04
J.H. Otey, Jr. v. Commr.	1403.02
J.J. Finch v. Commr.	106.04
J.K. Johnson v. Commr.	408
J.R. Moore	802.09
J.R. Parks v. U.S.	402.03
J.T. Finlen v. F.J. Healy	802.05
J.W. Hambuechen v. Commr.	903.01
J.W. Yarbro v. Commr.	503.19
Jackson Investment Co. v. Commr.	1502.04
Jackson Investment Company v. Commr.	1502.04
Jacobs v. Commr.	1104.02
Jade Trading LLC	907.01
Julian E. Jacobs v. Commr.	1502.04
K.D. Dorzback v. N. Collison	903.01
K.E. Lipke v. Commr.	801.03
Kenneth E. Lipke v. Commissioner.	801.03
Kimbell	802.09

Finding Lists

This table lists all Internal Revenue Code Sections, Regulations, Proposed Regulations, Temporary Regulations, and all rulings of the Treasury Department that are cited as authorities in *Practical Guide to Partnerships and LLCs.* The citations appear at the paragraphs indicated.

References are to paragraph (¶) numbers.

Code Sec.	Paragraph No.	Code Sec.	Paragraph No.	Code Sec.	Paragraph No.
IRC Section		83(a)	302.01	120(d)(1)	503.27
1	501; 1403.03	83(b)	302.01; 303; 304.01; 304.03	120(d)(2)	503.27
1(g)	802.01			125	503.27
1(g)(7)	802.01	83(b)(1)	302.01	127(b)(3)	503.27
1(h)	503.05; 1105.02	83(h)	304.02	127(c)(2)	503.27
		101(b)	503.27	127(c)(3)	503.27
1(h)(1)(D)	1105.02	104	503.22	129(d)(4)	503.27
1(h)(3)	503.05	105	503.22	129(e)(3)	503.27
1(h)(4)	1105.01	105(b)	503.27	129(e)(4)	503.27
1(h)(5)(B).	1101; 1105.01	105(g)	503.27	132(b)	503.27
1(h)(6)(B).	1101	106	503.27	132(c)	503.27
1(h)(7)(A).	1101	108	503.19	132(d)	503.27
1(h)(11)(B).	503.05	108(a)	503.19	132(e)	503.27
33	503.19	108(a)(1)(A)	503.19	132(g)	503.27
50(c)(5)	1602.05	108(a)(1)(B)	503.19	132(h)(5)	503.27
55	503.14	108(a)(2)	503.19	152(f)(1)	503.27
56	503.14	108(b)(2)(A)	503.19	162	404.02; 407; 408; 408.01; 408.02; 503.10; 503.17
56(a)(1)	503.14	108(b)(2)(C)	503.19		
56(a)(2)	503.14	108(b)(4)(A)	503.19		
56(a)(3)	503.14	108(b)(5)	402; 503.19		
56(a)(4)	503.14	108(c)(2)(B)	503.19	162(1)	404.02
56(a)(5)	503.14	108(c)(3)	503.19	162(a)	1502.04
56(a)(6)	503.14	108(d)(6)	503.19	162(m)	503.03
57	503.14	108(d)(7)	503.19	163	404.02
62	502	108(d)(7)(A)	503.19	163(d)	503.08; 503.17
63	502	108(e)	503.19		
63(d)	503.28	108(e)(1)	503.19	163(d)(4)(C)	503.08
64	1104.02; 1204.03; 1208; 1302.02	108(e)(2)	503.19	163(d)(5)	404.02
		108(e)(4)	503.19	165	408.03; 408.04
		108(e)(5)	503.19		
67	503.28	108(e)(11)	503.19	168	705.03; 1301.05
67(a)	503.28	108(g)	503.19		
67(c)	503.08	108(i)	503.19	168(f)(5)	1302.02
67(c)(1)	503.28	111	503.18	170	401; 503.11
79	503.27	116(a)(3)	802.03	170(b)	503.11
83	304.02	119	503.27	170(e)(1)	1107
				172	503; 503.20

References are to paragraph (¶) numbers.

References are to paragraph (¶) numbers.

Code Sec.	Paragraph No.	Code Sec.	Paragraph No.	Code Sec.	Paragraph No.
704(c)	202.01; 203; 206.01; 206.02; 206.03; 206.04; 302.02; 407.02; 601; 607.06; 701; 702.01; 702.02; 703; 704; 705.01; 705.02; 705.03; 705.04; 705.05; 906.01; 906.04; 907.01; 907.02; 1005.03; 1103.02; 1104.02; 1301.05; 1301.07; 1302.01; 1302.02; 1402.02; 1404; 1405	704(d)	206.06; 503; 1001; 1002.01; 1002.02; 1003; 1302.02; 1604.06	706(c)(2)	801.02; 801.03
		704(e)	601; 802; 802.01; 802.02; 802.05; 802.08	706(c)(2)(A)	801.01
				706(d)	302.02; 601; 801.02
		704(e)(1)	802.02; 802.03; 802.05	706(d)(1)	801.02
		704(e)(2)	604.02; 802.02	706(d)(2)	801.02
		704(e)(3)	802.02	706(d)(2)(A)(i)	801.02
		704/731	404.03	706(d)(2)(A)(ii)	801.02
		705	202.01; 501; 503.19; 801.01	706(d)(2)(B)	801.02
		705(a)	205; 1103.01; 1103.02; 1103.03	706(d)(2)(B)(iv)	801.02
				706(d)(2)(C)	801.02
		705(a)(1)(A)	503.19	706(d)(2)(D)(i)	801.02
		705(a)(2)	1103.01	706(d)(2)(D)(ii)	801.02
		705(a)(2)(B)	503	706(d)(3)	801.02
		705(a)(3)	205.01	707	1403.03; 1405; 1503
		705(b)	205.02; 1103.01; 1103.02; 1103.03	707(a)	302.01; 404; 404.01; 404.02; 404.03; 404.04; 503.03; 503.24; 503.25; 802.02; 1404.05; 1502.04
704(c)(1)	1404.01				
704(c)(1)(A)	701; 503.29; 1404.05	706	402; 801.02; 801.03		
704(c)(1)(B)	1204.03; 1205; 1212; 1403.01; 1403.03; 1404.01; 1404.04; 1404.05; 1404.06; 1405.06; 1405.07	706(a)	405.01; 501; 1502.03	707(a)(1)	805; 1403.02
		706(b)(1)	405.01	707(a)(2)	1403.03
		706(b)(1)(B)	404.02	707(a)(2)(A)	404.03; 805
		706(b)(1)(B)(i)	405.01	707(a)(2)(B)	805; 1212; 1403.01; 1403.02; 1403.03; 1404.02; 1405.07
		706(b)(1)(B)(ii)	405.01		
		706(b)(1)(B)(iii)	405.01		
		706(b)(4)	405.01		
704(c)(1)(B)(i)	1404.01	706(b)(4)(A)	405.02	707(b)(1)	1402.02; 1404.02
704(c)(1)(B)(ii)	1404.01	706(b)(4)(B)	405.02; 405.05	707(b)(2)	1402.01; 1404.02
704(c)(2)	1404.05	706(c)(1)	801.01	707(b)(3)	1402.02

References are to paragraph (¶) numbers.

References are to paragraph (¶) numbers.

Code Sec.	Paragraph No.	Code Sec.	Paragraph No.	Code Sec.	Paragraph No.
751(a)	.... 503.16; 1101; 1104; 1104.01; 1104.02; 1104.04; 1104.05; 1105; 1105.01; 1106; 1107; 1206; 1208; 1501	752	.... 104; 204; 503.19; 902.01; 902.02; 903; 903.02; 904; 905.02; 906; 907.02; 1103.02	754	.... 202.01; 203; 204; 402; 607.01; 1103.02; 1104; 1104.05; 1204.02; 1206; 1208; 1209; 1211; 1212; 1301; 1301.01; 1301.02; 1301.03; 1301.04; 1301.05; 1301.06; 1301.07; 1301.08; 1301.09; 1302; 1302.01; 1302.02; 1303; 1304; 1305; 1305.01; 1305.02; 1305.03; 1404; 1405; 1501; 1502.04; 1502.05; 1502.07; 1502.10
751(b)	.... 902.01; 1104; 1104.02; 1204.04; 1205.01; 1206; 1207; 1208; 1209; 1212; 1304; 1305.01; 1404.05; 1405; 1502.03; 1502.05; 1502.07	752(a)	.... 206.01; 903.02; 1103.01; 1110; 1205.01; 1405; 1502.06		
		752(b)	.... 503.19; 1107; 1108.01; 1208; 1302; 1502.03; 1502.06		
		752(c)	..... 204; 902.02		
		752(d)	... 1102; 1103.01		
751(b)(3)	 1208				
751(b)(3)(A)	 1208				
751(b)(3)(B)	 1208				
751(c)	.......1104.01; 1207; 1208; 1301.05; 1502.03; 1502.09				
751(c)(2)	 1106				
751(d)	.... 902.01; 1104.02; 1104.03; 1208			754(c)	.... 1402.02
				754/734(b)	 1212
				755	.... 607.02; 801.02; 1301.02; 1301.05; 1301.06; 1301.09; 1305.02
751(d)(1)	. 1104.02; 1208				
751(d)(2)	......1104.02; 1204.03; 1208				
751(d)(2)(D)	 1208			755(a)	.... 1305.02
				755(a)(2)	...... 1305.02
751(d)(3)	. 1104.02; 1208			755(b)	.......1301.05; 1305.02
751(d)(4)	. 1104.02; 1208			761	.... 106.01
751(f)	.... 1104.03			761(a)	.... 106.02; 1404.05

References are to paragraph (¶) numbers.

Code Sec.	Paragraph No.	Code Sec.	Paragraph No.	Code Sec.	Paragraph No.
1366(d)(1)	1603.04	1374(d)(7)	1602.01	3301	503.03
1366(e)	802.02; 1603.02	1375(a)	1602.02	3402	404.02
		1375(a)	1602.02	5112	1105.01
1366(e)(3)	802.02	1375(b)(1)	1602.02	6012(a)	402
1366(f)(2)	1603.02	1375(b)(2)	1602.02	6031	402
1366(f)(3)	1603.02	1375(b)(4)	1602.02	6031(b)	503.28
1367(a)	202.01	1375(d)	1602.02	6037	1606
1367(b)(2).(B)	1603.04	1377(a)(1)	501; 1601.01; 1603.01	6050K	1104.04
1368	1604.01			6050K(a)	1104.04
1368(a)	1604.01	1377(a)(2)	1601.01	6050K(b)	1104.04
1368(b)	1604.02	1378	405.01	6050K(c)(1)	1104.04
1368(b)(1)	1604.02	1398(a)	503.19	6050K(c)(2)	1104.04
1368(b)(2)	1604.02	1398(f)	503.19	6063	503.28
1368(e)(1).(A)	1604.04	1399	503.19	6072	1502.04
1368(e)(1).(C)	1604.04	1401	503.27	6072(a)	102
1368(e)(3)	1604.02	1402	104	6222(b)	1606
1371(d)	1602.05	1402(a)	104; 1502.11	6231	104
1372	503.27; 1601.01	1402(a)(1)	404.02; 503.12	6231(a)(1).(B)	104; 503.28
				6231(a)(7)	104
1374(a)	1602.01	1402(a)(10)	503.12; 1502.11	6501(e)	402
1374(b)(2)	1602.01			6698	503.28
1374(b)(3)	1602.01	1402(a)(13)	104; 503.12	6699(a)	1602.04
1374(c)(1)	1602.01	1402(a)(16)	503.16	6699(b)	1602.04
1374(c)(2)	1602.01	1402(f)	503.12	7519(a)(2)	405.07
1375	1604.03	2031	1301.01	7519(b)	405.07
1374(d)(2)	1602.01	2036	802.09	7519(d)(1).(B)	405.07
1374(d)(2).(B)	1602.01	2036(a)	802.09	7519(d)(4)	405.07
1374(d)(3)	1602.01	2036(a)(1)	802.09	7701	104
1374(d)(4)	1602.01	3004	1405	7701(a)(43)	202.01
1374(d)(5)	1602.01	3101	503.03	7701(a)(44)	202.01

Regulation No.	Paragraph No.	Regulation No.	Paragraph No.
Regulations		1.132-1(b)(1)	503.27
1.1(h)(1)(b)(2)(i)	1105.01	1.132-1(b)(2)(ii)	503.27
1.1(h)-1(b)(2)(ii)	1105.01	1.132-1(b)(3)	503.27
1.79-0	503.27	1.132-1(b)(4)	503.27
1.83-1(a)(1)	302.01	1.132-9	503.27
1.83-2(b)	302.01; 303	1.179-1(f)(2)	503.10
1.83-2(c)	302.01	1.179-1(g)(2)	503.10
1.83-2(d)	302.01	1.179-1(h)(2)	503.10
1.83-6(a)(2)	302.02	1.179-2(c)(1)	503.10
1.83-6(c)	304.02	1.179-2(c)(2)	503.10
1.108-2(c)	503.19	1.179-2(c)(6)(i)	503.10

References are to paragraph (¶) numbers.

References are to paragraph (¶) numbers.

Regulation No.	Paragraph No.
1.743-1(g)(2)(ii)	1204.02
1.743-1(g)(3)	1301.06
1.743-1(g)(1)	1204.02
1.743-1(h)(1)	1302.01
1.743-1(h)(2)(ii)	1301.07
1.743-1(h)(2)(iii)	1301.07
1.743-1(h)(1)	1301.07
1.743-1(j)(2)	1301.08
1.743-1(j)(4)(i)	1301.05
1.743-1(j)(4)(ii)	1301.05
1.743-1(j)(4)(ii)(B)	1301.05
1.751(d)(2)(iii)	1208
1.751-1	1104
1.751-1(a)(1)	1104
1.751-1(a)(2)	1104
1.751-1(a)(3)	1101
1.751-1(b)(2)	1208
1.751-1(b)(2)(ii)	1208
1.751-1(c)(1)(i)	1104.01
1.751-1(d)(1)	1208
1.751-1(d)(2)(ii)	1104.02; 1208
1.751-1(d)(2)(iii)	1104.02
1.751-1(g)	1207
1.752-1	1102; 1103.01
1.752-1(a)(1)	902.01; 904; 1103.03
1.752-1(a)(2)	906; 606.01
1.752-1(d)	905.02
1.752-1(e)	1102; 1103.01
1.752-2	606.01; 606.04; 1004.01
1.752-2(a)	904
1.752-2(b)(3)	905
1.752-2(b)(5)	905.02
1.752-2(b)(6)	905; 905.02
1.752-2(c)(1)	905; 905.02; 906
1.752-2(c)(2)	905.02; 906
1.752-2(d)(2)	905.02
1.752-2(e)(1)	905.02
1.752-2(e)(2)	905.02
1.752-2(e)(3)	905.02
1.752-2(g)(1)	905.02
1.752-2(g)(2)	905.02
1.752-2(j)	905.02

Regulation No.	Paragraph No.
1.752-2(j)(2)	905.02
1.752-2(k)	1004.01
1.752-3	905.02
1.752-3(a)	104
1.752-3(a)(3)	906.01; 906.04
1.752-3(b)(1)	906.05
1.752-3(b)(2)	906.05
1.752-4(a)	903.02
1.752-5	1102; 1103.01
1.752-7	903.02; 907; 907.01; 907.05
1.752-7(b)(2)(ii)	907.02
1.752-7(c)(1)	907.02
1.752-7(e)(1)	907.03
1.752-7(f)(1)	907.04
1.752-7(f)(2)	907.04
1.752-7(g)(1)	907.04
1.752-7(g)(4)	907.04
1.752-7(h)	907.03
1.752-7(i)	907.04
1.754-1(b)	1301.04
1.754-1(b)(1)	1301.04
1.754-1(c)	1301.04; 1305.01
1.755-1(a)	1301.05
1.755-1(a)(1)(i)	1305.02
1.755-1(a)(1)(iii)	1305.02
1.755-1(b)(1)	1305.02
1.755-1(b)(1)(ii)	1301.05
1.755-1(b)(2)	1301.05
1.755-1(b)(2)(i)	1301.05
1.755-1(b)(3)(i)	1301.05
1.755-1(b)(3)(ii)	1301.05
1.755-1(b)(5)	1301.05
1.755-1(c)	1301.06; 1305.02
1.755-1(c)(1)(i)	1305.02
1.755-1(c)(1)(ii)	1305.02
1.755-1(c)(2)(i)	1305.02
1.755-1(c)(2)(ii)	1305.02
1.755-1(c)(3)	1305.02
1.755-1(c)(4)	1305.02
1.757-2(e)	1405.07
1.761-1(a)	106.01; 106.03; 106.06; 1108.02
1.761-1(c)	1502.04

References are to paragraph (¶) numbers.

References are to paragraph (¶) numbers.

Index

References are to paragraph (¶) numbers.

References are to paragraph (¶) numbers.

T